FROM IBERIA TO DIASPORA

BRILL'S SERIES
IN JEWISH STUDIES

VOL. XIX

FROM IBERIA TO DIASPORA

STUDIES IN SEPHARDIC HISTORY AND CULTURE

EDITED BY

YEDIDA K. STILLMAN

AND

NORMAN A. STILLMAN

BRILL
LEIDEN · BOSTON · KÖLN
1999

This book is printed on acid-free paper.

Library of Congress Cataloging-in-Publication Data

From Iberia to diaspora : studies in Sephardic history and culture / edited by Yedida K. Stillmanand Norman A. Stillman.
    p.   cm. — (Brill's series in Jewish studies, ISSN 0926-2261 ; vol. 19)
    English, French, and Spanish.
    Includes bibliographical references and index.
    ISBN 9004107207 (alk. paper)
    1. Sephardim—History.   2. Sephardim—Intellectual life.
3. Ladino philology.   I. Stillman, Yedida Kalfon,. 1946–1998.
II. Stillman, Norman A., 1945–   .   III. Series.
DS134.F76   1997
909'.04924—dc21   96–48611
                                                                CIP

Die Deutsche Bibliothek - CIP-Einheitsaufnahme

From Iberia to diaspora : studies in sephardic history and culture / ed. by Yedida K. Stillman and Norman A. Stillman. – Leiden ; Boston ; Köln : Brill, 1997
    (Brill's series in Jewish studies ; Vol. 19)
    ISBN 90–04–10720–7
    NE: Stillman, Yedida K. [Hrsg.]; GT

ISSN 0926-2261
ISBN 90 04 10720 7

PRINTED IN THE NETHERLANDS

to

David Boren

and

Russell Postier

To whom we owe so much that words
fail to express our indebtedness—
this volume is gratefully dedicated

CONTENTS

PART TWO

INTELLECTUAL HISTORY

PART THREE

LITERATURE AND FOLKLORE

PART SIX

CONCLUSION: EDUCATION AND THE FUTURE
OF SEPHARDIC STUDIES

PREFACE

The field of Sephardic studies has flourished in recent years in North America, Israel, and Europe, and has become a major subdiscipline of Jewish studies. The 1992 Quincentennial commemoration of Ferdinand and Isabella's Edict of Expulsion and of Columbus's discovery of the New World stirred interest in Sephardic history and culture beyond the limited confines of researchers engaged in the field to broader circles within academe and within the wider public. The year 1992 and the years immediately preceding and following it witnessed an unprecedented number of international and regional conferences, museum exhibitions, films, concerts, and other cultural events dealing with Sephardim. There also appeared an impressive number of new publications, both scholarly and popular.

This book adds to the growing body of work in Sephardic studies and presents in a single volume a rich selection of some of the best and most up-to-date research in the field by scholars from all over the world. The chapters of this book are the outgrowth of papers presented at the Second International Conference on Sephardic Studies, which was held at Binghamton University (State University of New York) in 1991. The first conference, held there in 1987, also resulted in a volume of essays.[1]

The contributors to this volume come from Spain, Portugal, Italy, France, England, Israel, Morocco, the United States, and Canada. The subjects of their essays are even more geographically diverse, covering both pre-Expulsion Iberia and the far-flung Sephardic diaspora. The essays also represent the interdisciplinary nature of the field of Sephardic studies. The largest group of papers are historical—either social or intellectual history. The next-largest group are literary studies. The other disciplines include folklore, linguistics, musicology, and art history. The volume concludes with an important discussion of education and the future of Sephardic studies. Most of the essays are in English, but several are in French or Spanish.

We did not impose a "house style" on the individual contributors,

---

[1] New Horizons in Sephardic Studies, eds. Yedida K. Stillman and George K. Zucker (State University of New York Press: Albany, 1993).

and thus there is a variety of transcription systems for rendering Hebrew, Arabic, and Judeo-Spanish. There is also variation in the forms of personal and place names. To facilitate the reader search for names and subjects in the index, we have imposed a single, common form for the listing in the index.

Yedida K. Stillman* and Norman A. Stillman

*Yedida Stillman died on February 21, 1998 during the final editing of this volume. It was she who organized the conference upon which this collection of essays is based, and it was she who was the moving force that saw it through all but the final stage of publication.

PART ONE

SEPHARDIC AND ORIENTAL COMMUNITIES: PAST AND PRESENT

THE BLENDING OF JEWISH AND TURKISH IDENTITY AMONG THE JEWS IN TURKEY

Walter F. Weiker

Rutgers University
Newark, New Jersey

The concept of identity is complex. In broad social science terms it can be said that many people are confronted with the obligation to choose among "traditional" associations, i.e., adherence to the aggregate into which one is born, whereas fully "modern" people ideally select their associates on the basis of voluntary, rational choice. Of course there are many complexities to this. One is that traditional groupings vary in the degree to which one might be able to escape from them even if one wanted to; physical characteristics are good examples. Another is that the concept of the involuntary association includes groups like the family, from which most people have decided that they do not really want to escape, and that the very fact of having so decided may endow membership in the family with some aspects of a voluntary association.

One kind of group which presents problems of choice is the ethnic group. Simply defined, it is a collection of individuals based on characteristics which may include language, race, religion, various degrees of kinship, and shared history; in the United States and Israel, at least, the term is also used to include national origin. In much of the world most ethnic groups are minorities within a larger society or country. While for some groups in such situations it is not possible to transcend ethnicity completely, for others significant assimilation is conceivable. Relatively few individuals, however, have gone to the extent of voluntarily "melting" completely, though some groups have ostensibly tried to do so to a significant extent. Among Jews a good example was that of many German Jews, who sought to become, as the saying goes, more German than the Germans. In France, too, Jews were exhorted to conceive of themselves as Frenchmen of the Jewish persuasion.

It is instructive that the United States, once thought of as the ideal place for there to be a "melting pot," has not become so, and there does not seem to be any prospect of it, despite many enabling factors. These include a high level of education, a great deal of individual social as well as geographic mobility, a common language, little religious discrimination, a high rate of intermarriage, and so forth. On the other side, what we may call public policy, or America's general ideology, has come to celebrate "cultural pluralism," to a large extent in answer to the desires of most Americans. (While I certainly do not mean to imply that there is no ethnic tension in the United States, I think we must concede that among the higher social strata it is relatively mild in comparison with many other societies.)

For many of the Americans for whom identity based on ethnicity was expected by social scientists to disappear (i.e., those in the upper social strata), what has happened is that it has, instead, taken on a new character which has been labeled by the sociologist Herbert Gans as "symbolic ethnicity,"[1] and by others simply as the "new ethnicity." Instead of ethnicity held together by structural factors, such as residential proximity, distinct language, concentration in particular occupations, or ethnic churches, the new ethnicity is based on the celebration of cultural characteristics, such as great artists (Italian-Americans point to Michelangelo and Dante), ethnic foods, or holidays (St. Patrick's Day). It has the advantage that it is possible for individuals to choose the favorable manifestations of their ethnicity, while not having to make significant commitments to ethnic institutions and activities.

There are many factors which influence the degree to which an ethnic group will seek and/or be able to succeed in persuading many of its potentially marginal members to maintain ethnicity as one of their identities. These include:

1. The degree, if any, to which ethnicity restricts or facilitates economic, social, or political mobility.
2. The strength of the traditions, history, and overall culture of both the ethnic group and the larger society.
3. The amount and kind of contact with several levels of surroundings. The levels which are most important for the purposes of this study are the particular country in which a group lives, and the

---

[1] Herbert Gans, "Symbolic Ethnicity: The Future of Ethnic Groups and Cultures in America," *Ethnic and Racial Studies* 2 (1979): 1–20.

members of the ethnic group in other parts of the world. The history of these contacts is important as well. Jews are a major example.

4. The views toward the ethnic group held by other members of the society, the society's openness, and the possibilities for individual social mobility.
5. The attempts by the group and its leaders to retain its members.
6. The economic level of the society.

This paper will discuss these topics in reference to the Jews of Turkey. To summarize their situation briefly, they have borrowed liberally from Turkish culture and share many cultural tastes with Turks, but over the centuries of living in Turkey in considerable isolation, they were able to create enough Jewish variations on Turkish themes so that they can feel comfortable in sharing in both identities. There is, however, some opinion that subtle undercurrents in Turkish society continue to make being a non-Muslim at least a mild liability in terms of material and social opportunities, so that Jewish distinctiveness will disappear except in directly religious matters (and even here, as in much of the modern world, many Turkish Jews are becoming less observant). Though the Turkish Jewish community has a long history, and continues to have a network of communal social institutions, the activity connected with the five-hundredth anniversary of Sephardim in Turkey can, in the view of some, have the by-product of providing an opportunity to retain its potential defectors by creating some foundations for the kind of symbolic ethnicity mentioned above. These projects include the restoration of synagogues in Turkey, the establishment of a Jewish museum in Turkey, the revival of Judeo-Spanish music, and such activities in Israel as the recent exhibition staged by the Israel Museum, and the work of MORIT, the Foundation for a Cultural Center of Turkish Judaism. (One of the habits of the Turkish Jewish community in the past has been its "silence," i.e., that it was careful not to be too visible, and, therefore, that its culture was to a large extent a "private" one. This habit has been largely carried on among Turkish Jews in Israel.)[2] (How much blending, if any, there has been in the other direction,

² Walter F. Weiker, *The Unseen Israelis: Jews from Turkey in Israel* (Jerusalem Center for Public Affairs and University Press of America, 1988).

i.e., Jewish influence on Turkish culture, is beyond the scope of this paper.)

Before examining blending in several spheres of Turkish and Jewish culture, a brief summary of relevant historical phenomena will set the stage. Sephardic Jews came to the Ottoman Empire and to the areas of Turkish culture after the expulsion from Spain and Portugal in 1492 from what has been called the most brilliant medieval Jewish community. Their strong institutions of scholarship, religion, and general culture were transferred, often almost intact.

For a long time contact with Turks (the term Turks is used here to refer to Turkish Muslims) was very uneven. The Jewish luminaries who frequented the sultan's court and Ottoman economic and social circles were only a few, in contrast to the larger part of the Jewish community, which was poor, lived in particular quarters of Turkish cities, and was often concentrated in a few occupations. In these circumstances they continued the use of Judeo-Spanish and Hebrew, and perpetuated Sephardic culture through institutions of religion and internal self-government. The latter, under the *millet* system, allowed them, for example, to regulate many aspects of their economic affairs and to settle many kinds of disputes through their own system of courts, which had wide, if not total, authority. Thus most Jews had contact with Turks only when it became necessary for economic activity or when it happened "accidentally," such as those who lived at the edges of the Jewish quarters or who traveled. Of course there were exceptions even among the lower classes, but they were few.

There were no essential changes in this picture until the mid-nineteenth century, when both Turkish and Jewish society began to open up. The main spheres of change were in education and the economy. Both Turks and Jews began to go to secular schools in increasing numbers, and while few Jews went to Turkish schools (until the twentieth century), many met Turks in the foreign schools that opened in several major cities. The general quickening of economic development also put Jewish entrepreneurs and manufacturers, as well as workers, into contact with Turks. One result was the rapid increase in the number of Jews conversant in Turkish.

Integration became much more rapid after the Young Turk Revolution of 1908 and the founding of the Turkish Republic in 1923. Perhaps the most important single development was the nationalization of education in 1924, which made it compulsory for all

Turkish citizens to attend Turkish schools at least through elementary school. Even in the absence of this action, however, it is likely that the rapid growth of Turkish education would have attracted a high proportion of Jewish children, in large part because it was clear that attending Turkish secondary and higher schools could bring important career advantages. In the economy, growing industrialization attracted many Jews, who often went into business with Turkish associates, while Jewish workers increasingly found employment in Turkish establishments. The same was true of commerce. Soon Jews were also rapidly moving out of Jewish residential neighborhoods into more affluent Turkish ones, and as their knowledge of Turkish grew they began reading Turkish literature and newspapers, going to Turkish places of entertainment, and so on. Today there are few Jews who are not at home with Turkey and Turks, though for many their patterns of personal associations and close friendships are still concentrated, in considerable degree, in Jewish circles.

There was also a political aspect. In contrast to other non-Muslim minorities (specifically Greeks and Armenians), Jews were always known for their political loyalty to the Ottoman Empire, and since the revolution they have continued to be loyal to the Turkish state. To some extent this was a result of luck; the Jews never had a realistic prospect of founding a separate state within the empire, and so did not develop separatist ambitions. They also found loyalty to be important in that the Ottoman government often protected Jews from Christians, with whom there were often troubles deriving from blood libels and similar causes. There were, to be sure, periodic anti-Jewish incidents, but at official levels and among the elites, the image of Turkish Jews was generally positive.

Thus a number of favorable factors were present: a strong Jewish tradition, a modernizing Turkish state, a relatively favorable view of Jews among most upper- and middle-class Turks. In addition, as we shall now discuss, despite the long period of considerable separateness of the Jews, the two communities had enough cultural contact so that the Jews did not find Turkish ways altogether strange, and Muslim Turks did not see the Jews as totally different. On this basis, let us look at several manifestations of culture and the patterns of blending.

Language

As already mentioned, the isolation of the large majority of Jews resulted in the retention of Judeo-Spanish as the community's language for close to four centuries of residence in Turkey. Nevertheless, as Abraham Danon observed, "the quarters were not hermetically sealed to outside linguistic influence, and . . . Turkish penetrated through all the pores." He identified Turkish expressions in Jewish writings from as early as 1639. The earliest interest in Turkish, he observed, appears to have been as a result of the need for non-Jewish eyewitnesses to a death so that the widow could remarry, and he found evidence as well that Jews in Bursa learned Turkish as far back as the time of Orkhan (mid-14th cent.) to show their attachment to the conquerors, and that the same was true in Edirne during the reign of Murad I (1360). Turkish words usually received distinctive Jewish pronunciation and modification, and he further concluded that adoption of Turkish words and phrases was done by all classes of Jews, not only by the common people but also by the upper classes, who were "relatively cultivated and claimed some 'purism.'" (The latter, he notes, replaced some pure Castilian words, which they had forgotten, with borrowings from French and Italian.)[3]

More recent research into the period before large numbers of Jews began to be conversant in Turkish has pointed out two major forms of language blending which took place: the names of everyday items, which were either adopted entirely or as variants on Judeo-Spanish or Sephardic terms, and the use of Turkish endings on words used by Jews. The first is typical of adaptation in most such situations, the second is probably more specific, although I must leave this point to linguists.

As expected, the list of terms taken over all but verbatim consisted to a large extent of things in everyday use which were adopted in the form available on the local market. Avner Levi has compiled a list of terms adopted with only small linguistic changes, such as the addition of an *a*: *canak/canaka* ("pot"); *bakkal/bakkala* ("grocer"); *çorap/corapa* ("stocking"); *çarik/carika* ("peasant sandal"); *kundura/kundurya* ("shoe").[4] Karen Gerson has also listed fifty Jewish food names influ-

---

[3] Abraham Danon, "Essai sur les vocables dans le Judeo-Espagnol," *Revue Orientale* 4 (1903) and 5 (1904).
[4] Avner Levi, "The Turkish Element in Ladino Suffixes," in *Miqqedem Umiyyam (Studies in the Jewry of Islamic Countries)* (University of Haifa, 1981), p. 157 (Hebrew).

enced by Turkish ones, such as *portakal/portokal* ("orange"), *fasulye/ fasulyas* ("bean"), and *ispanak/ispinaka* ("spinach").[5]

The use of Turkish word-endings is also interesting. Levi's research points in particular to the use of the Turkish suffix *-ci* or *-cu* (pronounced *dji* or *dju*, though modified in Jewish adaptation to *gi*), which signifies someone who does a particular job. For example, in Turkish a *locantaci* ("restaurant owner or proprietor") or a *sucu* ("water carrier"). Jewish usage is illustrated by such terms as *heshbongi* ("accountant"). Another example is the suffix *-lik*, meaning the quality of being something. Levi cites, for example, *benadamlik* ("being a good human being"), and the attachment of this suffix to particularly Jewish terms such as *purimlik*.[6]

Another sphere of intermixing of words is in expressions. Karen Gerson has compiled a list of them. For example:

1. *Mereses una **medalya** de patata* ("You deserve a medal of potatoes").
2. *A **pisin** ke te vide, a **pisin** m'ennamori* ("I fell in love with you at first sight").
3. *Soz **rendesiz mese** odunu* ("You are an absolute blockhead").
4. *Ez kara de **kösele*** ("He has a face like coarse leather").
5. *Al rey un **yesil yaprak*** ("For the king a green leaf").
6. *Kada una a su **boy*** ("To each according to his stature").
7. *No es **yabanci**, es **konu komsu*** ("Not a stranger, a neighbor").[7]

Foods

This is often a major area of adaptation, in large part because of the availability of local raw materials. Not surprisingly, therefore, a Turkish-Jewish cookbook published in 1985 by two Istanbul women, Viki Koronyo and Sima Ovadya, entitled *Sephardic Foods* (*Sefarad Yemekleri*), with the recipes given in both Turkish and English, contains dishes which make much use of the many staples of general Turkish diet, including eggplant, lamb, fish, and a variety of nuts and spices. But they often have special Jewish touches and Jewish

---

[5] Karen Gerson, "Language Change as Influenced by Cultural Contact, A Case: Ladino" (M.A. thesis, Bogaziçi University, 1983).

[6] Levi, "Turkish Element in Ladino Suffixes," p. 159.

[7] Gerson, "Language Change," Appendix V. I thank David Altabé for helping me with the Judeo-Spanish.

names. One of the best-known examples is the what the Turkish
Jews call the *böreka*, a pastry filled with spinach, eggplant, ground
meat, etc., which in Turkish is called a *börek*. Another is a variety
of meatball dishes.

Music

A sphere where there was strong Turkish influence on Jewish culture was music. This is not surprising. Music is a medium in which
practitioners have an especially strong need to be original, in contrast to literature, in which there are more set forms into which
authors can fit variations of plots and topics.

Turkish and other local melodies appear to have found their way
into Jewish life, including synagogue rituals, at an early date. Israel
Zinberg found that Solomon ben Mazzal Tov's "religious poems and
song of Zion are constructed according to the rhythmic form and
melody of Turkish and Arab folk songs."[8] Stamatka Kaludova has
also given several illustrations, mostly from the early Ottoman period,[9] and Karen Gerson has identified numerous Jewish poems and
romancas which were borrowed from Turkish, as well as synagogue melodies which were taken from *makams*.[10] The Istanbul musical ensemble Los Pasharos Sefaradis, organized in 1978, specializes
in Judeo-Spanish songs; its repertoire includes many numbers with
Turkish themes and Turkish melodies, many of which go back to
Ottoman times. One of my favorites portrays Jews marching along
with the Turkish army and is entitled "We Are All Ottomans" ("He-
pimiz Osmanliyiz").

This is also a sphere in which Jewish performers attracted attention among Turks. (I do not know to what extent they sang Jewish
songs.) Franco noted that "Jewish musicians are highly regarded, as
are Jewish doctors and soothsayers."[11] Galante named several who
were so popular that they had Turkish nicknames: Rabbi Yomtob

---

[8] Israel Zinberg, *A History of Jewish Literature* (New York: Ktav, 1974), vol. 5,
p. 89.

[9] Stamatka Kaludova, "Sur la poésie et la musique des Juifs de la Peninsule
Balkanique du XVe au XXe siècle," *Etudes Balkaniques* 6 (1970).

[10] Gerson, "Language Change," pp. 9–10.

[11] M. Franco, *Essai sur l'histoire des Israélites de l'Empire Ottoman* (Paris, Librairie
A. Durlacher, 1897), p. 256.

Danon, known in mid-eighteenth-century Izmir as "the little rabbi"; Abraham Aryas, composer of more than eighty works in the early nineteenth century, who was called *hadji berjuzar*, the "consummate master"; Elia Levi, known as *santuri Elia*; and Isaac Barki, or "Little Isaac."[12] Hayyim Cohen similarly found that before World War I several Jewish composers, singers, and instrumentalists had become famous in Turkey.[13]

Folklore

In the sphere of folklore we find both integration and distinctiveness. In regard to the former, there is a large body of Turkish-Jewish folklore which is taken from Turkish themes. A recent collection of Judeo-Spanish folktales edited by Matilda Koen-Sarano (in Judeo-Spanish and Hebrew) includes many which are set in Turkey, refer to interaction with Turks ranging from sultans to ordinary townsmen, and use numerous Turkish words transliterated into Judeo-Spanish as well as Turkish endings on Judeo-Spanish words.[14] Samuel Armistead has also cited many such examples in his extensive work.[15] The best-known are the Nasreddin Hodja stories, moral anecdotes about a legendary village teacher/preacher which are familiar to every Turkish child. Karen Gerson has written that this figure, called Coha in Judeo-Spanish, "has become so familiar to the Jews that there are quite a few proverbs, idioms, and expressions with Coha, who was assimilated into the culture with relish."[16]

At the same time, there was a strong effort to preserve traditional Jewish forms. One of the clearest instances of such activity took place in Rhodes in the nineteenth century. Marc Angel found that due to the work of several Rhodian authors and editors who were assiduous in compiling local folklore and literature, "the romance tradition was

---

[12] Avraham Galante, *Les Juifs d'Izmir*, reprinted by Isis Yayincilik, Istanbul, vol. 5, pp. 120–124.

[13] Hayyim J. Cohen, *The Jews of the Middle East, 1860–1922* (New York: John Wiley and Israel Universities Press, 1984), p. 134.

[14] Matilda Koen-Sarano, *Kuentos del Folklor de la Famiya Djudeo-Espanyola* (Jerusalem: Kana, 1986).

[15] Samuel G. Armistead and Joseph H. Silverman, *The Judeo-Spanish Ballad Chapbooks of Yacob Abraham Yona*, Folk Literature of the Sephardic Jews, no. 1 (University of California Press, 1971).

[16] Gerson, "Language Change," p. 10 n. 4.

particularly vibrant among the Jews of Rhodes. Alberto Hemsi noted the astonishing fidelity of the Rhodeslies to the Spanish musical heritage. Professors Armistead and Silverman found that the Sephardim of Rhodes preserved the old Spanish *romances* in vitality, more so than Sephardim of the cities in Turkey. Jewish women of Rhodes origin, aged 45–55, could sing in general fifteen *romances*; the older women knew many more. By contrast, among the old women of Istanbul it was difficult to find one who knew more than three or four."[17] Among the factors to which Angel attributed this particular fidelity was the Rhodian Jews' "genuine love of singing. Moreover, one of their general cultural characteristics was a concern for detail and precision. Since the *romances* were often sung at family gatherings and public celebrations, the singers and audiences could check one another and would correct any deviations from the traditional words and/or melodies. The community was relatively small in number and close-knit, factors which also tended to strengthen their cultural traditions."[18]

One way in which folklore may have directly influenced relations between Jews and Turks is in the images of Jews found in proverbs. Galante has analyzed some of this in terms of general "oriental" proverbs, with which he found Turkish ones in agreement. He concluded that the Jews were portrayed as (1) intelligent, (2) tenacious, (3) avaricious, (4) having foresight, (5) fearful and timid. He asserted that some of these traits were tied to particular conditions, and that the images tended to change; e.g., that the fearful and timid impression became less prominent as the Jews became more emancipated (as after the French Revolution). He observed the same about another image that sometimes appeared, that of the Jew being "dirty," which had two components: a physical one, which Galante ascribed to the miserable conditions in which poor Jews often lived, and one meaning "of decadent intellect," which tended to fade as Jews acquired more education in the nineteenth century. Some samples are:

1. *Yahudi bile degilsin* ("You are not even like a Jew").
2. *Yahudi gibi kazan, Bulgar gibi sarfet* ("Earning like a Jew, spending like a Bulgarian").

---

[17] Marc D. Angel, *The Jews of Rhodes* (New York: Sepher-Hermon Press, 1980), pp. 137–138.
[18] Ibid.

3. *Evi yanmis Yahudi gibi yaygara eder* ("He cries out like a Jew whose house has burned").
4. *Yahudinin bastigi yerde ot bitmez* ("Where a Jew has trod the grass lasts").
5. *Bir Yahudi kasa, iki Yahudi banka, üç Yahudi havra* ("One Jew has a safe, two Jews have a bank, three Jews a society").
6. *Seytan ölünce, aklini Yahudilere, ayaklarini da Haleplilere miras birakmistir* ("When Satan died he willed his mind to the Jews, his feet to the people of Aleppo").
7. *Yillanmis yahudi akli gibi* ("Like the mind of an aged Jew").
8. *Açik gözlu Yahudi* ("A Jew with open eyes").
9. *Yahudi bereketi* ("Jewish abundance").
10. *Yahudi dini gibi kavi* ("Strong as the Jewish religion").
11. *Yahudi pazarligi* ("Jewish bargaining").[19]

Whatever the balance between favorable and unfavorable popular opinions about Jews (and many of the proverbs may well have been taken either way depending on circumstances and particular relationships), it is certainly clear that Turks and Jews of many social classes were known to each other and that all were probably aware of these images. It would be interesting to learn whether there were Jewish images of Turks; and it is not unlikely that Jews would have tried to change the negative images and thus "blend" better into Turkish culture and society.

Decorative Arts

We are only beginning to have research into the use of Turkish art forms by Jews, although there is no doubt that it was plentiful. Miriam Katz and Esther Juhacz of the Israel Museum in Jerusalem, and Vivian Mann of the Jewish Museum in New York have recently demonstrated the extensive use of Turkish motifs in decorative religious objects, such as Torah mantles, and in home furnishings and clothing for both general use and on special occasions like weddings. Examples include tapestries, which have many features of Turkish prayer rugs, such as design lay-out, floral decorations, colors, and

---

[19] Galante, *Le Juif dans le proverbe, le conte, et la chanson orientaux*, Isis Yayincilik, vol. 9, pp. 138–143, 143–146.

portrayal of lamps and lights; Torah finials topped by variations on
the Turkish star-and-crescent symbol; "customs similar to those of
the Muslims, for example the use of an embroidered set of towels
with which to wrap the bride as she emerged from the *hammam*
waters in preparation for her wedding"; the use of gold embroidery
in a manner similar to that of their neighbors, "but also for specific
purposes associated with Jewish custom and tradition . . . like ceremonies connected with marriage, as among Moslems"; "Tambour
embroidery should be given special mention, as it was rather popular in both Turkish and Jewish needlework"; "The hanging lamp
motif is widespread in Ottoman ark curtains of all periods. In the
early stages it always appears together with the portal pattern, and
the source of both is the Muslim prayer rug." (The hanging lamp
is also a Jewish iconographic motif, of course.)

There were also many similarities in costume; it would not infre-
quently have been difficult to distinguish Jews from Muslims except
for the restrictions on the colors which non-Muslims could wear.
"Intracommunal pressures not withstanding, by the end of the nineteenth century the Sephardic Jews were already well-rooted in contemporary Ottoman culture, and their lifestyle reflected the prevalent
one in the Empire."[20]

Superstitions

There are also some accounts of Jews' superstitions. Some are wider
than either the Jewish or the Muslim culture, e.g., ideas about the
evil eye and a large variety of ways to escape it.[21] Marc Angel has
described that on Rhodes Friday was a popular Jewish wedding day,
something which he attributes to the fact that Muslims also found
Friday auspicious, and he remarks that the "traditional Jewish value
[of respect for elders] was reinforced by a similar attitude among the
Turks."[22] Joseph Levi related that in contemporary Izmir no mar-

---

[20] *Sephardi Jews in the Ottoman Empire*, catalogue of the recent exhibitions at the
Israel Museum, Jerusalem, and the Jewish Museum, New York, passim.
[21] Angel, *Jews of Rhodes*, pp. 132–124, tells of a number of ways in which the
Jews of Rhodes sought to do this.
[22] Ibid., pp. 120–121.

riages are held in the second half of the month, that weddings must begin before sundown, and that change of residence should take place only on a Monday or a Thursday (the latter a Jewish idea, of course).[23] Karen Gerson observed that among the Turkish superstitions shared by Jews is the sacralizing of certain famous persons after their deaths whose graves were visited by Muslims, Christians, and Jews alike. An example is Telli Baba.[24]

Paul Dumont found indications in the Alliance Israélite archives that many Jews believed in folk remedies. Alliance reports often denigrated "superstitions," "prejudices," and "chimeras" as "obstacles to a spirit of progress."[25] Mair José Benardete also noted that superstitions were "universal" among the Jewish inhabitants of Salonika. "Amulets against evil spirits and sicknesses were worn by children and adults," he writes, and "Recourse was often had to Mohammedan women and dervishes for all kinds of illnesses."[26]

On the whole, it is unlikely that these arts and their integrational aspects had a great diluting effect on the Jewish consciousness of the Jewish lower classes, many of whom remained traditional and largely inward-oriented almost until they emigrated to Israel after 1948, but surely some of what they saw around them which was similar to things Turkish helped them to feel more at home in their adopted country. In regard to the Jewish middle and upper classes, these aspects of culture probably had greater effect (though unfortunately we have only sketchy and anecdotal life-style information) because they were another part of the general integration which many were experiencing through education, literature, and economic life. For all Jews, though, these cultural features were also setting the stage for the rapid social change in which the Jews would soon participate.

---

[23] Joseph Levi, "The Jewish Community of Izmir" (Paper presented to Dr. S. Della-Pergola, Hebrew University, Institute of Contemporary Jewry, 1976), handwritten (Hebrew).

[24] Gerson, "The Relationship of Language, Ethnicity and Ethnic Group Identity, A Case: Judeo-Spanish" (M.A. thesis, Reading University, 1986), p. 11.

[25] Paul Dumont, "Jewish Communities in Turkey during the Last Decade of the Nineteenth Century in the Light of the Archives of the Alliance Universelle," *Journal Asiatique* 17 (1979): 117 (French).

[26] Mair José Benardete, *Hispanic Culture and Character of the Sephardic Jews*, 2nd corrected ed. (New York: Sepher-Hermon Press, 1982), pp. 142–143.

A Recent Survey

The only attempt at directly measuring some aspects of Turkish identity which has come to my attention is a 1990 project by Boğaziçi University history student Lorans Tanatar Baruch. In a survey of 107 Istanbul Jews she included questions about naming children, about attitudes toward the Jewish school, and about feelings of being Eastern or Western.

On the first of these topics, she found that 23 percent of women and 29 percent of men preferred giving their children Turkish names, 42 percent and 46 percent favored "other" names, and the remainder thought two names side-by-side were desirable. In tabulating the names of Jewish children as reported in the Turkish Jewish weekly *Shalom*, she found that Turkish and other names were about fifty-fifty. In probing further with her respondents, she also discovered that the identity problem had additional dimensions in that there were times when French names were in fashion (Robert, Jak, Röne), as well as times when a fad resulted in names like those of Hollywood stars (Betsi, Ralf, Rudi, Mark, Sindi). (I have not commented on a possible additional complication of the Turkish Jews' identity situation, namely, the attachment to French culture that was a by-product of the schools of the Alliance Israélite Universelle, which educated many Turkish Jews in the late nineteenth and early twentieth centuries. It is outside the scope of this paper.)

She also asked about her respondents' thoughts regarding sending their children to the new Jewish school which is under construction in Istanbul. She found that 26.5 percent said definitely not, while 46 percent of the women and 35 percent of the men replied that the new school would be more attractive than the current one. The younger respondents were more suspicious of the idea than were their elders, but the majority asserted that if they were assured that their children would get a good education there, and it was impossible to send them to a better school, they would agree to have them attend the Jewish school. (This is important because, as I noted earlier, Jewish children have gone to Turkish schools not only because it was required by Turkish law for many years but also because many Jews were convinced that doing so would be an important advantage for their future careers.)

The survey also included questions on self-views, that is, whether the Jews, "who had lived in the East for 500 years but had continually had economic and cultural relations with the West," considered themselves Western or Eastern. As she had anticipated, she said, 65 percent of the men and 59 percent of the women saw themselves as closer to Muslim society. (She said that unfortunately she was not able to determine whether this was in reference to work relationships or to private social ones).[27]

Efforts to retain Jews through Social Clubs, Programming, and other Communal Activities

The Jews of Turkey are aware of the prospects for the assimilation of their youth. On one of the major measures of assimilation, intermarriage, the majority of the estimates which I got from various members of the community centered around 5–10 percent, which one observer characterized as low in comparison to Jews elsewhere, but high for Turkey. (On a more informal level, the young Jews whom I met agreed that the social pressure which the community asserted on them not to intermarry was very heavy, but that a problem was presented by the small size of the Jewish marriage pool.)

In response, Jewish social and cultural clubs are making increased efforts to stress programming with Jewish content, and their leaders assert without hesitation that combatting assimilation is the major reason for this. In 1988 I received estimates that at least half of the Jewish young people were members and attended frequently. Jewish identity also remains strong if measured by such things as holiday observance and the attendance at rites of passage.

Conclusion

The Jews of Turkey appear to have been quite successful in blending Jewish and Turkish identity. Several important factors have helped in this process: (1) their Jewishness and their Judeo-Spanish culture were preserved for a long time and were deeply imbedded; (2) the two communities were not completely strange to each other, and when blending increased during the modern age, formulas were available in such spheres as foods, decorative arts, and linguistics whereby

---

[27] "Istanbul Yahudilerine bir Bakis," *Shalom*, 27 February and 6 March 1991.

the Jews were able to fashion Jewish variations on Turkish culture; and (3) there was relatively little popular anti-Semitism, at least on the middle-and upper-middle-class levels where most Jews are found. (Lower-class Jews, most of whom moved to Israel shortly after the founding of the state in 1948, were often less successful at integrating with Turkish culture.) It would be instructive to assess the role of these factors in the situations of Jews elsewhere.

THE JEWISH COMMUNITY IN THE AZORES FROM 1820 TO THE PRESENT

FÁTIMA S. DIAS

University of Açores

I

The slim bibliography on the history of the Jewish community in the Azores Islands obliges us to found our investigation solely on archival sources.[1] These are dispersed amongst numerous Portuguese archives, where they await adequate study and, for this, a researcher who can dedicate himself solely to the study of the Jews.

For this study, I consulted all of the public and private sources regarding Jews in the Azores, but there remain gaps difficult to fill, because the existing documentation does not shed light on the activities of all of the Jews in the Azores archipelago.[2] Several Jewish families, for example, are known only from tombstones or death registers, the other aspects of their lives in the islands having gone undocumented.[3] (For a complete list of Jews living in the Azores in the nineteenth century, see *Table 1*.)

Finally, one must admit that the lack of a serious study on Azorean society and the economy of the Azores in the nineteenth and twentieth centuries makes it impossible, at this time, to present a definitive

---

[1] Alfredo Bensaúde, *A vida de José Bensaúde* (Porto: Litografia Nacional, 1936); Marcelino Lima, "Os judeus na ilha do Faial," *Boletim do núcleo cultural da Horta* 1, no. 1 (December 1956); Pedro Merelim, "Os hebraicos na ilha Terceira," *Atlântida* 8, nos. 1–4 (1964); 9, nos. 1–2, 4–5 (1965); 10, no. 2 (1966), Manuel de Mello Correa, *Subsídios para a geneologia da Família Bensaúde* (Lisbon, 1976).

[2] Ponta Delgada: Arquivo da Camara Municipal, Arquivo da Alfandega, Fundo Notarial, Núcleo Judicial; Horta and Angra do Heroísmo: Câmaras municipais, Alfândega e Fundo Notarial. Biblioteca Pública e Arquivo de Ponta Delgada (BPAPD), Biblioteca Pública e Arquivo de Angra do Heroísmo (BPAAH), Biblioteca Pública e Arquivo da Horta (BPAH), Arquivo Comercial Bensaúde e Ca. e Ldt., Arquivo José Bensaúde e Herdeiros, Arquivo Nacional da Torre do Tombo (ANTT), and Arquivo do Ministério das Obras Públicas (AMOP).

[3] Santa Clara cemetery on São Miguel, also at Angra do Heroísmo, Terceira island, and at Horta, Faial island.

interpretation on the present theme. This paper must be viewed as but a small contribution to the larger concept of the study of the Jews in the Azorean archipelago.

II

It is an indisputable fact of Portuguese historiography that large numbers of *Cristãos-Novos*, or New Christians, banished ones and commoners, helped to people the Azores Islands. Nonetheless, the Jews who resided in the Azores in the nineteenth century had little in common with the New Christians who much earlier had been forced to settle in the archipelago.[4]

The Jews who passed through the islands beginning in the 1820s were all originally from Morocco, and are known and referred to in contemporary documents as Moroccan Jews. It is thought that the motivation for their exodus from Morocco was rooted in the ethno-religious conflicts they faced there, as well as in economic hardships. What is certain is that from the beginning of the nineteenth century, Portuguese documents register a "flood of those men, especially of Jews, throughout the Algarve,"[5] and soon afterwards, throughout the rest of the Portuguese kingdom, including the Azores.

The provisional nature of the settlement of these Moroccan Jews in the Azores is attested to by the fact that the men arrived first, sending for their wives and families later. Moreover, some of the Jewish arrivals apparently settled temporarily in other locations after leaving Morocco and before deciding to call the Azores home. Many who settled in the Azores claimed British citizenship initially, and

---

[4] António Ferreira de Serpa, "Os judeus na ilha de S. Miguel," *Instituto* (Coimbra) 61 (1914) and "Algumas habilitações de naturais da distrito da Horta para ministros e oficiais da inquisição," ibid., 62 (1915); Isaías da Rosa Pereira, "A inquisição nos Açores. Subsídios para a sua história," *Arquipélago*, Série Ciências Humanas, no. 1 (Janeiro, 1979) and no. 2 (Janeiro, 1980); António Maria Mendes, "Práticas e crenças Cripto Judaicas nos Açores (Achegas)," in *In Memoriam de Luis da Silva Ribeiro* (Angra do Heroísmo: Secretaria Regional da Educação e Cultura, 1982); José Olívio Mendes da Rocha," Súbsídios para o estudo das gentes de nação (cristãos-novos) nos Açores na 1ª metade do século XVII," *Boletim do Instituto Histórico da Ilha Terceira* 45, no. 1 (1987).

[5] Arquivo da Assembleia da República, secção I and II, cx. 41, no. 58 (2), # 77, cited in David Justino, *A formação do espaço económico nacional, Portugal 1810–1913* (Lisbon: Vega, 1989), 1:380.

only later chose to adopt Portuguese citizenship, among them Abraham Bensaúde and Fortunato Abecassis.[6]

The first arrival of Jews in the Azores occurred sometime between late 1818 and early 1819. (The only two registries noting the Jewish settlement on São Miguel give conflicting information.)

There is no doubt, nevertheless, that increasing public notice was being taken, as of the second half of 1820, of the immense profits being reaped in the Azores by itinerant Jewish merchants.[7] Their success began, even at this early date, to attract the envy and resentment of the established local merchants, who soon focused their energies on putting an end to this new source of competition.

The arrival of Jews of Moroccan ancestry took place in waves. In the earliest wave came Abraham Bensaúde, Solomon Buzaglo, Aaron Ben Ayon, Jacob Matana, Isaac Sentob, and Aaron Aflalo.[8] But even with this group the documentation is sketchy as to their lives, mainly constituting information on the residence of their families in town, court actions brought by them to collect debts, announcements in the local press of newly arrived goods, and, finally, their names on tombstones in the Jewish cemeteries (Fig. 1). However, in the majority of cases, we do not know the date of arrival in the islands or the date of death. The arrival of the Moroccan Jews is also noted because, in their capacity as itinerant vendors, they traveled extensively, often installing themselves far from the main towns. For the most part, though, they concentrated in Horta, Angra, and Ponta Delgada, the three largest and most developed towns of the Azores archipelago.

The first authoritative document attesting to the presence of Moroccan Jews in the islands, specifically in São Miguel, is dated August 19, 1820. This document, almost twelve pages long, is a response from the Ponta Delgada town hall to a request for information from the commercial judge regarding a mayoral decision not to renew the Jews' peddling licenses. In this document, the town hall defends its decision by completely refuting the validity of the complaints presented by the Jews, and secondly, by invoking laws dating from the

---

[6] Bensaúde, *A vida de José Bensaúde*, pp. 44–45 ("Abraão Bensaúde naturalizado português em 22/11/1830"). *Livro de Registo da Câmara da Horta* (BPAH), no. 17, fols. 53–53v ("Fortunato Abecassis é naturalizado português em 18/006/1832"); ibid., fols. 108v–109 ("Salomão Bensabat é naturalizado português em 15/09/1831," etc.).
[7] *Livro de Registos da Câmara de Ponta Delgada, 1816–1823* (BPAPD), fols. 175v, 176v.
[8] Ibid., fols. 182–182v.

sixteenth century and by affirmations both racist and xenophobic in character.[9]

The Jews argued that they were Moroccan subjects and that Portugal had signed a commercial treaty with Morocco which granted all Moroccans the same rights, duties, and benefits as Portuguese merchants. The Jews further objected to the requirement that they pay for the importation of textiles with farm products locally produced, arguing that this requirement was not imposed upon other merchants. Lastly, they complained that the town parliament had unjustly prohibited them from taking money out of the country when that money, a product of their business transactions, was of foreign origin.[10] The town parliament, as the supreme representative organ of local mercantile interests, was firm in its decision, invoking, as previously stated, both "moral" grounds and legal precedent.[11] The judge, however, not convinced of the validity of the town's case, determined that the licenses ought to have been granted, and had in fact been denied because the Moroccan Jews were able to sell their products at prices lower than either the indigenous merchants or other foreign businessmen.[12]

The response of the commercial judge reveals the extent to which the Jews were so quickly able to threaten the preexisting commercial order and pose strong competition for established local merchants. The rivalry in effect between the established merchants and the newly arrived merchants can also be viewed in the context of the rivalry between monopolistic practices and free trade.

The success of the Jewish merchants was mainly founded in their policy of quick stock turnover and, concomitantly, in their creating a series of financial and economic innovations in the insular economy. By infiltrating all of the island, selling at lower prices, and offering a variety of goods, the Jews contributed to the "reconfiguration of the market by generalizing new forces of competition in the sense of a greater liberalization of prices," as David Justino described it when he identified the same phenomenon (confrontation between established merchants and recently arrived merchants) in the province of Algarve in southern Portugal in the early 1820s.[13]

---

[9] Ibid., fols. 159v, 164v.
[10] Ibid.
[11] Ibid.
[12] Ibid., fols. 166–166v.
[13] Justino, *A Formaçao do espaco ecónomico nacional* 1:380.

On January 19, 1821, Moroccan Jews presented a new legal process to the town government, explaining why they had not met the requirements established in the first license they were issued (market prices had been ruinous, and beyond this, they still had not understood the laws of the country or the Portuguese language). They were now soliciting a renewal of the license so as to sell the remainder of their stock, recoup the money dispersed throughout the island, and then leave the islands for good.[14]

The downfall of Portugal's *ancien régime* and the inauguration of the constitutional monarchy in 1821 does not seem to have resolved the issue of whether the Jews would be permitted to remain in the islands. Although the "constitutional courts" proclaimed free trade and abolished the last vestiges of the Inquisition, prejudice against Jews did not disappear from the Azores. It is thus that we are able to understand the directive issued by the Angra town hall, dated August 4, 1831, barring "Jewish merchants" from continuing to sell their goods at retail (invoking the law of November 19, 1757).[15]

Revealing the same sentiment of animosity toward Jews is the decree of 1834 in the city of Ponta Delgada, prejudicial to the property of the Jews and, in turn, to the individuals themselves. Anti-Jewish agitators, however, were dissuaded from taking hostile action because, since many of the Jews in the islands had British nationality, there was concern that the British authorities would reciprocate with economic reprisals. Beyond this, what with the United Kingdom being the principal buyer of oranges from São Miguel, it seemed unwise to jeopardize the entire São Miguel economy.[16]

The difficulties experienced by the first Jewish merchants in the islands continued for several decades. Without a doubt, accusations of fraudulent currency transfers to pay for the importation of "luxuries" were the most common complaint against them, and evidence of this complaint is found in a variety of documents.[17]

Beginning in the 1850s, one notes a gradual integration of the

---

[14] Arquivo da Cámara Municipal de Ponta Delgada, *Livro de Registo de Ofícios, 1816–1823* (BPAPD), bk. 8, fols. 182–182v.

[15] ANTT, M.R., Maço 259–260, *Província dos Açores, Comarca de Angra*.

[16] Arquivo do Governo Civil de Ponta Delgada (BPAPD), *Copiador de Correspondência do . . . às Autoridades Eclesiásticas*, 1833–1842, bk. 141.

[17] Cf. *Livro de Registos da Câmara Municipal da Horta* (BPAH), no. 14, fols. 98 (oficio dirigido ao Provedor do Concelho, a 2 de Maio de 1835); *Consultas das Juntas Geraes dos districtos Administrativos do Reino e Ilhas Adjacentes do anno 1848* (Lisbon: Imprensa Nacional, 1849), Distrito da Horta, pp. 2–3 exige, nomeadamente: "Providências

Jewish community in the social fabric of the Azores. While mixed marriages may not have been common,[18] Jewish social ties to the community were numerous. For example, there is evidence of Jews contributing funds to aid victims of local catastrophes,[19] donating funds for the founding of the public library in Ponta Delgada,[20] becoming members of local recreational societies,[21] and finally, representing mercantile interests in the various chambers of commerce.[22]

The common use of clerks and servants of local origin who lived with their masters would also have contributed to the bonding of Jews to the island culture. In fact, we find wills in which deceased Jews bequeath some of their possessions to their servants,[23] and legal documents in which Jewish men acknowledge paternity of illegitimate children of non-Jewish women.[24]

In 1836, Abraham Bensaúde, with other Jewish merchants (Elias Bensaúde, Salom Buzaglo, Joséph Azulay, and Fortunato Abecassis), bought a building for the purpose of converting it into a synagogue (Figs. 2a, b, c). The Jewish community now had a meeting place and could begin to design a common strategy of integration into the Azorean world.[25]

---

prohibitivas sobre a saída de moeda que os hebreos arrebatam destas pobres ilhas inroduzindo o luxo (através) fazendas superfluas."

[18] We only know the example of Raquel Bensaúde, Abraham's daughter, who was married to José Maria do Couto Severim on Nov. 2, 1854, cited in Bensaúde, *A vida de José Bensaúde*, p. 63.

[19] "Nomeadamente para as vítimas indigentes do incêndio da Faja de Cima em 1841, contribuiram José Azulay, um anónimo hebreu, Elias, Abraao e Joaquim Bensaúde, Moisés Sabat, David Conquy, Salão e Abraão Buzaglo e Isaac Zafrany." Cf. *O Acoriano Oriental*, no. 331 (Aug. 21, 1841).

[20] "Contribuiram José Azulay (pai e filho), Salomão Bensaúde, Issac Zafrany, Abraão Bensaúde, Jacob Nahon e Joaquim Bensaúde." *O Acoriano Oriental*, nos. 384 and 385 (Aug. 27 and Sept. 8, 1842).

[21] O Clube Michaelense, fundado em 1857, contava entre os seus membros Abraão, Jacob, Salão e José Bensaúde, tal como mais tarde o Ateneu Comercial de Ponta Delgada terá como sócios José Bensaúde, Joaquim Sebag, Fortunato Absidid e Salomão Delmar.

[22] Nomeadamente na Associação Comercial de Ponta Delgada, criada em 1835. Contavam-se entre os seus 167 sócios, quinze de credo israelita. Cf. Arquivo da Câmara de Comércio de Ponta Delgada, *Livro de Correspondência expedida*, 1841–1857, fols. 5–6v.

[23] Arquivo das Finanças de Ponta Delgada, *Processo de Imposto Sucessório de Mery Sabat* (Testamento de 1898), fols. 1–5.

[24] Arquivo das Finanças de Ponta Delgada, *Processos Antigos*, vol. 1 (1842–53), Maço 58.

[25] *Liro de Notas de José Jacinto de Sousa Moniz* (BPAPD), bk. 502, no. 91, fols. 131v, 154.

Fig. 1. The Jewish cemetary on São Miguel.

2 a

Fig.2 a–c. The Ponta Delgada synagogue.

Fig. 2 b

Fig. 2 c

III

The arrival of Moroccan Jews, as previously stated, came in waves, beginning in 1818–19. The first nucleus settled on the island of São Miguel; but soon afterwards we find Jews living on Terceira, Faial, and Graciosa. Jewish merchants never set down roots in Santa Maria, São Jorge, Pico, Flores, and Corvo. The reasons they did not settle on these islands include the paucity of local markets, the weak purchasing power of the populace, the absence of adequate ports, the prevalence of local "bosses," and finally, the peripheral nature of these islands in relation to regional decision-making centers.

Notarial records are fundamental for the study of the settlement and manner of survival of the Jewish community in the Azores. By referring to these records, we note the following:

1. The Jews began by renting buildings for a period of three, six, or nine years, which rent was payable annually, in advance. The clauses in the rental contracts on the cleanliness and maintenance of the buildings are specified in great detail, always favoring the interests of the landlord. The buildings rented by the Jews were located on the main streets of the city, and were considered to be "highly, desirable multistory houses." These buildings, while residential, in almost also every case also had a ground-floor commercial enterprise.
2. The most prosperous merchants, beginning in the early 1830s, a little over ten years after their initial arrival on the island, began to buy their own homes. These homes were also located on the main streets of the city. In addition to this investment, some of them began to buy and rent small second homes outside the town.[26]

In this manner, the Jews who arrived in the Azores in the 1820s were, within only ten years, enjoying, if not wealth, at least a degree of financial ease.

The predominant characteristic of the Jews in the Azores in this

---

[26] *Livro de Notas de José Pacheco de Almeida* (BPAPD), bk. 491, no. 89, fols. 90–91: Compra de uma pequena propriedade agrícola por Abraão Bensaúde a 30 de Dezembro de 1831; *Livro de Notas de José Jacinto de Sousa Moniz*, bk. 513, no. 93, fols. 5, 7v, compra de um prédio urbano por Issac Zafrany a 13 de Dezembro de 1839, etc.

period was their constant mobility, as evidenced by frequent changes in residence, periodic voyages to other islands of the archipelago and beyond, and countless writings about their voyages. This characteristic mobility, the source of their ability to maintain strong ties to the exterior, distinguished the Jewish community from the local Azorean community, which was so closed in upon itself.

The voyages of the Jews, once settled in the Azores, were as often business-related as for matrimony, both means by which they were able to further cement their bond with the Azores.

The example of Abraham Bensaúde reflects the combination of commercial and matrimonial interests. Abraham Bensaúde was the brother of Elias, cousin of Solomon, brother-in-law of Isaac Zafrany and of Jacob Nahon, father-in-law of Fortunata Azulay (daughter of José Azulay), and grandfather of Luis Bytton. As a result, various commercial houses, through matrimony, became interrelated.[27]

IV

The registry books in the Ponta Delgada town hall indicate that the newly arrived Jews were dealers in domestic and foreign handicrafts and in second-hand clothes. The practice of selling at low prices, the common use of credit, and the broad geographic distribution of sales were the principal characteristics of the early Jewish merchants. These practices motivated, without doubt, the consumption of imported goods, thus favoring the Jewish go-betweens, who based their commerce on the rapid turnover of their stock, as previously mentioned.

The same registry books also show that Jewish merchants customarily stored their goods at home, since they were only allowed to be itinerant peddlers. The conflicts between Jewish peddlers and established local storekeepers reveal the extent to which the competition between them took its toll.

The first customs registry of products imported by a Jewish merchant was that of Solomon Buzaglo, who, on December 12, 1821, unloaded, through the Ponta Delgada customs, goods valued at more than 4,500 réis off the British ship *Sector*, coming from Gibraltar.[28]

---

[27] Cf. the genealogies presented by Alfredo Bensaúde in *A vida de José Bensáude*.
[28] Fundo Ernesto do Canto, *Livro de direitos reais de 15% cobrados na Alfândega de Ponta Delgada* (BPAPD), 1821, bk. 10, fols. 50v ff.

In the following years, new British imports were registered by various Jewish merchants, but the bulk of these imports occurred after 1824,[29] when the rivalry between Solomon Buzaglo, Abraham Bensaúde, and Aaron Mor José was at its peak. These three men owned important retail shops, selling such critical products as codfish, rice, and sugar, handmade goods, hardware (iron strips and arcs), simple goods made out of fabrics, and pots and pans. At the outset they were independent merchants, but as competition increased they began to organize commercial partnerships among themselves as well as with third parties. Solomon Buzaglo associated himself with Jacob Hassan (established in London), Abraham Bensaúde combined with Ricardo Halloran, and Aaron Mor José formed a number of partnerships of short duration with small Jewish merchants who began to arrive in the Azores in the 1820s. The creation and dissolution of these various mercantile partnerships are reported in the notarial records and the regional press throughout the 1830s. It was in this context that Solomon and Elias Bensaúde founded Solomon Bensaúde and Co., on December 5, 1835, later to become the House of Bensaúde and Co. Ltd.

The documentation supports several conclusions regarding the tendencies that more or less permanently characterized the Jewish community residing in the Azores archipelago since the beginning of the 1820s. More than anything else, the Jews in the islands dedicated themselves to commerce. Established as merchants either in their own names or working through others, they always favored this form of economic activity. Even when they diversified their investments, commerce continued to be their business of choice.

There is no record of Jewish families making a living from agriculture. The primary sector only constituted a form of investment for the Jews, never a means of economic survival.

Similarly, before the end of the 1860s the secondary sector benefited little from Jewish investment. The only example available in this area is that of Jacob Bensaúde and José Azulay, who owned a nail factory (indispensable for the crates in which oranges, the main export of the Azores in this period, were shipped).

However, after the construction of the seaport of Ponta Delgada, beginning in 1861, the main investors in the secondary and tertiary sectors were Jews, who dominated (almost monopolized, through the

---

[29] Ibid., 1824, Cota. 18, fols. 5v ff., 22v–23v, 34 ff.

House of Bensaúde) the principal sectors of the Azorean economy. This situation only came about in the latter half of the nineteenth century, when the number of Jewish families in the Azores had decreased drastically after the painful economic reform mandated by the ruinous crisis in the production of oranges. By this time, the number of Jewish families spread throughout the archipelago was less than a dozen, compared to the almost 200 families settled in the Azores in the mid-1850s. The Azores archipelago again became the home of some Jewish families during the Second World War, but when the war ended, these new families left the Azores for good, and today there are only three families of Jewish ancestry left: the Adrahis, the Bensaúdes, and the Delmars.

Returning to the golden age of the Moroccan Jews in the Azores, one finds a certain hierarchy of power and wealth within the Jewish community. On the island of São Miguel, the preeminent families were the Bensaúdes, the Buzaglos, and the Mor Josés; on the island of Terceira, the Bensabats and the Levis; and, lastly, on the island of Faial, the Bensaúde and the Sabat families.

From the beginning of a Jewish presence in the Azores, the Bensaúdes were the community's most powerful and respected family. Their supremacy was due, among other things, to the fact that three independent male Bensaúde heads of families (two brothers, Abraham and Elias, and one cousin, Solomon) generated three separate families and, more significantly, three independent commercial houses, although these enterprises, over time, became interconnected through the creation of mercantile partnerships.

From the outset, the Bensaúde commercial houses also benefited from the strategic location of their businesses on São Miguel and Faial, these islands being the commercial hubs of the archipelago. The Bensaúde business strategy was in the classic scheme of massive importation of manufactured goods from Portugal and Great Britain, distribution throughout São Miguel, and then redistribution to the central and eastern islands. The Bensaúde imports were paid for, initially, in cash, but quite early on this was substituted by exchanges in kind. Thus, the principal interest in redistributing merchandise to the other islands was not just to realize greater profits, but also to take merchandise that had been paid for in kind and resell it for cash. Goods were moved to Faial, in particular, because its internationally renowned port had made it the principal site of the archipelago's foreign-exchange reserves. The comings and goings of North American whaling ships in the seas of the archipelago, the seasonal work that Azoreans found on these ships, and the important ship-repair facilities operated by the American Dabney family all made Faial the Bensaúde family's principal source of foreign exchange. This concern over access to foreign exchange is the underlying explanation for the interest and care with which the Bensaúdes handled their Faial commercial enterprises.

Thus, from early on, the Bensaúde commercial house began to compensate its exports to the other islands with wine and local spirits (from the westernmost islands), and with cereals and vegetables (from the central islands and from Santa Maria). Whereas the wine and liquors were destined for local consumption on São Miguel, the cereals and vegetables, in contrast, were exported to Portugal and to the island of Madeira. Interestingly, the Moroccan Jews were not permitted to export oranges, the most lucrative Azorean export at the time (see *Table 2*), and it was with great difficulty that they were able to penetrate this market, reserved for the British and for local merchants. It was not until the 1830s that the first exports of citrus by Jewish merchants were registered, and then it was Solomon Bensaúde & Co. which was responsible for these exports. There are no other records of Jewish firms in the orange-exporting business.

Again using the example of the Bensaúdes, one discovers that though the Jews were denied a direct role in the orange-export business, they still found a way to benefit from it. The papers of the principal Azorean orange traders include numerous bills of exchange that went to the Bensaúde agent in London (William MacAndrew & Sons), who cashed them as payment for orders made by the Bensaúde houses in São Miguel and Faial. This scheme, though simplified, well reveals the business strategy of the principal Jewish merchants in the Azores.

Contrary to the myth that the Jews were usurious moneylenders, one can count on the fingers of one hand the number of times that private moneylending appears in the notarial records. By contrast, as noted in the local records, this activity was practiced by the two principal non-Jewish merchants of the time, Nicolau Maria Raposo do Amaral and Jacinto Inácio Rodrigues da Silveira.[30]

---

[30] Fernand Braudel, *La civilisation matérielle, Economie et Capitalisme XVe–XVIIe siècle* (Paris: Armand Colin, 1979), vol. 3, p. 29: "Le critère le plus simple, sinon le meilleur, le plus immédiatement accessible en tout cas, c'est la présence ou la non-

V

The early commercial successes of the Jews in the Azores were the result of their use of more aggressive business methods than were previously found in the islands. The aggressiveness of the newly arrived merchants manifested itself in all the commercial enterprises in which they were engaged. Beyond this, the rapid adaptation of the Moroccan Jews to the Azores in the nineteenth century was facilitated by their exercise of a different business culture, or ethos, related to the ancient intermingling of money and bills of exchange, their use of elaborate accounting systems, their lack of prejudices regarding the retail trade and peddling, the absence of any instinctive rejection of the inconvenience and unpredictability of long voyages and sales on credit, as well as an elaborate pattern of commercial and family interconnections. Nevertheless, their initial success did not survive, because the competition was great, and local merchants eventually adopted the innovative business practices that characterized and distinguished the Jews in the 1820s to 1830s.

Sombart's thesis, therefore, does not seem applicable to the commercial fabric of the Azores, because the examples of Jewish commercial failure in this era were manifestly greater than those of other national and foreign merchants residing in the archipelago.[31] The great upheaval in the Portuguese economy in the 1840s and 1850s caused the Jewish merchants irremediable harm. The documentation of bankruptcy decrees and commercial failures is vast. During this same period, one discovers innumerable examples of first-born and second-born sons of Jewish merchants emigrating to Brazil or to parts unknown.

In the business world of the nineteenth-century Azores, the examples of business failure exceed the number of successes. The survival down to the present day of the firms of Bensaúde & Co., Domingos Dias Machado, and Azevedos & Sucessores and Co., all of which were created in the first half of the nineteenth century, is the exception rather than the rule. Of the roughly 300 commercial houses

---

précense, en telle ou telle région, de colonies marchades étrangères. S'il tient le haut du pavé en une ville donnée, en un pays donné. Le marchand étranger signale, à lui seul, l'inferiorité de la ville ou du pays par rapport a l'economie dont il est le representant ou l'emissaire."

[31] Werner Sombart, *Le bourgeois* (Paris: Payot, 1966) and *The Jews and Modern Capitalism* (New Brunswick: Transaction Books, 1951).

present in a census of the island of São Miguel in the 1830s, only these three survive today. Of the three, only one is of Moroccan Jewish origin.

Up until the Portuguese nationalizations in 1975, the Bensaúde company was the largest holder of investments in the Azores, towering over other local businesses. However, following the revolution of 1974, Portugal nationalized the tobacco, banking, and securities industries. These nationalizations were a terrible blow to the Bensaúde company. Yet the Bensaúde "group" survives. The present-day Bensaúdes, owing their genealogy to Abraham and his son José, Elias and his sons Henry and Walter, and Solomon and his sons Abraham and Salom, pioneered the principal Azorean industries (tobacco, pineapple, alcohol, and sugar beets), banking (Banco Michalense), securities (Açoreana de Seguros), maritime and air transport (Empresa Insulana de navegação and Sociedade Açoriana de Transportes Aéreos), and tourism (Sociedade Terra Nostra). By the first half of the twentieth century, they were one of the leading companies in all of Portugal. Now, with the challenge of Portugal's integration into the European Community, new horizons are opening up to the Bensaúde group, allowing it to overcome the nefarious effects of the savage nationalizations of 1975.

Table 1. Jews in the Azores: 19th cent.

NAME	LOCALE
Abuderham	Graciosa
Absidid	São Miguel and Faial
Abohobot	São Miguel, Terceira
Abecassis	São Miguel, Terceira, Faial
Adida	Terceira
Adrahi	São Miguel
Aflalo	São Miguel
Albo	São Miguel
Allias	São Miguel
Alchuscera	Terceira
Anahory	São Miguel, Terceira
Aquinine	São Miguel
Asseric	Terceira
Athias	Terceira
Azancote	Terceira, Faial
Azulay	São Miguel
Baroch	Terceira
Benhamon	Terceira
Benarus	Faial, Terceira
Ben Ayon	São Miguel
Benevalide(?)	Terceira
Benchanuse	Terceira
Benchimol	São Miguel, Faial
Beneditto	São Miguel
Benithe	Terceira
Benjamin	Terceira
Ben Mohel	Terceira
Bensabat	São Miguel, Terceira, Faial
Bensadon	Terceira
Bensaton	Terceira
Bensaúde	São Miguel, Terceira, Faial
Benshoha	São Miguel
Bensimol	São Miguel
Bensliman	São Miguel
Benzaquim	Terceira
Bergel	Terceira
Bernaton	Terceira
Bitton	São Miguel
Bunguer	Terceira
Buzaglo	São Miguel
Caim	Terceira
Cohen	São Miguel, Terceira
Conquy	São Miguel, Terceira
Dande	Terceira
David	Terceira

Table 1 cont.:

NAME	LOCALE
Delmar	São Miguel, Terceira
Farrache	São Miguel, Terceira
Hanachach	Terceira
Hanon	Terceira
Hellazar	São Miguel, Terceira
Levi	Terceira
Lewinsohn	São Miguel
Locy	Terceira
Lousoy	São Miguel
Losquy	São Miguel
Matana	São Miguel
Mendes	Terceira
Miguellis	Terceira
Mor José	São Miguel
Nahon	São Miguel, Terceira
Nehmas or Namias	São Miguel, Terceira
Nathan	São Miguel, Terceira
Oulman	São Miguel, Terceira
Pinto	Faial
Rito	Faial
Sabat	Faial, São Miguel
Sabon	Terceira
Sarraf	São Miguel
Sayague	São Miguel, Faial
Sebag	São Miguel
Seeamin	(?)
Sentob	São Miguel
Seriqui	Terceira
Silva	São Miguel
Siriey	Terceira
Smo'h	Terceira
Strauss	São Miguel
Zafrany	Terceira
Zagori	Terceira

Table 2. Azorean orange exports: 19th cent. (in crates)

YEAR	SÃO MIGUEL	TERCEIRA	FAIAL
1833	23,585	22,983	6,462
1834	52,234	17,942	5,362
1835	38,664	18,326	12,611
1836	63,939	14,231	4,695
1837	35,944	15,156	16,385
1838	62,478	9,562	3,695
1839	76,064	17,269	10,233
1840	73,000	20,794	11,321
1841	84,385	14,914	10,158
1842	65,130	21,822	8,006
1843	91,500	12,775	3,998
1844	123,005	30,903	5,689
1845	108,140	26,944	3,482
1846	100,266	13,053	1,333
1847	161,077	27,773	1,567
1848	88,774	17,139	2,848
1849	197,669	30,253	3,374
1850	80,271	16,898	1,658
1851	185,137	37,552	4,174
1852	115,275	35,037	—
1853	134,453	16,909	4,300
1854	130,452	20,048	7,660
1855	128,586	25,162	6,850
1856	100,519	25,874	1,980
1857	215,519	22,343	6,820
1858	141,703	34,569	2,360
1859	261,772	19,101	10,200
1860	211,592	27,904	6,400
1861	198,350	29,090	10,700
1862	161,867	17,851	3,035
1863	225,559	25,407	12,836
1864	199,536	36,095	4,200
1865	207,104	22,045	12,865
1866	217,167	32,690	6,700
1867	154,409	23,461	10,800
1868	222,347	48,669	5,200
1869	232,494	26,731	10,600
1870	279,407	36,754	8,105
1871	—	35,000	7,920
1872	—	44,706	—

Source: A. Gil and Augusto Ribeiro, *Almanach Insulano orico e Literário para o ano de 1875*, 2nd year (Angra, 1874), pp. 61, 51, 103.

Note: All quantities have been converted to units of "big crates" by equating 3 "small crates" to 2 "big crates."

THE DISSOLUTION OF SEPHARDIC CULTURE IN BULGARIA

Guy H. Haskell

Both political independence and the ideological basis of nationalism which supported it were in many ways foreign imports to Bulgaria. The country had been shielded by Ottoman domination from the ideas and changes created by the Reformation, Renaissance, and Enlightenment. With the defeat of Turkey by the Russian army and the liberation of Bulgaria in 1878, an independent country reemerged in Europe which had not existed for five hundred years.

In a sense, Bulgaria had been left out of a series of developmental phases in European history, and this fact produced a nation, for a time at least, in many ways unique on the continent. The same may be said for Bulgaria's Jews. Although winds of change had been blowing from the West and Russia for decades, they were unable to effect a substantive reawakening of Jewish creative potential until after liberation. More than a century of conflict and cleavage produced by radical modern thought in Jewish communities throughout Europe left Bulgarian Jewry largely untouched and unmoved. The Jewish community of Bulgaria remained homogeneous and unremarkable. It could not boast the cacophony of irreconcilable beliefs and philosophies which both enlivened and threatened European Jewry as a whole. With few exceptions, Bulgaria had no Hasidim and Mitnagdim, no Masortiyim and Maskilim, no socialists and communists and Bundists and Zionists of a dozen persuasions. Bulgarian Jewry in the nineteenth century could boast of no great thinkers, scientists, philosophers, or rabbis; it could, however, boast of a united and well-organized community in control of its destiny and certain of its identity.

The Turnovo Constitution (1879) set down the principles for the governance of religious communities in the country. Bulgarian Jewry was to be governed by a democratically elected committee, headed by a chief rabbi who was, in effect, an employee of the state. According to Bulgarian law, the Jewish community was a voluntary organization of citizens of the Mosaic faith. Failure to pay tax to the organization, however, would result in the denial of various services: marriage, burial, circumcision, a place in the synagogue, and various certificates and permissions. Thus, although the Jewish community organization was never officially recognized by the government, it was in reality the representative power, and was not interfered with until the promulgation of anti-Jewish legislation during the Second World War.

The story of the democratization and consolidation of Bulgarian Jewry is the story of the development and eventual dominance of Zionism in Bulgaria. The total Zionization of the Jews of Bulgaria was the result of the development of an original, native philosophy which predated the emergence of Zionist ideology in the rest of Europe. As Vicki Tamir wrote, "No phenomenon in Bulgarian Jewish history represents a more organic, authentically Jewish development than the emergence and ascendancy of organized Zionism earlier than in any other European country."[1] In fact, organized Zionist activity appeared in Ruse as early as 1864.

On his way to Constantinople in 1896, Theodor Herzl was surprised by the multitude of Bulgarian Jews who greeted him enthusiastically in Sofia. "Even before Herzl's appearance, there were Zionist societies like Ezrat Akhim in Sofia, Carmel in Plovdiv (Philippopolis), and Dorshei Zion in Khaskovo. Bulgarian Jews founded the settlement of Hartuv in Erez Israel as early as 1896."[2]

One of the fascinating developments in the Zionization of the Bulgarian Jewish communities was the support received from the religious authorities. In contrast to the development of Zionism elsewhere in Europe, where it was often considered foreign and antithetical to Judaism, and where there were bitter struggles between religious and Zionist Jews, Bulgarian Jewry perceived no contradiction between Zionism and Judaism. In fact, they were viewed as complementary and integrated bases for Jewish existence. Marcus Ehrenpreis, who succeeded Gabriel Almosnino as chief rabbi, played an active role in preparing the Bulgarian delegation to the First Zionist Congress in Basel in 1897, which he also attended. The rabbis strongly supported the Zionist movement, and in effect vol-

---

[1] Vicki Tamir, *Bulgaria and Her Jews: The History of a Dubious Symbiosis* (New York: Sepher-Hermon Press, 1979), p. 143.
[2] Aharon Zwergbaum, s.v. "Zionism," *Encyclopaedia Judaica* (1972), vol. 16, col. 1108.

untarily subordinated themselves to the democratically elected committees despite their superior legal status in the eyes of the Bulgarian government.

The First National Congress of Bulgarian Jewry was held in 1900. Its most significant contribution was the transformation of synagogue congregations into organized communities. The twenty years between this First Congress and the Second in 1920 would see the total transformation of organized Jewish life in Bulgaria, and the end of the struggle for its soul. The Second Congress, with its Zionist majority, "proclaimed the religious and national solidarity of all Jewish inhabitants of the country, regardless of origin, language or citizenship."[3] This proclamation, its implementation and connotations, resulted from a unified ideology and purpose which pervaded all levels and sectors of Bulgarian Jewish society, and would give it the strength to weather the travails of the coming two decades, and the unity and determination to make the exodus to Israel and there succeed and prosper. There is perhaps no arena in which this conflict and transformation was more significant and symbolic than in the struggle for the destiny and souls of the children.

The liberation of Bulgaria from Turkish rule found education in the country in a dismal state. Even thirty years following liberation, 53 percent of Bulgarian men and 83 percent of Bulgarian women were still illiterate,[4] and over 80 percent of the population were peasants.[5] The Jewish population, involved in trade, concentrated in the cities, and following its education-oriented tradition, fared somewhat better, having the highest literacy rate of any group in the country.[6] Nevertheless, by Jewish standards its educational system was totally inadequate in both the religious and the secular fields. The traditional form of Sephardic school, the *meldar*, was incapable of adapting to the new conditions, and could not satisfy the needs of a community thirsting for education. The rapid secularization of Bulgarian Jewry would require a completely new approach to Jewish education. Ya'akov Nitsani described the decline of religion and religious education as follows:

---

[3] Ibid.

[4] William F. Russel, *Schools in Bulgaria* (New York: Teachers College, Columbia University, 1957), p. 33.

[5] L.A.D. Dellin, ed., *Bulgaria* (New York: Frederick A. Praeger, 1957), p. 229.

[6] Stoyan Omarchevsky, "The Jews in Bulgaria," *Reflex* 4 (May 1929): 49.

[The teachers in the meldar] taught Ladino writing and told the pupils
many legends from the commentaries and the Book of Yosippon and
other books and folk legends. They knew how to tell these stories with
great conviction in flowing Ladino . . . the synagogues and study houses
were empty. Only with difficulty could they scrape together a few quorums. Even on the Sabbath the number of worshippers wasn't large.
Only those celebrating a wedding, a birth or, God forbid, a funeral
would bring their families to the synagogue. The synagogues only saw
a crowd on the High Holidays . . . the tower of strength of the Jews
was destroyed.[7]

If the tower of religious strength of Bulgarian Jewry was destroyed,
there would quickly be attempts to rebuild it in a new mold. The
first, unsuccessful attempt was made by the Alliance Israélite Universelle, which sought to replace traditional piety with Francophile human-
ism sprinkled with a minimum of Judaica. The second, successful
attempt was based on the awakening of Jewish nationalism animated
by Zionism, with its bedrock of Hebrew schools and youth movements.

The light of day which shone on Bulgaria after liberation glar-
ingly exposed the backwardness and inadequacy of Jewish education.
The enlightened leadership of the community urgently sought ways
to improve the education of Jewish children and expose them to the
benefits of modern Western learning and science. At the same time,
the elimination of Ottoman obscurantism revealed to the Jews of the
West the inadequate level of education prevailing among the Jews
of the East. This led to the birth of the Alliance Israélite Universelle.[8]

The popularity of the Alliance schools led to an interesting development. Most Jews at the time of liberation had only a cursory
knowledge of Bulgarian. Ladino was their first language, followed
by Turkish and Greek, the languages of trade. With the founding
of the Alliance schools, however, many Jews learned French before
Bulgarian. By the turn of the century, however, Bulgarian had become
the first language of the Jewish youth, and, as pointed out by both
Jewish and Bulgarian informants, the Jews were known for their particularly fine, if accented, Bulgarian. Nevertheless, the multilingual
and cosmopolitan education of the Jewish children would continue
to differentiate them from the largely unilingual Bulgarians.

---

[7] Ya'akov Nitsani, "Kehilat Plovdiv: 'Em Ha-Tsiyonut Be-Bulgariyah" [The Jewish
community of Plovdiv: mother city of Zionism in Bulgaria], *Reshumot*, n.s. 5 (1953):
48–49.
    [8] Shlomo Swirsky, "The Oriental Jews in Israel: Why Many Tilted Toward
Begin," *Dissent*, Winter 1984, p. 78.

This was also a period of large-scale publishing activity in the
Jewish community, and numerous journals appeared in Ladino. An
example of the evolution of linguistic competence can be seen in the
development of the daily *Ha-Shofar*. It was originally published in
Ladino, but ceased publication during the First World War. When
it resumed in 1919 it was published half in Ladino and half in
Bulgarian. By 1924 it was published entirely in Bulgarian. In addition, there were a number of Hebrew periodicals.[9]

The impact of the Alliance and of French language and education on Bulgarian Jewry should not be underestimated. The Alliance's
disparagement of Ladino as being the crude dialect of the uneducated and its refusal to teach it in its schools was an important factor in the demise of the language as the mother tongue of Bulgaria's
Jews. French opened the doors to better jobs and the liberal professions, and allowed the Jews to enter the worlds of international commerce and diplomacy.[10] In many countries of the former Ottoman
Empire, however, it increased the alienation of the Jews from the
majority population. In addition to being Jewish, they were now considered francophile and part of the foreign elite. For many Jews this
double alienation, both from traditional Jewish culture and from the
indigenous society, led to a greater sense of anomie and the further
breakdown of Jewish communal cohesion. The Jews of Bulgaria,
however, consciously and forcefully halted this process in midstream.

The rejection and eventual expulsion of the Alliance Israélite Universelle from Bulgaria by the united Jewish communities was a most
significant event in postliberation Bulgarian-Jewish social history.
The decision to oust the Alliance was the result of two seemingly
contradictory trends, one toward independent Jewish nationalism,
the other toward greater identification with Bulgaria and Bulgarians.
Although the influence of Alliance education would be significant
and lasting, it was the expression of these two trends which would
prove paramount in understanding the nature of Bulgarian Jewish
identity in Israel following the mass emigration.

The generation which was raised in the Alliance schools soon
became their adversaries, accusing them of fostering one of the
greatest sins against Zionist ideology—assimilation. Preceding the
Hebraization of Jewish schools came the formation of numerous and

---

[9] Nitsani, "Kehilat Plovdiv," p. 33.
[10] Tracy K. Harris, "The Decline of Judeo Spanish," *International Journal of the
Sociology of Language* 37 (1982): 82–85, and Malinowski, p. 17.

powerful Zionist youth movements, such as the sports-oriented Maccabi, the leftist Shomer Ha-Tsa'ir, and the Revisionist Betar. They were perhaps the most influential institutions in Jewish education, and provided a social outlet and a center of activity for most Jewish children. Outside of school, the youth movement was the social center of Jewish youth until emigration. Avraham Ofek, a sculptor living in Jerusalem who left Bulgaria at age fourteen in 1949, described his childhood in the movement:

> I didn't have a life outside of it [the youth movement]. You understand, from morning until night only that. And in actuality, really in the end, when we had already packed our things and emigrated, there couldn't have been a more settled decision, more complete or more desired.[11]

By the turn of the century agitation for the replacement of French by Hebrew in the schools was intense. In 1906 Pazardzhik was the first community to elect a Zionist-controlled school board. In 1910 Sofia followed suit.

The universality of Hebrew instruction in Jewish schools in Bulgaria was a unique development outside Israel. At the same time, the first language of the home had become Bulgarian, and Bulgarian Jewry was thus linguistically divided by generations. The generation which had been educated under the *meldar* system spoke Ladino as its first language; the generation of the Alliance was gradually turning to Bulgarian, but also knew French; the generation of the Hebrew schools spoke Bulgarian first, knew Hebrew, and was acquainted with Ladino in varying degrees of competence. Of course, knowledge of these languages varied from town to town and from family to family, often depending on economic and educational level (Ladino being the language of the old and the poor) as well as the availability of Jewish schools. Interview data consistently demonstrate this basic generational differentiation. Lili Avrahami, secretary of the office of the Bulgarian old-age home in Rishon Le-Tsiyon, remembered her childhood in Pazardzhik: "In our house two languages were spoken, both Ladino and Bulgarian, because we had a grandmother at home."[12]

Zionism in Bulgaria became far more than an ideology to which a sector of the Jewish population adhered, as was the case in other

---

[11] Ofek, p. 11.
[12] Avrahami, p. 4.

European countries. Zionism became indistinguishable from Judaism, it became part of the way of life, tradition, *Weltanschauung*, culture, and even folklore of the Jews of Bulgaria. This was a synthesis of outstanding significance in the development of Bulgarian Jewish identity. Isidor Toliko, a retired postal clerk, stated this feeling clearly: "The Zionist idea was identified with our nationalism, that is, a Jew had to be a Zionist, and if one wasn't a Zionist then one was a traitor, one who is assimilated."[13]

The interview data show that the worldview of the young-adult generation of the mass immigration was centrally affected by life in the youth movements. At a developmental stage rife with rebellious tendencies, the youth movements offered the Jewish children a complete social life, purpose, and an adventurous vision of the future away from school and parents.

In Bulgaria Jewish nationalism drew inspiration and strength from Bulgarian nationalism, but remained true to itself. What we see, then, are two parallel national movements with many similarities, but which would by their very natures diverge in their ultimate fulfillment. The youth movements provide an illuminating and concrete example of this development.

The most widespread and popular of the Zionist youth movements was Maccabi, which was primarily a confederation of Jewish athletic clubs without affiliation to a particular Zionist party or ideology. The founding members of Maccabi walked on foot to attend the First Zionist Congress in Basel in 1897, and the first Maccabi club was founded the same year in Plovdiv.[14] Maccabi was formed after the model provided by Yunak, the Bulgarian athletic youth movement, which was like the Sokol organizations in other Slavic countries. It followed the Zionist ideologue Max Nordau's teachings about "Jews of Muscle" (*Yahadut Ha-Shririm*).[15]

> National feeling was turned into symbols, armbands, movement uniforms, etc. . . . [Maccabi's uniform] was in the colors of the Zionist flag: white shirt, blue pants, decorated with a ribbon in the Bulgarian

---

[13] Toliko, p. 6

[14] Albert Versano, ed., *Maccabi Bulgariyah* (Tel Aviv: Albert Kiyoso Circle, 1976), p. 8; see also Albert Romano, "Agudot 'Maccabi' Be-Bulgariyah" [The Maccabi Organizations in Bulgaria], in *Yahadut Bulgariyah*, eds. Albert Romano et al. ( ), pp. 319–356.

[15] Nitsani, "Kehilat Plovdiv," p. 37.

colors. The hat was also blue and white. Two flags fluttered over all
festivities and marches: the Zionist flag and the Bulgarian national
flag.[16]

Isidor Toliko expanded on this phenomenon:

> There was a Jewish organization, the Maccabi, and the Jews would
> lift the blue-and-white flag and march in the main cities, and the Bul-
> garians accepted that as normal. Something like that couldn't happen
> in Vienna or Berlin or Paris, not in St. Petersburg, not in Moscow . . .
> those are the roots of Zionism in Bulgaria.[17]

Ha-Shomer Ha-Tsa'ir ("The Young Guard") was founded in Bulgaria
in 1923 for a different, if related purpose. By that time Hebrew education had been firmly established, but it was now felt that in order
for the language to become truly revitalized a framework would have
to be developed for fostering it outside of the classroom. Ha-Shomer
Ha-Tsa'ir was intended to provide a vehicle for continuing Hebrew
education, and its first motto was, "Hebrew: at Home, in the Street,
in the Schools."[18]

In 1929 former Bulgarian Minister of Education Stoyan Omarchevsky wrote: "It is very doubtful whether there is so great a tolerance regarding education for minorities in any other country in
the world."[19] The development of an independent Jewish educational system could not have occurred without the tolerance and support of the national government. By 1927 there were nine schools
for children five to seven years of age, with sixteen teachers serving
525 pupils; twenty-two schools for children seven to ten years, with
seventy-one teachers serving 2,139 pupils; and seven schools for
children ten to fourteen, with forty-seven teachers and 674 pupils.[20]
As one can see from the numbers, there was a severe shortage of
teachers, especially for the younger grades. Dozens of teachers were
brought in from Palestine to fill this need, and the ties between the
Jewish communities in Bulgaria and Palestine were thereby strengthened. In addition, attempts were made to have the curriculum in

---

[16] Ibid., p. 38.
[17] Toliko, p. 21.
[18] Zvi Einfeld, "Batei Sefer Ha-'Ivriyim Be-Sofia" [Hebrew Schools in Sofia],
Ha-'Olam (London) 17, no. 4 (January 1929): 74; Nitsani, "Kehilat Plovdiv," p. 40.
[19] Omarchevsky, "Jews in Bulgaria," p. 50.
[20] Ibid., p. 51. For a complete set of statistics on the enrollments and budgets
of the Jewish schools in Bulgaria, see Romano et al., *Yahadut Bulgaria*, pp. 643–661.

the Bulgarian Jewish schools match that of the Yishuv.[21] Hours were lengthened, and the entire government curriculum was taught in Bulgarian, in addition to Hebrew studies; Hebrew language and grammar, Bible, and Jewish history were taught eight to ten hours a week.[22] Almost 80 percent of all Jewish children attended Jewish schools, for which most of the funding was collected from the community. The national and municipal governments also contributed to their upkeep, covering 13.3 percent of the costs.[23] Of all my informants, not one attended a state school where there was a Jewish school available.

The society and culture of the Jews of Bulgaria during the period between liberation and emigration were possessed of the usually incompatible qualities of stability and dynamism. Drastic changes occurred in the life of Bulgarian Jewry during that seventy-year span, yet the core of group identity and purpose remained intact and, in fact, was substantially strengthened and focused. This reinforcement took place both in the realm of both social organization and cultural development.

The year 1878 found in Bulgaria a Jewish community which was similar in many respects to the Sephardic communities which existed throughout the lands of the former Ottoman Empire. As Bulgaria was a backwater of the cultural life of Europe, Bulgarian Jewry was obscured from developments in the rest of the Jewish world. Ritual religious life had so declined that services had to be held in the homes of several of the notables, complete with ark and Torah scrolls. "... when religion and tradition began to weaken, these quorums ceased to function and the religious objects passed into the hands of the community."[24]

Both to Jews and Bulgarians, however, national identity was not a function of the degree of religious belief or practice. Just as a Turk who failed to practice the rites of Islam was no less a Turk, or a nonpracticing Bulgarian no less a Christian, so a nonpracticing Jew was no less a Jew. Thus, for the Jews of Bulgaria, the decline of faith did not automatically result in the assimilation so widespread in western Europe. Nevertheless, a gap was left with the atrophy of

---

[21] Einfeld, "Batei Sefer Ha-'Ivriyim Be-Sofia," p. 74.
[22] Nitsani, "Kehilat Plovdiv," p. 35.
[23] Haim Vital, "The Jews of Bulgaria: A Survey of Jewish Ruin," *Congress Bi-Weekly* 8, no. 37 (1911): 12.
[24] Nitsani, "Kehilat Plovdiv," p. 27.

religion which needed to be filled in order to ensure the vitality of the community. That gap was filled by the awakening of Jewish nationalism. This new ideology became as much a part of Jewish culture in Bulgaria as religion had been previously. Lili Avrahami felt that "the root of Jewish existence was because I was a Zionist and not because I was religious."[25] Isidor Toliko said: ". . . in the Jewish tradition I was completely ignorant, everything that I knew was from what the Zionist movement translated and published in Bulgarian."[26]

The dramatically swift eclipse of a language and culture was, naturally, most difficult for the older generation, the "grandmothers and grandfathers," to accept. In his novel *Farewell, Salonika*, Leon Sciaky captures this anguish in his description of the feelings of an old Jewish woman viewing the changes taking place:

> Life had changed enough about her. Had not the Jewish woman discarded the veil? Had not Western fashions come into the city to change the appearance of the younger generation? New schools had been opened and were now teaching in foreign tongues. The young people were forgetting the traditions of their fathers and made little of age-old customs. God preserve us. She did not want to live the day when Spanish, the language of our ancestors, would be forgotten.[27]

The rapid-fire advent of Westernization, Bulgarianization, and Zionization would obliterate the major institutions of traditional Sephardic culture. Emigration would deliver the knock-out punch.

The Zionist revolution in Bulgaria went beyond the politics of the community, beyond cooperative economic activities, and even beyond the education of the children. The ultimate goal of Zionist ideology is aliyah and the rebuilding of the Land of Israel. But preparations for that ultimate fulfillment required the metamorphosis of the Jewish community and its members. This metamorphosis was to change the "diaspora mentality" and fundamentally alter the nature of Jewish society and culture. Of all the nations of Europe, only in Bulgaria did reality come to resemble ideology.

The language, symbols, holidays, dances, songs, images, longings, and goals of the movement suffused the community, supplanted many

---

[25] Avrahami, p. 9.
[26] Toliko, p. 8.
[27] Leon Sciaky, *Farewell Salonika* (New York: Current Books, 1946), quoted by Benardete, p. 167.

of the Sephardic traditions withering from exposure to modernity, and filled some of the spiritual emptiness left by the fading of traditional religious observance and belief. Lili Avrahami described her perception of tradition and nationalism:

> Our concept of Judaism is only national, even though I know that my grandfather . . . sat in the synagogue every day and read books. I didn't even know what it was, what he was doing there. He studied. We knew that he studied, that he believed, but we didn't pay attention to it, we weren't interested in what he was studying and what he was doing. With us Judaism doesn't have any relationship to religion.[28]

All the major Jewish holidays were celebrated in the home, with the exception of Rosh Ha-Shanah and Yom Kippur, which were for many Jews the only days on which they would enter the synagogue.[29] Yet the most important Bulgarian Jewish holiday had little to do with Judaism. Yom Ha-Shekel ("Shekel Day") was celebrated on Lag Ba-Omer, a religious holiday. Although Yom Ha-Shekel has its roots in Jewish tradition and philanthropy, in Bulgaria it was a celebration originally intended to help raise money for the Jewish National Fund.[30]

The holiday took place around May 11, Saints Cyril and Methodius Day, which was the national celebration of the Bulgarian cultural renaissance, and was influenced significantly by it. Although originally intended merely as a way to help encourage donations to buy land for the Yishuv, Yom Ha-Shekel became a celebration of Jewish solidarity and independence, as well as an occasion to demonstrate solidarity with the Bulgarian state. Marches were held in every town with a Jewish community large enough to support a parade. The day was packed with assemblies, sporting events, picnics, speeches, ceremonies, and memorials.[31] The marches, uniforms, symbols, and significance of the day became such a central part of Jewish consciousness that its origins seemed almost irrelevant. It served as a handy vehicle for a community greatly in need of an occasion to congratulate itself and show off its accomplishments. In addition, the task of contributing to the building up of the Yishuv was for the Jews of Bulgaria more of a mitzvah than keeping kashrut or attending

---

[28] Avrahami, p. 7.
[29] Arditi, Yehudei Bulgariyah, pp. 44–48.
[30] Ibid., pp. 102–104.
[31] Nitsani, "Kehilat Plovdiv," p. 42.

synagogue. Lili Avrahami related this story from the period she
worked for the Department of Corrections in Lod:

> There was always an argument. The Poles [Jews from Poland in Israel]
> always told the Bulgarians: "You're gentiles. What do you have to do
> with Judaism, you don't know anything! You're gentiles!" So one
> [Bulgarian] Jew, a man who worked there as a prison guard, one day
> almost got into a fight. And I saw it. He said: "What are you talking
> about!? What? We aren't Jews? Do you have any idea what kind of
> holidays we had? We had Yom Ha-Shekel!" And they laughed: "What
> is Yom Ha Shekel?" "It's a day for the Jewish National Fund." "What
> is it?" "It's the big holiday!" So afterwards, and until today, they get
> together sometimes and say: "Oh, what great Jews you are, you
> have Yom Ha-Shekel!" But that's our holiday. Yom Ha-Shekel, that's
> our holiday.[32]

The task of determining the relative significance of the various cultural influences which shaped Jewish society in Bulgaria during this
period is not an easy one. Sephardic, Bulgarian, European, and
Zionist influences all converged to create something new and composite. Nevertheless, both the historical record and the interview data
point consistently to the fact that Zionist influence, as an ideology,
political power, cultural force, and prime shaper of worldview, was
the most compelling of all. This does not mean that the other elements of this cultural complex were weak or insignificant. It does
mean that, from the perspective of attitudes, value systems, and
actions, Zionist influence was by far the most significant.

By the 1930s the Jews comprised perhaps the most urbanized and
cosmopolitan sector of Bulgarian society. Yet at the same time that
Zionism was supplanting Judaism in the spiritual realm, it was developing its own symbols, traditional behavior, and expressive culture
in the folkloric area. Originally, my study was intended to examine
the ways in which Bulgarian culture was altered by Israeli culture.
It soon became evident that the real problem was how Sephardic
culture became altered and replaced by Zionist culture. In essence,
a significant portion of the acculturation process had taken place
before the Jews of Bulgaria boarded the boats that would take them
to Israel. The Sephardic roots of Bulgaria's Jews are still much in
evidence, but they are confined to specific areas of Bulgarian Jewish

---

[32] Avrahami, p. 19.

life. The Zionists provided a mythology, customs, songs, holidays, dances, a meaningful social context, and even the dreams of the youth. The area in which Sephardic culture remained unchallenged was in the kitchen.

The confluence of neo-Messianism and the beginning of Ottoman decline affected Jewish intellectual and communal life to such an extent that it never fully recovered, and the bright star of the Balkan Sephardim gradually faded into obscurity. The two centuries between Shabbetai Tsevi and the liberation of Bulgaria from Turkish rule saw the atrophy of Jewish life in the Balkans, especially in matters cultural and spiritual. The lively intellectual atmosphere which had thrived for centuries in Salonika and Constantinople became dull and mechanistic, and Bulgarian Jewry, always on the fringes, sank further into anonymity. By the end of the Ottoman period, Jewish education, which is the very core of Jewish national life, was described as follows:

> The Jews of the Ottoman Empire were permitted to do business throughout the empire, and dealt more with matters of substance than of spirit. That influenced the education of boys. The rabbi would enter a few youths into his seminary and teach reading and writing: I never heard from the elders of the community that they had studied Talmud. Most would be satisfied with learning prayers and the portion of the week with Ladino translation. Girls were prohibited from all study. Ignorance reigned supreme.[33]

This spiritual and educational decline created a vacuum in Jewish life which threatened the very existence of Balkan Jewry. The ways in which this vacuum was filled differed substantially among the various communities of the Ottoman Empire, depending on differences in environment and historical, economic, political, and social circumstance. It was the way in which Bulgarian Jewry filled this vacuum which differentiated it from the other Balkan Jewish communities, and set it on a unique course toward a surprising destiny. Whereas other communities continued to decay in the rubble of the Ottoman Empire, the Jews of Bulgaria chose to transform the very definition and course of Jewish existence, infusing it with a new meaning and purpose. At the precise moment in history when Bulgarian Jewish life could no longer draw the sustenance and strength vital to its

---

[33] Nitsani, "Kehilat Plovdiv," p. 30.

continuation from its traditional sources, it found new wellsprings of inspiration—it reinterpreted and adapted itself to the realities of a new and rapidly changing world. Traditional Judaism was replaced by Jewish cultural, social, and political nationalism as embodied in the Zionist movement, which became the creed of the Jews of Bulgaria; and they emerged from five centuries of Ottoman rule completely changed, strengthened and revitalized.

Dramatic changes occurred within Bulgarian Jewry during the fifty years following independence which transformed it in fundamental ways. Language, culture, politics, religion, worldview, and basic communal structure were all involved in this metamorphosis, and the changes in each of these areas influenced the changes in the others. Examining this in historical isolation might lead the researcher to conclude that a basic alteration of Jewish character had taken place during the later part of the nineteenth and the early twentieth centuries. In a sense, this observation would be accurate, for the observer in 1930 would meet a very different people from that which existed in 1880. But this conclusion would be only partially correct. The revolutionary changes which occurred within Bulgarian Jewry were not without roots and not the result of foreign influence alone. They were an outgrowth of a Bulgarian Jewish experience which was unique, and they represent the transformation of this experience to accommodate a new reality rather than a complete departure from it.

The dark clouds of fascism which were rolling across Europe in the 1930s found a Jewish community in Bulgaria unlike any other. Introverted and self-assured, yet involved in the life of the nation, Bulgarian Jewry had both unity and direction. Although anti-Semitism was relatively mild in the country, the Jews nevertheless embraced an ideology which viewed it as endemic, the only solution to which was Jewish territorial and national independence. In the 1930s Bulgarian Jewry held its fate firmly in its own hands, but not for long. Zionist predictions would soon come true in unimaginably hideous form.

A RITUAL BLOOD LIBEL
IN NORTHWESTERN GREECE

Annette B. Fromm

Oklahoma Museum of Natural History

One particularly impervious legend which has been revived periodically by non-Jews at the time of Passover is known as the ritual
murder, or blood, libel. "The blood libel began to spread in the
thirteenth century. It was charged that Jews killed Christian [or
Muslim] children to get blood for the baking of matsos."[1] The misguided conception that the Jews hated non-Jews and mankind in
general dates at least to the time of Josephus, who recorded the alle-
gation that Greeks were used for sacrifices in the Jerusalem Temple.
From the Middle Ages to the middle of the twentieth century, it led
to the torture, trial, and massacre of Jews. Most recently it was
revived and utilized in the rhetoric of the Nazis. Almost two hundred cases of the ritual blood libel exist in Jewish literature, including forty-two cases in the nineteenth century.

A report of a ritual murder accusation which occurred in 1919
in the Greek village of Pogoni, north of Ioannina, appears in the
correspondence sent to Paris from the Alliance Israélite Universelle
school in Ioannina,[2] but not in the literature about ritual blood libels.
This paper will introduce this account. It will also present a historical, ethnographic, and demographic overview of the Jews in northwestern Greece to place the account in several contexts. Finally, the
narrative motifs of the account will be discussed. The ritual blood
libel of Pogoni is yet one more account of the interethnic conflict
which has permeated the Jewish experience worldwide.

Jews have lived in Ioannina, the provincial capital of Epirus in
northwestern Greece, since at least the twelfth century. The Byzantine Golden Bulls (Chrysobulla) of Andronicus II, dated 1319 and

---

[1] Hayim Schauss, *The Jewish Festivals: History and Observance*, trans. Samuel Jaffe
(New York: Schocken Books, 1938), p. 58.
[2] N. Sarfati to Paris, 9 May 1919, Alliance Israélite Universelle Archives (hereafter cited as AIU), Grèce IV.E.56.

1321, are the earliest documentary evidence of a Jewish population in Ioannina. Between 1318 and 1319, Andronicus II united Ioannina and Epirus with the Byzantine Empire and reaffirmed the rights of Jews there. Charanis characterized his "attitude toward the Jews [as] that of absolute toleration."[3] The earlier Golden Bull is considered to be the most important document regarding Christian-Jewish relations in the Balkans because it asserted that Jews had equal rights with other citizens.[4]

A review of the sparse literature about the Jews of Ioannina, however, displays a lack of agreement as to the earliest dates of settlement because of the insufficiency of documentary evidence. Legend places the origins of the community somewhere between the fall of the Second Temple and the expulsion of the Jews from Jerusalem (70 c.e.) and the ninth century.[5]

The city of Ioannina gained its commercial and administrative significance in the Byzantine period. It was located on trade routes which connect the Adriatic to the Mediterranean and northwards into Albania, thus serving as a center for trade connections outside of Greece. Ioannina also served as a gathering point for raw materials from the surrounding countryside. Jews found a niche in both mercantile and manufacturing sectors of the society.

The Jewish population of Ioannina grew in the sixteenth century with the influx of Sephardic Jews expelled from Spain and Portugal as well as Jews from Italy, Sicily in particular.[6] Unlike what happened in most other Greek cities with Jewish populations, however, the Sephardic immigrants to Ioannina assimilated to the Greek vernacular and to the liturgical ritual of the local Jews. The persistence of the Greek language as vernacular is important not only in the shape of the traditional culture of the community, but also in the

---

[3] Peter Charanis, "The Jews in the Byzantine Empire under the First Palaeologi," *Speculum* 21 (1947): 76.

[4] Nikos A. Bees, "Übersicht über die Geschichte des Judentums von Janina (Epirus)," *Byzantinische-neugreichische Jahrbucher* 2 (1921): 164.

[5] D. Salamanka, *Touristikos Odegos Ioanninon* (Yiannina: n.p., 1959), p. 6. See also *Megale Ellenike Enkeklopaidia* (1926–34), s.v. "Ioannina"; B. Schreutman, "Communautés juives de Grèce," *Dispersion et Unité* 10 (1970): 217–227; *Encyclopaedia Judaica* (1972), s.v. "Ioannina."

[6] See Joseph Matsas, "Ta Onomata ton Evraion Sta Yiannina," in *Afieroma es ten Eperon. Eis mnemen Christon Soule 1892–1951* (Athens: n.p., 1955), pp. 95–102; Rae Dalven, "The Names of Jannina Jews," *Sephardic Scholar* 3 (1977–78): 9–23; *Megale Ellenike Enkyklopaidea*, loc. cit.

nature of the business and social relationships between Jews and non-Jews in Ioannina.

One of the most important periods during the era of Ottoman rule in Ioannina was the governorship of Ali Pasha Tepelini (1788–1820). It was a period marked by a complete change in circumstances for non-Muslims. All freedoms were rescinded. Rich Jews were heavily taxed and consequently emigrated primarily to Corfu, Zante, Tripolis, Larissa, Volos, and Salonika.[7] On the other hand, Ali Pasha was lenient with the poorer Jews. This attitude attracted impoverished Jews from other parts of Greece to Ioannina. The prevalent attitude maintains that this ambivalence helped to stabilize the Jewish population by discouraging unrest.[8]

The population of Ioannina in the period of Ali Pasha and earlier was made up of Greek Christians, Muslim Turks, Albanians, Arabs, Greek Jews, Europeans, and others. The population figures for the city as a whole and for its Jewish community vary greatly in existing records. The city's population was between 20,000 and 40,000, with the number of Jews somewhere between 1,200 and 2,000.[9]

Karpat's excellent analysis of Ottoman records cites 3,334 Jews there in 1883. He also found that sixteen Jews lived in the smaller town of Pogoni and 197 in Prevesa.[10] These were Jews from Ioannina who settled there for business purposes. Jewish peddlers from Ioannina had been trading with Paramithia since 1830; six Jewish families moved there in 1878 and remained until the Italian occupation.[11] Other villages in which Jewish merchants from Ioannina settled included Filiates, Vostina, Margariti, and Delvino.[12] These particular villages were chosen because their populations were predominantly Turkish and did not compete commercially with the Jews as in the

---

[7] Bees, "Übersicht über die Geschichte des Judentums von Janina," p. 169.

[8] Ibid.

[9] Thomas Smart Hughes, *Travels in Sicily, Greece, & Albania*, vol. 2 (London: J. Mawman, 1820); F.C.H.L. Pocqueville, *Voyages de la Grèce*, vol. 1, 2nd ed. (Paris: F. Didot, 1826–27); L.I. Vranousi, "Dyo Ypomnemata tou Psalida pros tou Kopodistra," *Epirotike Estia* 1 (1952): 463–470; William Leake, *Travels in Northern Greece*, vol. 4 (London: J. Rodwell, 1835).

[10] Kemal M. Karpat, "Ottoman Population Records and the Censuses, 1881/82–1883," *International Journal of Middle East Studies* 9 (1978): 272.

[11] Basil J. Krapsiti, "I Evrai tes Paramythias," *Chronika* 63 (1983): 5; see also N.T. Ziakou, *Fedouarchike Eperos & Despotato tes Ellados, Symmbole sta Neo Ellenismo* (Athens: n.p., 1974), p. 257.

[12] M. Lahana to Paris, 20 January 1910, AIU, Grèce IV.E.48.

Christian villages.[13] By the first decade of the twentieth century, between 3,000 and 4,000 Jews, or perhaps 600 to 700 Jewish families, lived in Ioannina. This was the peak of the Jewish community.

Under the Ottomans, interethnic relations among the plurality of
ethnic groups in Ioannina showed little evidence of extreme dissension or discrimination. All ethnic groups fit into prescribed categories
which were determined by both the economic and social controls.
Isolated incidents of anti-Semitism took place, most of them carried
out by individuals and not directed against the entire community.

Banditry was a common occurrence throughout the late Ottoman
period in Greece. Greek Christian and Jewish peddlers were frequently kidnapped while traveling. Reports of brigands attacking
Jewish merchants from Ioannina were given as early as 1881[14] and
as recently as 1942.[15] While Greek Christian merchants were also
stopped and robbed by brigands, in most cases they were neither
held for ransom nor injured. For example, in 1912, Moses Samuel
Moshe was returning from Prevesa in the company of Greek Christian merchants. The party was stopped, the Christians relieved of
their money and allowed to continue their journey. Moshe, however, was held for at least ten days before the bandits communi-
cated with his family.[16]

The anti-Jewish riots of 1872 stand out as an event of interethnic
interaction which was out of the ordinary and was also perpetrated
by an unbalanced individual. On Holy Saturday, April 15, 1872, a
Jewish youth trampled a tray of Christian holy breads in one of
the alleys of the city. The Greek Christian populace was incensed
and proceeded to attack Jewish homes. The Turkish governor and
the archbishop were called in to quell the disturbance. As a result, the
Jewish merchants were boycotted by the Christian population.[17] The
point is, however, that these riots along with the incidents of brig-
andage were isolated activities which did not reflect deep-rooted sen-
timents of anti-Semitism in northwestern Greece.

---

[13] Personal communication, J. Matsas, 18 June 1984.
[14] A. Decastro to Paris, 8/20 May 1881, AIU, Grèce I.C.12.
[15] Krapsiti, "I Evrai tes Paramythias," p. 6.
[16] M. Benveniste to Paris, 18 March 1912, AIU, Grèce III.37.
[17] *Encyclopaedia Judaica*, s.v. "Ioannina." See also Kons Fotopoulou, "Palies Yannio-
tikes Mikroisteries, mia dramatiki sunkrousi Christianon ki 'Evraion,'" *Epirotike Estia*
18 (1969): 203–204; Moïse Franco, *Essai sur l'histoire des Israélites de l'Empire Ottoman,
depuis les origines jusqu'à nos jours* (1897; reprint ed., Hildesheim: Georg Olms Verlag,
1973), p. 277.

Ioannina was liberated from the Ottomans at the end of the First Balkan War in 1913, six years before the ritual blood libel of Pogoni. The Jews hailed the Greeks as their liberators. No other Jewish community in Greece was as politically amenable with the Greeks. According to Bees, they had supported the idea of Greek nationhood while under Ottoman rule because they were aware that they would be able to maintain their freedom under the Greeks.[18] The Greek Christians, however, did not immediately accept the Jews as equals and fellow-citizens because of their open business dealings with the Ottomans before liberation. Thus, Jews began leaving the city to resettle in other cities in Greece, as well as in Jerusalem and the United States.

Several reasons led to the decline in population of the Jewish community of Ioannina after the liberation. Economic concerns were a primary reason. The new frontiers separating Greece from Albania and the customs tariffs imposed by the Greek government paralyzed business transactions which had previously occurred with no restrictions.[19] Furthermore, after the liberation Greek Christians entered actively into commercial activities. Their businesses slowly grew at the expense of the Jewish-owned businesses.[20] New laws instituted by the Greek government forbade the opening of stores on Sunday. Business opportunities for observant Jews became restricted as they lost not only Saturday but also Sunday business. The imposition of mandatory military service also led to the emigration of Jews from all over Greece, including Ioannina. Therefore, the Jewish community of Ioannina decreased by about one half, to 2,000, in the first two decades of the twentieth century.

This was the setting in which the ritual blood libel in Pogoni took place. The Jewish community of Ioannina remained vitally active, though it had declined in population. It supported two synagogues with smaller attached chapels, a number of *hevrot*, a Zionist organization, Alliance Israélite Universelle schools for both boys and girls, and other social and cultural organizations. Commerce in Ioannina remained primarily in the hands of the Jews, although there was a rising Greek Christian commercial class. Satellite Jewish communities in the surrounding villages as well as in Albania also carried out successful mercantile activities.

---

[18] Bees, "Übersicht über die Geschichte des Judentums von Janina," p. 177.
[19] M. Benveniste to Paris, 19 May 1913, AIU, Grèce III.E.37.
[20] Report to Paris, 6 December 1936, AIU, Grèce I.C.21.

Pogoni was a village of about 300 homes including five Jewish merchant families, about thirty people, from Ioannina. One of the ways in which the families retained contact with Ioannina was through the presence of "rabbis" who were sent to conduct religious services. Several untrained men were "appointed" to serve the merchants and their families living in neighboring villages. They traveled to the mountains to lead Sabbath and holiday services. This tactic may have relieved some men from their military obligations. In one case, however, two "rabbis" in Pogoniani were reported as impostors. One fled to Albania and then to Palestine. The other served a short jail term.[21]

In May of 1919, Mr. N. Sarfati, the director of the Alliance school in Ioannina, wrote that early on the eve of the feast of unleavened bread, two Muslim girls, no more than twelve years old, had gone to the fields to collect greens. Around noon, one returned home saying that she had lost sight of her companion. "The people of the village accused the Jews of having killed this child to use its blood in a ritual purpose."[22]

On the first night of Passover, the police and townspeople rudely interrupted the Jewish residents of the village, questioning them about the disappearance. Later in the evening they were again interrupted and questioned, causing them to pass the evening filled with terror. The next day, the corpse of the girl was found and Jews were no longer in suspicion of foul play. "One more time the idiotic libel of ritual murder troubled the Jewish Passover," concluded the writer.[23]

Joseph Matsas told me that he had heard about the incident from his uncle. The uncle was familiar with the villages of northern Epirus because he and another young Jewish man from Ioannina regularly led services on major holidays for the Jews living there. It was his understanding that the local police chief in Pogoni at the time of this incident was originally from the Peloponnese, the southern part of Greece. Anti-Semitism was held to be more pronounced there. Matsas's uncle thought that the libel had been initiated by the imported policeman.[24] This interpretation is plausible, as there appear to be no other reported cases of the blood libel or community-

---

[21] Personal communication, J. Matsas, 18 June 1984.
[22] N. Sarfati to Paris, 9 May 1919, AIU, Grèce IV.E.56.
[23] Ibid.
[24] Personal communication, J. Matsas, 18 June 1984.

sanctioned discriminatory acts against Jews in northwestern Greece.

The ritual blood libel narrative, in general, follows a standard pattern. "A person, most often a child, disappeared, or was found dead. Someone recalled that the deceased was seen in the vicinity of the Jewish quarter, or that the Jews were about to celebrate a holiday . . . accusations followed."[25] The earliest recorded incident of the libel occurred in 1144. It involved a four-year-old boy in Norwich, England, who was found dead on Good Friday. This account, therefore, involved the death of a child near to the time of the Jewish Passover. Another prevalent motif of the libel is that of torture and murder. This motif persisted at least through the thirteenth century. In the incident under study here, as in the Norwich case, a child disappeared outside of the village on the eve of Passover.

The written account of the ritual blood libel which was sent to the Paris office of the Alliance mentions several other motifs. Two girls, under the age of twelve, were involved. They went outside of the village proper to collect greens. Only one returned. The Jews were accused of responsibility for the disappearance. The next day, the corpse was found and the accusation dropped. After the motifs of the disappearance of the child and the proximity of Passover, one other motif is most important in this narrative. According to the writer, the presumed intent of the Jews in carrying out this deed was to drink the blood for some ritual purpose.

Blood and its use remains a critical motif which is found in many of the ritual libel narratives. In fact, the entire existence of this category of narratives is based upon the "accusation that the Jews . . . require and employ Christian blood for purposes which stand in close relation to the ritual."[26] According to the perpetrators of the libel, blood served a variety of purposes. The first written reference to the use of blood related that Jews decided by lot which congregation would distribute Christian blood to be' used for medicinal purposes.[27] We find this to be the outstanding belief in two thirteenth-century cases. Jews in Munich in 1286 were accused of simply drinking blood. In Fulda in 1235 they were alleged to have used blood for medicinal purposes. The belief that blood was a necessary ingredient in the unleavened bread around which the

---

[25] *Universal Jewish Encyclopedia* (1943), s.v. "Blood Accusation."

[26] *Jewish Encyclopedia* (1904), s.v. "Blood Accusation."

[27] Ibid.

celebration of Passover centered was not widely circulated until the seventeenth century.

Allegations by Christians of the use of blood by Jews for any purpose are both absurd and point to the relative ignorance of biblical scripture. Distinct and clear prohibitions of the consumption of blood are stated in several places in Leviticus and Deuteronomy. For example, "I will set My face against that soul that eateth blood" and "No soul of you shall eat blood" are verses found in Leviticus (17:10, 14). The validity of the charges made in the recurrent blood ritual libels was repeatedly denied by religious and civic leaders. Finally in 1928, in response to a libel in New York State, the Permanent Commission on Better Understanding Between Christians and Jews in America stated that "there is no custom, ceremony or ritual among Jews anywhere . . . and nothing in their traditions and literature, which calls for the use of human blood for any purpose."[28] Despite that publication, the ritual blood libel continued to appear in the twentieth century.

Another motif presented by Sarfati was that the Jews of Pogoni "had passed the night in deep terror." In an incident which occurred in the early 1930s in Cavalla, "A Jew was falsely charged with ritual murder. His innocence was proved, but not before Jewish-owned shops had been attacked and the entire Jewish population terrorized."[29]

Other motifs found in variants of the ritual blood libel narrative which do not appear in the Pogoni narrative include the presence of witnesses, the extraction of confessions through torture, and the fact that the false confessions do not refer to so-called rituals which the accusers believed the Jews enacted. The general pattern following the emergence of a blood ritual libel was the destruction of Jewish property and the massacre or the dispersion of a particular Jewish community. There is no evidence provided, however, that the small settlement of merchant families in Pogoni were in anyway harmed, beyond the imposition of mental stress. In fact, after the body of the missing child was found, "the thirty Jews of [Pogoni] could breathe again."[30]

---

[28] *Universal Jewish Encyclopedia*, loc. cit.
[29] Ibid., s.v. "Greece."
[30] N. Sarfati to Paris, 9 May 1919, AIU, Grèce IV.56.

The examination of the ritual blood libel which took place in Pogoni in 1919 serves several purposes. First of all, and most simply, this particular incidence of the recurrent belief is now entered into the scholarly record. Minor as it may seem, it is indeed yet another example of this libel which has affected Jewish communities worldwide. Secondly, it provides a bit more data about the life of Jews in northwestern Greece. Scholarly focus on Greek Jewry tends to emphasize the more prominent Judeo-Spanish-speaking Sephardic communities. The Greek-speaking Jews of Ioannina and their satellite merchant communities in the northwest are little documented. This discussion of the ritual blood libel of Pogoni illustrates the existence of documentation which refers to these communities and remains to be researched and pieced together with known resources. Finally, the exploration of the ritual blood libel of Pogoni shows that even in the twentieth century, this persistent narrative has remained alive in non-Jewish popular culture.

THE EUROPEANIZATION OF THE
SEPHARDIC COMMUNITY OF SALONIKA

YITZCHAK KEREM

Aristotle University
Thessaloniki, Greece

The purpose of this paper is to show how Europeanization infiltrated and influenced the Sephardic Jewish community of Salonika in the latter half of the nineteenth century. In order to analyze this point, the paper will describe the traditionalist state of Salonikan Jewry in the earlier part of the century, the sometimes obstructive attitude toward European ideas and ways on the part of many Salonikan Jews as well as the Ottoman authorities, and the role played by educational institutions, industrialization, and commerce. In particular, it will show who was affected by the Europeanizing transformation, how the community, with its Judeo-Spanish culture, was advanced by this development, the consequences for the spiritual condition of Salonikan Jewry, and what social classes were alienated from the process. Finally, the paper will treat the effects of Europeanization on social mobility, emigration, and interdenominational relations.

Over the centuries since the expulsion from Spain in 1492, Salonikan Jewry had lived as an autonomous Judeo-Spanish-speaking traditional community. The mass of the community's populace was uneducated and traditional. Rabbis constituted its literate, learned class. The masses received barely six years of rote didactic instruction in the overcrowded *hedarim* and *hevrot*, barely sufficing them to read the prayerbook and the Bible, learn about the Jewish holidays, and attain the rudiments of simple mathematics.[1] Most of the community was plagued by poverty and the rigorous conditions of everyday life.

In the era which we are considering, the second half of the nineteenth century, the religious leadership of Salonika's Jewish community comprised a rabbinic triumvirate headed by Chief Rabbi Shaul

---

[1] Baruch report, Alliance Israélite Universelle Archives (AIU), Paris. Grèce, VII.B.27. Aaron Jacques Baruch to President of AIU, Salonique, 21 Avril 1914.

Molho (1835–1854), who personally enforced a tightly centralized authority in the name of communal advancement. So far as he and his colleagues were concerned, there was no place for modern European ideas. Molho strictly enforced social and religious order, even issuing excommunication decrees when necessary, and as a result, all elements of the Jewish community still adhered to the traditional communal course and norms.[2] Congregational affiliation based on Judeo-Iberian points of origin and local traditions was a point of reference, and not Northern or Central European Christian-derived ideas, whether religious or secular in nature.

The Ottoman Tanzimat reforms, on paper, "guaranteed life, honor, and property" for all of the sultan's subjects, but in practice government officials were very slow in permitting freedom of speech and the press, or the right to public political expression.[3] The parliamentary democracy of Northern Europe was not a part of the reforms, but the Hatti-i Cherif of Gulhane, or Noble Rescript of the Rose Chamber, declared by Mustafa Reshid Pasha on November 3, 1839, was a step toward "Europeanization, administrative centralization, modernization of the state apparatus, and secularization."[4] The 1839 Tanzimat called for the abolition of tax-farming, the regularization of tax assessments, and, moreover, the application of the judicial process for all subjects irrespective of religion. "The Jews now had the right to testify in court against a Muslim, the torture of the accused was outlawed, property could not be confiscated, anyone causing harm against the Jews (or any other non-Muslims) would be punished, and the Jews now received civil rights parallel to those of the Muslims."[5] Elements of liberty and equality for all before the law, emanating from the French Revolution, had thus been accepted

---

[2] Paul Dumont, "La structure sociale de la communauté juive de Salonique à la fin du dix-neuvième siècle," *Revue Historique* 263, no. 2, pp. 351–393.

[3] A. Almaleh, *Letoldot Hayehudim Besalonik* (Jerusalem, 1924), p. 5.

[4] Esther Benbassa, *Un Grand Rabbin Sepharade en Politique, 1892–1923* (Paris: Presses du CNRS, 1990), p. 19.

[5] Yitzchak Kerem, "The Effects of the Enlightenment on the Jews of Salonika: Political or Socioeconomic Advancement?" Paper given at the Conference on the Jews of the Middle East in Modern Times, under the auspices of the Jewish Theological Seminary of America, Ta'ali—World Movement for a United Israel, and the Seminary of Judaic Studies, January 15, 1991 (in press). See also Carter V. Findley, "The Acid Test of Ottomanism: The Acceptance of Non-Muslims in the Late Ottoman Bureaucracy," in *Christians and Jews in the Ottoman Empire: The Functioning of a Plural Society*, eds. Benjamin Braude and Bernard Lewis, vol. 1 (New York: Holmes & Meier, 1982), pp. 339–368.

in principle, complemented by well-established elements set by the Dutch legal tradition.

The Jewish community of Salonika in this period was blessed with three social reformers, Saadi Betsalel Halevi Ashkenazi, Rabbi Juda Nehama, and Dr. Moïse Allatini. Each encountered obstacles among the Jewish community's conservative rabbinic and communal leaders and sometimes also among the Ottoman authorities. Ashkenazi belonged to a 300-year-old family of reformers and printing-house owners originating in Amsterdam. Born in 1820 in Salonika, in an age of ignorance and illiteracy, he risked his life as a co-founder of Salonika's first French-speaking school, twenty years before the Alliance Israélite Universelle school was founded in 1873.[6]

Nehama (1824–1899), a descendant of a rabbinic family and himself a nonpracticing rabbi, befriended the city's rabbinate and luckily met with no opposition from the organized Jewish community. However, he was plagued by the authorities. In order to counteract the vehement religious fanaticism and ignorance of the Jews in the Salonika region, he founded a printing house in 1859. Compelled to work clandestinely and illegally due to difficulties in acquiring a permit, he opened a school and in 1861 translated for his students, from English to Judeo-Spanish, the *Universal History* of Peter Parali. Soon afterward Governor Hifzi Pasha angrily broke into Nehama's printing establishment and put a ban on it, announcing that Nehama would be hung on a cross beneath the Arch of Galiere, his death to serve as a warning and an example for violators of the public order. Fortunately for Nehama, the English consul in Salonika brought the case to the attention of the United States minister in Istanbul, and as a result the sentence was rescinded.[7]

Dr. Moïse Allatini had to overcome great difficulties in his ultimately successful campaign to bring Europeanization to Salonika. The grandson and namesake of an Italian physician who had settled in Salonika, Allatini studied medicine in Italy. On his return to Salonika he opened a medical practice and soon became the Jewish community's wealthiest philanthropist and most active educational innovator. Allatini knew that he could not attack the city's archaic

---

[6] Sam Levy, "Mes Memoires," *Otsar Yehudei Sefarad* 8 (1965): 51, and Yitzchak Kerem, "Toldot Yehudei Saloniki Bemayot 19 ve 20," in *Pinkas Kehilot Yavan* (Jerusalem: Yad Vashem, 1992).

[7] M.D. Gaon, *Yehudei Hamizrah Be'eretz Yisrael* (Jerusalem, 1938), pp. 463–464.

Talmud Torah head-on, but he wanted to transform this bastion of traditionalism by introducing instruction in foreign languages, which he regarded as the essential tools for acquiring modern knowledge and Western culture. He refrained from attacking backward beliefs and superstitions, and instead quite ingeniously came up with the idea of adding an independent wing to the Talmud Torah that would serve as a model educational institution.[8]

In 1855 Allatini began his campaign to update the Salonika Jewish community with the ways of Northern Europe and its Jewish communities. Together with his brother-in-law, Solomon Fernandez, the Tuscan consul and a highly regarded and influential figure in government circles, he set out to bring this project to fruition. Toiling constantly to counter the objections of the rabbis and the religious establishment, he had to combat their laziness, personal interests, and passivity. Fortunately, he derived great personal power from his knowledge, his wealth, and his prestige throughout the country and in the eyes of Ottoman officials and foreign consuls. Allatini's focus on educational reform was deeply embedded in his daily agenda. The community objected to his establishing a school because they saw instruction in foreign languages as a dejudaizing force, but Allatini's persistence eventually paid off. While on a trip to Istanbul, he met with a member of the Rothschild family, who was impressed by the idea of a modern school in Salonika. On his return to France Rothschild agreed to recruit a Hebrew and French teacher, and reported affirmatively on Allatini's project to the Consistoire. He also helped Allatini to obtain a *firman* ordering the opening of a school that would provide instruction in French and Turkish. The *firman* required the communal leaders and rabbis to accept the establishment of the school. The document was read at a colorful ceremony in the presence of the Ottoman governor, the urban notables, and the rabbis. While the process of establishing the school had now begun in earnest, however, the communal opposition did not end.[9]

Nonetheless, in 1856 the school opened, and Baron Rothschild sent Dr. Albert Cohen to help Allatini organize it. In addition, the Consistoire sent Rabbi Joseph Lippmann from Strassbourg to teach and to serve as principal. Allatini also received assistance from Rabbis

---

[8] Joseph Nehama, *Histoire des Israélites de Salonique*, vols. 6 and 7 (Thessaloniki: Communauté Israélite de Thessalonique, 1978), pp. 658–663.

[9] Kerem, "Effects of Enlightenment on the Jews of Salonika."

Juda Nehama and Avraham Gattegno, secretary of the rabbinate,
who in 1858 jointly founded the Hesed Olam philanthropic society
with the specific purpose of backing Allatini's project and aiding the
city's poor, orphans, and widows. In order to overcome objections
by the rabbinate, Allatini allocated funds from Hesed Olam's treasury to charitable institutions. Although Chief Rabbi Asher Covo did
not especially treasure Allatini, he consented to Allatini's communal
reorganization plan and invited fifty of the community's notables to
assess it. The plan, under the direction of twenty-four delegates,
determined that a tax of 10 piasters would be imposed on every
item of merchandise coming into or leaving Salonika that in any
way passed through Jewish hands.

In its first year, Lippmann, a modern rabbi, succeeded in running
the school fairly well. Following the devastating fires of 1856 and
1857, however, the community ran into financial difficulties.[10] After
Hesed Haolam was founded, the communal council assisted the
school financially. In 1861, after four years of service to the Salonikan
Jewish community, Lippmann returned to France. He left because of
interference from fanatical religious elements that opposed the introduction of European ideas and accused him of "spreading infested
ideas that could choke any religious feeling in the hearts of the
Jews."[11] Denounced as an agent of dejudaization, Lippmann was condemned as a "Franco," as if he were a stranger. Due to the difficult economic situation, he had not received his regular salary. Many
Jewish merchants were unable to pay the taxes demanded by the
Ottoman government. As the treasury of Hesed Olam dwindled, what
money it had was allocated exclusively for the poor and the needy.
Once Lippmann was gone the school closed its doors. Lippmann
had, however, succeeded in training a number of students to work
as accountants and scribes in the city's economic institutions. He
had also provided a few diligent students with a mastery of Turkish
and French. The knowledge and education they attained enabled
them, on the one hand, to improve relations with the Ottoman Army
and, on the other, to comfortably correspond with European merchants. Until then Jewish merchants had been dependent on publics

---

[10] See *L'Univers Israélite* 11, no. 12 (August 1856): 567; *Jewish Chronicle and Hebrew
Observer* 13, no. 88 (August 22, 5616–1866): 701; and David Recanati, ed., *Zichron
Saloniki, Gedulata Vehurvata shel Yerushalayim Debalkan*, vol. 1 (Tel Aviv: Havaad Lehotsaat
Sefer Kehilat Saloniki, 1972), p. 122.

[11] Baruch report, AIU.

scribe to fulfill that function. One of Lippmann's students, Haim Shalem, together with his brother Solomon, reestablished the school in 1866, and it continued to function until 1904.

After Lippmann's departure, Allatini abandoned any further attempt to revitalize the Talmud Torah. In 1862, with his encouragement, his brother-in-law Solomon Fernandez founded a school that was subsidized by the Italian government. The instruction was in Italian, and the principal was an Italian teacher named Frederico Filardar. Rabbi David Boton was responsible for Hebrew and religious instruction.[12]

In his study of Jewish schools in the Ottoman Empire, Aron Rodrigue placed the above experiment in the framework of a general trend in which new schools offering European languages were established in Sephardic communities throughout the region. He offered this description of Europeanization in the Ottoman Empire:

> The principal impetus for the increasingly Western orientation of the leadership of Turkish Jewry was the growing European economic and financial penetration of the Ottoman Empire. The lucrative consequences of the acquisition of the knowledge of European schools and languages were all too apparent to a community suffering from the social ills of economic backwardness. It was this necessity that created the base of support for modern schooling.[13]

The establishment of the Alliance Israélite Universelle's school system was a landmark in this process. After Allatini failed to reform the Talmud Torah, he and Solomon Fernandez joined forces to establish an AIU school. As in the earlier project, Allatini's influence in government circles was an asset. Rabbis Juda Nehama and Abraham Gattegno continued their financial and spiritual assistance. A local AIU committee was organized in 1862, but because of financial difficulties was unable to found a school.

Sometime in this period Chief Rabbi Samuel Nahmias died and Chief Rabbi Covo was left as the sole leader of the rabbinic triumvirate. The feuds between the Nahmias and Covo rabbinical clans finally ceased, and in consequence communal action under the auspices of the chief rabbi took on a more decisive course.[14]

In 1864 the president of the Alliance Israélite Universelle, Adolphe

---

[12] Kerem, "Effects of Enlightenment on the Jews of Salonika."

[13] Aron Rodrigue, *French Jews, Turkish Jews: The Alliance Israélite Universelle and the Politics of Jewish Schooling in Turkey, 1860–1925* (Bloomington: Indiana University Press, 1990), p. 45.

[14] Dumont, "La structure social de la communauté de Salonique," p. 369.

Crémieux, invited Chief Rabbi Covo to accept the concept of establishing a new school.[15] The AIU promised that the new institution would rest on strong foundations thanks to funding by the French government. The rabbi gave his consent, moved by the notion of the spread of knowledge and the popularization of languages. Similarly, in 1873, Covo supported the school's establishment. Rabbi Nehama's role in the founding of the school played an important part in inducing the chief rabbi to take a positive stance toward the project. Allatini overcame the financial difficulties and convinced the wealthy members of the community, many of whom were foreign subjects and felt no obligation to fund communal activities, to help finance the establishment of an AIU school.

The cornerstone of European French-oriented education in Salonika was laid on August 20, 1873, when the AIU boys' school finally opened with 200 pupils.[16] The school was to have been a joint effort of the Alliance and the Regie Scola Italiana, but in the end, although the latter closed its school, it refused to merge. In any case, the students from the Italian school, overwhelmingly Jewish but including three Catholics, were among the first youngsters to enroll in the AIU school. A continuation of the Italianization process was seen with the founding of the AIU girls' school in 1874, when sponsors of the project in Livorno sent two teachers and the instruction was in italian.

In 1875, when there were already 210 male students and 150 females studying under AIU auspices, Baron Hirsch visited Salonika and promised to donate a sum for the construction of a school building equal to whatever the Jewish community could raise on its own. Allatini swung into action, collecting contributions from several wealthy local Jews as well as from the well-known Jewish philanthropists Reuvain Sassoon, Frederick David Mocatta, and the Comte de Camondo, and even from two Turkish non-Jews. Baron Hirsch kept his promise, and in 1876 the building was dedicated in a ceremony attended by Chief Rabbi Abraham Gattegno, who had succeeded Covo in 1874.[17]

In 1877 the Alliance began an apprenticeship program, thus adding another dimension of vocational training. To complement the new generation of Jewish students who would become Europeanized

---

[15] AIU, III.B.20, Salonique.
[16] *Bulletin de l'Alliance Israélite Universelle*, 2e semestre, 1873, p. 30.
[17] Kerem, "Effects of Enlightenment on the Jews of Salonika."

merchants, physicians, dentists, lawyers, pharmacists, journalists, and engineers, the apprenticeship students prepared to become shoe-makers, carpenters, locksmiths, and tailors. In 1878 sixteen Jewish youths entered the program, but by 1898 the AIU apprenticeship program counted a total of 116 students, including eight young men studying chairmaking, seven shoemakers, twenty-two blacksmiths, thirty carpenters, six typographers, four tailors, and seven stove re-pairers.[18] Moreover, sixty young women had completed apprentice-ship training as lacemakers, and this training created a revolution, in and of itself, for them and for the role of women in the community. Women now began to have careers and to work, although still in a limited capacity, in fields other than the traditional ones of domes-tic servant, washerwoman, laundress, and governess. The AIU also provided avenues for them in embroidery, sewing, and ironing, and in 1887 opened a workshop for young girls.[19]

The next challenge in the pedagogic sphere was to revitalize the Talmud Torah. In 1877, David Morpurgo, an agent for the North British Insurance Company and president of the local AIU com-mittee, published an article in the *AIU Bulletin* condemning the dete-rioration of the Talmud Torah, its neglect and contamination. The article attracted strong feedback and almost led to a scandal.[20]

The vigorous Dr. Allatini did not hesitate to act and received the help of Nehama and Fernandez. Nonetheless, the older generation, sunk in their Old World outlook and objecting to change, continued to be an obstacle. Allatini formed a reorganization committee consist-ing of Yisrael Danon, former local AIU principal; Avramino Varius, Italian-language teacher; Haim Shalem, private school principal and former student of Rabbi Lippmann; and Rabbi Juda Nehama, who was quite learned and very aware of modern developments in the European Jewish world.[21]

In 1878, in the name of the AIU local committee, Allatini promised

---

[18] Dumont, "La structure social de la communauté de Salonique," pp. 359–363.

[19] Paul Dumont, "Jewish Communities in Turkey during the Last Decades of the Nineteenth Century in the Lights of the Archives of the Alliance Israélite Universelle," in *Christians and Jews in the Ottoman Empire*, ed. Braude and Lewis, pp. 209–242. By 1908 the AIU girls' apprenticeship program had 350 students in Salonika.

[20] David Morpurgo, *Bulletin de l'Alliance Israélite Universelle*, 1877; and Nehama, *Histoire des Israélites de Salonique*, pp. 644–645.

[21] Nehama, *Histoire des Israélites de Salonique*, p. 645; *Saloniki, Ir Ve'em Beyisrael* (Tel Aviv: Hamahon Leheker Yahadut Saloniki, 1967), p. 62; Recanati, *Zichron Saloniki*, p. 136.

to allocate 1,000 francs annually to the Talmud Torah, which at that time had a student body of 1,500, on condition that a new director with a modern outlook would be appointed, and the curriculum revised. An additional 300 lira were allocated from the communal revenues of the meat *gabelle*. As a result, the Talmud Torah's students no longer had to sit on a wet floor, but could enjoy sitting on benches in a remodeled building. Chief Rabbi Arditti presided over the ceremony concluding the remodeling.

In order to provide enough space to overcome the Talmud Torah's overcrowding, a new lot was purchased for future construction. In the meantime several teachers were fired, and more experienced ones took their places. In 1880, Dr. Moshe Yaakov Ottolenghi, the Talmud Torah principal of Livorno, was brought to Salonika to supervise and run the Talmud Torah. He belonged to the school of ultra-religious enlightened Italian intellectuals, and during the two decades until his death in 1900, he transformed one of Salonika's last bastions of religious traditionalism into a school that was modern and Europeanized, but still religion-oriented.[22]

In 1884 the cornerstone was laid for the construction of the two buildings that would house the Talmud Torah.[23] In his remarks, Rabbi Yaakov Covo, the committee chairman, acknowledged the generosity of the deceased Dr. Allatini and Gvir Shaul Modiano. Without their financial help, he said, none of this would have been possible. In 1885, two two-story buildings were dedicated, and the institution was on its way to help elevate and educate coming generations to the ways of Europe.

In general in the Ottoman Empire, modernization and secularization of the state became pronounced through changes in the general education system in the latter half of the nineteenth century. Although the Ottoman state's educational apparatus lagged behind and was highly unsatisfactory, one of its impressive achievements was the founding, in the latter quarter of the nineteenth century, of a string of higher schools for professional training. Among these were the military schools, the school for management, and several high schools, the foremost being the Lycée Galata Sarai.[24]

---

[22] Kerem, "Effects of the Enlightenment on the Jews of Salonika."

[23] L. Danon to President of AIU, August 13, 19, and 22, 1884, September 23, 1884, October 2 and 24, 1884. AIU, Grèce, VII.B.27, Salonique.

[24] Haim Gerber and Yaakov Barnai, *Yehudei Izmir Bemeah Hatsha-Esray: Teudot Turkiyot Mibeit-Hadin Hasharai*, Sidrat Mekorot 1 (Jerusalem: Misgav Yerushalayim, Hamahon Leheker Moreshet Yahadut Sefarad Vehamirah, 1985), p. 6.

The schools had an impact on the elite of the Istanbul Jewish community, and to a lesser extent on Salonika's Jewish community. In 1877 Salonikan Jewish students were already studying medicine and pharmacy in these schools.[25]

Industrialization drew Salonika's Jews closer to Europe and Europeanizing forces. Jews were in the forefront of the city's industrial revolution. The spinning mill founded by the Saias family in the latter part of the eighteenth century was the largest and most sophisticated of its kind in the city. In 1858, Dr. Allatini established a large flour mill. Several years later he opened a beer brewery, and then followed by establishing brick and tile factories. In 1883 the Allatini Ceramics factory was founded. Moreover, by 1875 the Company for Silk Spinning was well established, and there were other Jewish-owned spinning mills belonging to Torres and Mizrahi, Shabetai Hasid, and Sidis. In 1898 Yosef Modiano established a factory for women's scarves and silk spinning.[26]

Not only were Jews the first to import fabrics and other items from Europe, but they also imported industrial equipment, such as steam engines, pumps, and motors. The Fratelli Tiano were machinery importers. In 1868, Joseph Covo opened a printing-supply firm.[27]

Juda Nehama was instrumental in Salonika's industrial advancement. He conceived, initiated, and brought to the city a gas company, a petrol company, a water company, and the electric railroad. In the words of M.D. Gaon, "For all of these he was an active and loyal agent."[28] In September 1887 he received the concession for the production and distribution of illuminating gas. In November 1883 he obtained the concession for installing a water-distribution system. Afterward he passed the concessions on to European companies.

The Jews of Salonika, like the other inhabitants of the Ottoman Empire, benefited from the improvements in communications that marked the nineteenth century. During the reign of Abdul-Hamid II (1876–1909), as part of the changes in urban life in the main cities of the empire, Istanbul, Izmir, Edirne, and Salonika, "the myriad of post offices, telegraph lines, and steamships provided internal as well as external communication."[29]

---

[25] AIU, Grèce, Salonique, IV.B.21.
[26] Kerem, "Effects of the Enlightenment on the Jews of Salonika."
[27] Ibid.
[28] Moshe David Gaon, *Yehudei Hamizrach Be'eretz Yisrael*, pt. 2 (Jerusalem, 1938), pp. 463–464.
[29] Stanford J. Shaw and Ezel Kural Shaw, *The History of the Ottoman Empire and*

The Jews of Salonika prospered from the improved transportation in the city and in the region. In 1871 Salonika was connected to Mitrovitsa by railroad. The line was extended to Belgrade in 1880, and by 1888, dubbed the "Orient Express," it reached Vienna.[30] Salonika was connected by train to Monastir in 1893 and to Istanbul in 1895. In 1891 horsedrawn tram service was inaugurated in the city. In 1899 France began to build a secure multi-pier port for large ships to dock in Salonika. Jews were noted for being very active in loading and unloading, as shipping agents, and in the area of insurance.

Other technological improvements helped the city and its residents, with the Jews naturally benefiting, since they were a majority of the population in this period.[31] In 1898 a Belgian company provided the city's residents with a supply of live running water coming from the Hortiachi Mountains. In 1899 electricity was installed in Salonika. Most of the projects of this nature were initiated by European companies, with Salonikan Jews participating as investors and stockholders.[32]

The increase in commercial activity led to an increase in European influence. Salonikan Jews, employed as maritime agents, insurance agents, or even tobacco agents for large European firms, introduced numerous Europeanizing lifestyle changes. Economic affluence and changes in taste and style brought changes in dress. In *Michtevei Dodim Miyayin*, Rabbi Yehuda (Juda) Nehama remarked how, with the advent of the infiltration of European fashions among the Jews of the city, "more than sixty boys changed their dress and removed the *haduim* (?) from their wives and will dress them in charming European clothes."[33] Large commercial houses like the Allatinis and Fernandez formed branches in European commercial centers and became well integrated and exposed to European business techniques and ways.

Modern Turkey, vol. 2, *Reform, Revolution and Republic: The Rise of Modern Turkey, 1808–1975* (Cambridge: Cambridge University Press, 1978), p. 241.

[30] *Salonika, Ir Ve'em Beyisrael*, pp. 3, 20.

[31] The subject of the Jewish population and its percentage of the general population is a vast one. In 1862 the *Jewish Chronicle* reported that of Salonika's 70,000 inhabitants, 38,000 were Jews (6,200 families). In 1880 Michael Hatzi Ioannou noted that there were 15,000 Greek Orthodox, 20,000 Turkish Moslems, and 50,000 Jews. See "The Jews of Salonika," *Jewish Chronicle*, no. 371 (January 24, 1862), p. 7; and N.K. Moutsopoulos, *Thessaloniki, 1900–1917* (Thessaloniki: M. Molho, 1980), pp. 24–25.

[32] Recanati, *Zichron Saloniki*, p. 156.

[33] Juda Nehama, *Michtevei Dodim Miyayin*, bk. 1 (Salonika, 1893), p. 127.

Jews controlled the commerce of the city, and even administered the railroads. Jews also began an active upsurge in banking and gained great prominence in the field. The director general of the Bank de Salonique, A. Ben-Nahmias, was a Jew. The city had several Jewish banks—Bank Shaul Amar, Bank Moseri, Bank Benveniste; and Jews were a majority of the employees of the Bank Commercial, the Ottoman government bank, which actually was owned by a French company.[34]

The Alliance school system, through its educational program, and the accompanying advances in industry, communications, and commerce, produced a new Jew in Salonika—one much closer to the ways of Europe, and speaking either French or Italian. A new petit-bourgeois class developed, but despite AIU scholarship assistance and a wide range of communal philanthropic organizations, most of the city's Jewish populace remained poor, and many could not benefit from an AIU education. The numerous children who attended the overcrowded and old-style Fusion schools and *hedarim* were still ignorant and economically backward.[35] Unable to better themselves by becoming lawyers, doctors, and merchants, they remained fishermen, peddlers, stevedores, and tobacco workers.[36] The children studied in dilapidated conditions and lived in the poor neighborhoods surrounding Salonika, such as Regie Vardar, Kalamaria, 151, and Toumba.

Nonetheless, the formerly closed traditional religious culture of Salonikan Jewry was now open to secular European forces, thanks to the Alliance Israélite Universelle. Although much of Salonikan Jewry remained religiously observant in varying degrees, the secularization process caused a transformation of printed material from Ladino, used in Bible translations and rabbinical exegesis, to a modernized Judeo-Spanish appearing in novels, translated classics, and the press.

In 1864 Nehama published Salonika's first Judeo-Spanish newspaper, *El Lunar*. Although it was more of an encyclopedic journal, containing information about science, translations from noted rabbinic works, stories, historical pieces, folkloric tales, and articles on business matters, it served, during its short life-span of six issues, as a format and introduction for future Judeo-Spanish newspapers that

---

[34] Kerem, "Toldot Yehudei Saloniki."
[35] Baruch report, AIU, VII.B.27.
[36] Dumont, "La structure sociale," p. 379.

would report the news of the region and the world to Salonika's Jewish populace.[37]

The creation of a Judeo-Spanish press in Salonika was an expression of a Judeo-Spanish cultural renaissance. Through Judeo-Spanish newspapers like *La Epoca*, founded in 1876 by Saadi Halevi Ashkenazi, not only could the Jews of the city and the region read about the world in their own language, but the local Judeo-Spanish culture began to flourish. There were musicians and Judeo-Spanish theater.[38] *Romansas* and poetry were popularized for the Jewish masses. Salonika became a haven for Judeo-Spanish culture and a beacon to the Sephardim of the Balkans and the entire Mediterranean region. Previously Salonika had been renowned as a community of astute and revered rabbinic authorities, as manifested in the city's golden age in the sixteenth century following the Spanish and Portuguese expulsions. Now the city became a cultural center.

La Epoca was important not only as a daily paper reporting the news, but because it guided it readers in dealing with the problems of the time, and attracted them to education and the attainment of knowledge in a clear and open manner, as a first step in regularizing their economic and social situation. Michael Molho, in *Contribution a la Istoria de Salonika*, noted that "the newspaper systematized the Ladino language in the course of time in order to fit the modern European speech and thought of the era."[39] Ashkenazi's student proteges, working under him as journalists, elevated the level of the newspaper and translated treasures from the wide resources of Western literature, in particular from French and Italian. The language used was one of the first examples of the transition from the embedded literary language of rabbinic works and biblical translations to the modern language of Judeo-Spanish.

In *La Epoca*, endorsed by Allatini and supported by the AIU, Ashkenazi tried to promote propaganda for the progress and reorganization of the community. In 1875, Ashkenazi established the French newspaper *Journal de Salonique* together with his sons Betsalel, Daout (David) Effendi, and Shmuel.

Hebrew had been the prime language of rabbinic works published in Salonika until about 1880–1890, when it was replaced by Judeo-

---

[37] Gaon, *Yehudei Hamizrah Beeretz-Yisrael*.
[38] Elena Romero, *El teatro de los sefardies orientales*, 3 vols. (Madrid, 1979).
[39] Michael S. Molho, *Contribution a la Istoria de Saloniko* (Salonika, 5692), pp. 76–78.

Spanish secular works. The schools of the Alliance Israélite Universelle, which emphasized instruction in French, contributed greatly to the development of a Spanish jargon and its literary spread throughout Turkey.[40] Talmud and other religious texts ceased being the main focus of attention for Salonikan Jewish youth, as well as throughout Sephardic Jewry, except in Eretz Israel.

Several Salonikan Judeo-Spanish authors enriched their readers with a few fairly worthy works written in the language of Spaniolit (Judeo-Spanish). Through their writings they elevated the "jargon"-filled vernacular language to a literary language.[41]

In Salonika, as within the general flourishing of Judeo-Spanish literature and publishing in the second half of the nineteenth century, those who spread the phenomenon were Jewish journalists and a few young men from the "intelligentsia." As Hebrew religious and rabbinic texts dwindled toward the end of the nineteenth century and the monopolies of the rabbis on printed books and published works loosened, a new generation arose.[42] A few young men began to supply their readers with compositions and stories in Spaniolit, and as time passed, they began translating novels, historical works, and plays from Hebrew, French, German, Greek, and other languages to Judeo-Spanish. The weight of the latter process led to a stagnation in the writing of original creations in Judeo-Spanish. Nonetheless, in Salonika during the last decade of the nineteenth century, there did appear many books in Spaniolit on the history of the Jews in the Ottoman Empire, biographies, poetry collections, travel accounts, storybooks for schools, and so forth. The energetic young writers, in their effort to create a new literary style, greatly increased the Europeanization of Salonikan Jewry.

Another obstacle to the development of Judeo-Spanish literary expression in print was Ottoman censorship. The old-fashioned regime of Abdul-Hamid strangled the freedom of the Judeo-Spanish press. Any article with the least bit of a political idea was thought of as

---

[40] Avraham Almaleh, *Letoldot Hayehudim Beselanik* (Jerusalem, 1924).

[41] Ibid.

[42] See Avraham Yaari, "Od Dfusei Saloniki," *Kiriyat Sefer* 7 (1930–31): 290–309, and *Rishimat Sifrei Ladino Hanimtzaim Bebeit-Hasefarim Heleumi vehauniversitai Beyerushalayim*; Shlomo Avraham Rozanes, *Korot hayehudim Beturkia Veartzot Hakedem*, pt. 5 (Sophia: Imprimerie "Amichpat", 1937–38), pp. 346–364, and pt. 6 (Tel Aviv: Hotsaat Dvir, 1930); M. Franco, *Essai sur l'histoire des Israélites de l'empire Ottoman depuis les origines jusqu'a nos jours* (Paris: Centre d'études Don Isaac Abravanel USIF, 1980), pp. 270–275.

treason to the Porte. Even scientific articles were eliminated and crushed if the ignorant Ottoman censor did not agree with their most minute details. The first vestiges of a Salonikan Zionist movement, found in the city as early as 1897, and remaining clandestine until the 1908 Young Turk Revolution, were internalized. The Judeo-Spanish newspaper *El Avenir*, founded in 1897, and edited by the ardent Zionist David Florentin, showed no signs of expressing political Zionist sentiment at the end of the nineteenth century.

As early as 1869 the government organ for commerce and agriculture, *Selanik*, was appearing in four languages: Spaniolit, Turkish, Greek, and Bulgarian. Its founder and editor was Rabbi Yaakov Ouziel. Midhat Pasha, the governor of Salonika and a liberal reformer, backed the papers. In 1873 he planned to publish a constitutional proposal in Turkish in *Selanik*, but the sultan's spies uncovered the plan. He was removed from his post. Later, as minister of justice, he worked for the establishment of constitutional government and the downfall of Sultan Abdul-Aziz. This movement laid the groundwork for the granting of a constitution by the new sultan, Abdul-Hamid II, in 1876, shortly after he had gained power by sending his emissaries to execute his predecessor. Jews were not among the leaders, but in the years to come they actively participated in the Young Turk movement. Their political activism was an expression of the European political culture they had attained through their AIU education and exposure, and through the influence of Western-educated Turkish Muslim reformers in the region.

Meanwhile, the poorer classes, consisting of porters, tobacco workers, and peddlers, were pushed aside by the newly emerging European-educated elements of the Jewish community. The politicization of the poor did not occur until the twentieth century, with prompting from the Bulgarian socialist movement and migratory activists like Avraham Ben Aroye. They did not benefit economically from the AIU schools and the industrialization toward the end of the nineteenth century, as did the merchants and those working in the free professions. Later, in the next century, they would improve their condition through the Socialist Federation of Salonika, led in part by intellectuals educated in Salonika's AIU schools.

Herzlian political Zionism in its early stages had an influence on a active core group of individuals at the end of the nineteenth century. This European "ism" would also wait until the next century before taking full effect.

Increased educational opportunities in the era of this late-nine-teenth-century Europeanization brought upward social mobility in their train. As the Jews of Salonika obtained more materially, their expectations increased. Those who had attended the French-oriented AIU schools became aware of the possibility of studying abroad in France and later working there. The great fire of 1890 was a major setback to the populace and caused much Jewish homelessness.[43] At this time, rumors of economic possibilities in the United States reached Salonika. Poor youth who felt they had no future concluded that they could make their fortunes on the other side of the ocean in the United States. Also, the economic slump in the Ottoman Empire in the 1890s made the future bleak for many young people. At this stage, however, only small numbers of youth departed. The general Jewish population increased in size. By 1900 some reports stated that Salonika's Jewish population was high as 80,000.[44] Although this is probably a bit exaggerated, one sees a basic stabilization in the community.

With the advent of the AIU in Salonika, relations with the Greek Orthodox improved. A few Greek Orthodox students attended the AIU school, and it is worthy of note that there was more Greek than Turkish instruction in the school. When Dr. Allatini began to hire Greek Orthodox workers in his tile factory, his brewery, and his tobacco factories, relations between Jews and Greeks in the city improved.

In conclusion, at the halfway point of the nineteenth century, the Jewish community of Salonika was in a state of underdevelopment. Through the Frenchification of the populace, promoted by the Alliance Israélite Universelle, Europeanization infiltrated into the Jewish community and advanced it. A new petit-bourgeois class was formed, while the poor stagnated in their traditional one-room *hedarim* and traditionally unskilled occupations. While French language motivated the youth pedagogically, it prompted the flourishing of the Judeo-Spanish press, drama, and translation of novels. At the end of the century, French itself threatened the role of Judeo-Spanish as the means of expression. Part of the Europeanization process also

---

[43] Recanati, *Zichron Saloniki*, pp. 161–162. At least 2,000 Jewish homes were destroyed within an area of 250 acres. See also Sam Levy, "Mes Memoires, Salonique à la fin du XIX siècle," *Tesoro de los Sefardies* (Jerusalem), bk. 6, pp. 32–51.

[44] AIU, Grèce, IV.B.24 (1893–1900). J. Zehiprunt to President of AIU, pp. 42–44.

strengthened the role of Italian, which was the ceremonial language
of the community. French and Italian, as the keys to European culture, were the means for the infiltration of the AIU school system,
the development of the Salonikan Jewish petit-bourgeois commercial
class, and future tools for political activity. The AIU and industrialization advanced the Jewish community greatly after nearly two
centuries of spiritual and communal depression in light of Sabbatea-
nism. Whereas the Salonikan Jewish community did not need the
French Jewish Enlightenment to attain political rights in the Ottoman
Empire in the Tanzimat era, it was aided by the AIU, the educational tool of French Jewry, in order to promote economic and social
development.

LES SÉFARADES D'ESPAGNE EN ALGÉRIE
AUX XIIIᵉ ET XIVᵉ SIÈCLE

Richard Ayoun

Lorsque les Juifs d'Espagne prennent à nouveau le chemin de l'exil, l'élégie d'Ibn Ezra sur la terreur almohade est encore dans leur coeur:

> Comment fut détruit le Maghreb et furent affaiblies toutes les mains
> Hélas un malheur s'abattit du ciel sur l'Espagne
> Et mes yeux pleurent. . . .

Il est fréquent de décrire les Juifs d'Afrique du Nord comme d'obscurs rejetons d'une diaspora imprévisible, que seule l'arrivée des *megorashim* (les exilés) évolués auraient arrachés à leur sort lamentable. Pour les historiens français de l'Algérie comme Charles André Julien, les vrais fondateurs du Judaïsme d'Algérie seraient ces exilés. Les *megorashim* ressentent certes, à quel point les moeurs africaines sont en général, moins policées que celles des riches cités ibériques. Cependant ces historiens n'oublient-ils pas la grande proximité culturelle, affective et matérielle qui dés le Haut-Moyen-Age unit ces deux communautés dans l'adversité comme dans la réussite?

A trop vouloir encenser le raffinement, voire la sophistication des Juifs venus d'Espagne, à trop desservir le Judaïsme maghrébrin par des descriptions apocalyptiques, on court le risque de l'absurde: comment deux expériences humaines aussi diamétralement opposées auraient-elles pu, en l'espace de quelques années, se fondre et s'harmoniser?

Avant 1391

Les rabbins d'Alger, installés après l'immigration de 1391 évoquent dans leurs écrits des individus et des communautés résidant dans la région frontière du Sahara, à Biskra, à Touggourt et Warghlan, à Honaïne.[1] Ces sources rabbiniques n'expliquent pas comment les Juifs

---

[1] Rabbi Isaac ben Sheshet (1326–1408) dit Barfat, RIBaSH, *Responsa*, 1ère éd. (1546/47), 2nd éd. (1559), nos. 16–19.

indigènes sont parvenus à survivre pendant l'époque des tribulations.

Les écrivains arabes mentionnent les Juifs comme une réalité établie. Quant aux sources européennes, elles montrent que les états occidentaux et les cités indépendantes maintiennent des relations commerciales avec les communautés juives du Maghreb central. Des motifs politiques et économiques jouent un rôle primordial dans la restauration des communautés juives, dans les ports maritimes et les capitales.

Bougie (Béjaïa),[2] Tenes et Honaïne deviennent d'importants ports marchands, mais également des centres de piraterie. En même temps, la navigation marchande se développe. Le rythme de croissance de ces villes est accéléré à partir du milieu du XIIIe siècle par le flux des réfugiés musulmans qui viennent d'Andalousie. Les représentants des pays chrétiens qui établissent des relations avec les ports du Maghreb central sont chargés selon leurs possibilités, de prendre soin de leurs ressortissants, parmi lesquels se trouvent des Juifs.

Les marchands juifs de la Péninsule Ibérique établissent des relations commerciales avec les villes côtières de l'Afrique du Nord. Aux XIIIe et XIVe siècles, Tlemcen jouit d'une appréciable position économique grâce à l'influence grandissante des Mérinides. Cette ville devient un croisement des routes marchandes de l'Est, de l'Ouest et du Nord au Sud. La communauté juive s'y développe en 1287 lorsqu'un groupe de Juifs de Minorque immigre après la conquête de l'île par les Chrétiens et essentiellement après les persécutions de 1391 en Aragon et à Majorque.[3]

Vers 1250, la famille Ferrusol, dont certains membres ont vécu à

---

[2] Bougie, ville déjà prospère à l'époque romaine est en 1184 prise par l'almoravide Ali Ibn Ghaniya qui débarque des îles Baléares et reconquiert tout le Maghreb central, d'Alger au chott Dherid. Vers 1230, Bougie est soumise par le premier souverain hafside de Tunis, Abou Zakarya, mais devient en 1284, la capitale d'un royaume indépendant, amenant ainsi une rivalité entre les deux souverains hafsides de Tunis et de Bougie. Cette dernière connaît alors un grand rayonnement intellectuel. C'est l'époque où la visite le théologien Raymond Lulle (1235–1315) dont la doctrine est mal accueillie par les docteurs musulmans. L'unité hafside est rétablie par Abou Bekr au début du XIVe siècle, qui sauve son royaume des tentatives d'attaque des souverains zianides de Tlemcen, en réussissant à faire occuper cette dernière ville par les Mérinides de Fès, lesquels s'emparent d'ailleurs à la mort d'Abou Bekr, de Bougie et de Tunis en 1347. C'est entre 1366 et 1390 qu'Abou El Abbas reconstitue de nouveau l'unité de l'Empire hafside.

[3] Charles Emmanuel Dufourcq, *L'Espagne catalane et le Maghreb aux XIIIe et XIVe siècles, de la bataille de Las Navas de Tolosa (1212) à l'avènement du Sultan mérunide Abou-l-Hassan (1331)* (Paris: P.U.F., 1965; réédité en 1966), pp. 141–143, 149–153 321–336, 371–375.

Bougie, est établie à Marseille. Elle commerce avec d'autres ports du Maghreb central comme Bougie et Tenes dont les correspondants sont des Juifs. C'est ainsi qu'en 1248, la plus grande partie de la cargaison de deux navires, est envoyée par cette famille de Marseille, à des Juifs de Bougie. C'est le cas aussi, de la famille Manduel de Marseille spécialisée dans le commerce avec l'Afrique du Nord. Sur les relations entre les Juifs de Bougie, de Majorque, et de Marseille, à la fin du XIIIᵉ siècle et au début du XIVᵉ siècle, des documents existent.[4]

Quelle que soit l'importance des liaisons entre le Maghreb central, et les républiques portuaires du Nord de l'Italie et du Sud de la France, leurs liens avec les Baléares et les villes d'Espagne chrétiennes, distendus au XIIIᵉ siècle, sont plus significatifs à cette période. La raison en est la longue tradition de contacts entre les Juifs du Maghreb central et l'Espagne musulmane, et les Juifs. A partir de la deuxième moitié du XIIᵉ siècle, il y a de plus grandes relations avec les royaumes chrétiens d'Aragon et de Castille.

Les états musulmans du Maghreb central, sont confrontés à l'expansion et au renforcement de l'Aragon. Jacques Ier (1213–1276) et ses successeurs Pierre III (1276–1285), Alphonse III (1285–1291) et Jacques II (1291–1327) conquièrent et prennent le contrôle des Baléares[5] ainsi d'importantes régions sur la côte sud-ouest de la Péninsule pyrénéenne (Valence en 1238 et Murcie en 1296). Ils se rendent maîtres également de la Sicile en 1282, de la Sardaigne en 1297 et deviennent tour à tour les voisins, les ennemis et les alliés du Maghreb central.

Des Juifs du Maghreb central s'établissent essentiellement à Majorque, depuis 903, après la conquête de l'île par les Musulmans. Leur nombre augmente à la suite des persécutions des Almohades. Ils s'ajoutent à ceux venus des villes européennes. En 1291, Jacques II envoie Abraham Abengelel chez le roi de Tlemcen, sa famille l'accompagne.[6]

En 1293, le médecin de la cour, Bondavi, quitte l'Aragon avec sa

---

[4] Raoul Busquet, Régine Pernoud, *Histoire du Commerce de Marseille* (Paris: publiée par la Chambre de Commerce de Marseille, 1949), t. I, ch. IV: les relations commerciales de Marseille avec l'Afrique du Nord, pp. 169–180, pp. 171, 175, et p. 292.

[5] Majorque en 1230, progressivement d'autres îles jusqu'en 1235 et Minorque en 1286.

[6] Jean Régné, "Catalogue des actes de Jaime Ier, Pedro III et Alfonso III, rois d'Aragon, concernant les Juifs (1213–1291)," *Revue des Etudes Juives* (Paris), 60 (1910):

famille pour une mission secrète.[7] Sa tache consiste à conclure un traité de paix avec Othman, roi de Tlemcen. Cette ambassade échoue, comme avaient échoué les précédentes tentatives entreprises dans le même objectif.[8]

Des Juifs du Maghreb central s'installent en Espagne grâce à Jacques Ier, roi d'Aragon, de Majorque Valence. Jacques Ier ordonne que l'on facilite l'émigration des familles juives depuis l'Afrique du Nord vers ses territoires européens. Par exemple, le 11 juin 1247, il autorise tout juif et juive de Sijilmasa à venir s'installer à Majorque, Barcelone, Valence ou tout autre lieu sous son commandement.[9]

Dans les relations commerciales entre l'Aragon, Majorque et le Maghreb central, les Juifs sont à cette époque des partenaires efficaces. Du fait de leur connaissance des conditions de vie et de la langue locales, il est possible d'utiliser leurs relations avec les Juifs indigènes du Maghreb central aussi bien qu'avec ceux qui viennent de s'y installer. Ils développent le commerce en ouvrant des agences de courtage commercial pour les échanges entre les commerçants chrétiens dans les *funduqs* et les détaillants juifs et les colporteurs dans les oasis des steppes du sud, à la limite du Sahara.

En 1276, Pierre III inclue dans une mission diplomatique au Maghreb central, des commerçants juifs, de façon à ce qu'ils puissent bénéficier de l'immunité durant leur séjour en Afrique et continuer leur négoce sans difficulté.[10] En septembre 1296, les autorités de Tlemcen se plaignent auprès du roi Jacques II que le capitaine d'un navire de Valence a confisqué en mer certains biens rapportés (de Valence) par le Juif Maymon ben Atar, habitant de Taount (Nemours), un port maritime près de Honaïne. . . . Selon des traités signés entre les gouvernants de Tlemcen et les trois prédécesseurs de Jacques II, les sujets de la couronne d'Aragon ne sont pas autorisés aux gens de Tlemcen ni sur terre, ni sur mer.[11]

161–201, 61 (1911): 1–43, 62 (1911): 38–73, 63 (1912): 245–268, 64 (1912): 67–88, 215–235, 65 (1913): 6–88, 196–224, 66 (1913): 252–262, 67 (1914): 53–81, 195–224, 68 (1914): 198–221, 69 (1919): 135–220, 70 (1920): 74–87, 195–208. Réédité par Haïm Beinhart, Jean Régné, *History of the Jews in Aragon, Regesta and Documents 1213–1327* (Jérusalem: Magnes Press, Hebrew University, 1978), Hispañia Judaïca 1, 744 pp., pp. 1–208.

[7] Dufourcq, *L' Espagne catalane*, pp. 225, 329–335.

[8] *Ibid.*, p. 331.

[9] Jaime Villanuea, *Viage literario a las iglesias de España*, vol. 22 (Madrid: Impr. de la Real academia de la historia, 1852), p. 327.

[10] Dufourcq, *L'Espagne catalane*, p. 313 et note 4.

[11] *Ibid.*, p. 347, notes 4 et 5; p. 348, note 2.

En 1302, un traité est signé entre Bougie et Majorque. Il donne au Consul de Majorque, juridiction sur tous les sujets du roi, y compris les Juifs. En effet, en 1303, le consul Benet Blancas arrête à Bougie quelques Juifs de Majorque accusés de pédérastie.[12] En 1304 et 1305, des navires arrivent de Majorque dans les ports de Taount, de Cherchel, de Tenes, et d'Alger, en dépit d'un sérieux conflit qui oppose cette cité d'Aragon. Le Juif Salomon Ben Zequi sert d'intermédiaire dans des négociations d'ordre commercial avec Breshk.[13] Lors d'un conflit entre Majorque et Bougie en 1304, les Juifs ne prennent pas part à l'armement de la flotte de Majorque qui va attaquer Bougie, à cause des liens amicaux établis avec cette cité dans les relations commerciales. En 1330, selon un rapport, le prêtre catalan de Tenes rédige une procuration pour un Juif majorquin qui vit dans cette ville.[14]

Pour l'année 1327, la valeur des marchandises importées de Barcelone, Valence et Majorque à Tlemcen est de 15000 à 20000 dinars, et les dettes des marchands de Tlemcen envers les Juifs de Majorque, dépassent 100000 dinars.

Majorque et la Catalogne achètent des céréales au Maghreb central. Bougie exporte le papier de Fez, la peau et la fourrure d'animaux domestiques variés et différemment traitées. Parmi les autres produits exportés nous relevons du poisson, du corail, des dattes et du coton. Les exportations du Maghreb central consistent donc essentiellement en produits agricoles et leurs dérivés, ainsi qu'en matières premières.

D'Europe sont importés au Maghreb central, des vêtements, des tissus, des bijoux, des armes, du cuivre, du plomb et du fer blanc et, de manière assez étonnante du sel et de l'huile, alors que ces produits sont disponibles en grande quantité localement. Une grande partie des biens exportés du Maghreb central sont apportés vers les ports de sortie, lointains, par des marchands ambulants juifs, qui les vendent à des agences et reçoivent en retour des "produits industriels" et de "luxe", ensuite revendus à l'intérieur du pays.[15]

Aux XIII⁰ et XIV⁰ siècles donc, la situation au Maghreb central a un effet favorable sur les développements au sein de la population

---

[12] *Ibid.*, pp. 420–422, p. 422, note 4.
[13] *Ibid.*, p. 369, note 4.
[14] *Ibid.*, p. 141, note 3.
[15] *Ibid.*, p. 547.

juive. La règle, selon laquelle un pays en inimitié avec ses voisins ne doit pas avoir tendance à asservir sa communauté juive à une oppression persistante et difficilement supportable, est de nouveau confirmée. Les Juifs ont continué à vivre dans la Péninsule ibérique. De même, les Juifs sont exposés à de graves dangers quand un simple et puissant royaume apparaît, comme au temps des Almoravides, des conquêtes Almohades et de l'union des rois catholiques de Castille et d'Aragon. La division politique s'accompagne fréquemment de la fragmentation ethnique et sociale.

Les personnes de diverses origines, de coutumes sociales et religieuses distinctes et de langues différentes, vivent côte à côte. Cela apparaît au Maghreb central avec les conquérants politiques et commerciaux venant d'Europe. La dynastie des Mérinides[16] au pouvoir à cette époque, est un facteur d'accalmie de la tension religieuse. Cette dynastie n'appartient pas aux familles aristocratiques *Shurafa* de la maison du prophète Mahomet. De plus, cette famille ne montre pas un grand enthousiasme à l'égard des dernières réformes religieuses des Almohades.

L'Immigration de 1391

Les communautés juives du Maghreb central connaissent une véritable mutation avec, notamment, l'arrivée d'immigrants de Majorque et de la Péninsule ibérique en 1391, à la suite des soulèvements meurtriers d'artisans, de paysans, de marins, de bourgeois et de chevaliers, du 6 juin au 13 août, en Castille et en Aragon, contre les quartiers juifs.[17] Leur établissement dans la ville d'Alger marque le début de sa prospérité économique et de son développement en tant que centre administratif.

Au Maghreb central l'accueil n'est pas aussi sinistre que celui subi

---

[16] Cette dynastie berbère du groupe des Zanatas règne temporairement sur le Maghreb, du XIIIe au XVe siècle. L'intervention des Mérinides en Espagne contre les rois chrétiens de Castille permet seulement de maintenir au pouvoir les Nasrides de Grenade jusqu'à la fin du XVe siècle. En Afrique du Nord, Abû al-Hassan (1331–1351), qui est le plus grand souverain mérinide, occupe Tlemcen en 1337. Après sa défaite à Kairouen en 1348, il doit se réfugier au Maroc. Son successeur Abû Inan (1351–1358) entreprend de nouveau la conquête du Maghreb. Les rébellions provoquent la chute de ce peuple de grands bâtisseurs.

[17] Philippe Wolff, "The 1391 Pogrom in Spain: Social Crisis or Not? Past and Present," *Journal of Historical Studies* 50 (février 1971): 4–18.

au Maroc par certains exilés, comme le rapportent l'auteur du *Shebet Yehuda*[18] et le rabbin Ephraïm Enkaoua (Ibn al-Nakawa 1359–1442).[19] De Tolède, Ephraïm Enkaoua s'exile à Marrakech. A la suite d'expériences pénibles dans cette ville, il part pour Honaïne. Quant aux jours difficiles, mentionnés par le rabbin Isaac bar Sheshet, que subissent les exilés lors du siège et de la capture d'Alger durant un des conflits armés entre les dynasties rivales, ils affectent la population dans son ensemble.[20] L'afflux de réfugiés de 1391, vers certaines régions et le non-établissement dans d'autres, reflète la stabilité ou l'instabilité de la situation politique générale des régions concernées. Ils illustrent également les conditions de vie des Juifs dans les différents lieux.

Un des récits d'Isaac bar Sheshet (1326–1408), évoque les fugitifs de la manière suivante: "Un jour, un bateau arriva ici en provenance de Majorque, avec quarante cinq convertis forcés de Majorque, de Valence et de Barcelone. Le gouverneur voulut les admettre dans la ville pour des raisons de propre intérêt, car il voulait leur prélever un doublon par tête, un arrangement suggéré par une certaine personne. Ils furent originellement admis libres de toute charge, et le cadi Ibn Mehrez blâma quelques arabes qui vinrent le voir et lui demandèrent de ne pas les laisser débarquer à cause de la montée des prix; il les expulsa de sa maison, en colère, disant: Je pensais que vous étiez de vrais croyants, mais maintenant je vois que vous êtes des infidèles. Est-ce que Dieu est incapable de nourrir ceux qui sont à côté du reste de l'humanité? Est-ce que l'homme ne vit pas de chaque mot qui provient de la bouche du Seigneur? Mais cette personne demanda au peuple d'inciter le gouverneur à ne pas les laisser débarquer, afin qu'ils puissent retourner à Majorque et qu'aucun d'entre eux ne vienne ici."[21]

---

[18] "Mais ceux qui allèrent dans des pays arabes, supportèrent en chemin une souffrance passée sous silence, comme ils l'écrivirent à leurs parents, restés chez eux. Ce fut spécialement les villageois qui se soulevèrent contre eux (disant qu'ils protégeaient leur religion) et les enchaînèrent jusqu'à ce que le fait fut connu du roi. Une partie d'entre eux se sauva en fournissant du travail et de l'argent à leurs persécuteurs, et une partie fut incitée à dire en fonction de leurs tribulations: 'laissez-nous nommer un capitaine, et laissez-nous revenir chez nous.'" *Nombres* 14, 4, chapitre 27.

[19] Ce rabbin médecin est l'auteur de *Sha'ar Kevod Hashem* (Tunis, 1901). Son pére, Israël Al-Nakaoua, est l'auteur de *Menorat Hamaor* (New York, 1928). André Elbaz, *Folktales of the Canadian Sephardim* (Toronto: Fitzhenry et Whiteside, 1982), pp. 106–107.

[20] RIBaSH, *Responsa*, nr. 154.

[21] *Ibid.*, nr. 61.

Au début, l'autorité musulmane permet aux réfugiés de débarquer libres de toute charge, et seulement à l'instigation d'un certain juif, il ordonne une taxe d'entrée d'un doublon par personne. Ce juif étant lui-même un réfugié venant de Majorque, comme le fait remarquer Isaac Bar Sheshet, avant d'évoquer ce texte. Le cadi réprimande d'abord les Musulmans, qui craignent que l'afflux de plusieurs réfugiés ne provoque une montée des prix, puis il blâme le Juif, qui cherche à persuader des personnes de dissuader le magistrat musulman d'épargner les réfugiés.

A Tenes, une réduction de la taxe de capitation, et de la taxe du roi, est octroyée aux réfugiés, ce qui provoque des manifestations des habitants.[22] Selon la tradition orale, l'autorité médicale Ephraïm Enkaoua, qui guérit notamment la fille du roi de Tlemcen, permet aux Juifs de venir vivre dans sa capitale. Il leur attribue le droit d'agrandir le faubourg de Tlemcen, nommé Agadir.[23] Les exilés s'installent le long de la côte, de Honaïne (le port de Tlemcen), à l'ouest, en passant par Oran, Mostaganem, Tenes, Breskk, Alger[24] et Bougie où Simon Duran évoque deux communautés distinctes.[25] La majorité des exilés s'établit à Tlemcen et un plus petit nombre dans les villes de la plaine comme Miliana, Médéa et Constantine.

Les conditions de vie des exilés sont plus favorables, à la fin du XIVe siècle, au Maghreb central, sous les princes musulmans, qu'en Europe. Dans leurs quartiers de villes ou de villages, ils mènent leur propre existence, administrant leurs affaires, exerçant de nombreux métiers et pratiquant leur religion à leur manière.

Certains exilés deviennent propriétaires de biens fonciers étendus et d'esclaves; d'autres, font partie de caravanes arabes. Ils consentent des avances aux Musulmans, avec ou sans intérêt, sur un simple billet de crédit la plupart du temps et sans aucune autre garantie. Les Musulmans empruntent de l'argent aux Juifs et en rembour sent le montant avec leurs récoltes. Au moment des semailles, les Musulmans achètent des semences aux Juifs, ou leur empruntent la somme nécessaire pour s'en procurer. Les Musulmans font souvent abattre

---

[22] Siméon ben Sémah Duran, *Responsa* (Amsterdam: Nephtali Hirz Lévi, 1738), t. III, nr. 46.

[23] A. Sershman, *Perfet* (Jérusalem, 1956), p. 162.

[24] Cf. Shalom Bar-Asher, "Basic Trends in the History of the Jews of the Maghreb and the Rise of the Center in Algiers, 1391–1492," *Pe'amim* (Jérusalem) 31 (1987): 22–39.

[25] Siméon ben Sémah Duran, *Responsa*, nr. 568.

leurs agneaux par des sacrificateurs juifs, et donnent la préférence aux mets préparés par les Juifs.

Les exilés, comme les autres Juifs dans leur grande majorité, s'adonnent au commerce, à la revente et au colportage. Ils négocient essentiellement la laine naturelle ou manufacturée, la soie, les textiles, les teintures, la cire et les plumes d'autruche. Le commerce des métaux précieux et des pierres précieuses nécessite une licence, elle provoque fréquemment de fortes amendes.

Une des grandes spécialités des exilés est la distillation des vins et autres liqueurs. Les autorités rabbiniques interviennent dans leur Import-Export, leur interdisant d'acheter des vins étrangers, notamment ceux de Majorque et de Valence, et des vêtements confectionnés en Europe, pour éviter que certaines lois religieuses ne soient violées. A l'importation, les Juifs exilés acquittent, comme tous les autres commerçants, un droit de 10% "ad valorem". A Honaïne, les exilés se livrent aussi à la pêche, une entente est intervenue entre pêcheurs juifs et non-juifs, qui règle les conditions et les moments de la pêche, et fixe les salaires de l'ensemble de l'équipage du bateau.

Ces communautés du Maghreb central, comment sont-elles organisées? Un *Cheikh* (chef) est nommé par les responsables gouvernementaux sur la base du statut social et familial.[26] Dans les différends d'ordre civil et religieux, lui est conféré le droit de décision. Il juge les affaires matrimoniales, commettant souvent des erreurs à cause de son manque de connaissances. Il cumule les fonctions, nomme les fonctionnaires, les lecteurs, et a le droit de les congédier. Sa charge de trésorier lui permet d'administrer les revenus de la communauté pour l'achat de vivres aux pauvres et l'octroi d'autres secours. Les exilés d'Espagne font perdre au *Cheikh* une partie de ses pouvoirs; ses décisions sont âprement discutées. Les exilés sont administrés par un conseil de *Nè'émanim*, régulièrement élu. Ils introduisent au Maghreb central, les taxes rituelles sur la consommation de la viande et du vin. Les *Nè'émanim* rendent la justice. Le conseil des Marchands s'occupe des différends d'ordre financier, il a sa propre procédure et suit des règles bien déterminées dans l'examen des affaires qui lui sont soumises. Sa grande réputation d'impartialité fait que souvent dans des cas difficiles, les tribunaux musulmans, les

---

[26] Menachem Weinstein, "The Jewish Communities in Algeria between the Years 1300–1830" (Thèse d'Histoire juive, Université Bar-Ilan, Israël, octobre 1974/5735), pp. 46–67.

tribunaux rabbiniques et même Simon ben Sémah Duran, ont recours à sa compétence. En contrepartie, lorsque le Conseil de Marchands a des cas compliqués relevant de la jurisprudence religieuse, il transmet le dossier à l'autorité rabbinique. C'est le cas à Mostaganem et à Cherchel.

Les Séfarades d'Espagne s'élèvent contre l'interdiction qu'ont les lecteurs et rabbins, d'avoir le droit de mettre en interdit, tout laïc qui les offense. Ils n'acceptent cette interdiction qu'à la condition qu'elle soit reconnue valable par les *Né'émanim*. Leur souhait est que ce droit des lecteurs et des rabbins ne devienne pas un moyen d'oppression.

En cette fin du XIVe siècle, le rituel n'étant pas encore fixé, de fréquentes disputes éclatent à ce sujet au cours des offices, puisque la liturgie comporte des différences entre la communauté des exilés et la communauté des indigènes.

Annexe

La *"Loi de Castille"* règle le partage-des biens en cas de décès du Mari ou de la femme.[27]

Art. 1er.—Si la femme meurt laissant son mari et des enfants, tous les biens meubles ou immeubles appartenant à l'un ou l'autre des époux seront partagés en deux portions égales, l'une sera dévolue au mari et l'autre aux enfants.

Art. 2.—Il en sera de même si le mari meurt à la survivance de sa femme et de ses enfants. Tous les biens que possédaient les époux au moment du décès, formeront une masse qui sera divisée en deux parties égales, l'une sera attribuée à la veuve et l'autre aux enfants. La veuve dans ce cas, n'aura à réclamer ni la dot légale, ni l'augment, ni la *nédounia* (son apport de la maison paternelle).

Art. 3.—Si le père et la mère laissent, à leur décès, des fils et des filles, et que celles-ci n'aient jamais été mariées, les fils donneront aux filles ce qui leur appartient.

Art. 4.—Si le mari meurt laissant une veuve mais pas d'enfants, sa veuve reprendra tous les biens qu'elle aura apportés et qui composaient sa *nédounia* et le surplus des biens laissés par le mari sera divisé

---

[27] Abraham b. Mordocai Anqawa (AnrkaVa), *Ordonnances des Rabbins de Castille, Kerem Hemer II* (Livourne: E. Benamozegh, 1869).

en quatre parts, une de ces parts sera attribuée à la veuve et les trois autres aux héritiers du mari.

Art. 5.—Si la femme meurt à la survivance de son mari, ne laissant pas d'enfant issu de son mariage, ses héritiers prélèveront, sur les biens appartenant aux deux époux, la moitié de la *nédounia* et le surplus restera au mari.[28]

---

[28] La Loi de Castille apporte aux règles de la loi générale rabbinique des dérogations importantes et établit entre les époux un régime de communauté de biens. Cependant, cette communauté n'est effective qu'après la mort de l'un des époux, auquel cas le montant de la *Kétoubah* dont la femme est créancière légale, ainsi que tous les biens qu'elle a pu acquérir après le mariage vont avec la fortune entière du mari, constituer la masse des biens communautaires. Ces biens seront alors partagés conformément aux articles 1 et 2.

MOROCCO, ENGLAND, AND THE END OF THE SEPHARDIC WORLD ORDER (THE SULTAN'S JEW, MEIR MACNIN)

Daniel J. Schroeter

University of California, Irvine

Some years ago, in an address to the Jewish Historical Society of England, Cecil Roth suggested the possibility of a new area of Anglo-Jewish research which could contribute to a wider understanding of Jewish history. "We all know," said Roth, "the accepted patterns of the development of the new Jewish communities that were set up in Northern Europe from the seventeenth century. First there came surreptitious Marrano settlers from Spain and Portugal ... later they slowly threw off the veil of secrecy, and thereafter these places became the centres for an ever-increasing immigration of refugees from the Inquisition, to be reinforced in due course from other segments of Jewry." Roth continued that "this picture is only partially true," since "almost from the beginning, these new Sephardic communities—in particular perhaps that of London—were swollen by Sephardic settlers from Northern Africa, more precisely from Morocco." Roth points out how these families became absorbed both in the life of Anglo-Jewry and in English life more generally. Referring to his own research on the notorious Buzaglo family, who settled in London in the second quarter of the eighteenth century, Roth suggested that he did "not desire for the moment to discuss the respectability of this family, but only to point out how at this relatively early period they began to cut something of a figure in London life, not as picturesque Orientals, but as members of occidental society."[1]

This present study examines the activities of Meir Macnin in London. Macnin was a Moroccan Jewish merchant who arrived in London in 1800. On a number of occasions, over the next three

---

[1] Cecil Roth, "Why Anglo-Jewish History?" *Transactions of the Jewish Historical Society of England* 22 (1970): 24.

decades, he served as the sultan's Jewish agent in Europe. In fact, he was often practically the only intermediary between Morocco and Europe.

A number of studies by Roth and others have examined the activities of Jewish merchant-emissaries from Morocco who arrived in London in the eighteenth century as representatives of the sultan.[2] Among these prominent Moroccan Jews, some settled in London. Research on this period of Anglo-Jewish history has also revealed that important numbers of North African Jews were settling in London. But none of these discussions have attempted to answer the question that Roth himself suggested was important—how this chapter in Anglo-Jewish history can contribute to a wider understanding of Jewish history. The reason that this has not been done perhaps has to do with research agendas which have invariably limited the kinds of questions asked. Motivated, as Roth himself suggests he was, by an "untiring search for picturesque scallywags," scholars have seen these influential Oriental Jews as rather exotic vestiges of a bygone age. By underlining the fact that the elite of these Sephardic Jews were perfectly capable of acculturation to the norms of English society, Roth reinforces a belief that the Eastern culture of their origins was not really relevant. As Roth tells us, the Moroccan Jews who settled into London life were not simply "picturesque Orientals," but became full members of Western society. It is, after all, Sir Moses Montefiore who comes to represent the prototype of the Westernized and Anglicized Sephardic, who left behind the Sephardic world at the time when Anglo-Jewry nervously entered the post-emancipation age.[3] Sephardic history in England is expropriated by an almost obsessive fixation on the venerable philanthropist and community leader. This Montefiore-centrism has limited our understanding of the Sephardic world at the period of

---

[2] Cecil Roth, "The Amazing Clan of Buzaglo," *Transactions of the Jewish Historical Society of England* 23 (1971): 11–22; idem, "Jacob Benider: Moroccan Envoy at the Court of St James' (1772)," *Miscellanies of the Jewish Historical Society of England* 2 (1935): 84–90; also on Benider, and on Jewish intermediaries generally, see H.Z. (J.W.) Hirschberg, "Jews and Jewish Affairs in the Relations Between Great Britain and Morocco in the 18th Century," in *Essays Presented to Chief Rabbi Israel Brodie on the Occasion of His Seventieth Birthday*, eds. H.J. Zimmels, J. Rabbinowitz, and I. Finestein (London, 1967), pp. 153–181.

[3] See, e.g., V.D. Lipman, "The Age of Emancipation, 1815–1880," in *Three Centuries of Anglo-Jewish History*, ed. V.D. Lipman (Cambridge, 1961), p. 69.

time when Anglo-Jewry was still only making its first, hesitant steps into civic society.

As Roth indicated, a significant proportion of the Sephardic Jewish immigrants in England during the late eighteenth and early nineteenth centuries were from North Africa, especially Morocco. Often Jews of Moroccan origin reached England by way of Gibraltar, which had been occupied by the British since 1704.[4] A large segment of Gibraltar's population was composed of Moroccan Jews, and it often served as a springboard for Moroccan Jewish emigrants.[5] In 1826, for example, Gibraltar had a population of 15,503; of that population, 1,203 are listed as native Jews, and 456 as Barbary Jews.[6] However, most of the "native" Gibraltarian Jews were of Moroccan origin. The 1803 aliens register from Bevis Marks (the synagogue of Spanish and Portuguese Jews in London) reveals that about 16 percent of the new arrivals came from the Maghreb or Gibraltar.[7]

Not all of the North African Jews came from economically privileged backgrounds. Many came to seek opportunities in England as the economic position of much of the Sephardic diaspora continued to deteriorate. A wave of immigration from North Africa and Gibraltar started in the 1770s. A large number of Gibraltarian Jews arrived in England after the evacuation of the population in 1781 as a result of the French siege between June 1779 and February 1783 (most of these Gibraltarian Jews were of Moroccan origin).[8] The famous journalist Henry Mayhew gives an account of an elderly rhubarb and spice seller who left Mogador at about age seventeen. He sold dry goods in Gibraltar for about six years, then moved to England, having previously heard in Morocco about Moroccan Jews making money selling dried rhubarb in London.[9] Some of the congregation of Bevis Marks tended to have a disparaging image of the *berberiscos*, as the new Jewish members from the Maghreb were known. Disputes over

---

[4] A.M. Hyamson, *The Sephardim of England* (London, 1951), p. 97.

[5] Cf. Hirschberg, "Jews and Jewish Affairs," pp. 158–159.

[6] CO 91/90, Gibraltar, 11 November 1826 (Colonial Office, Public Record Office).

[7] Todd M. Endelman, *The Jews of Georgian England, 1714–1830: Tradition and Change in a Liberal Society* (Philadelphia, 1979), p. 170.

[8] R.D. Barnett, "The Correspondence of the Mahamad of the Spanish and Portuguese Congregation of London during the Seventeenth and Eighteenth Centuries," *Transactions of the Jewish Historical Society of England* 20 (1964): 15.

[9] Endelman, *Jews of Georgian England*, p. 171, quoting from Henry Mayhew, *London Labour and the London Poor*, vol. 1, pp. 507–508.

liturgy sometimes occurred between the relative newcomers from
North Africa and the older members.[10] In the folk tradition of
Sephardic Jews today, Moroccan Jews are remembered for their
obstreperous conduct in the synagogue.

But the Sephardim in London as a whole, of whom the Moroccans were certainly considered a part, were viewed by Gentiles as
the elite Jews of London. Much as in France, they had achieved a
certain legitimacy before the influx of Ashkenazim began. In the
eighteenth century, the Sephardim were outstripped by Ashkenazic
immigrants. By 1800, the Sephardim in London numbered about
4,000, only about a fifth of all of London's Jews.[11] As a generaliza-
tion, the Ashkenazim were regarded as poor, relatively uneducated,
peddlers, petty thieves, and swindlers. Wrote one London observer
in 1791: "The praise which is due to the generality of the Portuguese
relative to their manners and morals, cannot be bestowed upon the
majority of the German Jews. They are great sticklers for their old
tenets and usages; but they allow themselves great liberties in regard
to their morals. I believe few burglaries, robberies, and false coinages
are committed, in which some of them are not, in one shape or
other, concerned."[12]

The French Revolution and the Napoleonic wars contributed to
the economic deterioration of continental Sephardic Jewry. London
was considered a place of opportunity. Already the largest city in Europe in the eighteenth century, during the Napoleonic wars London
was in the process of becoming the most important financial center
of the world, overtaking the preeminent position formerly held by
Amsterdam.[13] Commercial speculation in foreign markets was boom-
ing, and tremendous wealth in London was derived from foreign trade.

At the center of England's international trade and banking was
the Sephardic community. For over a century, Sephardic Jews had
been prominent as merchants, stockholders in the Bank of England,
and contractors for the king.[14] Jews were prominent in the stock

---

[10] Moses Gaster, *History of the Ancient Synagogue of the Spanish and Portuguese Jews*
(London, 1901), p. 169.
[11] Hyamson, *Sephardim of England*, p. 222.
[12] F.A. Wendeborn, *A View of England Towards the Close of the Eighteenth Century*
(London, 1791), vol. 2, p. 471. This view is echoed by Patrick Colquhoun, *A Treatise
on the Police of the Metropolis*, 7th ed. (London, 1806), pp. 119–121, 319–322.
[13] George Rude, *Hanoverian London, 1714–1808* (Berkeley, 1971), pp. 33–36.
[14] *Ibid.*, pp. 53–54.

exchange, so much so that the profession seemed, to some Christian observers, to be dominated by them.[15] Jewish merchants were to be found frequenting the coffeehouses of the City, where much business was transacted.

The Sephardic merchants were located at the heart of the City of London, where the Bevis Marks synagogue was located. Increasingly, Moroccan Jews were to be found settled in this financial district. In the first two decades of the nineteenth century, representatives of some of the most prominent Moroccan families settled in London and became members of Bevis Marks: Abitbol, Afriat, De Lara, Massiah, Cohen Solal, Abecassis, Levy BenSusan, Sebag, Guedalla, Zagury, Aflalo, and Hadida, to name several of them. The Sephardic congregation of Bevis Marks maintained an elaborate network of relations with Sephardic communities in Europe, North Africa, and the New World. Noted Moroccan spiritual leaders, such as Rabbi Haim Pinto of Essaouira, maintained a correspondence on halakhic questions with the chief rabbi of the congregation, the Haham Raphael Meldola, who was appointed in 1805, and with his son, David, who succeeded him upon his death in 1828.[16]

It was into this world that Meir Macnin entered. It was a cosmopolitan world of traders and businessmen of all descriptions. Even a few Muslims from Morocco trickled into the City. On this semi-neutral ground of international commerce, Moroccan Jews and Muslims intermingled with Christians. Muslim merchants, upon arriving in London, resided with Jews. Take, for example, the case of al-Hajj 'Abd as-Salam Buhillal from Tangier. The Buhillals were among the most prominent Fasi families, whose mercantile interests stretched from Timbuktu to Europe.[17] In 1799, 'Abd as Salam Buhillal petitioned the duke of Portland concerning some lost cargo. On a commercial trip to Amsterdam, he had been captured by a French privateer, then freed after a British frigate captured the French ship. Buhillal claimed that the cargo, instead of being restored to his possession, had been sold. Some thirteen years previously he had been

---

[15] Robert Southey, *Letters from England*, ed. Jack Simmons (London, 1951), p. 397.

[16] Archives of the Spanish & Portuguese Jews' Congregation, MS 755, vol. 2. On the Meldolas, see R.D. Barnett, "Haham Meldola and Hazan de Sola," *Transactions of the Jewish Historical Society of England* 21 (1968): 1–10; Gaster, *History of the Ancient Synagogue*, pp. 160–164

[17] On the Buhillals, see Daniel J. Schroeter, *Merchants of Essaouira: Urban Society and Imperialism in Southwestern Morocco, 1844–1886* (Cambridge, 1988), p. 53.

to London, and now he claimed that he was in the service of the sultan. Buhillal resided at 7 Castle Street, the residence of Abraham Benjamin, next to where Bevis Marks was located. He and other Muslim merchants who were taken at sea and made their way to London in 1800, used Bevis Marks as their address.[18]

Our story begins on July 26, 1799, when the Jewish agent of the governor of Essaouira, Meir Macnin, left the Moroccan port for London on board the ship *Aurora*.[19] The *Aurora* originated in London, sailed to Gibraltar, and from there it continued to Essaouira, arriving on June 1. It remained in port for nearly two months. On June 27, it began loading its cargo and set sail about a month later. The cargo was a typical one—the products among the standard exports in the Moroccan trade: calf and goat skins, almonds, and gum arabic. Rarely would more than a dozen ships a year call at the port of Essaouira. In general, Morocco was of no great commercial or political interest to Europe, except insofar as the British wanted to protect and supply their garrison in Gibraltar. England had dominated the Mediterranean trade ever since Napoleon's invasion of Egypt in 1798 and the subsequent victory of the British fleet under Nelson. With the outbreak of the naval war with France in 1793, the French Mediterranean trade had declined, and the demand for English goods grew. Napoleon's subsequent occupation of much of Western Europe crippled the trade of the Dutch and Italians, Morocco's other principal trading partners.[20] By the first decade of the nineteenth century, England had become practically the only country trading with Morocco.

What was of much greater concern to the British authorities than trade was the fact that the *Aurora*, together with two other ships from Essaouira, had come to England from Morocco, where a horrible epidemic of the bubonic plague was decimating the population. The British authorities feared the spread of the epidemic if the ships' crews, passengers, and cargoes were allowed to land. The *Aurora* reached England on August 27, anchoring at Standgate Creek, where it remained for several months. On January 7, 1800, after protracted parliamentary debate on the matter, the British authorities ordered

---

[18] FO 52/14, 17 June 1799, and 6 March 1800, Petitions to Duke of Portland (Foreign Office, Public Record Office).

[19] Parliamentary Papers, House of Commons, Reports, vol. 28, 1799–1800, no. 169.

[20] Alfred C. Wood, *A History of the Levant Company* (New York, 1964), pp. 180–187.

that the crews and passengers be taken on board other vessels and placed under quarantine for fourteen days. On January 18, the three ships were sent out to sea, burned, and sunk in deep water. The value of the ships, cargoes, and personal effects was assessed so that all interested parties could be compensated for their losses. Meir Macnin and his fellow passengers had been aboard the ship for nearly six months.

The reasons for Meir Macnin's departure in 1799 for London are nowhere disclosed in the sources at hand. Undoubtedly, Macnin's commercial ties with London would have guaranteed him the means to establish himself there. Soon after the establishment of the royal port of Essaouira in 1764, which rapidly became Morocco's foremost commercial entrepôt for trade with Europe, Moroccan Jewish merchants began traveling to Europe, and especially to England, where they made increasingly lengthy sojourns. A number of Moroccan Jewish merchants had already settled permanently in London. The timing of Macnin's departure suggests that he may have used the opportunity to accompany his large and valuable shipment of goods, which was assessed at £5,375 (some 39 percent of the value of the cargo on the *Aurora*), as a means of escaping the approach of the plague to Essaouira.

Not surprisingly, Macnin took up residence in the City, a few streets from Bevis Marks, which was also in the vicinity of the commercial district. His arrival in London in 1800 coincided with the rise to prominence of a coterie of Moroccan Jews in England's Sephardic community. Aboard the three ships that left Essaouira in the summer of 1799 were some of the port's leading Jewish merchants. Apart from Meir Macnin, members of two families related to him by marriage were aboard the *Aurora*: Abraham and Solomon Sebag, and Abraham and David Pinto. Other Jewish merchants included Afriat, Coriat, Aflalo, Abensur, and De Lara. Another representative of the leading Muslim merchant family, Buhillal, was also on board. Under normal circumstances, special authorization was needed to travel abroad, and often only after agreement was reached and signed on the amount of deposit to be pledged as security.[21] This was because the Moroccan merchants in Essaouira were trading with the money of the royal treasury, and were, in theory, in-

---

[21] Jean-Louis Miège, *Le Maroc et l'Europe, 1830–1894* (Paris, 1961–62), vol. 2, p. 23.

debted to the sultan. The plague in Morocco led to general pande-
monium in the ranks of the military, and in all probability government officials abandoned their duties. The governor of Essaouira
sent for troops from Agadir to guard the town.[22] With local authority collapsing, there would have been little effort to prevent Macnin
and the other merchants from absconding.

Meir Macnin straddled two different worlds which were rapidly
growing farther apart. Macnin's rise to prominence in London can
be attributed, not only to his acumen and cunning, but to the relative weakness and unimportance of Morocco to Europeans. Moroccan merchants in London did not initially have the capital at their
disposal to enter the world of commerce on British terms. With the
absence of an autonomous group of capitalist merchants, Moroccan
merchants were dependent on their ties to the sultan and the ruling class.

Powerless to compete with the expanding capitalist market of Europe, and fearful of seeing Morocco embroiled in the Mediterranean
conflict, Sultan Mawlay Sulayman implemented a policy of strict
control which hoped to maximize profits for the Makhzan, and min-
imize involvement in European affairs.[23] The export of various items,
such as olive oil, sheep, dates, tallow, and honey, was periodically
prohibited.[24] Mawlay Sulayman was also well aware of events to the
east.[25] In the year before the plague, Napoleon invaded Egypt, causing alarm throughout the Islamic world. Ripples of fear undoubtedly shook the Muslim state of Morocco. The sultan of Turkey wrote
an appeal to the Moroccan sultan to come to the aid of Egypt and
the defense of Islam.[26] Mawlay Sulayman, who had only recently
secured the throne after six years of dynastic struggle, hardly wanted
to get embroiled in the European conflict. Mediterranean traffic
was hampered, not only by the departure of European merchants
during the plague, but by the consequences of the Napoleonic wars
in Europe.[27]

---

[22] FO 52/11, Gibraltar, 13 September 1799, Matra.
[23] FO 174/13, 17 May 1802.
[24] FO 174/13, 14 October 1803.
[25] Muhammad ad-Du'ayyif ar-Ribati, *Tarikh ad-Du'ayyif* (Rabat, 1986), p. 313.
[26] FO 174/2, 3 Rabi' I 1213/15 August 1798. Translation of a dispatch from
the Ottoman sultan to the Moroccan sultan.
[27] See Mohamed El Mansour, *Morocco in the Reign of Mawlay Sulayman* (Wisbech,
Cambridgeshire, 1990), pp. 56–57, 60–61.

Morocco had not been so isolated in decades, and the foreign threat loomed large. Yet if the Moroccan government was to maintain its army in order to consolidate its authority from within, it needed military hardware and other supplies from Europe. A few Moroccan Jewish merchants, with their already established network in Europe, were the solution. By the time the plague broke out in Essaouira, Meir Macnin and his brother Solomon had considerable assets, close connections with the local government of Morocco's most important seaport, and numerous debtors with considerable obligations to their commercial establishment. On this basis, Meir Macnin was able to become Morocco's indispensable agent in Europe.

With his close contacts with the Moroccan administration, Meir Macnin had no difficulty attracting credit in London. His commercial operations there were mostly financed by the governor of Essaouira. Meir would dispatch cargos to his brother, Solomon, and to Essaouira's leading merchant, Judah Guedalla (who was also the uncle of his wife, Zohra née Pinto).[28] These cargoes, for the most part, were advanced on credit by British merchants. But the Macnins' financial links with the governor of Essaouira left them in a vulnerable position. The governor and Solomon Macnin were arrested. Apparently, some half million dollars of Makhzan funds were missing, used by the governor for commerce through the two Macnin brothers. Merchandise dispatched to Morocco was sequestered by the Makhzan.[29] Ultimately the issue was resolved between the Macnins and the Moroccan government. But the over fifty British creditors were unable to recover their goods.[30] The British government was clearly unwilling to act, apart from sending a few formal protests to the Makhzan.[31] The Moroccan trade was too insignificant for much attention to be paid to such a minor matter.

Macnin's status in London's mercantile circles did not seem to be unduly tarnished by his wheeling and dealing. He continued to attract English lenders, as well as contracts with the Moroccan sultan. Macnin also arrogated for himself the position of official representative

---

[28] Monsieur S. Levy clarified these marital links to me in an oral communication in Paris in 1985.

[29] FO 52/11, Tangier, 1 August 1801, Matra to Duke of Portland; 18 September 1801, Matra.

[30] FO 52/14, 26 Muharram 1217/29 May 1802; FO, 52/14, 10 June 1801, Petition to Duke of Portland.

[31] FO 52/11, Tangier, 2 October 1801, Matra.

of the Moroccan government in London. It is doubtful that Mawlay Sulayman had issued him a *carte blanche* to act on behalf of the
Makhzan, although periodically he was used as the sultan's agent.
Nevertheless, Macnin used his office in London not only on behalf
of coreligionists from Morocco, but also for Muslim merchants. For
instance, in 1808 he writes to Lord Castlereagh on behalf of Sidi
Mubarak Qasim of Marrakesh, asking that he be granted a passport
to embark on a British ship.[32]

For about sixteen years after his arrival in England, Macnin pursued his import-export business from London with his brother in
Essaouira. The European-Moroccan trade remained extremely limited in these years because Europe was in the throes of the Napoleonic
wars and the Moroccan sultan was still struggling to assert his authority over both the mountainous interior and the coastal plains. In
1798, prior to the plague, some sixty European trading vessels reached
the port of Essaouira, while in 1812, this number had dwindled to
twenty-four. Only four European trading firms engaged in commerce
with Europe were to be found in Morocco's principal seaport.[33]
Practically the only Jewish mercantile establishments in Essaouira
directly involved in the European trade during these years were Haim
Guedalla, Solomon Macnin, David Macnin, Mordecai Zagury, David
Pinto, and Salem Abitbol (the latter was in partnership with Semtob
Ben Attar and was known also as the Bel Capitain because of his
official position as appointed head of the corps of merchants in the
port).[34] All of these merchants had relatives in London and were
active in the Spanish & Portuguese Jews' Congregation.

In March of 1808, Mawlay Sulayman initiated efforts to obtain a
ship from the British. The *qa'id* of Essaouira, Ahmad b. 'Abd as
Sadiq, was ordered to write Macnin to purchase a brig cutter equipped
with twelve brass cannons, stipulating that it should be delivered to

---

[32] FO 52/14, 10 October 1808.
[33] El Mansour, *Morocco in the Reign*, pp. 62–65. Reference to merchant firms
in Essaouira during these years is found in FO 174/13, December 1808, 1 June
1809, Gwyn to Green; FO 174/20, 4 May 1814, Dupuis to Green, 1 February
1810, 5 April 1810, 1 March 1811, 2 July 1811, 3 April 1812, 29 April 1812,
Gwyn to Green.
[34] Reference to merchant firms in Essaouira during these years is found in FO
174/13, December 1808, 1 June 1809, Gwyn to Green; FO 174/20, 4 May 1814,
Dupuis to Green, 1 February 1810, 5 April 1810, 1 March 1811, 2 July 1811,
3 April 1812, 29 April 1812, Gwyn to Green.

Essaouira within three months.[35] With the recent French occupation of Portugal, the Moroccans were becoming increasingly alarmed. The British agreed to the request.[36] In 1816, the British were still demanding repayment for the ship. Some £10,256 of an account dating from 1809 remained unpaid. Meir Macnin's nephew, D.C. Macnin of London (35 New Broad Street), requested in September that a new arrangement be made. Meir at the time was in Livorno (or Leghorn, as it was known to the English), and his nephew requested that he complete half the payment, stipulating that the other half would be paid by J. and D. Guedalla of Finsbury Square, who were awaiting further instructions from Essaouira. David wrote that Meir was undergoing some commercial difficulties, and he asked that the Foreign Office delay communication to the sultan until advice and remittance arrived. "The proposed communication to the Emperor would most probably be followed by his displeasure at Mr. Macnin's not having immediately obeyed his orders without reference to Mr. Macnin's circumstances, as such displeasure would be highly detrimental to his family and interests in Morocco (the bulk of his property lying there)."[37] Numerous other letters were exchanged on this matter, with Meir stalling for time by offering to meet the payment in dollars at the exchange rate. The British, however, demanded that interest be paid.[38] Partial payment for the brig was only remitted by Judah Guedalla and D.C. Macnin in early 1817.[39]

It seems that Meir Macnin left the country about this time, as evidenced by information provided by Yosef Ben Ribuh, a petitioner to the British government. According to his petition, Ben Ribuh went to Gibraltar in 1811, and was en route to England, but was shipwrecked in the Bay of Biscay. He was able to reach London, where he worked for Macnin until the latter left the country. The petitioner asked the British government to help him pay for his passage to Livorno, where he had some relatives.[40] Meir's nephew, David, continued to represent the Macnin interests from London, in close

---

[35] FO 52/14, 28 Dhu al-Hijja 1222, Sultan to Ahmad b. ʿAbd as-Sadiq; 16 Rabiʿ I 1223, Abd as-Sadiq to Principal Secretary of State; 26 April 1808, Meir Macnin to Castlereagh.

[36] FO 174/13, 24 May 1808, Downing Street, E. Cooke to Meir Macnin.

[37] FO 52/17, 18 September 1816, D.C. Macnin to Earl Bathurst.

[38] FO 52/17, 28 December 1816, Navy Office.

[39] FO 52/18, 11 February 1817, J. Guedalla and D.C. Macnin to Earl Bathurst.

[40] FO 52/19, 8 June 1818, Ben Ribuh to Bathurst.

association with Judah Guedalla. In 1818 both write to Earl Bathurst regarding some letters transmitted from the sultan through their houses in Essaouira.[41]

Back in Morocco, Meir Macnin successfully cultivated his ties with the prince and future sultan, Mawlay 'Abd ar-Rahman, who served as governor of Essaouira for a period of time before Sultan Sulayman's death.[42] The close ties forged became evident when 'Abd ar-Rahman succeeded to the throne in 1822. Shortly thereafter, Meir Macnin became the sultan's Jew. Perhaps never before in Moroccan history had a Jew received such a grandiose mandate. Macnin was granted control of most of Morocco's export trade and appointed ambassador-at-large with the authority to appoint representatives both in Moroccan seaports and in Europe.[43]

After a few years, Macnin's influence in Morocco waned. In 1827, Meir Macnin, quite advanced in age, returned to London, claiming to be entrusted with a diplomatic mission to King George IV.[44] The British refused to receive him in any official capacity, in light of the trail of debts he had left (allegedly about £70,000 in England). The British official who inspected his documents discovered that the *dahir* from the sultan was dated from 1823. Despite threats that he would be subject to arrest,[45] Macnin was able to take up residence and resume commercial activities for a few years, after coming to an agreement with one of his principal creditors.[46]

In the last years of his life, Macnin's financial problems accumulated. In 1831, David Cohen Macnin, with whom Meir had previously been closely associated, was declared bankrupt, with debts amounting to £21,729. Meir was among the largest creditors, claiming some £4,932,[47] but nonetheless continued to incur large debts of his own. In 1832 his creditors, through the Foreign Office, attempted

---

[41] FO 52/19, 2 November 1818, J. Guedalla and D.C. Macnin (now of 110 Fenchurch Street) to Earl Bathurst.

[42] Ahmad b. Khalid an-Nasiri, *Kitab al-istiqsa' li-akhbar duwal al-Maghrib al-Aqsa*, 2nd ed. (Casablanca, 1956), vol. 9, p. 3.

[43] FO 52/28, 22 Safar 1239/27 October 1823, Sultan 'Abd ar-Rahman to King George; Archives du Ministère des Affaires Etrangères, Paris, Correspondance Consulaire et Commerciale, Maroc 28, 22 Safar 1239/19 November 1823, Sultan to Consular Corps; National Archives, Washington, D.C., Despatches from U.S. Consuls in Tangier, Record Group 84, T61, 22 November 1822, Mullowny.

[44] FO 52/28, 25 October 1826, Sultan 'Abd ar-Rahman to King George IV.

[45] FO 52/38, Standgate Creek, 29 April 1827, Smith to R.W. Hay.

[46] FO 52/58, London, 17 May 1827, R. Burchall.

[47] PRO B3/3615 (Bankruptcy Commission Files).

to compel the Makhzan to place an attachment on his property in Morocco. The sultan claimed that Macnin had little property and no significant debts owed to him in Morocco, and that what it amounted to would be insufficient to pay the debts he owed the Makhzan.[48] Again some sort of agreement was reached. Meir Macnin returned to Morocco in about 1833, and died in his city of birth, Marrakesh, in 1835.

In the non-Jewish commercial circles of London, Meir Macnin could only have been regarded with derision. His questionable, seemingly duplicitous business practices could only have served to confirm the well-established, stereotypical preconception of the swindling Jew, coupled with the disparaging image of the Oriental from Barbary. A popular playwright, Richard Cumberland, better known for his philosemitic drama, *The Jew*, wrote a comic farce, *The Jew of Mogadore: A Comic Opera in Three Acts*, in which one of the principal protagonists was allegedly based on Macnin.[49] The play revives the theme of the benevolent Jew found in his previous work, though the setting is Morocco. The theme in both plays is that the miserliness of the Jew is justified by his incredible charity, which of course did little to dispel the negative stereotype. The play opened at the Drury Lane Theatre in 1808, and was poorly reviewed by the critics.[50]

Macnin had therefore clearly become quite notorious in some circles, but within the Sephardic community, he maintained a dignified, aristocratic respectability. It was of course natural that Meir Macnin gravitated toward Bevis Marks. In the year of his arrival in London, 1800, he became a member of the synagogue. His *finta* (a requirement of all members which supported the expenses of the synagogue) was assessed at £6. He was also assigned a prominent seat (*gaveta*) in the synagogue, allocated according to his high rank.[51] In subse-

---

[48] FO 174/126, 8 Muharram 1248/8 June 1832, Sultan 'Abd ar-Rahman to Drummond Hay. The numerous deeds in the family collection prove that the sultan was protecting the family's assets. For many years, the Makhzan looked after the interests of Meir Macnin's daughter, Blida.

[49] This assertion is made by the British consul in Tangier. FO 52/24, 29 November 1823, Douglas.

[50] See Richard J. Dircks, *Richard Cumberland* (Boston, 1976), p. 86; Louis Zangwill, "Richard Cumberland Centenary Memorial Paper," *Transactions of the Jewish Historical Society of England* 7 (1915): 170–173; Gerald Reitlinger, "The Changed Face of English Jewry at the End of the Eighteenth Century," *Transactions of the Jewish Historical Society of England* 23 (1971): 38–39.

[51] Minutes of the Spanish & Portuguese Jews' Congregation, MS 108, fols. 257, 288, 296. Macnin is listed either as Meir Cohen Macnin or as Meir Cohen.

quent years, Macnin's *finta* increased considerably.[52] In 1814, Meir Macnin was elected *parnas*, and the following year he became the *presidente* of the executive council, the Mahamad (election was for one year).[53] Once elected to the Mahamad, a former *parnas* often continued to play a leading role in the congregation, and that seems to have been the case with Macnin.

Meir Macnin rapidly became integrated into the upper echelons of the Sephardic elite of London, his wealth and status clearly over-shadowing the disdain that some of the Sephardim may have had for the *berberiscos*. Eleven days after her marriage to Moses Montefiore, the most prominent leader of Anglo-Jewry for much of the nine-teenth century, Judith Montefiore (the daughter of Levi Barent Cohen) wrote in her diary: "Mr. Macnin, Mr. Sebag and Mrs. Sebag (?) dined with us, and we spent a very agreeable evening."[54] Marital ties were a key for entering the Sephardic upper class, and indeed, the Mahamad of the Spanish and Portuguese Synagogue prohibited its male members from marrying below their social rank without permission.[55] The following year, Moses Montefiore's sister married Solomon Sebag, a relative of Macnin, born in Essaouira in 1783,[56] and arriving in England with Macnin on the *Aurora* in 1800. The Guedallas also became linked to Montefiore and Macnin in mar-riage: Judah Guedalla's son Haim, who became one of the most prominent Jews in England, married a daughter of Solomon Sebag.[57]

Meir Macnin, therefore, was able to rapidly ascend the Sephardic hierarchy, not because he achieved "respectability" in occidental soci-ety, but because he was still a part of a Sephardic world order which transcended one's affiliation to the nation state. In many respects, London became the epicenter of the Sephardic world, ironically at a time when a significant number of Jews were becoming accultur-ated to English society. Despite his many years in England, Meir

---

[52] In 1809, the congregation decided to increase the maximum *finta* of a single member to £56 (4 percent of £1,400); Hyamson, *Sephardim of England*, p. 241.

[53] Minutes of the Spanish & Portuguese Jews' Congregation, MS 110, fols. 128, 156.

[54] Lucien Wolf, *Essays in Jewish History*, ed. Cecil Roth (London, 1934), p. 246.

[55] Hyamson, *Sephardim of England*, p. 190.

[56] *Diaries of Sir Moses and Lady Montefiore*, ed. L. Loewe (London, 1891), vol. 1, p. 9; Wolf, *Essays*, p. 246, n. 1. In the quotation from Lady Montefiore's diary, who Mrs. Sebag would have been is unclear (perhaps why Wolf inserted a ques-tion mark).

[57] Paul Goodman, *Think and Thank* (London, 1933), p. 119.

Macnin only spoke a rudimentary English; his Spanish and Arabic were all he needed for his dignified communal and social activities. Schools for Sephardic children still taught in Spanish and Portuguese in the early nineteenth century. The records of the Spanish and Portuguese synagogue were kept in Portuguese until 1819, when English began to be used. At about that time, English was also becoming the language of instruction in the schools. In the 1830s, sermons in English were introduced in the liturgy.[58]

By the time Meir Macnin returned to England in 1827, a new generation of communal leaders was emerging. The new Sephardic elite attained prominence, not because of the international Sephardic network, but because of their ability to enter into English high society.[59] Prominent members of the Jewish community were obtaining baronetcies, the lower rank of the English hereditary nobility.[60] Conservative observers were mourning the decline of the traditional English gentry as commercial wealth became the avenue to reach the ranks of nobility.

Macnin's demise symbolically marks the end of a Sephardic world order where descendants of Spanish and Portuguese Jews had maintained a network of connections and ties in conducting the Mediterranean and Atlantic trade. By the time of the Damascus Affair in 1840, Jews felt that they had attained respectability in English society, and their identity had shifted away from the Sephardic world and toward a civic, national English identity. Moroccan Jews, and for that matter Jews throughout the Middle East and North Africa, were henceforth regarded as backward, waiting for the beneficial effects of European Jewish civilization.

Macnin's position as a Moroccan court Jew and his activities in London are representative of a specific conjuncture in Sephardic history. The era in which Macnin lived was the last age in which affiliation to the Sephardic world still transcended one's national affiliation. Despite the fact that the gap between Moroccan and English economic and military power was obvious in the early nineteenth century, the Sephardic Jewish merchants who frequently trav-

---

[58] Hyamson, *Sephardim of England*, pp. 159–260, 269–272.

[59] This process led many prominent Sephardim to abandon Judaism altogether. See Todd M. Endelman, *Radical Assimilation in English Jewish History, 1656–1945* (Bloomington, 1990), pp. 15 ff.

[60] Ibid., p. 75.

eled between Europe and North Africa demonstrate that there was a kind of parity between Anglo and Moroccan Jewry. There was as yet hardly a sense of a dichotomous relationship between a superior, Western, modern Jew, and the Oriental. The sense of parity was undermined when English Jews increasingly become a part of national civic society. Emancipation, in this sense, brought an end to Sephardic history. Henceforth, the Jewish world was divided between a new set of juxtapositions: East versus West, modern versus traditional, and so forth. In the last few years of Macnin's life, the sultan's Jew had become an anachronistic symbol of a bygone era.

ASPECTS OF THE EFFECTS OF JEWISH PHILANTHROPIC SOCIETIES IN MOROCCO

M. Mitchell Serels

Yeshiva University

The *hebrot*, or beneficial societies, were essential elements of every traditional Jewish community organization. One of the most important of these societies was the *hebra qadisha*, or burial society. The need to obtain and maintain a cemetery or other burial place was exemplified in Jewish history by the patriarch Abraham's purchase of the cave of Machpelah as a final resting place for the matriarch Sarah.[1] The Bible extends a prohibition on ritual defilement of the *cohanim*, the priestly caste, by contact with the dead or their graves.[2] Graves, therefore, had to be marked and the markings maintained.

The Talmud reports that in Iraq there were societies to tend to the dying and the dead, thereby freeing all others from the obligation to provide for the terminally ill and for funeral needs.[3] As a consequence, in Jewish communities everywhere, including Morocco, there were *hebrot qadisha* which acted as burial societies. These societies and other beneficial societies faced the demands for modernization with varying degrees of success.

Formal regulations governing the conduct of the *hebrot*, and defining the scope of their activities, were established early in Spain. The Aljma of Lérida drew up regulations for the *hebra qadisha* and charged an entrance fee for its members. Members were required to serve lifelong unless there was a mitigating illness. The *hebra*'s regulations were to be reviewed every five years. Funds were to come from subscriptions and from endowments. They were to be invested, rented, or lent to non-Jews at interest. The monies generated thereby were to be used to bury the poor. Surplus revenue could be disposed of by providing additional services to the poor.[4]

---

[1] Genesis 23:4.
[2] Leviticus 5:2.
[3] Moed Katan 23b, Sanhedrin 47a.
[4] Isidore Epstein, *Studies in the Communal Life of the Jews of Spain* (New York: Sepher-Hermon Press, 1968), pp. 66–68.

Some Spanish communities did not have their own burial societies, either because they were too small or because a land allotment for a cemetery had not been granted. Cervera was one town which did not have a *hebra qadisha* but relied on the society in a neighboring community.[5]

The need for welfare benefits provided the stimulus for the development of various specialized *hebrot* not related to burial. These regulations were brought to Morocco by the *megurashim* upon their exile from Spain in 1492.

The impetus for the specific *hebrot* was a desire to eliminate begging amongst the Jews in various Moroccan towns and villages. The mutuality of the Jews dates to the Talmud's requirement for the development of the *tamhui*, or charitable distribution of food to the hungry and the homeless. Monies were collected in a designated container called a *hupa*, a term extended to mean the funding as well as the alms box in which the funds were collected.[6]

In addition to the burial societies and the groups that provided for the immediate feeding of the hungry, there were *hebrot* that performed many other necessary social functions. All in all, the *hebrot* fulfilled a number of important social needs.

First, they were a source of status for the wealthy individuals who funded them, thereby obtaining positions of power and importance. The post of *sheikh el-yehud* was hereditary in most communities. Next in importance were those who endowed synagogues if there was a need;[7] but directly after this came the *parnassim*, or wardens, of charitable organizations.

Second, the *hebrot* provided work for the poor in charitable surroundings. Often they hired the poor to dig graves, distribute food, or run other errands. The societies also provided for the voluntary redistribution of wealth within the Jewish community. As funding for these organizations was voluntary, donations took the form of cash or endowments of land and property (*heqdesh*). The community was required to collect the taxes to pay the *djizia*, but had to tax meat and wine in order to raise funds. Donations facilitated the transfer of funds.[8]

---

[5] Ibid.

[6] Baba Batra 8b.

[7] The *sheikh el-yehud* served as the leader of the local Jewish community, often a hereditary position. The major task of the *sheikh el-yehud* was the collection of the *djizia* (poll tax), which was paid annually to the local ruler.

[8] The Hebrew term *heqdesh* signifies sanctified property.

Taken together, the *hebrot* provided the necessary social welfare structure for the semi-autonomous Moroccan Jewish communities. As Moroccan Jewry, until the most modern period, had little mobility within the sultanate, the needs of the individual became the needs of the community.

The societies provided an outlet for individuals seeking power within the community but unable to obtain it, and simultaneously they maintained the stability of the communal establishment. Individuals could establish new *hebrot* or rise to power in established ones, thereby acting in leadership roles without threatening to overturn the established Jewish leaders. The *hebrot* thus were a training ground for potential leaders.

In some Moroccan communities the *hebra qadisha* assumed various tasks related to the community's welfare needs beyond providing burial for the poor. In other communities, these tasks were assumed by specialized *hebrot*.

In the Rif Mountains, where the graves of various *sadaqim* are located, *hebrot* were established to organize the *hilula*, the pilgrimage to these various graves. These *hebrot* provided candles for sale at the graves, maintained the gravesites, and established decorum in the area. Often they coordinated their activities so that there would be no conflict of scheduling in order to maximize the donations to the poor who often crowded the gravesites during the *hilula*.[9]

In some communities the burial society was called the *hebra qadisha*, in others it was the *hebra geummelout hasadim*. In Tangier, the burial society was known by the latter name.[10] In Sefrou, it was called *Hebrat Eliahu Hanabi*.[11]

The other societies in Sefrou included the *qeren linsoe yetomim*, which funded the marriages of orphans; the *hebrat bikur holim*, which provided sick visitation and medicine for the poor; and the *moshab zeqanim*, which provided home care for the elderly poor.[12]

In 1938, the *Hebrat Eliahu Hanabi* expanded its activities to include hospitality by providing bed and board to male or female visitors; it also gave funds to a poor father to pay for the circumcision

---

[9] Issachar Ben-Ami, *Haaretset Haqedoshim beqereb Yehudei Moroqo* [Saint veneration among the Jews in Morocco] (Jerusalem: Magnes Press, 1984), p. 147.

[10] M. Mitchell Serels, *History of the Jews of Tangier* (New York: Sepher-Hermon Press, 1991), p. 41.

[11] David Ovadia, *Qehilat Sefrou* [Community of Sefrou]. (Jerusalem, 1975), p. 276.

[12] Ibid., pp. 317–318.

of his son and made *masot* for the destitute. In addition, it continued to provided shrouds and graves for the poor.[13]

In 1932, Sefrou's *hebrat moshab zeqanim* was headed by David Simon Elkaslassi. It served four or five elderly indigent men. They were required to attend synagogue and then read the Zohar until *minha*. While they studied they would receive packages of tea and sugar every two days. Funds were collected from Jewish storekeepers, and each of the men was given 75 francs a week for reading the Zohar. These elderly Jews were therefore useful and received some financial benefit, albeit limited.[14]

The Sefrou *biqur holim* society was organized into an effective body in 1926. However, it was continually plagued by small-scale thinking and limited finances. On January 20, 1949, the society wrote to the French Protectorate government requesting that it be reorganized. The society had a positive cash flow, although services had been severely curtailed. Its assets (all amounts given in francs) included:

cash on hand	49,677.50
men's contributions	106,738.00
women's auxiliary	43,435.00
donations	133,027.50
subventions from Jewish Committee for French Aid	15,000.00
receipts from medicines	33,961.00
Total assets	421,839.00 francs

The expenditures included:

doctor and nurse	89,250.00
purchase of medicines	110,656.50
food supplies	66,358.00
financial aid of 24 February	22,150.00
travel to Fez	8,760.00
rent & office supplies	2,749.00
accounting	7,675.50
miscellaneous expenses	3,333.00
Total expenditures	310,932.00 francs
Cash on hand	110,977.00 francs

---

[13] Ibid., p. 380.
[14] Ibid., p. 386.

However, the *biqur holim* society never founded a hospital or a meaningful medical-care program, despite its nearly half-million-franc budget.[15]

The Sefrou burial society fared less well. It broke up into four groups, each claiming legitimacy, and each led by a different aspirant for communal leadership—Abraham Assouline, Judah Harosh, Pinhas Benelbas, and Haim Itah. A compromise solution was worked out, whereby no women, married or single, were permitted to attend interments, and each group was put in charge of a different area of the society's activities: one took care of digging the graves, another of reading the Zohar, a third of celebrating the *hilula* of the deceased, and the fourth of providing the consolation meals. Each group was to have eleven members and to be headed by one of the four rival leaders. Thus the political rivalry led to a less effective society.[16]

In most communities of the French Protectorate, the *biqur holim* societies did not develop into systematic health-care providers unless they received outside assistance from the occupying power.

In Meknès, in addition to the usual *hebra qadisha*, *bikur holim*, *guemmelout hasadim*, and *hakhnasat orhim* societies, other groups were organized to meet the needs of the community's poor, including *em habanim*, *matan beseter*, *ezrat nesuin*, *yetumim ve almanot*, and *lemudei tora*.[17] The Meknès *hebra qadisha* was known locally as *Hebrat Shimon Bar Yohai* after the rabbi who is most closely identified with the Zohar, read in memory of the deceased.[18]

The Meknès *matan beseter* society, like the other societies of the same name that developed in various localities throughout Morocco, arose and disappeared frequently. Usually it was set up by relatives of the person who was to receive the aid. The purpose of the society was to provide assistance in a secret manner for someone who was embarrassed to ask for charity. Once the indigent individual was again on his feet financially, the society disappeared, only to be reborn when some other wealthy person wanted to provide discrete assistance to a needy relative.

While the *hebra hakhnasat orhim* satisfied the mishnaic injunction of *eshel: akhila, setia ve lina* ("food, drink, and lodging"), the community opened a *mahlon le orhim* (guest-house) under the influence of the pro-

---

[15] Ibid., pp. 380–382.
[16] Ibid., pp. 40–47.
[17] Gaby Levi, *Yehudei Meknes* [Jews of Meknès] (Tel-Aviv: Alef, 1982), p. 49.
[18] Ibid., p. 68.

tectorate, although the initial funding came from wealthy individuals.[19]

The *em habanim* society developed as a women's auxiliary organization to supervise the religious school, feed and clothe poor students in the Talmud Torah, and assist in raising funds for teachers' salaries.

Hebrat yetomim ve almanot provided tefillin for *bar misva* boys and helped widows to remarry. Whenever an important person married off a son or a daughter, he financed the marrying off of a widow. When an important individual celebrated the *bar misva* of his son, he would also arrange, through this society, for the *bar misva* of an orphan. All the poor would be invited to the *seuda misva* (festive meal) tendered in honor of the fulfillment of the precept.[20]

Other societies which rose and dissipated in Meknès included *qimha de pesha*, *malbish anivim*, and *gebliot*. By 1912, there were forty Talmud Torah societies, including *Ets Haim*, *Bet El* (which included the synagogues they founded), *Qorei Zohar* (comprised of elderly people), *Qorei Baqasot* (whose members returned to the synagogue after midnight on Friday nights), and *Lomdei Midrash*. These societies provided traditional education centered around the reading of traditional texts even with limited understanding.[21]

In Tetuán, there were several beneficial societies primarily concerned with caring for the needy. In 1889, the local charitable organizations supported 160 families.[22] In the decade from 1940 to 1950, the city's voluntary societies fed and clothed as many as 6,000 people, including 400 children receiving supplemental food. Funds during this period were raised from playing bridge, rummy, and canasta. When activities of this kind were later taken over by the Joint Distribution Committee, Oeuvre de Secour aux Enfants, and ORT, the societies were abandoned.[23] The *hebra biqur holim* developed a maternity and disease-prevention clinic.[24]

The *hebra qadisha* was the most important society in Tetuán, and it maintained its secretive character throughout the life of the city's

---

[19] Ibid.

[20] Ibid.

[21] Ibid., p. 70.

[22] Sarah Leibovici, *Chronique des juifs de Tetuán, 1860–1896* (Paris: Editions Maisonneuve & Larose, 1984), p. 277.

[23] Alegria Bendelac, *Los Nuestros* (New York: Peter Lang, 1987), p. 268.

[24] Ibid., p. 269.

Jewish community. The sheikh of the *hebra* was often at odds with the president of the Jewish community, for the *hebra* was politically autonomous and resisted all attempts by the Community Council to control it and absorb its funds.[25]

The Tetuán burial society held its annual banquet on the seventh of Adar, the traditional commemoration of the death date of Moses. Membership in the burial society, often called by its Judeo-Spanish name, Sancta Hermanidad, was a great honor. Fathers would often designate newborn sons to be members of the *hebra*. The father would state at the circumcision: *le meti en la hebra*. The sheikh of the *hebra* would accept the child into the society by enunciating the phrase: *este es para Rebbi Shimon*. The child would then be given his name and the sheikh would pronounce the customary blessing for the newly circumcised child, adding the words: *Bueno, esta ya es hebri*. When the young man reached maturity, he would be initiated into the *hebra*.[26]

In Tangier, operating under the umbrella of the Jewish governing council, or Junta, the various societies set up a sophisticated welfare organization—a kind of Federation of Jewish Philanthropies. The Tangier organization sought to provide the poor with food, clothing, free schooling, and health care. The goal was to ensure that no one suffered; the poor would continue to be poor but would not be miserable.

The Jews of Tangier were concerned about their world image even prior to the internationalization of the port city.[27] Tangier was one of the newest of the Moroccan Jewish communities, and consequently the development of its *hebrot* and the formation of the Junta occurred in close temporal proximity. The four major *hebrot* in Tangier were the *aniyim*, *biqur holim*, *guemmelout hasadim*, and *obrim ve shabim* societies. In 1850, these *hebrot* were headed by Messod Abecassis, Joseph Ashriqui, Joseph Toledano, and Jacob Toledano respectively.[28] When the Junta was formed in 1853, these four men were invited by Chief Rabbi Bengio to serve on it. Thus, from the inception of the Junta, the *hebrot* were included.

The *biqur holim* society was headed by a very wealthy businessman. The latter two *hebrot* were headed by members of the Toledano

---

[25] Ibid., p. 276.
[26] Ibid., p. 274.
[27] Ibid., pp. 266–267.
[28] Serels, *History of the Jews of Tangier*, pp. 38–41.

family, originally from Meknès. It was the Toledanos who led the fight to free Tangier from the rabbinical jurisdiction of Tetuán and establish the independence of the local Jewish community.

Funds for the Tangier *hebrot* came from the traditional sources: alms boxes (usually collected during the daily recitation of the morning prayer *Vayebareh David*), *nedabot*, subscriptions, and legacies. In 1861, the Junta took steps to ensure that the societies were completely accountable to it. Money raised by the societies was to be handed over to the Junta, which would then allocate funds on a percentage basis: 50 percent for the *aniyim* society, 25 percent for *biqur holim*, and 25 percent for *obrim ve shabim*.[29] The burial society raised its own funds from traditional subscriptions and from legacies. It also kept its own records, which need to be studied. The Tangier Junta's board included a number of bankers who were closely affiliated with these societies. In 1860, a *malbish arumim* society was founded to clothe Jewish refugees from the Spanish-Moroccan War.[30]

In 1863, there was a challenge to the traditional burial society by Salomon Abuzaglo. He founded a rival burial society named *Hebrat Hesed Ve Emet*. The Junta, supporting the *Hebrat Guemmelout Hasadim*, summoned Abuzaglo to a meeting. Summonses were issued on May 19, 1863 and August 2, 1863. They remained unanswered. The Junta then bypassed Abuzaglo and spoke directly to the members of the new society.[31] They agreed to abide by the Junta's decisions. The Junta then issued the following directives:

1. The Junta is supreme over each and every *hebra*.
2. The new society will continue to function but will limit its duties to comforting mourners and saying the *Mismara*.[32]
3. The new society is accountable to the Junta.
4. It is to open a synagogue called *Bet Qeneset Hebra Hesed Ve Emet*.
5. The society may use its funds for no other purpose.
6. The society will be reorganized in a democratic fashion.[33]

---

[29] Ibid., p. 47.
[30] Ibid., p. 48.
[31] Ibid., p. 58.
[32] The *Mismara* is a specific service held in memory of the deceased. The service includes a reading from the Zohar and recitation of segments of Psalm 119, spelling out the name of the deceased and his/her mother in Hebrew.
[33] Serels, *History of the Jews of Tangier*, pp. 59–60.

The only other threat to the consolidation of the societies in Tangier came from Judah Assayag, who founded the *Hebrat Rodef Sedaqa Ve Hesed* charitable organization in March 1864. Assayag was community-minded, but claimed that the Junta had no jurisdiction over him because he had been born in Algeria and therefore was not a native Jew but a French protege. The Junta objected to the unauthorized new society and ordered its members to remit all funds; 50 percent was to be given to the school for poor girls, and 50 percent to be used for dowering poor girls. The society was then to disband.

The members objected to the distribution of funds laid down by the Junta, arguing that they had specified other purposes for the money when soliciting contributions. The Junta insisted and the society was disbanded. There were no other objections to the Junta consolidating the work of the *hebrot* as subcommittees of the Junta.[34] All further welfare assistance would come as a communal effort channeled through existing societies.

The most dramatic changes occurred in the *biqur holim* society. In the decade 1850–1860, it was led by Joseph Ashriqui, who had given the synagogue named Shearith Joseph to the community. The *hebra* ran a lying-in clinic in Holland House. When the British consul, Thomas Reade, objected to the quality of health care as not up to European standards, Ashriqui reorganized the society as a hospital along the following lines:

1. All patients were to receive hospital and nutritional care. Home care was to be provided if possible. There was to be coordination between the parnas of the hospital and the parnas of the poor fund.
2. The hospital would provide beds, linen, etc.
3. The society would hire a doctor, preferably French. If a French doctor was unavailable, the society would hire a Spanish physician.
4. The hospital would have its own special account.
5. No one could be employed by the hospital without the express permission of the parnas.
6. The hospital was responsible to the Junta, and the parnas was required to report frequently to the Junta.

---

[34] Ibid., pp. 72–73.

7. Donations pledged at the Torah for the hospital fund would be paid directly to the hospital committee.
8. All patients would be accepted regardless of religion.
9. The sum of 1,000 frances would be used to purchase a building for the hospital.
10. Two members of the Junta would visit the hospital every month and report to the Junta independently of the parnas of the hospital.[35]

Haim Benchimol, a wealthy banker and member of the Junta, donated a trust fund including cash and property to perpetually endow the hospital, which was then named the Hôpital Benchimol in his honor. The Junta granted funds to the hospital to cover any deficit that might develop.[36] For more than sixty years, *Benchimol Hôpital* was the only Jewish hospital in Morocco. Together with its affiliated old-age home, it continues to function.

The *Hebra Obrim ve Shabim* changed its name in January 1866 to *Hebrat Hakhnasat Orhim*.[37] This society continued to offer assistance into the 1950s. During the period of World War II, it served as a channel for Joint Distribution Committee aid to European Jewish refugees who found a haven in Tangier. In 1956, with Moroccan independence, some Jews from the south of Morocco were stuck in Tangier while trying to leave for Israel. The society provided them with assistance, although some remained for nearly two years.

In 1918, there were rivalries among the members of the Tangier burial society. There were challenges to the parnas from other individuals who wanted the status that accompanied the post. The Junta allowed for expanded power by dividing the burial society into five subcommittees: *rehissa*,[38] cemetery, *velas*,[39] treasury, and secretariat.[40] This society continues to function.

More research needs to be done on the influence and effectiveness of these societies. As they were rivals of the Alliance Israélite Universelle, the AIU reports used to analyze Moroccan Jewish life are slanted

---

[35] Ibid., pp. 80–82.
[36] Ibid., p. 38.
[37] Ibid., p. 94.
[38] *Rehisa* (Hebrew for "washing") is part of the preparations of the body for interment.
[39] Distribution of Candles.
[40] Serels, *History of the Jews of Tangier*, p. 228.

at best. The officials who wrote the reports to the AIU headquarters in Paris often portrayed Moroccan communal leaders in a negative light. Unfortunately, all too often researchers rely heavily on the AIU's records and therefore fail to develop a complete picture of the communities.

Bibliography

Actas de Hebra Qadisha Geumellout Hasadim de Tanger.

Actas de la Junta de Tanger.

Ben-Ami, Issachar. *Haaretset Haqedoshim beqereb Yehudei Moroqo.* Jerusalem: Magnes, 1984.

Bendelac, Alegria. *Los Nuestros. Sejina, Letuarios, Jaquetia y Fraja.* New York: Peter Lang, 1987.

Epstein, Isidore. *Studies in the Communal Life of the Jews of Spain.* New York: Sepher-Hermon Press, 1968.

Ovadia, David. *Qehilat Sefrou.* Jerusalem, 1975.

Serels, M. Mitchell. *History of the Jews of Tangier.* New York: Sepher-Hermon Press, 1991.

Vilar, Juan Bautista. *Tetuán en el Resurgimiento Judío Contemporaneo.* Caracas: Biblioteca Popular Sefardi, 1985.

MORES AND CHORES AS DETERMINANTS
OF THE STATUS OF JEWISH WOMEN IN LIBYA

RACHEL SIMON

Princeton University

Changes in the position of women may serve as indicators for developments within the society at large. Their status, similar to that of other segments of the population, is shaped by the combined influence of internal and external forces. Furthermore, when dealing with a minority which has strong connections with similar groups abroad, the range of influences may involve the authorities and majority society in the country of residence, the traditions of the minority group, and the influence of its counterparts abroad.

Women's status in different Jewish communities is a function of environmental, socioeconomic, and political forces as well as the dictates of Jewish culture, tradition, and religion. Consequently, changes in Jewish women's status may be instigated by factors originating outside the Jewish community, but it is imperative that what is regarded as fundamental be kept intact, and that people feel the need for change. This paper examines the reasons for changes in the status of Jewish women in Libya during the late nineteenth century and the first half of the twentieth.

The late nineteenth century was an important turning point in the status of Jewish women in Libya due to changes in economic conditions, the social and cultural involvement of the Ottoman state (which ruled Libya from 1551 to 1911), and the penetration (mostly cultural and economic) of European powers (mainly Italy and France).[1] The Italian occupation (1911–1942/43), followed by the British military administration (1942/43–1951), included large-scale Italian colonization and the presence of European (Italian, German, and British) military forces and administrators, all of which influenced the behavior and beliefs of the indigenous population.

---

[1] For a detailed examination of the subject, see R. Simon, *Change Within Tradition Among Jewish Women in Libya* (Seattle: University of Washington Press, 1992).

The move from an environment which was predominantly Muslim
and Jewish to one in which the political and military power was in
European hands did not fail to have an impact on the Jewish community and the status of its women. The growing Italian settlement
in Libya and the fact that most of the Jews lived in cities, which
served as administrative centers, also strengthened the contacts of
Jews with Europeans, and increased the latter's impact upon them.

The Jewish minority in Libya was a loyal component of the population as long as its own traditions and existence were not threatened. In keeping with this tradition, the Jews turned their allegiance
to Italy once it became the sovereign power in Libya. But even
before the Italian occupation, a large number of urban Jews influential
in communal affairs had been European (mainly Italian) citizens and
had close economic and social contacts with Europe. Thus, Italian
influence over important segments of the Jewish community had
started to take root long before the actual occupation.[2]

Although the majority of the Jews lived in the urban centers, a
significant number were villagers.[3] This environmental divergence
had implications for the penetration of external influences and brought
about different economic patterns, which in turn had an impact on
the condition of women. Moreover, once external influences began to
cast their mark on the indigenous society, they were stronger in the
big coastal urban centers than in the rural hinterland. Consequently,
developments were not equal in various parts of the country due to
different starting points, proximity to the centers of change, and the
existence of diversified role models.

Traditional Status of Jewish Women in Libya

The norms of the Muslim majority society coupled with Jewish traditions shaped the status of Jewish women in Libya until the late
nineteenth century, and even afterwards to some extent. Muslim

---

[2] For details see R. Simon, "The Relations of the Jewish Community of Libya
with Europe in the Late Ottoman Period," in *Les relations intercommunautaires juives en
Méditerranée occidentale XIIIe–XXe siècles*, ed. J.-L. Miege (Paris: CNRS, 1984), pp.
70–78.

[3] Libyan Jewry numbered some 20,000 at the end of the Ottoman period, and
some 35,000 before the mass emigration of 1949–51. Most of the country's Jews
lived in the big coastal urban centers of Tripoli and Benghazi, but a large number lived in small towns and villages in the countryside.

norms had a significant impact on the division between the public, male domain and the home, female domain, whereas Jewish tradition influenced women's roles in the Jewish community and at home and also their cultural experiences.

Urban Jewish women were usually kept at home—first in their fathers' and later in their husbands' houses.[4] When they left their homes, it was usually to visit relatives or go to the synagogue. Since in most towns the Jews lived in special neighborhoods, the possibility of meeting non-Jews was small, until the late nineteenth century, when Jewish families started to move out to mixed neighborhoods. Women were responsible for all the work at home, but in town, those chores which required stepping out (e.g., shopping, bringing water, etc.) were performed by men. Urban women past the age of thirteen were veiled when in the presence of nonrelated males, and wore long-sleeved, long-skirted dresses.[5] They were married at a young age (usually around twelve), and had hardly any say in the selection of their husbands.[6] There was, however, a special event in Tripoli, the Feast of the Roses (Hag ha-Shoshanim) on the last day of Passover, when unveiled and nicely dressed young women presented themselves in front of their homes for marriageable Jewish men to choose from.[7] This selection required parental approval, but not necessarily the bride's consent.

The definition of household work was broader in the village than in the town.[8] Village women had more work to do in a wider area, but this in turn increased their freedom of movement and action, including their contacts with nonrelative males. Thus, women went each day to draw water, and since at times, especially in the summer, this could be a lengthy process, it enabled them to meet nonrelated males, a process which often led to marriage.[9] In addition, once a week women went to fetch wood, and in doing so had to

---

[4] D. Arie, Tripoli, to AIU, Paris, 1 June 1898, AIU Archives, Libyan Series (hereafter cited as AAIU), file IC-12.

[5] M. Ha-Cohen, *Higgid Mordecai* (Jerusalem: Ben-Zvi Institute), pp. 47–48, 336.

[6] H.E. Goldberg, "The Jewish Wedding in Tripolitania: A Study in Cultural Sources," *Maghreb Review*, 3, no. 9 (September–October 1978): 1–6; Ha-Cohen, *Higgid Mordecai*, pp. 274, 305.

[7] T. Sutton, "Usages, moeurs et superstitions des Israélites tripolitains," *Revue des écoles de l'Alliance Israélite Universelle* 2 (1902): 154–155; F. Zuaretz et al., *Yahadut Luv* (Tel Aviv: Va'ad Qehilot Luv be-Yisra'el, 1980), p. 378.

[8] Ha-Cohen, *Higgid Mordecai*, pp. 49–50, 193–194, 303–309; N. Slousch, *Travels in North Africa* (Philadelphia: Jewish Publication Society, 1927), pp. 63–64, 159.

[9] Ha-Cohen, *Higgid Mordecai*, pp. 274–275.

wander in the fields and the woods for several hours, far from the supervision of their male guardians. Their work also had an impact on their clothing; they were usually unveiled and their arms were bare.[10] It was regarded as shameful for rural women to be idle, and as a result they did all the work themselves; even when technological developments could ease their lives, they were reluctant to take advantage of them, or might not have had the means to procure them. When they had surpluses, they would sell them privately to neighbors, but their work continued to be connected with the house.[11]

Only a few Libyan Jewish women worked at waged jobs outside their households, whether widely or narrowly defined, and these were mostly in a female environment. The most common occupations were midwifery and cosmetics (mainly for brides).[12] They were usually kept in certain families, and taught by the older to the younger generation, similar to the manner in which household skills and male professions were transmitted.

Libyan Jewish women were traditionally deprived of any formal Jewish education that could have prepared them for participation in religious activities, because according to Orthodox Judaism women have no role in public religion. Nonetheless, there were women who received some education, mainly when their male relatives chose to teach them in private. The education of most women consisted of no more than learning from their female relatives how to run the household along with various oral traditions, some of which were unique to women. Thus, until the late nineteenth century most Libyan Jewish women remained illiterate and ignorant of the spiritually prestigious subjects.

Agents of Change

Politics

Political developments instigated changes in the legal system, ideas, attitudes, and modes of behavior that in turn left a mark on the status of Jewish women in Libya. Under Ottoman rule, the external

---

[10] Ibid., p. 291.
[11] Ibid., pp. 290, 308.
[12] Ibid., pp. 272, 370; D. Noy, *Shiv'im Sippurim ve-Sippur mi-pi Yehudey Luv* (Jerusalem: Bi-Tefutzot ha-Golah, 1967), p. 109.

influence of the majority society and the authorities was based on customs prevalent among Muslims. To a large extent, this influenced urban Jewish women to be veiled, locked at home, and have little role in mixed-gender society, even among Jews. Toward the end of the Ottoman period, the authorities began to advocate Western ideas (including some changes in the attitude toward women, such as female education), but this had little effect on the local population in Libya. Those Jews who were influenced by Western ideas belonged mainly to the rich urban mercantile class, and looked for their inspiration to the original source of the ideas (i.e., European models) and not to Westernized Ottomans. Due to their growing contacts with Europe, they gradually started to view Europeans, and not Muslim Libyans and Ottomans, as their external societal role models.[13]

From 1911 on, Libyan Jews lived in a Muslim society that was ruled by Italy, and was increasingly influxed by Italian settlers. This, and the attitudes of the rich mercantile class, brought increasing numbers of Libyan Jews to view Italy, and not Muslim society, as the external model to emulate. But because many Jews lived in predominantly Muslim towns and villages, they had to keep in mind the possible reactions of their Muslim neighbors to their contacts with the Italians, whom the Muslims resisted as occupiers.

The Europeanization of Libya's Jews was further strengthened because the Italian regime, especially after the Fascist party came to power in 1922, had as one of its declared aims the "civilizing and advancing" of the country's "primitive" society, including a change in the attitude toward women. The authorities advocated female education, approved of women working outside their households, and regarded adult women, especially Italian citizens, as independent human beings who were free to decide on their own futures. When it was in line with official policy, the authorities involved the courts and the administrative apparatus to protect Jewish women's rights during conflicts within the family regarding the right of women to marry against the will of their fathers.[14]

The growth of Zionism in the Jewish community of Libya in the twentieth century brought forth yet another political force which had an important influence on the position of women. Although the

---

[13] For more details on these contacts, see Simon, "Relations of the Jewish Community of Libya with Europe."

[14] R. De Felice, *Jews in an Arab Land: Libya, 1835–1970* (Austin: University of Texas Press, 1985), pp. 119–120, 155–160.

Libyan Zionist movement was small in size, its cultural and social influence far exceeded the boundaries of its membership. The Zionists advocated the notion of a complete change in Jewish life and behavior, with the creation of a "new Jew" (not excluding women from this definition) with new roles in the future society; and to this end they began to integrate women in their activities in the 1930s, with the establishment of Hebrew courses by the Ben-Yehuda Society in Tripoli. This involvement grew in the 1940s, with the foundation of Hebrew schools, the pioneering youth movement He-Halutz, and communes, when Jewish soldiers and emissaries from Palestine gave a strong push and support to these tendencies. All these ideological, administrative, and structural changes were important in setting the ground for social, economic, and cultural changes in the position of Jewish women.

Economics

Just as the economic demands on rural women increased their freedom, so did changes in the economic structure of Libya toward the end of the nineteenth century. Among the major factors causing these transformations were shifts in the trans-Saharan trade between sub-Saharan Africa and Europe, which influenced economic life all along the trade routes in North Africa. Several of these trade routes passed through Libya, and Libyan merchants, some of whom were Jews, provided pack animals, men, food, and shelter for the caravans. The suppliers of these services generated additional economic activities in their own communities. The Jewish merchants involved in this trade were the backbone of the communal welfare system. When fluctuations started to affect the trans-Saharan trade in the latter part of the nineteenth century, many people lost their jobs, merchants went bankrupt, and the communal budget was drained just when the number of those who needed assistance was growing substantially.[15] As a result, families became dependent on every source of income, and were even ready to accept female participation in the workforce.

Regular waged work (in contrast to midwifery and cosmetics) started

---

[15] R. Simon, "The Trans-Saharan Trade and Its Impact on the Jewish Community of Libya in the Late Ottoman Period," *Proceedings of the American Historical Association*, 1987 (Ann Arbor: University Microfilms International, 1988).

with skills that girls acquired as part of their basic training; women became servants in the homes of the rich. Although families preferred that their daughters work in Jewish households (married women were usually still kept at home), this was not always possible, especially following the increase in the foreign Christian presence. Throughout the nineteenth and twentieth centuries Jewish maids performed hard work, were often treated badly, and received poor wages—which usually went to their male guardians.[16] During the first half of the twentieth century, the Jewish community tried to establish vocational programs to enable these servants to find other jobs: this was done mainly because of moral problems (e.g., sexual harassment and contacts with non-Jews) rather than working conditions.[17]

The trans-Saharan trade also opened economic opportunities for women. One of the major commodities in the late nineteenth century was ostrich feathers, and the fluctuations in the demand for them by the European fashion industry was one of the main causes for serious shifts in the trade. The need for this commodity necessitated a large workforce in Libya to prepare the feathers for shipment, and many women were involved in cleaning, sorting, and packing them. Because of the strong Jewish involvement in this trade, Jewish women who needed work often ended up in these workshops. When bad times came, however, many of them were dismissed, as happened in 1906, when some 400 Jewish women in Tripoli were laid off by the feather-processing industry.[18]

Domestic workers and feather processors did not have to acquire new skills, but their wages were low, and their chances to ascend economically and socially were negligible. They could not obtain better jobs because there were no institutions in Libya where women could be vocationally trained, due to the structure and character of female work.

This situation changed as a result of the European penetration, one of whose channels was education. In 1890, the Paris-based

---

[16] A. Benchimol, Tripoli, to AIU, Paris, 11 March 1907, AAIU, file IIIE-10; Ha-Cohen, *Higgid Mordecai*, p. 157; De Felice, *Jews in an Arab Land*, p. 85.

[17] S. Yelloz, Tripoli, to the American Joint Distribution Committee, New York, 17 August 1946, Central Zionist Archives (hereafter cited as CZA), file S6/1984; S.U. Nahon, "Yehudey Luv," *Yalqut ha-Mizrah ha-Tikhon* 1 (January 1949): 23–24; *Nitzanim* 24 (Elul 5707 [Summer 1947]): 5; F. Zuaretz and F. Tayyar, *Hokhmat Nashim* (Tel Aviv: Va'ad Qehilot Luv be-Yisra'el, 1982), p. 16.

[18] N. Slousch, *Sefer ha-Masa'ot: Masa'ay be-Eretz Luv* (Tel Aviv: Devir, 1938), 1:24; idem, *Travels*, p. 7.

Alliance Israélite Universelle (AIU) established its first educational
institution in Libya with the opening of a vocational workshop
for boys in Tripoli. The Jewish community was interested in the
AIU initiative due to the difficult economic conditions among the
Jews of Tripoli at the time and the prospect of better-paying jobs
as a result of entering new European occupations. Six years later,
this experiment was expanded to include a girls' school, and it, too,
focused on vocational training, but neither institution neglected
academic studies.[19]

The innovation of sending boys to the AIU schools rested mainly
in putting them in a European, although Jewish, environment, leading to the acquisition of vocational skills; having boys in an educational institution was in itself nothing new. Sending girls to school,
however, was quite a new phenomenon in Tripoli, and it occurred
mainly in European families or those with close economic and social
ties with the northern Mediterranean. Due to the difficult economic
conditions and the chance of improvement by acquiring modern and
well-paying occupations, many poor families were ready to send
daughters to the AIU school, where they knew the girls would remain
in a Jewish, and predominantly female, environment. The occupations taught at the AIU girls' school in Tripoli were sewing, cutting,
embroidery, knitting, and ironing. Thanks to the AIU programs,
growing numbers of poor Jewish women entered these fields. This
improved the economic condition of the whole family, and also the
status of the women, who thus learned job skills and joined the erst-
while almost exclusively male group of income providers.

The AIU did not long remain the sole provider of vocational training for Jewish women. The Italian educational network, which
started operating in Libya in 1876, added needlework to the curriculum of its female institutions shortly after the establishment of
the AIU girls' school, as part of its competition with the AIU institutions.[20] Nonetheless, the emphasis in the Italian schools, which were
attended mainly by upper-class children, was not on vocational training but on Italian culture and preparation of the boys for an economic future in mainly European-style commerce and finance. There

---

[19] On the AIU and female vocational education in Libya, see AAIU, files IIE-5,
IIE-6, IIIE-6, IIIE-10, IVE-22; Ha-Cohen, *Higgid Mordecai*, p. 239.
[20] Ha-Cohen, *Higgid Mordecai*, p. 167; D. Arie, Tripoli, to AIU, Paris, 18 December
1895, AAIU, file IIE-6a. On the Italian schools, see below.

was no intention to provide the pupils with vocational skills in the manual crafts that interested the lower classes. The Italian educators decided to include needlework in their girls' schools only because of their competition with the AIU. Later on, under Italian rule, several indigenous Jewish women's organizations[21] and the Tripolitan Ben-Yehuda Society[22] opened courses in needlework for lower-class Jewish girls. These developments, like the AIU programs, had economic benefits for the whole family and facilitated the entrance of women into the formerly all-male body of income providers. The number of young Jewish women who could make a living in European-style needlework grew steadily, mainly in the big coastal urban centers.

The establishment of Italian rule over Libya improved the atmosphere and opportunities for women to work outside their homes. The impact of this was felt mainly by European settlers and indigenous Jews, because Muslim women, including urban ones, continued to stay at home until the 1950s and 1960s. Since many Italians settled on farms, the new economic opportunities in the towns were utilized mainly by Jews, including women. Among the results of this was that most of the female factory workers, especially in the tobacco industry, and most of the nurses in the Jewish and Muslim hospital wards, were Jewish women.[23] These developments not only brought Jewish women into additional work fields, but also increased their contacts with non-Jews.

The Ben-Yehuda Society was influential in opening the educational profession to women. Shortly after its establishment in 1931, women were admitted first as students, and soon after as tutors and teachers, who were chosen from the graduates of the society's Hebrew courses. This was an important turning point, because the jobs held by indigenous Jewish women until then were basically manual ones; becoming teachers brought them into the cultural-spiritual realm, which had hitherto been reserved for men. This was still only a partial development, because it was not until the early 1940s that women were admitted as teachers and students to the communal

---

[21] Mme. Levy, "Tripoli," *Bulletin des écoles de l'Alliance Israélite Universelle* 44 (April 1914): 207.

[22] Zuaretz, *Yahadut Luv*, p. 149; De Felice, *Jews in an Arab Land*, p. 98. On this society, which aimed to revive the Hebrew language, see below.

[23] De Felice, *Jews in an Arab Land*, pp. 172–173. They received only rudimentary training in the workplace.

educational network (Talmud Torah schools and yeshivot); the Ben-Yehuda Society was not an official communal body, although shortly after its establishment it became responsible for the education department of the Tripoli community. This process was strengthened with the establishment of the Hebrew school system in Libya (to which girls were admitted) in the 1940s, when a growing number of women became teachers in the communal system, especially in Tripoli and Benghazi. At least in a few cases, however, female teachers received lower wages than male teachers with similar qualifications.[24] Another development around the same time was the establishment of a professional representative body: a Jewish teachers' union in Tripoli and its environs. Since so many teachers were women, the union was a mixed one, and women served on its board, but not in proportion to their membership.[25]

The spread of Zionism affected the professional life of Libya's Jewish women. Pioneering youth movements became active in Libya, especially in Tripoli, in the 1940s. In keeping with the Zionist ideology, these organizations admitted women as members and guides (*madrikhot*). And when agricultural and industrial communes were established near Tripoli, they were eager to include women among their members, so as to transform them, as well as the men, into cooperative farmers and workers. It was, however, difficult for most young men, and even more so for young women, to leave their homes and live an unmarried life within a mixed-gender group of nonrelatives, in order to acquire what most community members regarded as despicable professions. As a result, the communes were relatively small, and women started to join them as full members only toward the end, shortly before the last commune was evacuated due to an Arab attack in June 1948; even then women tended to join the commune when they had brothers or other relatives there. Moreover, despite many proclamations to the contrary, female members were occupied mainly in cleaning and cooking.[26]

---

[24] F. Khalfon, Benghazi, Report on the community, January 1944, CZA, file S/4582; Report on the budget of the Benghazi Hebrew school in 1945, CZA, file S25/5217.

[25] J. Fargion, Tripoli, to Youth Department, Jerusalem, 8 Tammuz 5704 [29 June 1944], CZA, file S32/1068; P. Shakir, Zliten, to Youth Department/Religious Division, 23 Heshvan 5707 [18 November 1946], CZA, file S32/123; *Ha-Tzofeh*, 8 December 1946; *Hayenu*, 9 September 1949.

[26] Tayyar, Tripoli, to Youth Department, Jerusalem, 9 Adar 5708 [17 February

Despite all these developments, the percentage of Jewish women who worked outside their households remained low until the mass emigration of 1949–51. Women's decisions to join the workforce were dictated mainly by economic constraints; many worked in low-paying and unskilled jobs, and fewer were in the more prestigious professions like teaching. Nonetheless the gradual emergence of women as income providers improved their status and increased their independence and contacts with non-kin and gentile society, thus exposing them to new ideas and life patterns.

Education

During most of the Ottoman period in Libya, education was provided by the various religious establishments. With the Ottoman reforms (*Tanzimat*) that began in 1839, the state adopted a new approach to its role in social and cultural services, and starting in the 1860s state schools were opened in Libya. The indigenous population, however, hardly attended them; they usually preferred their own educational institutions, and the Ottoman schools were frequented mainly by the children of Ottoman administrators and of local dignitaries close to the regime. Most of the Jewish boys went to the communal Talmud Torah schools, which were geared to prepare them for full participation in Jewish religious life. This did not change until the 1940s, and thus, Jewish female education in Libya was connected during most of the period with extracommunal educational initiatives.

Not all of Libya's Jews approved of the attitude of the spiritual leadership toward female education. This was mainly so among the significant number of wealthy Jewish merchants who had taken Europeans as their external role models and had become aware of the new roles women were beginning to play in Europe, and especially of their cultural and social development. Members of this class, in order to feel somewhat equal to their European role models, tended to emulate at least some European customs. Among the first influences they adopted were those in the field of education.

Opportunities in Libya were, however, very limited, and for a long

1948], CZA, file S32/123; Yariv, Summer 1944, CZA, file S6/1984; Report from Tripoli, early 5705 [Fall 1944], CZA, file S32/1068; *Hayenu*, Tammuz 5704 [June–July 1944], pp. 3–4.

time the only institutions for female education were Christian or
Ottoman. Since those Jews who were interested in educating their
daughters wanted them to become Europeanized, they preferred
European to Ottoman schools, even if the former were Christian.
Some Jewish girls (about 30 in 1875) were sent to the Christian girls'
school in Tripoli (established in 1846), where general studies and
music were taught, and to its kindergarten, which was run by nuns.[27]
Still, a Christian school was out of bounds for most Jews, who remained very traditional and observant, including those with strong
economic and social contacts with Europe.

Some rich Tripolitan Jews, in an effort to provide their children
with European education in a Jewish environment in Libya and to
prepare their boys for careers in the family businesses, contacted the
Jewish community of Livorno for help in establishing Italian schools
in Libya that would be suitable for Jews. In 1876, an Italian Jewish
teacher, Giannetto Paggi, settled in Tripoli and started the Italian
Jewish educational network. A year later, the system opened a girls'
school in Tripoli, headed by an Italian Jewess, Carolina Nunes-Vais.
By the end of the Ottoman period, the network had twelve schools,
three of which were for girls (in Tripoli, Homs, and Benghazi).[28]

The Italian schools in Libya were primarily aimed at the commercial urban upper middle classes, and intended to instill Italian
culture and loyalty to Italy in their students. Accordingly, the curriculum included Italian language and literature and some general
studies, as well as commercial training for boys, in answer to the
wishes of the mercantile class which had initiated the whole project.
Most of the girls who attended the Italian schools during the Ottoman period were from the same social classes, aiming to improve
their cultural and social skills, and become more "European," and
not in order to learn a profession.

The establishment of the AIU girls' school in Tripoli in 1896
changed the character, socioeconomic background, and size of the
Jewish female student body in Libya.[29] The AIU pioneered education among the lower classes in Libya. Although its declared pur-

---

[27] E. Hazzan, *Ta'alumot Lev* (Livorno, 1879), 1:14b.

[28] On the Italian educational network in Libya, see Ha-Cohen, *Higgid Mordecai*,
pp. 53–54, 129, 167, 324; Zuaretz, *Yahadut Luv*, pp. 166–167; M. Levy, Tripoli, to
AIU, Paris, 10 September 1911, AAIU, file IVE-22c.

[29] On AIU female education in Libya, see AAIU, files IIE-5, IIE-6, IIIE-6, IIIE-
10, IVE-22.

pose was vocational training, the AIU school also provided academic studies (French, Hebrew, and arithmetic). As it turned out, the AIU continued to provide vocational training, but an increasing number of girls from the lower classes wanted to attend its school because they believed that academic skills, and especially European languages, were imperative for upward social mobility.[30]

Under Italian rule, the state educational system became Italian and included "metropolitan" schools, where the curriculum was identical to that in Italy, and "indigenous" ones for the Muslim population. The traditional Jewish educational system continued to operate independently, and was hardly influenced by external developments in the parallel non-Jewish educational systems. Since the Italian metropolitan schools were secular and provided skills that growing numbers of Jews regarded as necessary, many Jews attended them, including girls.[31] This brought Jewish girls into closer contact with the non-Jewish society; during the Ottoman period most of the pupils in the Italian educational network were Jewish, but this changed under Italian rule due to the increase of Italian settlement in Libya. Whereas most of the Jewish boys who went to the Italian schools were sent in the afternoons to complementary studies at the traditional Talmud Torah, this opportunity was not open for girls, who thus received (with the exception of the AIU pupils) only general, and no Jewish education. Although most of the girls had to stay home in the afternoons and help with the household work, many managed to develop contacts with their non-Jewish schoolmates and thus got some first-hand knowledge of Italian Christian family life. As a result, not only were they exposed to modern European education, but also to European lifestyles.

Another educational development in the 1930s strengthened the influence of modern Judaism. In 1931, the Ben-Yehuda Society, whose main purpose was to revive the Hebrew language as part of the national revival, was established in Tripoli, and girls began to attend its afternoon Ha-Tiqvah school.[32] Because the AIU network did not grow beyond its two Tripolitan schools, Ha-Tiqvah was the

---

[30] E. Arie, Tripoli, to AIU, Paris, 28 January 1897, 20 January 1898, 14 May 1899, AAIU, file IIE-5.

[31] De Felice, *Jews in an Arab Land*, pp. 85–86, 321 n. 15.

[32] For details on the revival of the Hebrew language in Libya, see R. Simon, "Ha-Tenu'ah ha-'Ivrit be-Luv," *Shorashim ba-Mizrah* 2 (1989): 173–209; Zuaretz, *Yahadut Luv*, pp. 148–152; De Felice, *Jews in an Arab Land*, p. 98.

main means for Tripolitan Jewish girls to learn Hebrew and Jewish studies. Consequently, their numbers there often exceeded those of the boys. Moreover, the all-male administration regarded it as extremely important that girls should study there in order to safeguard the future of the Jewish people, because they believed that mothers would have a dominant role in the upbringing of the new generation. The administration advocated that girls should be taught by female teachers, because it believed that women had more effect in female education. The Ben-Yehuda Society was also effective in the modest beginnings of intergender relations. Classes were gender-segregated and boys and girls attended on alternate days, but some cultural and social activities were mixed, mainly those focusing on the holidays and national Zionist events. All in all, a few thousand Tripolitan Jewish girls studied in these courses during the 1930s, and were imbued with Zionism and a growing feeling of self-value. In 1939, however, as a result of Italy's racial legislation, the society was outlawed.

The education of Libya's Jews came to a partial standstill during World War II, for Jews were expelled from the state schools, while "enemy" institutions (i.e., the AIU schools) were closed, and various societies (such as Ben-Yehuda) were outlawed.[33] Jewish communal education continued when conditions allowed, and even expanded, to accommodate those boys whose studies in the Italian and AIU schools had been interrupted. The community, however, did not at this time concern itself with female education, and there was no schooling for Jewish girls from 1939 until 1943.

Jewish education in Libya underwent fundamental changes in orientation and composition in 1943. It now became a Hebrew educational network, increasingly drawing in content and form from the Hebrew network in Palestine, and including girls among its students.[34] Female education could become an integral part of communal education only when the latter was ready for radical conceptual changes. This happened as a result of the events of World War II and the presence of Palestinian Jewish soldiers in the British army which occupied Libya in 1942/43 and liberated the indigenous Jews from the racist Italian regime and the Nazi threat. Many local Jews had

---

[33] On the condition of the Jews of Libya during World War II, see R. Simon, "It Could Have Happened There: The Jews of Libya During the Second World War," *Africana Journal*, 16 (1994): 391–422.

[34] For details, see Simon, "Ha-Tenu'ah ha-'Ivrit."

become disappointed with Italianization due to the war events, and the presence of the Palestinian Jews strengthened another option for Westernization which had some following even before the war— Zionism. The weakness of the local Jewish leadership after the war, coupled with the presence of the Palestinian Jewish soldiers, brought about changes in various fields, including education, in line with Zionist ideology. Consequently, Hebrew schools with a curriculum based on that of the Hebrew educational network in Palestine gradually spread across Libya, and female education was from the beginning an integral part of them.

Although this development did not involve all the Jewish communities of Libya, it included the two major ones (Tripoli and Benghazi) as well as several minor ones. Thus most of Libyan Jewry was affected by an educational process which lasted until the mass emigration to Israel in 1949–51. Still, large numbers continued to attend the Italian network and the AIU school, which reopened in 1947 and was no longer anti-Zionist. The new Hebrew schools followed in the direction that had been started by the Ben-Yehuda Society, stressing different subjects and ideas in preparation for the creation of a new social order composed of a new type of Jew, emphasizing time and again the new role of women in that order. In most places, however, there was no coeducation, although intergender extracurricular activities increased.

One characteristic feature of Jewish female education in Libya was that, being rejected by local traditional Jewish educational systems, it could develop only within external frameworks that were ready to accept women among other nontraditional modes of behavior and thought. Consequently, it was connected from the very beginning with trends of Westernization and modernization on the European or Zionist models. Thus, whereas numerous Jewish boys only attended traditional Jewish schools, those Jewish women who received a formal education obtained it only within modern, Westernized systems. Libyan Jewish women succeeded in entering formal education when their families felt the need for it, due to sociocultural or economic reasons, and when the appropriate institutions were established. Until the 1940s this occurred only outside the Jewish communal education systems. This process improved the women's cultural and economic standing, but changes were slower in the social and political fields.

Conclusion

Economic necessity was a very important factor in changing the status of Libyan Jewish women in the late nineteenth century and the first half of the twentieth. To this were added educational opportunities, the attitude of the authorities and the leaders of the Jewish community, and changes with regard to role models. Changes in the status of Jewish women in Libya occurred in various interrelated spheres, the most important of which were education and work. Developments in one field were not necessarily equal to those in other realms, and in certain areas change was slower than in others. Wherever the initiative was personal and depended on the individual's ability (e.g., education and work), women gradually managed to achieve impressive results. In those spheres, however, where society's approval was required (e.g., leadership, involvement in mixed-gender activities, family roles), advances were much slower and sporadic.[35] It was not enough for women to want to change, and even to take actual steps to that end; society at large had to change its perceptions with regard to women's capabilities and roles. As it turned out, changes in perception were very slow to take place.

---

[35] Thus, for example, women were never leaders of the Jewish communal council or of the Zionist movement; they were represented in the Jewish teachers' union, but not in proportion to their numbers (see n. 25 above); they ate separately from men even in the 1940s (see Zamir and Yariv, Tripoli, to Yosifon and Ben-Yehuda, 7 November 1943, CZA, file S25/5217; for the earlier period, see Ha-Cohen, *Higgid Mordecai*, pp. 190, 289; Slousch, *Travels*, p. 159); they hesitated to voice their opinions in mixed-gender groups; and men took the seats in the overcrowded Hebrew classes for adults on the eve of the mass emigration (see *Hayenu*, 10 August 1950).

THE YEMENI MESSIAH IN THE TIME OF
MAIMONIDES: PRELUDE FOR FUTURE MESSIAHS

BAT-ZION ERAQI-KLORMAN

The Open University,
Tel Aviv, Israel

Thanks to Maimonides and his *Epistle to Yemen* (*Iggeret Teman*), the Jewish messiah who arose in Yemen in the twelfth century became famous. His renown is even greater than that of the messiahs who inflamed the hopes of nineteenth-century Yemeni Jewry. The twelfth-century messianic movement in Yemen was the first in that country, both chronologically, as the foremost in a series of Yemeni Jewish messianic movements, and in the thematic sense, as the initial expression of some of the characteristics of Yemeni Jewish messianism that would recur in similar circumstances in the future.

Present-day study of Yemeni Jewry recognizes the impossibility of understanding the history of this community, as of any other Jewish community, in isolation from the society in which its members lived. Political, social, economic, and other developments which influenced the Muslims of Yemen necessarily left their impact on the Jews. Religious and messianic matters are no exception. Therefore, prior to discussing the twelfth-century Jewish messiah and his movement, I will outline the political and religious circumstances of Muslim society in Yemen which preceded and paralleled the messiah's appearance and activity.

ʿAli Ibn Mahdi and ʿAbd al-Nabi Ibn Mahdi

In Islam, as in Judaism and many other religions and cultures, there is a belief in a redeemer who will appear during the eschatological era at the End of Time and establish a new era, restoring religion, justice, prosperity, and welfare.[1] The title of this redeemer is generally

---

[1] For the concept of the mahdi in Islam, see D.B. MacDonald, s.v. "Al-Mahdi,"

al-mahdi, i.e., "the one who is guided [by God] in the right way." Mahdist claims have at various times been the moving force and the legitimizing factor for political movements in Islam. Among the most famous were the Fatimids in the early ninth century, the Muwahhidun (Almohads) led by Muhammad ibn Tumart in the Maghrib in the mid-twelfth century, and more recently, the mahdist state established in Sudan in the last quarter of the nineteenth century under the leadership of Muhammad Ahmad ibn Abdallah.

Mahdist movements are also known in Yemen. Among them are the movement of 'Ali ibn al-Fadl in the late ninth century,[2] the movement which grew around the Zaydi Imam al-Husayn ibn al-Qasim in the eleventh century,[3] and, of particular interest in this essay, the movement of 'Ali ibn Mahdi and his son 'Abd al-Nabi in the twelfth century. Also known are two nineteenth-century Yemeni mahdist movements: the movement of Faqih Sa'id in 1840 and that of Sharif Isma'il in 1846.[4]

As is often the case, 'Ali ibn Mahdi's movement combined religious ideals and political ambitions. He began his career as a religious preacher in A.H. 531 (1136) in the village of 'Anbarah near the town of Zabid in the Tihama and later became the founder of one of the short-lived local dynasties which governed parts of Yemen before the Ayyubid period (1173–1229).

In his preaching, 'Ali ibn Mahdi employed typical eschatological language, saying that the Time was near. In allusion to the model he was imitating and implying his own role in history, 'Ali ibn Mahdi

---

Encyclopaedia of Islam, 1st ed. (1913), vol. 3, pp. 111–115; D.S. Margolioth, s.v. "Mahdi," *Encyclopedia of Religion and Ethics* (1916), vol. 3, pp. 336–340; P.M. Holt, *The Mahdist State in the Sudan* (Oxford, 1970), pp. 21–31; and especially W. Madelung, s.v. "Al-Mahdi," *Encyclopaedia of Islam*, new ed. (1986), vol. 5, pp. 1230–1238. For the political and social background of the development of the mahdi concept, see Jan-Olaf Blichfeldt, *Early Mahdism: Politics and Religion in the Formative Period of Islam* (Leiden, 1985); cf. H. Lazarus Yafeh, "Is There a Concept of Redemption in Islam?" in *Types of Redemption*, eds. R.J. Zwi Werblowsky and C. Jouco Bleeker (Leiden, 1970), pp. 168–180, and "On the Messianic Idea in Islam," in *Messianism and Eschatology*, ed. Zvi Baras (Jerusalem, 1984), pp. 169–176 [Hebrew], who belittles the importance of the messianic idea in Islam, especially among the Sunnis.

[2] See 'Abd al-Wasi' ibn Yahya al-Wasi'i, *Tarikh al-Yaman* (Cairo, A.H. 1346 [1927]), pp. 22–23.

[3] Al-Hakami 'Omarah, *Yaman: Its Early Mediaeval History*, original texts with translation and notes by H.C. Kay (London, 1892), pp. 228–229; Madelung, "Al-Mahdi," p. 1237.

[4] See B. Eraqi Klorman, "Jewish and Muslim Messianism in Yemen," *International Journal of Middle East Studies* 22, no. 2 (May 1990): 202–210.

applied to his people certain terms that had been used during the time of the prophet Muhammad. The word *muhajirun*, which originally referred to the Meccan emigrants who followed Muhammad to Medina, was applied to those who followed 'Ali ibn Mahdi from the Tihama to the territory of Khawlan in the central highland. Similarly, his supporters in the mountains were called *ansar*, as had been Muhammad's helpers in Medina.[5] Undoubtedly, this parallel usage of terms embraced messianic connotations and had a strong appeal.[6]

The people who were attracted to 'Ali ibn Mahdi formed a large army that eventually took over the Tihama and the neighboring highlands. His most significant victory was the capture of the important town of Zabid (at the time governed by an Abyssinian dynasty) in A.H. 554 (1159), but a few months afterwards he passed away.

Once he became a sovereign ruler, 'Ali ibn Mahdi's messianic pretensions were revealed again. One of the titles he assumed in the *khutbah* (Friday sermon), in addition to commander of the faithful, was *al-mahdi*. Ibn Khaldun notes that Ibn Mahdi's followers believed that he was infallible (*fihi al-'isma*), a quality sometimes assigned to the expected mahdi (especially among the Shi'i's). 'Omarah, a Yemeni historian and Ibn Mahdi's contemporary, adds that he could foresee the future. He, therefore, was able to create a community that was totally submissive to him. His supporters transferred all of their possessions to him, and he furnished them with their needs. Even the warriors, in contrast to older practice, were not permitted to keep their own horses and weapons; they were supplied according to need from 'Ali ibn Mahdi's stables and arsenals.

Like other mahdist pretenders before and after him, and in accordance with expectations of the anticipated mahdi, 'Ali ibn Mahdi introduced a religious reform. It was based on a strict and rigorous interpretation of the law and sought to bring Islam back to what Ibn Mahdi believed to be its pure and true essence. 'Omarah, who

---

[5] 'Omarah, Arabic original pp. 93–94, English trans. pp. 124–126; Ibn Khaldun, *Ta'rikh Ibn Khaldun* 4 (Beirut, n.d.), pp. 219–220. For more on the political history of twelfth-century Yemen, see G. Rex Smith, "The Early and Medieval History of San'a' ca. 622–1382/1515," in *San'a': An Arabian Islamic City*, eds. R.B. Serjeant and R. Lewcock (London, 1983), pp. 59–60.

[6] It is no surprise, therefore, that precisely the same parallel resounded during the nineteenth-century movement of Muhammad ibn Abdallah in the Sudan. See Holt, *Mahdist State*, pp. 54, 119–122; and Haim Shaked, *The Life of the Sudanese Mahdi* (New Brunswick, N.J., 1978).

personally knew 'Ali ibn Mahdi, says that he belonged to the Hanafite school of law (one of the four orthodox legal schools in Sunni Islam), "but he added to its fundamental articles of faith the doctrine that regards sin as infidelity and punishable with death." This interpretation is reminiscent of the radical beliefs held by the Kharijites, who deviated from mainstream Islam in the mid-seventh century. Thus, Ibn Khaldun, who read 'Omarah, accuses Ibn Mahdi of being a Khariji. 'Omarah continues that in his application of the law, 'Ali ibn Mahdi made a distinction between his warriors and the rest of the people. It was only from the former that he demanded impeccable moral behavior and absolute obedience to the law, thus making them a model of emulation for all. Consequently, those warriors who "drank intoxicating liquors suffered death, and death was the penalty for listening to songs, for adultery, and for absence from the Friday prayer or from the two assemblies at which he preached to the people, on Thursdays and Mondays."[7] All other people, however, were subject to more lenient laws.

Enforcement of the law in compliance with 'Ali ibn Mahdi's exegeses continued, if sometimes less strictly, during the reign of his son 'Abd al-Nabi (1159–1173). He succeeded in taking control of almost the whole of Yemen, thereby expanding the influence of his father's religious and legal legacy. It was during his government that there appeared in Yemen another messianic contender, this time from among the Jews.

The Jewish Messianic Movement

The Increase in Messianic Hopes

It is no coincidence that messianic hopes intensified among the Jews when Yemen was governed by a dynasty of rulers who had mahdist pretensions and worked for the coming of the messianic age. This is represented by the activity of the Yemeni Mourners of Zion (*Abele Zion*), i.e., people who believed that mourning over the state of exile might precipitate the End of Time. Such mourners, with their lamentations and ascetic habits, especially the practice of abstaining from

---

[7] 'Omarah, *Yaman*, Arabic pp. 98–100, English trans. pp. 131–134; and cf. Ibn Khaldun, p. 220. For the Kharijites, see, for example, Montgomery W. Watt, *Islamic Philosophy and Theology* (Edinburgh, 1962), p. 12.

meat and wine, were discernible in Palestine as early as the second century, not long after the destruction of the Temple. In the eighth century they surfaced again in Palestine and Babylonia, and during the ninth century they were joined by a group of Qaraite Abele Zion who settled in Palestine. In the twelfth century, Rabbi Binyamin of Tudela, who traveled in the Middle East (1169–1172), heard about the Yemeni Mourners of Zion:[8]

> Their land is wide and there are sages among them. And they give a tithe of whatever they possess to the sages who study in the synagogues, and to the ascetics of the generation who are the Mourners of Zion and the Mourners of Jerusalem. And they do not eat meat, and they do not drink wine, and they put on black clothes, and they live in caves or in concealed houses. And they torment themselves their entire lives except for the Sabbath and the holidays. And they ask the Holy One, blessed be He, for compassion for the exile of Israel, and that He have mercy upon them for the sake of His great name.[9]

Apparently some of these customs of lamentation continued to be associated with acute messianic expectations in Yemen and reemerged during the Sabbatian movement.[10]

But the clearest evidence for the intensity of messianic hopes in twelfth-century Yemen is spelled out in Maimonides' *Iggeret Teman*.[11] The *Epistle to Yemen* is Maimonides' reply to a letter sent him by Rabbi Jacob ben Nathanel al-Fayyumi of San'a', seeking his opinion in regard to the messiah who had arisen in Yemen. In his letter, Rabbi Jacob detailed the signs that had been perceived in Yemen as announcing the commencement of the messianic age: (a) several Yemeni calculations of the End had revealed that the messianic appearance was due to happen at this time;[12] (b) recent motions of

---

[8] A.Z. Aescoly, *Jewish Messianic Movements* (Jerusalem, 1956), pp. 109–111 [Hebrew]; and cf. Moshe Zuker, "Teguvot li-tenu'at Abele-Zion ha-qara'im ba-sifrut ha-rabanit," *Sefer Hayobel le-Rabbi Hanokh Albeck* (Jerusalem, 1963), pp. 348–401; as there were never any Qaraites in Yemen, Mourners of Zion there could only have been Rabbanites.

[9] M. Adler, ed., *Sefer massa'ot shel Rabbi Binyamin* (London, 1907), pp. 70–71; and see Jehoshua Prawer, "The Hebrew Itineraries of the Crusader Period," *Cathedra* 40 (July 1986): 45–46.

[10] See B. Eraqi Klorman, "The Sabbatian Movement in Yemen," *Pe'mim* 15 (1983): 49 [Hebrew]; *The Jews of Yemen*, pp. 40–41.

[11] All references are to Kafih's edition, Maimonides, *Iggeret Teman*, and cf. A.S. Halkin's edition, *Iggeret Teman by Maimonides* (New York, 1952).

[12] Maimonides, *Iggeret Teman*, p. 40; in order to justify calculations of the End taken in Yemen, Rabbi Jacob points to similar calculations by Rabbi Sa'adia Gaon.

the celestial bodies, observed by Yemeni astronomers, had been explained as harbingers of the messianic days;[13] and (c) current political and religious developments were regarded as premessianic tribulations. Similar to what had happened on other occasions when Yemeni leaders had championed Muslim religious fervor, the ruler ('Abd al-Nabi ibn Mahdi) had forced Jews in his territory to accept Islam (though the extent of the forced conversions is not clear).[14] In addition, there were some instances of Jews converting to Islam as a result of missionary efforts by a Jewish apostate.[15]

Rabbi Jacob, whose letter quotes Rabbi Sa'adia Gaon's *Book of Belief and Opinions*, might have interpreted these cases of apostasy, in accord with Sa'adia's predictions, as "pangs of the messiah." At one stage, Sa'adia writes, many Jews will abandon their faith, and thereafter Elijah will appear and redemption will come.[16]

No doubt these "signs" prepared the setting for the arrival of the Jewish messiah and contributed to the support which he enjoyed during the days of his activity.

The Jewish Messiah and His Activities

All our information concerning the Yemeni messiah derives from Maimonides' writings, first in his *Iggeret Teman* and then in an epistle he wrote in 1194 to the sages of southern France.[17] The Yemeni messiah was known for his modesty and honesty; he was a learned person but not a sage. In Rabbi Jacob's words, "he had some knowl-

---

See Sa'adia Fayyumi, *Sefer ha-nibhar ba-emunot u-ba-de'ot* [Book of beliefs and opinions], trans. into Hebrew and annotated by Yosef Kafih (Jerusalem, 1970), pp. 241–244.

[13] Maimonides, *Iggeret Teman*, p. 42.

[14] Ibid., p. 17; and cf. the Mawza' exile (1679), during the reign of Imam Ahmad al-Mahdi, when Jews were offered the choice between conversion and exile; see Y. Ratzabi, "The Mauza' Exile," *Sefunot* 5 (1961): 341–342; and cf. Yosef Sadan, "A New Text on Jewish Messianic Movements in Yemen in the Second Half of the Seventeenth Century—Background and Hebrew Translation," *Pe'amim* 43 (1990): 111–135 [Hebrew]; and see the forced apostasy decreed by Sharif Isma'il in 1846 in Eraqi-Klorman, "Jewish and Muslim Messianism," p. 209.

[15] Maimonides, *Iggeret Teman*, pp. 18, 31.

[16] Sa'adia, p. 246.

[17] See Maimonides' letter in B.Z. Dinur, *Israel ba-golah*, vol. 2 (Jerusalem, 1962), p. 429 [Hebrew]. In the epistle dated 1194, Maimonides mentions the messianic movement in Yemen which occurred "about twenty-two years ago." The time of the movement was established, therefore, to be 1172; and cf. Halkin's introduction to *Iggeret Teman*, p. v.

edge." It seems that at first he appeared as a messianic forerunner, "and he said that he is a messenger who prepares the way for the King Messiah." He wandered about in the Yemeni highlands, going from one Jewish settlement to another, and asking the people to awake and repent. Before long he was being followed by many who believed first in his message and later in his messianic role. They joined his camp and spread their testimonies of his "wonders." The extent of their support can be deduced from what Maimonides says in the last paragraph of *Iggeret Teman*. After dismissing the signs of the messianic days given by Rabbi Jacob and refuting the messiah's claims one by one, Maimonides expresses the wish that his explanations will be heard all over Yemen. He writes, therefore, to Rabbi Jacob: "I request that you send a copy of this book to each and every congregation in the towns and villages." Maimonides did indeed have cause for concern, since the messiah had become a genuine religious authority for the inhabitants of the country's Jewish settlements. Like other Jewish messianic pretenders, he introduced his admirers to new religious usages and new prayers.[18]

In his letter to France, Maimonides notes that some of the messiah's followers were Muslims. This phenomenon was not restricted to the twelfth century. In nineteenth-century messianic movements as well, there were many Muslims who accepted the belief in the eschatological role assigned to Jewish messiahs. This behavior obviously reflects the close social contacts between Jews and Muslims in Yemen. These contacts also produced a reverse effect, namely, Jewish adoption of Muslim eschatological traditions and images.[19] Nonetheless, Muslim affiliation with Jewish messiahs apparently did not

---

[18] Dinur, *Israel ba-golah*; and cf. Abu 'Isa al-Isfahani, who established seven prayers a day, Aescoly, *Messianic Movements*, p. 118; Sabbatai Sevi's alterations of the calendar, e.g., the abolition of the Fast of the Ninth of Ab, G. Scholem, *Sabbatai Sevi, the Mystical Messiah* (Princeton, 1973), pp. 616–622; and Yosef 'Abdallah's new prayers, B. Eraqi Klorman, *The Jews of Yemen*, pp. 158–164.

[19] See Klorman, "Jewish and Muslim Messianism." A few works that explore other implications of the close social contacts between Jews and Muslims in Yemen are S. Geridi, "Demons and Spirits in the Beliefs of the Jews of Yemen," in *Shebut Teman*, eds. Y. Yesha'yahu and A. Zadoc (Tel Aviv, 1945), pp. 155–165 [Hebrew]; David Semah, "On the Formal Origins of the Yemenite *Muwashah*," *Tarbiz* 57, no. 2 (1989): pp. 239–260 [Hebrew]; and Carmela Avder, "Dress and Appearance of Jewish Women in a Yemenite Village as an Expression of Their Status," *Pe'amim* 41 (1989): 134–153 [Hebrew].

depend only on messianic excitement among the Jews but was, rather, related to existing messianic desires in Muslim society, a phenomenon which increased with the rise of a Muslim messianic personality. This seems to have been the case during the twelfth century following the activities of 'Ali ibn Mahdi.

Jewish attachment to Muslim religious and messianic trends is even recognized in the Jewish messiah's actions. His preaching resembles 'Ali ibn Mahdi's call to repent and to return to the "pure" form of religion. Also, the messiah's emphasis on the virtue of charity echoes the Muslim commandment to give alms as well as its integration and use by 'Ali ibn Mahdi. In Islam, charity was formalized in the *zakat*, the only tax imposed on the early Muslim community. The *zakat* money was intended first to support the needy and then to finance public necessities. Thus the Jewish messiah, in an obvious parallel to 'Ali ibn Mahdi, ordered his supporters to give all their possessions to charity. He probably intended the property to be kept in the public treasury and to be distributed from there. This similarity did not escape Maimonides, who writes about the believers: "And they thought that he [the messiah] would succeed, as did Ibn Mahdi."[20]

Nevertheless, the messiah's fate did not match that of 'Ali ibn Mahdi. A year after Maimonides wrote his *Iggeret Teman*, the messiah was captured by the authorities.

> And a king from among the Arabs who caught him said to him, "What did you do?" He said, "I did right, and I followed God's command." He said to him, "What is your proof?" He said, "Cut my head off, and I will immediately resurrect." He said to him, "There is no better sign than this one . . .," and at once they killed the poor soul.[21]

The death of the messiah, however, did not completely eradicate his movement. Although the Jews in many settlements had to pay considerable fines for the messianic stir, and their messianic excitement generally calmed down, yet twenty-two years later Maimonides notes: "And until now there are some ignorant people who say that he will soon resurrect, and will succeed." Expectations of the reappearance of a dead messiah reoccurred in the nineteenth century after the killing of another Jewish Yemeni messiah, Shukr Kuhayl I (1861–65),

---

[20] Maimonides, *Iggeret Teman*, pp. 50–51.
[21] Dinur, *Israel ba-golah*.

and they certainly reflect the intensity of the belief in these messianic claimants.[22]

The twelfth-century messianic movement definitively shook and disturbed the life of Yemeni Jewry, so it is perhaps surprising that when Maimonides writes to Yemen, his strongest criticism is not of the messiah, whom he calls a "madman," nor of the masses, who were attracted to him, as he says, on account of their "ignorance in matters of the messiah." Maimonides' sole criticism is directed at Rabbi Jacob and through him at the other Yemeni rabbis: "I was astonished at your words—for you are a learned person, and you are acquainted with the teachings of the sages—[in that you said] perhaps it is true."

Rabbi Jacob's words mirror the perplexity in which the rabbis were caught. On the one hand, they perceived themselves as living on the verge of the messianic days; on the other, they were not certain as to the merit of their "messiah" and the truthfulness of his claims. The rabbis' perplexity led to hesitation and to their reluctance to take a clear stand for or against the messiah. This lack of decisive leadership certainly contributed to the willingness of the masses to join the messiah. Maimonides, however, maintains that any messianic eruption should be met with rabbinic skepticism. He believed that his own time was one in which the messianic age was imminent. But this period, he says, is characterized by the rise of numerous messianic pretenders, and therefore it is the role of the rabbis to criticize and suppress all false messiahs.

As further messianic situations developed, the rabbis of other Jewish communities followed the indecisive stand detected by Maimonides, and their weakness was especially evident during the Sabbatian movement. However, in contrast to the rabbis of other Jewish communities, the Yemeni rabbinic leaders pursued the passive mode of conduct first revealed in the twelfth century even after the Sabbatian movement.[23]

---

[22] Such beliefs can also be found, for example, among the first Christians and the various sects of the Shi'a (e.g., the Twelver Shi'ites, who expect the reappearance of their twelfth imam, Muhammad al-'Askari [d. A.H. 878]), and were held about the Jewish messiah, Abu 'Isa al-Isfahani (mid-8th cent.), and the messiah Shukr Kuhayl II. For the latter, see B. Eraqi Klorman, "The Messiah Shukr Kuhayl II (1868–75) and His Tithe (Ma'aser): Ideology and Practice as Means to Hasten Redemption," *Jewish Quarterly Review* 79, nos. 2–3 (October 1988–January 1989): 199–217.

[23] Maimonides, *Iggeret Teman*, pp. 50, 55, and see Amos Funkenstein, "Maimonides:

In any event, the movement of 1172 represents several patterns of messianic behavior which were to be repeated with variations. This messianic behavior was characterized by frequent messianic eruptions, indecisive rabbinic conduct, and parallels both in time and motif between Jewish and Muslim messianic movements. The Yemeni Jewish community shared its messianic hopes with all Jews in the diaspora but developed as well its own mode of messianic expression, which depended on the community's unique historical context and its social situation in the Islamic society of Yemen.

Political Theory and Realistic Messianism," *Miscellanea Mediaevalia* 11 (1977): 84–85; and B. Eraqi Klorman, "The Attitudes of Yemenite Rabbis Towards 19th Century Jewish Messianic Figures," *Proceedings of the Tenth World Congress of Jewish Studies, Division B*, vol. 2 (Jerusalem, 1990), pp. 355–362.

STREAMS OF IMMIGRATION:
SEPHARDIC IMMIGRATION TO
BRITAIN AND THE UNITED STATES

Walter P. Zenner

State University of New York at Albany

In this paper, I compare two communities that were produced by the small Sephardic streams of immigration to Britain and the United States during the nineteenth and early twentieth centuries.[1] Both are heterogeneous in nature. The Sephardim in both places came to major industrial centers. In both cases, they were outnumbered by larger waves of Ashkenazic, especially East European, immigrants. The results of these migrations, however, were quite different. The Chicago Sephardim were marginalized until fairly recent times, while the Manchester Sephardim became part of the Jewish elite of Britain.

Streams of Immigration

Early Jewish history in the United States is usually divided in terms of three major waves of immigration, the Sephardic (really Dutch and English), the German or Central European, and finally the huge East European wave which began in 1881 and ended with the Immigration Act of 1924. This picture is a gross oversimplification. The first wave, which lasted longer than the other two, was really much smaller and more a series of rivulets than a wave. Indeed, by

[1] This paper is based on two different studies. One was fieldwork carried out in Manchester, England, in 1987 and funded by the Research Foundation of the State University of New York. The second project was carried out in Chicago in 1988 with assistance from the Dolores Kohl Educational Foundation. I would like to acknowledge the aid of these institutions, as well as the patience and cooperation of present and former Chicagoans and Mancunians that made this work possible. Some of the interviews utilized in this study were conducted in the 1950s and 1960s. None of the foundations or interviewees are responsible for any errors made here. I would also like to thank participants in the Second International Sephardic Studies Conference for their comments and criticism.

the late eighteenth century, it included as many Ashkenazim as Sephardim. Figures in early American Jewish history were of mixed ancestry, like the colorful Mordecai Noah, who had both Marrano and German ancestry.[2]

This picture also neglects the many rivulets and streams which became part of the waves of Jewish immigration in the nineteenth and twentieth centuries. For instance, some Caribbean, Dutch, and English Jews, as well as Central Europeans, arrived on these shores during the nineteenth century. They include both Ashkenazim and Sephardim. Judah P. Benjamin and Samuel Gompers were among the immigrants from these communities. In various northeastern cities, such as New York, Buffalo, Chicago, and Albany, we find a small rivulet of Dutch Jews, both Sephardim and Ashkenazim. A small cemetery on Church Road outside of Albany is a monument to this group.[3]

In the late nineteenth century, Jews from the Mediterranean basin and Southwest Asia joined both their fellow countrymen of other faiths and their coreligionists in the great migration to the West and the New World. While substantial proportions from many communities in North Africa, the Balkans, and the Fertile Crescent immigrated, their numbers were much smaller than those of the East European Jews who arrived in the Americas. Thus it might be better to view these groups of immigrants as a stream rather than a wave.

The Mediterranean and Middle Eastern Jews joined other streams of emigrants from these countries. In the case of those from the Ottoman Empire, they included Greeks, Turks, Bulgarians, Armenians, Assyrians (Nestorians), and Arabic speakers from all religious groups.[4]

They wended their ways to a wide variety of countries, including all parts of the Americas from Canada to Argentina and Chile, South and East Asia, as well as important trading centers of Europe. Records

---

[2] See Jonathan Sarna, *Jacksonian Jew: The Life and Times of Mordecai Manual Noah* (New York: Holmes & Meier, 1985). Also see J. Huehner, s.v. "Phillips," *Jewish Encyclopedia* (1905): 10:2–5.

[3] On Albany, I am using material from an ongoing study of Albany Jewish cemeteries, including the Church Road cemetery, and city directories. Also see Selig Adler and Thomas E. Connally, *From Ararat to Suburbia: The History of the Jewish Community of Buffalo* (Philadelphia: Jewish Publication Society, 1960), pp. 68, 79, 134, 174, 238, 348, 368, 444.

[4] Cf. Kemal H. Karpat, "The Ottoman Emigration to the Americas, 1865–1914," *International Journal of Middle Eastern Studies* 17 (1985): 175–209.

of their presence are often found in surprising contexts, as in Paul Theroux's short story "A Burial at Surabaya," in which Jews of European and Middle Eastern origin gather to bury a fellow member of their once-substantial community.[5]

The Manchester Sephardim

When it became the center of the Lancashire cotton industry in the eighteenth century, Manchester became a magnet for merchants from many parts of the world. By the late nineteenth century, thirty pages of the Manchester city directory were devoted to what was termed "shipping merchants." Among these were a significant number of such agents from the Mediterranean and Southwest Asia, including Moroccans, Greeks, Turks, Syrians, Iraqis, and Armenians.[6] Many of the merchants from these regions were Christians or Muslims, but a significant number of them were Jews following the Sephardic rite. In fact, with few exceptions, the Sephardim in Manchester until the mid-twentieth century began their lives in Lancashire as shipping merchants.[7]

Shipping merchants were brokers who sold cotton goods from Lancashire and Cheshire and woolens from Yorkshire to the rest of the world. They were a large segment of the business community of Manchester. In pre-World War I days, the city directory of Manchester-Salford contained a special subdirectory for shipping merchants. This section took up close to thirty pages of the directory. By 1965, it had been reduced to five pages. The shipping merchants included businessmen with British surnames and with foreign surnames. There were Germans, Greeks, and Armenians as well as Jews. Most had their offices in Manchester Centre. Many also spent one day a week at Bradford to handle the trade in woolens.

---

[5] Paul Theroux, "A Burial at Surabaya," *Sinning with Annie and Other Stories* (New York: Ballantine Books, 1990), pp. 153–166.

[6] Bill Williams, *The Making of Manchester Jewry, 1740–1875* (Manchester: Manchester University Press), pp. 319–326, 428. Also see Y.J. Frangopulo, "Foreign Communities in Victorian Manchester," *Manchester Review* 10 (1965): 189–206; B. Jenazian, "Armenians in Manchester: A Commercial Community" (original appeared in Sevan; mimeographed copy in Manchester Central Library).

[7] See City Directory for Manchester and Salford. The "Shipping Merchants" section was for many years a subdirectory within this directory. I used the directories for 1885, 1912, 1925, 1935, 1955, and 1965.

The directory indicates where they did business and where they exported. In the beginning, most of the Middle Easterners shipped goods to the Levant, from where they had come. By the 1920s, however, many were doing business with other regions, especially Latin America, but also West Africa. Several Syrian Jews from Latin America whom I met had lived in Manchester as children in the 1930s. Several Mancunian Syrians mentioned family members who had been sent to Jamaica or Argentina.[8]

Manchester was viewed by Middle Eastern Jews as a place where one could prosper easily. One rabbi said that when a baby boy was born in Aleppo, his father would slap him on his rear and say, "Go to Manchester and make your fortune."

Although the Sephardic shipping merchants were recent immigrants, they quickly adjusted to an upper-middle-class way of life. They bought houses in middle-class suburbs. While first living to the north of central Manchester, later they were concentrated in areas to the south, especially West Didsbury near Palatine Road. They had homes there with servants and often sent their children to schools run by the Church of England. Their children sometimes reported a discrepancy between their foreign appearance and Jewishness, and the very English and Christian character of their education.[9]

The Sephardim also formed congregations separate from those of the Ashkenazim in the 1870s. The first of these was on Cheetham Hill Road in northern Manchester, but later two congregations were established in West Didsbury. Two of the three used the term "Spanish and Portuguese" in their names, thus linking them with Bevis Mark, the veteran synagogue in London. The prayerbook used, the manner of conducting services, and the general decorum make one feel that one is in a synagogue of veteran British residents rather than newcomers.

As relatively prosperous residents of Manchester, the Sephardim quickly moved to enter the elite of Manchester Jewry alongside veteran residents descended from older Anglo-Jewry or from German immigrants. In the period from 1881 until World War I, when Manchester became a destination for many Russian Jews, Sephardim

---

[8] See the post-World War I directories, which show more and more Syrians listing Latin America as a market territory. Also see the unpublished manuscript by Hayyim Nehmad, which was copied for me by Mrs. Mary Nehmad.

[9] Fieldnotes, 1987.

were among the officers of the Jewish philanthropies in what became Britain's second-largest Jewish community. Russian Jews came to see the Sephardim as exotic and aloof. Such is the description in Maurice Samuel's *The Gentleman and the Jew*.[10] The poorer Russians were concentrated in the northern parts of the city, and their upwardly mobile descendants, in contrast to the Sephardim, have tended to disperse in the northern suburbs of the city, for which reason they still sometimes say that one needs a passport to go from north to south. By the 1920s many of the descendants of the German Jews who had been the leading families of the Manchester community had assimilated or moved away. So the Sephardim formed a special elite that did not interact much with their coreligionists. Even the wealthier Ashkenazim of that period continued to live in the northern part of the metropolitan area, while the Sephardim lived more in the south.[11]

West Didsbury was home not only to Mediterranean Jews, but to other Middle Easterners as well. One grocer in the area, by the name of Mansour, was a Lebanese Christian who stocked foodstuffs for his Middle Eastern clientele. St. Aidan's Reformed Church has a stained-glass window with an Arabic inscription indicating that it was contributed by Fadlo Hourani. Fadlo Hourani was a Lebanese Christian shipping merchant and a Presbyterian. He served as Lebanese consul in Manchester. His sons Albert, Cecil, and George became prominent in Middle Eastern studies. When I asked a scion of one of these Lebanese families about the interaction between the Middle Eastern Jews, Christians, and Muslims in Manchester, he said that they maintained the kind of social cordiality and distance that had prevailed in the Middle East.[12]

Jews participated actively in the philanthropic and other activities of the community. Much of this was concerned with relief on behalf of the Russian Jews who were pouring into the poorer sections of the city. One congregation, the Withington Congregation, was the one in which Neville Lasky, a member of a prominent Ashkenazic family, participated.[13]

Early on, the Sephardic congregations had hazzanim who followed the Spanish-Portuguese liturgical tradition. One congregation, Shaare

---

[10] Maurice Samuel, *The Gentleman and the Jew* (New York: Knopf, 1950).
[11] Fieldnotes, 1987. Also see Oral History tapes at Manchester Jewish Museum.
[12] Fieldnotes, 1987. Fred Halliday, "The *Millet* of Manchester," *British Journal of Middle East Studies*, 19 (1992), pp. 159–176.
[13] Oral History tapes at Manchester Jewish Museum.

Sedek, also had leanings toward certain Eastern, especially Aleppian and Baghdadi traditions. This congregation and its neighbor, the Withington Congregation of Spanish and Portuguese Jews, were once rivals, and their early leaders often disliked each other, on Friday evenings they hold a single Kabbalat Shabbat service, though they meet separately on Saturday mornings.[14] In 1997, they merged.

The Sephardim of Manchester were adversely affected by the decline of Manchester as capital of the Cotton Kingdom and by the economic depressions of the interwar period. Many of the families which had kept up sumptuous households had to let servants go, take children out of private schools, and take in lodgers. Young women began to enter the labor force, which they had not done previously.

Both as a result of the economic decline and because of education, increasing numbers of Manchester Sephardim eschewed the role of cotton broker and entered other occupations and professions. While some sons of a family might enter the family business either in Britain or abroad, others became barristers or university professors or real estate agents. This process was accelerated by the Second World War. During this period, women especially were encouraged to enlist and to enter extra-domestic occupations.[15]

There were some who left Manchester for London. For instance, a woman who became a professional early on was Elizabeth Abadi, the daughter of Abraham Abadi, a native of Aleppo. She received her education at Abertswyth. She became headmistress of a Jewish school in London at the turn of the century and is mentioned in the "Who's Who" in the *Jewish Yearbook* for several years (1901–1910). Leslie Hore-Belisha, whose father came from a Gibraltarian family, but whose mother intermarried, was a prominent Liberal politician in the 1920s and 1930s.[16]

I have no statistics on intermarriage, either between different Jewish-origin groups or between Sephardim and Gentiles. I have not seen any statistics for England which deal with Sephardim and Ashkenazim on this score. While the first generations of Sephardic

---

[14] Fieldnotes, 1987.
[15] Joseph A.D. Sutton, *Aleppo Chronicles* (Brooklyn: Thayer-Jacoby, 1988), pp. 425–433. Oral histories at Manchester Jewish Museum.
[16] *Jewish Yearbook*, 1901–1911.

immigrants tried to prevent marriages with Gentiles, there were instances of marriages among different Sephardic groups. For instance, one prominent immigrant from Aleppo married a woman from a Corfiot family early in this century. I know of several other such marriages. There were few marriages with Ashkenazim. Certainly the class difference between the mass of Russian immigrants and the suburban Sephardim inhibited such unions. Today the situation is quite different. Even some of the older members of the community have Ashkenazic wives.

The congregations also have some Ashkenazic members. In fact, the northern congregation, which used to be on Cheetham Hill Road, is now in Kersal and has a largely Ashkenazic membership. The rabbis of all the congregations, however, have been either Sephardim or Sephardicized Ashkenazim.

Despite its decline, Sephardic families continued to migrate to Manchester during the past half-century. Some were Middle Eastern Jews who had businesses on the Continent but became refugees during the Second World War. Some recent immigrants came from the Middle East directly, either as immigrants or as refugees. One of the most prominent of these is David Alliance, an Iranian who was a noted entrepreneur in the 1980s.

Less newsworthy individuals have also immigrated to Manchester. For instance, in 1987, Withington had a Middle Eastern restaurant which was owned by a Yemenite-Sephardic Jew from Jerusalem and his Lebanese-born wife. Across the street from their establishment, I found the Chicago Cafe, which served American hamburgers and humous, owned by a Lebanese non-Jew.[17]

The Chicago Sephardim

Among the tens of thousands of Jews who poured into Chicago as part of the huge wave of immigration in the early twentieth century, one finds three small streams of Jews from the Near and Middle East. Like most of their East European coreligionists, they were concentrated on the West Side and moved, alongside the much more numerous Ashkenazim from the near West Side, to Lawndale and

---

[17] Fieldnotes, 1987.

then to the North Side. For the most part, these immigrants were poor and unskilled.

The immigrants from the Near and Middle East were preceded by small numbers of Sephardic individuals. Sephardic organizations appear only after the turn of the century and are associated, in particular, with the immigrants from the Ottoman Empire.

By 1920, Chicago had representatives of three Middle Eastern groups. The largest were Spanish Jews, Ladino-speaking Jews from the Balkans and Anatolia. They also were the ones most associated with a variety of voluntary organizations. There were Arabic-speakers, primarily from Aleppo. Finally, one found Persians, Aramaic-speakers from Urmia and other parts of Iranian Azerbaijan.[18]

As in Manchester, Gentiles came to Chicago from the same areas as the Jews. One could find Greek, Serbian, Armenian, Assyrian, and Syrian (Lebanese) Christians, and Palestinian, Albanian, and Turkish Muslims in Chicago in the period of mass immigration. It is noteworthy that Chicago, one of the few American cities to have a congregation of Aramaic-speaking Jews, also was home to a substantial Assyrian community, also speaking Aramaic, from the same region of Azerbaijan. The Jews and their non-Jewish compatriots lived apart, however. Especially in the wake of World War I, relations between the Jewish and Gentile ex-neighbors were often hostile and animosities from the old country were carried over to the new one.[19]

The occupations of Sephardic immigrants, like those of their Ashkenazi coreligionists, were generally in light industry and petty commerce. Spanish women worked in factories, though members of the other two speech communities generally did not. Many of the men were peddlers, especially installment dealers. While many of the Ashkenazi installment dealers sold to immigrants from Slavic lands, Ladino-speakers often dealt with Italians.

Some, especially among the Persians and Syrians, specialized in the sale and later the manufacture of lingerie and other forms of women's wear. In the 1920s and 1930s, some of the Syrians in

---

[18] Walter P. Zenner, "Chicago's Sephardim: A Historical Exploration," *American Jewish History* 80 (1990–91): 221–241.

[19] Edith M. Stein, "Some Near Eastern Immigrant Groups in Chicago" (M.A. thesis, University of Chicago, 1922). Also see Zenner, "Chicago's Sephardim," pp. 225–229.

Chicago were part of the Aleppian trade network which specialized in the sale of table linen and children's clothing. In fact, some of these families continued in these businesses into the 1980s.

The Sephardim gradually became more diversified in their occupations. Spanish women in particular often worked as secretaries. Some men opened shops on the South Side. Several Persians became manufacturers of women's wear, especially nightgowns. One family moved from women's wear to men's wear and continues in that business to this day. The next generation included many who went into the professions and moved away from Chicago. The Syrians in particular included many who moved away. However, one Syrian family owns several car dealerships. Many younger people are going into the professions.[20]

Intermarriage between the different Sephardic speech communities was common from the beginning. In part, this was a product of an immigration pattern in which single men pioneered the migration to Chicago. The outbreak of the First World War and the disorder in the countries of origin interrupted immigration. There also were instances of marriage with Ashkenazim early on. Today intermarriage with Ashkenazim is common. I have no statistics on marriage, including mixed marriages with non-Jews.

The residential mobility of the Sephardim from the West Side to the North Side and to the northern suburbs is parallel to that of the East European Ashkenazim. Despite some social distance because of the unfamiliarity and prejudices of the Ashkenazic majority, the Sephardim have accompanied the Ashkenazim from one region to another. During the interwar period the Sephardic congregations met in buildings in Lawndale, while today they are found in West Rogers Park, South Evanston, and Skokie.[21]

The three Sephardic congregations were small. One, the Persian congregation, owned its own building from 1920 on. Possibly the Syrian congregation, whose history is the hardest to document, did too. The congregation of the Spanish Jews evidently was a guest of the Romanian synagogue in Lawndale for a long time. The organization which provided a corporate existence for this group was the Portuguese Israelite Fraternity.

---

[20] Zenner, "Chicago's Sephardim," p. 228; Fieldnotes, 1988.
[21] Zenner, "Chicago's Sephardim," pp. 235–237.

The early spiritual leadership of these congregations appears to have been a part-time affair. There were Sephardic teachers, one of whom was Syrian. In fact, one individual read the Torah for both the Syrian and the Spanish synagogue. The leadership of the Spanish group received a boost when Shalom Nadoff, a Yemeni silversmith from Palestine, came to Chicago for the Century of Progress Exposition in 1933. He had sufficient knowledge to serve as a rabbi, which he did for several decades thereafter. He was both a Hebrew teacher and a rabbi, and in addition invested money in real estate.

Of the three congregations on the West Side, the Syrian congregation disappeared a long time ago. The Persians had their own building on the West Side but sold it during the 1950s. They built a new building in Skokie in the early 1960s. This small congregation has opened its doors to Ashkenazic members and was served by an Ashkenazic rabbi in 1987, although its membership has also been augmented by the post-Khomeini immigration of Iranians.

The "Spanish" congregation opened its synagogue on Howard Street, on the Chicago-Evanston border, in 1970. This congregation restricts membership to Sephardim and their spouses. It has a Sephardic rabbi, a native of Seattle. It very deliberately maintains Sephardic liturgical traditions. Both of these congregations are Orthodox, and men and women are seated separately. The Sephardic congregation today has some of the older Chicago residents as members, but it also has many post-1950 immigrants.[22]

Chicago has had a more diverse and flourishing economy than many other Great Lakes cities and the old industrial centers of northern England. It is thus fairly attractive to new immigrants. Sephardic Jews have been among these, including Egyptians, North Africans, Israelis, and Iranians. In addition to the Sephardic congregation, a small new congregation was founded in the 1980s in West Rogers Park about a mile and a half south of the Sephardic congregation. This congregation is also assertively Sephardic in maintaining liturgical traditions. Its members are mainly newer immigrants, many of whom are professionals. Increasingly it will be new immigrants who bear the Sephardic torch, as the descendants of earlier immigrants are assimilated into the American Jewish population.

---

[22] Ibid., pp. 228, 229, 231, 233, 236–237, 238–239.

Conclusion

In this paper, I have suggested that much Sephardic immigration must be considered as small-scale immigration of small numbers of people. Trickles and streams of immigration are subjected to greater assimilatory pressures than are larger waves. Such groups remain proportionately small, even when concentrated in large metropolitan areas.

Sephardim of a variety of origins were attracted to Manchester and Chicago, two cities which grew rapidly as a result of industrialization in the eighteenth and nineteenth centuries. Both communities were small in number. It is likely that neither numbered more than 1,000 up to the 1940s, though Manchester's Sephardim formed a larger proportion of the city's total Jewish community than those of Chicago.

Still, there is a contrast. From the start, the Manchester Sephardim constituted an upper-middle-class aggregate and were able to be part of the elite of that city's Jewish community. They were quite prominent and visible. In fact, a Sephardic synagogue building now serves as a monument to the Jewish past in Manchester. In addition to their occupational advantages as shipping merchants, several Sephardic firms were well-established in Manchester by 1881, when the massive Russian immigration began.

The Sephardim of Chicago, who had similar regional origins to those of Manchester, were barely noticed among the teeming masses of East European immigrants on Chicago's West Side. They certainly were not part of the Jewish elite of Chicago. In this, they were like the other eastern Sephardim in North America for the greater part of the twentieth century. Only at the end of the twentieth century have they become visible.

Were the Chicago Sephardim poorer in origin than those who went to Manchester? I do not have a definitive answer. Certainly many of the Sephardim in Manchester arrived as representatives of well-to-do merchants, often connected to the rabbinic elites in Aleppo and other cities. Such families can be seen as "tribe-families,"[23] parts

---

[23] The term "tribe-family" is derived from Stewart G. McHenry, "The Syrians of Upstate New York: A Social Geography" (Ph.D. diss., Syracuse University, Department of Geography, 1973; Ann Arbor, University Microfilms, No. 74-8660). He uses the term to describe families involved in large-scale family firms. On this

of an ancient trading diaspora. But such families were also represented in the immigration to the United States. Yet the American
Sephardim generally had a more difficult time than those who went
to Britain. The Sephardic immigration to Manchester and the United
States included both rich and poor. Consideration of family histories, tracing them from Mediterranean and Middle Eastern trading
centers to the West offers to solve some of these quandaries.

phenomenon, also see Walter P. Zenner, "The Cross-National Web of Syrian-Jewish
Relations," in *Urban Life*, ed. G. Gmelch and W.P. Zenner (Prospects Heights, Ill.,
1988), pp. 381–390.

THE NORTH AFRICAN JEWS IN TORONTO TODAY: ASSIMILATION OR SURVIVAL

Sarah Taieb-Carlen

York University
Toronto, Ontario

The North African Jewish community of Toronto counts over 8,000 people. This number does not include Israelis of North African origin, who are estimated at 5,000 to 25,000 people. The data analyzed in this paper were obtained by interviewing the eleven leaders of the community and a social worker at the Jewish Family and Child Services (JFCS) who deals with the North African cases, as well as 108 North African Jews now living in Toronto. The results of our data analysis show that two sets of external factors have pushed the North African Jews to organize internally; these are the general characteristics of Canadian society and those of the larger Jewish community.

External Factors

General Characteristics of Canadian Society

Canada's political ideology

Ontario's official policy vis-à-vis its various ethnic groups is cultural pluralism, whereby each group is encouraged to keep its specific culture. This liberal environment and legislated tolerance are highly appreciated by the North African Jews, who endured thirteen centuries of *dhimmi* status under Muslim rule and were also exposed to Christian anti-Semitism during the era of French colonization.[1]

---

[1] The Arabic word *dhimmi* literally means "protected citizen." The status of *dhimmi*, however, was for Jews in Muslim lands an official and legalized state of second-class citizenship. For more details, see Stillman (1979).

Heterogeneous character of Canadian society
In North Africa, the Jews were usually one of two or three ethno-religious groups.[2] Today in Toronto, the North African Jews are one of many cultural, religious, racial, and ethnic groups, all of which are equal before the law. This engenders a feeling of great security and self-confidence among the North African Jews.

Availability of free education
Education was most instrumental in modernizing and secularizing the Jewish communities in French North Africa. Education and teaching in the French schools were generally excellent, expensive, and opened many more doors to the students than the best religious education. In Toronto, education in Jewish schools is supposedly better than in the public schools. This might explain the high percentage (60 percent) of North African Jewish children registered in Jewish day schools.

Existence of numerous ethnic residential areas
In Toronto, ethnic districts such as Chinatown, Little Italy, Rosedale, and Baby Point Crescent constitute homogeneous, mainly ethnic, non-Jewish enclaves. Other districts, however, are mixed, without necessarily being exclusively non-Jewish. As well, there are some areas which are very heavily populated by Jews, such as the select neighborhood of Forest Hill and the Bathurst/Sheppard area, dominated by the Orthodox Jewish community.

Government-funded cultural programs
The Ontario government finances such programs as Heritage Languages, which includes Ukrainian, Chinese, Armenian, Italian, Portuguese, etc.; English as a second language (ESL), which encourages non-English-speaking adults to learn English; the week-long Caravan program, during which each cultural group exhibits its folklore, foods, and artifacts in its booth; and the Caribbana weekend, which includes Caribbean songs, dances, and parade in August. All these programs indicate to North African Jews not only that they can freely express

---

[2] For more details, refer to Sarah Taieb-Carlen, "Assessment of a Small Group Ethnic Identity: The Jews in North Africa and the North African Jews in Toronto" (Ph.D. diss., York University, 1989).

their Jewishness, but also that they could and should preserve their North Africanness.

Characteristics of the Larger Jewish Community

Heterogeneity

In North Africa, the Jewish community was quite homogeneous, except for the few immigrant waves following the expulsions from Portugal, Spain, and Italy. In Toronto, North African Jews found a long-established Jewish community of Eastern European origin; and recently, a substantial number of Jews from Israel have added even more cultural and geographic diversity to the community.

Network of institutions

The long-established Jewish community of Toronto has founded and maintained a very impressive network of institutions which cover almost all domains of Jewish life from the recreational to the educational. Therefore, whenever their own community cannot be a proper resource (Breton 1974), the North African Jews turn to the institutions of the larger Jewish community.

Attitudes and behavior toward North Africans

The Eastern European Jews' pronunciation of Hebrew and use of Yiddish in the synagogues made the North Africans feel uneasy and alienated. The North African leaders stated that, at first, the Eastern European Jews relegated them to the basements of their synagogues, instead of welcoming them in the main sanctuary. Moreover, according to a few leaders, because the North Africans could not speak Yiddish, some Eastern Europeans asked them if they were "really Jewish."

Board of Jewish Education

A few North African leaders said that, following several unsuccessful meetings with the teachers and administrators of their children's schools about the absence of Sephardic content in the curricula, they met with Board of Jewish Education (BJE) officials. The meetings were very frustrating because "they [the BJE officials] did not seem to be able to acknowledge that there was a problem, and consequently they could not address it." This led to the foundation of the

Or Haemet Sephardi School in 1979. This conflict is an example of one which results "from institutional states rather than from individual predispositions" (Jackson 1975, p. 162).

Reaction of the North African Jews: Institution Building

Synagogues

The North Africans founded a few synagogues. In 1975 Petah Tikva Anshe Castilla, which counts 320 families, mostly Hispanophones, and Magen David Sephardic Congregation, which counts 220 families, mostly Francophones, were inaugurated. Around 1977–78, there was a return to stricter observance of Shabbat; and a few families, Francophones and Hispanophones, branched out into Minyan Sepharade, which counts 130 families, and Tiferet Israel, which counts 80 families.

So, whereas Petah Tikva and Magen David share a common desire to preserve their respective languages, Minyan Sepharade and Tiferet Israel share a common desire "to go back to our roots, our Torah, to respect the Fourth Commandment." This "renaissance of observance," as one leader called it, seems to be growing, especially among the young people. More recently, two synagogues, Rabbi Shimon Bar Yohai (1985) and Lemaan Shemo Beahava (1987), were founded, respectively, by a Tunisian and a Turkish rabbi; each has a mostly North African congregation of about 120 people.

Do the synagogues fill the same crucial role as in North Africa, and do the rabbis still enjoy the *zekhut avot*?[3] None of the synagogues has a school or a cemetery, but they all have kosher catering services. They offer almost exclusively religious services. One of them has a brotherhood and a sisterhood, a youth group, and a senior group, but no social activity takes place regularly. The others boast of many activities apart from prayer, such as "weddings, Bnei-Mitsvah, oneg Shabbats, births, deaths, *hilloulot*."[4]

As for the rabbis, a leader said that "synagogues here do not have a spiritual leader, like in North Africa. They have committees. These

---

[3] *Zehkhut avot*, literally "the privilege of the fathers," means, by extension, the respect due to elder or learned people.
[4] *Hilloulot* (sing. *hilloula*) are celebrations of the death anniversaries of saints or great Jewish scholars.

are our leaders today, the committees." Another leader noted that the rabbis "come from the Old Country, but they are educated and trained in New York, in Ashkenazi yeshivot. It really does not matter, because they do make an effort to preserve all which is typically North African: the accent in Hebrew, the pronunciation, certain prayers, all the habits and customs, so it's O.K."

A few people disagree strongly with this opinion; one of them said: "These rabbis lost many important features of Sephardi Judaism, such as leniency and tolerance. They impose very strict rules of Orthodoxy in and out of the synagogues, with the result that many of our Sephardi synagogues are losing their members to Ashkenazi Conservative synagogues and even to Reform temples. It's very, very sad. They dress like Ashkenazim who dress like Polish gentlemen of the seventeenth century. Those people hated the Jews more than any other group in the history of anti-Semitism. And why should a Sephardi rabbi dress like them? Ridiculous!"

Besides the unfriendly attitudes of the Ashkenazim, language was also a major reason for founding Sephardi synagogues, since, as Breton (1974, p. 151) noted, "language is relevant in two ways: as a symbol of ethnic identification, and as an instrument of communication."

The North Africans felt that by speaking Yiddish, the Ashkenazim were emphasizing their origins, from which the North Africans were excluded, as well as communicating among themselves and therefore again excluding the North Africans. Whether they were actually being excluded is not relevant here; what is relevant is that the North Africans believed they were excluded, or even at times dominated, since, in Breton's words, "Language is an instrument of institutional control, [and] he who imposes the linguistic rules in a particular situation has established ascendancy in that situation" (1974, p. 153).

Schools

The important role of education in preserving Jewish identity in young children has been emphasized by many authors (Kallen 1977; Davids 1982; Liebman 1983; Waxman 1983; Himmelfarb 1984). As Goldstein and Goldscheider (1968, p. 211) wrote: "One of the many reasons for the great interest in education is that not only does it contribute to a more meaningful participation in religious services and to a greater familiarization with religious rituals, but it has taken on the significant task of creating a sense of identification with Jewish culture, history and tradition." The North Africans have created Or Haemet. Or Haemet receives no grant from the Ministry of Education and not enough money from the Board of Jewish Education. A leader explained "the ambivalence of the Board of Jewish Education towards Or Haemet. . . . They [the Toronto Jewish Congress] say we [the North Africans] do not give enough money. So, their perception of the whole thing is: 'If you don't give, should you get?'"

There are only 300 children enrolled, 45 percent boys and 55 percent girls. Boys and girls study together up to grade 4, after which they are separated.

According to most of the leaders, approximately 30 percent of Toronto's North African children attend Or Haemet, 30 percent attend other Jewish day schools, and 40 percent attend non-Jewish schools. Most of the boys in the last category are provided with a supplementary Jewish education up to their Bar Mitzvah, after which it is usually dropped. Most North African Jewish girls do not cele-brate their Bat Mitzvah, at least not in the synagogue like the boys. When they leave Or Haemet, most of them go to Ulpanat Orot, a Bnei Akiva Orthodox high school for girls.

Some boys who leave Or Haemet after grade 8 go to Associated Hebrew Day Schools, and subsequently many go to CHAT (Com-munity Hebrew Academy of Toronto), a traditional high school for boys and girls, or to Or Haim, an Orthodox high school for boys. So, after age thirteen, a North African Jewish boy in Toronto may still receive a Jewish education in a Jewish school, but his North African Jewish heritage is hardly mentioned. He will have to rely on the synagogue or his family to teach him about the sages, the history, and the writings of his ancestors. This may lead to what Epstein (1978, p. 111) has termed "cultural erosion," which is what many parents said they feared: "If they do not learn about their specific North African heritage at school, where will they learn it? At home, who has the time to teach the children? Besides, frankly, I do not think me or my wife know enough to teach our children. You see, we know what we know because we lived it. And also because our parents or grandparents told us about it, you know, about life in their younger years. We did not learn it in books."

When students leave Or Haemet for some reason, they usually keep in touch with their old classmates if they are related, if their parents are friends, if they live nearby, or if they belong to the same synagogue. Usually, we were told, at least one of these conditions does prevail. We can therefore assume that leaving Or Haemet does not necessarily mean losing social contact with North African Jewish youth.

These are the institutions that the North African Jews have built in Toronto. We shall now review how much they participate in the life of the Jewish community and whether they manage to keep their Jewishness and their North Africanness.

Community Life, Jewishness, and North Africanness

Community Life

In the literature, the community is often cited as a crucial feature of Jewish life, and involvement in the community as a highly regarded activity. In *Ethnic Identification Among American Jews*, Dashefsky and Shapiro (1974, p. 121) remind the reader of the great importance that the community has for the individual Jew: "One of the most famous rabbinic aphorisms admonishes the Jew: 'Do not separate yourself from the community.' The rabbis were well aware of the importance of being Jewish within the framework of the organised Jewish community and of the consequent effects of the community on the individual."

Over 60 percent of our sample are not involved in community affairs, apart from belonging to and attending the synagogue.[5] Unlike the larger Jewish community, the North Africans have no newspaper, no radio program, no theater, no summer camp, no Primrose Club. This is due to their limited resources, relatively recent arrival, small number, and maybe mostly the availability of excellent non-North African Jewish institutions.

A majority of North Africans belong to a synagogue (81 percent); most of them are members of a North African synagogue (62 percent), while a minority belongs to a non-North African synagogue (19 percent). In the latter group, many families were already members of a synagogue before there were North African ones in Toronto.

---

[5] A Canadian Jewish Congress official told us that the percentage was the same among Ashkenazim.

As for the other families, they are usually not Moroccan but Algerian or Tunisian, and since the Moroccan tunes, liturgy, and ritual are different from their own, they felt that a non-North African synagogue was adequate, especially when it was located near their home or if many of their friends belonged to it.

About two-thirds of the North African Jews do not belong to any social club or organization (60 percent). Slightly more than half of the remaining 40 percent belong to non-North African Jewish clubs (21 percent) and some to Canadian clubs (15 percent).

Almost half the respondents (48 percent) feel at ease only in their own institutions. Some of them stated that they had suffered humiliation and discrimination on the part of the Ashkenazim and said that they were "very happy" when their own community started to organize and built the synagogues and school. More than a quarter of our subjects do not feel out of place in non-North African institutions (27 percent), and 14 percent said that they were "quite at ease" in organizations with North African and non-North African members.

There is not much concerted action emanating from the various leaders of the North African institutions because there is no real leader. Also, the North African institutions are mostly owned or run by Moroccans; although Algerians and Tunisians are welcome to use them as members or as clients, they are not invited to join the leadership. Within the Moroccan community there is a linguistic division between the Francophones and the Hispanophones. The latter often accuse the former of not being religious enough and of tailoring Judaism to their needs or tastes, whereas the Francophones ridicule the austerity and strictness of their Spanish-speaking brothers and sisters. But both groups agree that they are more religious than the Tunisians and the Algerians, and the Moroccans and Tunisians agree that the Algerians do not have much religion left.

Despite these differences, one cannot write about any great conflict within the North African Jewish community, but it seems there is just enough of it to confirm Dahrendorf's axiom that "there is no community without conflict, there is no conflict without community" (1965, p. 225).

There is no deep-seated animosity, and the children of the two Moroccan linguistic groups and those of the three North African subcommunities intermarry frequently.

Retention of Religious Practice

Holiday and kashrut observance
On the whole, most North African Jews in Toronto are still quite observant, although their migration to Toronto has caused an average decrease of 16 percent in religious practice, calculated from the observance of all the religious holidays and of kashrut (see *Table 1*).

Synagogue attendance
As an index of religiosity, synagogue attendance has remained quite similar to what it used to be in North Africa. Interestingly, 22 percent of our subjects stated that they were not members of any synagogue, whereas only 3 percent said that they never went to synagogue. It seems, then, that 19 percent go to synagogue without being members. This is to be explained by the fact that some North African Jews in Toronto do not seem to have gotten used to the idea of "pay in order to pray" or to paying membership fees in order to belong to clubs and other social organizations. In North Africa, it was accepted by all that a few wealthy families would take complete care of the needs of the community, including the creation and maintenance of certain institutions, especially synagogues.

Here is how one of our subjects expressed a view stated by many others: "You can't know what it does to me to pay to pray. I don't mind paying for day school, buying Israel Bonds, giving *tzedaka* [charity] every single Friday, but paying for the synagogue, buying my right to pray—never!" Since we are studying the immigrant generation, it seems evident that perhaps the 19 percent of unaffiliated North African Jews still abide by the norms of the Old Country.

Schools
Although the data seem to reveal a general tendency on the part of the respondents to send their children to Jewish schools, the type of school the parents went to in North Africa has little influence on the their choice of a school for their children in Toronto (see *Table 2*).

Most of the 39 percent of parents who send their children to public school, with or without a Sunday school supplement, stated that for them, general studies are more important than Hebrew studies. Others said that religion is a private matter which should be taught in the privacy of one's home. Although the Board of Jewish Education provides free schooling for needy families, some North African Jews refuse, out of pride, to accept any kind of financial aid.

Intermarriage

By intermarriage, we mean a marriage in which one of the spouses was not born Jewish and did not convert. A great majority of our respondents are against intermarriage (90 percent). This is not surprising, since exogamy has always been regarded as the ultimate danger for Jews, and in the Eastern European ghetto it was even considered a sin (Kallen 1977). This fear is due to the small size of local communities and to a very sharp desire of the Jewish people to survive as a distinct and homogeneous group. This view is reinforced by the high percentage of North African Jews who gave the future of the community and the spiritual and psychological balance of the children as reasons for their opposition to intermarriage (83 percent).[6]

North Africanness

Observance of North African customs

The North African Jews in Toronto are gradually giving up most of their specific customs. For example, only 50 percent of them still celebrate birth, circumcision, Bar Mitzvah, engagement, and marriage the North African way. Many said that doing so was too costly in time and/or money; and more significantly, some added: "There is [*sic*] not enough people to invite who would appreciate and understand. Here, it just does not fit the context." This implies that these customs are being lost irreversibly, since the reason for the loss is the context, i.e., Toronto and the non-North African Jews.

The North African Jewish holidays (Mimouna, Fête des Filles, Fête des Garçons, etc.) are still observed by 55 percent of our subjects. The others, explaining their failure to observe them, gave reasons very similar to the ones stated above.

More than a third of our subjects (38 percent) still believe in the superstitions and other popular beliefs which permeated their daily life in the Maghreb. The most common answer given by the other 62 percent was: "Everybody was superstitious there, the teachers, the doctors . . . everybody. Here, nobody is. So it's stupid to believe in all these things."

---

[6] In Montreal, however, according to Lasry and Bloomfield-Shachter (1975), the rate of intermarriage among Jewish North African males was over 50 percent.

Language

Language has often been cited as a most important component of ethnic identity. However, among some groups, such as the Jews, "language . . . is . . . not . . . ideologized" (Fishman 1965, p. 10).

Under Muslim rule, the Jews of North Africa spoke a Judeo-Arabic dialect and/or Arabic, and received their Jewish education in Hebrew. During the French and Spanish colonizations, they learned French and/or Spanish. In Toronto, 53 percent of the immigrant North African Jews have adopted English as their home language, and almost all of their children speak only English (and Hebrew for those who go to Jewish schools) (see *Table 3*).

Although Canada is officially an English-French bilingual country, the Canadian-educated children of North African Jews do not usually speak French, and they are even less eager to learn and speak Arabic, Judeo-Arabic, or Spanish, since these languages are not particularly useful in Toronto or in Canada.

Writing about Yiddish, Davids (1984, p. 95) explains that its replacement by German or English "is taken to mean that modernization has taken place and the speaker no longer functions within the mental and social framework of the highly isolated, very religious and traditionalist culture of East-European Jewry." The same pattern applies to the languages of the North Africans, as indicated by this answer by an interviewee: "Our kids often say, 'Why should we speak Arabic or Judeo Arabic? These were the languages you spoke when you were in North Africa and you were scared of the Arabs. Here we are in Canada, and we are not afraid of anybody.'"

Residential area

Residential concentration is usually considered to encourage ethnic solidarity.[7]

In Toronto, most North African Jews live near the institutions of the larger Jewish community, which indicates that it is important for them to live among Jews, even Jews who are not North Africans (see *Table 4*).

The North African Jews seem to cluster in the area stretching from Bathurst and Wilson to Leslie and Don Mills, in the northern part of the city. In sum, except for the Forest Hill area (a wealthy

---

[7] See, for example, Balakrishnan (1976 and 1982), Borhek (1970), Drieger & Church (1974), Reitz (1980), and Richmond (1972).

Jewish neighborhood where only five of our subjects live), most of
the North African Jews can be found in all the Jewish neighborhoods in the city.

Some of the interviewees mentioned that they would rather live
in an apartment in a Jewish district than in a house in a non-Jewish
district even when they could financially afford to buy the house.
This shows that they are quite willing to sacrifice a certain degree
of comfort and social prestige in order to live near their fellow Jews
and their own institutions and organizations.

Commercial enterprises
Some North African men and women have successfully opened their
own businesses. Those which serve a North African clientele are two
bakeries and a Judaica bookshop.

World Jewry and Israel
In the twelfth century, Maimonides wrote to Jews in North Africa
to ask their financial help to free Jewish captives. This shows that
traditionally the ransoming of captives was a highly respected value
among North African Jews. Similarly, today in Toronto, the North
Africans seem genuinely concerned about the Jews of Ethiopia, Iran,
Russia, Syria, and Yemen. As yet they have not developed a program to help them because "we do not have the resources."

How about all the Israelis of North African origin now living in
Toronto? Do the North Africans have programs for them which
would safeguard their roots? The leaders believe that the local Israelis
have very little Judaism left in them, and many blame Israel for this.

As one interview subject exclaimed: "How can we? Look what
Israel did to our flowers, our young people: no respect for religion,
for mother or father. They are ashamed of their culture, of their
Arabic language, of their grandparents because of their North African
clothes, their way of talking, and their very large families. I know,
I lived there for twelve years. But now what happens? The Israelis
have introduced Arabic as a compulsory language in the schools,
they are crying for more children. Eh! All the characteristics of our
culture that they forced us to give up, to unlearn, now they are
spending a fortune trying to give them to all the Israelis. Don't talk
to me of Israel!"

Another interviewee said: "They feel more Israeli than North
African, therefore they are closer to the Ashkenazi culture and norms.

Most of them haven't even kept their religion, so how can we draw them back to their culture?"

There is a yearly organized trip to Morocco after Pesah. It is usually well attended. Some go in order to visit the cemetery where members of their family are buried (100 percent), others to alleviate a "very strong nostalgia" (92 percent), or to visit relatives still living there, especially old ones who cannot travel (68 percent). They like to go as a group because "it's safer" or because "the leaders of the Jewish community give us the red-carpet treatment."

They are very proud of the Moroccan king, Hassan II, whose birthday they celebrate and who is quite protective of his Jewish subjects, but they do not know "what will happen to the Jews in Morocco when Hassan II no longer reigns, so it's almost a must for us to go and visit Morocco now."

There is also a yearly organized trip to Israel, but it is less popular. This may be due to the fact that "all year round, we go to Israel. We don't need an organized trip." Those who go usually "have family to visit" (85 percent), "want to see what it's become since we left" (80 percent), "feel every Jew should go at least once in their life" (54 percent).

Would the North African Jews or their Canadian-born children like to live in Israel? "Not at all; except for me, no one thinks of living in Israel in the congregation." Or, "Look . . . their parents invest in Israel, worry about Israel, travel there, send the kids to study there, but they would sit *shiva* [mourn] if the kids decided to live there." Or, "Practically 100 percent of them want to stay here or go to California, that's their new promised land."

However, a minority disagreed. "I would say 30 percent of the North African Jews consider Toronto only as a stopover to make some money and assure our children of a good education that, as Sephardim, they unfortunately could not get in Israel. Then, once more, we'll pack up and go home to Israel."

We must emphasize that for the Jews of Muslim lands, Zionism was not an intellectual, leftist, politico-social movement, but a messianic hope and belief wrapped up with some very strong religious mysticism. Therefore, when religion lost much of its importance and meaning, love for Israel and the ancestral wish to live there also lost much of their importance and meaning.

According to Sklare (1974, p. 77), for American Jews "Israel has become the major unifying symbol in the community, in effect replacing traditional religious values as the binding tie linking Jews of varying persuasions and interests."

As for the North African Jews, however, only the religious among them are still attracted by Israel, which means that they have kept both their religion and their love for Israel. Sklare adds: "Indeed, Israel has become, de facto, the authority-giving element in Jewish life today, in the way that the Torah was in the pre-modern world" (1974, p. 78).

For North African Jews, the premodern world had already changed into a quasi-modern one in North Africa, through the French colonization of the region. As a result, even before they emigrated to Canada the Torah had already lost much of its authority without being replaced by anything else.

Nowadays, what would make Toronto's North African Jews move to Israel? "[The certitude of being] treated there like I am here, fairly, according to my capacities and not depending on where I was born or what my name is" (91 percent). "Another Hitler, worldwide anti-Semitism" (87 percent). "Peace between Israel and its neighbors" (85 percent). "If all our relatives and friends were there" (76 percent). "If I win the lottery, if I can save enough money for my three children's education, if I were sure of a good job" (70 percent).

Conclusion

To sum up: the North African Jewish community of Toronto is far from being institutionally complete. A few synagogues and a school are the only communal institutions it has built. Internally, linguistic, ritual, and regional rivalries weaken the community. Externally, free access to the institutions of the larger Jewish community probably satisfies the other nonreligious and noneducational needs of the North Africans, who may thereby remain Jewish but will most probably lose their North Africanness. Nationally, exogamic marriages are frequent and usually welcome, most parents expressing a sense of relief along these lines: "Let them marry whoever they want, provided he/she is Jewish!" The external and internal factors of identity maintenance which kept them Jewish for so long in North Africa, especially before the advent of French rule,[8] are all but gone.

---

[8] For more information, see Taieb-Carlen 1989.

Table 1. Holiday and kashrut observance

OBSERVANCE	PERCENTAGE OBSERVING		DIFFERENCE
	North Africa	*Toronto*	
Shabbat	95	91	- 4
Yom Kippur	97	90	- 7
Rosh Hashana	96	82	- 12
Sukkot	94	82	- 14
Simhat Torah	94	76	- 18
Hanukkah	95	76	- 19
Pesah	96	74	- 22
Purim	95	73	- 22
Tu Bi-Shvat	94	73	- 21
Shavuot	95	71	- 24
Kosher home	94	82	- 12
Average	95	79	- 16

Table 2. Type of school attended by children
and parents (percentage)

PARENTS' SCHOOLS

		Jewish schools		
	Non-Jewish schools (N = 35)	Day schools (N = 36)	Supplementary schools (N = 12)	All subjects (N = 83)
CHILDREN'S SCHOOLS				
Non-Jewish schools:	51	31	43	43
Jewish schools:				
Day schools	21	14	14	18
Supplementary schools	28	55	43	39
Total	100	100	100	100

Table 3. Language spoken at home (percentage)

LANGUAGE	NORTH AFRICA	TORONTO
English	0	53
French	76	39
Spanish	21	7
Other	3	1
Total (N = 108)	100	100

Table 4. Residential patterns (percentage)

TYPE OF AREA	NORTH AFRICA	TORONTO
Jewish	53	56
Mixed	11	23
Non-Jewish	36	21
Total (N = 108)	100	100

References

Attal, R. 1973. *Les Juifs d'Afrique du Nord Bibliographie.* Jerusalem.
Balakrishnan, T.R. 1976. "Ethnic Residential Segregation in the Metropolitan Areas of Canada." *Canadian Journal of Sociology* 1:481–498.
———. 1982. "Changing Patterns in Ethnic Residential Segregation in the Metropolitan Areas of Canada." *Canadian Review of Sociology and Anthropology* 19:92–110.
Borhek, J. 1970. "Ethnic Group Cohesion." *American Journal of Sociology* 76:33–46.
Breton, R. 1974. "Institutional Completeness of Ethnic Communities and Personal Relations of Immigrants." *American Journal of Sociology* 70:193–205.
Dashefsky, and Shapiro. 1974. *Ethnic Identification Among American Jews.*
Dahrendorf, R. 1965. *Class and Class Conflict in Industrial Society.* Stanford University Press.
Davids, L. 1982. "Ethnic Identity, Religiosity and Youthful Deviance." *Adolescence* 17, no. 6:673–684.
———. 1984. "Yiddish in Canada: Picture and Prospects." *Canadian Ethnic Studies* 16, no. 2:89–102.
Driedger, L., and G. Church. 1974. "Residential Segregation and Institutional Completeness: A Comparison of Ethnic Minorities." *Canadian Review of Sociology and Anthropology* 11:30–52.
Epstein, A.L. 1978. *Ethos and Identity: Three Studies in Ethnicity.* London: Tavistock.
Fishman, J.A. 1965. *Varieties of Ethnicity and Varieties of Language.* Georgetown University Monograph, no. 18.
Goldstein, S., and C. Goldscheider. 1974. "Jewish Religiosity: Ideological and Ritualistic Dimensions." In M. Sklare (ed.), *The Jew in American Society*, pp. 203–221. New York: Behrman House.
Himmelfarb, H.S. 1980. "The Study of American Jewish Identification: How It Is Defined, Measured, Obtained, Sustained and Lost." *Journal for the Scientific Study of Religion* 19:48–60.
Kallen, E. 1977. *Spanning the Generations: A Study of Jewish Identity*, Longman's, Canada.
Lasry, J.C., and E. Bloomfield-Shachter. 1975. "Jewish Intermarriage in Montreal, 1962–1972." *Jewish Social Studies* 37, no. 3:261–278.
Liebman, C.S., and E. Don-Yehiya, *Civil Religion in Israel*, Berkeley, 1983.
Reitz, J. 1980. *The Survival of Ethnic Groups.* Toronto: McGraw-Hill, Ryerson.
Richmond, A.H. 1972. *Ethnic Segregation in Metropolitan Toronto.* Toronto: York University, Institute for Behavioral Research.
Sklare, M. 1974. *The Jew in American Society.* New York: Behrman House.
Stillman, N.A. 1979. *The Jews of Arab Lands.* Philadelphia: Jewish Publication Society.
Taieb-Carlen, S. 1989. "Assessment of A Small Group Ethnic Identity: The Jews in North Africa and the North African Jews in Toronto." Ph.D. diss., York University.
Waxman, C.I., *America's Jews in Transition*, Temple University Press, Philadelphia, 1983.

THE JUDEO-SPANISH COMMUNITY IN PARIS

ANNIE BENVENISTE

University Paris 8
Paris, France

The itineraries of Jewish immigrants in France since the end of the nineteenth century have their own specific character, that of a significant social mobility and an enduring sense of particular identity distinct from the national identity. Mobility and reference to Jewishness are not contradictory, for Jewish immigration has been conducive to social ascension and to different forms of solidarity. Whatever their origin, whether driven out by pogroms or simply obliged to leave their adopted country for political or economic reasons, Eastern European and Mediterranean Jews emigrated in waves containing all social classes. These waves constitute an almost complete spectrum of socioeconomic roles. Although this variety was sometimes a source of conflict, it also facilitated mobilization and concentration of resources in community networks.[1]

This double model of mobility (implying integration) and resistance to complete assimilation is therefore indispensable to an understanding of Jewish immigration to France. The latter phenomenon is attributed by Phyllis Albert to a double recognition of ethnicity and solidarity and is already present among nineteenth-century French Jews.[2]

Throughout their processes of integration, Jewish immigrants have kept alive a feeling of Jewish identity, comprising the concepts of people, family, and nation, particularly by means of local, national, and international solidarity. The biological aspect of this sentiment,

---

[1] For a study of community inner relationships, see David Weinberg, *Les Juifs à Paris de 1933 à 1939* (Paris: Calmann-Lévy, 1974); Paula Hyman, *De Dreyfus à Vichy* (Paris: Fayard, 1985); Nancy Green, *Les travailleurs immigrés juifs à la Belle Epoque* (Paris: Fayard, 1985).

[2] Phyllis Albert, "Ethnicity and Solidarity Among French Jews in the XIXth Century," in *Mystics, Philosophers and Politicians: Essays in Jewish Intellectual History in Honor of Alexander Altmann*, ed. Jehuda Reinharz and Daniel Swetschinski (Durham: Duke University Press, 1982).

referred to as ethnicity by Phyllis Albert, weighs as heavily as do its cultural and historical aspects. As applied to immigrants, this term, transposed to the French context, connotes an American view of dividing migrant populations into minorities. I prefer the term *appartenance* ("belonging to a community"), as used by Dominique Schnapper in *Juifs et Israélites*,[3] in which the sense of belonging is the minimal form of Judaic perpetuation. This preference reflects certain anthropologists' reactions to the term "ethnicity," criticized as "the image projected by a group or assigned to them by other groups."[4]

Oriental Jews and Occidentalization

Jewish immigrants to France from the Ottoman Empire, who have come in several waves and are referred to as Judeo-Spanish, do not seem to fit the model defined above.[5] A very strong wish for integration at the moment of their arrival in France, combined with a more or less successful acculturation to French values, led to an assimilation which seemed foreordained.

The acculturation of Oriental Jews is generally associated with the creation of the Alliance Israélite Universelle (1860) and its network of schools. Conceived as a "regeneration" of Oriental Jews through the diffusion of modern values, its programs had enormous influence. In fact, the process of the occidentalization of the Ottoman Empire began in the *tanzimat*, or reform, period (1839–1876) and is part of the history of struggles with Western European countries, in which each of their victories led to a new Western penetration.

European economic and financial influence contributed to the emergence of a middle class composed of importers, bankers, and agents belonging to the minorities. "The Turk still preferred the three professions of religion, government and war, and left commerce, with its degrading infidel associations, to the Christians and Jews."[6]

The reform and the European penetration produced a gradual

---

[3] Dominique Schnapper, *Juifs et Israélites* (Paris: Gallimard, 1980).

[4] Jean-Loup Amselle, "L'ethnicité comme volonté et comme représentation: A propos des Peul du Wasolon," *Annales ESC* 2 (March–April 1987): 466.

[5] For a more thorough study of the Judeo-Spanish community in Paris, see Annie Benveniste, *Le Bosphore à la Roquette* (Paris: l'Harmattan, 1990).

[6] Bernard Lewis, *The Emergence of Modern Turkey* (London: Oxford University Press, 1961), p. 448.

secularization of the empire's Jewish communities. The French influence, with its "civilizing mission," was particularly strong. In the ensuing communal reorganization, the power of the lay leaders supplanted that of the religious leaders. These changes led to conflict in the Jewish community among partisans of modernization, advocates of French values, and conservatives.

However, the modernists won and the spirit of Enlightenment sweeping the Orient renewed the Jewish communities caught up in the decline of the empire. Edgar Morin coined the term *neo-maroon* to describe this situation, in which Jews became bicultural through appropriation of Gentile secularity.[7]

This situation explains why the reforms did not facilitate the integration of non-Muslim communities. Violent conflicts arose between Christian communities and the central power. The Jews, who had no territorial claims, did not wish to participate in the Turkish national project. The situation of the Jewish communities after the Balkan Wars and the creation of nation-states on the ruins of the Ottoman Empire must be analyzed specifically for each country. But the responses were virtually unequivocal: play the "stateless-person card" or adopt a new identity.

The Young Turk government's decision to make military service obligatory for the entire Muslim and non-Muslim population is of key importance in the history of Jewish emigration from the Ottoman Empire. In the life-stories told to me, the survivors of immigration in France often cite it as the starting point. "I had to leave because of military service" is the beginning of the story of the man who, fleeing the army, leaves for France. But the emigration candidate had to submit to numerous dissimulations before making the trip. Why did Jews interpret the equality in bearing arms, later transformed into obligatory military service, as a discriminatory measure? When the first measure was passed, minorities were able to avoid conscription by paying an exemption tax called the *bedel*.

Avoiding military service or refusing to bear arms was considered a privilege. When the draft became obligatory, it was seen as the abolition of a privilege or as a constraint forcing minorities to integrate into the Turkish nation. In order to escape, one had to change one's age, name, and even nationality, thus recovering a privilege by obtaining a protective nationality from a Western embassy, or,

[7] Edgar Morin, *Vidal et les siens* (Paris: Seuil, 1989).

during the First World War, the identity of *Israélite du Levant* issued by French consulates. In the life-stories, the identity changes are interpreted as a change of condition as well as a passage from Orient to Occident, from a country which abolishes privileges to one which grants them. This passage, symbolized by crossing the Mediterranean, represents a return to the former rule, with its separation between the Muslim and non-Muslim worlds. Bearing arms remains the duty of Turks, just as commerce, an itinerant profession, is that of the Jews.

Immigration Itineraries

When the Judeo-Spanish arrive in France with their borrowed identity, ready to serve under the French colors after having fled the Ottoman army, are they already assimilated? The answer is no— but they are no longer Turks either (or Greeks or Bulgarians), in the sense that they rapidly lose the language, if they ever possessed it. The fact is, their domestic language was Judeo-Spanish and their external communication was in French or, more rarely, German, English, or Italian. Other than family ties, they maintain no link with the Old Country. They will seek to correct this identity flaw; despite their mobility, their immigration itineraries will become itineraries of integration. Unlike the Ottoman Empire, composed of a mosaic of peoples, France is not a multi-ethnic nation. Social or territorial positions are not attributed according to ethnic origin, even if certain places and economic activities become poles attracting immigrants in the period between the two world wars.

In *Les Etrangers en France*, Georges Mauco analyzes the professional and geographical distribution of the different groups of foreigners during the interwar period.[8] He notes that the groups least attracted to manual work are the most attracted to Paris, and suspects them of being parasitic. He points at the Levantines and the Jews.

The group whose immigration itinerary I have studied, found in the Roquette quarter of Paris during this period, is one of the targets of G. Mauco's accusation. They are Levantine Jews, a great number of whom have settled in this hard-working quarter of the 11th arrondissement, with its gridlock of courtyards full of workshops

---

[8] Georges Mauco, *Les Etrangers en France* (Paris: Armand Colin, 1932), p. 130.

specializing in wood and ironwork. They represent the poorest of the waves of immigrants from the Ottoman Empire, where they were artisans—tailors or shoemakers—and often ambulant tinkers or tin-plate workers. Many were small-business employees, shop assistants, porters, or peddlers. The wealthier groups settled in other districts (the Sentier or the Faubourg-Montmartre).

The Community Space

In the Roquette quarter, the spatial concentration of a population group of the same socioeconomic origin took place as a process of aggregation of several families around a central nucleus (Place Voltaire).

Instead of a concentric installation around the Place Voltaire, a selective occupation of four streets or parts of streets came about "spontaneously." In these *juderias* the Sephardic population was extended outward from the center in thinner and thinner branches. In this space that I call the "Oriental block," the immigrants created the fundamental institutions of a Jewish community: the Oriental Jewish Cultural Association of Paris (oratory and Talmud Torah), founded in 1909; mortuary assistance and mutual-assistance organizations; and athletic and youth associations. Along with businesses and Judeo-Spanish cafes, these institutions defined the community space, functioning on a solidarity basis. The creation of charitable organizations in the quarter reflected a policy aimed at local efficiency through the establishment of specific institutions serving the community. The Consistory's failure to unify the existing societies is explained by the immigrants' desire to preserve a degree of independence. This failure can be seen as an episode of the struggle between immigrant communities and the central Consistory, dominated by French Jews.[9]

Groups such the Association of the Faubourg-Montmartre, motivated by a desire to melt into the French Jewish community, had much stronger links with the Consistory. The fracture between this group and that of the Roquette quarter corresponded to socioeconomic differences. The former was more dispersed. Upward social mobility went in its direction. It attracted "winners" and became the heart of the Sephardic Cultural Association of Paris, founded in

---

[9] Weinberg, *Les juifs à Paris.*

1930. This union of diverse associations was presided over by Rabbi Ovadia from Vienna. Can we interpret this situation according to the Chicago School's model of urban ecology, in which the appropriation of different spaces conforms to community lifestyles? In France communities like that of the 11th arrondissement did not correspond to the image of segregation, the ghetto, described by Louis Wirth. Geographical concentration did not exclude interrelations with the rest of the city; community identity was more the result of relations woven with other groups than a fixed, homogeneous quality. There were a certain number of levels of appropriation and privatization of public space.[10] The interior court, the stairwell, and the street were a series of markers on the path of everyday life.

When a building projected an image of concentration in the two senses of overpopulation and immigrant visibility, community religious practices started there. Under a carriage entrance, a space/frontier between public and private, a rabbi came on each eve of Yom Kippur to publicly sacrifice chickens. The carriage entrance became the scene of collective practices unknown to the street, but common to a majority of the building's residents, a distinguishing feature of the Jewish quarter. When the Sephardim were dispersed, the process of recognition and distinction did not go beyond the home or other closed spaces such as shops. In this way, what Pierre Mayol calls *convenance*,[11] a group of implicit rules governing behavior within a neighborhood, was respected. These rules varied from one place to another; from drinking and eating places to workplaces and social places—a system of rites, codes of what to say and what not to say, and of contracts structuring exchange.

The Storekeeper Figure

Did the Sephardic community correspond to a Consistory notable's definition as "the most apt to assimilate"? He added, "the unattractive aspect of the Oriental Jew's character changes from a flaw to

---

[10] Isaac Joseph, *Le Passant considérable. Essai sur la dispersion de l'espace public* (Paris: Librairie des Meridiens, 1984).

[11] Pierre Mayol, *L'invention du quotidien*, vol. 2, *Habiter* (Paris: Union générale d'éditions, 1980), pp. 26–28.

a quality, making him more malleable." One might expect such a small and permeable population to become almost invisible. However, the census and patent-registration figures of workers specializing in the linen and hosiery trade indicate a definite presence in the Roquette space. Economic activity, rather than the network of associations, was what distinguished the Sephardic population from the other inhabitants of the quarter and identified it as a minority. The statistics concerning declared professions seem to confirm the judgment of interwar historians. The predominance of commercial activities is clear: 30 percent of active Sephardim in 1926, growing to 52 percent in 1936. At this point, they are proportionally twice as numerous in commerce as the Parisian working population.

The tradesmen specialized in textiles, haberdashery, and, above all, linen hosiery. The merchants were often manufacturers employing men and women working at home. The percentage of the Sephardic population registered in the garment industry (as tailors, couturieres, confectioners, modistes, shoemakers, etc.) is relatively high—21 percent, twice that of the Parisian working population.

These figures imply a rather limited integration in Parisian professional life. With the textile and linen-hosiery businesses, an "immigrant economic territory" is emerging. It was to develop further after the war and become a full-fledged Jewish commercial center, gradually eating away the previous artisanal space. However, in the 1930s the textile emergence corresponds to an ethnic division of labor. Sephardic immigrants rarely fit into the economic context of the quarter as wood and iron workers. The vast majority of the population is concentrated around activities destined for foreigners, and which they are used to: the textile/garment business and industry.

Professional specialization of minority groups, of which the Jews are a typical example, is a phenomenon with several historical applications.[12] Their role as middlemen is especially significant. The style of integration of the middleman minorities—Jews from Europe and Muslim countries, Indians from East Africa, Chinese from Southeast Asia—explains their professional specialization and success. Their stay can be prolonged indefinitely, but it is the myth of the Return, including the Jewish Return to the Promised Land, which gives these groups their particular structure. They keep their distance from the

---

[12] Edna Bonachich, "A Theory of Middleman Minorities," *American Sociological Review* 38 (October 1973): 583–594.

society as a whole and possess a strong internal organization, combining a concentration of human and financial resources in certain areas with the development of networks of mutual aid and concern.

Therefore, there is a system of horizontal and vertical relations within the Judeo-Spanish community. On one hand, storeowners, artisans, and small merchants were supplied by wholesalers. Besides the merchandise, they received "tips" on sales circuits. The wholesalers were also symbols of successful careers. They went from being godfathers to being bosses when they directly hired salesmen, warehousemen, and accountants from the community. On the other hand, they were linked to the poor through solidarity, expressed by the administration of community resources and their redistribution as charity. Economic activity played a greater role in community functioning than the permanence of cultural practices by its way of occupying space and creating a clientele and alliance network within and outside of the neighborhood.

This system of horizontal and vertical relations between members of Jewish communities goes beyond a strategy of "settling" into the nation's society. The totality of the community's economic activities has a double function of integration and differentiation. The Sephardic immigrant personifies the foreigner who "appears everywhere as a shopowner,"[13] and who, for Simmel, is a condensation of integration and otherness This character is at the heart of the life-stories similar to picaresque tales describing immigration itineraries. Whether these stories tell of leaving the Ottoman Empire, described as a voyage of adventure, or of their insertion in France, characterized by continuous breaking apart and reconversions, mobility remains a central feature of the itineraries. The discontinuities and changes stem from the typical wandering of the merchant-traveler. Their accounts, apparently placing greater value on individual stories than collective destiny, are in fact in perfect harmony with the prevalent integration modes of the immigrant group in the Parisian space.

Translated by Evan Chandlee

---

[13] Georg Simmel, "Digressions sur l'étranger," in *L'école de Chicago*, presentation Y. Grafmeyer et I. Joseph (Paris: Aubier, 1984), p. 54.

PART TWO

INTELLECTUAL HISTORY

THE BEGINNINGS OF A SCIENTIFIC THEORY
OF RACE? SPAIN, 1450–1600

JOHN EDWARDS

University of Birmingham
Birmingham, England

In the early years of the nineteenth century, any student who applied for a scholarship at the Colegio Mayor Fonseca in the University of Santiago de Compostela would receive a printed form containing seven questions to be answered on his behalf by five witnesses. These witnesses had to tell the local judge whether the student was who he claimed to be, whether any brother of his had received a scholarship from the same institution, and whether he was the legitimate son of his parents; but the primary purpose of the questionnaire was to be found in question 4: "If [the witness] knows that the said college-member elect, as well as his parents, grandparents, and great-grandparents, have been and are held and reputed to be Old Christians, without race or mixture of Jew, Moor or *converso*; and that they have not been condemned or made to do penance by the Holy Office of the Inquisition as heretics or suspicious in the faith."[1]

In 1935, the *Reichsgesetzblatt* of November 14 stated that, according to laws passed in Nuremberg, "An individual of mixed Jewish blood [*Jüdischer Mischling*] is one who descended from one or two grandparents who were racially full Jews. One grandparent shall be considered as a full Jew if he or she belonged to the Jewish religious community [*jüdischen Religionsgemeinschaft*]" (Article 2). In addition, "A Jew is anyone who descended from at least three grandparents who were racially full Jews" (Article 5).[2]

The aim here is to provide a commentary on Spanish "purity of blood" (*limpieza de sangre*) laws, and indicate some of the predecessors

---

[1] Printed form for those elected as scholars of the Colegio Mayor de Fonseca, University of Santiago de Compostela, kindly provided by Dr. David Mackenzie.

[2] Official English translations for the Nuremberg trials, in *The Holocaust: Selected Documents in Eighteen Volumes*, eds. John Mendelsohn and Donald S. Detwiler (New York and London, 1982), 1:27–30 (German text) and 31–32 (English trans.).

of the legal productions of the Third Reich. It will begin with an outline of the introduction and spread of the Spanish blood laws in the period between 1449 and about 1550, and then turn to the theory and intellectual activity which underlay these laws. After this the detailed working out of purity of blood laws will be examined, and then an attempt will be made to compare fifteenth- and sixteenth-century Spanish views of Jews and race with those of the twentieth century.

In May 1449, a document known at the time and hence to history as the Sentence-Statute (*Sentencia-Estatuto*) was drawn up in Toledo by the constable of the royal castle, Pero Sarmiento. The gist of the lengthy text was: "that all the aforesaid *conversos*, descendants of the perverse lineage of the Jews, in whatever guise this may be . . . should be had and held, as the law has and holds them, as infamous, unable, incapable and unworthy to have any public and private benefice and office in the aforesaid city of Toledo, and in its land territory and jurisdiction."[3]

Although Sarmiento was a royal official, he and the city had been in rebellion against John II of Castile since the beginning of that year, when the king's chief minister, Don Alvaro de Luna, had demanded direct taxation from the city, and the latter had responded by attacking a *converso* tax-collector, Alonso Cota, and other *conversos*. The rebellion did not spread to the outlying territories named in the Sentence-Statute, and by March 1451 John II felt able to issue a general pardon to the citizens of Toledo, but the concept of purity, or cleanliness, of blood, first publicly enunciated in this context, was to become a motif of Spanish history for several centuries thereafter.[4]

To begin with, the debate about the Toledan concept of excluding individuals from public office on account of their racial origin was confined to literary and propagandistic activity, but important political and religious figures were involved, both at the Castilian royal court and in the papal entourage at Rome. Some of these were Christians of Jewish origin, and others were not, but all were discussing what was increasingly perceived to be a political and social problem in the crown of Castile, that is, the rapid advance, both in the church and in society as a whole, of the more able and intelli-

---

[3] Eloy Benito Ruano, *Toledo en el siglo XV. Vida política* (Madrid, 1961), p. 194.
[4] Ibid., pp. 33–81 for a full account of the rebellion.

gent of the descendants of those who had converted from Judaism to Christianity, under pressures of violence, missionary activity, and restrictive legislation against Jews, in the period between 1391 and about 1420.[5] While the intellectuals debated, and proposed various solutions, such as an Inquisition to test the *conversos'* orthodoxy, various public bodies around the country began to follow the Toledan rebels' example.

As the product of an illegal government, the 1449 Sentence-Statute was repealed as soon as the royal government regained control, and it was more than fifteen years before another such law was enacted in Castile. However, before outlining the spread of purity of blood laws up to about the year 1600, it is necessary to note the legislative context in which they were produced. Firstly, there was never any *national* blood law in Castile, or indeed in any other Spanish kingdom when these were eventually brought under Habsburg rule in the period after 1516. Thus the Castilian Cortes never passed a blood law, and neither did the royal administration make any regulation to that effect, as became increasingly its practice in other matters, in the reigns of Ferdinand and Isabella and their successors. Instead, purity of blood statutes appeared piecemeal, and each applied only to a specific corporate group, in a specific place, such as a cathedral chapter or private chapel, a military order, a university college, or a guild, whether the last was a religious confraternity or (and the difference was frequently obscure) a trade association, Eventually, late in the day, the Inquisition itself adopted blood criteria for its "familiars," or lay spies and supporters. The important point is that Spain, like other late medieval and early modern societies in Europe, saw itself as a set of diverse corporate entities under God and the king, each jealous of its particular liberties and privileges, and this fact inevitably had a vital influence on the development of blood laws in the country and in its empire. The contrast with the monolithic nature of Nazi government and society seems obvious, even though both systems met serious problems in the implementation of laws concerning the genetic origin of individuals.

It was not Toledo but the Andalusian city of Córdoba, with its tradition of multifaith coexistence, which first followed the example of the Sentence-Statute, according to the evidence which has appeared

---

[5] Albert A. Sicroff, *Los estatutos de limpieza de sangre. Controversias entre los siglos XV y XVII* (Madrid, 1985), pp. 51–85.

so far. In 1466, the precentor of the cathedral and former mosque in Córdoba, Don Fernand Ruiz de Aguayo, established a statute for the six chaplains and two sacristans who were to serve the altar of his new family chapel, which was dedicated to the apparently mythical martyr, Saint Acacius, whose cult had been popular in the crusading period in the twelfth century. The precentor decreed that no one of Jewish blood should occupy any of these posts, "notwithstanding that in this generation of *conversos* there are many virtuous and good persons, and of good conscience and life." He explained that he nonetheless wished to exclude such people because, so he claimed, two of his cousins, members of lesser noble families in Córdoba which were prominent in politics locally, had suffered in unspecified ways at the hands of unnamed converts from Judaism.[6]

By 1471 at the latest, a new confraternity, called the Brotherhood (*Hermandad*) of Charity, had been established in the city, and its statutes explicitly excluded those of Jewish origin. It is probably no coincidence that it was a procession by this confraternity, in honor of the Virgin Mary, which led, in Lent 1473, to an outbreak of violence against Córdoba's *conversos*. Nobles, workers, and artisans fell upon the *conversos* after water, or some said urine, had fallen on a statue of Mary from the balcony of a *converso*'s house. As a result, many prosperous members of Córdoba's business community who were of Jewish origin either died or were injured, had their goods looted, and in many cases fled to other towns where they received more protection. In addition, though, the city council, which was at the time under the control of the leader of Córdoba's largest noble faction, Don Alonso de Aguilar, who had been quite unable to quell the riot, passed a law which excluded all those of Jewish origin from any public office in the city or its lands. This law, too, was quickly suppressed, when Isabella, together with her consort Ferdinand, succeeded in reasserting royal authority in the region, which had been largely lost by 1473–74, thanks to the ineffectiveness of her predecessor, Henry IV. Nevertheless, the purity of blood statutes continued their slow and erratic march through the institutions of the country.[7]

---

[6] Manuel Nieto Cumplido, "La revuelta contra los conversos de Córdoba en 1473," in *Homenaje a Antón de Montoro en el V centenario de su muerte* (Montoro, 1977), pp. 35–36; David Hugh Farmer, *The Oxford Dictionary of Saints* (Oxford, 1978), p. 1.

[7] Nieto, "La revuelta," pp. 41–45; John Edwards, *Christian Córdoba: The City and Its Region in the Late Middle Ages* (Cambridge, 1982), pp. 183–184.

In 1486, the blood law affected, for the first time, a religious order in the Catholic Church. The new Castilian Inquisition had claimed to find extensive Jewish belief and practice among the Hieronymite friars, who stressed a solitary or hermitlike, rather than a communal, life. Henceforth, no one of Jewish blood was to be allowed to join the order. Attempts to introduce similar measures into the Dominican order in the 1480s failed to spread beyond a single priory, and even there the provisions were soon diluted.

Slow and piecemeal progress was, however, to continue among the religious orders and cathedral chapters during the sixteenth century. Thus the famous Catalan reformed Benedictine house of Montserrat acquired a statute in 1502, the Spanish province of the Observant Franciscan friars in 1515, and Córdoba cathedral in 1530. Here, as later in Toledo, the experiment in a single chapel was spread, in this case after more than sixty years, to the institution as a whole. At the same time, blood statutes were beginning to appear in trade guilds, such as that of the candlemakers of Barcelona in 1498, but the only geographical area to exclude *conversos* was the lordship of Vizcaya in the Basque country, which banned all immigrants of Jewish origin after 1482.[8]

Ironically, it was not until 1547 that Toledo cathedral, in the city which had started the whole process, copied the private chapel of the "New Kings" (*Reyes Nuevos*) within it, and adopted a purity of blood statute, However, the archbishop, Juan Fernández Silíceo, had great difficulty in achieving this result, not only because of personal interest on the part of *converso* clerics, but also at the level of intellectual controversy. The issues which had been debated in 1449–51 were still very much alive a century later, and were to continue to be so in the early seventeenth century, when some thinkers began to blame the declining political and economic influence of Spain in that period on the pernicious influence of the blood laws.[9] However, it is necessary at this stage to look more closely at the theories and ideas which lay behind measures of this kind.

There were two main sources for Spanish thought in this period

---

[8] J.N. Hillgarth, *The Spanish Kingdoms, 1250–1516*, vol. 2, *Castilian Hegemony, 1410–1516* (Oxford, 1978), pp. 465–466.

[9] Sicroff, *Los estatutos*, passim; Edwards, "From Anti-Judaism to Anti-Semitism: Juan Escobar del Corro's *Tractatus*," in *Proceedings of the Ninth World Congress of Jewish Studies, Division B*, vol. 1, *The History of the Jewish People from the Second Temple Period until the Middle Ages* (Jerusalem, 1986), pp. 143–150.

concerning the relationship between blood, or genetic origin, and human behavior. One was, of course, the Bible, together with the works of the fathers of the early church and the contributions of the medieval scholastics. The Hebrew and Greek Scriptures display, on occasion, a deep concern with human genealogy, and also with the idea of a person's sins being visited on his or her descendants, including those still unborn at the time of the original commission.[10] It is arguable, therefore, that the Scriptures of the church, apart from any later commentary upon them, already blurred the distinction between biological and moral or religious categories, as for example in the New Testament attitude to the supposed moral dimensions of illness.[11]

The religious aspects of the thought behind the blood laws will be considered in due course, but such measures were also an expression of medieval theories and knowledge concerning human reproduction, In Noonan's wise words, "A knowledge of biology, everyone would agree, was not included in Christian revelation"; therefore the deficiency had to be made up from elsewhere and, as was usual in the period, the main source was ancient Greek science and medicine.[12]

All classical theories, in both the Hippocratic and the Aristotelian traditions, accorded the major role in procreation to the male.[13] Aristotle asserted that woman provided the matter for the embryo, while man gave it form and motion. He provided an image to illustrate the point. "Compare the coagulation of milk. Here the milk is the body, and the fig juice or the rennet contains the principle which causes it to set."[14] Menstrual blood was the prime matter, while

---

[10] For genealogical preoccupation, see, for example, Gen. 4–5, 9–11 and the (conflicting) statements concerning the human ancestors of Jesus in Matt. 1:1–17 and Luke 3:23–38. For the visitation of sins on the descendants of sinners, see Deut. 23:3–5, referring to the Ammonites and Moabites, and the notorious supposed admission by Jews of communal and perpetual guilt for the death of Jesus in Matt. 27:25, "His blood be on us and on our children."

[11] In the story of the paralyzed man, who was lowered through a house roof to be healed by Jesus, both he and his opponents among the "lawyers" and Pharisees appear to have assumed that the healing would inevitably involve the forgiveness of the patient's sins (Luke 5:17–26).

[12] John T. Noonan, *Contraception: A History of Its Treatment by the Catholic Theologians and Canonists* (New York, 1965), p. xvii.

[13] Helen King, "Making a Man: Becoming Human in Early Greek Medicine," in *The Human Embryo: Aristotle and the Arabic and European Tradition*, ed. G.R. Dunstan (Exeter, 1990), pp. 10–19.

[14] *On the generation of animals*, bk. 1.

semen contained no material substance, in fact evaporating after the quickening and forming of the blood. Greek philosophy generally showed a deep contempt for material or matter, and made a sharp distinction between "form," which was noble and male, and "matter," which was degraded and female. Even though late classical authors tended to blur the distinction, the implications for sexual stereotyping are obvious, and carried on in full form into the medieval and early modern worlds. Thus the female role in reproduction appeared animal and inferior, while the male performed "the spiritual, noble and infinitely superior function of imparting life."[15] Aquinas believed this, and so, as late as the seventeenth century, did the pioneer of studies of the circulation of the blood, William Harvey.[16]

However, despite the sexual stereotyping which apparently followed from these theories, there was a sense in which the mother was seen as having a more than physical role in the formation of a new human being. As Balme puts it, "When Aristotle comes to explain family resemblances in *Generation of animals*, bk. 4 ch. 3, he argues that these are due to different movements in the fetal matter. The movements introduced by the male semen fashion the matter in the direction of the father's characteristics, but if these movements are weak they may be overcome by the female movements which already exist potentially in the matter, and may relapse into them, so producing resemblances to the female." Aristotle, significantly, works out the balances of character of offspring likely to have been caused by more active or less active parents, grandparents, and even ancestors further back, Balme notes that "people have remarked upon the resemblance between this theory and modern genetic coding theory, but of course Aristotle attempts no more detailed physical explanation."

It has to be observed, firstly, that this belief did not work to the advantage of mothers in general, or of Jewish and *conversa* mothers in particular, Secondly, although it would be wrong to assume from the foregoing that modern modes of scientific thought were quite unknown to medieval people, it has to be acknowledged that many ideas and considerations entered the minds of those who took seriously matters of genetics and gynecology which would not, rightly or wrongly, find a place in such discussions today. Plays on the

---

[15] Marina Warner, *Alone of All Her Sex: The Myth and the Cult of the Virgin Mary* (London, 1976), p. 40.
[16] Noonan, *Contraception*, pp. 116–118; Warner, *Alone of All Her Sex*, pp. 40–42.

similar sound of words, such as the *vulva* (which was used as a general term for all female genital organs) *volvendo*, were regarded as serious contributions to biological discussion, while contrasts, such as "hot-cold" or "left-right," were accorded considerable importance, as was astrology.

In addition, one of the most deep-rooted beliefs of medieval physicians and scientists and hence of theologians and legislators, was that women had sexual organs which were exact equivalents of those of men, but inside the body instead of outside. Thus, not only did women, as Galen had surmised, give birth to one or more children according to the number of receptacles in the womb which had been filled with sperm—this in turn depending, as seen above, on the potency of the male—but they were also held to possess testicles of their own, inside the body, which produced a female sperm, which had to combine with the male's sperm in order to engender a child. The male sperm was believed to originate in the brain, traveling by means of veins to the testicles, but already white, rather than the normal red color of blood. These veins would in turn supply the brain with nourishment in the form of whitened blood, sperm thus being the "quintessence" of the ultimate "nourishing fluid," that is, blood. The female's "sperm," on the other hand, was held to be coarser and more humid than a man's, the humor of humidity being regarded as sexually unattractive.[17]

However, there was another aspect of medieval scientific thought which was to prove extremely significant in the intellectual background to the Spanish blood laws. This was the perceived link between blood and mother's milk. This too has proved to be a tenacious belief in Western European society, as three examples should indicate.

Firstly, in the small Aragonese town of Teruel, in about 1480, an Old Christian serving-lad, Jaime Palomos, gave evidence to the Inquisition at the trial of his former employer, the *conversa* Brianda Besant, wife of the merchant Luis Santangel, who was also a *converso*, and told the story of what had happened one day in his mistress's kitchen. A Jewish wet-nurse was feeding Brianda's daughter, Aldolica. Seeing this, the lad said to Brianda, "Why are you giving your daughter the milk of this Jewish bitch?" She replied, "She's not

---

[17] D.H. Bahne, "Human Is Generated by Human," in *The Human Embryo*, pp. 20–23.

a bitch." Jaime responded, no doubt in accordance with what he had heard at home and church, "Yes she is, and the Jews killed Our Lord!" Brianda's reply, "*If* they killed him, it was he who wished it," of course raises questions about the Christian view of the divine plan which are, to say the least, provocative, but the important point here is the implication of Jaime's comments, that drinking the Jewish wet-nurse's milk could somehow transmit Jewish, and therefore evil and anti-Christian, qualities to the child.[18]

The second case comes from Florence, where, despite misgivings, many better-off parents entrusted their children to wet-nurses, often in villages in the surrounding countryside, but worried about the consequences. They were influenced by conventional medical opinion, which stated that, as mother's milk was directly derived from menstrual blood, a nursing-mother, like a natural mother who suckled her own child, would continue to shape the child in her own image, despite the dominant male role in its conception. These notions were clearly believed in by the artist and anatomical experimenter Leonardo da Vinci, who, in a drawing done in 1492, shows veins leading from the upper part of a woman's uterus to take the menstrual blood to her breasts.[19]

Lest it be thought that modern scientific knowledge put an end to such ideas, it should, thirdly, be noted that in 1943, the Reich Ministry of Justice reported to Adolf Hitler that a Jewish woman had sold her milk to a pediatrician without revealing her racial origins. The clients whose children received this milk were held by the ministry to have been "wronged" because the milk of a Jewish woman could not be considered "food for German children" (*weil die Muttermilch einer Jüdin nicht als Nahrung für deutsche Kinder gelten kann*), though in this case nothing was done, so as to avoid "alarming" the parents of the children concerned.[20]

Such beliefs, which accorded with the science of the day, clearly

[18] Claude Thomasset, "Le représentation de la sexualité et de la génération dans la pensée scientifique médiévale," in *Love and Marriage in the Twelfth Century: Medievalia Lovanensia*, ser. 1, Studia, VIII (Louvain, 1981), pp. 1–17; Bahne, "Human Is Generated by Human," *passim.*

[19] Archivo Histórico Nacional, Madrid, Sección Inquisición, legajo 535 no. 13, quoted in Manuel Sánchez Moya and Jasone Monasterio Aspiri, "Los judizantes turolenses en el siglo XV," *Sefarad* 32 (1972): 335.

[20] Christiane Klapisch-Zuber, "Blood-Parents and Milk-Parents: Wet-Nursing in Florence, 1300–1530," in *Women, Family and Ritual in Renaissance Italy*, trans. Lydia G. Cochrane (Chicago, 1987), pp. 161–162.

lay behind not only the Sentence-Statute of Toledo but also the writings of later Spanish chroniclers and theorists. Thus the Andalusian priest and chronicler Andrés Bernáldez expressed the view, in his history of the reigns of Ferdinand and Isabella, that, contrary to the view of the popes and theologians, Jewishness was transmitted through blood and therefore could not be removed by baptism.[21]

At about the same time, the *Dictionary of the Inquisitors*, published in Valencia in 1494, stated, under the heading of "Apostasy," that "the Jews transmit to each other from father to son, with the blood, the perfidy of the old Law."[22] Similarly, the sixteenth-century writer Juan de Pineda urged the avoidance, by the relevant political authorities, of a situation in which, "a Moorish woman, or one of Jewish blood, might nurse the child of Old Christians, because although their original blood might be known, to the credit of their ancestors, the children, without any fault of their own, might be reminded of their origins by those who wished them ill; and many times I have heard it said about a person of good intellect and conversation that, if he was only one-eighth a Jew, they would never cease to beg him to convert to Judaism."[23] As Julio Caro Baroja has observed, here there is definitely a link "between a moral and a religious criterion, or rather, between religion and pathology."[24]

This "pathology" has been examined by R.I. Moore in a study which concludes that the mentalities which appear in the fifteenth and sixteenth centuries were products of earlier developments. In the years between about 1050 and 1200, "Persecution became habitual. That is to say not simply that individuals were subject to violence, but that deliberate and socially-sanctioned violence began to be directed, *through established governmental, judicial and social institutions*, against groups of people defined by general characteristics, such as race, religion or way of life, and that membership of such groups in itself came to be regarded as justifying these attacks."

---

[21] *The Holocaust*, 13:143–144.

[22] Angus MacKay, "The Hispanic-*Converso* Predicament," *Transactions of the Royal Historical Society*, 5th series, 35 (1985): 168.

[23] *Dictionnaire des inquisiteurs, Valencia, 1494*, ed. L. Sala Molins (Paris, 1981), quoted in Josette Rondière de la Roche, "Du discours de l'exclusion des juifs: antijudaïsme ou antisemitisme?" in *Les problèmes de l'exclusion en Espagne (XVI\u1d49–XVII\u1d49 siècles)* (Paris, 1983), p. 62.

[24] Juan de Pineda, *Diálogos familiares de la agricultura cristiana*, III, *Biblioteca de Autores Españoles*, CLXII, 103b.

The groups which Moore considers are Jews and Christian heretics, but also male homosexuals and lepers. To these may be added, in the fifteenth and sixteenth centuries, female prostitutes, gypsies, American Indians, and even animals and plants, which were crudely seen in this period as subordinated to, and at the mercy of, mankind, and not, according to the values of the time, womankind.[25]

The case of lepers is particularly relevant to the theory and practice of blood laws. There appears to have been a male obsession, in the Middle Ages, concerning women and the "sperm of a leper" (*sperma leprosi*), according to which, if a man had sexual intercourse with a woman who had previously had sex with a leper, the second lover would contract leprosy as well. Thus leprosy came to be connected (for example, in the confession of Arnaud de Verniolles, a student who was interrogated by Bishop Fournier of Pamiers in the early fourteenth century) with the sexual act as well as the cardinal sin of "luxury." In particular, the woman, rather like the HIV-positive woman of today, was believed to be able to transmit the disease of leprosy without contracting it herself. In this context, the "internal" nature of female sexual organs only increased suspicion of women, in that there was little more than a five percent chance that a male would be able to see that his female partner was infected.[26]

The idea that leprosy was a punishment for sin appears in Christianity, Islam, and Hinduism, though in Judaism (Lev. 13:45–46) it was seen just as one of many causes of ritual impurity, rather than innate sinfulness. However, by the twelfth century, skin diseases which may or may not have corresponded to the modern diagnosis of leprosy were commonly associated not only with sexual misconduct but also with religious heresy. When Count Raymond of Toulouse appealed, in 1177, for help in suppressing the Cathar heresy in his territories, he described it as the "*tabies* of heresy," a *tabies* being a putrid sore, normally acquired as a result of venereal disease. Thus "leprosy was believed to be sexually transmitted and inherited, to

---

[25] Julio Caro Baroja, *Las formas complejas de la vida religiosa. Religión, sociedad y carácter en la España de los siglos XVI y XVII* (Madrid, 1978), p. 489.

[26] R. I. Moore, *The Formation of a Persecuting Society* (Oxford, 1987), p. 5; Leah L. Otis, *Prostitution in Medieval Society: The History of an Urban Institution* (Chicago, 1987), passim; Anthony Pagden, *The Fall of Natural Man: The American Indian and the Origins of Comparative Ethnology*, 2nd ed. (Cambridge, 1986), pp. 15–26; Keith Thomas, *Man and the Natural World: Changing Attitudes in England, 1500–1800* (Harmondsworth, 1984), pp. 17–36.

increase sexual appetite and to cause swelling in the genitals." However, in the twelfth century, Jews were already associated with lepers
and heretics, in their ceaseless efforts to undermine society. "Jews
were also held to resemble heretics and lepers in being associated
with filth, stench and putrefaction, in exceptional sexual voracity
and endowment, and in the menace which they presented in consequence to the wives and children of honest Christians."[27]

Behind these fears, which were projected onto so many marginal
and underprivileged groups in late medieval and early modern society, was a deep Christian suspicion and fear of women, which was
closely related to Christian teaching on "original sin." The paradox of Christian teaching on the relationship between the sexes has
always been that, while Christianity proclaims the equality of men
and women in a text from Paul's Epistle to the Galatians, which
was also used by the papacy and Spanish *conversos* alike to defend
the right of baptized Jews to take a full part in fifteenth-century
Spanish society: "In Christ there is neither Jew nor Greek, there is
neither bond nor free, there is neither male nor female, for you are
all one in Christ Jesus" (Gal. 3:28), the same religion has always
appeared to hate and fear sex.

In particular, the Christian fathers, such as Augustine of Hippo
and his teacher Ambrose of Milan, adapted the Genesis stories of
the Garden of Eden to ascribe the responsibility for a definitive fall
of all human beings to Eve, because she partook of the fruit of the
knowledge of good and evil, when it was offered by the serpent, and
persuaded Adam to eat it too. Thus Augustine saw marriage as no
more than a device to control lust, while Ambrose asserted that "virginity is the one thing that keeps us from the beasts." Thus, for
Augustine, although a Christian was, as Paul said, saved by baptism,
he was still plagued by "concupiscence," as Augustine's jargon had
it, which means taking pleasure in created things, and in particular
in sexual relationships, rather than in the Creator himself.

This meant that "every child born into the world has sin passed
on to it by its copulating parents, and is thus doomed to eternal
damnation. Sex is the means whereby Original Sin is transmitted
(like a venereal disease which infects man's deepest nature) because
it is now impossible for people to have sex without concupiscence."[28]

[27] Thomasset, "La représentation," pp. 9–10.
[28] Moore, *Formation of a Persecuting Society*, pp. 61–65.

It is thus the Christian development of the doctrine concerning the result of the behavior of Adam and Eve in the Garden of Eden, rather than the original story in Genesis, which mainly influenced the thinking behind the Spanish blood laws.

The degradation of women, as a result of Christian teaching, also distorted Jewish ideas about purity and holiness, in that states of ritual impurity, in terms of the possibility of access to the Tent of Meeting or the later Temple, were converted, in the Christian tradition, into a permanent, and even a genetic, exclusion from the new "Temples," that is, Christian places of worship. Also, in political language, *limpieza*, which may be translated either as "purity" or as "cleanliness," came to be an important term, which might be used to express old and hallowed feelings about social and constitutional propriety.

In Córdoba, for instance, resentment of the ever-increasing demands of the crown for manpower, military material, and taxation revenue, in the period between Isabella's death in 1504 and the defeat of the Comunero rebellion in 1521, was expressed in the repeated assertion that the city had not only done its duty in the recent Granada war, but was also "clean" (*limpia*) of the stains on its honor (this being another emotionally significant word in Spain in this period) which were implied by those, such as the failed inquisitor Lucero, who had accused the town of harboring illegal synagogues in the period up to 1508. In 1521, the municipal authorities indignantly rejected a proposal from the regent, Cardinal Adrian, that genealogies of the local *conversos* should be compiled for the purposes of the Inquisition.[29] Thus, while the authorities of Córdoba might despise and degrade women, and profoundly suspect, in particular, the power and influence of Jewish and *conversa* women in particular, they could also see their own city as a "violated" and abused woman, in terms of the governmental attitudes of the day.

The material which has been considered so far will very probably have given the impression that the Spain of Ferdinand and Isabella and of their successors, Charles V and Philip II, was increasingly intent on the elimination of people of Jewish descent from public life. Delays in carrying out this process might thus be put down to

---

[29] Karen Armstrong, *The Gospel According to Woman: Christianity's Creation of the Sex War in the West* (London, 1987), pp. 1–33; Warner, *Joan of Arc: The Image of Female Heroism* (London, 1983), pp. 154–157.

inefficiency rather than any lack of will. However, an examination of the application of individual purity of blood statutes indicates, not only that there were considerable practical difficulties in the way of ideological efficiency, but that many other considerations were also brought into the process. The early statutes, such as those in Toledo in 1449 and Córdoba in 1466 and 1473, excluded all those who had any Jewish blood at all, but it soon became clear that a meticulous enforcement of such laws would be quite impossible in a country in which Jews and Christians had coexisted for so many centuries. The first statute to specify the methods which would be used to inquire into the origins of candidates for office was that of the cathedral chapter of Córdoba, which was adopted in 1530.

This city's preoccupation with the "purity" of its blood, and its honor in the service of the crown, has already been noted, so it is no surprise that the cathedral saw itself as "the church cleaner of this stain [i.e., Jewish or heretical blood] than any other church in these kingdoms." However, the new statute, which was highly controversial and did not receive approval from Rome until 1555, and then only after the intervention of Juan de Toledo, who had been bishop of Córdoba at the time of its promulgation, descended from the heights of language concerning blood and honor to procedural details. A candidate for any kind of cathedral office was to swear, on his knees and with his right hand on a crucifix placed in a missal, that he was not descended from Jew or Moor. He had to supply the names and places of birth of his parents and grandparents, and all these details were then to be investigated by the ordinary entrusted with the case, as well as two men delegated by the cathedral chapter. If necessary, similar investigations would take place outside Córdoba, due expenses being paid to the individual entrusted with the task. It should be noted that the witnesses were all chosen by the candidate, and therefore likely to be favorable to him, but even more interesting is the procedure which the cathedral chapter was to follow when this evidence had been collected. Having heard the evidence, the chapter was to vote, and a simple majority was sufficient to admit the candidate to office. In addition, no further investigation of blood purity was required if he attempted to advance in the cathedral hierarchy.[30]

---

[30] Rafael Gracia Boix, *Colección de documentos para la historia de la Inquisición de Córdoba* (Córdoba, 1982), pp. 97, 99–101; John Edwards, "Trial of an Inquisitor: The

In the same year, similar conditions were imposed in the Reyes Nuevos chapel of Toledo Cathedral. Again, all those who had "race" of Jew or Moor were to be excluded even from the most menial office.[31] However, it was here that the obvious problem of false applications was first overtly mentioned. As a result, when Archbishop Silíceo proposed a similar statute for the cathedral as a whole, he was fully aware of the danger of *conversos* illicitly passing the *limpieza* test. He used the image of mother's milk when he stated that cathedral offices should not be held by those "who still had on their lips the milk of the recent perversity of their ancestors," but less conventionally, he also compared the situation of cathedral dignitaries, when they attempted to judge the racial origins of a candidate for office, to that of a dealer buying a horse. He wrote to Pope Paul III in 1547 that such a dealer would not accept an imperfect animal, even if it were offered free of charge, because the animal's race (*raza*), or pedigree, was more important than anything else.[32]

However, the theoretical arguments put forward to justify selection according to religious and "racial" origin can increasingly be seen to have fallen down in practice, and to have been supplemented, or even replaced, by considerations of a totally different order. Examples from a variety of sixteenth-century corporate institutions will illustrate the point.

It has already been noted that the candlemakers' guild in Barcelona excluded Muslims, Jews, *conversos*, and their descendants as early as 1498; and the 1557 statutes of the surgeons' guild there appeared to be faithful to this tradition, in that they excluded all descendants of "infected persons" (how appropriate that surgeons should employ this venerable image!), even on the remotest suspicion, and as a result of secret investigation. However, Molas Ribalta concluded from his

---

Dismissal of Diego Rodríguez Lucero, Inquisitor of Córdoba, in 1508," *Journal of Ecclesiastical History* 37 (1986): 240–257; *Colección de Documentos Inéditos para la Historia de España*, CXII, 94–97; Augustin Redondo, "Le discours d'exclusion des 'deviants' tenu par l'Inquisition à l'époque de Charles Quint," in *Les problèmes de l'exclusion*, p. 31 and note.

[31] Sicroff, *Los estatutos*, pp. 120–122.

[32] Ibid., pp. 129–131. The earliest known use of the word *raza* in Castilian, probably derived from the Latin *ratio* or *rationis*, meaning "calculation" or "account," is to be found in 1438 in the archpriest of Talavera's *El Corbacho*, where the author finds it necessary to add the synonym *linaje*, or "lineage" (Martín Alonso, *Diccionario medieval espagñol. Desde las glosas Emilianenses v Silenses (siglo X) hasta el siglo XV*, 2 vols. [Salamanca, 1986], 1:1544a).

study of Barcelona guilds that this and other guilds in the crown of Aragon were operating, in this period, "a mechanism of social segregation which used purity of blood or lineage and contempt for manual work."[33]

The conjunction of these apparently distinct phenomena is significant, in that it illustrates the manner in which tests for noble, or *hidalgo*, status provided a precedent for investigations into purity of blood. In both cases, details of parents and grandparents were sought, but the decision in practice depended on the willingness or otherwise of witnesses to testify on the candidate's behalf.[34] Claude Chauchadis came to a similar conclusion concerning Spanish religious confraternities. For him, purity of blood was just one among many constraints on those who wished to join one of these pious and charitable bodies, the others being cash, spare time, education and culture, social rank, and the *numerus clausus*. Increasingly, in the case of such brotherhoods, the cost of the necessary investigations replaced the ostensible object, that is, racial purity and religious orthodoxy, as the main practical barrier to membership.[35]

It may seem remarkable that religious corporations, such as the military orders and even the Inquisition itself, did not actively concern themselves with blood laws until about 1550. This was certainly so in the venerable Order of Santiago, in which individual merit still had priority over religious and racial origin into the reign of Philip II, though orders such as those of Montesa and Alcantara had been trying to exclude *conversos* by statute since 1468 and 1483 respectively. Even in the later sixteenth century, the possession of nobility (*hidalguía*) seems, in practice, to have mattered more then *limpieza de*

---

[33] Pere Molas Ribalta, "El exclusivismo en los gremios de la Corona de Aragón: limpieza de sangre y limpieza de oficios," in *Les sociétés fermées dans le monde ibérique (XVIᵉ–XVIIIᵉ siècles). Définitions et problématique (Actes de la table ronde des 8 et 9 février 1985)* (Paris, 1986), pp. 69–70, 78.

[34] On the clear connection between *limpieza* statutes and *pruebas de hidalguía*, see Pierre Chaunu, "La société espagnole au XVIIᵉ siècle. Sur un refus collectif de mobilité," *Bulletin Hispanique*, 4th series, 1–2 (1966): 104–115; Antonio Domínguez Ortiz, *La sociedad española en el siglo XVII* (Madrid, 1963), p. 289; Ricardo Sáez, "Hidalguía: essai de définition. Des principes identificateurs aux variations historiques," in *"Hidalgos" et "hidalguía" dans l'Espagne des XVIᵉ–XVIIIᵉ siècles* (Paris, 1989), pp. 38–39.

[35] Claude Chauchadis, "Los modalités de la fermeture dans les confréries religieuses espagnoles (XVIᵉ–XVIIIᵉ siècle)," in *Les sociétés fermées*, p. 94.

sangre.[36] Such pragmatism went right back to 1449, and the original Sentence-Statute.

It has recently been demonstrated that even while this law was in force during the rebellion, Toledo Cathedral continued to employ Jews as tax-farmers, even as replacements for *conversos* who were no longer eligible for such contracts. Such actions hardly suggest that religious or racial considerations were paramount.[37] Accordingly, it perhaps seems less surprising that investigations of the *limpieza* of potential Inquisition familiars, which were only systematized, on the lines of the cathedral statutes, in Córdoba and Toledo after 1550, became mechanisms of social, rather than religious or racial, exclusivity. As Jean-Pierre Dedieu has concluded, in the case of Toledo, "I do not deny that the concept of purity of blood may have played, in consciousness of the actors, a capital role. But I am obliged to observe that its verification served as the pretext for the putting in place of a test which, more than origins, tested ever more severely the social power of the candidate. It remains to discover why the theological-racial detour through purity of blood was considered necessary."[38]

Further studies will probably confirm this conclusion over and over again, and demonstrate how far Golden Age Spain was, in fact, from the totalitarian racial policies of Nazi Germany, despite a terrifying blend of biological and theological theory which affected learned and unlearned alike. However, it may also prove that the preoccupation of modern French and Spanish scholars with the manipulation of *limpieza* statutes to mask the exclusion of individuals from corporations for quite other reasons may also fail to tell the full story of the Spanish blood laws, as did Sicroff's excellent and venerable study of the intellectual controversy surrounding the question. Research, for example in Córdoba, is beginning to reveal that the criteria of *limpieza* could be, and frequently were, used to include rather than

[36] Martine Lambert-Gorges, "Le bréviaire du bon enquêteur, ou trois siècles d'information sur les candidats à l'habit des ordres militaires," *Mélanges de la Casa de Velázquez* 18 (1982): 186–188.

[37] Mark Duggan, "Jewish Life in Christian Society: The Kingdom of Toledo, 1436–51" (B.A. diss., University of Birmingham, 1987), pp. 41–44.

[38] Jean-Pierre Dedieu, "Limpieza, pouvoir et richesse: conditions d'entrée dans le corps des ministres de l'Inquisition (tribunal de Tolède), XVIᵉ–XVIIᵉ siècle," in *Les sociétés fermés*, p. 187.

exclude. Thus Jewish or Muslim origins could be shed, just as in other cases they might be found and publicized, if personal and pragmatic reasons dictated that they should be forgotten.[39] By a paradox, blood laws might become an instrument of assimilation as well as segregation. It may be asked whether the same may also prove to have been true in later, and much more terrible, cases than that of sixteenth- and seventeenth-century Spain.

---

[39] José Antonio Martínez Bara, *Catálogo de informaciones genealógicas de la Inquisición de Córdoba conservadas en el Archivo Histórico Nacional*, 2 vols. (Madrid, 1970); John Edwards, "Los conversos de Córdoba en el siglo XV: un proyecto de la historia social," in *Andalucía entre Oriente y Occidente. Actas del V Coloquio Internacional de Historia Medieval de Andalucía* (Córdoba, 1988), pp. 581–584.

L'ARGUMENT DE L'HISTOIRE DANS LA TRADITION ESPAGNOLE DE POLÉMIQUE JUDÉO-CHRÉTIENNE D'ISIDORE DE SEVILLE À ISAAC ABRAVANEL, ET ABRAHAM ZACUTO

J. Genot-Bismuth

Université de Paris III

L'engouement pour l'histoire qui caractérise l'Espagne au moins depuis Alphonse le Sage, et qui a sa véritable source dans le *Cronicon*[1] d'Isidore de Séville, se marque par un développement de la littérature

---

[1] *Chronicon D. Isidori Archiep. Hisp. emendatum, scholiisq; illustratum, per garciam* [*sic*] *De Loaisa, sacrae theologiae D. Archidiaconum de Guadal Ecclesiae Toletanae Canonicum. Tavrini, apud lo. Baptistam Bevilaquam,* MDXCIII (1593). Le texte s'en achève en l'an 5814 de l'ère de *creatio mundi,* ce qui donne la date de 2054 selon la concordance de l'ère de *yeẓira* du comput hébraïque avec le comput de l'ère commune; sur ce point cf. infra; en fait il s'agit de la 5e année du règne d'Héraclius et de la 4e de Sisebut, roi visigoth régnant à Tolède (*Chronicon,* p. 94), soit de l'an 615. L'écart entre, le décompte effectif de *creatio mundi* et celui, manipulé, d'Isidore s'élève donc à 1439 ans (cf. infra). Il n'est pas possible de fixer avec certitude si la rédaction du *Contra Judaeos* est antérieure ou postérieure à celle du *Chronicon.* Toutefois on remarquera que les modèles déclarés d'Isidore sont en particulier le *Canon des Temps* d'Eusèbe de Césarée publié en 303, et la chronique de Jérôme, éditée par Rudolf Helms, *Die Chronik des Hieronymus* (Leipzig, 1913). Or chez Eusèbe, le *Chronicon* était une préparation à l'*Histoire Ecclésiastique* (*Sources Chrétiennes,* tome I, I, 6 p. 5), il est vraisemblable qu'Isidore se soit inspiré de la méthode, et en ce cas le *Chronicon* serait antérieur. Le titre complet du traité de polémique anti-juive publié par Migne est exactement: *De fide catholica ex veteri et novo testamento contra Judaeos, Patrologia Latina* 8, 449 sq. Sur la fortune du *chronicon* d'Eusèbe en Espagne au XVᵉ–XVIᵉ cf. Abraham Zacuto, *Sefer Yuḥasin,* Filipovski, p. 245: *'Isibio sofer divre hayamim*; et ibid., p. 247: *ze 'asa sefarim batekhuna, te'ologya weqosmografya wedivre hayamim me'Adam we'ad zemano.* C'est à travers la version latine de Jérôme (vers 382) que la chronique d'Eusèbe s'est diffusée en terre de latinité. Une édition bilingue des chroniques d'Eusèbe et d'Isidore est en préparation au Centre de Recherche sur la Culture de l'Israël Ancien et Médiéval. On notera encore la *Chronica Gothorum* ou *Historia Gothorum wandalorum suedorum suevorum* attribuée à Isidore, cf. *Crónica seudo-isidoriana* (Valencia, 1961). Sur la notion fondamentale de *seder* comme ordre logique ou chronologique linéaire, restitué dans l'histoire de la matière scripturaire, cf. *Sefer haYašar,* pseudo-préface (Venise, 1625), 6*r* (reproduction, Editions de la Sorbonne Nouvelle, Service des Publications [Paris, 1986], tome II, p. 13) qui justifie le titre "biblique" de "*yasar*" (retto, droit ou linéaire par le respect intégral de l'ordre chronologique de la matière. En monde rabbinique cette préoccupation remonte au début de l'époque tanaïtique et s'exprime dans le *Seder 'Olam* attribué traditionnellement au *tana*' Yose

des *Cronicas*[2] au XIVe–XVe. Il s'agit, de fait, d'une historiographie officielle des rois de Castille qui se conçoit comme une continuation de la *Première Chronique Générale d'Alphonse le Sage*[3] et qui fait donc remonter l'histoire de l'Espagne à celle des origines de la Création et d'Adam. Cette vogue est à l'évidence partagée par les intellectuels juifs qui comme Zacuto se réfèrent aussi bien aux *Canons des Temps* d'Eusèbe de Césarée (*Yuḥasin* 6, 243) qu'au *Chronicon* d'Isidore qui s'en inspire (*Yuḥasin* 6) ou encore à la *Chronique d'Alphonse le Sage* (*Yuḥasin* 4: "et le roi susnommé a fait composer un livre de chronique d'Adam à son temps" *sefer divre hayamim*). Chez ces derniers cette vogue espagnole est enrichie du branchement sur une autre tradition bien plus prestigieuse,[4] celle des *Livres des Chroniques* de la Bible

---

ben Halafta, réputé pour ses goûts et ses curiosités en matière d'histoire ancienne (*Shabat* 16b, *Sanhedrin* 97a, *'Avoda Zara* 5b, 9a entre autres); elle se poursuivra à l'époque gaonique avec des ouvrages comme le *seder* (*Sefer* ou *Yiḥus*) *Tana'im we'Amora'im*, composé en 887 et faussement attribué au rabbin français du XIe Yosef Tov 'Elem. Cf. *Seder Tana'im we'Amora'im* (Prague, 1839; Breslau, 1911), Alexander Marx, ed. Toutefois, en matière d'exégèse prescriptive ou narrative, les maîtres fondateurs ont établi le critère de la non-pertinence de la linéarité logique ou chronologique du texte scripturaire (principe "*'en muqdam u-me'uhar ba-tora*", *Pesahim* 6b); argument de polémique dans les milieux convertis d'Espagne ou *conversos*, cf. Alfonso de Zamora, *Libro de la Sabiduria de Dios* (titre calque de l'hébreu: *Sefer hokhmat Adonay*, 40–41 citant en outre le *Midras Tehilim*. La question des infractions à la linéarité chronologique des récits scripturaires paraît être une spécificité de l'exégèse juive d'Espagne; elle est marquée chez Bahyé ben 'Ašer, et particulièrement sensible chez Abravanel qui présente de ce point de vue une remarquable convergence avec l'auteur du *Sefer haYašar* (cf. supra). Ce souci de l'ordre, logique ou chronologique, "corrigé" ou "remis en ligne droite" se marque dans la méthode d'Abravanel: *Commentaire de la Tora*, Genèse I, 15b: "la question demeure du motif pour lequel toute la chose n'a pas été mentionnée à sa place, conformément à l'ordre convenable et régulier"; ibid. *péricope Ha'azinu* I, 13b: "Ainsi donc les choses ne sont pas à leur place si l'on se fonde sur ce qui a été dit plus haut (dans le texte)."

[2] Cf. en particulier les textes publiés par Ramon Menendez Pidal (Madrid, 1906, 1918, 1955); D. Cayetano Rosell (Madrid); Juan Mata Carriazo (Séville, 1951, Madrid, 1943); J. Puyol (Madrid, 1934). Sur l'origine de la vogue du terme de "chronique" lui-même, v. infra note 54.

[3] Cf. Ramon Menendez Pidal, *Primera cronica general de Espana que mando componer Alfonso El Sabio y se continuaba Bajo Sancho IV en 1289* (Madrid, 1955), 2 vol.

[4] Opinion intéressante d'Abravanel sur l'existence d'annales royales ou chroniques (*divre hayamim*) déposées en archives dans lesquelles les prophètes auraient puisé des développements pour l'intelligence historique de leurs prophéties; d'où les doublets entre *Isaie* et les *Rois*, ou encore *Jérémie* et les *Rois*, cf. préface du *Commentaire au livre de Josué*, II, p. 11. Sur la censure de la matière des *Chroniques* par Samuel auteur de ses livres, Cf. préface au *Commentaire de 1 Samuel*, II, p. 163. On notera aussi un grand souci à reconstituer l'ordre chronologique quand celui-ci lui paraît perturbé, cf. *Commentaire du livre de Jonas*, III, 128b: "*'im ken haketuvim šelo' keseder beqadima we'i-hur*". D'autre part Abravanel s'étonne que les *Chroniques* soient complètement négligées par la tradition exégétique rabbinique et confesse qu'il n' à pas encore lu les

ou d'*Esther*;[5] ainsi Zacuto encore voit-il dans ce qu'il appelle la Chronique d'Assuérus le modèle de sa propre chronique des origines du monde jusqu'à son temps, et écrit-il en justification de son ouvrage:

> Il est inutile d'insister sur l'utilité de ce livre (Chronique d'Assuérus) c'est pourquoi j'en ai relié la matière avec celle d'un livre des saints, ou *Sefer Yuḥasin*, que j'ai composé pour en faire connaître les saints sages d'Israël, cet ouvrage nécessitant qu'y soient relatés tous les événements qui se sont produits depuis la création. Et c'est là la grande différence qu'il y a entre nous et les livres de chroniques des nations, rapport du bon grain à l'ivraie.

> (*Yuḥasin* 6, 232)[6]

Et Yosef d'Arevalo,[7] un auteur du XIVe lecteur lui aussi d'Isidore et des auteurs espagnols, pratique même une manière embryonnaire d'histoire au sens moderne du terme en procédant au recoupement et à la comparaison des chroniqueurs espagnols qu'il nomme *kotve*

---

deux livres au moment où il compose son commentaire du livre de Samuel (préface II, 164).

[5] Les intellectuels juifs de culture espagnole réalisent donc une manière de synthèse de leur double univers de référence en en faisant agir une face sur l'autre; cf. a ce sujet la méthode "comparatiste" d'Abravanel, préface au *Commentaire de 1 Samuel*, II, 164. On notera toutefois que tant Eusèbe ou Isidore bien évidemment, mais aussi la chronique d'Alphonse le sage, se rattachent à la Genèse et aux temps patriarcaux.

[6] Rapprocher d'Abravanel: "je dirai que ce prophète (Samuel), en relatant ce qui se rapporte à David et à ses actions, ne l'a pas fait avec pour seul objectif le récit simple des faits comme c'est le cas dans les livres des chroniques que les nations composent en ne relatant que ce qui se rapporte à elles; il ne l'a fait que dans le but d'édifier et d'éduquer dans le culte de Dieu" (préface au *Commentaire de 1 Samuel*, II, 164).

[7] *Chronological Notes* (Oxford, 1887–1895, 2 vol.; Amsterdam, 1970 [reproduction de 1887–1895]), I, pp. 85–100. On notera que l'auteur reprend la périodisation du *Chronicon* selon laquelle Isidore classe l'histoire en six âges. Le *Sefer Yuḥasin* de Zacuto, compte, quant à lui, treize âges du monde; cependant il convient de préciser que le manuscrit d'Oxford, base de l'édition du texte, est inachevé. Cette tradition qui remonte apparemment à Eusèbe de Césarée paraît en écho de celle, isolée, conservée dans *Sanhedrin* 97a et qui prend vraisemblablement origine dans l'entourage d'Abahu de Césarée. Polémiste anti-chrétien tenant école à Césarée, Abahu était un contemporain déculé d'Origène, lui-même installé à Césarée à partir de 232; initié de la *paideia*, il était rompu à la culture grecque en laquelle baignaient alors les pères de l'église d'orient; il n'est donc pas fortuit qu'il soit le père du maître (Avimi) qui enseigna que le septième millénaire serait celui de l'ère messianique (*Sanhedrin* 99a–b). Abraham bar Hiyya, avant Yosef ibn Zadiq, avait explicitement emprunté à Isidore sa théorie des six âges du monde fondée sur le parrallélisme entre les six jours de création et les six jours de durée du monde, un jour de durée en échelle divine étant de mille ans d'après Ps. 90:4. Cf. *Chronicon* et *Etymologies* V, 13, XXXVIII.

zikhronot hamelakhim ou *koteve khronot be'umot ha'olam* (*Zekher Zadiq*, Neubauer II, 89). Yosef ibn Verga lui-même n'hésite pas à y avoir recours en signalant qu'il a utilisé un *sefer me'ora'ot malkhe Edom* (*Shevet Yehuda*, fin, 146).[8] Le phénomène est si courant que même le fragment de chronique retrouvé par Neubauer dans un manuscrit d'Oxford (Mss F. Mich 138)[9] fixe la date du début du christianisme à partir des *divre hayamim lemalkhe Edom* (ibid. 194).

Ainsi la valeur d'arme idéologique de l'histoire n'échappe à personne.[10] Tous ont clair conscience en Espagne que le récit du passé,[11] exaltant le peuple qui en est le héros, a pour mission d'affirmer la légitimité et la prééminence d'une confession sur les autres puisqu'autant alors confession et nation coïncident.[12] L'arme n'est d'ailleurs

---

[8] L'ouvrage composé par Yehuda ibn Verga, fut ensuite complété successivement par son parent Šelomo et le fils de ce dernier Yosef ibn Verga; il a été publié par Wiener en 1855 à Hanovre.

[9] Cf. Neubauer, *Fragments and Notes*, I, 194–195.

[10] Cf. *Anales Breves*, Cayetano Rosell, p. 535, sur la fonction d'édification de la littérature des *crónicas*: "la costumbre y uso del escribir historias y corónicas, asi en tiempos; pasados como en los presentes, paresce . . . celebrada y confirmada por todas las naciones y. gentes capaces de razon . . . porque si en el escribir se guarda lo que se debe, no solo se nos da manera para bien y virtuosamente vivir, pero tambien somos instruidos en el fin que debe mos seguir . . . porque entonces la corónica tiene autoridad para ser imitada y seguida". Sur la notion de *to'elet* ou "utilité" de l'histoire, cf. *Sefer haYašar*, pseudo-préface (Venise, 1625), fol. 7*v* (1986), p. 15. Cf. aussi *Etymol.* I, XLIII: *De utilitate historiae*. Cf. supra.

[11] Ainsi pour Abravanel l'existence d'un *seder 'olam* est-il la preuve que le monde a été créé et a bien eu un commencement, une chronologie ne pouvant se concevoir sans un point zéro, Cf. *Commentaire de la Tora*, péricope *Ha'azinu* I, 13b; argument déjà avancé dans le *Sefer haKuzari*, premier traité. Désormais le comput de création (*minyan hayezira*) a pris le pas sur les anciens computs relatifs: *minyan hašetarot* (textuellement: comput des documents) désignant l'ère séleucide à point zéro en 312 avant notre ère, ou encore *minyan haḥurban* (comput de la destruction du Temple) commençant en 67–68 ou 70. L'expression symétrique chez les pères est de *creatio mundi* ou *anno mundi*. Sur l'éternelle querelle judéo-chrétienne et les accusations mutuelles de manipulation de chronologie Cf. infra et plus spécialement Alfonso de Valladolid, *Mostrador de Iuticia* VII, Mss BN Fonds espagnol 43; cf. *Revue des etudes juives* 18 (1889): 59.

[12] Initiée chez Isidore de Seville, la manipulation chronologique qui démarre à Adam vise à "vieillir" le monde afin de démontrer que les prévisions messianiques de *Daniel* coïncident bien avec l'avénement de Jésus, alors qu'on argue en milieu juif que le décompte historique conduit à l'appréciation d'un événement encore à venir. Chez Isidore, alimentant l'essentiel de la démonstration du *Contra Judaeos*, le lecture de *Daniel* comme se rapportant à la venue de Jésus qualifié de Christ, vise spécialement à combattre en Espagne le retour des convertis au judaïsme, en une terre où ce dernier était particulièrement vivace et attractif. D'où l'"actualité" de la relecture d'Isidore à l'époque du mouvement *marrane*. Sur le vieillissement systématique des patriarches et la critique qu'en fait Zacuto, cf. *Chronicon* 1er et 6e âges, *Sefer Yuḥasin* 6, Filipovski, p. 249; cf. aussi Abravanel, *Ma'yene haYešu'a* 10, 7, 375–376.

pas nouvelle[13] elle explique la rédaction du *Yosifon*,[14] et avant lui des oeuvres de Joseph Flavius[15] qui en sont la source, mais surtout en Espagne les oeuvres d'Abraham ibn Daud comme le *Zikhron divre Romi* ou les *Malkhe Yisra'el bevayit hasheni*[16] dont il est superflu de souligner la fonction apologétique dans la controverse judéo-chrétienne que les débuts de la *reconquista* commencent à rendre suraiguë. Le recours à l'histoire—nous dirions mieux l'historiographie—est donc le recours à une arme de combat.[17] J'ai récemment montré dans un

---

[13] C'est tout l'enjeu d'une terminologie qui, du côté hébraïque, emprunte une phraséologie scripturaire et désigne successivement par *"Edom"*, *"Yišma'el"* et *"Yisra'el"* la chrétienté, l'islam et le monde juif; cela est particulièrement net dans l'usage que fait Abravanel de ces ethniques, cf. J. Genot-Bismuth, "Le mythe de l'orient dans l'eschatologie les Juifs d'Espagne à l'époque des conversions forcées et de l'expulsion", *Annales* 4 (juillet–août 1990).

[14] Selon la thèse de David Flüsser, l'ouvrage est rédigé en 952–953 en Italie méridionale, alors sous la domination de Byzance, cf. *"meḥaber sefer hayosifon, demuto u-tequfato"*, *Zion*, 1953, 1–2, et *Sefer Yosifon*, tome II (Jérusalem, 1980), 74–84.

[15] Sur la vogue de Joseph Flavius à l'époque de l'essor de l'imprimerie cf. infra. Destiné à faire l'apologie d'Israël dans l'entourage de sa *gens* d'adoption, les Flaviens, et dans le but de conduire l'empereur à adoucir le régime répressif en Judée au lendemain de l'écrasement de Jérusalem, la version revisée qui nous est parvenue de la *Guerre des Judéens*, parue sous Vespasien entre 75 et 79, prétend rétablir la véracité des faits, garantie par le récit d'un acteur, et nuancer le tableau manichéen qui a cours à Rome. L'oeuvre est, en effet, destinée "aux Grecs et à ceux des Romains qui, n'ayant pas pris part à la campagne, continuent d'ignorer 'la réalité des faits' parce qu'ils n'ont lu que des relations inspirées par la flatterie ou le mensonge" (*Guerre* I, 6). Composées bien plus tard, en 93/94 en la 13e année de Domitien, alors qu'après la mort de Titus Joseph se trouve privé du patronage impérial et a trouvé salut dans la clientèle d'Epaphrodite le Grammairien, les *Antiquités* sont destinées à un lettré, lui-même lecteur et commentateur d'Homère dans le but de gagner sa sympathie à la cause ethnique de son client, cf. André Pelletier, Flavius Josèphe, *Autobiographie* (Paris, 1959), introduction, XI–XIII.

[16] Le *Sefer haQabala* ne représente en fait que le tiers d'un ouvrage historique composé de trois parties, par la suite dissociées en textes indépendants: (a) *Sefer haQabala* ou chronologie de la tradition rabbinique d'inspiration vraisemblablement anti-karaïte, (b) *Zikhron divre Romi* (Mémorables de Rome), imprimé à Mantoue (1514) ou histoire d'Israël depuis la fondation de Rome et jusqu'à l'islam: la principale thèse tient à ce que le Christ est présenté comme n'étant qu'une forgerie de l'époque de Constantin. Cf. aussi Abravanel cité in Genot-Bismuth, op. cit., 833–834. (c) *Malkhe Yisra'el bevayit hašeni* (Histoire des souvrains à l'époque du Second Temple), compilation de la recension longue du *Yosifon* (Constantinople, 1512) et *Midraš 'Eser Galuyot*. L'ensemble est une trilogie apologétique destinée à lutter contre les ennemis du judaïsme dominant: pêle mêle Karaïtes, Chrétiens et Juifs doutant de l'espérance eschatologique; c'est dans le climat de compétition de la nouvelle Tolède chrétienne, où il s'était réfugié chassé de Cordoue par la conquête almohade, qu'il faut comprendre cette oeuvre de combat rédigée vraisemblablement aux alentours de 1160. Il est de reste significatif que, victime d'abord du fanatisme musulman, il ait fini en martyr, victime du fanatisme chrétien en 1180.

[17] Cf. supra note 10 et infra note 45.

article paru dans les *Annales* que l'usage apologétique de l'histoire qui s'intensifie avec la diffusion de l'humanisme, s'explique très largement par la conviction, alors partagée par tous, Juifs ou Chrétiens, que c'est bien Dieu qui décide des événements du monde, bref que l'histoire n'est jamais que l'écriture, dans la réalité du monde, du dessein providentiel.[18] Alors chacun s'applique, preuves du passé à l'appui, à tirer à soi la faveur divine pour justifier de sa supériorité sur les autres. Isaac Abravanel lui-même, engagé dans le combat, projetera de composer une chronique universelle d'Israël pour dresser l'inventaire des nations persécutrices d'Israël:

> Et si nous faisons le décompte des nations qui ont persécuté Israël nous en trouvons bien plus que les quatre empires[19] (de Daniel), ainsi de bien des nations qui les suivirent qui se nourrirent de la destruction de Jud à (Tosef. B.M. 7:19 d'apres Lev. 19:16) par toutes sortes de persécutions dans l'exil. Qui racontera tous les maux terribles et les persécutions excessives commises par les Arabes, les Ismaéliens,[20] à l'encontre de la diaspora, ainsi que j'ai l'intention de le narrer dans le *Livre des jours du monde* que j'ai commencé à écrire et dans lequel je ferai le récit, avec l'aide de Dieu, de l'histoire depuis le jour de la naissance du premier homme jusqu'au jour d'aujourd'hui.
>
> (*Ma῾yene haYešu῾a* 288)

Son but est bien évidemment de tirer l'histoire réelle—celle de la défaite juive devant le pouvoir conjugué de la royauté et de l'Eglise d'Espagne—dans le sens d'une histoire providentielle consolante pour les Juifs, et des fameuses prophéties de *Daniel* pour y déchiffrer le

---

[18] Cf. supra note 13.

[19] Cf. *Ma῾yene haYešu῾a* 10, 7, 375–376 où Abravanel combat l'interprétation chrétienne qui prétend prendre appui sur les *Antiquités*, et telle qu'elle est formulée par Nicolas de Lyre. Sur Abravanel utilisateur des gloses de Nicolas de Lyre cf. ibid. 10, 7, 376 et infra note 61. Or on observera qu'on venait de publier à deux reprises la Bible latine avec les commentaires de Jérôme et de Nicolas de Lyre: Nüremberg, 1487 (Bibliothèque de l'Université de Barcelone, Incunables no. 186) et Venise, 1489 (Barcelone no. 66). Nicolas de Lyre est d'autre part l'auteur d'un traité anti-juif publié à Venise en 1481, le *Contra Perfidiam Judaeorum disputatio*.

[20] Sur la phraséologie ethnique cf. supra note 13. A l'heure où le traumatisme des persécutions polarise les esprits sur l'Espagne chrétienne et où nombre d'expulsés on tenté de trouver un asile souvent tragique en Afrique de Nord, Abravanel qui, lui, a choisi Naples et l'Italie comme terre d'asile contrairement à Zacuto réfugié à Tunis, se singularise par une attitude très nettement anti-islamique, travaillant à mettre ses coréligionnaires en garde contre le piège d'une migration en terre arabe et plus largement en pays musulman; d'où sa distinction des Arabes, maîtres du Maghreb, et des Ismaéliens de l'empire ottoman. Sur toute cette question cf. Genot-Bismuth, op. cit.

prochain anéantissement des Chrétiens et des Musulmans; telle est sa lecture du grand affrontement de l'époque entre camp chrétien et turc, l'Espagne se faisant le champion de la Chrétienté et, pour donner l'exemple, ayant chassé enfin de son territoire musulmans et juifs.[21]

La chronique anonyme publiée par Hacker montrera de son côté comment l'histoire fournit modèle de déchiffrement et références en appliquant à Ferdinand le Catholique l'histoire du mauvais pharaon de l'Exode.[22]

C'est en quelque sorte la réponse polémique à un argument du camp adverse, très bien formulé par exemple dans la *crónica* du chroniqueur des rois catholiques Fernando de Pulgar:

> Pero escriveremos con el ayuda del muy alto Dios, la verdad de las cosas que pasaron. En las quales veran los que esta corónica leyeren los efectos de la Providencia[23] en sus obras, çerca la subçesion desta prinçeça (Isabel) en los reynos de Castilla y de Leon...
>
> (*Crónica de los reyes católicos, version inedita*, Juan Mata Carriazo, 2 vol. [Madrid 1942], I, 3)

Au coeur du débat, et déjà depuis au moins Abraham ibn Daud[24] se trouve la question de l'ancienneté du peuplement de l'Espagne: qui des Juifs ou des Chrétiens est de souche la plus ancienne et peut prétendre à l'occupation légitime du pays? C'est toute la tradition de *"galut Yerushalayim 'asher bi-Sefarad,"*[25] du débat sur la descendance

---

[21] Cayetano Rosell, Chronique de Hernando de Pulgar 518; Andres Bernaldez, *Historia de los Reyes Catolicos*, 651; cf. *Anales Breves*, 546: "Ano 1492: A dos dias del mes de énero de este ano ganaron y entraron los Reyes la honrada y gran ciudad de Granada, y la pusieron a obediencia de nuestro Señor Jesu Christo, y sua en su nombre, honra y gloria de Dios ... Este ano mandaron los Reyes desterrar de todos sus reinos de Castilla y Leon oa los Judios."

[22] Yosef Hacker, "Qroniqot hadašot 'al geruš ha-Yehudim mi-Sefarad, sibotaw wetoza'otaw", *Sefer Zikaron le-Yizhaq Baer* (Jérusalem, 1979).

[23] Même thèse sur la providentialité de l'histoire que celle qui sous-tend le *Sefer haYašar*, cf. pseudo-préface (Venise, 1625), 1986, II, fol. 5r–8r, 11–17.

[24] Cf. essentiellement *Zikhron divre Romi* (Mantoue, 1514).

[25] *Ovadia* 20. Cf. la chronique dite *Seder 'Olam*, Neubauer I, 175, qui attribue à Hadrien (contrairement à ibn Daud qui la fait remonter à Titus) la déportation des Judéens en Espagne, en réalisation de la prophétie d'*Ovadia*: "... il les emmena et les déporta en *Sefarad*". Et pourquoi (l'Espagne) porte-t-elle le nom de "*Sefarad*"? Parce qu'à la fin (*ba-SoF*) ils y "descendirent" (émigrèrent) (*RaDu*), et c'est d'eux que le prophète a parlé (en disant): "*we-galut Yerušalayim 'ašer bi-Sefarad*" ("et la déportation de Jérusalem qui se trouve en Espagne-*Sefarad*"). L'identification de *Sefarad* à l'Espagne date effectivement de l'époque de domination romaine puisqu'elle se trouve déjà dans le Targum (Targum dit de *Yonatan ben 'Uzi'el*): "*we-galut Yerušalayim*

de Yafet et Tubal que déjà Isidore de Séville assigne à l'origine du peuplement des Ibères et d'Hispan (*Etym.* IX ii,29,109).[26] La *Chronique d'Alphonse le Sage* reconduira ce mythique Hispan[27] à la figure d'Hercule (Ramon Menendez Pidal, *Primera Crónica General de Espana* [Madrid, 1955], 5–8).

C'est directement de la *Chronique d'Alphonse le Sage* qu'Abravanel tire lui-même son histoire du peuplement de l'Espagne qui sert d'épilogue au *Commentaire du deuxième Livre des Rois*:

---

di-be-Ispamia". Abraham ibn Ezra et David Kimhi, dans le sillage d'Abraham ibn Daud, en commentant *Ovadia* 20, identifient aussi le peuplement juif de l'Espagne aux déportations de Titus. Le fait est d'ailleurs historique: la mise en valeur des provinces ibériques (Bétique et Narbonnaise) nécessitait une main d'oeuvre servile que la Guerre de Judée alimenta par la constitution d'une masse de plus d'un million de captifs qui provoqua un effondrement des prix sur les marchés d'esclaves, notamment dans la zone occidentale de l'empire; les Judéens ont donc effectivement eu une part active à la constitution de l'Espagne. Sur les cinq régions de l'Europe, qui correspondent de fait aux grandes provinces de l'empire romain, où furent repartis les captifs judéens déportés, v. Yosef ibn Yahya, *Commentaire des Psaumes* (Ps. 120:5) (Bologna, 1538); *malchut 'Edom* (nom de l'empire romain, puis par dérivation de toute la chrétienté après Constantin) s'y répartit en *Sefarad* (Espagne), *Zarfat* (Gaule, France), *Germanya* (Germanie), *'Erez Yawan* (Grèce), *'Italya* (Italie). Sur les transferts de sens d'*"Edom"*, cf. Genot-Bismuth, *op. cit.*, note 7.

[26] De *Gen.* 10:2. Cf. *Yosifon* 1 qui fait des *Bene Tuval* la souche du peuplement de la Toscane, les *Bene Kitim* étant identifiés aux populations ayant occupé la Campanie; l'épisode de l'enlèvement des Sabines y est interprété comme le rapt par les *Bene Tuval*, fondateurs de la cité de Sabina, des femmes des *Bene Kitim*; les *Bene Tuval* sont en fait assimilés aux Etrusques, maîtres de l'artisanat (témoignage de Tatien), par une confusion entre *Tuval* (*Gen.* 10:2) et *Tuval Cain* (*Gen.* 4:22), maître fondateur de l'art du bronze et du fer. Une autre tradition qui s'origine aux *Chroniques de Yerahme'el* (Moses Gaster, *The Chronicles of Jerahmeel* [Londres, 1899], 66) et qu'on peut dire espagnole, à la différence de celle, italienne, du *Yosifon*, fait des *Bene Tuval* les premiers habitants de l'Espagne; elle est partagée aussi bien par les *Chrétiens* (*Chronique d'Alphonse le Sage*, 6; Florian de Ocampo, *Los cincos libros primeros* [Alcalà, 1578], I, 4, 16; Alonso Morgado, *Historia de Sevilla* [1587], 4) que par les Juifs (Abraham ibn Daud, *Zikhron bene Romi*; Abravanel, *Commentaire de Gen.* 10:2 et *Ez.* 32:27; Zacuto, *Sefer Yuhasin*, 5 et 6: "*Tuval hu' Sefarad*". Sur toute la question voir l'étude érudite de Yehuda Rosenthal, "*Tuval*", *Mehqarim u-meqorot* [Recheches et Sources], 2 vol. (Jérusalem, 1966), I, 93–100. Cf. Jérôme, Migne, *Patrologia Latina* XXIII, 99: Thubal Iberi qui et Hispani a quibus celtiberi licet quidam Italos suspicentur; parcontre dans la traduction d'*Isaac*, 66,19 (Vulgate): "*In Italiam et Greciam*". On notera que le *Sefer hayašar* s'aligne sur la tradition du *Yosifon* et non sur la tradition espagnole, ce qui est idéologiquement compréhensible dans la perspective de la thèse selon laquelle l'auteur occulté de l'ouvrage est un expulsé d'Espagne réfugié à Naples, cf. J. Genot, "Censure idéologique et discours chiffré: le *Sefer hayašar*, oeuvre d'un exilé espagnol réfugié à Naples", *Revue des études juives* CXL, 3–4 (juillet–décembre 1981): 433–451; cf. Venise (1625): 1986, fol. 22*r* p. 45. Cf. Abravanel, *Commentaire de la Tora*, péricope *Noah*, I, 33a–b.

[27] "*Espan*" en *romance*, Menendez Pidal 11. "*Ispamiya*" du Targum est une adaptation d'Hispan. "*Ispamiya*" et "*Afriqua*", comme provinces romaines de peuplement judéen, cf. Saadia ibn Danan, *Hemda Genuza* 28b, 30b.

Il est nécessaire de savoir que bien des rois accompagnèrent le roi de Babel marchant contre Jérusalem,[28] rois et princes du reste des nations, et qu'ils ramenèrent des Judéens dans leurs pays, et parmi eux Peros[29] qui était roi d'Espagne. En effet Hercule le grand qui était originaire de Grèce, était parti à la conquête du monde; par sa force et sa sagesse qui était très grandes, il s'étendit en terre d'occident; et après avoir accompli de nombreuses prouesses au cours de ses conquêtes, il arriva avec une grande flotte et une forte armée en Espagne où il se fixa et régna sur tout le pays d'Espagne. Et quand il se languit de sa terre et de sa patrie, il retourna en Italie et de là en Grèce ... et quand cet Hercule quitta l'Espagne il laissa la royauté au fils de sa soeur Hispan, et c'est de son nom que tout le pays de *Sefarad* tire son nom en langue de peuple étranger soit *Hispania*.[30] Cet Hispan n'avait qu'une fille qui épousa Peros, lui-même un prince de Grèce. Il participa à la première destruction (du temple) et en ramena des fils de Juda, Benjamin et Simon,[31] de même que des lévites et des prêtres qui étaient à Jérusalem, un peuple nombreux qui l'accompagna de son plein gré et qu'il ramena par mer sur des navires jusqu'en Espagne où il les installa dans deux régions, l'une que l'on appelle aujourd'hui l'Andalousie[32] ... et l'autre le pays de *Tulitula*[33] en allusion au *tiltul*[34] (tribulation) qu'ils effectuèrent en venant de Jérusalem jusque là, car auparavant, selon les Chrétiens, le nom de la contrée était Ferrizuela, et ce sont les Judéens qui arrivés plus tard la nommèrent Tolède ... et il ne fait pas de doute qu'en ce temps-là ils baptisèrent toutes les villes proches de "Tolède" de nom de cités d'Israël, mais avec le temps les noms se

---

[28] Tradition d'origine non identifiée.

[29] Pyrrhus, personnage historique, roi d'Epire ayant pris part aux guerres puniques, cf. Polybe, *Histoire* III, 1, 26, 191–192, 198. Lors des deuxième et troisième traités entre Rome et Carthage se situe la "victoire à la Pyrrhus". *Mastia* et *Tarseion* (future région de Carthagène) et le Beau Promontoire constituent la limite interdite aux Romains pour la piraterie ou la fondation de villes, mais Carthage se prémunit contre une éventuelle alliance du roi avec Rome qui lui donnerait la liberté de passage en Sicile, voire en Afrique; ce sont ces épisodes, romancés après une chaîne souvent mal identifiable d'avatars, qui aboutissent dans le *Sefer haYašar* au cycle de *Zefo* fils d'Esau-Edom et d'*Angias*, roi d'Afrique, fol. 118*v*–125*v*, 136*v*–137*r*. "Pirus" en *romance* (Menendez Pidal 12–14), d'où *Piro* et "Pireneos" nom donné aux "Monts Cethubales", homilétiquement rattachés au nom de "*Thubal*" (*Tuval*).

[30] Cf. supra note 27.

[31] Cf. Yosef ibn Zadiq, op. cit. 94 et Zacuto, op. cit. 4: tradition propre aux Juifs de Grenade selon laquelle le peuplement judéen de l'Espagne se serait fait de déportés de Jérusalem issus des tribus de Juda et Benjamin.

[32] *Andalucia*, transposition de *Andaluç* (nom arabe de l'Espagne, ou pays des Vandales).

[33] Comparer avec la chronique de Bernaldez, Cayetano Rosell 654–655. "*Tulitula*" ou "*Toletola*" est une adaptation hébraïque de la forme latine *Toletanus*.

[34] Cf. *Sefer haYašar*, pseudo-préface, II, 5*v*, 12.

perdirent et changèrent, et il n'en resta jusqu'à ce jour que trois en
témoignage et preuve de l'ensemble (*Tulitula, Maqeda, Eshkelona*).[35] Et
depuis les juifs sont installés dans le royaume d'Espagne jusqu'à présent
et se sont répandus dans toutes ces cités; ils ne sont pas rentrés à
l'époque du second Temple car ils ont pensé que ce n'était pas là la
grande convocation parfaite puisque l'arche était absente, que la
prophétie avait cessé et que le reste des saintetés faisaient toujours
défaut à Israël.[36] C'est pourquoi ils ne firent pas retour car seulement
au vrai retour de Dieu à Sion tous ses enfants rentreraient des limi-
tes d'Assur, de Cush et des Iles de la mer[37] ainsi que tout le récit en
est fait dans le *sefer divre hayamin haqedumim 'asher le-malkhe Sefarad* (dans
le livre des chroniques anciennes des rois d'Espagne).[38]

(*Commentaire de 2 Rois*, II, 680–681)

On ne pouvait mieux souligner l'intégration culturelle des Juifs en
Espagne. Cette participation à l'engouement général pour le passé
n'est pas, de reste, le fait de seules quelques grandes figures d'intellectuels, mais d'un très large public ainsi qu'en témoigne Abraham
Zacuto qui justifiera ainsi sa volonté, une fois l'expulsion accomplie,
de redonner à ses corélégionnaires d'Espagne, désormais dispersés,
une nouvelle relecture de leur histoire: Ainsi déclare-t-il composer
son *Sefer haYuḥasin*[39] (à Tunis entre 1497 et 1515) "... pour satisfaire
le désir de ceux de notre nation qui veulent savoir ce qui a été écrit
sur l'histoire qui les concerne et sur ce qui est advenu à Jérusalem,
en Terre sainte, en Italie, en Grèce, en Egypte, en Babylonie, en
Turquie et partout où se concentre un fort peuplement juif, comme
Tyr ... la Tiro des Chrétiens ... où étaient installés autrefois les
Vénitiens"[40] (*Yuḥasin* 6, 231b).

---

[35] *Escalona*, cf. chronique de Bernaldez, Cayetano Rosell 632.

[36] Cf. *Baba Batra* 12a, *Yoma* 21b. Cinq privilèges sacrés ont disparus entre le premier et le second Temple: *'aron* (arche), *parokhet* (tenture originelle du Saint des
Saints), *keruvim* (chérubins gardiens de l'arche), *'eš* (feu sacré originel), *ruaḥ haqodeš*
("esprit saint", inspiration quasi prophétique dans la langue rabbinique), *Urim* et
Tumim.

[37] D'après *Isaac* 11,11.

[38] Référence à la *Chronique d'Alphonse le Sage*, en paraphrasant le nom hébraïque
des deux livres des *Chroniques*. A rapprocher au pseudo-titre *Sefer haYašar* en "latin"
(*romance*) "*Libro de las palabras de los dias di feitos de los grandes, de los guerres despues morir
Yehošu'a*" (Venise, 1625), fol. 62 (Paris, 1986), p. 13.

[39] *Sefer Yuḥasin hašalem*, Zevi Filipovski ed. (Londres-Edimburgh, 1857), sur la base
du Mss d'Oxford, *Catalogue de la Bodléienne* fol. xxxvii.

[40] Tyr, *Ẓur* des textes scripturaires; conquis par les Croisés en 1124, le port de
Tyr fut investi par des colonies de marchands conduits par les Vénitiens. Les Juifs
vivaient dans le quartier vénitien, directement sous le contrôle des autorités de la

Mais l'analyse de Zacuto est plus fine encore. Elle dénote une claire conscience de l'enjeu idéologique, et une volonté de manier le récit dans un but manifeste d'apologie et d'édification: "Ainsi est-il très utile à Israël, installé au sein de la nation chrétienne (de connaître l'histoire générale) afin de combattre les Chrétiens plus efficacement dans la controverse religieuse" (ibid. 231a).

Mais c'est surtout l'histoire biblique qui met le plus en valeur la portée idéologique et les objectifs édifiants de la connaissance de l'histoire: ". . . Etant donné que la connaissance des faits advenus à toutes les époques pour toutes les nations, comme ceux qui concernent la génération du déluge et les épisodes similaires (concernant l'humanité entière). . . et en particulier la connaissance des événements advenus à la nation d'Israël, nous conforte en la foi en la puissance divine comme en sa providence . . ." (ibid. 231a).

Or on observera que cette thèse générale est, par ailleurs, exactement celle de l'auteur du *Sefer haYashar* telle qu'elle est formulée dans la pseudo-préface éditoriale.[41] On peut donc la tenir pour un des traits de mentalité les plus fondamentaux de l'époque.

L'on pourrait citer encore bien d'autres auteurs comme Yosef ibn Zadiq d'Arevalo, auteur du *Zekher Zadiq* signalé plus haut, ou encore Abraham de Torrutiel,[42] lui-même auteur d'un *Sefer haQabala* qui se veut en somme la continuation de la chronique d'Abraham ibn Daud et encore publié par Neubauer,[43] mais à l'évidence le nombre des

République de Venise; mais après la conquête mamelouque en 1291, la colonie juive cessa d'exister, d'où l'intérêt particulier de Zacuto pour ce comptoir de la côte phénicienne. D'une façon plus générale la question du synchronisme entre faits d'histoire dite sainte et faits d'histoire profane était débattue dès avant Eusèbe, avec Théophile d'Antioche, Hippolyte et Jules l'Africain, Eusèbe de Césarée, *Hist Eccl.* I, I, 6, p. 5.

[41] *Op. cit.* fol. 7r, p. 15. Le récit de l'histoire générale ("histoire des nations") y est justifiée par un argument d'apologétique: celui de la différence de nature entre victoires militaires des nations, effet du hasard, et victoires militaires d'Israël dues à l'intervention divine, d'où les notions complémentaires de *bitahon* et de *devequt*, qui relèvent depuis Bahye ibn Paquda du courant d'ascétisme mystique espagnol, *Sefer Hovot haLevavot*, version de Yehuda ibn Tibbon (Jérusalem, s.d.); David Kapah (Kafih, ed), *Torat Hovot haLevavot*, édition critique et nouvelle traduction hébraïque à partir de l'original arabe (Jérusalem, 1973). Cf. aussi Georges Vajda, *La Théologie Ascétique de Bahya Ibn Paquda* (Paris, 1947) et Ramos Gil, *Homenaje a Millas Vallicrosa*.

[42] Cf. supra note 7.

[43] *Op. cit.*, 101–114. Abraham ben Selomo de Torrutiel en complète le texte d'additions et le pourvoit d'une "suite" jusqu'en 1497. Cf. Fidel Fita, *Boletin de la Real Academia de Historia*, IX fasc. 4 (avril 1867): 245.

chroniques anonymes espagnoles de l'époque retrouvées, fut-ce en
fragments, est là pour prouver que les Juifs d'Espagne étaient quasi
tous sans exception des lecteurs avertis de la littérature des *Crónicas*
dont ils sentaient parfaitement bien les objectifs idéologiques qui les
plaçaient au premier cercle de la cible. Mais pour finir, je voudrais
me concentrer sur le cas d'Isaac Abravanel.[44] Intellectuel humaniste
de grande exigence, comme le montre sa lettre au comte de Faro,[45]

---

[44] Attestée au moins depuis 1300, la famille des *Abravanel* (*Abravaniel* ou *Brabanel*,
en diminutif de la forme espagnole *Abravan*); le premier de ses membres à se dis-
tinguer est Yehudà Abravanel de Cordoue, puis dit ensuite de Séville, trésorier et
collecteur d'impôts sous Sanche IV (1284–1295) et Ferdinand IV (1295–1312);
assumant probablement la charge d'*almoxarife* de Castille (percepteur de revenus),
on le voit en 1310, avec d'autres Juifs, garantir un prêt à la couronne de Castille
pour le financement du siège d'Algeciras. En 1391, au moment de la vague de persécutions, il se convertit sous le nom de Juan Sanchez de Séville et reçoit la charge
de contrôleur en Castille. Plus tard réfugié au Portugal, d'abord au service de l'in-
fante pour la gestion de ses finances, puis à celui du Duc de Bragance; ce qui
explique sans doute les liens de son fils avec cette grande famille de princes du
sang, et le péril de complicité en lequel il se trouva lors du complot manqué du
Duc de Bragance. Yehuda, grand négociant international était en relation avec les
Flandres. Isaac Abravanel appartient donc au milieu aristocratique des Juifs de la
cour du Portugal par sa naissance et son éducation et représente un cas typique
d'intégration sociale et culturelle bien que le phénomène n'ait affecté qu'une très
mince élite du judaïsme ibérique. Le soupçon d'avoir trempé dans la conjuration
des ducs de Bragance et de Faro contre Jean II (1481–1495), hostile au pouvoir
de la noblesse, le contraindra à la fuite en 1483; et il sera condamné à mort tout
comme l'illegible de complot, Don Alfonso, duc de Bragance, dans un procès *in
absentia* tenu à Lisbonne en 1485. Soucieux de sauver sa fortune, il s'installe à
Segura, à la limite de la Castille et du royaume du Portugal. Sans doute, contraint
comme Machiavel à brusquement se retirer des affaires, il occupe ses loisirs forcés
à une réflexion sur le pouvoir qu'il conduira en commentant les quatre livres historiques, cf. supra. Mais après quelques mois à peine il entre au service de Ferdinand
et Isabelle de Castille (1484). On le retrouve à Alcalá de Henares en 1488 et à
Guadalajara en 1491, associé au puissant Abraham Señor de Segovie dans la ferme
générale des impôts. L'expulsion le surprendra au faîte de la puissance et de l'influence
auprès des rois catholiques.

[45] Don Alfonso conde de Faro, est le troisième des fils du duc de Bragance; ami
personnel d'Abravanel, il trempa dans la conjuration de son père, et l'affaire des
soupçons qu'il attira sur Isaac Abravanel reste obscure. Abravanel, quant à lui, s'en
disculpe totalement mais son témoignage doit être replacé dans le contexte; briguant
le service des monarques, il avait à soigner une image de serviteur fidèle et loyal,
cf. *Commentaire du livre de Josué*, préface II, 2. Né en 1437 à Lisbonne, Abravanel a
47 ans au moment de sa fuite en Espagne, il aura 55 ans en 1492.

Le texte de la lettre a été publié par Joaquim de Carvalho à partir du Mss 297
de la Bibliothèque Nationale de Lisbonne (*Revista de Estudos Ebraicos* 1 [1928],
231–233), après une première édition par Janette Schwerin, "Ein Brief Don Isaak
Abarbanels in portugiesischer Sprache", *Magazin für Wissenschaft des Judentums* (Berlin),
1891, 133–145. Sur la culture gréco-latine d'Isaac Abravanel cf. J. Guttmann, *Die
Religions-philosophischen Lehren des I. Abravanel* (Breslalu, 1916), 41–43 (inventaire des

chez lui, en effet, la conscience aiguë de ce que l'on appellait alors l'utilité de l'histoire,[46] à la suite de Polybe (*Histoire* I, préface, ou Thucydide I,22), comme la conscience des exigences que requière son étude marque un état d'esprit humaniste neuf qu'on a jusque là mal mesuré. Lisant couramment le latin (il va même jusqu'a traduire en hébreu une très longue citation des *Etymologies* d'Isidore de Séville, *Ma'yene* 3, 7, 462), il montre ainsi une familiarité avec les classiques de la culture humaniste qu'il rencontre à Naples d'abord puis en Italie et à Venise puisque Polybe et Thucydide viennent d'être traduit du grec en latin sous le pontificat de Nicolas V (1447–1455); ainsi la traduction de Polybe due à Perotti et celle que Lorenzo Valla vient de donner de Thucydide sont désormais des classiques de la culture humaniste diffusés en terre italienne, tout comme Hérodote également traduit par Valla (Venise 1474 et 1494[2]) et mis en italien par Boiardo entre 1478 et 1479; sans compter Plutarque, Tacite et Tite-live qui font l'objet d'éditions imprimées (Plutarque Venise, 1478; Tite-Live, Venise 1481, *Decades I–IV*, Venise 1498, *Historiae romanae decade*).[47] On notera que nombre de ces oeuvres sont éditées à Venise au moment même où Abravanel écrit sa trilogie: *Ma'yene haYeshu'a*, *Yeshu'ot meshiho* et *Mashmi'a Yeshu'a*,[48] composés à Monopoli sur deux années (1497–1498). Dans le même temps les oeuvres de Flavius Joseph commencent à être publiées dans leur

citations d'auteurs classiques dans son oeuvre). Sur sa maitrise consciente de la rhétorique et de la littérature latin, cf. *Ma'yene* 10, 4, 385 où "*divre hayamin 'ašer la-latinim*" réfère apparemment aux *Annales* de Tacite; ou encore ibid. 8, 5, 368: "*hokhmat ha-davar ha-niqr'et 'ezlam 'oratoria*" (la science du discours appelée chez eux *oratoria*). Il arrive que la culture latine lui permette d'élargir les horizons de l'exégèse comme à propos du châtiment de Nabuchodonosor, ou encore de Cyrus (*Yešu'ot Mešiho* [Konigssberg, 1861], 55a). On le voit encore citer les *Métamorphoses* d'Ovide, ou Virgile en même temps qu'Albert le Grand (ibid.). Enfin ses sources sur la guerre de Judée sont autant Joseph Flavius que les *Histoires* de Tacite qu'il résume pour ses lecteurs qui n'ont pas son accès au latin. Cette méthode de la citation textuelle en traduction, donnée avec sa référence dénote l'humaniste de la Renaissance et atteste la conscience qu'avait Abravanel de disposer, sans doute exceptionnellement, d'une culture profane de vaste étendue qu'il entendait diffuser parmi ses coréligionnaires.

[46] Cf. supra note 10.

[47] Tacite, *Histoires*, texte établi et traduit par Henri Goelzer (Paris, 1963); Thucydide, *Histoire de la Guerre du Péloponèse*, traduction, introduction et notes de Jacqueline de Romilly (Paris, 1990).

[48] *Ma'yene haYešu'a* (Ferrare, 1551), colophon donnant la date d'achèvement: 1er tevet 5257 (1497). *Yešu'ot Mešiho*, colophon en date du 20 tevet 5228 (1498) (Königsberg, 1861). *Mašmi'a Yešu'a*, colophon du 4 adar 5258 (1498) (Salonique, 1526). Les trois oeuvres ont été composées à Monopoli, dans le Royaume de Naples après la fuite devant l'occupation française.

version latine (*Antiquités*, version de Rufin, Venise 1481, 1486, 1499; *De bello* et *Contra Apionem*, Vérone 1480 dans la version de Petrus Mauser). Dès 1484 et les débuts accidentels de sa carrière littéraire, Abravanel choisit l'histoire, et l'on a sans doute été abusé par le fait que ce choix se fait par le biais d'une relecture de la quadrilogie biblique *Josué, Juges* et les 2 *Samuel*.[49] On a pris cela pour de l'exégèse quand il s'agissait de toute autre chose. Il suffit pour cela de relire la préface au *Commentaire de Josué*:

> Je dirais, en ce qui concerne leur finalité, que le premier objectif commun à ces quatre livres, est de nous délivrer des enseignements et des renseignements utiles à la connaissance d'idées vraies et à l'apprentissage des dispositions positives et des vertus ainsi que les montrent leurs récits.[50] Et l'une des finalités qui leur est commune à tous les quatre c'est la connaissance des temps du monde, des durées et des générations, car nous n'avons d'autre moyen de connaître la durée du passé sinon à travers celle du décompte de l'époque des juges et des rois qui se sont succédés les uns aux autres sans solution de continuité. Et si chaque Etat, chaque nation dans sa propre langue s'est efforcé de fixer et de connaître les débuts et les limites temporelles des générations successives afin de connaître les époques historiques et leur durée, *a fortiori* doit-il en être pour les enfants d'Israël à qui il convient de connaître et de comprendre les ramifications des générations depuis l'origine de la création jusqu'à l'exil de Jérusalem, dans l'attente de l'échéance.[51] ... Et c'est pourquoi il était nécessaire que soient décomptées les années des juges et des rois[52] et racontés les faits qui les concernent car ainsi nous parvenons à établir la durée des années du monde.
>
> (*Préface au Commentaire de Josué* II, 6a)

[49] Sur la foi des colophons la chronologie des premiers commentaires est la suivante: Josué (du 10 au 26 marhešwan 5244/1483–84) soit un travail de deux semaines; Juges (1–25 kislew 5244/1483–84), en 25 jours; 1 & 2 Samuel (1er tevet–13 adar 5244/1484) soit en deux mois et demi. Les Rois, à peine entamés à la suite, attendront leur achèvement à Naples en 1493. L'ensemble a donc été produit de l'automne 1483 au début du printemps 1484; la baisse de productivité laisse pressentir que c'est sans doute à la fin de l'hiver de 1484 qu'Abravanel est vraisemblablement entré au service des rois catholiques.

[50] Noter la convergence d'objecfifs avec le *Sefer haYašar*, cf. inventaire des 13 utilités de la pseudo-préface fol. 7r–v; plus particulièrement utilités là 9.

[51] Confirmation que l'enjeu essentiel de la connaissance et de l'établissement de la chronologie universelle est, en milieu juif comme en milieu chrétien, de nature eschatologique.

[52] Cf. Abraham ibn Daud, *Sefer haQabala*, I, Cohen pp. 3–4.

Ainsi le principal argument de l'histoire est d'abord la bonne chronologie,[53] clef de l'exacte appréciation des prophéties et de leur accomplissement, déjà réalisées ou à venir. Or c'est là l'esprit du *Chronicon*[54] d'Isidore de Séville qui n'est du reste qu'une manière de préparation de son traité contre les Juifs. Une thèse parcourt en effet le *Chronicon* qui soustend toute l'argumentation du *Contra Judaeos*:[55] elle consiste, par la récapitulation du décompte des années en comput de *creatio mundi*, à prouver que les prophéties de *Daniel* concernant les soixante-dix semaines d'années se sont bien accomplies avec l'avènement de Jésus ainsi prouvé en sa messianité, et à combattre la thèse juive du messie à venir.[56] Or cette démonstration n'est possible que par une manipulation chronologique des temps patriarcaux, opérée par Isidore sur le *Canon des temps*[57] d'Eusèbe de Césarée qui sur ces points suivait la chronologie du *Seder 'Olam*. C'est à Abraham Zacuto qu'on doit la clef de ce trafic de décompte des âges:

> Sache que selon la Tora et les 70 sages qui la traduisirent pour Ptolémée, et telle est aussi l'opinion de Jérôme, de mémoire bénie pour avoir traduit la Tora en latin, entre la création et le déluge il y a 1656 ans. Mais Isidore prétend qu'il y en a 2242 et Augustin, que maudit soit son nom, qu'il y en a 2262, il est donc infondé de se baser sur Isidore. Ainsi prétendent-ils (le camp espagnol adverse chrétien) qu'en la 5499e

---

[53] *Ma'yene* 10, 7, 375a sq.: Abravanel y réfute l'interprétation chrétienne de *Dan.* 8:13 et 9:25–26. Et sur la chronologie comme argument décisif dans le débat messianique, Cf. *Yešu'ot Mesiho* 18v.

[54] *Etymol.* V, xxviii: "De chronicae vocabulo. Chronica Graece dicitur quae latine temporum series appellatur, qualem apud Graecos Eusebius Caesariensis episcopus edidit et Hieronymus presbyter in Latinam linguam convertit. Xronos enim Graece, Latine tempus interpretatur". Isidore justifie donc une tradition d'usage calquée du grec en se rattachant à ses deux plus grands prédécesseurs. Première édition Turin, 1593, cf. supra note 1; réédition in Migne, *Patrologia Latina* 83, 1040 sq.

[55] Migne *PL* 83, 449 sq.

[56] *Contra Judaeos* I, V, par interprétation de *Dan.* 9:23–26. La "démonstration" que les 70 semaines représentent effectivement le temps écoulé entre Daniel et Jésus, conduit Isidore à conclure: "Mais ô dureté du coeur des Juifs! parce qu'eux-mêmes ont tué le messie, il en résulte qu'ils ne croient pas qu'il est venu". Cette tradition, qui est déjà celle de Bède el de Jules l'Africain, est combattue par Abravanel, cf. *Ma'yene* 5, 4, 302a–303b; 10, 7, 375a sq. V. aussi Abraham ibn Daud, *Sefer haQabala* I, 8–9.

[57] Dans son introduction, Isidore se réclame de ses prédécesseurs Jules l'Africain dont l'oeuvre est perdue, Eusèbe de Césarée, Jérôme et Victor de Tunis (*Chronicon* [Turin, 1593], p. 1). Cf. Rudolf Helmed, ed., *Die Chronik des Hieronymus* (Leipzig, 1913). La chronique de Victor évêque de Tunis (de l'an 444 à Justinien) est publié par Migne, *Patrologia Latina* 68, 941–962: *Victoris Chronicon*.

année de création est né Jésus le chrétien, ce qui ne s'est produit qu'en l'an 3760 de la création selon l'opinion des Juifs et la différence est de 1439 ans car on a décidé que Caïn est né en l'an 15 de la création, Abel son frère en l'an 30 et en 130 Seth,[58] lui qui fut le premier à connaître les trajectoires célestes.

(*Sefer Yuḥasin*, Filipovski, p. 232)

L'enjeu était donc majeur et central, il était au coeur du procès intenté par l'Eglise espagnole et l'Inquisition aux Juifs d'Espagne.[59] Cela nous fait ainsi mieux saisir les motifs qui ont conduit Isaac Abravanel à infléchir sa production, à partir de 1496, quittant le terrain de l'exégèse proprement dite pour la rédaction de véritables traités d'apologétique comme le *Maʿyene hayeshuʾa* fondé précisément sur Daniel[60] ou le *Yeshuʾot meshiho*, traité polémique essentiellement

---

[58] Naissance de *Šet* en 130 (vie d'Adam) selon le *Seder ʿOlam* vs 230 selon le *Chronicon* d'Isidore. Toutefois une oeuvre anonyme, l'*Abbreviatio Chronicae*, datée de 809 et éditée par Migne, *Patrologia Latina* 29, 871–874, contemporaine de Charlemagne, ne diverge pas du *Seder ʿOlam*.

[59] Cf. Disputation de Tortose, J.D. Eisenstein, *Ozar Wikuhim: A collection of Polemics and Disputations* (New York, et Jérusalem 1969/2), 105–108; le champion chrétien y était Geronimo de Santa Fe, l'ex-rabbin Yehošuʿa haLorqi, disciple du talmudiste Šelomo HaLevi converti sous le nom de Pablo de Santa Maria ou Paulus Burgensis, évêque de Burgos. Geronimo est l'auteur du *De Judaeis erroribus ex Talmuth*, imprimé à Augsburg en 1468, puis à Zurich (1552) et à Frankfort (1603), dans la *Bibliotheca Maxima Veteram Patrum Hebraeomastrix*, vol. 3. Les polémistes apostats sont surtout un phénomène particulier à l'Espagne chrétienne du XVᵉ; Abravanel les désigne par l'expression *"perize ʿamenu hamitpaqrim"*, d'après *Dan.* 11:14, ce qui peut se rendre par "les brigands de notre nation devenus apostats" (*Yešuʿot Mešiho* 16v); il vise particulièrement Pablo de Santa Maria el Burguense (1350–1435) et son disciple Geronimo de Santa Fe. Le talmudiste, Šelomo haLevi, après sa conversion, alla faire sa théologie à Paris où il fut ordonné prêtre en 1394. Il devient le favori Benoît XIII et séjourne Avignon où il s'éveille à l'action anti-juive, incitant plus tard Jean Ier d'Aragon à promulguer des décrets anti-juifs. En 1396 il est arhidiacre à Trevino, en 1403 évêque de Carthagène, et parvient au faîte avec sa nomination comme évêque de Burgos (1415–1435). En outre, à partir de 1407 il devient le *canciller mayor* du roi de Castille. Ses deux frères, également convertis, feront de brillantes carrières, illustrant ainsi la rapidité du processus d'intégration des notables juifs dans l'aristocratie espagnole, ce qui n'alla pas sans susciter par choc en retour le mouvement de réaction anti-*conversos* bien connu. Quant à son fils Gonzalo García, il fit une carrière, dans les hautes sphères de l'Eglise, d'abord évêque de Carthagène, puis successeur de son père comme évêque de Burgos; il composera une apologie en faveur des *conversos* pour tenter d'enrayer la réaction des vieux chrétiens, *Defensorium unitatis christianae*. Le premier de ses frères Alvar Garcia, choisissant la carrière des hautes charges royales, exercera le commandement militaire des rois de Castille. Et le second Alva Sanchez de Carthagena fera, quant à lui, une carrière diplomatique au service de la couronne de Castille. Cf. P.L. Serrano, *Los conversos Pablo de Santa Maria y Alfonso de Cartagena* (1942); F. Cantera, *La conversion del celebre talmudista Salomon Levi* (1933); *Alvar García de Santa Maria y su familia de conversos* (1952); *Homenaje à Millás Vallicrosa* I (1954): 301–307.

[60] Il apparaît à l'évidence que la finalité n'est pas exégétique, mais qu'il s'agit

dirigé contre l'apostat Paulus de Burgos auteur du *Scrutinium Scrip-turarum*[61] et—ce n'est pas un hasard—un poème historique inspiré des six âges du *Chronicon* de Isidore intitulé *Las siete edades del Mundo* ou *Edades trovadas*.[62] Zacuto lui, prendra une autre voie, on l'a vu en produisant sa propre version de l'histoire du monde "rectifiée," et Abravanel commença, selon son témoignage, un ouvrage du même genre dont la trace nous est perdue.

Ainsi on voit à quel point toute cette production de la généra-tion des expulsés de 1492 est à réinterpréter comme une réponse d'actualité en rapport dialectique avec l'intense activité idéologique missionnaire de l'Eglise d'Espagne—le clergé régulier en l'occurrence—surtout alimentée par l'afflux d'anciens rabbins devenus apostats, très au fait de l'approche juive et focalisant l'essentiel de l'affrontement sur la question décisive de la venue du messie.[63]

Ce n'était là que quelques jalons, quelques indications pour nous faire prendre conscience que sans doute tout est à reprendre dans l'approche que nous avons traditionnellement naïvement en abor-dant l'ensemble de la production de la génération des grands auteurs de l'expulsion. C'est singulièrement vrai d'Isaac Abravanel dont il est habituellement donné une image bien fade, alors qu'il s'agit, on le pressent, d'une oeuvre forte et combattante, plus encore en réplique à l'influence déstabilisante de l'activité missionnaire des convertis, qu'à usage strictement interne.

---

bien d'une réponse à l'offensive des clercs apostats qui, dans la ligne d'Isidore, pren-nent appui sur *Daniel* pour mener leur combat sur ce qu'ils estiment être le prin-cipal point de résistance du Judaïsme à la christianisation: la reconnaissance de la messianité de Jésus.

[61] *Scrutinium Scripturarum recognitum ac restitutum per Magistram F. Christophorum Sanctotisium. Augustinianum Burgensem* achevé en 1432 et paru à Strasbourg en 1471, Cf. Bibliothèque de l'Université de Barcelone, Incunables no. 66; 2e édition à Burgos (1591). Paul de Burgos est également l'auteur d'*Aditiones ad Postillam Magistri Nicolai Lyra*, com-posés en 1429. Oeuvre lue et citée par Abravanel, Cf. *Ma'yene* 10, 7, 376: "tu trou-veras encore une seconde objection formulée par le grand évêque espagnol nommé chez eux Bispo de Burgos et dont le nom ci-devant dans le sein d'Israël était Šelomo Halevi qui a composé des additions (*tosafot*) et des interprétations inédites (*ḥidušim*) au commentaire des vingt-quatre livres saints de Nicolas (de Lyre), le meilleur et le plus distingué de leurs commentateurs. Cf. supra note 19.

[62] Poème historique qui donne une manière de version littéraire de son histoire de l'Espagne jusqu'en 1412 intitulée *Suma de la cronicas del mundo*.

[63] Sur le tournant décisif que représente l'entrée en force des *clerigos* dans le dernier combat de la *reconquista*, et l'offensive contre les Juifs et les musulmans, et en particulier sur le rôle décisif d'Alonso de Espina, cf. J. Genot-Bismuth, v. supra note 13.

MONTAIGNE'S ESSAY ON VANITY AND KOHELET

T.A. Perry

Ben-Gurion University of the Negev
Beer-Sheva, Israel

Three factors qualify Montaigne for a conference on Sephardic Jewry. The first is the fact, acknowledged by all and then promptly dismissed, that he was of Sephardic origin through his mother.[1] The second is the possibility that some of his most stunning intellectual formulations and especially his skepticism have striking affinities with the medieval Spanish rabbis.[2] The third is his interest in the Hebrew Bible. In this paper I shall focus on the third of these, in particular Montaigne's reading of what was perhaps his favorite book, Kohelet, or the Book of Ecclesiastes. I would especially like to explore Montaigne's method of essayistic exegesis in "De la Vanité" (*Essais* III:9), a meditation that constitutes a most interesting interpretation of that impenetrable biblical book.

Montaigne's Interest in Jews and Jewish Scripture

There are two curious absences in Montaigne scholarship: his Jewish connection and his biblical interests. The first is perhaps the more understandable, for Montaigne does not make many explicit references to Jews. Yet, in view of his Jewish mother and the fact that around 35 percent of the faculty of his prep school, the Collège de Guyenne in Bordeaux, was of *marrano* origins, according to the estimate of Richard H. Popkin, we may wish to ponder the following

---

[1] On Montaigne's mother, see Donald Frame's biography, *Montaigne* (New York, 1965), p. 28. Interestingly, it seems that Montaigne's Jewish connection comes up for discussion only with reference to Jewish stereotypes. Thus, Thibaudet attributes a subtle remark to Montaigne's "Jewish genius." Albert Thibaudet, *Montaigne* (Paris: Gallimard, 1963), p. 252.

[2] For Montaigne's intellectual affinities with the Spanish rabbis, see my *The Moral Proverbs of Santob de Carrión* (Princeton University Press, 1987).

comment regarding King John of Portugal's treachery toward the Jewish exiles from Spain:

> [Those who did not die] could do nothing but return to slavery. Some turned Christian; of their faith, or of that of their descendants, even today, a hundred years later, few Portuguese are sure, though custom and length of time are far stronger counselors than any other compulsion.
>
> (*Essais* I:14, p. 36)[3]

From our scholarship on the *marranos*, it is well known that explicit reference is precisely not the best method of inquiry into this matter, in fact not a good way at all, since their purpose was not to divulge but to hide. It may be that Montaigne, like other *marranos*, had to resort to defensive writing and facade techniques, and this likelihood is increased by the fact that some of Montaigne's heterodoxical opinions were of great interest to the Office of the Inquisition.

As far as the Bible is concerned, Montaigne's explicit references make up a judicious mixture of Hebrew and Christian Scripture, and this would have been no cause for alarm, especially since the Hebrew references were few and well scattered.[4] There is one body of evidence that has been known for years, however, but not at all understood or even interpreted. I refer to the discovery of the quotations inscribed on the walls of his library, constant reminders in appropriately epigrammatic form of how he daily wished to condition himself to think and live. The library, in its personal centrality and privacy, seems a good analogue of the *marrano* woman's kitchen, where, upon returning home from church on Good Friday, she secretly lit the Sabbath candles.

There were fifty-seven such epigrams on his walls, twenty-three in Greek and the rest in Latin. Twenty are from the Bible:

St. Paul: 4 (the only Christian author)
Psalms: 1
Isaiah: 1
Proverbs: 1
Ecclesiasticus: 1

---

[3] I quote from the translation of Donald M. Frame, *The Complete Essays of Montaigne* (Stanford University Press, 1965). All references are to this translation (here = F) unless otherwise noted. For the French text I use Pierre Villey's edition, *Les Essais de Michel de Montaigne* (Paris: Presses Universitaires de France, 1965).

[4] On this subject see especially Marianne S. Meijer, "Montaigne et la Bible," *Bulletin de la Société des Amis de Montaigne*, 5th series, no. 20 (1976): 23–57.

All the rest, the twelve remaining biblical quotations, are from Kohelet, making up almost one forth of the entire corpus. Of these, ten are identified by the author,[5] and two are conjectural.

Montaigne's selection of the book of Kohelet is not surprising, given its lack of explicitly Jewish reference, its universalistic appeal, and undoubtedly its skeptical method. It appears that Kohelet is definitely not a Catholic favorite, and if this was indeed the case in sixteenth-century France, then Montaigne's choice gains further in interest. But the concept of the world's vanity was a Catholic preoccupation, as we shall see, and Montaigne's attack against vanity can thus be interpreted as a critique with very contemporary undertones.

The Title Theme: Vanity

That Kohelet was Montaigne's favorite biblical book is suggested not only by his library inscriptions but by the fact that it is the only book of the Bible that forms the subject of an essay, and one of the major ones. It is widely held that "De la Vanité" is exemplary in its lack of thematic unity. Thibaudet, for example, believed that the essay rambles out of control, while R.A. Sayce lists no less than eleven themes, "all in some way interconnected," and with vanity "the most distant of all."[6] Montaigne was, of course, the first to make this claim, but we have missed the joke, or rather we have failed to uncover the elaborate and typical exercise in defensive writing. I therefore propose that we pause to examine the implications of the crucial opening passage.

> Of Vanity . . . There is perhaps no more expressive example than to write about it so vainly. What the divine word divinely expressed about it should be carefully and continually meditated upon by sensible people. Who cannot see that I have chosen a route along which, without end and without labor, I shall travel for as long as the world has ink and paper.
>
> (my translation)

---

[5] Montaigne indicated both Ecclesiasticus and Ecclesiastes as "Eccl." but did not always distinguish carefully between them. For example, in 1:39 (Villey ed., p. 238) he incorrectly designates Kohelet (verse 7:28) as "L'Ecclesiastique."

[6] "Vanité du discours, qui n'a jamais été aussi décousu, aussi fait de lopins" (Thibaudet, cited in R.A. Sayce, *The Essays of Montaigne: A Critical Exploration* (London: Weidenfeld & Nicolson, 1972), p. 270.

The first point of note is the careful allusion to Kohelet at the very start of his essay, an invitation to close intertextual criticism and to meditation on the original message of Kohelet. My second point is exemplified by the unusual syntactic continuity between title and text, pointing to the inversion or self-inclusion of method and topic. Montaigne is to write about vanity, and vanity is to be illustrated and constituted by the very writing. Note also that travel is a metaphor for writing; he refers to the "route" he "travels" as a writer, just as further on his writing is termed "vagabond" (p. 946). The two become different but substitutable expressions of a deeper point, the very theme of the essay, which is, as proposed at the outset by the biblical allusion, not travel or writing or home economics or the civil wars or Rome but vanity, and all other topics are subsumed under this. The originality of the essay "On Vanity" is that it proposes a new interpretation of vanity, or perhaps it simply returns to a healthier and more primitive reading of the biblical text.

Montaigne, as already seen, presents his topic as biblically motivated and exemplifies his theme in himself: "stupidity, vanity, idleness" (F722) and lack of usefulness. As traditionally understood, vanity thus means that our lives are emptiness and wind and bereft of real substance and value. Montaigne begins with this expected view, giving the impression that vanity's emptiness has all the density of a real substance (scribbling, stupidity), but he then proceeds to cut the definition in two, agreeing only that vanity is an absence and a distance—this is why travel is so appropriately its metaphorical expression. The real and unifying theme is therefore absence, but in what is perhaps the boldest maneuver of the essay, Montaigne views vanity as the absence of evil rather than simply the absence of positive value. Rather than being simply neutral, therefore, vanity comes to be defined as the negation of a negation and thus a strong positive value.[7] Before developing this concept, however, it is well to examine how and why Montaigne uses titles that deliberately misrepresent their subjects.

---

[7] On the important subject of what I call Montaigne's negative morality, see my "Just Say No: Montaigne's Negative Ethics," in *The Teaching of Montaigne's "Essays"*, ed. Patrick Henry (New York: Modern Library Association, 1992). While it would be hazardous to argue rabbinic influence on Montaigne's thought here, in the absence of explicit textual proof, one is still tempted to recall such rabbinic evaluations of vanity as the following: "This world subsists only because of the breath [*hebel*, lit. vanity] of schoolchildren" (Resh Lakish in the name of Rabbi Yehudah

Facade Titles, Defensive Writing

A facade title is one that does not correspond to the true subject of the work it introduces. Clear examples of this deceptive practice in Montaigne's *Essays* include the following: "A Custom of the Island of Cea" (II:3), a free discussion of suicide; "On Some Verses of Virgil," a recommendation of eroticism in senior citizens; "Of Coaches" (III:6), a bold political critique; "Of Cripples" (III:11), a critique of superstition and judicial torture. The purpose here is to avoid the scanning glare of church censorship, since none of these titles would arouse suspicion and invite further scrutiny.

There is another group of facade titles that misrepresent the contents in a more interesting way, not by foregrounding an insignificant detail at the expense of a more dangerous subject matter but rather by taking a theologically important topic head-on and then going on simply to disregard it or, more subversively, redefine it. Again, the given title would not arouse suspicion, and one could hardly object if such a "vain" writer of fantasies simply changed the course of the discussion. In this category are the following: "Of Solitude" (I:39), "Of Repentance" (III:2), "Of Vanity" (III:9).

The first is the clearest example and is in fact paradigmatic of the rather original approach. Immediately following the harmless but misleading title, Montaigne takes his distance from the subject as traditionally understood, putting aside as irrelevant the time-honored distinction between the active and contemplative ideals so dear to Aristotelian philosophy but also to Christian monasticism. Similarly, the essay "On Repentance," despite the promise of its title, actually focuses on regret and dismisses as inappropriate the religious call to repent and be born again by destroying the "old" man in order to create a "new" one. "Of Vanity" proceeds in like manner, for from the title one expects the usual discourse on the world's insubstantiality. Thus, Montaigne is careful to specify that "I have no philosophical disdain for things transitory and mundane: my tastes are

---

haNasi, in B.T. Shabbat 119b). Such views led to the important distinction between "vanity that has sin in it and vanity that doesn't" (ibid.). Montaigne will go on to view vanity alternately as the virtue of the weak and the absence of evil, and in this latter instance he recalls the "vanity" of the Spartan warriors, who pared their nails and did their hair before launching into battle. For further comment, see my *The Dialogues of Kohelet* (Penn State Press, 1992).

not so refined, and I value these at least to their full worth" (my translation, p. 953).

The comparison with "Of Repentance" is instructive, for just as in that essay he argues against those who for pseudo-religious reasons despise and neglect their being, here he attacks those who apply their hatred and disenchantment to the world and their daily lives. He proposes that, just as repentance should be a reflection upon the goodness of our being rather than an attempt to replace it, the sense of vanity or despair over God's creation is here interpreted as an awareness, a constant acknowledgment of limitation, a backdrop for reflection and action rather than their substitute. In short, in all three essays Montaigne opposed an entire tradition of moralizing, one that used texts such as Ecclesiastes to support their stance of self-hatred and world-hatred and contempt for wisdom.

Other defensive tactics can be mentioned, notable more for what they do not say than for what they do: his rhetoric of submission, his total neglect of key Catholic doctrines (on the Virgin, on the saints), in an entire essay on education not the slightest mention of the church's role in teaching virtue.[8] Another notable tactic of his defensive writing is his willing assumption of the role of children, women, fools. And, most crucially, Montaigne's insistence that his writing is pure vanity.

Vanity as a Positive Value

It is true that Montaigne did not always attach so high a price to negativity. Thus he complains that "our well-being is but the privation of being ill" (F364). But neither did Montaigne ever see such a positive value in vanity. What all this has to do with vanity can be seen in his attempts, throughout the opening section of the essay, to define it by saying what it is not. Thus, vanity is (at least) *not* utility, narrowly conceived, or political activism (p. 946), and not evil either. The thread connecting vanity to writing and travel (and to all other absences to be noted throughout the essay) is *non-doing*, whence the association between "vagabonds and idlers" (F721), "vanity and idleness" (F722). It is true that these are projected as

---

[8] See especially Patrick Henry, *Montaigne in Dialogue* (1987), esp. chap. 1. I am much indebted to this excellent study for much of Montaigne's defensive techniques.

strengths only against the backdrop of the times: "It seems to be the season for empty things, when harmful ones weigh upon us. In a time when it is common to do evil, it is practically praiseworthy to do what is merely useless" (F722). But these same characteristics return with more positive valuations, as in the almost synonymous "idleness and freedom" (F741) and "freedom and laziness" (F759), now listed as his "favorite" and "ruling" qualities. Vanity is now viewed as a freedom to act, not out of useful motives but for its own sake (p. 977), it is a distancing from petty obligations, self-imposed and useless. Nondoing is now seen as noninterference in matters that can get along quite well by themselves (cf. pp. 952, 956 f.). The space of absence is now conceived not only as room or freedom for oneself but also as room for events and especially other people: let your servant do his job (p. 996, Kohelet 7:21), let your wife run the house as she sees fit, let the kids grow and have their own lives (p. 970, Kohelet 2:18 f.), don't weigh too heavily upon the emotions of others (e.g., the evocation of dying scenes in which the patient tries to milk sympathy from relatives and friends), especially through exaggerated claims of wisdom (pp. 988, 995, and Kohelet generally).

But are the little "vain" things of life so unimportant? I recall the remark of a friend: "I can get through the big things of life, it's the little ones that get me down." Montaigne's version: "Trivial pin-pricks: sometimes trivial, but always pinpricks. The pettiest and slight-est nuisances are the most acute; and as small letters hurt and tire the eyes most, so do small matters sting us most" (F725). Thus, van-ity is so important, as Montaigne's and Kohelet's paradox would have it, precisely because it is so unimportant.

Vanity as Otherness: The World, Fortune, Friendship, God

Book III of the *Essays*, and the Vanity essay in particular, introduces a third element to the title/signature dialectic of the outset, the author/self diad "The Essays of Montaigne," which is now tested by what Montaigne, following the Stoics, has called *l'étranger*, what is outside us and radically different, whether it be fortune or the alterity of the Other. Here all the examples of travel (travel to Rome, in time through the study of history, toward other cultures and value-systems, toward friendship especially, which is potentially the most alienating of all forms of travel): all kinds and levels of travel come to be viewed as absence from the self, the value of each is now measured by the distance that the self takes from itself, notably the scary act of extending one's feelings and interests. And just as (perhaps to the degree that) self-discovery, through negative definition, had been abstract (both general and a withdrawal from the nonself), the return to the world and toward otherness is particular, it takes place only at the level of concrete experience and intimate knowledge. "Possession" of the other, by which Montaigne means enjoyment of otherness, even in erotic enjoyment (III:5), is thus a paradoxical reality, paradoxical because one cannot possess another freedom; it is imaginable and approachable, nevertheless, because the method is truly dialectical, it incorporates the absence and distance of the negative phase. Whence those paradoxical formulations such as "we only possess through absence, etc."

Montaigne's famous formula of friendship ("parce que c'était lui, parce que c'était moi") stresses not similarity but difference. Friendship in his view is the opposite of self-love, not in a moral sense but a metaphysical one. I love a friend (as opposed to my neighbor) not out of duty or altruism but because it takes me away from myself, sets me at another's distance. Just as one does not travel to Rome to find Paris, one does not travel toward a friend to discover one's own self. This distance from the self, morally speaking—and here is the deep connection with Kohelet—is viewed as "vanity," a free and risky alliance with alterity/fortune (the nonself) at the expense of those obligations that tie down our freedom and self-development. This is the context for understanding Montaigne's desire to be loved rather than feared (p. 970). There is an art of pleasing, superior to the requirements of duty in that it requires a knowledge of the other in his particularity, whereas duty is based on principle and the general notion of mankind.

We can perhaps now resolve what has always appeared to me as one of the great puzzles of the *Essais*. In the very opening essay (I:1), the author ascribes the virtue of unconditional forgiveness to only two groups: the Stoics, who do so out of principle, and women and common folks, out of "softness." Montaigne's astonishing self-identification with the latter group seems overly apologetic but in reality can be related to a developing sensitivity to the presence of the other (what Lévinas refers to as the other's "face"), here the persons begging mercy. This is superior to Stoical principles because it is available to general humanity. This interpersonal sensitivity is not part of Kohelet, but it can be related to that adventure common to both Kohelet and Montaigne to "travel" toward the other, to live through the world's "vanity" by taking on those scary absences through which, for example, an author becomes Michel de Montaigne. Thus, one's styles of writing and of living must "let themselves be tossed in the wind" (F761), in *hebel*, or vanity.

SEPHARDIC TRADITION ON GALUT AND POLITICAL ZIONISM: THE HALAKHIC POSITION OF RABBI YA'AKOV MOSHE TOLEDANO

ZVI ZOHAR

Shalom Hartman Institute, Jerusalem

In this paper I present and analyze the concepts of Galut and of the modern Return to Zion found in a seminal responsum composed by Rabbi Y.M. Toledano. Born in Tiberias, scion of an illustrious Sephardic family of Meknès. Rabbi Ya'akov Moshe Toledano (1880–1960) served as rabbi in Malta, Cairo, and Alexandria, subsequently returning to Eretz Israel and serving as Sephardic chief rabbi of Tel Aviv from 1942 until his decease. For a brief period toward the end of his life he also served as minister of religious affairs of the government of Israel.[1] In his creativity and career he may be seen as reflecting attitudes and values common to a significant but insufficiently studied group, the Old Sephardic Yishuv, whose members identified with the Zionist movement while remaining loyal to their traditional heritage.[2]

Rabbi Toledano's central halakhic publication was a collection of responsa entitled *Yam HaGadol* (Cairo, 1931). Several of these responsa express his deep identification with the Zionist Yishuv and his belief that halakha entailed supporting the Yishuv in various ways. Thus, he takes up the question whether halakha requires a Jew in Eretz Israel to employ only Jews and to buy only Jewish produce even if non-Jewish labor or produce is cheaper—and answers in the affirmative. Moreover, he stresses that this halakhic determination applies also with regard to the labor and produce of nonobservant Jews.[3]

---

[1] There is no biographical and intellectual study of Rabbi Toledano. A brief but informative biographical article can be found in *Encyclopaedia Judaica* (1972) 15:1197–1198.

[2] On the attitude of the elite of the "old" Sephardic leadership in Eretz Israel to Zionism, see Penina Moraq-Talmon, "The Status of Jerusalem" [Hebrew], in *Jerusalem in Zionist Thought and Praxis* [Hebrew], ed. H. Levski (Jerusalem, 1989).

[3] *Yam HaGadol*, no. 92 (pp. 165–169).

In another responsum, he determines that under current conditions halakha forbids the sale of weapons to non-Jews, especially in Eretz Israel. Only when a state of true peace prevails between Jews and Gentiles can such sales be permitted.[4]

In a third decision, Rabbi Toledano discusses the possibility of restoring a Sanhedrin-type institution. Coming out in favor of the position typical of the more radical wing of religious Zionism, he advocates the establishment in Jerusalem of a (halakhic) High Court for the whole Jewish people; a court which would also, if possible, restore *semikha*.[5]

However, it is a yet another of Rabbi Toledano's responsa which I wish to analyze in my presentation. In 1929 there occurred a wave of Arab violence against the Yishuv which included a pogrom in the old Jewish quarter of Hebron in which many yeshiva students were massacred. In *Yam HaGadol*, published soon afterward, the following question is posed:

> Does the mitzvah of settling Eretz Israel apply in our times in a manner which obligates all Jews to obtain possession of the Land by all possible means? And, is it not halakhically forbidden to teach the sons of Israel military tactics and methods of defense, so that they might fight and defend themselves against their enemies, should the necessity arise?[6]

A close reading of the question reveals an important conceptual differentiation that is further explicated in Rabbi Toledano's response. Two very distinct questions are being asked. Only one of these questions, that concerning the parameters of settling Eretz Israel, is presented as relating specifically to current reality. The second question, regarding halakha's opinion on the correct self-defense posture Jews should adopt, is understood to be one of basic principle, not contingent upon current context; it is precisely because of this that Rabbi Toledano's position on the matter is so striking.

Attitudes toward self-defense stem, in his analysis, not from Jews' concepts of Eretz Israel but rather from their concept of Galut. An understanding of Galut that was fundamentally mistaken, theologically and morally, had come to prevail in rabbinic circles; in

---

4 Ibid., no. 57 (pp. 91–92).
5 Ibid., no. 21 (pp. 43–49).
6 Ibid., p. 180.

consequence, many rabbis preached that Judaism advocated a passive-submissive response to persecution. The Jewish masses had followed the teachings of these rabbis, reacting to pogroms not by defending themselves but by allowing themselves and their families to be slaughtered "for the sanctification of the Divine Name." Rabbi Toledano feels that although it is not an easy thing to say, the truth must be stated outright: those rabbis who have furthered this attitude bear direct and unequivocal responsibility for the Jewish blood that was unnecessarily spilled due to their misguidance. Here is the relevant paragraph, in full:

> Many of our great rabbis, both in former generations and in current times, erred—and misguided the simple masses of our people—in the belief that as long as we are in this hard exile we are forbidden to lift up our heads. Rather, we are commanded to bow ourselves down before every tyrant and ruler, and to give our backs to the smiters and our cheeks to them that pluck off hair (Isa. 50:6); as if the blood of Israel had been forfeited, and as if He, blessed be He, had decreed that Jacob be given for a spoil and Israel to the robbers (Isa. 47:24). They thought that the decree of exile and servitude to the nations included slavery and lowliness, and that, as a matter of sanctifying the Name even at the price of one's life, a Jew must forfeit his life and surrender himself like a slave or a prisoner of war to Israel's enemies, even in a situation in which it would have been possible to resist them and to retaliate in kind.
>
> Let me, then, state outright that—begging their pardon—they have caused the loss of individual lives and of entire communities of the Jewish people, who in many instances might have saved themselves from death and destruction, had the leaders and rabbis of the generation instructed them that they were obligated to defend themselves against aggressors, according to the rule "If a person comes to murder you, kill him first."[7]

Further reading of the responsum clarifies Rabbi Toledano's understanding of the nature of the exile ordained by God. Galut, it emerges, is a political category; the Jewish people were deprived of sovereignty, and compelled to live as subjects of Gentile governments, in the various lands in which they sojourn. To be the subject of a state, says Toledano, entails that one obey the duly enacted laws promulgated by the authorities, pay taxes, and the like; not that one

[7] Ibid.

be the object of insult and torture, and even less that one willingly
acquiesce in such a role.

Rabbi Toledano states that such a conception of Galut is indeed,
the one borne out by classic Jewish sources. What exile, he writes,
was more directly and specifically ordained than that of the children
of Israel in Egypt? Why, Abraham was clearly informed that the
Divine plan was for his descendants to be enslaved and afflicted by
the Egyptians for four hundred years.[8] Yet when Moses saw an
Egyptian attacking an Israelite, he struck the Egyptian down, for he
realized that such an attack could not possibly have been ordained
as part of Israelite bondage. So, too, Esther and Mordecai regarded
it as only natural that the Jews not only be saved from Haman's
genocidal plan, but also that they retaliate against those who had
planned to destroy them.[9]

In addition to biblical instances, Rabbi Toledano cites two other
types of sources. One is Sephardic folk-tradition, according to which
Don Isaac Avrabanel and other leaders of Spanish Jewry planned
together to organize their communities to confront their enemies and
fight against them (a plan foiled by a treacherous *converso* who revealed
it to the authorities).[10] The other comprises the descriptions by historians of the Jewish uprisings against Rome during the period after
the destruction of the Second Temple. Most of the events to which
he refers in this context (i.e., the uprisings in Mesopotamia, Egypt,
and Cyrenaica) could not have been known to Rabbi Toledano from
traditional Jewish historiographical works. His acquaintance with
the findings of modern historiography is noteworthy.[11] Special notice
should be taken of his halakhic methodology, which enabled him
to regard these findings as valid sources in the halakhic decision-
making process.

---

[8] Genesis 15:13.

[9] Esther 8:11, 9:1–5.

[10] This startling tradition, referred to by Toledano as a commonplace, is, to the
best of my knowledge, not cited elsewhere. In his introduction to his commentary
on the Book of Kings, Avrabanel relates dramatic aspects of his attempts to fore-
stall the expulsion but makes no mention of a planned uprising. Two sixteenth-
century historical works which deal with the expulsion, Capsali's *Seder Eliyyahu Zuta*
and Ibn Verga's *Shevet Yehuda*, also do not record it. Similarly silent on the topic
are modern works, such as Netanyahu in *Don Isaac Abravanel* (Philadelphia, 1972)
and Shmueli in *Don Yitzhak Avrabanel v'Geirush S'pharad* (Jerusalem, 1963).

[11] Toledano was a pioneer of modern Sephardic historiography, his most famous
book-length work being an encyclopedia of Moroccan rabbis entitled *Ner Hama'arav*
(Jerusalem, 1911). In addition, he also wrote many articles on historical and Judaic
topics, utilizing contemporary historical and philological approaches.

Toledano maintains that an uncowed defensive posture was the original and correct orientation advocated by Judaic tradition and practiced by Jews in biblical and postbiblical times. Deviation from this primal norm originated within a specific historico-geographical framework: "It was only in France, Ashkenaz, and Russia that they so demeaned themselves, and never attempted to resist and defend themselves."[12] In recent generations, he adds, this attitude spread to many Sephardic communities, including Morocco, Persia, and Turkey. In other words, the ideology of submissiveness, widely regarded in traditional rabbinic circles as the truly normative one ordained by Torah for Jews living in a pre-messianic reality, is nothing but an "Ashkenazic heresy" which subsequently corrupted many Sephardic Jews, whose own ancestors (e.g., Avrabanel) had never stooped to such levels.

In its fully developed form, the religious glorification of this perverted notion of Galut had turned back against the heroes of the pre-exilic era and attempted to mold their images in consonance with the supposedly eternal values exemplified in the figure of the submissive Jew.

> When one reads works of homilies and musar composed by several recent rabbis, one finds that they believe Jews are religiously obligated to submit to all forms of suffering, insult, and physical degradation. They thought that this followed from [the ideal of] Galut or humility. As a result, some of them regarded as problematic the attitude of the patriarch Jacob, who said, "With my sword and bow,"[13] and of Caleb, who said, "As was my strength then, so is it even now,"[14] and they asked: "How could such saintly men boast of physical prowess?!"[15]

In characterizing this attitude, Rabbi Toledano employs a literary allusion of extreme force that could not fail to evoke a powerful reaction on the part of readers acquainted with classic talmudic culture. This posture, he says, calls forth the rabbis' devastating critique of Zechariah ben Avkiles: "The piety of Rabbi Zechariah ben Avkiles destroyed our Temple, etc." Toledano is alluding, of course, to the well-known talmudic historical myth outlining the chain of

---

[12] *Yam HaGadol*, p. 181.
[13] Genesis 47:22.
[14] Joshua 14:11.
[15] *Yam HaGadol*, p. 181. Rabbi Toledano refers specifically to the homiletical work *Sha'ar Bat Rabim* by R. Haim Aryeh Leib (Jerusalem, 1891), p. 39, adding that similar statements by other recent rabbis could easily be cited.

events that led to the destruction of the Second Temple.[16] Perhaps best-known today is the first part of the tale, often referred to as "Kamzah and Bar-Kamzah," which illustrates the moral and social callousness of Jerusalem's Jewish elite on the eve of the first revolt. In the second part of the story, the offended Bar-Kamzah maneuvers the Roman emperor into sending an imperial sacrificial offering to the Temple of Jerusalem—an offering that Bar-Kamzah secretly disfigures in a manner rendering it unfit for sacrifice according to Temple norms.

It is the third part of the story, however, to which Toledano alludes. Having received the animal sent by the emperor, the rabbis of Jerusalem convene to decide upon a course of action. Most, realizing the disastrous effects of noncompliance, favor having the animal offered up on the Temple altar despite its ritual unfitness. One, however, Rabbi Zechariah ben Avkiles, speaks out in a different vein: sacrosanct rules should not be set aside because of an imperial whim lest a precedent be set. Abashed by his devoutness, the other rabbis swing round to Zechariah's position—and Jerusalem's fate is sealed.

In the talmudic story, Zechariah appears as the advocate of a non-propitiatory policy, with the other rabbis tending toward a "weaker" line of "appeasement." In what sense, then, can Toledano, who supports a bold defensive posture vis-à-vis enemies of the Jews, identify his opponents, who preach Jewish submissiveness, as analogous to Zechariah? The answer lies not in the similarity of their specific proposals, but rather in their concept of value and norm; both identify true devoutness with unswerving commitment to set patterns of behavior, without the broader consequences of such behavior being recognized as a prime consideration in the decision-making process. In both cases, this narrow sense of what commitment to Torah entails led to the virtual ruin of the Jewish people. As Toledano puts it, with regard to the "Ashkenazic" glorification of submissiveness:

> This faulty humility, which rabbinic leaders instilled in the hearts of the multitude, caused an intensification of Galut, and postponed its end. And, alas for our sins, we recently saw this with our own eyes here in our Holy Land; for in the riots and disturbances which occurred in the year 5689 [1929], the number of deaths was especially great

---

[16] Bavli, Gittin 55b–56a.

among our brethren who were yeshiva students or of the simple folk, who were educated to agree to suffer insult, to be dragged about, and to be victimized.[17]

Misguided religious attitudes toward Galut thus affect mass behavior and contribute in no small measure to the perpetuation of the exile. Rabbi Toledano's conclusion is clear.

> Regarding the second question, then, "Is it not halakhically forbidden to teach the sons of Israel military tactics and methods of defense, etc.?" why, according to the above, not only is it not halakhically forbidden, but it is a mitzvah and an obligation incumbent upon all rabbis and leaders of Israel, to institute mandatory daily lessons in these matters in all yeshivot and institutions of Torah study, so that the students and young men be prepared to fight, in case an hour of need arises.[18]

According to Toledano, then, renewed acknowledgment of the Torah's positive attitude toward self-defense must lead to a revised notion of Torah study; the curriculum of Torah institutions should reflect the role which their students are expected to fulfill as defenders of Jewish lives. As he noted previously, however, this was not at all the actual praxis of these institutions; current yeshiva students—and, of course, their teachers—were far from exemplifying the values of Judaic tradition in this crucial matter.

Until this point, Rabbi Toledano's analysis and rhetoric have unfolded purely as a discourse on Galut. His critique of the "Ashkenazic" sanctification of Israel's suffering in exile derives from the self-evident nature of the imperative of self-defense, and is supported by the citation of scriptural and historical instances. His conclusion is that self-defense is "a mitzvah and an obligation" incumbent upon all Jews, wherever they reside. In other words, there is no inherent connection between the mitzvah of self-defense and any geographical locus, e.g., Eretz Israel.

Eretz Israel, however, is squarely on the agenda of Toledano's responsum. The first question posed by the inquirer was, we recall, whether the mitzvah of settling Eretz Israel applied in our times in a manner which obligated all Jews to obtain possession of the Land by all possible means. Thus, in the second part of his *teshuva*, Toledano

---

[17] *Yam HaGadol*, p. 182.
[18] Ibid.

proceeds to discuss halakhic perspectives on the conquest and settlement of Eretz Israel. Relating, in his lengthy, detailed, and technical analysis, primarily to the opinions of medieval halakhists, he concludes that the two leading authorities, RaMbaM[19] and RaMbaN,[20] both agree that Jews are at all times obligated in principle by Torah to do what they can to develop the potential of Eretz Israel, settle there, and gain possession of the Land.[21] To be obligated in principle does not always entail obligation in practice. With regard to Eretz Israel, a specific question obtained. According to a midrashic tradition cited in the Talmud, three vows were Divinely ordained in conjunction with the exile:

> *Lo la'alot kahomah.* Forbidding the Jewish people to initiate a collective campaign to regain sovereignty in Eretz Israel against the will of the nations of the world.
> *Lo limrod beumot haolam.* Forbidding Jews to revolt against sovereign powers in the lands of exile.
> *Lo lehisht'abed beyisrael yoter midai.* Forbidding the nations of the world to overly oppress the Jews.[22]

To what extent were the primary norms on the settling of Eretz Israel curtailed or suspended due to the first of these vows?

Rabbi Toledano argues that under contemporary conditions, the first vow cannot be construed as applying to the Zionist project, for two reasons. (1) It is quite probable that the limitations originally imposed by the vows should be understood as mutually contingent. Thus, should the nations not fulfill their obligation to limit the oppression of the Jews (and they have not done so, notes Toledano), the Jews would be freed from their limitations under the first two vows, and might try to regain Eretz Israel even in the face of Gentile opposition. (2) The preceding claim, regarding the reciprocity of the vows' validity, is (while correct) unnecessary for halakhic justification

---

[19] Rabbi Moshe ben Maimon (Maimonides), 1135–1204, Spain, North Africa, and Egypt. Codifier and philosopher.
[20] Rabbi Moshe ben Nachman (Nachmanides), 1194–1270, Spain. Halakhist and mystic.
[21] Interestingly, Toledano holds that analysis of the medieval sources reveals that they differentiate between two discrete obligations: *yishuv eretz israel*, i.e., the development of the country so it is fit to support a viable Jewish population; and *yeshivat eretz israel*, i.e., living in the country. One may thus live in the land without developing it, just as one may contribute to its development without living in it.
[22] Bavli, Ketubot 111a.

of the contemporary Zionist enterprise. The vow *Lo la'alot kahomah* related only to a collective Jewish move opposed by the nations of the world, whereas in the twentieth century the nations have endorsed political Zionism through the Balfour Declaration and the Mandate of the League of Nations.

What I think should be stressed, in analyzing Toledano's position, is the absence of messianism from his presentation of Zionism. His halakhic rationale for Zionism is not based on the claim that current events with regard to Eretz Israel represent a new phase or mode of history, or a materialization of prophetic promises of Israel's restoration to Zion.[23] In an important sense, Toledano's understanding of Zionism stems from his understanding of Galut: Galut was not an expression of a Divine decree obligating Jews to deny their group's dignity, or forbidding them to affirm that dignity through activist reaction to persecution. Even in the depths of Galut, Jews were always expected to regard themselves as a nation, in the most conventional, political sense of the term. Galut simply meant that the Jewish nation might not unilaterally attempt to avail itself of the usual instrument for safeguarding a polity, i.e., sovereignty.

Given such a notion of Galut, it follows that political Zionism does not involve or require any redefining or rethinking of previously held concepts regarding the place and role in history of the Jewish people. Rather, Zionism requires only that Jews realize that the political limitations imposed by Galut, expressed in the three vows, do not apply in contemporary reality. No longer constrained by these limitations, Jews can legitimately (as far as halakha is concerned) attempt to achieve that ultimate political expression of nationality, i.e., sovereignty, to which they had always aspired. In and of itself, there is nothing miraculous in the shift and ebb of international political constellations; thus, there is nothing in the emergence of a political moment favorable to Zionism which requires explanation or justification in terms of messianism or of Divine intervention in the course of history. Religiously, one need not claim that Zionism's validity is contingent upon current events being understood as *reishit zemihat geulatenu*, the inception of eschatological reality.

Yet Rabbi Toledano does allude to an aspect of recent developments as reflecting Divine involvement—not directly in history, but

---

[23] In contradistinction to Rav Kook, and to certain other religious Zionist ideologies.

in the realm of the psyche: God has enabled certain Jews to free
themselves from the false consciousness of Galut propounded by the
rabbis and thus to reappropriate the authentic Judaic posture of self-
defense and self-assertiveness. This psychological shift has enabled
those Jews to seize the opportunity, provided by international politics, for the Jewish people to regain sovereignty in Eretz Israel. As
Rabbi Toledano puts it:

> Let me praise the flowers of this new generation[24] who "awoke and
> wakened"[25] to revive oppressed hearts,[26] to engirdle themselves with a
> courageous spirit, and to restore the crown of Israel's honor to its pris-
> tine glory. And it is with regard to this that the Bible says: "And I
> will give you a new heart, and instill in you a new spirit."[27]

There is thus a two-pronged irony here—both prongs directed at
the rabbinic establishment. On the one hand, God's involvement
serves precisely to eliminate the psychological attitude which had
been explicitly extolled by rabbis as the essence of correct Jewish
conduct. On the other hand, his involvement is manifest specifically
within the hearts and minds of the secular *halutzim* of the New Yishuv.
Paradoxically, it is those whom the yeshiva world would tend to
identify as furthest from Torah, whose hearts and spirits reflect God's
concern for Israel. Indeed, God works in mysterious ways unac-
knowledged by the rabbinic "establishment."

An Agenda for further Research

Rabbi Toledano's understanding of Galut, self-defense, and Zionism
are fascinating in their own right. In addition, several significant
directions for additional research and reflection emanate from his
responsum. These include:

---

[24] I.e., the Zionist youth of the New Yishuv; most of them did not follow a life-
style characterized by commitment to religion, and many of them identified with
ideologies which regarded Zionism as antithetical to traditional religiosity.

[25] This phrase is a direct allusion to Song of Songs 2:7 (and 3:5) as traditionally
interpreted to signify the awakening of God's love for Israel expected in the messianic era. These are the very same verses in Song of Songs interpreted by midrash
as enjoining the "daughters of Jerusalem" not to unilaterally "awaken" love.

[26] An allusion to Isaiah 57:15.

[27] An allusion to Ezekiel 36:26.

Analysis of his halakhic methodology

Toledano integrates biblical, rabbinic, and historiographical sources in his discussion, and makes extensive use of reasoned arguments that are not contingent upon proof-texts (*s'vara*). It would be of great interest to flush out the underlying methodological and conceptual assumptions which make possible such halakhic writing, and to explicitly develop their philosophical and religious implications.

Authority, commitment, and critique

Rabbi Toledano is writing within the classical genre of halakhic responsa, which is based upon the acceptance of tradition and recognition of the authority of previous scholars who created within that framework. Yet Toledano directs a powerful attack upon what had become a pillar of convention in the rabbinic community, indeed, in the Jewish community at large—the interpretation of Galut as requiring submissiveness and as justifying suffering at the hands of the nations. Obviously, then, Toledano does not hold that to be within the halakhic tradition means to accept as binding everything that has been justified by halakhic masters of the past, or to refrain from explicit criticism of generally accepted opinions. How, then, does he understand the relationship between halakhic authority and halakhic independence, between working within a tradition and subjecting it to a direct critique?

Continuity and change

Toledano claims that his perception of Galut harks back to a classic tradition that was accepted by Sephardic Jews up to the expulsion from Spain. Are there real grounds for this claim? If so, what are they, and why and how were they subsequently supplanted by "Ashkenazic" submissive attitudes? If not so, then what does Toledano's adoption of a novel understanding of Galut indicate regarding the integrative and transformative capacity of the halakhic system vis-à-vis cultural and social change?[28]

---

[28] For an analysis of varied modes of response to social and cultural change, see Eisenstadt, *Tradition, Change and Modernity*, 2nd ed. (New York, 1983), esp. chap. 15, "Major Types of Response to Change."

Is Toledano representative?

Toledano's views are not those usually identified as the views of the "halakhic world." Why so? One answer might be that his attitude is idiosyncratic: interesting, but totally nonconformist. Another answer, however, would be that Toledano is not alone, but rather his positions reflect a currently neglected stream of opinion within halakha, which he did not originate, and which was accepted by a significant group of modern halakhic masters. If so, who were they? One fruitful avenue would be, I think, to search first among Toledano's teachers and peer group: Sephardic scholars who were born or grew up in Eretz Israel in the century preceding Word War I. My own impression, based upon still insufficient survey of the material, is that unhappiness with a quietistic posture and openness to Zionist moves were not at all a rarity within that group. But much remains to be done before such an impression can be argued for—or rejected.

SEPHARDIC ALCHEMISTS

RAPHAEL PATAI

Forest Hills, New York

The study of the work done by Jews in alchemy has been grossly neglected until now. To remedy the situation, I began about ten years
ago to investigate the contribution Jewish alchemists made to the
field, beginning with Maria the Jewess, who lived in the second century c.e. in Egypt, and was considered by later Hellenistic alchemists
as well as by their Arab heirs as the founding mother of alchemy.
I published a paper about her, and went on to publish several more
articles on various aspects of the position of Jews in and on alchemy,
the books they wrote on the subject, and the reputation they enjoyed
in the Gentile world as masters of the "great art."

At an early stage of my work I found not only that little was
known about Jewish alchemists, but that all the Jewish scholars who
discussed it, in encyclopedia articles and other brief papers, were
unanimous in going on record with statements such as "Traces of
the connection of Jews with the science of alchemy are very scanty
in Hebrew literature" and "The number of Jews who practiced the
art of alchemy was apparently relatively small,"[1] to mention only
two of many. As my own studies progressed, I recognized that these
negative statements were due to two factors. One was that as a
heritage of the Haskalah, the Jewish Enlightenment, everything in
the Jewish past which smacked of superstition was frowned upon,
considered embarrassing, and therefore underplayed, and alchemy
definitely belonged to this disconcerting category; and the other was
actual ignorance of the true situation, because no Jewish historian
had ever undertaken a systematic search of the available printed and
manuscript sources with a view to piecing together a history of Jewish alchemy.

Once I recognized the situation, the attraction the subject had for

---

[1] Moses Gaster, in *Jewish Encyclopedia* (New York, 1901); Bernard Suler, in
Encyclopaedia Judaica (Jerusalem, 1972).

me to begin with increased, and whatever time I had left over from
taking care of more urgent literary projects, I devoted to studying
the Jewish contribution to alchemy throughout the ages. In the course
of my work,[2] I found that Jewish alchemical activity began slowly
in the Hellenistic world, gathered momentum in the early Arab environment, and then became an important Jewish preoccupation in
Muslim and Christian Spain and the countries to which Jews moved
from the Iberian Peninsula both before and after the 1492 expulsion. That is to say, while there were quite a number of non-Sephardic
Jewish alchemists as well, alchemy can be considered a Sephardic
Jewish specialization. In the following I propose to present briefly
and in a summary manner what I have found out about Sephardic
rabbis, scholars, and physicians who were alchemists, about several
unknown anonymous individuals of whom nothing is known except
that they were alchemists, as proven by the Hebrew manuscripts
they left behind, and about likewise unknown Jews of whom we
know only that they were the masters from whom Christian alchemists
acquired their knowledge of the "royal art."

However, before embarking upon this rapid historical voyage, a
few words, I believe, are in place on what alchemy is all about, since
the general conception, or rather misconception, of alchemy is that
it is nothing but a misguided and of necessity useless effort to transmute base metals into gold. The fact is that alchemy, as it reached
its full development in the Middle Ages, was a worldview and a philosophy which held that all forms of the mineral, vegetable, and animal world, including man, were but varied manifestations of one
identical basic substance. Underlying the innumerable forms contained in the physical world there must be a common essence, referred
to in Latin as the *quinta essentia*, or "quintessence," also known by
other names, such as "elixir of life" (*samma dihaya* in talmudic Aramaic),
which to find was one of the great aims of alchemy. The quintessence, once found, could be used to cure illness, give perpetual youth,
and transmute base metals into gold. However, since minerals were
believed to ripen gradually in the bosom of the earth until they
reached their most perfect form, that of gold, the alchemists also
believed that they could duplicate the process in the laboratory and
achieve in a few days or even hours that which in the body of the
earth took eons to transpire.

Much more could, and should, be said of alchemy, but these few

[2] Completed in *The Jewish Alchemists* (Princeton: Princeton University Press, 1994).

words will have to suffice to indicate that the alchemists, among whom were not only leading Jewish scholars of the Middle Ages and the Renaissance, but also such great minds as Newton and Goethe, were not misguided fools, but men of a serious, searching bent of mind intent on delving into the secrets of the natural world. And now to our Sephardic alchemists, whom we shall present in chronological order, and whom we shall let, occasionally at least, speak in their own words. I shall have to be very selective, for I have gathered material on some two dozen Sephardic alchemists who lived in the tenth to seventeenth centuries, and since I do not want this to be a dry catalogue, I shall have to concentrate on but a few of them.

Let me start with Bahya ibn Paquda, the famous Jewish religious philosopher who lived in Muslim Spain in the second half of the eleventh century. He wrote his major work, which assured his lasting fame, around 1080, in Arabic. It was translated into Hebrew by Judah ibn Tibbon in 1161, under the title *Hovot haLevavot*, or "Duties of the Heart," and had a profound influence on all subsequent Jewish moralistic-ethical literature, In chapter 4 of this book Bahya underpins his argument that the best way of life is to trust in God by comparing the life of the pious man who trusts in God with that of the alchemist, and enumerates the advantages of the first. While doing so, he paints a detailed picture of the work of the alchemist, and shows not only great familiarity with it, but also an unquestioning belief in the alchemist's ability to transmute base metals into gold. Moreover, the very fact that of all the possible careers open to talented individuals (including Jews) in Muslim Spain, he selects that of the alchemist as a foil to point up the superiority of putting one's trust in God, indicates that the work and social position of the alchemist were the most appealing and rewarding.

A younger contemporary of Bahya was Abraham ibn Ezra (1089–1164), one of the greatest figures of Spanish Jewry, of whom I wish to mention only in passing that an explanation he appends to Exodus 32:2 indicates clearly that he too believed in the reality of alchemical manipulation of gold.

When we come to the work of Moses de Leon, the greatest kabbalistic author of all times, who lived in Spain in the thirteenth century, we are faced with a rather complex situation. In both his magnum opus, the Zohar, and his small but important book, the *Sheqel haQodesh*, he repeatedly speaks of the various kinds of gold and other metals in a manner that leaves no doubt that he was well acquainted with alchemical practice and theory. He says, for instance, that "the glance of the sun and its power made the dust turn into gold,"[3] which is an unmistakable reference to the alchemical theory of the relationship between the sun and gold (the common *Deckname* in alchemy for gold was "sun"), and of the gradual maturation and ennobling of telluric elements into gold. De Leon also has much to say about the four elements of fire, air (which he calls wind), water, and earth (which he calls dust), and about the four properties of warmth, cold, dryness, and moisture, and discusses in detail how these factors go into the production of the four basic metals, gold, silver, copper, and iron, in the bosom of the earth[4]—all concepts and ideas figuring prominently in alchemical theory and practice. In his *Sheqel haQodesh* De Leon evinces familiarity with the alchemical practice of using copper as the base metal to be transmuted into gold, and lead for transmutation into silver, when he comments on the similarity between copper (which he calls *metal*) and gold, on the one hand, and that between lead and silver, on the other.[5] In passages such as these De Leon shows himself a true alchemist in the sense of having internalized the alchemical view of the universe and the genesis of earthly substances.

On the other hand, De Leon, with his genius for mysticism, infused every alchemical idea he borrowed from his cultural environment with a mystical meaning, a procedure which those out of sympathy with mysticism will call mystification. Thus the four primordial elements of fire, air, water, and dust are for him far from being simply what they were for the alchemists; they are "a mystery (*sod*) of faith: they are the fathers of all the worlds, and are the mystery of the supernal Holy Chariot. . . . They are a supernal mystery."[6] As for the element of air, which De Leon terms *ruah*, he makes full use of the opportunity given by the double meaning of this Hebrew word. For him the physical phenomenon of the *ruah*, the wind, which he characterizes as being hot and moist, has a mystical relationship to the *ruah*, the spirit, and he asserts as a basic axiom which needs no proofs that "if the *ruah* [spirit] were to be removed even for one moment, the soul could not exist." And, of course, this too is "a

---

[3] Zohar 1:249b–250a.
[4] Ibid. 2:23b–24a.
[5] *Sheqel haQodesh*, pp. 120–122.
[6] Ibid.

great mystery." In general, one is struck by De Leon's incessant use of the word *sod*, which means both "secret" and "mystery." He repeats many times, not only such formulations as "the supernal mystery of faith," "the mystery of supernal wisdom," but also phrases like "mystery of the four metals," "mystery of gold," "mystery of silver," and so forth.

A contemporary of De Leon was Gershon ben Shlomo of Arles, Provence, of whose work only one book, the *Sefer Sha'ar haShamayim* ("Book of the Gate of Heaven"), has survived. This book is a popular compilation summing up the sciences as was their status in the thirteenth century, including astronomy, meteorology, mineralogy, alchemy, zoology, botany, anatomy, physiology, medicine, as well as psychology, heredity, and theology. Gershon was widely read; he cites a great number of Greek, Latin, Arabic, and Jewish authors, and quotes many of them.

He discusses alchemy at length,[7] but peculiarly, does not identify the source from which he took his description. Several modern Jewish scholars have dealt with the *Sha'ar haShamayim* (there is even a full English translation of it), but none of them has even raised the question of the source of this passage. In the course of my own researches, I found that Gershon lifted his entire discussion of alchemy from an eleventh-century Hebrew book (preserved in manuscript in the London British Library) titled *Em haMelekh* ("Mother of the King"). Its *incipit* attributes it to a certain Abufalah the Saraqusti (i.e., of Syracuse, Sicily), who is credited also with the authorship of another work, *Sefer haTamar* ("Book of the Palm Tree"). Both of these books are preserved only in their Hebrew versions. However, numerous Arabisms and other signs in the text of *Em haMelekh* indicate that the Hebrew is a translation from the Arabic.

The *Em haMelekh* is an interesting composite work. It contains two entirely different parts. One is a folktale (or legend) telling how the Queen of Sheba acquired the philosophers' stone, came to visit King Solomon, and, seeing his great wisdom, entrusted the stone to him. The other part is pure alchemy; it tell about the influence of vapors on the telluric substances, including the metals, a description of the metals, of the properties of quicksilver, sulphur, minium, verdigris, saltpeter, naphtha, sal ammoniac, arsenic, vitriol, the processes of

---

[7] Venice, 1547 ed., pp. 9b–10b.

whitening and coloring, and, of course, the methods of transmuting copper into gold and silver, and of producing the "great theriac" (panacea, elixir). All in all, this manuscript is a good practical introduction to alchemical theory and practice as was their status in the eleventh century. The fact that such an Arabic work was translated into Hebrew at that time, and that it remained in circulation for centuries (this is shown by its utilization by Gershon ben Shlomo in the thirteenth century) is one testimony to the keen interest Jews had in alchemy.

That this interest was not merely theoretical, but that Jews actively engaged in the practice of alchemy, is shown by historical documents from the fourteenth century that survived in Spanish archives. From them we learn that in 1345 a certain "Magister Menaym [Menahem] Judaeus," who is described as "a great experimenter and necromancer," had to stand trial in Majorca for counterfeiting gold and silver. He seems to have been able to prove that the gold and silver he produced were the real thing, for a year later King Pedro IV of Majorca concluded an agreement with him concerning certain experiments and "*opera*," whose nature is not stated in the surviving royal letter patent, but which could have been nothing but alchemical in character. Magister Menahem became the personal physician of the king, as well as his confidant and master in alchemy and astrology.[8] Regrettably, this is all I have been able to find about Master Menahem, who, to judge from the contemporary documents, must have been the outstanding alchemist of his age in Majorca.

The second practicing Jewish alchemist of the period was Saracosa Samuel, one of the heads of the Jewish community of Perpignan, at the time under the rule of the same King Pedro IV, and his successor, King John I, who, like Pedro, was a patron of the arts and an aficionado of alchemy. On April 5, 1396, King John issued a decree addressed to "Saracosa Samuel, Jew of the city of Perpignan," and stating that "we concede to you that you have the right to, and can experiment with, the art of alchemy anywhere in our territories, without incurring anyone's penalty; you may freely use, and try through experimentation to the fullest degree, whatever you think fit in this art; you may fabricate each and every thing which is con-

---

[8] Cf. *Bolleti de la Societat Arqueologica Luliana* (Palma), January 1914, p. 6; Curita, *Los Cinco Libros*, vol. 2 (Saragossa, 1610), p. 389a.

sonant with, necessary to, and convenient in whatever manner to, the said art and to its practice and exercise."[9]

This document reveals a lot. It shows that alchemy was an honored profession among the Jews of Perpignan (and certainly elsewhere too), since otherwise they would not have elected an alchemist to be one of the heads of their community. It shows that the Jew Saracosa Samuel was considered a leading expert in the profession of alchemy, for otherwise the king would not have granted him such a comprehensive license, which, incidentally, threatens with royal "wrath and indignation" anybody who would dare put any obstacle in the way of Saracosa Samuel exercising his art. And it shows that crowned heads believed in the ability of masters of the "great art" to make gold, and, as in the case of King Pedro IV, were not averse to studying it, learning it from Jews, and practicing it.

Next we turn to the remarkable documentation of Jewish alchemical activity in the fourteenth century contained in the writings of Nicolas Flamel (ca. 1330–1418). Flamel was a Parisian scribe who became one of the most famous medieval French alchemists due to his autobiographical book, his claim that he had succeeded in producing large amounts of gold, and the endowments of churches and cemeteries for which he used his fortune. In his autobiographical *Hieroglyphic Figures*, begun in 1399 and completed in 1413 (in French), Flamel describes how years earlier he had acquired a "very old and very large gilded book," written in Latin and titled *Abraham the Jew. Prince, Priest, Levite, Astrologer and Philosopher to the Nation of the Jews Scattered by the Wrath of God in the Gaules* [France], *Salvation*. He describes in careful detail the contents of this work, and on that basis it is possible to determine that the book in question has been preserved in several manuscripts in various French libraries. The most important part of the book consists of seven symbolic pictures (it is these to which Flamel refers as "Hieroglyphic Figures"), and from the added explanations it becomes clear that they were to serve as pictorial guides to alchemical procedures. It is also clear that the extant manuscripts underwent considerable Christian and Christological reworking, although it is not clear whether this was the case with the manuscript that was in Flamel's hands or was done later.

---

[9] Antoni Rubio y Luch, *Documents per l'Historia de la Cultura Catalana Mig-eval* (Barcelona, 1921), 2:346–347. Translated from the Latin by Prof. Joseph Salemi.

In any case, the book made such an impression on Flamel that he decided to become an alchemist. He spent the next twenty-one years trying to understand the book and get its explanation from Parisian alchemists. When all this proved to be in vain, he decided, with the concurrence of his wife, Perrenelle, to whom he was greatly beholden, to go to Spain and "seek their interpretation from some Jewish Priest in some Synagogue." This piece of information indicates that by the late fourteenth century the fame of the alchemical expertise of Spanish Jews had spread to Paris, and that they were considered greater masters in it than the Parisian alchemists.

In Spain Flamel succeeded in his quest. In León he made the acquaintance of "a physician, Jewish by nation, but now a Christian, living in said León, who was very knowledgeable in the sublime sciences, called Master Canches [probably Sanchez]," who instantly recognized the sample pictures Flamel had brought. Master Canches agreed to explain the pictures to Flamel and even to accompany him back to France for that purpose. However, when they reached Orléans Master Canches fell ill and died. Fortunately for Flamel, while they were on the way he managed to learn enough from Canches to be able to continue studying the book, and another three years later (in 1382) he began a series of successful "projections," as he calls the transmutation of mercury first into silver, and then into gold. In this manner, Flamel writes, he acquired a fortune, and with it "built Churches, Cemeteries, and Hospitals" in Paris. Let me add in conclusion that, on the one hand, the actual source of Flamel's riches has remained a matter of contention among scholars down to the present day, and, on the other, that Flamel himself had by the eighteenth century acquired the reputation of being still alive thanks to the power of the philosophers' stone, the preparation of which he had learned from the book of Abraham the Jew.

A generation after Flamel lived R. Shim'on ben Tzemah Duran (1361–1444), a prolific and many-sided author who lived in Majorca, where he worked as a physician and surgeon, and later in Algiers, whose Jewish community elected him chief rabbi. One of Duran's most important books is his *Magen Avot* ("Shield of the Fathers"), an encyclopedic work treating astronomy, natural sciences, animal and human physiology and pathology, and psychology. In this book Duran manifests a thorough knowledge of alchemical theory and his unquestioning acceptance of it, while at the same time expressing himself critically on the alchemists' claim of being able to transmute base metals into precious ones. To quote only one passage from him, where De Leon attributed the transmutation of telluric substances into gold to the power of the sun, Duran attributes it to fire. He writes: "Were it not for the element of fire which ripens them, all the substances would remain like the potter's clay, but by reason of the element of fire they divest themselves of that form and assume other forms according to the nature of the mixture."

A younger contemporary of Duran was Abraham ben Shim'on of Worms (1369–ca. 1450), a magician and alchemist, who left behind a work titled *The Book of Sacred Magic which God gave to Moses, Aaron, David, Solomon & to Other Saints, Patriarchs & Prophets, which Teaches the true Divine Wisdom, Left by Abraham to Lamech His Son. Translated from the Hebrew 1458.* The book is not extant in Hebrew, only in the German and French translations (the date 1458 seems to refer to the year of the French translation), which contain some Christian and Christological additions. Since a Jew of Worms was probably an Ashkenazi, Abraham would have no place in the present context except for two factors. One is that he claims to have acquired his knowledge of the Secret Magic from a Jewish hermit by the name of Abramelin who lived in a desert location in Egypt, and whose faithful disciple Abraham became; and the other, that all of the many Hebrew words which appear in his book are transliterated according to the Sephardic pronunciation of Hebrew, which can be interpreted as indicating that he actually did learn what he knew from a Sephardic master in Egypt.

Jewish alchemical interest and activity continued unabated after the fourteenth century. In the fifteenth century, Solomon Trismosin, one of the most popular German Christian alchemists, claimed to have been a disciple in Italy of a Jewish alchemist, whose name he does not mention. In the same century Johanan Alemanno, who introduced Pico de la Mirandola to the Kabbalah, has some remarkable things to say about the possibility of "transmuting the whole world into silver and gold and precious stones." In the sixteenth century Shim'on Labi, a North African kabbalist, philologist, and liturgical poet, speaks about the common origin of all metals, and theorizes that the metals ripen in the bosom of the earth under the influence of the heat of the sun. In the same century Abraham Hamawi, a Moroccan rabbi and rain-maker, offers a method of transmuting lead into silver with the help of a mysterious herb. His contemporary, R. Joseph Taitazak, who lived in Salonika, terms alchemy "the divine science which enables the adepts to produce at will any of the seven metals." Also in the sixteenth century lived Hayyim Vital (1541–1648), one of the leading Safed kabbalists, who, according to his own testimony, devoted several years, first in his youth and then again in his old age, to alchemical work and experimentation, and wrote about it in detail. In the seventeenth century Leone Modena (1571–1648), the well-known Venetian rabbi and author, tells in his autobiography about the death of his uncle Shemaya due to alchemy, about his own work in alchemy, and about the death of his son Mordecai, at the young age of twenty-six, of poisoning as a result of protracted alchemical work with which he and his father were able to earn a thousand ducats in a year.

I conclude with a one-sentence summation: my research, in which much has still to be done, has convinced me that alchemy was a favorite and high-prestige occupation among the Jews, and especially among the Sephardic Jews, in the Middle Ages and for some two centuries thereafter, when Jewish alchemists occupied a position similar to that of Jewish physicians in Jewish and Gentile society and in royal and princely courts.

PART THREE

LITERATURE AND FOLKLORE

WHAT CONSTITUTES SEPHARDIC LITERATURE?

Norman Roth

University of Wisconsin (Madison)

Although my research is primarily on the culture of the Jews of medieval Spain (history, literature, philosophy, science), and, perhaps even worse, I am definitely of Ashkenazic background rather than Sephardic, it is possible that an "outsider" may bring some new insights to the field.

The question of what we mean by Sephardic literature (incidentally, I suggest we drop the archaic transliteration of "Sephardic" in conformity with modern transliteration rules) may at first glance seem to have an obvious answer.[1] However, upon reflection it will be seen that it is not obvious at all.

First of all, it has to do very much with what we mean by "Sephardim" in the first place. The origin of the term we all know; it comes from the Bible, Obadiah 20, and the term was applied in the medieval period to Spain. However, only a few Jews in Spain, and then mostly in the late medieval period, referred to themselves as Sephardim. Basically, the term refers to those Jews who left Spain, at whatever period, to settle in other lands, carrying with

---

[1] There is no bibliography of Sephardic literature, even if we confine the term to Ladino literature. The best one can do is to consult bibliographies of Ladino books, which include many religious, legal, and other nonfiction works: Meyer Kayserling, *Biblioteca española-portugueza-judaica* (Strasbourg, 1891; reprint ed. with additions and corrections, New York, 1971); H.V. Besso, *Ladino Books in the Library of Congress* (Washington, 1963; essentially the same list appeared as "Bibliography of Judeo-Spanish Books in the Library of Congress," *Miscelánea de estudios árabes y hebraicos* 8 [1960]: 55 ff.; cf. also *Bulletin hispanique* 54 [1952]: 412–422); Abraham Yaari, *Sifrey Ladino* (Jerusalem: Jewish National Library, 1934). M. Studemund, *Bibliographie zum Judenspanischen* (Hamburg, 1975) is helpful only for the *romanceros*, etc., while the bibliography of Marius Sala, published as part of a series described as "state-of-the art reports," is inadequate, comprising perhaps less than a fourth of the published works, *Le judéo-espagnol* (Paris, 1976). It is the only one which attempts to deal with history, literature and language, however. There is no book which offers even an adequate introduction to the total topic of Sephardic culture and history. The best of a bad lot is Raymond Renard, *Sepharad* (Mons, 1966), one of the works ignored by Sala.

them their uniquely Spanish traditions, and then also to the descendants of those Jews.

Obvious, you say? Not at all. Almost every history dealing with
Sephardim, almost every work dealing with aspects of Sephardic
literature or language, and certainly modern works dealing with
aspects of Sephardic culture or religion, automatically include all
the Jews of Iran, Iraq, North Africa, and sometimes even Egypt.
Only a minority of writers in Israel have chosen to use the more
appropriate term 'edot ha-mizrah to refer to these Jewish communities, for which they often come under severe attack from ill-informed
Sephardic apologists. The fact is that only a very small minority
of the Jews of these countries could conceivably be described as
Sephardim.

At the other end of the spectrum are those communities which
historically did have more or less significant Sephardic populations
which today have nearly been forgotten. Among these are the communities of Germany, India, the Caribbean, South Africa, and isolated but nonetheless important communities in Eastern Europe. For
that matter, only recently has there been any substantial interest in
the Sephardic Jewish communities of Bulgaria, and the generally
informative book by Vicki Tamir is unfortunately marred by the
mistaken impression that all the Jews of Bulgaria, virtually, were
Sephardim.[2] On the other hand, we still await a solid monographic
treatment of the Sephardic Jews of Yugoslavia. Most amazingly, the
work on the Jews of Turkey, with the exception of a few fine articles, is deplorably sloppy.

Lest what I am saying here sound like the trivial carping of an
overly pedantic historian, let me call your attention to a recent work
which I am sure most of you have received, if not actually read,
Rabbi Herbert C. Dobrinsky's recent book, *A Treasury of Sephardic
Laws and Customs*.[3] Certainly there is a desperate need for such a

---

[2] Vicki Tamir, *Bulgaria and Her Jews* (New York, 1979). The most serious prob-
lem is that the author makes no distinction between Bulgaria and the Ottoman
Empire, so that most of the information in the book is on the Jews of Sofia and
Constantinople, not Bulgaria.

[3] (Hoboken, N.J., and New York, 1988). This is apparently the only study of its
kind, in any language, however unsatisfactory. Since the rabbi did not mention,
nor even include in his bibliography, the most important and widely used work
of Sephardic halakhah, let me call attention here to Joseph Hayyim, *Ben ish hay*
(Jerusalem, 1957; my copy, at least; I believe there are other editions), and also
his *'Od Yosef hay* (Jerusalem, 1949/50).

work, particularly one which takes into consideration the wealth of important Sephardic halakhic texts. Unfortunately, this book is not that study. Forgetting for the moment the numerous errors and omissions, the focus of the book is what I wish to mention, for the introduction says it is concerned with "preserving the heritage" of four groups of Sephardic Jews in America: Syrian, Moroccan, "Judeo-Spanish" (from the Balkans), and "Spanish-Portuguese" from Amsterdam. Never mind, for the moment, that this ignores the heritage of a good many Sephardic Jews in America who originate from none of these places; in fact a majority of the customs (there is very little of "law" in the book) are from Syria and Morocco. They reflect not Sephardic traditions at all, but the traditions of the indigenous Jewish populations of those two countries.

The same sort of problem is frequently encountered in studies purporting to deal with the history, language, and literature or even folklore of such communities. Little or no effort is made to distinguish truly Sephardic culture from that of the non-Sephardic *majority* culture of these communities, nor is there much of an attempt to take cognizance of such things as the "corrupting influence," if you will, of the French Jewish impact on North Africa, through the activities of the Alliance Israélite Universelle schools, for example. In the areas of literature and language, little or no effort has been made to distinguish and analyze Arabic influences on Sephardic patterns, and none whatsoever has been given to the undoubted influence of modern Spanish.

The second problem which confronts us is also one which may seem to be obvious, and that is what we mean by "literature." In addition to my research on the history, philosophy, and other aspects of the culture of the Jews of medieval Spain, I also do a considerable amount of work on medieval Hebrew poetry and literature. Thus I became aware early on of the shocking lack of understanding, particularly among Israeli scholars, of what constitutes literature. In fact, this is a problem which goes back to the last century in Jewish scholarship. Moritz Steinschneider, for example, that indefatigable scholar to whom all medievalists of whatever culture are forever indebted, wrote his magnificent study of "Jewish literature" and included every conceivable type of writing from biblical commentaries to science to poetry, etc. David Kaufmann wrote a more specialized book on "Hebrew literature of the Middle Ages," actually a collection of papers, in which not a single one dealt with any work which possibly could be considered "literature."

One could multiply such examples endlessly, to the point of the absurd suggestion made by a widely recognized scholar in the *Encyclopaedia Judaica* that any work written by a Jew in any language should be considered "Hebrew literature"; not Jewish literature, mind you, but Hebrew literature. Thus, Einstein's work on the theory of relativity must rank as one of the great masterpieces of modern Hebrew literature!

Such, obviously, is not my understanding of what is meant by "literature." I rather understand by this term what I believe the world generally does; creative or imaginative narrative, whether prose or rhyme, which is essentially fictional.

Given this not entirely too technical definition, but one which I think we can work with, it now becomes our task to consider what we mean when we refer to "Sephardic literature." When one turns, again, to the work that has been done in the field, it becomes all too obvious what so far has been meant by the term. Without getting into the ridiculous debate over the attempt to force the use of the highly questionable expression "Judezmo" on certain Sephardic dialects, generally the word "Ladino" is what has been used to describe Sephardic literature.[4]

While I do not, indeed, want to get into the linguistic debate, suffice it to say that the term "Ladino" is quite authentic, and has a history which goes back to early medieval Arabic, where *latino* meant "Romance," and so it was used already in Hebrew, by Moses Ibn 'Ezra, for example. In the fifteenth century we find the term *ladino* employed at least by *converso* authors. Thus, Diego de Valera, an important chronicler, reports that during the siege of Malaga in 1487 a certain Muslim from the city who came to the Christian camp with the intention of killing the king and queen "could not

---

[4] Note that Haïm Vidal Séphiha, for example, describes Ladino as "judéo-espagnol-calque," a "dead" language limited to the period prior to 1620, and so-called Judezmo as a "living" vernacular ("Hispanité de Ladino," in *Hispania Judaica*, ed. Josep M. Solà-Solé et al. [Barcelona, 1984], vol. 3, pp. 87–88; cf. also his *Le Ladino, judéoespagnol calque* [Paris, 1973]). David Bunis, one of the strongest advocates of "Judezmo," incorrectly writes in the same collection that Ladino is restricted to "that special calque variety of Judezmo [!] used in translating sacred or liturgical Hebrew (-Aramaic) texts." He further adds that it has only been reported "in a small number of Ottoman communities," an equally false statement (ibid., p. 11, n. 3). David L. Gold is the most dogmatic; for a typical statement of his views, see his "Myths About the Glottonym *Judezmo*," *Jewish Language Review* 4 (1984): 126–141. Errors are obvious.

speak *ladino*"; i.e., Romance.[5] The *converso* poet Antón de Montoro, at the same period, writes about two drunks, one of whom was his servant, speaking incoherently, which he expresses by saying they were speaking "Latin, Hebrew, Chaldean [Aramaic], and all of it bad *ladino*," i.e., Romance.[6]

I do not know when the first use of the term "Ladino" is found in a text of that dialect, but Moseh Altaras, a Sephardic rabbi of Venice, published in 1609 the *Libro de mantenimento de la alma*, a translation of Joseph Caro's *Shulhan ha-Panim*, and in his prologue said that it was translated into *ladino* because many now know no other language.

Contrary to the claims of so-called "authorities," however, Ladino is neither dead nor was it used exclusively for translations of Hebrew works (note, incidentally, that even Caro's book can hardly be described as "liturgical"). Modern twentieth-century authors, in fact, continued to employ the term "Ladino," and not "Judezmo," on the title-pages or introductions to their works. Nor is it correct that the term "Judeo-español," or "Judeo-Spanish," is a "pseudo-scientific term, imposed on the [Sephardic] community from without," as David Bunis has written.[7] A mere glance at the titles of Ladino books in Besso's bibliography, for example, reveals the terms "Gudeo-espaniol" and "Zudeo-espaniol" (note such other terms as "Espaniol" and "Sephardit"). On the other hand, not one single book catalogued either by Kayserling or by Besso has the term "Judezmo," which in fact is a proper term only for the spoken vernacular chiefly of the Balkan countries in the modern period only.

It will come as no news to this audience, of course, that there has been a tremendous "Ashkenazic bias" in Jewish history and culture, dating indeed to the initial contacts between Ashkenazim and Sephardim in Renaissance Italy, and particularly in Turkey, with later manifestations of intolerance on the part of both communities in Amsterdam and elsewhere. With the single exception of halakhah (one could hardly ignore the contributions of Joseph Caro, Jacob Berav, and others), and even that limited almost entirely to the sixteenth-

---

[5] *Crónica de los reyes católicos*, ed. Juan de Mata Carriazo (Madrid, 1927), p. 258.
[6] Antón de Montoro, *Poesía completa*, ed. Marithelma Costa (Cleveland, 1990), p. 61.
[7] Bunis, loc. cit. (this reflects also the views of Séphiha). See the bibliographies cited in n. 1 above.

century scholars, there has been little interest in Sephardic culture
until the present day.

It is, therefore, almost entirely due to the interest of Spanish writers and scholars that the field of Sephardic studies emerged at all.
Reports by Spanish travelers as early as the sixteenth century of the
nearly perfect archaic medieval Spanish still spoken by Jews in Turkey
or parts of North Africa aroused the imagination of linguists and
the romantic curiosity of the general public in Spain. By the nineteenth century great Spanish scholars such as Menéndez Pelayo were
already making significant contributions to the exploration of the
Spanish language and literature of the Sephardim. The major nov-
elist of that era, Pérez Galdós, spent a mere nine days in Tangiers,
where it has been surmised that he picked up something of the
Sephardic dialect. In addition, he was probably influenced by the
recent important work of Angel Pulido Martín on the Sephardim,
and in any case soon began depicting Sephardic life in his novels.[8]

Rodolfo Gil compiled his anthology *Romancero Judeo-Español* in 1911,
and some other work was done, culminating finally in the important work of Menéndez Pidal, now being continued by his grandson, and Manuel Alvar and other Spanish scholars. This in turn
stimulated the important research of Armistead and Silverman and
what may be termed their "school" in this country, the work of some
French Jewish scholars, and a few in Israel and other countries.

The point is that the concentration has been exclusively, or almost
so, on Ladino literature, and in fact almost entirely on ballads or
"*romanceros.*" To such an extent has been this concentration that
otherwise-informed scholars like Séphiha and Bunis can write that
Ladino was only used for the "translation" (not even original composition is recognized) of purely liturgical works and Bibles! The very
existence of Ladino secular literature is not even suspected by such
scholars, and this in spite of the exhaustive bibliographical researches
of Kayserling, Besso, and Yaari. Of course, it is perhaps not so surprising that scholars pay little or no attention to these bibliographies
when one discovers that the published catalogue of the Sephardic
Reference Room of Yeshiva University's library, presumably the fore-

---

[8] See Robert Ricard, *Etudes hispano-africaines* (Tetuán, 1956), p. 178 (it should be
noted that Galdós's interest in Sephardim goes back to his early novel *Gloria* [1876],
however). Pulido's work referred to is *Españoles sin patria, y la raza sefardi* (Madrid,
1905); see on him especially Manuel L. Ortega, *Figuras ibéricas, el doctor Pulido* (Madrid,
1922), pp. 259–283 and 325 ff.

most research center in the field in this country, does not even list any of them![9]

Yet another problem, and one would think this would be obvious to Sephardic scholars, is that we must distinguish carefully between Ladino and Spanish. The former, of course, refers to Spanish written in Hebrew characters. No one speaks, or ever has spoken, Ladino; the spoken language, however dialectical it may be, is Spanish. Yet one still hears not only ordinary people refer to "speaking" Ladino, one finds references to Ladino in scholarly literature as a "language" in the spoken sense.

Worse errors occur, however, in failing to identify (possibly because the author has not actually examined) works which are written in Spanish, and not Ladino. This was apparently the case, for example, in Tamir's previously cited book on the Jews of Bulgaria, where she talks about a "Ladino periodical," and yet elsewhere says that it was printed in Spanish and read by non-Jews.[10] If it was Ladino, it could not have been read by non-Jews, of course. I have also seen other references to works as being in Ladino when in fact they are in Spanish, or even in Hebrew with perhaps a Ladino title. Indeed, there is a tendency sometimes to refer to Ladino as the supposedly "dialectical" Spanish of Sephardic Jews. A word of caution here about such generalizations. Not only is modern Spanish marked by a great deal of dialectic variation in different regions of the country, but so also were medieval and "Golden Age" Spanish. Very little research has been done on this, and in fact we are far from having even an adequate understanding of "standard" medieval Spanish. All of this should serve as a caution to those attempting to consider the dialectic nature of Spanish among Sephardim. Such research must be done in close collaboration with a variety of experts on general Spanish dialect.

To turn again to the question at hand, what constitutes Sephardic literature, it would appear that the experts have given little or no thought to the issue. Thus, Iacob Hassan has stated, for example,

---

[9] Yeshiva University (New York), Sephardic Reference Room, Jacob E. Safra Institute of Sephardic Studies, Unified Catalogue (mimeographed, 1982). It should be noted that this is so far the only attempt at any such bibliography, although unfortunately very inadequate.

[10] *Bulgaria and Her Jews*, pp. 109, 270, n. 253. Similarly, in Gibraltar in 1843 was published the Ladino newspaper *Ha-Mazkir*, but was the periodical *Esperanza Israelitica* in Spanish or Ladino?

that Sephardic literature must be considered only as that written in Judeo-Spanish, from the time of the Expulsion until recent decades.[11] Yet there are obvious problems with this. First of all, why should only Judeo-Spanish writing *after* the Expulsion be considered, but not that of medieval Spain? Indeed, would not our understanding of the development of both spoken Spanish and written Ladino among Sephardim after the Expulsion benefit greatly from careful study of Judeo-Spanish and of Spanish writing by Jews in medieval Spain?

Secondly, and this is the point of my present remarks, by what logic should Sephardic literature be limited only to Judeo-Spanish?

It would seem apparent that this hitherto-unchallenged definition of Sephardic literature is the result of two obvious factors. One of these we have already discussed, and that is the fact that the entire field of research was introduced by non-Jewish scholars and, at least in the area of literature (which is to say almost exclusively poetry and ballads), is even today dominated by scholars whose only training is in Spanish literature and language. They have no interest whatever in, and no knowledge of, Hebrew poetry and literature, for example.

The second factor is a purely historical one. The Sephardic Jews after the Expulsion did, in fact, compose secular poems and ballads in Ladino and did also translate religious and liturgical works, including the Bible, into Ladino. The first land of Sephardic settlement after 1492 (discounting, of course, those Spanish Jews who already had gone to North Africa, Italy, Crete, and elsewhere even in the previous century) was Italy. It is interesting to observe that, aside from some well-known Bible translations, prayerbooks, etc., the only Ladino works published in Italy were Joseph Caro's previously mentioned work in Ladino translation (Venice, 1609, 1712–13); a translation of Jacob Berav, *Zimrat ha-ares* (Mantua, 1745; Livorno, 1820); Isaac de Moses de Fas, *Sefer me'irat 'einayim* (Livorno, 1753); and Joseph Farhi, *Sefer aligoriah di Purim* (Livorno, 1875, 1902). Nothing else! All these, it will be noted, were religious or quasi-religious works.

Yet Italy was the center of the Renaissance precisely at the time not only of the initial arrival of Jews expelled from Spain and Portugal, but of a more or less continuous influx of "Marranos" from Portugal during the sixteenth century. Thanks to the important research of

---

[11] "Vision panorámica de la literatura sefardí," in the above-cited collected papers *Hispania Judaica*, vol. 2, p. 27.

Hayyim Schirmann, we know that the Spanish Hebrew secular poetic tradition was continued, if somewhat impoverished, in Italy. The rise of Hebrew drama in that country was also almost certainly influenced by the development of modern drama in Spain, with the famous *Celestina*, the work of at least two *conversos*, which incidentally was translated into Hebrew by Joseph b. Samuel Sarfati, the famous doctor and son of the physician of Pope Julius II. The Hebrew translation, however incomplete and poorly done, of the popular Spanish novel *Amadís de Gaula* is another example of the continued influence of Spanish literature, as is, of course, the translation of Cervantes.[12] All of these works, as well as the poetry and plays of numerous Jewish writers in Italy not only in the Renaissance but up to the modern period, must be examined carefully for inclusion in our broader understanding of Sephardic literature.

One of the difficulties, of course, and this applies equally to the Hebrew and even, possibly, the Judeo-Arabic literature of other countries, such as Turkey and the North African lands, is that the few scholars who have written anything at all concerning this literature have shown little or no interest in determining the cultural background of the authors. One cannot assume that any author is a Sephardi, of course, without convincing evidence. For this reason, it is absolutely essential that future research make careful and thorough use of historical documentation as well as the literary sources.

In the above cases, we know certainly that Joseph Sarfati and the other translators were Sephardim (the family name Sarfati, incidentally, was a common one in medieval Spain).

Such is also the case with Judah Zarco of Rhodes, author of an important Hebrew *maqamah*, or rhymed prose work of fiction, recently reprinted but totally ignored by scholars.[13]

In Amsterdam one of the very few Hebrew works produced by Sephardim was a translation of the Erasto tradition of the "Seven

---

[12] On Sarfati's (lost) translation of *Celestina*, see M.D. Cassuto, "Me-shirey Yosef ben Shmuel Sarfaty," in *Jewish Studies in Memory of G.A. Kohut* (New York, 1936), pp. 124–128. Schirmann's important studies on Hebrew poetry and, especially, drama in Italy are now conveniently assembled in his (posthumous) *Le-toldot ha-shirah ve-ha-dramah ha-ʿivrit* (Jerusalem, 1979), vol. 2. The Hebrew translation of *Amadís de Gaula* has been edited by Zvi Malachi (Tel Aviv, 1981); see my review in *AJS Newsletter* 31 (1982): 19.

[13] *Sefer lehem Yehudah*, photo reprint with introduction by A.M. Habermann (Jerusalem, 1970).

Sages" literature by the chief rabbi (17th cent.), Isaac Uziel.[14] This, too, deserves further study.

The difficulty of determining the Sephardic background of authors is particularly evident with regard to poetry. In medieval Spain, for example, I have been able to discover the names of over 150 Hebrew poets, and for many of these we have a considerable amount of information. Schirmann has estimated that there were about the same number of Hebrew poets in Italy, and yet we know next to nothing about most of them. This is also true of those who wrote in Italian, most of whom, but perhaps not all, were "Italianate" Jews and not Sephardim. Such was the case with the famous Rachel Morpurgo, a member of the Luzzatto family. However, was the equally fascinating (though hardly known) poetess Deborah Ascarelli "Italian" or Sephardic? Why is there no study of her, much less an edition of her work?[15]

With Turkey and the Ottoman Empire we come, surprisingly, to even more serious problems. In spite of the fact that a tremendous amount has been written on this subject, most of it is superficial and of little value (the few exceptions being articles by such scholars as Heyd, Hacker, Benayahu, and some few others). The oft-cited books of Abraham Galante, for example, are nearly worthless, as are other monographic studies, including volumes of collected papers. In many respects the most useful work of all remains that of Solomon Rosanes, although there are numerous errors and the volumes are extremely scarce.

The main difficulty, among many, with the research so far in this

---

[14] *Mishley Erasto*, ed. Abraham Elmaleh (Jerusalem, 1945). See his "Una traducción hebraica de los proverbios de Erasto," *Sefarad* 6 (1946): 95–108, and "Les Proverbes d'Erasto," in *Les cahiers de l'Alliance Israélite Universelle* (supplement to *Mahberet*) 14 (1960): 244 ff.

[15] On Morpurgo there is the work, which I have not seen, of Nina Salaman, *Rachel Morpurgo and Contemporary Hebrew Poetry of Italy* (1924). On Deborah Ascarelli, see briefly M. Cassuto, "Bibliografia delle traduzioni giudeoéitaliane della bibbia," in *Festscrhift Armand Kaminka* (Vienna, 1937), pp. 139 ff. (article: pp. 129–141). For Hebrew poetry in Italy, etc., see generally Schirmann, *Mivhar ha-shirah ha-'ivrit be-Italiah* (1934; recent reprint ed.); A.B. Rhine, "Secular Hebrew Poetry of Italy," *Jewish Quarterly Review*, n.s. 1, pp. 341 ff. and 2, pp. 25 ff.; Leon Weinberger, ed., *Jewish Poets in Crete* (Cincinnati, 1985). General surveys of Hebrew literature focusing on Italy include Simon Bernfeld, *Storia della letteratura ebraica*, trans. Enzo Sereni (Turin, 1926), and Umberto Cassuto, *Storia della letteratura ebraica postbiblica* (Florence, 1938). Not to be overlooked either are Steinschneider's important articles (see his bibliography in *Festschrift... Moritz Steinschneider* [Leipzig, 1896; photo reprint, Jerusalem, 1970], vol. 1, p. xxiv, no. 14 and p. xxxiii, no. 49).

area is that it has focused almost exclusively either on the economic conditions of Jewish communities or on the history of rabbis and their works. There is also precious little that deals with periods beyond the eighteenth century. To date, there has not been one single study of the literature or poetry of Jews in the Ottoman Empire or Turkey, excluding again those done strictly of Ladino (or "Judezmo," if you must) ballads. The one Hebrew poet who has received some attention is Israel Najara, the importance of whom was already pointed out by Rosanes.[16]

In addition to Najara, other major poets of the sixteenth century mentioned by Rosanes include Nissim Ibn Sanji, Sa'adyah Longo, and our previously mentioned Judah Zarco.[17]

Another major question which remains to be explored is whether Jews wrote works in the vernacular in Turkey, Bulgaria, Greece, etc. Undoubtedly the answer must be in the affirmative; at least in the case of Bulgaria, in the modern era, we know this to be so. To the extent that any such literary production, poetry, fiction, drama, was done by Sephardic authors, they also should become a part of the investigation of Sephardic literature. With regard to Bulgaria, it would seem that not even the Ladino work of Sephardic authors has received any serious attention. Tamir mentions, for example, Aaron Menachemov, an important modern playwright, and Yosef Papo, a poet. I have been unable to discover any information on either of them.

Other significant Sephardic writers of the sixteenth through the eighteenth centuries who merit more attention than they have so far received, which is to say virtually none, include David Abenatar Melo, a Marrano who was tortured in Madrid, and went finally to Germany, where he became rabbi of Frankfurt. There in 1626 he composed a poetic paraphrase of the Psalms in Spanish. Daniel Israel López Laguna of Portugal, who lived for a time in France and then in Spain, where he also suffered at the hands of the Inquisition,

---

[16] See, e.g., Israel Davidson, "Shirey tiqvah min *Sherit Yisrael* le-R' Yisrael Najarah," in *Sefer ha-yovel le-Shmuel Krauss* (Jerusalem, 1936), pp. 193–210; Aaron Mirsky, "'Eseret shirim le-R' Yisrael Najarah," in *Ish ha-Torah ve-ha-ma'aseh* (*Moses Ostrovsky Jubilee Volume*) (Jerusalem, 1946), pp. 125–132, and "Shirey geulah le-R' Yisrael Najarah," *Isaiah Sonne Memorial Volume* (*Sefunot* 5 [1961]), pp. 207–234.

[17] Rosanes, *Divrey yemey Yisrael be-Togarmah* (Hosietin[?], 1914), vol. 3, pp. 22–23. On Najara, see also pp. 304 ff. Excerpts of poems by Longo, Zarco, Najara, and others such as Joseph Bibas, with English translations, may be found in T. Carmi, *Penguin Book of Hebrew Verse* (New York, 1981), pp. 460 ff. (unfortunately, he does not indicate his sources).

going finally to Jamaica where he embraced Judaism, was another who composed a Spanish version of the Psalms. Duarte Gómez, or Solomon Usque, translated Petrarch into Spanish and wrote plays.[18] Antonio Enríquez Gómez, poet and philosopher of Portuguese origin, poet, philosopher and playwright, escaped to Rouen, where he lived as a Jew and published his plays. He has recently been the subject of considerable study.

Moses Mendes of England (d. 1758) and the poet Abraham López-Penha of Curaçao, who in 1887 settled in Colombia, are examples of those whose work needs further investigation.[19] In modern Latin America, of course, one has to be very careful, inasmuch as there are poets or authors who write in Spanish and have adopted Spanish names, and yet are not Sephardim but European Ashkenazim. The same is obviously true in Israel, where many Ashkenazic Jews have taken Sephardic-sounding names.

The Netherlands, and particularly Amsterdam, was unquestionably the site of the most productive development in literature by Sephardic Jews, primarily those who had been Christians and were descendants of Jews of Spain and Portugal. Their knowledge of Judaism was virtually nil, as they fled the threat of the Inquisition to seek freedom in one of the few places willing to grant them, if certainly not "tolerance," at least a measure of liberty. They knew little or no Hebrew, of course, and this is reflected in the literature which they produced, which was almost entirely in Portuguese or Spanish (not Ladino).

The most famous was, of course, Daniel Lévi, or Miguel de Barrios as he is better known, whose mother, Sara, was a member of the famous Valle family originally of Catalonia. Miguel was born in Montilla in Spain, and the family then lived in Portugal and in Algiers. His work, all written in Amsterdam, was entirely in Spanish.[20]

---

[18] Very brief and inconsequential information may be found on some of these in Cecil Roth, *A History of the Marranos* (Philadelphia, 1932), pp. 329–332. Translations of one or two poems may be found reproduced in Nathan Ausubel and Marynn Ausubel, *A Treasury of Jewish Poetry* (New York, 1957), pp. 286 (Melo), 279 (Antonio Enríquez Gómez).

[19] See ibid., pp. 40, 421, 422 (Mendes) and 233 (López-Penha).

[20] The writings of de Barrios are discussed extensively in various volumes of *Hebraische Bibliographie* (1, 2, 6, 7). Some of his poetry is translated in the important work of Timothy Oleman, *Marrano Poets of the 17th Century* (1979); see also his "Contra la verdad no hay fuerza," trans. in Moshe Lazar, ed., *The Sephardic Tradition* (New York, 1972). See especially I.S. Révah, "Les escrivains Manuel de Pina et Miguel

In spite of the importance, at least quantitatively, of the literary output of the Sephardim of Amsterdam, there is still no attempt to deal with this subject. Even though the scholarly work on the history of the Jews of the Netherlands in general, and of Amsterdam in particular, is generally vastly superior to that so far done on Turkey and the Balkan region, it also concentrates on religious and economic factors. For that reason, it may be well here to at least give the names of a few of the more outstanding Sephardic authors. These include Jacob Israel Belmonte, co-founder of the first synagogue, who wrote poetry attacking the Inquisition. One of his sons, Manuel, founded a Marrano poetic academy at Amsterdam.[21]

Mosseh Pinto Delgado is fairly well known, and is the only poet aside from de Barrios to have merited significant study.[22]

Others who bear investigation include doña Isabel Henriques, greatly admired as a Christian writer in Madrid, who became a Jew in Amsterdam and continued to write poetry.

David Franco Mendes is another poet who is now better known, thanks to the work of Melkman.[23] Of course, to some extent even Menasseh ben Israel may be included in the list of literary figures.

Unfortunately, it appears that the less romantic period of Dutch Jewish history beyond the seventeenth century has received far less attention, again with the exception of some purely socioeconomic historical studies. Therefore, at the present time we can only guess at what may remain to be discovered of Sephardic literary and poetic contributions in the modern era.

From Amsterdam we should turn our attention to Belgium and to the Sephardic communities of Germany and even Austria, for example, to say nothing of the "New World." Surely here, as well as in England, there were examples of literature and poetry produced through the years. We have, however, little or no information about them. For example, there is still, disgracefully, no decent history of American Jewish literature. The few anthologies and attempts

---

de Barrios," *Otzar yehudei Sefarad* (so the Library of Congress spelling), vol. 8, pp. lxxiv ff. of the vernacular section; and Kenneth Scholberg, "Miguel de Barrios and the Amsterdam Sephardic Community," *Jewish Quarterly Review* 53 (1962): 120–159, and his *La poesía religiosa de Miguel de Barrios* (Ohio State University Press, sans anno).

[21] Information on these writers chiefly in Kayserling, *Biblioteca española-portugueza-judaica*.

[22] The bibliography is fairly extensive; I shall be glad to send it to anyone interested.

[23] Joseph Melkman (Michman), *David Franco Mendes: A Hebrew Poet* [Hebrew] (Jerusalem, 1952; and also Amsterdam, 1952 [English?]).

at such a history have predictably focused on Henry Roth, Saul
Bellow, and even Philip Roth—to say nothing of such great Jewish
"writers" as Groucho Marx, no less! We may recall that Emma
Lazarus was a Sephardic Jew, but aside from the memorable verses
on the Statue of Liberty, what does anyone know of her work?

Let us consider also North Africa. While the Judeo-Spanish ballads and folklore have been studied *ad nauseum*, practically nothing
is known of the Hebrew poetry of North African Jews. Only recently
has some important research begun.[24] It is clear from even so
unscientific investigation as merely glancing at the names of poets
that many of them were, in fact, Sephardim, and yet this simple
fact has not been recorded, much less has this poetry been considered part of Sephardic literature. Further research in this area is
certainly essential.

Perhaps even more surprising is the apparently total lack of interest, or nearly so, in literature produced by Sephardim in Israel.
David Altabe did his doctoral dissertation on the Sephardic novel,
but aside from that I am unaware of a single study, in this country
or in Israel.

This is perhaps less surprising when we realize that not one single
study, whether it is one volume or a multivolume series, of the history
of modern Hebrew literature (Zinberg, Waxman, or the more recent
critical essays of Kurzweil or Shaked, for instance) even mentions
Sephardim or discusses the work of a single Sephardic author! Thus
not only schoolchildren but even potential scholars in the field are
taught that modern Hebrew literature began in Russia, Lithuania, and
Galicia and then magically jumped across to Israel, where the Eastern
European immigrants and their children continued the tradition.

One could reasonably argue, I would submit, that not only the
deteriorated status of Sephardic culture, subjected to innumerable
forms of discrimination, but also the deterioration of the quality of
Hebrew literature and poetry today in Israel is due in no small measure to this failure to take cognizance of the *totality* of the Jewish
experience, of the *totality* of Hebrew literature and its traditions.

The suggestion which I am making here is, therefore, simple: that

---

[24] Notably in the work of Haim Zafrani; see, e.g., his *Poésie juive en Occident musulman* (Paris, 1977); pt. 2 of *Etudes et recherches sur la vie intellectuelle juive au Maroc*. To
be sure, this focuses on Morocco, and there is no comparable research on Tunisia
or Algeria.

future research on Sephardic literature not concentrate exclusively
on the Judeo-Spanish variety but include whatever has been written
by Sephardim in any language. Furthermore, it is obvious that a
special effort needs to be made to recover Hebrew poetry and literature by Sephardim particularly, and to ensure that this receives
its proper place in the overall history of Hebrew literature.

Suggestions for future Research

The purpose of this paper has been to expand our understanding
of what we mean by "Sephardic literature." Of course, it is entirely
possible that specialists in the field will choose to ignore these suggestions and continue in the narrowly conservative position that
Sephardic literature is only what is written in a so-called dead language, Ladino. Such a decision would, I believe, be unfortunate.

For those who may decide to pursue the alternatives suggested
here, let me suggest some paths for possible research.

With respect to Hebrew literature and poetry written by Sephardim,
inasmuch as not one single study has ever been written on the subject, this is truly virgin territory. Every effort will have to be made
to determine who among the Hebrew writers of a particular country
were, or are, Sephardim. Careful study of relevant historical works
concerning a particular land or city may prove beneficial, although,
as already mentioned, few of the historical writers bother to mention secular literature at all. The extant catalogues of Hebrew books
and manuscripts, and particularly those dealing with printing in a
specific city or country, must be carefully analyzed.[25]

For works by Sephardic authors in other vernacular languages,
such as Spanish, Portuguese, Italian, French, the task is even more
difficult. Little work has so far been done on Jewish writers in these
languages, and it is all of very poor quality. Here it may be most

---

[25] Again, I will be glad to assist any inquiries for bibliographic specifics. Generally, consult such work as A. Yaari, *Defus ha-'ivry be-mizrah* (Jerusalem, 1936), and
his "Defus ha-'ivry be-Izmir," *Areshet* 1 (1958): 97–223; Abraham S. Yahuda, *Defus
ha-'ivry be-Qushta* (Jerusalem, 1967), with additions by Yaari in *Areshet* 5 (1972): 457–
493; Leo Fuchs, "Amsterdam: Hebrew Printing," *European Judaism* 5 (1971): 17–20,
and Herbert Zafren, "Amsterdam, Center of Hebrew Printing in the 17th Century,"
Jewish Book Annual 35 (1977): 47–55; L. Fuks and R.G. Fuks-Mansfield, *Hebrew
Typography in the Northern Netherlands, 1585–1815*, 2 vols. (1984, 1987).

useful to work cooperatively with specialists in particular areas of the relevant literature, who may perhaps be able to assist in identifying possible Sephardic authors. Generally, more cooperative research than currently is reflected in Jewish studies in any area would be a welcome novelty.

Finally, it seems to me that we are missing a tremendous opportunity in field research. I refer to the kind of thing which so far has only been done, and that on a limited scale, with respect to the Ladino ballads: personal interviews with Sephardim from various countries. Were such research expanded to include discussions of the whole spectrum of literature read by the older immigrants in their home communities, the results might be very significant.

Along these lines, I shall again say what might appear obvious to some. Those of us who are professors perhaps miss an important opportunity in not discovering the cultural backgrounds of our own students. Over the years I have found that some of my students were descended from very famous Jewish figures. Unfortunately, no major discoveries of long-lost letters of Rashi, for example, have yet come to light. However, dramatic family archives, letters, and records have done so. Many of my students, even in the "wilderness" of Wisconsin, happen to be Sephardim.

The danger that confronts us if we persist in ignoring such possibilities may be illustrated by an example I have encountered just this semester. One of my students suddenly revealed to me that he is from Iran. This is only the second Jewish student I have had from that country (I have had at least one non-Jewish Iranian student). He already has lived here for three years, and speaks fluent English now. Our conversation revealed that his parents had made, and continue to make, every effort to integrate totally into American culture—not even particularly Jewish culture. It is easy to predict that the future of this family will be near-total assimilation, and there is no chance that this young man's own children will continue to know Farsi, as he does, or have any knowledge of Iranian Jewish traditions.

Our "melting pot" works all too well, and those of us who care about preserving Jewish cultural diversity need to act quickly before it is too late.

Addendum

In the interesting discussion which followed the presentation of the abbreviated version of this paper, it was mentioned that in France recently there have been some publications, and the publication of some novels by modern writers who are said to be Sephardim (are they, or are they North African Jews?). It hardly needs to be said that these examples, however commendable in themselves, in no way affect what has been stated in this paper; namely, that we generally have little or no idea of what constitutes the total picture of Sephardic literature, a field in which little or no research has been done. Nor does the work of Jews of medieval Spain properly belong to that field.

In this regard, it is interesting to observe that close to half, perhaps more, of the presentations at this conference dealt with the Jews of medieval Spain, to say nothing of papers on Jews of Yemen, and thus had nothing to do with Sephardim at all.

JEWISH TRADITION IN ARABIC FORM IN THE WAR POETRY OF SHEMUEL HA-NAGID

A. Sáenz-Badillos and J. Targarona

Universidad Complutense
Madrid, Spain

I

Shemuel ha-Nagid is doubtless a very particular case of a medieval Jew who adapted himself in the highest degree to his Arabic or Muslim environment. From the point of view of his activity as a politician, and from the point of view of his literary creativity, he represents one of the most complete examples of symbiosis that we can find in Andalusian Jewry. His background in both Islamic and Jewish culture, and his integration in the political situation of his epoch are well known, and we will not now discuss those aspects of his personality or of his outlook. We do not know with certainty whether his road to the heights of the political administration was adequately described by such historians as Abraham ibn Daud and Se'adyah ibn Danan, but the fact is that he attained a very significant position in the Bereber court of Granada, first under Habbus and later on under his son Badis. There, he conformed to the social and political atmosphere of the kingdom and served his masters in an extraordinarily efficient way.

Like other Jewish intellectuals of the epoch, Shemuel ha-Nagid had occasion to write in the Arabic language in all his prose works, especially those dedicated to polemics with Muslim philosophers, Jewish law, and philology. But even if, as his chroniclers maintain, he once wrote a poem in seven different languages,[1] his complete poetic output was in the language of the Bible. His poetry, nevertheless, was elaborated in accordance with the norms of Arabic patterns and technics, and it may even be stated that very few medieval

---

[1] Cf. Se'adyah ibn Danan, "Ma'amar 'al seder hadorot," ed. and trans. J. Targarona, *Miscelanea de Estudios Arabes y Hebraicos* 35, no. 2 (1986): 96 and 137.

Andalusian writers were able to use the technics of Arabic poetry with the same expertise.

II

Our paper centers on the forty-one poems written by Shemuel ha-Nagid on the battlefield from 1038 to 1056. We have recently prepared a new critical edition of the text, with Spanish translation and commentary,[2] and we think that several aspects of these poems deserve some remarks.

War poetry was known in the oldest biblical traditions, but post-biblical Jewish poets no longer used the motifs of Deborah's or Miriam's songs. With the exception of the nonmetrical poem written by Menahem ben Saruq as introduction to the Letter to the Khazars, sent by his master, Hasday ben Saprut, to Yosef, the Jewish king of this Caucasian country, the Jewish tradition previous to ha-Nagid provides no sample of descriptions of troops or battles. As is well known, it was in the works of Arabic poets that Shemuel found his direct source of inspiration. Some years ago, Prof. Israel Levin disclosed in a very good analysis the possible parallels with the major Arab poets of the East who were probably known and imitated by ha-Nagid in this kind of composition.[3] More recently, I had occasion to study some Andalusian models that could equally have been employed by him.[4] And in a doctoral thesis presented at the University of Amsterdam in 1988 by Dr. Arie Schippers, new cases of contact between Arabic poets (particularly al-Mutanabbi) and ha-Nagid's war poetry are attractively collected.[5] We do not intend to repeat similar comparisons here, even though we will occasionally allude to some of them.

[2] *Semu'el ha-Nagid, Poemas 1, Desde el campo de batalla Granada 103–1056*, Edición del texto hebreo, introducción, traducción y notas por Angel Sáenz-Badillos y Judit Targarona Borrás (Córdoba, 1990). We quote the poems according to this edition.

[3] "The War Poetry of Shamuel Hanagid: Its Relation to Ancient Arabic Heroic Poetry" (Hebrew), *Hasifrut* 1–2 (1968): 343–367. See also his *The Embroidered Coat: The Genres of Hebrew Secular Poetry in Spain* [Hebrew] (Tel Aviv, 1980), pp. 40–76.

[4] A. Sáenz-Badillos, "La poesía bélica de Semu'el ha-Nagid: una muestra de convivencia judeo-musulmana," *I Congreso Internacional "Encuentro de las tres culturas", 3–7 octubre 1982* (Toledo, 1983), pp. 219–235.

[5] "Arabic Tradition and Hebrew Innovation: Arabic Themes in Hebrew Andalusian Poetry" (University of Amsterdam, 1988). Published recently as a book (hereafter cited as "Schippers").

It must be clearly stated from the beginning that for ha-Nagid, as for any Hebrew poet, to write in one of the genres cultivated by Arab poets, it was necessary to take from Arabic poetry the usual literary conventions connected to his topic, such as metaphors, comparisons, rhetorical figures, motifs, and so on, and try to integrate all those elements in his own Jewish universe. The greatest merit and originality of the Hebrew poet consisted in his selecting the appropriate words and meters, searching out adequate figures for expressing his own feelings, and blending, in the right proportions, elements taken from his own tradition with those provided by the literary history of the genre.

Even if Shemuel was a quite realistic poet, many of the descriptions of armies and of different moments in the fighting introduced in his war poems are well-known topics employed by Arabic poets in similar situations. Here are the main components or steps of a typical war-poem, in Arabic as well as in his Hebrew poetry:

1. The circumstances and causes of the war.
2. Description of the enemy and of the contending armies.
3. The advance of the armies.
4. Immediate preparations for the battle.
5. The battle.
6. The divine intervention.
7. The victory and a description of the defeated enemy.
8. Thanksgiving and diffusion of the good news.

In practically every one of these components there are almost "consecrated" images or motifs in Arabic poetry that can also be found in ha-Nagid's compositions, clearly imitating earlier poems in the genre and reflecting their Muslim origin. If I may mention a few examples: The soldiers of the poet's own army are like "lions."[6] The enemy, however, has great power and is numerous; their troops are "like the night."[7] "Their eyes, due to the dust of their chariots, were full of darkness, without any order,"[8] which can be compared with a poem by al-Mutanabbi.[9]

---

[6] No. 2, 67; no. 4, 2, 30; no. 33, 45; cf. Schippers, p. 272.
[7] No. 25, 26. Parallels in Ibn Darray, cf. M.J. Viguera, "La corte tuybi de Zaragoza en el Diwan de Ibn Darray," *Actas del IV Coloquio Hispano-tunecino, Palma de Mallorca, 1979* (Madrid, 1983), pp. 246 ff. (hereafter cited as "Actas").
[8] Cf. Job 10:22.
[9] Cf. Schippers, p. 268.

Moreover, the feelings of the men going into battle are permeated by a kind of fatalism.

> On a day of anger, fury, and revenge, men think that the angel of
> death is a lucre,
> And each seeks to purchase fame for himself though he sell his life in
> exchange.[10]
> Strong men were tired of life and chose death instead.
> Lions considered a fresh wound upon their heads as a crown. Death
> was, in their opinion, right, while to live was forbidden.[11]
> They all walked toward death like one who goes merrily to collect
> honey from honeycombs;
> They run to sacrifice themselves, and they shall awaken when bodies
> revive.[12]

This last is very similar to the spirit of the *jihad*. Both in the old Arabic
poets[13] and in al-Mutanabbi similar manifestations can be heard.[14]

The description of the battle does not inform us about particular
details, but usually takes already forged images, with extensive hyper-
bole. As in Arabic poetry, the marching of the armies and the battle
itself produce a kind of earthquake.

> During the day the heavens are boisterous due to the noise of the
> horses, and the earth quakes and shakes at their motion.[15]

Blood is frequently mentioned.

> Princes dressed in red silk become red with arrows, and the group of
> the sublimes is colored with blood.[16]
> And the horses ran and turned back like vipers thrown out of their
> caves.[17]
> And the arrows were like drops of rain.[18]
> The bows were serpents in their hands, and each spat a bee from his
> mouth.[19]

---

[10] No. 2, 53 f.
[11] No. 2, 66 ff.
[12] No. 25, 40 f.
[13] Cf. R. Blachère, *Histoire de la Littérature Arabe*, p. 411.
[14] Cf. E. García Gómez, *Cinco Poetas Musulmanes*, 2nd ed. (Madrid), p. 58.
[15] No. 8, 20; cf. Schippers, p. 267.
[16] No. 8, 21; cf. Schippers, p. 271.
[17] No. 2, 60; similar to al-Mutanabbi; Schippers, p. 268.
[18] No. 2, 62; Schippers, pp. 269 ff.
[19] No. 2, 63; Schippers, pp. 269 ff.

The sword upon their heads was like a torch; as it fell its light was dimmed.[20]

The consequences of the battle:

We left them in the steppe for the hyenas, the jackals, the leopard, and the wild boar.[21]
We conquered their cities and their land, and we demolished, in vengeance, wall and castle.
We took possession of villages and towns, and we conquered, by force, city and fortress.[22]
We left the earth colored with their blood and sliced with the corpses of their lords.
As you walked, you trampled with your feet upon bodies or skulls, and you heard the cries of the mortally wounded.[23]

Also similar to this:

They were amazed as the dwellers of large houses, found without the shade of house and roofs,
Who, in a day burning with heat, did not enter a palace of marble or a cool upper chamber.[24]
We felled their lords and king, their princes and servants were killed. They were like dung upon the face of the earth, their heads in the dust were like muck.[25]

Many of the rhetorical figures consecrated by the theorists of Arabic literature are present in ha-Nagid's poems. Among them, for instance, is the figure of "distribution."

She [the soul] teaches generosity to the noble man, cunning to the prince, to the teacher justice, and vigor to the old lion.[26]

---

[20] No. 2, 64; cf. Schippers, p. 269; M.J. Viguera, "Símiles sobre la espada en la poesía árabe," *Homenaje a Alvaro Galmés des Fuentes* (Oviedo-Madrid, 1985), vol. 1, pp. 675–683 (hereafter cited as *Homenaje*).

[21] No. 2, 107 ff.; no. 25, 54 ff. The description of wild animals and birds devouring the corpses of the enemy is very usual among Arab poets; cf. Schippers, pp. 280 f.

[22] No. 2, 115 f.; very similar to the words of Ibn 'Abd al Rabbihi, cf. J.T. Monroe, *Hispano-Arabic Poetry* (1974), p. 128; Schippers, pp. 279 f.

[23] No. 8, 25 f.; similar to descriptions of the defeated by Ibn al-Rûmi, cf. Schippers, p. 258 s.

[24] No. 2, 111 f.

[25] No. 4, 85 f. Similar images can be found in 'Amr ibn Ma'dikarib; R. Blachère, *Histoire de la Littérature Arabe*, pp. 407 f.

[26] No. 39, 10.

The figure of contrast and antithesis is also very frequent, particularly when the poet is comparing the two armies before the battle or describing the defeated enemy.

> While the vizier who planned and decided to slay me and proclaimed the sentence . . . I apprehended him and brought him with my rope to the jail and put him in fetters.[27]
> They came up in daylight, like warriors, on highways; they returned in the dark, like thieves, on byways.[28]

There is a fundamental coincidence between some of the themes of Arabic poetry and the following words of ha-Nagid, which accord with Jewish tradition:

> He sent a messenger who deflected their swords.[29]
> God ordered destiny to spoil the goods of some men and give them to others.[30]

In the last quotation, destiny is subordinate to God, and not an independent force. The angels of Sheol are its captives and obey him.

God sends the angels Michael and Gabriel to Shemuel.[31] Michael is the most important of the angels and, according to Jewish tradition, the "prince of Israel,"[32] the prince of the waters, in relation to the Exodus from Egypt.[33] Gabriel, in Jewish tradition, is "the prince of the fire,"[34] he who delivers the three young men from the burning furnace in Daniel 3.[35] Both angels are very close to the Messiah.[36] Shemuel applies to himself Isaiah's words: "When thou passest through the waters, I will be with thee; and through the rivers, they shall not overflow thee: when thou walkest through the fire, thou shalt not be burned; neither shall the flame kindle upon thee."[37]

Prayer to the angels is exemplified by the following:

---

[27] No. 2, 122 ff.
[28] No. 16, 23.
[29] No. 4, 72; similar in Ibn Darray; cf. Viguera, "Actas," p. 247.
[30] No. 25, 53.
[31] No. 1.
[32] Midrash 'Aseret ha dib. 1.
[33] Cf. Num. Rab. 2.
[34] T.B., Pesah 118.
[35] Cf. Pir. R. El. 33:7, Ber. Rab. 44.
[36] Ot. de-R.'A., shin.
[37] God speaks to Israel. Brought again to the context of Semu'el's life; no. 2, 88 f.; no. 3, 4 ff.; no. 7, 10, 19.

> Ye angels! Draw near and make war upon them, with the stars and the glowing sun.[38]

The angels pray for Shemuel and Granada's troops,[39] and help him against the enemy.[40]

> He ordered the ministering angels, and they were my help from the heavens, descending and ascending.[41]

We can compare all these references to the words of Ibn Darry:

> God helped you for it with the angels, who before had helped your ancestors, Muhammad's officers.[42]

Sometimes these motifs can also be found in the Bible, and then the Hebrew poet has a double justification for employing these images, being particularly fond of them.

The personification of death, similar to that of Sheol in Isaiah 5:14, frequent in ha-Nagid's poems,[43] is a well-known motif in Arabic poetry.[44]

> [The city] became a widow when its king died.[45]

Al-Mutanabbi describes the conquered city as a woman who has lost her sons.[46] This image is employed by ha-Nagid in a different context: if the son does not listen to his parents, "the country will cry like a mother who has lost her sons."[47]

The sun is obscured by the dust of the battle.

> The day was obscure and misty.[48]
> And the blood of men upon the earth ran like the blood of rams at the sides of the Temple court.[49]
> If he argues with me for my association with kings, I reply to him: "This is a portion of my inheritance and my lot."[50]

---

[38] No. 2, 93.
[39] No. 24, 36.
[40] No. 27, 73.
[41] Cf. Gen. 28:12, like Jacob; no. 4, 128.
[42] Cf. Viguera, "Actas," pp. 246 f.
[43] No. 10, 4; no. 21, 2 ff.; no. 39, 30.
[44] Schippers, p. 277.
[45] Ibid., p. 282.
[46] Cf. Lam. 1:1.
[47] No. 20, 23.
[48] No. 2, 57, close to Joel 2:2. Compare with the Arabic texts collected by M.J. Viguera, "Actas," p. 247.
[49] Cf. Ezra 43:20; no. 2, 65. Cf. Schippers, p. 271.
[50] Ps. 16:5; no. 7, 7. This is found also in 'Urwa ibn al-Ward. Cf. Blachère, *Histoire de la Littérature Arabe*, p. 411.

Who knows what is written in my book when I organize the battles with soldiers and troops?[51]
To write with a pen of iron[52] [on the skin of the enemy].[53]
The time of harvest arrived[54] [for the bodies of the enemy].[55]

Ha-Nagid praises his own verses, in accordance with Arabic usage, with frequent biblical allusions.[56] Many of his motifs are taken directly from biblical and Jewish tradition, but at the same time, they are not far from the topics of Arabic war poetry. Such is the recourse to prayer before or during the battle.

[Motivation of Shemuel's supplication:][57] Remember in my behalf the merit of Isaac and Abraham and Sarah![58]
praying for Granada's Muslim army and asking for the patriarchs' help].
There are those who make a covenant against me, but I, too, have the patriarchs' covenant to protect me.[59]
In times like these, the patriarchs pray in my behalf.[60]
And if, in Your judgment, I am not worthy, then do it for my son and my Torah.[61]
Will You do wonders for me each year as You did for the patriarchs and the saints?[62]
Enemies poured blood like water on a day of anguish while I pour forth prayer
To the God who abases and fells every evildoer into the pit which he by himself excavated and dug.[63]
God arises like a lion and disperses the enemy[64] [and gives the victory to Shemuel].[65]

A few examples of other typical Jewish motifs:

---

[51] Cf. Ps. 139:16; no. 22, 7.
[52] Cf. Jer. 17:1.
[53] No. 24, 44; cf. al-Mutannabi, Schippers, p. 269.
[54] Joel 4:13.
[55] No. 26, 32; cf. Schippers, p. 283. It is already found in Abu Tammam.
[56] No. 23, 33 ff.
[57] No. 2, 73 ff., 76 ff.
[58] No. 2, 81 ff.
[59] No. 2, 10.
[60] No. 4, 61 ff.
[61] No. 3, 10.
[62] No. 4, 1.
[63] No. 2, 70 f.
[64] No. 30, 17 ff.
[65] No. 20, 38.

With the voice of the seventy banners.[66]

[Israel's and Shemuel's election:] I will make your lines fall in pleasant places.[67]

And the foliage of thick-leaved trees made atonement for me like the burnt offerings or the shekels [alluding to the feast of Sukkot and the Temple].[68]

If you reward in this world for my merits and grant me a recompense according to my righteousness,

How shall I stand on the day of judgment?[69]

To the mighty God who appeared in the storm and in the whirlwind against the worshipers of idols.[70]

Rise up and read the Canticles, and draw not near to Lamentations.[71]

"I long for Hammot and Mefa'at"[72] is a whole song yearning for Zion and asking for a speedy restoration, full of biblical names and motifs.[73]

She [the wine] is chosen among Sadoq's sons . . . [among wine's other qualities].[74]

III

One of the most remarkable aspects of ha-Nagid's poetry is the projection of the biblical word onto the people and situations depicted in his war poems. Biblical names, for instance, are often applied to persons in his own epoch. Zuhayr, the king of Almeria, is referred to as Agag;[75] slaves, as Amalek;[76] Christian mercenaries as Edom and Arabs as sons of Keturah.[77] In addition:

The Philistine [Bereber] captains heed his words.[78]
Sons of the Philistines.[79]

---

[66] No. 4, 58. About the seventy angels of the peoples, cf. Pir. R. El. 24:4.
[67] Cf. Ps. 61:6; no. 4, 64.
[68] Cf. Lev. 23:40, Exod. 30:15; no. 4, 124.
[69] No. 4, 135 f.; see another allusion to "the day of judgment," no. 4, 144.
[70] Cf. Nah. 1:3; no. 4, 137.
[71] No. 6, 19.
[72] No. 8, 1–15.
[73] Similar to this: nos. 25, 1–17 and 31, 1–7.
[74] No. 20, 5.
[75] No. 2, 12, 102, 105; no. 4, 47; no. 12, 2.
[76] No. 2, 41, 104, 145; no. 12, 2.
[77] No. 2, 41.
[78] No. 4, 14, 102; no. 16, 16.
[79] No. 29, 12.

With the troops of Semari.[80]
The choice troops of Og and Sihon the Amorite.[81]
The sister of Uz[82] [probably the Christians].[83]
Ba'al-meri, Ahimelech[84] [Yaddayr, a rebel relative of the king].[85]
Bosrah . . . Teman[86] [cities of Edom, applied to the Christians].[87]
Girgashim, before Medanim, Emorim and Nibdalim[88] [the Girgashim
are the Granadan troops, mainly Berebers, and for this reason referred
to as "sons of Cain"].
Arabs and Hagarens, princes of the Philistines, Hittites and thousands
of eunuchs and Christians.[89]
The prince of Ephron[90] [Abu Nur of Ronda].
The prince of the Hittites and the king of Jebus[91] [Muhammad ibn
Nuh of Morón and Ibn Hazrun of Arcos].

Contemporary situations are often compared to incidents in the Bible.

The earth trembled from the foundation and was overturned, as in
the destruction of Gemorrah.[92]
As on the night of Abram and the night of Moses, as on Joshua's
afternoon, as on the night when the burdens were removed.[93]
I returned to my home with gladness, surrounded by God's angels,
who sheltered me like to Jacob in Mahanaim.[94]
And He blew upon them as on the day of the Sea of Reeds, and they
were destroyed by His storm.[95]
He then put on the costume of fury and went forth, as on the day
when Pharaoh and his troops were drowned.[96]
He magnified Himself by the waters [as in the Red Sea].[97]

---

[80] A descendant of Canaan, cf. Gen. 10:18, of difficult identification; no. 7, 24.
[81] Cf. Deut. 1:4; no. 7, 31.
[82] Cf. 1 Chron. 1:42; Lam. 4:21.
[83] But it could be an allusion to the Arabs too; no. 8, 13.
[84] 1 Chron. 9:40.
[85] No. 8, 16.
[86] Cf. Isa. 34:6, Jer. 49:7.
[87] No. 8, 15.
[88] Cf. Gen. 10:16, Deut. 7:1, Gen. 25:2, Esd. 6:21; no. 16, 17.
[89] No. 33, 30.
[90] No. 35, 18.
[91] No. 35, 19.
[92] Cf. Gen. 19:24, Deut. 29:22; no. 2, 55.
[93] Cf. Gen. 14:15, Exod. 11:4, Josh. 10:13, Isa. 10:27; no. 4, 111.
[94] Cf. Gen. 32:2 f.; no. 38, 16.
[95] Cf. Exod. 15:10, Isa. 40:24; no. 2, 96.
[96] Cf. Exod. 14:28; no. 4, 66.
[97] No. 4, 125.

> They stopped by the riverbank, while he stood facing them, as on the day when the brooks overflowed.[98]
> We came back as on the day of Arnon and the day of Mattanah.[99]

Allusions to Deborah's war include:

> Do to them as to Sisera, and to me as You did for Barak and Deborah.[100]
> Angels! Draw near and make war upon them with the stars and the glowing sun.[101]
> The wicked had already divided their spoils.[102]

Further allusions include:

> And I will feel strong as Samson with the tent-pin and the web.[103]
> I am the David of my age. . . . Mine is the heritage from Merari and from Assir, Elkanah and Asaph, and Mishael, Elzaphan, and Sithri.[104]
> My forebear was Jeduthun.[105]
> Like Mishael I went into the furnace and was not consumed, like Jonah I was submerged in the depth of the waters and did not die.[106]
> Formerly Agag perished at the hand of Samuel, and Haman by the wise man
> And in the past Amalek came to evil.[107]
> And call its name "Sister to the deeds of Ahasuerus and Esther the noble."[108]

What do all these identifications mean? Does Shemuel really consider himself so important in Jewish history as to compare his person with the great ancestors and heroes of the Bible? Should these passages be read in the light of the well-known Arabic *fahr*, the praise of oneself? We would say that Shemuel is simply trying to establish a parallel between the history of salvation and his own epoch, in this way magnifying the help he has received from God, as in the great moments of the life of the chosen people. Some scholars have seen a kind of Messianism in ha-Nagid's attitude, as if he thought

---

[98] Cf. Num. 21:15; no. 4, 45. According to Jewish tradition, it was a day of great defeat for Israel's enemies.
[99] Cf. Num. 21:13 ff.; no. 13, 30 f.
[100] Cf. Judg. 4–5; no. 2, 78.
[101] Cf. Judg. 5:20; no. 2, 93.
[102] Cf. Judg. 5:30, Joel 4:2; no. 4, 56.
[103] Judg. 16:14; no. 6, 50.
[104] Cf. Exod. 6:16 ff.; no. 7, 38 ff.
[105] Cf. Ps. 39:1; no. 7, 42.
[106] Cf. Dan. 1:7, 3, 19; Job 2:1 ff.; no. 38, 6.
[107] Cf. 1 Sam. 15:33; Esther 7, Mordecai; Exod. 17:8 ff.; no. 2, 105 f.
[108] No. 2, 148.

of himself as being the Messiah. But there is no real basis for defending such a view in his war poetry. It is true that his political and historical role was quite momentous, as such authors as Abraham ibn Daud understood perfectly, but we do not see any genuine Messianic aspiration in Shemuel, who knew his own limitations very well, despite his pride in his noble origins and his political and religious position.

Biblical allusions and expressions (generally not used by the Arab poets) are very frequent in ha-Nagid's war poetry, giving, in this way, a quite peculiar tone to his compositions, which are characteristically Jewish with a unique blend of different traditions. It will suffice to mention a few examples.

> Those who bore the bunch of grapes upon a pole.[109]
> Remnant and offspring, the woman giving birth and the one with child.[110]
> And He rode upon a cherub, and did fly: and He was seen upon the wings of the wind[111] [the words about God are used here to describe the enemy's military operations]; He hurried like a bird that rides the wings of the wind and appears.[112]
> Bitter destruction.[113]
> The offspring of ostriches will moan for them, the young daughter of the she-goat shall dance.[114]
> But its end was a day of redemption, a day of jubilation, as when the poor delight in the harvest.[115]
> [The vizier] was there shaved by the hired razor.[116]
> And God fulfilled the word of my father to his tribe, the children of song and offerers of incense.[117]
> And what Zeresh said to him who bought with his kikars the men that brought the gift of an agorah.[118]
> Filled with pearls like the Tummin, like the songs of Tehillim in number.[119]

---

[109] Num. 13:23 ff.; no. 2, 21.
[110] Jer. 31:7; no. 2, 23.
[111] 2 Sam. 22:11. The words about God are used here to describe the enemy's military operations.
[112] No. 2, 43.
[113] Deut. 32:24; no. 2, 80.
[114] Cf. Isa. 13:21; no. 2, 113.
[115] Cf. Isa. 9:2; no. 2, 119.
[116] Cf. Isa. 7:20; no. 2, 123.
[117] Cf. Deut. 33:11; no. 2, 128.
[118] Cf. Ezra 6:13, Isa. 18:7, Exod. 30:13; no. 2, 129.
[119] No. 2, 139.

His spies hastened to him with words like dross and adulterated drinks.[120]
I beheld with my eyes death's firstborn.[121]
He terrorized them and made them dance like young oxen, like a kid or like a calf.[122]
They fled in seven different directions.[123]
He put coverings of cords on their hearts.[124]
On the Thursday night we pursued them like a partridge, as does a swarm of bees.[125]
We captured our would-be captors, and those who thought to devour us were devoured.[126]
You made their bows resemble straw.[127]
The cup of salvation.[128]
I am a worm and not a man.[129]
Refresh yourself with apples.[130]
He will be an idol to you, and you to him, Micah.[131]
Like Tivni dying before his time or Zimri . . .[132]
. . . were buried like the Egyptian.[133]
Like the lever to its appendage.[134]
The hand upon the throne [the hand of God].[135]
Like deer on the mountains of Senir and Amanah.[136]
You shall be praised among your brethren like Joseph, blessed among sons like Asher.[137]
Like Samson's lion I was strong, but the blood of my body was sweet.[138]
The day of Korah.[139]
Let them consider me as David, and consider you as Kohelet.[140]

---

[120] Cf. Isa. 1:22; no. 4, 39.
[121] Jub. 18:3; no. 4, 57; no. 25, 46; no. 27, 80.
[122] No. 4, 69.
[123] Cf. Deut. 28:7; no. 4, 74; no. 16, 22.
[124] Cf. Num. 19:15; no. 4, 76.
[125] Cf. 1 Sam. 26:20, Deut. 1:44; no. 4, 84.
[126] Cf. Isa. 14:2, Jer. 30:16; no. 4, 88.
[127] Cf. Isa. 41:2; no. 4, 100.
[128] Ps. 116:13; no. 4, 109; no. 7, 16; no. 8, 33; no. 12, 4; no. 31, 50; no. 34, 21.
[129] Cf. Ps. 22:7, Jub. 25:6; no. 4, 132.
[130] Cf. Song of Sol. 2:5; no. 6, 17.
[131] Cf. Judg. 17–18; no. 6, 36.
[132] Cf. 1 Kings 16:15 ff.; no. 7, 12.
[133] Cf. Exod. 2:11 f.; no. 7, 13.
[134] Cf. Exod. 29:13; no. 11, 19.
[135] Exod. 17:16; no. 12, 2.
[136] Song of Sol. 2:17, 4:8; no. 13, 35.
[137] Cf. Gen. 49:24, Deut. 33:16 ff.; no. 14, 30.
[138] Cf. Judg. 14:5 ff.; no. 16, 27.
[139] Cf. Num. 16:32; no. 16, 48.
[140] No. 20, 20.

As did Mahol's sons, and not like those of Eliab, Yishar, or Peleth.[141]
The best language of Kedar and Ephah.[142]
I trusted him my soul, and he deceived me like Ziba.[143]
We inundated them like Noah's waters.[144]
[The troops of Granada resemble] the immensity of the Sihor and the Jordan.[145]
Like the fire of Nadab . . .[146]
She [my soul] is Moses in the day of prodigies, in time of speaking she is Aaron, and in time of singing see her like Miriam playing timbrels.[147]

IV

Ha-Nagid's war poems reflect many authentic aspects of Jewish life integrated with the classical Arabic patterns. There are, for instance, frequent allusions to Jewish traditions, festivities, or institutions.

> And the month of Av finished, with the ancient calamities . . .[148]
> The beginning of Friday on the first of Elul was to me like the ninth of Av or the tenth.[149]
> On the night of rejoicing with the precious Torah.[150]
> Now make a second Purim for the God who arose and cut off from Amalek blossom and branch.[151]
> And tell it to the masters of Pumbeditha and to the elders of the academy at Sura.[152]
> I will tell of Your wondrous deeds in the assembly of the pious, and of Your miracles among those clothed with fringes.[153]
> And you helped Ethan's son in the month of Ethanim against the worshippers of the Baals.[154]

---

[141] Cf. 1 Kings 5:11, Num. 16:1; no. 20, 25.
[142] No. 21, 1.
[143] Cf. 2 Sam. 16:4, 19:25–27; no. 22, 15.
[144] Cf. Gen. 6:1 ff., Isa. 54:9; no. 22, 26.
[145] No. 24, 12.
[146] Cf. Lev. 10:1 f.; no. 37, 12.
[147] No. 39, 13.
[148] No. 2, 45.
[149] No. 2, 118.
[150] No. 2, 127.
[151] No. 2, 145.
[152] No. 2, 147.
[153] No. 4, 8.
[154] No. 4, 103.

There was light for me on the eve of the festival of the Harvest Gathering [Sukkot].[155]

At the time that the people brought into their booths myrtle from the rock and branches of the palm tree [Sukkot].[156]

And when your sons will ask in the future: "What is that?" [as at the Seder of Pesah].[157]

Read them as on the Sabbath you read your Torah.[158]

Write all that your God has made to my soul and send it to the academy.[159]

[The celebration of the Sabbath:] Everyone, rich or poor, observes festivals and Sabbaths with banquets and dinners.[160]

God's dwelling [a very specific expression, probably alluding to the synagogue in Granada].[161]

Oral and written Torah, tradition, Mishnah, Talmud, etc.[162]

It shall be like the recitation of the Shema in the mouth of the people that thrice rounds God's Sanctuary celebrating the feasts.[163]

In my mouth is found the word of the Torah, that from the day of Sinai to the day of the Lord shall not change.[164]

Concrete references to Jewish law can also be found in these compositions.

The ordinance concerning all vessels keeping impurity in themselves is to break them instead of immersing them.[165]

And in respect to the rushing ox being not guarded, they said that to slaughter him is to guard him.[166]

I observed rightly the Lord's festivals . . . the Sabbath days and the day of the shofar and atonement, the days of the booth until the departure of the pilgrim feasts.[167]

God ordered that on the days that work is forbidden there are troops that refuse to work.[168]

The judgment for homicide must take place on the same day.[169]

---

[155] No. 4, 110.
[156] No. 4, 120 ff.
[157] No. 4, 147.
[158] No. 6, 55.
[159] No. 22, 20.
[160] No. 23, 4 f.
[161] No. 23, 2, 22.
[162] No. 27, 3 ff.
[163] Cf. Deut. 16:16; no. 37, 28.
[164] No. 39, 47.
[165] Cf. Lev. 11:33; no. 2, 135.
[166] Cf. Bab. Qam. 4:9; no. 2, 136.
[167] No. 4, 112 f.
[168] Cf. 1 Macc. 2:32 ff.; no. 4, 115.
[169] Cf. T.B. Sanh. 4a; no. 24, 38.

Various details about Jewish family relations can also be deduced from the poems written by ha-Nagid on the battlefield. His strong and loving relationship with his young son Yehosef is shown in poem no. 9, a reply to some verses sent to him by his son, where he states: "My love for you is attached to the walls of my heart and to its feelings,"[170] or in no. 10, a will to his son before the battle at Lorca: "Yehosef, all I suffer and endure, whenever I go into distress, it is on behalf of you,"[171] while no. 11 is an exultant message of victory to this same son. In no. 14 he expresses his sorrow during Yehosef's illness; no. 15 is an elegy on the occasion of the death of his sister: "the sorrow for the death of a brother is nailed and fastened in the heart forever."[172] No. 17 was written by Yehosef, regretting his absence. In no. 21 the father gives instructions to his son about the way to attain wisdom, and in no. 23 he offers further teachings about the proper way of life.

V

In addition, ha-Nagid's poetry also reveals a kind of ideological integration, since for Ibn Nagrella there is a perfect symbiosis between Granada's interests and the Jewish community. In a sense, we could call this a projection of Judaism on the daily life of a Muslim kingdom. For Shemuel, Granada's enemies are enemies of the Jewish people, and the destinies of Granada and the Jews are inseparably united.

Here are a few examples:

> There is One who looks after the humble of the scattered lambs.[173]
> Now make a second Purim for the God who arose and cut off from Amalek blossom and branch.[174]
> In his land wicked men stoned with the stones of their tongues the children of the living God.
> They conspired against them, and took weapons and purchased ropes,
> In order to destroy the principal city in Israel [the Jewish community] and lay waste both strong and weak, the suckling infant and those that had been weaned.[175]

---

[170] No. 9, 9.
[171] No. 10, 1.
[172] No. 15, 17.
[173] Cf. Jer. 50:17; no. 2, 94.
[174] No. 2, 145.
[175] Cf. 2 Sam. 20:19; no. 4, 25 ff.

> It is a praise to God who redeemed His beloved . . .[176]
> My son, pay attention to God's glorious hand,
> Rise up and recite my song of praise in the gatherings and assemblies
> of the people.
> Set it as a frontlet tied upon your hand,
> Inscribe it upon your heart with iron pen and lead
> [alluding to the victory at Lorca].[177]
> They proposed to destroy the sons of God [Jews and citizens of
> Granada].[178]

For this reason, the victories that God grants to Granada's army are an occasion of rejoicing for the whole community of Israel, all over the world, as we have already observed.

VI

Thus, Shemuel uses many elements and materials taken from the Arabic tradition, both older ones as well as some more representative of the modernistic or neoclassic Arabic poetry. This is true from the point of view of certain nuclear ideas generally included in such compositions and also from the point of view of the images, metaphors, and expressions which are usual in the genre. But all of these more or less conventional components receive, in ha-Nagid's poems, a new dress and a new orientation that could be described as truly Jewish and, at the same time, as original.

Shemuel is a sincere Jew, and he cannot forget the redemption of his people even if it would be difficult for him to leave his post at the Granadan court. For him, as a consequence of deep reflection, to be in the Temple of Jerusalem seems better than to dominate over all creatures.[179]

His role as a politician and as a military commander leading the troops of the kingdom of Granada may be stated succinctly thanks to a correction that we have introduced in our critical edition of these poems. "Through my mouth executed them the avengers of the blood of the oppressed"; that is to say, "according to my orders,"

---

[176] No., 4, 148.
[177] No. 11, 28 ff.
[178] No. 33, 41.
[179] No. 25, 10 f.

and not "My hands executed them," as it was possible to read the verse in Habermann or Yarden.[180] This is ha-Nagid's role in battle; he makes decisions, he gives orders, or is among the leaders of the troops, but he does not fight personally with his own weapons. He is, in a sense, above the cruel reality of the battle, and can write his own feelings about the situation in a realistic, unconventional way.

His personal role is better reflected in the final words of one of the poems he wrote during the battle in 1041 against Yaddair, where he describes himself as a singer of God's court:

> It is my duty in respect to God to make sweet His council with my songs, and His task toward me to embitter the
> hearts of my enemies.
> He shall overtake him to slay my adversaries, and I, to entreat Him with my poetry,
> And to work for Him like a hired worker every day, and He will pay my salary on time.[181]

---

[180] But not in Sassoon, 75; no. 29, 23.
[181] No. 7, 43 ff.

THE POETRY OF TODROS HA-LEVI ABULAFIA AS A REFLECTION OF CULTURAL CONTACTS: HEBREW POETRY IN CHRISTIAN SPAIN

Aviva Doron

Haifa University

A Hebrew Poet in Christian Spain

Todros ben Yehuda Ha-Levi Abulafia was born in Toledo, the capital of New Castile, in 1247. He lived about 100 years after the Jewish cultural centers were transferred from Muslim Andalusia to Christian Spain, and approximately 250 years before the expulsion of Spanish Jewry.[1]

During Todros Abulafia's lifetime, Toledo was a lively cultural center which drew poets and scholars from many different nations, and formed a meeting point for a broad range of artistic traditions and literary currents. The ranks of Toledo's poets included monks trying their hand at composing forms of the romance that had acquired great popular appeal (while still writing other texts in Latin), folk singers recounting tales of Spanish epic heroes, troubadours from the south of France, and even King Alfonso X, the Wise (El Sabio), whose innovative *cantigas* are considered to have made a great contribution to Spanish poetry. It almost goes without saying that Jewish poets functioned within this cosmopolitan milieu.

There have been virtually no studies of the Hebrew poetry composed in Christian Spain in this period, as scholars have generally shown greater interest in the earlier Hebrew poetry written in Andalusia and in the manifestations of cultural contact between Hebrew and Arabic poetry. I therefore would like to draw attention to one of the most interesting trends in the Hebrew poetry of thirteenth-century Christian Spain, focusing specifically on the verse composed by Todros Ha-Levi Abulafia.

---

[1] Yitzhak Baer, *The History of the Jews in Christian Spain* (Tel Aviv, 1959), pp. 45–51; Dan Pagis, *Innovation and Tradition in Secular Hebrew Poetry* (Jerusalem: Keter, 1976), pp. 173–175; Bernard Septimus, *Hispano-Jewish Culture in Transition* (Cambridge, Mass.: Harvard University Press, 1982).

Dan Pagis, the well-known Hebrew poet and student of medieval Jewish poetry, was one of the first modern scholars to call attention to the complexity of the Hebrew poetry written in Christian Spain in the thirteenth and fourteenth centuries.[2] As Pagis points out, in addition to preserving traditional elements, this poetry also introduced certain new elements. It is precisely these elements that I shall closely observe in this paper, indicating their relation to historical circumstances, changing social conventions, the poet's talent, and his self-perception as an individual and a poet. I thus hope to examine in detail the intricate nature and the historical formation of Hebrew poetry in Christian Spain, subjects which have generally been overlooked.

Born into a respectable Jewish family in Toledo, Todros ben Yehuda Ha-Levi Abulafia had a gift for self-expression that became evident at an early age, and as a boy he is known to have written poetry as a form of exchange with local Jewish notables. He soon made his way into the royal court as poet and attendant to Don Çag de la Maleja, a statesman serving Alfonso X. In this capacity he attended Don Çag on journeys, kept him company, and, in keeping with the social requirements of the time, flattered him with poems of praise. Within a short while Todros Abulafia had become a member of the king's inner circle, eventually acquiring economic security with his appointment to the post of tax inspector.

Several names recur in a number of thirteenth-century documents: Ha-Levy, Caballeria, Aboulafia, Porta Benvenishti, Alconstantini, Ibn Ezra, Ibn Shoshan, and Orhabuena. The bearers of these names were all representatives of well-known and powerful Toledo families which formed an oligarchical stratum basically governing the lives of Toledo's Jews. The same people also became courtiers to the king and were granted a variety of privileges.[3]

The emergence of a circle of Jewish officials in the court of a Catholic sovereign may be surprising, but can be explained in terms of their administrative and economic expertise, whereby they made substantial contributions to the royal government without posing any kind of threat to the king. In fact, their positions, like those of the non-Jewish courtiers, were precarious, for the king, had he wished, could divest them of all their privileges without notice. In a society

---

[2] Pagis, *Innovation and Tradition*, pp. 1–2.
[3] Luis Suarez Fernandez, *Judíos españoles en la edad media* (Madrid, 1980), p. 11.

rent by religious wars between Muslims and Christians, employing
Jews as a means of ensuring stability and economic security was an
insightful and practical move; it was, one might say, the "sensible"
thing for a king to do.

José Amador de los Ríos describes in detail how the Jews at court
rose to rank and honor, and how they expressed their gratitude for
these benefits by presenting the Christian king with a gold key made
especially for him. The key was inscribed with the Hebrew text "The
King of Kings will open," and the Spanish translation, "*Rey de los
reyes abrira.*"[4] Alfonso X is considered to have had a keen interest
in other societies, and his court has historically been depicted as
one of the intellectual pinnacles of medieval Europe. The Jewish
courtiers, all members of the wealthy Toledo families listed above,
were among the main beneficiaries of the king's penchant for cultural entertainment.

Baer notes that "Don Fernando and his son Alfonso X were aided
by the help and advice of learned and wealthy Jews, and these
received special treatment."[5] José Amador de los Ríos writes: "This
was a combination of the extraordinary trust of the Catholic kings
and the benefits which the Jews obtained daily in public administration. Thanks to their proximity to the king, and to the large sums
of money they brought to his treasury, some of these courtiers attained
noteworthy positions in the kingdom, some of which had strong political clout."[6]

Among the Jewish courtiers was Todros Abulafia. As a prominent
figure in Toledo, he led a turbulent life in the company of courtier
colleagues who were predominantly non-Jewish, but he maintained
firm ties with the leaders of the Jewish community. A respected and
well-known poet, he was a member of Alfonso X's entourage, a spir-
ited group of intellectuals, scholars, poets, and artists of all creeds
and races.[7]

Abulafia's poetry has certain distinctive features. While it is derived
from the classical tradition of Andalusian poetry, it also represents
contemporary literary developments and reveals an emergent poetics

---

[4] José Amador de los Ríos, *Historia crítica de la literatura española* (Madrid, 1969),
p. 372.
[5] Baer, *History of the Jews in Christian Spain*, p. 78.
[6] Amador de los Ríos, *Historia crítica de la literature española*, p. 324.
[7] Luis Alborg, *Historia de la literatura española* (Madrid, 1966), p. 154; Peter Dronke,
The Medieval Lyric (Cambridge, 1968), pp. 71–74.

that has its own unique and individual nature. Some of its more
interesting conventions are, for example, the use of a singular narrative stance and the poet's habit of addressing God in a personal,
intimate manner. The effect of the latter feature is intensified by the
use of a new stylistic line. Yitzhak Baer has noted in Abulafia's writings, which he refers to as "so-called devotional poetry," an innovation he deems "indecent," claiming that it discloses the poet's
egocentric personality. This, underscores Baer, attests to the fact that
the poet has "not the least interest in the nation's troubles."[8]

In his poetry Todros extracts phrases from the religious tradition
and works them into a secular context. Approaching God in a collective national idiom which has been recontextualized as religious
poetry, he addresses the Lord, requesting His intervention on personal, everyday matters, such as tax collecting, and asking that He
make the Christian king favor him.

> Before I approach flesh and blood
>   I will praise God, and hear of good.
> I shall rely solely on His grace.
>   Shall he who relies on the Lord want for anything?
> I shall place everything in the Lord
>   and all creation will heed me.
> And the heart of the king and his court
>   shall favor all of my wishes.
> He will destroy the lying fools
>   and He will preserve the wise and the just.
>   (poem 43)[9]

The poet's preparations prior to appearing before the king are
described in mundane terms and the occasion is reconstructed as an
everyday event, using elements generally characteristic of secular
rather than devotional poetry. Praise and glorification of God combined with declarations of faith in Him are traditionally held to be
features of devotional poetry. In the verses cited above, these elements are combined in a manner which is virtually unprecedented
in Spanish-Hebrew poetry; this is done by way of extending prayer
and thanks to the God of Israel in a manner which changes the

---

[8] Yitzhak Baer, "Todros ben Yehuda Ha-Levi and His Time," *Sion "b"*, 1937,
p. 55.
[9] The numbering of the poems follows the edition of David Yelin, *The Garden of
the Proverbs and the Riddles* (Jerusalem, 1932–35).

speaker's stance from one of self-flattery to one which valorizes God. Currying favor with the king is an element often found in troubadour verse, yet here it is placed in conjunction with words of contemplation alluding to the Book of Proverbs:

> May my king regard me with favor
> And turn his heart to me with love and kindness . . .
> And the Lord will command his attendants
> To commit all his wealth to my care.
>   (poem 644)

> Trust the Lord and seek His wisdom.
> All will be granted you in the house of the king.
>   (poem 645)

In "Many are the enemies in the court" (poem 641):

> Should you stand before flames, O my soul
> I shall teach you the road to walk . . .
> My heart, be strong and of good courage, and if the warriors
> Be many, cast yourself at the mercy of God.

These poems, evidently written before Todros Abulafia met with the king of Castile, illustrate the new stylistic line he established. We note in this trend a definite move away from the sphere of exalted and abstract expression to that of specific, concrete, intimate reality. The transition from one sphere to another is sudden, and usually occurs at the end of the poem, causing a unique poetic effect.

"My heart, take the rod of your tongue" (poem 672) is a clear example of the poet's use of elements appropriated from another context and worked into a new setting that violates the reader's expectations. The poem begins with words and phrases belonging to the elevated linguistic register characteristic of religious poetry:

> My heart! speak . . .
> And fill your song with gems of praise to God . . .
> And plead before Him . . .

A sudden change occurs in the last verse, when the elevated linguistic register gives way to a discussion of things as mundane and unaesthetic as boils and an irritation in the poet's eye.

> And He will cure your plague of boils
> And disease in your eye.

Any attempt to compare Todros Ha-Levi to the Andalusian Hebrew poets who preceded him only accentuates the differences between them, particularly with regard to the selection and ordering of linguistic elements and materials. The idioms and phrases that over the ages became the most fundamental and finely crafted building blocks of Spanish Hebrew poetry used in a rigidly ordered way, whereby the distinctions between the sacred and the profane, and between personal and national matters, are always upheld.

In devotional poetry a dialogue is constructed in order to express a situation in which man is addressing God; the motif, while personal, is also existential in nature. Generally speaking, the recurring motifs are contemplation on man's condition in the universe vis-à-vis God, and a plea for spiritual reinforcement enabling man to follow God's ways. In other words, these are universal and ongoing existential questions.[10]

The transference of certain idioms from secular love poetry to devotional poetry was extraordinary enough in its own right to attract the attention of scholars. (A similar transference is seen in the war poems of Shmuel HaNagid, but it was because Shmuel perceived himself as a leader of the community that he took it upon himself to insert phrases from religious poetry into a description of war.) The singularity of Todros Ha-Levi's concrete and personal understanding of divine assistance reveals a great deal about his unique relationship with God. Poems specifically addressing God indicate that the poet clings to God as a son does to his loving father: "Am I not your only son?" (poem A-84). The warm and loving relationship in which the poet develops an intimacy and a close affinity with "his" God is nothing new, since it is also found in the devotional writings of other poets, such as Shlomo Ibn Gabirol. Todros Ha-Levi's innovation lies in his ability to represent relationships not only in terms of grand and lofty situations, but in terms of simple, everyday concerns. His ability to turn an eye irritation or the everyday

---

[10] Ezra Fleischer, *Hebrew Devotional Poetry* (Jerusalem, 1975), pp. 395–412. The term "dialogical structure" refers here to a represented situation in which someone, usually God, is being addressed, and in which the addressee assumes that the addressor is listening to him and will respond. For a detailed discussion, see Aviva Doron, *A Poet in the Royal Court: Todros Ha-levi Abulafia, Hebrew Poetry in Christian Spain* (Tel Aviv, 1989), pp. 50, 67.

hardships involved in collecting taxes into poetic events requiring God's intervention is truly remarkable.

A relevant question would be whether this tendency is at times exaggerated to the point of irony. My response is that even if this is so, it does not detract, from a literary point of view, from the fact that these poems represent a striking poetic innovation.

The combination of poetic structures borrowed from the devotional sphere with descriptions of secular matters and manifestations of the poet's feelings with regard to daily occurrences brings to mind a literary phenomenon which took place in Castile during the lifetime of Todros Abulafia. This was a time during which new and exciting phenomena were occurring in Castilian literary life, where one finds precisely the fusion of elements from devotional poetry with those from secular, popular verse forms. In the overall context of the romance, the vernacular and the vocabulary of popular poetry, a new genre composed chiefly by classical devotional poets began to emerge. These poets, seeking to address the masses so as to confer values upon them and inspire them to faith, had to abandon Latin in favor of the more widely spoken vernacular.

Thus a new elitist poetry emerged in the form of the romance, which became known as *el mester de clerecía*. The first poet to be known by name in the context of the emerging poetry of twelfth-century Spain, Gonzago de Bereceo, calls himself *el juglar del creador* ("the folk bard of God"). Explaining his choice of the vernacular over Latin in order to write romances in a language accessible to all, he says: "Quiero fer una prosa em román paladino, en el qual suele el pueplo fablar a su vezino" ("I want to compose poetry in simple Romance, the language which people use to carry on a conversation with their neighbors").[11]

These poets continued to regard the written word with the utmost respect. Interesting testimony to this is provided by a *clerecía* poet who says the following about his work:

> Mester trago fermos, non es de ioglaria
> mester es sem pecado, ca es de clerezia
> fablar curso rimado por la quaderna via
> a silabas del cantadas, ca es grant maestria.[12]

---

[11] Carlos Blanco Aginaga and I.M. Rodriguez Puertolas y Zavala, *Historia social de la literatura española* (Madrid, 1978), p. 74.

[12] On *mester de clerecía*, see Francisco Lopez Estrada, *Introducción a la literatura medieval*

Freely translated: "My work is high art, not that of the *juglaría* [folk verse]; it cannot be faulted, for it is the *clerecía*" (taken from the second strophe of the introduction to *Libro de Alexandre*).

"On the other hand, we see that the juglaria (popular poetry), which for centuries had been handed down orally from one generation to the next, was just beginning to be written down, and certain distinctly religious topics had crept into popular poetry."[13]

Another phenomenon indicating a similar trend took place in the thirteenth century, when hymns of praise to the Virgin Mary began to be written in the provincial Gallego-Portuguese-style *cantigas de amor* and *cantigas de amigo*, that is, following the mode of secular poems of love and friendship. Alfonso X himself wrote approximately 430 *cantigas de Santa Maria*, in which he proclaims his devotion to, and love and passion for, the Virgin Mary.[14] Alfonso the Wise did not hesitate to combine the sacred with the profane, and this fact, which is of major significance in the overall literary context of thirteenth-century Castile, is greatly relevant to an understanding of the poetry of Todros Ha-Levi Abulafia.

Conclusion

The poetry of Todros ben Yehuda Ha-Levi Abulafia, Hebrew Castilian poet, is located at the site of intersecting literary traditions and styles of poetry. Todros Abulafia wrote in the language of the Bible and of the talmudic sages, and based his poetic style on the forms and motifs he inherited from his predecessors, the classical Hebrew poets who lived and wrote under Muslim rule. At the same time he was familiar with the king's *cantigas*, as well as with the works of all the other poets writing in the royal court, i.e., the *mester de clerecía* poets,

española (Madrid, 1974), pp. 220–221; Michel Gelri, prologue to Gonzalo de Bereceo, *Milagros de Nuestra Señora*; Fernado Diaz Plaja, *Nueva Historia de la literatura española* (Barcelona, 1974), pp. 17–39; Raymond S. Willis, "*Mester de clerecia:* A Definition of the *Libro de Alexandre*," *Romance Philology* 10 (1956–57): 212–224.

[13] Ramon Menéndez Pidal, *Poesia juglarezca y origenes de las literaturas, romanicas* (Madrid, 1957), pp. 334–337.

[14] Francisco Marquez Villaneueva, "La poesia de las cantigas," *Revista de Occidente*, no. 73, pp. 72–93; Marquez de Valmar, *Estudio historico, critico, y filologico sobre las Cantigas del Ray Don Alfonso* (Madrid, 1897); *Cantigas de Santa Maria*, ed. José Filguera Valverdo (Madrid, 1985), introduction, pp. xi–lix; *Algonso X "El Sabio", Cantigas*, ed. Jesus Montoya (Madrid, 1988), introduction, pp. 13–71.

the *juglares* operating in Castile, and the troubadours who came to the royal court afar. He was also keenly aware of the ongoing cultural processes at the time, of the emergent literary currents, and of the violation of traditional boundaries in all poetic forms.

The writings of Todros Abulafia manifest innovative features and original combinations. His work represents the fascinating integration of different cultures that took place in Toledo, the capital of New Castile, Casilla la Nueva.

MÁS SOBRE EL PRESUNTO JUDAÍSMO DE *CELESTINA*

Carlos Mota-Placencia

Universidad del País Vasco

Los años ochenta han sido pródigos en estudios sobre la *Celestina*. Baste recordar que al término del decenio ha cumplido catorce años de existencia el boletín *Celestinesca*, monográficamente dedicado a los más variados aspectos de la obra y de sus avatares. Y que, desde 1985, año en que se detiene la segunda edición de la bibliografía compilada por Joseph T. Snow,[1] han aparecido varios centenares de nuevas publicaciones sobre el tema.[2] De hecho, y debido a Alan Deyermond, ya contamos incluso con un útil balance general de la crítica del período comprendido entre 1979 y 1990[3]: es de notar que en tal balance, presidido por una voluntad de limitación y rigor selectivo considerables, Deyermond referencia no menos de setenta trabajos de diversa entidad.

Como no podía ser de otro modo, una parte sustancial de esa bibliografía toca a las permanentes cuestiones del problemático sentido de la obra de Rojas, de la moralidad y religiosidad presuntamente inherentes a él, de la relación de éstas con las del propio bachiller (en menor medida, con la del probabilísimo primer autor, demasiado a menudo descuidado),[4] y, por ahí, con la personalidad histórica de Fernando de Rojas. No obstante, pese a la amplitud y la variedad de la reflexión, si existe un capítulo en el que nada nuevo parece haber surgido es en el de los datos biográficos fundamentales

---

[1] Joseph T. Snow, *Celestina by Fernando de Rojas: An Annotated Bibliography of World Interest 1930–1985* (Madison: Hispanic Seminary of Medieval Studies, 1985).

[2] Como es bien sabído, en la revista *Celestinesca* van apareciendo puntualmente suplementos actualizadores de la obra citada en la nota anterior.

[3] Me refiero a "La *Celestina*", en Francisco Rico, *Historia y crítica de la literatura española*, 1/1: Alan Deyermond, *Edad Media. Primer Suplemento* (Barcelona: Crítica, 1991), 377–388.

[4] Y por ello no contemplado de facto ni como hipótesis de trabajo, pese a tratarse de una de las más probables y casi probadas de entre cuantas pueden formularse a propósito de *La Celestina*.

y la documentación relativa a Fernando de Rojas.[5] Sí se han apor-
tado en ese terreno, naturalmente, hipótesis: entre ellas destacaría
en especial la formulada por Miguel Marciales, que situa el nacimiento
de don Fernando hacia 1465 ó 1466, y su intervención en la composición de *La Celestina*, por tanto—de ser cierta tal hipótesis-, a una
edad sensiblemente más avanzada de la que suele suponérsele (a los
32 ó 33 años, siendo ya un *jurista* ['abogado', que no 'estudiante de
leyes'] en ejercicio).[6] Por otra parte, siguen siendo objeto de discusión determinados elementos históricos y posibles tradiciones contemporáneas de la realidad del oscuro primer autor y, sobre todo,
de Fernando de Rojas, las cuales, en algunos casos, podrían haber
dejado trazas en la obra: así las alusiones a las casas de Celestina,[7]
o las circunstancias relativas al ejercicio de la casamentería y de la

---

[5] Ténganse en cuenta a su respecto las importantes consideraciones de Peter E.
Russel, "Un crítico en busca de un autor; reflexiones en torno a un reciente libro
sobre Fernando de Rojas", en *Temas de "La Celestina" y otros estudios. Del "Cid" al
"Quijote"*. (Barcelona: Ariel, 1978), 341–375, especialmente, pp. 347–348, inicial-
mente publicado en en *Comparative Literature*, XXVII (1975), 59–74 como artículo
reseña de Stephen Gilman, *The Spain of Fernando de Rojas: The Intellectual and Social
Landscape of "La Celestina"* (Princeton: Princeton University Press, 1972).

[6] Véase Fernando de Rojas, *Celestina. Tragicomedia de Calisto y Melibea*, Introd. y
ed. crítica de Miguel Marciales, al cuidado de Brian Dutton y Joseph T. Snow
(Urbana y Chicago: University of Illinois Press, 1985), I, 269–280, especialmente,
269–275. Menéndez Pelayo, *Orígenes de la novela*, III, señaló como posiblemente
significativa para Rojas la edad que en la obra se atribuye a Calisto (veintitrés
años). En cualquier caso, Peter Russell, en reseña a Fernando de Rojas, *La Celestina*,
ed. de Dorothy S. Severin, notas en colaboración con Maite Cabello (Madrid:
Cátedra, 1987) aparecida en el *Bulletin of Hispanic Studies*, LXVII (1990), 294–296,
plantea resumidamente la cuestión del status (y la posible edad, en cierto modo)
de Rojas como *bachiller* en los siguientes términos: "as a *bachiller* of Salamanca in
his day, he must have (...) completed 9–10 years study in Arts and then Law,
done some teaching in the Faculty and was, by the statutes of the University, eligible to offer himself as a candidate for *oposiciones a cátedra*" (p. 295). Más audaz
parece la teoría que Marciales, *loc. cit.* desarrolla aneja a la que motiva esta nota,
en el sentido de que Rojas habría conocido a Rodrigo Cota, autor del auto I de
la obra para el mismo Marciales.

[7] Sobre la cuestión, véase ahora Peter E. Russell, "Why Did Celestina Move
House?", en Alan Deyermond & Ian MacPherson, eds., *The Age of the Catholic
Monarchs, 1474–1516. Literary Studies in Memory of Keith Whinnom* (Liverpool: Liverpool
University Press, 1989), 155–162). Nótese que la posible existencia de una *domus
Celestinae* en Salamanca "before *La Celestina* was ever written" es hipótesis que el
Prof. Russell afirma considerar "with ... reluctance since it would imply that, at
any rate for its first readers, *La Celestina* may have seemed to be, much more than
we are accustomed to suppose or want to suppose, what Menéndez y Pelayo disparagingly called an 'obra local'". Sobre las consideraciones de los antiguos lectores de la obra de Rojas. es clásico el trabajo de Maxime Chevalier, "*La Celestina*
según sus lectores", en su libro *Lectura y lectores en la España del siglo XVI y XVII*
(Madrid: Turner, 1976) 138–166. Recientemente, Francisco Rico, *Breve biblioteca de*

alcahuetería en la España medieval (esta última una verdadera preocupación social entonces, al parecer)[8] y aun de la prostitución en
la Castilla y en la Salamanca de los tiempos de los Reyes Católicos,
actividad cuidadosamente reglamentada por aquellos años por el gobierno de los soberanos;[9] o, en otro orden de cosas, el papel de la
universidad salmanticense y de sus enseñanzas (y paraenseñanzas)
erotológicas en la configuración de determinados géneros, obras, y
aspectos de la literatura española del siglo XV.[10] Así pues, resum-
iendo, nada nuevo en cuanto a documentos directamente referentes
a Fernando de Rojas; bastante en cuanto al entorno físico e intelectual más inmediatamente próximo al personaje.

Lógicamente, otro tanto—*nihil novum . . .*—, podría decirse respecto
al peculiar rasgo biográfico de la condición de converso de Fernando
de Rojas, tan elaborado desde 1902:[11] señalada por la documentación
en términos discutidos,[12] pero difícilmente cuestionables en absoluto,
sigue en pie el problema de cuál habría sido el grado de proximidad al judaísmo del Bachiller y la posible incidencia de ella
en su personalidad y en su obra literaria. Proximidad en términos
ético-religiosos, y también en los que podríamos llamar biográfico-
generacionales. (Por lo demás, y un tanto en paralelo con lo que
veíamos antes, cada vez es mayor nuestro conocimiento sobre la verdadera situación de judíos, conversos y criptojudíos en la España
medieval). Ahora bien, llegada a este lugar, la crítica no puede sino
despegarse de los datos y emprender el vuelo de las conjeturas, en
el mejor de los casos tratando de involucrar en sus argumentaciones
una mayor o menor porción de hechos documentados pero siempre
de significado poco inequívoco (y frecuentemente agregando a ello

---

autores españoles (Barcelona: Seix Barral, 1990), 81, insiste en que el lugar de la acción
de la obra es "una gran ciudad tan concreta como para resultarnos familiar y tan
imprecisa como para no inclinarnos a lecturas en clave anecdótica".

[8] Véase Francisco Marquez Villanueva, "*La Celestina* as Hispano-Semitic
Anthropology", *Revue de Littérature Comparée*, LX (1987), 425–453.

[9] Véanse varias observaciones al respecto en María Eugenia Lacarra, *Cómo leer
"La Celestina"* (Madrid: Júcar, 1990), 23–29, y el artículo citado en la n. anterior,
passim.

[10] En especial la literatura amorosa: véase el capital estudio de Pedro M. Catedra,
Amor y pedagogía en la Edad Media (Salamanca: Ediciones de la Universidad de
Salamanca, 1989), y también la reseña al mismo de Alan Deyermond publicada en
Insula, DXXXII (1991), 1, 4.

[11] Desde el artículo de Manuel Serrano y Sanz, "Noticias biográficas de Fernando
de Rojas, autor de *La Celestina* y del impresor Juan de Lucena", *Revista de Archivos,
Bibliotecas y Museos*, VI (1902), 245–298.

[12] Véase el trabajo citado de Márquez (1980) en n. 8.

la convicción de la existencia de una peculiaridad literaria de los
conversos):[13] así, en especial, los consabidos conflictos tenidos con la
Inquisición por el suegro de Rojas, Álvaro de Montalbán (1525–1526)
y los problemas surgidos en la probanza de hidalguía del nieto del
autor de la *Celestina* (en 1584), de un lado, o las circunstancias que
rodearon la aparentemente discreta y respetada existencia de la
madurez del Bachiller y su testamento, muerte y sepultura cristianas
(1541)—circunstancias tan aparentemente contradictorias con el
espíritu inquieto, no solo desde el punto de vista religioso, que se considera en el autor de la obra-, entre otros. En el peor de los casos (habría
grados intermedios), y en ello acercándose paradójicamente a los
puntos de vista más cerrilmente intolerantes, el vuelo de las conjeturas aludido se inicia dando por supuesta en Rojas la identidad
entre condición conversa, criptojudaísmo, incredulidad, heterodoxia
dentro de la vieja y la nueva religión, hipocresía, nihilismo, etcétera,
etcétera.[14] En lo relativo a la que llamábamos proximidad biográfico-
generacional de Rojas al judaísmo, todo se fundamenta ya en puras
hipótesis, pero lo cierto es que las más verosímiles parecen apuntar,
como es sabido, a que Rojas no era converso él mismo ni, posiblemente, descendiente de conversos recientes,[15] lo que constituiría un

---

[13] Que ha sido objeto de seria discusión: véanse los ensayos de Eugenio Asensio
ahora reunidos en su libro *La España imaginada de Américo Castro* (Barcelona: El Albir,
1976).

[14] Para una inteligente discusión de los muy variados tipos históricos de conversos, véase Julio Caro Baroja, *Los judíos en la España moderna y contemporánea* (Madrid:
Istmo, 1978²), en especial I, 291–316.

[15] Y menos hijo del converso Hernando de Rojas ejecutado en 1488 sugerido
por Stephen Gilman en la *op. cit.* (en n. 2), (antes en *Romanische Forschungen*, LXXVIII
(1976), 1–28). Resume los pertinentes argumentos cuestionadores Keith Whinnom,
"Interpreting *La Celestina*: The Motives and the Personality of Fernando de Rojas",
Mediaeval and Renaissance Studies on Spain and Portugal in Honour of P.E. Russell, edited
by F.W. Hodcroft, D.G. Pattison, R.D.F. Pring-Mill, R.W. Truman, (Oxford: The
Society for the Study of Mediaeval Languages and Literature, 1981), 53–68, concretamente, p. 58, n. 17. Whinnom tiene en cuenta Miguel Marciales, *Carta al Profesor
Stephen Gilman*, que no me ha sido accesible (e Ya Russell, más allá de las propias
dudas de Gilman (que le llevaron a postular una posible conversión antigua de la
familia de Rojas, quizás producto de la agitación siguiente a las atrocidades de
1391), había señalado que "no hay prueba alguna de ningún tipo de que Hernando
de Rojas tuviera ese final por sus actividades judaizantes, y, desde luego, ni es
siquiera seguro que ese Hernando de Rojas fuera el padre de nuestro Fernando"
(Peter E. Russell, "Un crítico en busca de un autor...", 375, n. 11.). Para la con-
traargumentación de Gilman, "Sobre la identidad histórica de Fernando de Rojas",
Nueva Revista de Filología Hispánica, XXVI (1977), 154–158, y en esa línea, "A
Generation of Conversos", *Romance Philology*, XXXIII (1979–1980), 87–101.

paliativo considerable a un entorno familiar próximo en el que ha quedado bien establecida la existencia de problemas con el Santo Tribunal.

En esas condiciones, se ha impuesto la atención prioritaria a la letra de la obra, también al objeto de atisbar vislumbres de la personalidad del autor. La mayor parte de las cosas se vuelven ahí árduas ambigüedades, incesantemente interrogadas, o demostraciones de ideas en buena medida preconcebidas.[16] Y así parece que habrá de seguir siendo mientras, cada vez más gerneralizado el escepticismo respecto a explicaciones de la obra completamente coherentes en sí mismas,[17] se procura ahondar en el conocimiento de los materiales primarios de la literatura y la cultura españolas del siglo XV a pie de los datos, de los conocidos de antiguo y de los no pocos nuevos que van surgiendo. Quizás provisionalmente, y por un designio pedagógico inevitablemente simplificador, la crítica ha advertido la alineación de quienes buscan claves interpretativas de universal (o de esencial) validez en dos posturas, que Dorothy S. Severin ha

---

[16] Sería el caso, entre los trabajos recientes, de Yirmiyahu Yovel, "Marranos in Mask and a World without Transcendence: Rojas and *La Celestina*", en *Spinoza and Other Heretics*, I: *The Marrano of Reason* (Princeton: Princeton University Press, 1989), 85–127; 217–226 (notas), en el que resulta llamativa—entre otras cosas, como su elección textual- su descuido de no poca parte de la bibliografía pertinente. Algo distinto es el trabajo de Manuel da Costa Fontes, "The Idea of 'limpieza' in *La Celestina*", *Hispanic Studies in Honor of Joseph H. Silverman* (Newark, Delaware: Juan de la Cuesta, 1988), 24–35, que establece un útil inventario y discusión de las apariciones y posibles usos equívocos en la obra de *limpio, limpiar, limpieza*, y concluye que "the disagreement concerning the role played by this concept in *La Celestina* shows that the aversion that Fernando de Rojas must have felt towards *limpieza de sangre* is not clearly reflected in his work" (p. 24), pero sin embargo, guiado por el propósito (enunciado literalmente en p. 24) de aplicar unas palabras de Américo Castro a *La Celestina* ("la literatura de los cristianos nuevos (. . .) no reconocía valor a la limpieza de sangre, la rechaza, la desdeña o ironiza", *Hacia Cervantes*, 22), le parece verlas confirmadas en la a su juicio exageradamente desproporcionada presencia del concepto de *limpieza* en los versos iniciales y finales de la *Tragicomedia* ("el autor, escusándose de su yerro en esta obra que escrivió, contra sí arguye y compara" y "concluye el autor"). La constatable frecuencia de la idea en esos lugares, tal vez desproporcionada pero atestada en usos no tan disímiles en cuanto a su presunta ambigüedad a los que detecta en los autos y le llevan a la conclusión antes citada, nos parece que obstaculizan afirmar tan tajantemente como lo hace el Prof. Fontes que "it (la abundante presencia del concepto de limpieza en los versos en cuestión) invalidates any possibility of a pure coincidence".

[17] Hasta plantear la práctica imposibilidad de tales coherencias integrales como hipótesis de base: así Whinnom, *art. cit.*, p. 66: "One of the greater obstacles to a proper interpretation of *La Celestina* is surely the presupposition that it is a masterpiece without flaws, a wholly self-consistent work which, in spite of its manifold ambiguities, reflects a unified version of life and one unswerving purpose".

etiquetado como "escuela judeopesimista" y "escuela cristianodidáctica."[18] Tras tantos decenios de discusión, cabe preguntarse si se trataría de la designación de dos líneas decididamente divergentes y comparables en cuanto a magnitud, y por ello, del reflejo de un cierto *impasse*. Parecería deseable que no fuera así, y más cuando en general, incluso la crítica no especialmente afin a orientaciones teóricas radicalmente textualistas parece tender a adherirse a la letra de la obra y a preterir la especulación "biografista"[19] (Por lo demás, es preciso subrayar el incomparablemente menor énfasis puesto en lo biográfico por la llamada "escuela cristiano-didáctica"). Sin embargo, recientemente ha sido dado un paso que cabría calificar como un intento de cortar el nudo gordiano: el artículo de Nicasio Salvador Miguel "Sobre el presunto judaísmo de *La Celestina*."[20] El propósito de dicho trabajo está claramente definido en sus últimas líneas: *La Celestina* (. . .) es obra de interpretación plural; así, descartar, con rotundidad, una de las presuntas lecturas significa adelantar no poco, pues deja abierto el campo para la exploración de otras vías más acertadas. No es cuestión de repasar ahora y aquí al pormenor los argumentos ajenos analizados por el Prof. Salvador, ni sus propias réplicas.[21] Pero podría afirmarse, en nuestra opinión, que esta aportación ha certificado como partes del museo de la crítica a la mayoría de dichos argumentos e interpretaciones "judaicas."[22]

---

[18] Fernando de Rojas, *La Celestina*, ed. de Dorothy S. Severin, notas en colaboración con Maite Cabello (Madrid: Cátedra, 1987), "Introducción", 23–24. Precisando (*ibid.*, en n.): "Para la primera de las categorías, véase Gilman [*Art* y *The Spain*]. Bataillon tipifica la segunda, y a él vienen a unirse [Otis H.] Green y sus discípulos, por ejemplo Morón Arroyo . . ."

[19] Es difícil, de todos modos, pronunciarse sobre la existencia en el plano diacrónico de sesgos claramente definidos y significativos en la ingente y pluralísima producción crítica más reciente. Además, en todo caso, y como señala Deyermond (*Historia y crítica*, 1/1, 385), en este campo de la especulación biográfica como en otros, falta sopesar con el debido detenimiento, por ejemplo, las hipótesis de Marciales.

[20] Publicado en *The Age of the Catholic Monarchs*, citado más arriba, n. , pp. 162–177.

[21] Éstas se sintetizarían en sus conclusiones: "la explicación del argumento de *La Celestina* como reflejo de un problema racial no se apoya en el más mínimo fundamento, tampoco existe base alguna para pensar que la *Tragicomedia* plantee una protesta social contra la situación de los conversos; la actitud del autor no deja al descubierto ningún flanco de supuesto ataque a la ortodoxia ni a la Inquisición; ningún aspecto de la obra se aclara desde la perspectiva del Rojas converso. Todo ello coincide, en definitiva, con lo percibido por los lectores durante siglos, de modo que, si no nos constara documentalmente tal origen del joven bachiller, sería imposible inferirlo de la obra, como atestigua el hecho de que nadie haya sugerido ninguna cuestión de este tipo con anterioridad a 1902" (*op. cit.*, 172).

[22] De todos modos, advierte el autor de dicho artículo la acusada tendencia a

Analizarlos en sí, ya no como instrumentos operativos, puede ser de interés. Porque es digna de nota la proximidad de algunos de esos argumentos o de sus fundamentos teóricos—sobre todo de los que Salvador considera los más "impresionistas",[23]—a determinados tópicos de la propaganda antisemita característica de los siglos XIX y XX (y en algún caso de la anterior a dichos siglos). Y ello a pesar del demostrable filojudaísmo de muchos de los postuladores de los argumentos en cuestión. Ejemplos: en las habituales consideraciones de las vacilaciones rojanas (reflejadas en los preliminares y partes finales y en los añadidos y supresiones variantes de unas a otras versiones) como *indudables* signos de desafíos o befas a la Inquisición (de la que, paradójicamente, el autor se ocultaría aterrorizado a otros propósitos), o como depósitos de mensajes encubiertos, ¿cómo no ver al menos la sombra de las fantásticas conspiraciones secularmente esgrimidas por los antisemitas como descripciones de las actividades judaicas por excelencia? O ¿cómo interpretar la tendencia a admitir acríticamente lo presuntamente inconcebible de la actividad mercantil de Pleberio en alguien no perteneciente al sector social de los cristianos nuevos, o incluso la atribución de un carácter *infamante* a ella? ¿O la negación del sentido del honor en los judíos (y por extensión en los conversos, abusivamente) por ejemplo a propósito de la opción por el suicidio? ¿O la propensión a considerar rasgo judío-converso la inclinación a blasfemar (que no a polemizar en materia de religión, éste sí, rasgo histórico de los judíos), o las no poco a menudo muy imaginarias blasfemias que proliferarían en el texto— más allá de las hipérboles sagradas, en su momento blanco predilecto de apreciaciones de tal naturaleza-? ¿O la aceptación de la tesis xenófoba de la no pertenencia, por definición, de los judíos (y de los conversos) a la comunidad nacional, monopolizada por los católicos? ¿O las asociaciones del tipo frialdad y cálculo igual a (presunta) naturaleza judía-conversa? ¿O, sin más, la relación: condición de converso igual a subversión (y al margen el calificativo que acompañe a esa subversión: siniestra o admirable)?

La posible coincidencia entre tópicos antisemitas y ciertas interpretaciones de esta obra (mayormente surgidas de la exageración, retorsión o reducción al absurdo de tesis sostenidas en su día por

---

resucitar de dichos argumentos. Estimamos que algunas secciones del capítulo del libro de Yovel antes citado podría considerarse una buena muestra de ello.

[23] Véase sobre todo, en *art. cit.*, sección 6, pp. 165–166.

Américo Castro o por Stephen Gilman, aunque no cabe descuidar
que otras nacieron y se desarrollaron en la época previa a la guerra
civil española), requeriría un tratamiento más extenso del posible
ahora: es aspecto sobre el que nos proponemos volver. Pero que,
prima facie, no creemos producto o reflejo de intenciones programáticas,
sino más bien de inconsecuencias lógicas en las argumentaciones o
de una peculiar propiedad de esos tópicos (y sus *razonamientos* ane-
jos) que sería su radical e insidiosa reversibilidad, que tiende a hac-
erlos ser, en el tiempo, como una banda de Moebius (del odio a la
filia y viceversa, las dos caras de una misma moneda a un tiempo).
No cabe descuidar, aunque aún falten bastantes cosas por averiguar
en ese ámbito la desvertebración del antisemitismo contemporáneo
español, sumamente lejano del antisemitismo *científico* de la Centro-
europa decimonónica y algo menos del católico ultraconservador
mayormente vigente en Francia, que enseñó su rostro a toda Europa
al hilo del affaire Dreyfus. En ese sentido, puede resultar emblemáti-
camente ilustrativo confrontar (de momento, sólo eso) determinadas
ideas de Ramiro de Maeztu que, aisladas de su contexto mayormente filojudaico, pueden parecer hasta estridentemente antisemíti-
cas (así la célebre caracterización de Celestina como "la trotaconventos
es un rabino por el conocimiento y la sutileza dialéctica" o "La
Celestina es un rabino que conduce el mundo no al imperio mesiánico,
sino al de su propio interés")[24] con un artículo periodístico del joven
Maeztu londinense y filofabiano, en el que, congratulándose de la
resolución del proceso al oficial Dreyfus, termina sin embargo escri-
biendo (en una muestra paradigmática del argumento antisemítico-
xenófobo por excelencia):

> Y tampoco es probable que la absolución de Dreyfus ponga defi-
> nitivamente término a la campaña antisemita. Actualmente, no cabe
> duda, los judíos son dueños de cuanto en Francia brilla (. . .), y la sen-
> tencia de Dreyfus viene a confirmar su poderío. Pero no se hagan ilu-
> siones, ni traten de abusar de su triunfo. La Francia, en su parte sólida
> y perdurable, la rica tierra, es aún de los franceses de raza francesa,
> raza testaruda y obstinada. A los judíos toca asimilarse a ella y no a
> los franceses parecerse a los judíos. Si éstos se empeñan en mandar a
> los otros, el resultado será el despertar del antisemitismo, que no dejará

---

[24] Ramiro de Maeztu, *Don Quijote, don Juan y la Celestina. Ensayos de simpatía* (Madrid:
Calpe, 1926), 270.

de manifestarse con alguna energía el día próximo en que Rusia se declare en bancarrota y acudan los padres de familia a las casas de banca judías que les aconsejaron la inversión de sus ahorros en fondos moscovitas, y pregunten a los banqueros:

—¿Qué habéis hecho de nuestros ahorros?[25]*

---

[25] Ramiro de Maeztu, "La absolución de Dreyfus", *La correspondencia de España*, no. 17688 (Madrid, 17 de julio de 1906), recopilado en Jesús Jareño Lopez, *El affaire Dreyfus en España (1894–1906)* (Murcia: Godoy, 1981), 296. Información fundamental sobre la peculiar trayectoria ideológica de Ramiro de Maeztu en: José Luis Abellán, "Ramiro de Maeztu o la voluntad de poder", en su libro *Sociología del 98* (Barcelona: Península, 1973), 141–160, Carlos Blanco Aguinaga, "La otra España de Maeztu", en su libro *Juventud del 98* (Barcelona: Crítica, 1978²), 157–175; José Carlos Mainer, "*La guerra del Transvaal* y los secretos del 98", *Camp de l'Arpa* XVII–XVIII (1975), 31–34; E. Inman Fox, Ramiro de Maeztu, *Artículos desconocidos* (Madrid: Castalia, 1978). Más recientemente, y con referencias bibliográficas amplias, José Miguel Fernández de Urbina, *La aventura intelectual de Ramiro de Maeztu* (Vitoria: Diputación Foral de Alava, 1990).

* Este trabajo se presentó como comunicación a la *Second International Interdisciplinary Conference on Sephardic Studies* en 1991 y pretendía ser una aportación con información bibliográfica muy al día ante una audiencia no dedicada primordialmente a la historia de la literatura española medieval aunque sí puntualmente interesada en ella desde otros ámbitos de estudio. Es claro que el posible valor de su actualidad se ha desvanecido en los años transcurridos, que también han sido abundantes en libros y artículos sobre *La Celestina*, aunque no particularmente sobre los temas que se tocaban en el artículo. En cierto modo, esos años transcurridos desde 1991 permiten reafirmar algunas de las cosas que se señalaban en él, como el valor de corte de un nudo gordiano que parece haber tenido el artículo de Nicasio Salvador de 1989, citado en la n. 20. Por otra parte, es muy importante el libro de Francisco Márquez Villanueva, *Orígenes y sociología del tema celestinesco*, Barcelona, Anthropos, 1993, como profundización en ciertas ideas apuntadas en su trabajo citado en la n. 8.

"JONEN DALIM," AUTO ALEGÓRICO DE MIGUEL (DANIEL LEVÍ) DE BARRIOS

Julia R. Lieberman

Saint Louis University

Introducción

Miguel (Daniel Leví) de Barrios nació en Montilla, Córdoba, en 1635, y salió de España antes de 1660. Después de residir brevemente en Francia, Italia y la isla de Tabago en América, hacia 1662 llegó a la comunidad de mercaderes sefarditas de Amsterdam. Desde su llegada, hasta aproximadamente 1674, mantuvo relaciones literarias con los españoles de la corte de Bruselas y escribió y publicó obras que iban dirigidas al público español en general. Hacia 1674 dejó de viajar a Bruselas y comenzó a escribir casi exclusivamente para los sefarditas de Amsterdam. Miguel de Barrios nunca volvió a España y murió en Amsterdam en 1701.[1]

Las obras de Barrios escritas en el primer período de su carrera literaria, aunque no muy bien conocidas de españoles e hispanistas en general, han recibido alguna atención y hay varios estudios críticos sobre su poesía y sus comedias de capa y espada.[2] Barrios, como poeta, está considerado un seguidor de Góngora y el poeta por

---

[1] Para la vida de Miguel de Barrios los estudios más importantes y completos son: Meyer Kayserling, "Une Histoire de la Littérature Juive de Daniel Lévi de Barrios," *Revue des Etudes Juives* 18 (1889): 277–281; Kenneth R. Scholberg, *La poesía religiosa de Miguel de Barrios* (Ohio State University Press, 1962); Wilhelmina C. Pieterse, *Daniel Levi de Barrios als geschiedschrijver van de Portugees-Israelietische gemeente te Amsterdam in zijn "Triumpho del Govierno Popular"* (Amsterdam: Scheltema & Holkema, 1968), y el capítulo III de mi tesis doctoral "El teatro alegórico religioso de Miguel (Daniel Leví) de Barrios y la colonia de sefarditas de Amsterdam en el siglo XVII" (diss., Yale University, 1990).

[2] Henry V. Besso, "Dramatic Literature of the Sephardic Jews," *Bulletin Hispanique* 39–41 (1937–39): 215–238, 37–47, 158–175 y 316–344. Charles Moolick, "The Poetic Styles of Miguel de Barrios" (diss., University of Southern California, 1964). Ervie Peña, "El español de Orán by Miguel de Barrios: A Critical Edition and Study" (diss., University of Southern California, 1971). José Luis Sánchez Fernández, *Poemas mitológicos de Miguel de Barrios* (Córdoba: Instituto de Historia de Andalucía, 1981).

excelencia de la comunidad de mercaderes portugueses y españoles de Amsterdam en el siglo XVII. La obra de Barrios es también conocida entre los historiadoress interesados por los judíos españoles en el exilio que hacen frecuentemente mención de ella y la consideran la primera crónica de los sefarditas de Amsterdam en el siglo XVII.[3] Pero apenas se sabe de sus dramas que siguen la técnica literaria de los autos sacramentales alegóricos de España, especialmente los escritos por Calderón de la Barca. Existen seis obras dramáticas de Miguel de Barrios que siguen esta técnica literaria y que además dramatizan los pasos de su vida de marrano a judío. Entre 1665 y 1672, Barrios escribió una comedia alegórica titulada *Contra la verdad no hay fuerza*. Esta obra es una apología de la religión judía. Además de que aproximadamente coincide con los años en que Barrios deja de relacionarse con los españoles de Bruselas, la comedia es una dramatización de la decisión del escritor de vivir dedicado al estudio de la religión judaica. Hacia 1684 Barrios escribió cinco autos alegóricos en un solo acto en los cuales evidencia su total dedicación al estudio de la ley de Moisés.[4] Lo que sorprende a primera vista es que Barrios escogió escribir todas estas obras siguiendo la tradición literaria de los autos sacramentales de España, considerados el género católico por excelencia, precisamente para expresar su identificación con el judaísmo. El género literario de estas obras es solamente una de las evidencias de que la vida de Barrios no está claramente dividida en dos etapas: vida como marrano y vida como judío, sino que entre los dos períodos se crearon lazos difficiles de romper. El teatro alegórico de Barrios explora aspectos de la religión, la judía y la cristiana; la nacionalidad, ¿qué es ser español,? y sentimientos ambivalentes, como es la fidelidad y

---

[3] Además del ya mencionado estudio de Wilhelmina C. Pieterse, véanse, por ejemplo, L. and R. Fuks, "Jewish Historiography in the Netherlands in the 17th and 18th Century," *Studia Rosenthaliana* 6 (1972): 137–165. Yosef Kaplan, "Isaac Orobio de Castro and His Circle" (diss., Hebrew University of Jerusalem, 1978); también de Yosef Kaplan, "The Portuguese Jews in Amsterdam: From Forced Conversion to a Return to Judaism," *Studia Rosenthaliana* 15 (1981): 37–51; Y. Kaplan, ed., "The Travels of Portuguese Jews from Amsterdam to the 'Lands of Idolatry' (1644–1724)," *Jews and Conversos: Studies in Society and The Inquisition*, págs. 197–224; *Proc. of the 8th World Congress of Jewish Studies, 16–21 August 1981* (Jerusalem: Magnes Press, 1985).

[4] El libro de Haydee Litovsky, *Sephardic Playwrights of the Seventeenth and Eighteenth Centuries in Amsterdam* (Lanham, Md.: University Press of America, 1990), incluye un breve estudio de la comedia alegórica de Barrios *Contra la verdad no hay fuerza*, pero su autora parece desconocer que Barrios escribió los cinco autos que yo he estudiado en mi tesis doctoral.

el rechazo a España, su país de nacimiento. La obra de Barrios es también representante de los sentimientos de otros muchos coetáneos de Amsterdam que en el pasado habían vivido como christianos en la Península.

Auto Alegorico "Jonen Dalim"

"Jonen Dalim," el auto alegórico que voy a analizar seguidamente, es uno de los cinco autos de hacia 1684 que se encuentran en un libro colecticio titulado *Triumpho del Govierno Popular y de la Antiguedad Holandesa*.[5] El título hebreo del auto, "Jonen Dalim," es también el nombre de una academia de estudios religiosos o *yeshivá*, en honor de la cual Barrios escribió el drama. El texto tiene indicaciones de que la obra fue representada en una reunión académica y suponemos que los actores, y aún su público, serían otros miembros de la academia. El título hebreo de la obra, "Jonen Dalim," está inspirado en varias citas del libro de Proverbios donde aparece la expresión hebrea "Jonen Dalim," el que se apiada de los pobres:[6] Proverbios 14:21, "Quien desprecia a su prójimo peca, / más quien se apiada de los desgraciados es feliz." 14:31, "Quien oprime al pobre escarnece a su Hacedor; / en cambio, le honra quien se apiada del necesitado." 19:17, "Presta a Yahveh quien se apiada del pobre, / y El le pagará su buena acción," y 28:8, "Quien multiplica su fortuna por usuras y logros, / para el que se apiada de los pobres las acumula."

Los personajes de la obra son abstracciones personificadas. La Ley, que representa la Torá judaica, Israel, el pueblo judío, Edom, personaje abstracto femenino enemigo de Israel que representa la cristiandad y España, Jonen Dalim, otra abstracción femenina que personifica la yeshivá o academia de estudios del mismo nombre y que, como su nombre hebreo indica, simboliza la caridad, dos personajes secundarios llamados el Socorro y el Anuncio, y dos coros de músicas que, según las indicaciones del texto, cantaban y tocaban instrumentos musicales desde detrás del escenario.

"Jonen Dalim, Auto Sacro," así llama Barrios a la obra, es en

---

[5] (Amsterdam: 5443–1683), Ejemplar Ros. 19G12. El auto se encuentra en las págs. 217–240. Las citas para este estudio son de la edición con versos numerados que se encuentra como apéndice a mi tesis doctoral, págs. 218–240.

[6] Cito siempre de la *Sagrada Biblia*, Biblioteca de Autores. Cristianos (Madrid: Editorial Católica, 1961), edición de José María Bover y Francisco Cantera Burgos.

principio difícil de parafrasear ya que carece de lo que comúnmente entendemos por trama o historia. Está formada por más de 67 breves citas de una variedad de libros bíblicos, que a primera lectura pueden parecer dispares, además de otras fuentes judías y literarias de España que Barrios adapta y entrelaza con su propia poesía. La obra, escrita en versos, consta de un solo acto dividido en tres partes separadas cada una por la salida al escenario de dos de los personajes: Israel y la Ley, en la primera parte; Socorro y Anuncio en la segunda y Edom y Jonen Dalim en la tercera. El auto comienza con las voces de los coros que desde detrás del escenario amenazan con arrojar a Israel al mar. Notas al margen del texto indican que la poesía que cantan los coros son citas bíblicas de los Salmos. Se corre la cortina y aparece al fondo la escena de un mar en tormenta y en el exterior ruinas y montañas. Israel, el protagonista, sale del mar y llega a tierra, vestido muy humildemente y acompañado de la Ley o Torá. Dialogan Israel y la Ley. Aquél expresa su cansancio y ésta le conforta diciéndole que la redención se aproxima. Israel se siente aliviado y acepta su culpabilidad por los pecados cometidos en el pasado. Compara su situación a la representación que hace el pobre en la comedia de *La Vida es sueño*. El rico de la comedia de la vida es Edom, que no tiene compasión de Israel. Se oyen las voces de Edom y Jonen Dalim. Aquél llama a Israel "mendigo asqueroso," Jonen Dalim dice que despreciar al pobre es ofender a Dios.

La segunda parte del auto comienza con la salida a escena del Anuncio y el Socorro describiendo a Jonen Dalim. El Anuncio la describe como: "El que pasage / da al Pobre en los alivios que le intima." El Socorro dice que Jonen Dalim es "El que de la Piedad blanco plumage / en la cabeça está que lo sublima," versos 234–237. Esta parte del auto no tiene citas bíblicas. Es en esencia la parte "real" de auto de ocasión. Describe la academia de estudios "Jonen Dalim," en honor de la cual está escrito el auto. Esta institución según nos dice el personaje Socorro, fue fundada en abril de 1667 y, en el momento en que se escribe el auto, se compone de un sanedrín o tribunal de sesenta hermanos. En la academia se hacen obras de caridad, siguiendo la tradición judaica y como decretaron los codificadores José Caro y el rabino Baxié.[7] El estatuto de la hermandad

---

[7] José Caro (1488–1575), es autor del *Shulhan Arukh*. Baya ben Joseph ibn Paquda, escritor de la España medieval del siglo XI, es conocido por una obra de ética escrita en árabe y traducida al español con el título de *Obligación de los corazones*.

rige a sus miembros y prescribe que se asista a los hermanos nece-
sitados, que se reparta pan semanalmente entre las viudas de la
comunidad y que se acompañe el cadáver de los hermanos que
mueren. El Socorro describe las reuniones de estudios de los miembros los domingos, las fiestas y los sábados. Alaba los miembros y,
finalmente, dirigiéndose a Israel, le dice que representa al pobre y
que el tesorero se ocupará de ayudarlo. Israel queda agradecido.

En la tercera parte del auto salen a escena de Jonen Dalim y
Edom. Como en la primera parte, las notas al margen indican que
la poesia que recitan los personajes son, a menudo, citas biblicas.
Jonen Dalim dice a Israel que siente piedad de él. Edom, por el
contrario, le dice que no se cansará de molestarlo. La Ley promete
consolar a Israel. Edom pregunta cómo puede hacerlo sino ha aceptado al mesías, La Ley responde que es Edom la que no la entiende.
Los coros de músicos anuncian la destrucción de los enemigos de
Israel. Al lado derecho del escenario aparece un campo de cadáveres
y al izquierdo una campaña frondosa. Los cadáveres representan los
miembros muertos de la hermandad Jonen Dalim, y la campaña la
estancia de Edom. La Ley explica que los que atraviesan la selva
quedan convertidos en aves, sierpes y brutos. El Anuncio identifica
las cuatro fieras del libro de Daniel con diversos países de Europa
y dice que en Hesperia, España, la Inquisición obliga a todos a
cometer idolatría. Israel dice que él es el único que permanece con
su forma humana. La Ley llama a Israel: Ulises del cielo, y compara a Jonen Dalim con la sacra paloma del Cantar de los Cantares.
Los coros musicales, desde dentro, alaban a Jonen Dalim, la hermandad, y sus miembros. Edom se identifica con Roma. Jonen Dalim
explica el significado de su nombre, "que del pobre se apiada," y
se identifica con aquellas naciones que sienten piedad de Israel y a
las cuales Dios premiará con victorias y conducirán al mesías a tierra
santa. Edom dice que ya entra en la selva. Jonen Dalim predice su
caída. Vuela un papel por el aire y lo alcanza el Anuncio y lo lee.
En el papel hay escrita una cita de Isaías 26:6, que predice a caída
de la ciudad, Roma. Un coro canta la permanencia de la Ley
frente a Roma, que todo lo entiende al revés. Un miembro de la
academia, Selomoh de Olivera, canta en hebreo una alabanza a
los otros miembros. Según se interpretan varias citas bíblicas, se
aproxima la llegada del mesías. La Ley, el Socorro, el Anuncio e
Israel expresan su reconocimiento a Jonen Dalim. El auto termina
con las palabras de Jonen Dalim: "Pues con repetidos gozos / Demos

a Dios puras loas, / para que en su Amor tengamos / aquí paz, y después gloria."

Uno de los aspectos más importantes de esta obra es la interpretación que Barrios hace de los textos bíblicos. Si bien, como veremos más adelante, la técnica literaria de la obra es la de los autos sacramentales de España, la lectura e interpretación de las fuentes en que se basa difiere en gran medida de la exégesis cristiana. Barrios era miembro de varias de las yeshivot o academias de estudios existentes en Amsterdam, entre ellas la llamada Jonen Dalim, en honor de la cual está escrito el auto. En estas instituciones los miembros se reunían frecuentemente para estudiar y discutir la Biblia.[8] Como es históricamente característico en la tradición judaica, la lectura de la Biblia supone el examen de breves versículos, a veces la base de una discusión pueden ser simplemente varias palabras, que se comparan y contrastan con versículos de otros textos y que se interpretan a la luz de comentarios de autoridades rabínicas. Como contraste a esta lectura de un texto o pasaje bíblico, la exégesis cristiana interpreta un texto, una selección del Nuevo Testamento, por ejemplo, como la confirmación de otro texto, a menudo el Antiguo Testamento. Siguiendo la exégesis místico-judaica, Barrios trata de descifrar significados secretos en los pasajes bíblicos que hace decir a los personajes del drama. Para ello reúne episodios que históricamente no tienen relaciones entre sí pero que en algunos casos comparten los mismos temas y en otros reconcilian ideas contradictorias.[9] Los temas del exilio del pueblo judío y el de la redención, por ejemplo, aparecen en muchas de las citas bíblicas del auto, a veces para

---

[8] Para más información sobre las actividades de las yeshivot de Amsterdam véase el capítulo II de mi tesis doctoral titulado: "Vida intelectual de la 'Jerusalem del norte.'"

[9] Además de la influencia de la tradición oral de las yeshivot de Amsterdam, Barrios, en el auto, verso 457, cita a Mennaseh Ben Israel, en su libro *Conciliador o de la conveniencia de los lugares de la Sagrada Escritura, que repugnantes entre si parecen* (Amsterdam, 1632). Véase la edición de E.H. Lindo (New York: Hermon Press), págs. 216–217. Creo que Mennaseh debió tener una gran influencia en la obra de Barrios, más de la que esta breve cita indica. El tema del mesianismo es evidente en muchas de las obras de Mennaseh y la lectura que este autor hace de ciertos pasajes bíblicos es muy similar a la que hace Barrios de los textos bíblicos en general. Véase, por ejemplo, el estudio sobre otra de las obras de Mennaseh, *Piedra Gloriosa* y su mesianismo: Avigdor W.G. Poseq, "Left and Right in Rembrandt's Defeat of Goliath," *Studia Rosenthaliana* 22 (1989): 8–27. El profesor Poseq brevemente estudia la lectura místico-cabalística que Mennaseh hace de los textos bíblicos, y sugiere como posible fuente de Mennaseh la obra de la cábala el *Zohar*, o *Libro del esplendor*.

referirse a Israel y otras a Edom, su enemiga. Barrios cita de los libros de Ezequiel, Zacarías, Jeremías y Levítico, como prueba de que el exilio y el sufrimiento del pueblo judío previstos en los libros bíblicos son castigos que Dios se ve forzado a imponer en su pueblo favorito ya que éste se ha olvidado de su pacto con él y ha cometido el pecado más aborrecible de todos, la idolatría.[10] Para el nombre del personaje Edom, Barrios se inspira en el libro profético de Abdias, donde Edom se llama también Esaú, hermano de Jacob, y es el padre de los edomitas, pueblo enemigo de Israel. Citando del libro de Isaías compara metafóricamente a Edom con un mar en tempestad. Otra vez Edom es comparado a Gog, el enemigo de Israel del libro de Ezequiel, refiriéndose a los terribles días que predecerán la llegada del fin de los días y, finalmente, identifica a Edom con la cristiandad, que, interpretando Génesis 49:10 y Deuteronomio 28:65, culpa a Israel de su propio exilio como consecuencia de no haber aceptado al mesías.[11] El tema del mesianismo del pueblo hebreo, culminación del tema del exilio, tiene un significado especialmente personal para Barrios. Durante el período del movimiento sabatiano que causó estragos en toda la diáspora judía, Barrios, por algún tiempo, fue uno de los seguidores del movimiento, creyendo que la redención del pueblo judío había llegado, o por lo menos, que se aproximaba eminentemente.[12] Aunque el auto "Jonen Dalim"

---

[10] Ezequiel 39:24, "Conforme a su inmudicia y sus crimenes los he tratado [a los israelitas], y he ocultado de ellos mi rostro" ("Jonen Dalim," versos 75 y ss.). Zacarías 2:6, "Huíd del país del norte—oráculo de Yaveh—." Jeremías 9:16, "Los dispersaré entre las gentes que no conocieron ni ellos ni sus padres, y enviaré tras ellos la espada hasta consumirlos." Levítico 26:33, "Y a vosotros os desparramaré por las naciones y desenvainaré la espada tras de vosotros; vuestra tierra quedará asolada, y vuestras ciudades, reducidas a escombros" ("Jonen Dalim," versos 125 y ss.).

[11] Abdias 14, "Por la mortandad, por la injusticia contra tu hermano Jacob, / te cubrirá la vergüenza y serás extirpado para siempre" ("Jonen Dalim," versos 217 y ss.). Isaías 57:20, "Son los impíos como el mar en tempestad" ("Jonen Dalim," versos 28 y ss.). Ezequiel 38:20, ". . . y [aquel dia en el país de Israel] temblarán ante mí . . . todos los hombres que existen sobre la superficie de la tierra" ("Jonen Dalim," versos 41 y ss.). Génesis 49:10, "No se retirará de Judá el cetro / ni la bengala de entre sus pies hasta que venga Aquél a quien pertenece / y a quien deben los pueblos obediencia" ("Jonen Dalim," versos 102 y ss.). Deuteronomio 28:65, "En aquellas naciones no disfrutarás tranquilidad ni tendrá punto de reposo la planta de tu pie, y Yahveh te dará allí un corazón trémulo, desfallecimiento añorante de ojos y congoja de espíritu."

[12] Por motivos de espacio no puedo detenerme aquí en detalles sobre el comportamiento de Barrios en relación al movimiento sabatiano. En una obra de aproximadamente la misma fecha que el auto que estudiamos, 1683, Barrios rechaza las

no tiene indicaciones ni del movimiento sabatiano ni de la creencia de la llegada del mesías, la preocupación por el tema mesiánico que revelan las numerosas citas bíblicas relacionadas con el tema, indican que la fe de Barrios seguía alimentada con la esperanza de la ansiada redención.

"Jonen Dalim" no parece estar basada en una obra literaria específica pero sigue la técnica de los autos sacramentales de Calderón de la Barca en cuanto a los personajes más importantes del drama, el paradigma histórico que tiene como fondo, y la técnica del desarrollo de la acción.

El lector familiariazado con los autos sacramentales de Calderón reconocerá que algunos de los personajes que más frecuentemente aparecen en sus dramas alegóricos: el Hombre (que representa un español católico), la Ley de Gracia (o la Iglesia católica), y el Judaísmo (llamado otras veces la Sinagoga), son también los personajes del auto que nos ocupamos, "Jonen Dalim," si bien desde la perspectiva de Barrios los papeles han sido invertidos: así la verdadera Ley en el drama de Barrios es la Torá judaica, su enemiga es Edom, identificada con Roma o la Iglesia, y otras veces con la Inquisición como símbolo de la España católica, y el protagonista es Israel, representante del pueblo judío en el exilio.

El paradigma de muchos autos sacramentales de Calderón está basado en el concepto de la ley natural, de procedencia clásica, que tuvo una gran influencia en el pensamiento político y en la literatura de la España barroca. La ley natural, como principio de orden moral, se expresaba metafóricamente representando a Dios como un dramaturgo y el mundo como un teatro. Muchos de los autos sacramentales de Calderón tienen como base el concepto de la ley natural y la historia de la humanidad se representa en estas obras dividida en tres etapas o las tres edades del mundo: la primera edad, en la que imperó el gentilismo como protagonista humano, estuvo regida por la ley natural. La segunda edad, en la que el protagonista fue el pueblo hebreo, estuvo regida por las Sagradas Escrituras, la ley escrita o revelada. La tercera edad comenzó con la llegada de Jesucristo y el mensaje de la Ley de Gracia que imperarará hasta el final de los días. Este paradigma histórico, basado en la ley natural, aparece como fondo en la mayoría de los autos sacramentales

---

pretensiones de Shabbatai Zevi como el mesías. Véase mi tesis doctoral, págs. 112–113.

de Calderón donde se desarrolla ampliamente la etapa de la Ley de Gracia, la era presente, y la edad de los gentiles y la de los hebreos aparece de fondo o simplemente se menciona. La ley natural es tan fundamental a muchos de los dramas de Calderón que sin una comprensión de su sistema filosófico es fácil que el lector no comprenda bien los temas presentados en el drama.[13]

Para Barrios y sus coetáneos de Amsterdam que habían vivido en España o Portugal como marranos, el concepto de ley adquiría una nueva dimensión al integrarse a la comunidad de judíos sefarditas. El concepto de la ley natural que había influenciado cada aspecto de sus vidas, incluyendo la concepción de obras de artes como los autos, tenía que ser rechazado a favor de la aceptación de la Torá judaica en su doble aspecto de escrita y oral. Las obras alegóricas de Barrios, incluyendo "Jonen Dalim," el auto que estudiamos, tienen como fondo el escenario de encuentro entre la segunda edad, el pueblo hebreo regido por la Torá, y la Ley de Gracia o la cristiandad.[14] En "Jonen Dalim" el protagonista, Israel, sale a escena acompañado de la Ley o Torá que a cada momento de debilidad está dispuesta a ayudarlo. Edom es la cristiandad que, desde la perspectiva judía de Barrios, es la enemiga del pueblo israelita y, además, la que no comprende los textos bíblicos. Jonen Dalim, la academia personificada que, como su nombre en hebreo indica, representa la caridad, es también el símbolo de las naciones gentiles que se compadecen del pueblo israelita. Así se auto-define el personaje Jonen Dalim:

> Yo en el teatro del mundo
> el papel hago de quantas
> naciones, dan a Israel
> hospicio con manos largas.
> Pues Jonen Dalim denota
> lo que del pobre se apiada,
> y los Pueblos, que tuvieren
> piedad de la desterrada

---

[13] Véase el estudio de Robert L. Fiore, *Drama and Ethos: Natural-Law Ethics in Spanish Golden Age Theater* (Kentucky: University Press, 1975), specialmente los capítulos uno y cuatro, de donde básicamente procede mi información sobre la ley natural.

[14] La comedia alegórica titulada *Contra la verdad no hay fuerza*, es un altercado entre el personaje la Verdad (la Torá judaica) y la Mentira (la cristiandad o España) que se disputan al protagonista de la obra, el Albedrío. Véase el studio que hago de esta obra en mi tesis doctoral, págs. 160–186.

Gente Electa. el Rey Empíreo
los apiadará, con tantas
victorias, que al redimido
lleven a su Tierra en Palmas,
                    (v. 527 y ss.)

iluminando detalles del mesianismo de Barrios: cuál será la función de las naciones gentiles en la era de la redención. La cita bíblica indicada al margen, Isaías 66:20, junto con otra cita de Mennaseh Ben Israel, se refiere al momento en que Dios, después de castigar a los impíos, congregará a los pueblos dignos de redención.[15]

La teoría dramática de Calderón alcanza su mayor grado de perfección en los últimos autos sacramentales que escribe. Según Alexander Parker, Calderón desarrolla su teoría dramática basándose en el sistema filosófico de la teoría de la imaginación de la tradición escolástica, especialmente el sistema de Santo Tomás de Aquino. Los autos calderonianos son obras de carácter conceptual donde el dramaturgo puede reunir en escena "fantasmas" o imágenes del mundo metafísico de la imaginación. Esta teoría dramática hace posible que aparezcan juntos en escena objetos, acontecimientos y personajes que en la experiencia ordinaria se hallan separados por el espacio y el tiempo. En algunos autos de Calderón, la acción de la obra es la representación de lo que ocurre en la mente del protagonista. Aunque todos los autos calderonianos dramatizan aspectos dogmáticos de la doctrina cristiana, las obras escritas con esta técnica tienden a subrayar temas morales y la acción de la obra es el desarrollo de las decisiones mentales que hace el personaje.[16]

El auto "Jonen Dalim" está escrito también con esta técnica literaria y la acción de la obra es el proceso mental que ocurre en la mente de Israel, el protagonista. Al comienzo del auto Israel aparece en escena saliendo de un mar en oleaje y llegando a un puerto, símbolo de uno de los momentos de su peregrinaje. Para representar

---

[15] Isaías 26:20, "Y traerán entonces a todos vuestros hermanos, de todos los pueblos, como ofrenda a Yahveh, en cordeles, y carros, y coches cubiertos, y mulos, y dromedarios, a mi santa montaña, a Jerusalén." En cuanto a la cita de Mennaseh Ben Israel, Barrios dice que viene de su libro "Nabucho." En su obra titulada *Conciliador*... Mennaseh identifica a Roma con los edomitas. Cuando Mennaseh se refiere a los gentiles, diferencia entre los idólatras y los justos. Estos se salvarán en la era de la redención. Barrios, con toda probabilidad toma la idea de Mennaseh. Para este autor, véase nuestra nota 9.

[16] Alexander A. Parker, *Los autos sacramentales de Calderón de la Barca* (Barcelona: Ariel, 1983), especialmente el capítulo II, págs. 45–96, "Los autos como drama."

el conflicto interior que experiencia Israel, la escena contiene los cuatro elementos básicos del universo: aire, agua, tierra y fuego, en estado de desarmonía. Se escuchan las voces de los coros de músicos. Una voz pide que se arroje Israel al mar, coro 1: "Precipitadle a las olas" y otra le incita a que llame a Dios para ver si acude en su ayuda, coro 2: "Llama a tu Dios, / y veremos si te acude" (versos 1 ss.). Las notas al margen del texto aclaran que estos versos son salmos bíblicos. La Ley alienta a Israel y éste se lamenta. Se oyen otra vez los cantos de los coros que se alternan versos de temas marítimos:

> *Coro 1.* Buelve (Ysrael) a mis golfos.
> *Coro 2.* Sigue tu estrella Jahacob.
> *Coro 1.* No daras en seco nunca.
> *Coro 2.* Yrás al puerto mejor.
> (v. 12 y ss.)

y luego todas las voces juntas cantan versos populares que en consonancia con los temas marítimos: el peregrinaje de Israel por el mar en oleaje, sirenas que acechan su paso y golfos que pueden servir de refugio, simulan gritos propios de los marineros y sus maniobras: "A la xarcia, a la bela, a la gavia, al timon, / que anda el mar por los cielos de Sion" (versos 16 y 17). Al final de los temas marítimos de los primeros 40 versos que culminan en una tormenta, los músicos introducen también cantos de tema bélico, citas del libro bíblico del profeta Ezequías, 32:2:

> *Música.* Al llanto, al ayuno, a la fuerza, al ardid,   que de Gog y Magog
> suena la lid.
> *Ysrael.* O, Ven David!
> *Música.* Al mar, al combate, al aljava al cañón   que apunta de Jehudá,
> y Joseph, la unión.
> (v. 41 y ss.)

que anuncian los temibles tiempos que han de preceder la llegada del Mesías. Después del énfasis en el exilio de Israel durante el cual nadie se apiada de su sufrimiento, el mesianismo utópico y escatológico de Barrios se nos presenta como la terrible justicia divina, de tono fuertemente vengativo, que se ocupará de dar el merecido castigo a los enemigos de Israel.

El tema del auto

"Jonen Dalim" es un auto que básicamente carece de trama ya que no está basado en una historia o fuente única sino que, como hemos visto, está formado por numerosas citas procedentes de diversos libros bíblicos. Una primera lectura de la obra puede incluso hacernos pensar que el auto no es más que una cadena de citas bíblicas recitadas por los personajes y sin un aparente sentido común que las una. Pero la lectura atenta del drama, y el examen de los temas de las citas bíblicas que lo forman, muestra que las tres partes del auto tienen una unidad y que su enlace depende de diferentes significados del término en que se basa el título: Jonen Dalim, el que se apiada de los pobres. El tema del auto es el de la caridad y la justicia desde la perspectiva judía: cómo debe el judío compartir los bienes que ha recibido de Dios, la caridad y justicia para con los pobres, y cómo imparte Dios justicia y caridad, al pueblo judío y a los pueblos gentiles, el tema de la justicia y piedad divina. El auto es una reflexión del significado del término tzedek, justicia y caridad, como uno de los atributos divinos que define un aspecto de Dios y que por su doble significado crea una tensión que sirve de conflicto dramático.

En primer lugar, como auto de ocasión, la obra es un elogio a la academia del mismo nombre y a sus miembros que, siguiendo la tradición judaica de tzedakah, practicaban actos de justicia y caridad hacia los pobres de la comunidad. En hebreo, el concepto de caridad es inseparable del de justicia. Tzedakah es el término que traducido al español tiene el doble significado de justicia y caridad. La palabra deriva de tzedek (justicia y piedad) y, además de ser uno de los atributos divinos, tiene dos significados: (1) dar a cada uno que tiene derecho a algo, aquello que le corresponde y (2) dar a cada ser lo que le corresponde según sus méritos. Tzedakah, justicia-caridad, es también un mandamiento positivo que todo judío está obligado a cumplir. Barrios, basándose en la obra del codificador José Caro, *Shulhan Arukh*, menciona en el auto ocho grados de hacer la caridad que van en nivel ascendente. El grado más elevado de hacer la caridad es cuando se hace en secreto o silencio, cuando se desconocen entre sí la identidad del donante y la del recipiente. Tzedakah implica que la caridad hacia los pobres es un acto de justicia y de distribución equitativa ya que las posesiones del hombre pertenecen en última instancia al propio Dios. En el auto, la caridad está representada por la abstracción femenina Jonen Dalim, símbolo de la academia del mismo nombre, donde los miembros llevaban a cabo obras de caridad-justicia hacia los pobres de la comunidad. Así termina el personaje Anuncio la descripción de la academia Jonen Dalim:

> La octava caridad, y más preciosa,
> tiene el rostro de empréstimo agradable,
> y se la premia Magestád gloriosa
> en mostrársele siempre favorable.
> Estas ocho piedades, generosa
> Ionen Dalim, ostenta en casa afable.
> y assí que apiada al Pobre se interpreta,
> voz de la fama, de la Ley trompeta.
>
> (v. 312 y ss.)

El significado más evidente del auto es el elogio a la academia del mismo nombre; pero si la obra fuera solamente una alabanza a la institución no podría considerarse más que una poesía devota sin conflicto dramático. Por medio de la alegoría, Barrios da otra dimensión y significado al auto. Como obra alegórica, la obra es la dramatización del exilio de Israel, el protagonista, y el encuentro con las dos abstracciones, Jonen Dalim y Edom, representando las naciones gentiles. Jonen Dalim es el símbolo de las naciones que sienten piedad del pueblo israelita y le dan cobijo. En contraste, la abstracción Edom representa los pueblos gentiles que no sienten piedad de Israel y lo desprecian. Aunque el exilio de Israel está fuera del control de los protagonistas humanos, Barrios de ningún modo exenta a Edom de su responsabilidad de asistir a Israel. Entre las diversas citas bíblicas se encuentra la metáfora de la vida como una comedia, aportada de la herencia española de Barrios. En la comedia de la vida humana Israel representa el papel del pobre, y Edom, o los pueblos gentiles, el del rico. Los gentiles, a su vez, pueden representar su parte como Jonen Dalim, que se apiada de los pobres, o como Edom, que no siente compasión de Israel y lo desprecia.

Los actos de justicia y caridad entre los humanos son a su vez los que generan en respuesta la justicia y caridad divina. En cuanto a Israel se refiere, las citas bíblicas claramente indican que el exilio es la respuesta divina al pecado de idolatría cometido por el pueblo favorito de Dios Israel. El protagonista así lo admite:

Dígalo yo, que en las prosperidades
crecí, rebelde a tus sagrados ritos,
árbol pomposo de las vanidades
hasta que me secaron mis delitos.
  No el bruto Rey de la cabeza de oro
(antes del tigre del error manchado)
cayó a los pies del Oso levantado;
cual yo, Perilo por el rubio toro
dos veces de mi hecho y adorado,
caí de tu gracia, donde sin cordura
labré en su adoración mi sepultura.

(v. 135 y ss.)

Y, de nuevo, las citas bíblicas anotadas al margen del texto indican el origen de la inspiración de los versos.[17] La dureza del exilio es conmesurable con el pecado a espiar. Pero Dios es también misericordioso y premiará la expiación de Israel con la ansiada llegada del Mesías. Inspirado en versículos de Isaías y Jeremías, Barrios hace exclamar al protagonista Israel:[18]

i O crezca ya la prodigiosa Vara
del mejor tronco! O ya con alta gloria
expire frutos de libertad clara
árbol de luz, en campo de victoria?
o alternése a su vista el de xara!

(v. 163 y ss.)

El momento tan deseado de la redención del pueblo israelita será también el de la retribución divina a Edom, por su falta de caridad a Israel. En el auto hay numerosos ejemplos de la implacable furia

---

[17] Esta sección del auto indica varias citas bíblicas todas ellas con temas relacionados con la idolatría. Por ejemplo, Deuteronomio 31:20, "pues le conduciré [al pueblo israelita] a la tierra que prometí con juramento a sus padres, y mana leche y miel, y comerá y engordará, y luego se volverá hacia dioses extraños, y los servirán, y me despreciarán, y quebrantarán mi alianza." Es importante aclarar que el tema de la idolatría no es de especial interés a la tradicción judaica. Las preocupación con el tema que muestra Barrios y otros de sus contemporáneos está sin duda relacionada a la situación especial de los ex-marranos y el remordimiento que sentían por su pasado fingiéndose cristianos.

[18] Isaías 11:1, "Ahora bien, saldrá un brote del tocón de Jesé / y un vástago sus raíces brotará." Jeremías 33:15 y 16, "En aquellos días y aquel tiempo suscitaré a David un vástago justo que ejercitará el derecho y la justicia en el país. En tales días, Judá será salvada y Jerusalén habitará en seguridad, y éste será el nombre con el que se le llamará: 'Yahveh, nuestra justicia.'"

divina hacia Edom por su falta de caridad hacia Israel. Así describe
Israel, el protagonista, sus relaciones con Seir o Edom, su enemigo:

> En la Comedia de la La vida es sueño,
> el pobre represento, tan al vivo
> como el Rico, Seir, que mi despeño
> trata con verme misero, y captivo:
> él, como aguila va donde el empeño
> Turquezco, derivarle intenta altivo:
> y yo con descender a la Pobreza,
> (o Ley!) te estimo mas que a la Riqueza.
>
> (v. 215 y ss.)

Y al margen del texto, Barrios da la cita bíblica aclaratoria donde
se inspira para su definición de Edom, que en este ejemplo identifica
con Seir, el tradicional enemigo del pueblo israelita: 43 Abdías 14
(el profeta abdías se dirige a Edom), "Por la mortandad, por la injusticia contra tu hermano Jacob, / te cubrirá la verguenza y serás extirpado para siempre."

Conclusiones

"Jonen Dalim" es un auto que en esencia carece de trama. El tema
de la obra está basado en un concepto abstracto que es lo que crea
el conflicto dramático y que en esencia se refiere al doble significado
de la palabra hebrea tzedakah, justicia y caridad. El concepto surge
cuando Barrios concibe un auto de elogio a la academia llamada
Jonen Dalim o "el que se apiada de los pobres," seguido de una
cadena de asociaciones que el término caridad-piedad evoca. En
última instancia el que se apiada de los pobres es Dios ya que tzedek,
justicia-caridad, es uno de los atributos que lo definen. Pero la
situación precaria de Israel, el pueblo favorito de Dios, desafía la
aceptación del término que define a Dios. ¿Cómo es posible que
siendo Dio; justo y piadoso permita el exilio y el sufrimiento de
Israel, su pueblo favorito? Barrios, inmerso en el estudio de la Biblia,
depende totalmente del texto al cual acude para encontrar una re-
conciliación al doble sentido del término hebreo. El modo de lectura que se llevaba a cabo en las yeshivot es evidente en la estricta
dependencia de las citas bíblicas que forman la estructura del auto.
"Jonen Dalim" es un drama internalizado que toma lugar en la

mente de Israel, el protagonista, y en realidad el único personaje de la obra. Teniendo en cuenta que el personaje Israel es en muchos aspectos idéntico al propio Barrios, el auto es una representación de las esperanzas y la desesperación del autor, inmerso en la lectura de la Biblia donde trata de encontrar respuestas que den sentido a su existencia.

JUDEO-SPANISH FOLKTALES FROM THE BALKANS AND ISTANBUL IN THEIR JEWISH AND NON-JEWISH SOCIETAL CONTEXTS

Rebecca Scherer

Providence, R.I.

In their introduction to *Christians and Jews in the Ottoman Empire*, Benjamin Braude and Bernard Lewis point out that "For nearly half a millennium the Ottomans ruled an empire as diverse as any in history. Remarkably, this polyethnic and multireligious society worked. Muslims, Christians and Jews worshipped and studied side by side, enriching their distinct cultures."[1] However, Jewish culture, Muslim Turkish culture, and so forth, were not watertight compartments. If, as another observer put it, the Ottoman Empire resembled "a block of flats inhabited by a number of families which met only on the stairs,"[2] these families may seldom have talked directly to each other, but a considerable amount of eavesdropping occurred, and the overheard narratives became part of their own family conversations.

A study of the Judeo-Spanish folktales in the three main collections gathered from Sephardim in the Balkans and Istanbul, and a comparison of these tales with those of other groups living in former Ottoman areas provide a useful perspective on traditional Eastern Sephardic society and its cultural relationship to the surrounding non-Jewish milieu.

The collections are: Cynthia M. Crews's *Recherches sur le Judéo-Espagnol dans les Pays Balkaniqes* (Paris, 1935), containing thirty-two tales, of which sixteen are from Monastir (Bitolj or Bitola), ten from Skoplje, four from Salonika (including two Djoha tales), and two from Bucharest; Max A. Luria's "A Study of the Monastir Dialect of Judeo-Spanish Based on Oral Material Gathered in Monastir,

---

[1] Benjamin Braude and Bernard Lewis eds., *Christians and Jews in the Ottoman Empire* (New York, 1982), vol. 1, p. 1.

[2] Sir Harry Luke, *The Old Turkey and the New* (London, 1955), p. 8; cited in Kemal H. Karpat, "Millets and Nationality: The Roots of the Incongruity of Nation and State in the Post-Ottoman Era," in Braude and Lewis, vol. 1, p. 162.

Yugoslavia,"[3] containing twenty-two tales (including a Djoha tale); and Max Leopold Wagner's *Beiträge zur Kenntnis des Judenspanischen von Konstantinopel* (Vienna, 1914), containing fourteen tales.[4] Wagner's tales were gathered over a three-year period concluding in the autumn of 1910, Luria's were gathered in 1927, and Crews's, in 1930.

Reginetta Haboucha's "Classification of Judeo-Spanish Folktales"[5] is a tale-type and motif classification of the sixty-eight Crews, Luria, and Wagner tales[6] and the 153 tales from Arcadio de Larrea Palacin's *Cuentos Populares de los Judíos del Norte Marruecos.*[7] In her preface, Haboucha expresses concern about "the degree to which the representation of a given category may be the result of the collectors' field methods, their criteria for the selection of raw field materials for publication, the tastes and preferences of individual informants and other factors which . . . must remain unknown to us."[8] I believe that the question of these collections' representative value is answered to a significant extent by a comparison of the sixty-eight with those in Larrea Palacin, in the Judeo-Spanish tale collection of the Max Grunwald Archives at the Hebrew University in Jerusalem, and with Turkish, Greek, and other Near Eastern tales.

The three collections differ markedly in style, theme, and content. In Crews, the majority are tales of magic and novellas. They are lengthy (on the average, about 1,800 words, although a few are much shorter and two are considerably longer, around 5,600 and 9,000 words) and rich in motifs and details. The Luria tales, with one exception, are fairly short and unembellished by details or motifs. Most are anecdotes, sometimes moralistic, if only by implication, which contrast rich/poor, clever/stupid, good/bad, often opposing poor/good to rich/bad. There is a wider variety of types in Wagner, although magic tales and novellas predominate. The tales here average about 1,300 words or less, and are generally devoid of motifs or details not contributing directly to the plot. A number are somewhat lacking in coherence, as though condensed from longer versions,

---

[3] *Revue Hispanique* 79 (1930).

[4] With German translations which are occasionally inaccurate or inadequate.

[5] Ph.D. thesis (Johns Hopkins University, 1973).

[6] Sixty-nine tales by her count, as she includes a short narrative in Luria about a fire which I do not regard as a tale and have omitted.

[7] Arcadio de Larrea Palacin, *Cuentos Populares de los Judíos del Norte de Marruecos* (Tetuan, 1952–1953).

[8] Haboucha, p. xiv.

or as though parts might once have belonged more appropriately to other tales.

Haboucha bases her classification on the widely used Aarne-Thompson[9] scheme developed for the European folktale, a decision which sometimes results in misleading or inappropriate classifications.[10] A number of tales could easily belong to more than one category. Haboucha classifies many anecdotes (mainly from Luria) as novellas because their plots coincide with certain AT types so classified. Despite these reservations, my assessment of both overall and relative tale-type distribution accords for the most part with that of Haboucha. Tales of magic are the most frequent, followed by novellas, then anecdotes; neither religious tales nor animal tales are well represented (see *Table 1*).

A comparison of Crews-Luria-Wagner and Larrea Palacin shows the type distribution for tales of magic and novellas following the same pattern, but diverging for the other types (see *Table 2*). Only eight of the Crews-Luria-Wagner tales—two Luria anecdotes, and an anecdote and five magic tales from Crews—are variants of Larrea Palacin tales. All eight represent AT tale-types widely encountered throughout Europe and/or the Near East.[11] There is also one motif common to a Crews, a Wagner, and a Larrea Palacin tale, the Sugar Puppet.[12] The degree of correspondence to details varies. They match to a large degree in shorter tales where they are an integral part of the type, as in AT 563 (Bitolj XI), "The Table, the Ass and the Stick," where a man receives from his animal son-in-law a food-producing utensil, a money-dropping animal, and a stick-like object that distributes blows until ordered to stop, or AT 1741 (Luria VI), "The Priest's Guest and the Eaten Chickens," where a wife eats a fowl (in Luria, a duck; in Larrea Palacin, two chickens) her husband bought, then invites a guest for dinner, scares him off, and tells the

---

[9] Antti Aarne, *The Types of the Folk-Tale: A Classification and Bibliography. Antti Aarne's Verzeichnis der Märchentypen* (FF Communications no. 3), trans. and enlarged by Stith Thompson (FF Communications No. 74). (Helsinki, 1928).

[10] For example, Bucharest VII (Crews) concerns golden twins removed from their mother at birth by an evil Gypsy woman, their subsequent magical transformations, eventual reunion with their parents and the Gypsy's punishment. Haboucha classifies this as 780D, "The Truth Comes to Light," which places it in the religious tale category; a more appropriate category would be magic tales, or even novellas. Conversely, the thrust of some Luria tales containing magic elements is moralistic; these would be more appropriately placed with religious tales than with magic tales.

[11] AT 480, AT 531, AT 563, AT 706, AT 879, AT 883A, AT 1415, AT 1741.

[12] See Wolfram Eberhard and Pertev Naili Boratav, *Typen Türkischer Volksmärchen* (Wiesbaden, 1953), p. 225.

witless husband that the guest ate the bird (the Luria version is a Djoha story). In the longer magic tales like the variants of AT 883A, "The Innocent Slandered Maiden," AT 706, "The Maiden Without Hands," or AT 879, "The Basil Maiden," only the basic plot-lines agree.

During World War I and the following decade, Max Grunwald collected Judeo-Spanish tales from Sephardim mostly in Vienna. Unfortunately, the original texts were not preserved; what exists are Grunwald's German translations, which in many cases are synopses only. The corpus consists of 150 tales, of which sixty have been published, and fifty-five Djoha stories, ten of them published.[13] Among these seventy published tales, there are forty-three from Crews-Luria-Wagner. Included are all of Wagner and all but six of Crews; the only Luria tales represented are three variants of Crews and/or Wagner tales. What is striking about the Grunwald tales is not only the number of Crews and Wagner tales represented, but the degree of correspondence in details; they are not variants, but virtually the same tales, even when occasionally parts appear recombined. It is not possible to draw any conclusions about the absence here of Luria tale variants without examining the remainder of the Grunwald corpus.

Variants for fifty-two Crews-Luria-Wagner tales have been found, fifty of which are Turkish, Greek, or other Near Eastern (see *Table 3*). A number of these appear as well in Heda Jason's "Types of Jewish-Oriental Oral Tales."[14] The numbers of such variants per collection are: Crews, twenty-one; Luria, fifteen; Wagner, ten. In addition, there is an East Slovak Gypsy variant of Crews Bit. VIII/Luria VIII, both themselves variants of the same tale.

Turkish variants predominate. W.R. Halliday drew the same conclusion with regard to Greek tales.[15] Of the twenty-five most frequent Turkish tales listed by Eberhard and Boratav in their *Typen Türkischer Volksmärchen*,[16] eleven are represented in Crews-Luria-Wagner, including the first five: "The Beautiful Children" (Bucharest VII), "The Beautiful Halva-Seller" (Bit. XV), "The Three Citron Maidens

---

[13] Max Grunwald, *Tales, Songs and Folkways of Sephardic Jews*, ed. Dov Noy, Hebrew University Folklore Research Center Studies, vol. 6 (Jerusalem, 1982), English summaries, pp. xvi–xxxv, Hebrew texts, pp. 20–86; annotations [in Hebrew] pp. 87–111.

[14] *Fabula* 7 (1965): 115–221.

[15] W.R. Halliday, "The Subject-Matter of the Folk-Tales," in *Modern Greek in Asia Minor*, ed. R.W. Dawkins (Cambridge, 1916), pp. 218–219.

[16] Eberhard and Boratav, *Typen Türkischer Volksmärchen*, p. 9, *Table 3*.

(Bit. II), "The Patience Stone" (Wagner XIV), and "The Ali Cengiz Spiel" (Luria XXI). The most popular Turkish tale-types are Type D, "Marriage with a Supernatural Animal or Spirit," and Type C, "Animal or Spirit Helps a Human."[17] These categories cover the majority of the Crews-Luria-Wagner magic tales.[18] In Marzolph's *Typologie des Persischen Volksmärchens*, magic tales and novellas rank second and third after jokes and anecdotes as the most popular categories;[19] however, among the first ten of the thirty-nine most frequent Persian tales are four from Crews-Luria-Wagner, including the first and second, "The Orange Princesses" and "The Patience Stone."[20]

Animal tales are not well represented among either Turkish or Greek tales,[21] as is the case in Crews-Luria-Wagner, as noted above. Eberhard and Boratav surmise that the paucity of such tales in their collection may reflect limitations of the field methods used rather than such tales' actual popularity.[22] Zamila Kolonomos, in *Proverbs, Sayings and Tales of the Sephardic Jews of Macedonia* (which includes five animal tales from Skoplje and two from Monastir), notes the popularity, particularly with the young, of such tales, mostly moralistic ones in which the humans are always smarter.[23]

Numerous motifs or characters in Crews-Luria-Wagner, particularly in the magic tales, are common to Balkan and Near Eastern tales: the Beauty of the World (Turkish: *Dunia Güzeli*); the Apple of Fertility given by a dervish or supernatural agent to a childless couple; the wife accused of bearing puppies instead of human children; punishment of an evil woman by tying her to wild horses which pull her to pieces; arrows shot to choose a spouse; a tavern or bath built by a protagonist which is free to customers in exchange for a story; the king's advisory council of twelve; the child lured down from a tree by an old woman pretending inability to correctly perform a

---

[17] Ibid., p. 8, *Table 2*.

[18] For a discussion of the Eberhard-Boratav classification vis-à-vis the AT classification, see H. Jason and O. Schnitzler, "The Eberhard-Boratav Index of Turkish Folk Tales in the Light of the New Revision of Aarne Thompson's Types of the Folktale," in *Folklore Research Center Studies*, eds. Dov Noy and Issachar Ben Ami, vol. 1 (Jerusalem, 1970), pp. 43–71.

[19] Ulrich Marzolph, *Typologie des Persischen Volksmärchen* (Beirut, 1984), p. 31.

[20] Ibid., p. 19.

[21] Eberhard and Boratav, *Typen Türkischer Volksmärchen*, p. 3; R.M. Dawkins, *Modern Greek Folktales* (Oxford, 1953), p. xix.

[22] Eberhard and Boratav, *Typen Türkischer Volksmärchen*, p. 3.

[23] Zamila Kolonomos, *Poslovice, izreke i price sefardskih Jevreja Makedonije—Proverbs, Sayings and Tales of the Sephardic Jews of Macedonia* (Belgrade, 1978), pp. 81–82.

task; a bone thrown at a windowpane, which breaks; the curse by an old woman, whose jug a prince has broken, that he must love a far-off princess; a hollow golden animal in which a protagonist hides to gain entrance to the beloved's bedroom; the scab-pate who wears an animal bladder on his head; the black giant whose upper lip stretches to heaven and lower lip to earth.

The majority of the tales manifest no Jewish content. In only fifteen (Crews, 6; Luria, 5; Wagner, 4) are characters identified as Jews; most of these contain other Jewish references as well. Eight others (Crews, 4; Luria, 2; Wagner, 2) contain such Jewish references as Gan Eden, alef-bet, "thin as a lulav," and Haman's hanging merely as narrative grammar, not as a means of "judaizing" the text. Eight of the fifteen have non-Jewish variants: a rich Jew finally succeeds in marrying his wastrel son to a poor girl who reforms him and later rescues him when he travels to the Indies and is jailed (Bit. V); a haham orders his son to kill his daughter, accused (falsely) by a Christian servant of adultery, who allows her children to be murdered rather than herself be raped (Bit. XV); a Jewish girl kills her mother at the suggestion of another Jewish woman, who marries the girl's father and ill-treats the girl, who is aided by a magic cow (Bit. XVI);[24] a Jew assesses correctly the value of a king's jewels or horse and reveals a secret: the king's lowly origin (Luria X, XXIII); a poor Jew joins in a thieves' song and is rewarded, while his greedy rich brother, who tries to do likewise, is killed (Luria XVIII); fish given to a queen by a Jewish fisherman spit at her; the fisherman's daughter eats the ashes of a magic head and gives birth to a baby who explains the fishes' behavior (Wagner X); poor Haham Avram's wife accidentally sneezes into her dough and is rewarded, while a rich neighbor woman sneezes deliberately and is punished on the testimony of the personified sneeze (Wagner XI); after staying

---

[24] See Warren Roberts, "A Spaniolic-Jewish Version of 'Frau Holle'," in *Studies in Biblical and Jewish Folklore*, eds. Raphael Patai, Francis Lee Utley, and Dov Noy (Bloomington, 1960), pp. 177–182. Roberts contends that the Near Eastern versions derive from the Spanish form brought by Sephardim in 1492. A version stating explicitly that the cow is the dead mother is recited as part of a women's Ismaili Muslim ceremony in eastern Iran. See Margaret A. Mills, "A Variant in the Context of a Muslim Women's Ritual," in *Cinderella: A Folklore Casebook*, ed. Alan Dundes (New York, 1982), pp. 180–192 and Margaret Mills, "Sex Role Reversals, Sex Changes, and Transvestite Disguise in the Oral Tradition of a Conservative Muslim Community in Afghanistan," in *Women's Folklore, Women's Culture*, eds. Rosan A. Jordan and Susan J. Kalcik (Philadelphia, 1985), pp. 201–212.

awake forty nights to win her bridegroom, a girl falls asleep and
another girl wins the youth, who eventually learns that the first is
his destiny, and tells the rabbis he will marry her instead (Wagner
XIV). The tale-types represented by Bit. XV and XVI, Luria XVIII,
and Wagner XIV are particularly widespread in the Ottoman area.

Of the six for which variants have not been found, removal of
the Jewish markers would affect the content significantly in only two
tales: a rich man's wife orders him to tell his poor brother to cease
having children because she is tired of supporting them; the poor
couple "makes a mistake," and when the child is born, the prophet
Elijah officiates at the *brit milah* and provides gold coins, and the
rich couple dies (Bit. XII); a Jewish peddler, too poor to afford
Passover food, is urged by his wife to steal; he steals from a Turk,
then from a rabbi, who persuades him to return the Turk's goods,
while the wife has him return the rabbi's horse (Luria XIX). Jewish
references, in addition to those mentioned above, are: food: *birmuelos,
boyos, bogaca*; holidays: Rosh Hodesh, Purim, Passover, especially the
last; customs: Seder, early morning synagogue service, minyan, *bodek*
(ritual slaughterer; this occurs in Bit. XVI, when the stepmother
decides to kill the girl's helpful cow), *shiva* after a funeral (also Bit.
XVI); names: Moshiko, Rahalika.

Judaization of the text in Bit. XV and XVI occurs particularly
where the non-Jewish variants supply distinctly non-Jewish markers.
In Bit. XV, the girl's father is a haham who decides to "go on a
pilgrimage" to Jerusalem; in Turkish versions, he goes on a pilgrimage to Mecca,[25] and in a Greek version from Chios, he is Hadji
Nicholas, who goes to the Holy Sepulchre (Jerusalem).[26] After persuading her brother not to kill her, the girl meets a prince, who asks
her to marry him, then tells her he is a Jew. Consistency with the
father as a haham is thus maintained. In Bit. XVI, after the mother
is buried, *shiva* is observed; in an Albanian version, the priest is called
in to bury the woman.[27]

Judeo-Spanish proverbs are not numerous in these texts either.
Only four have been positively identified (in Bit. III, Skop. I, a

---

[25] See Eberhard and Boratav, *Typen Türkischen Volksmärchen*, pp. 297–298.
[26] Philip P. Argenti and H.J. Rose, *The Folk-Lore of Chios* (Cambridge, 1949),
vol. 1, no. 1, pp. 429–433.
[27] Johann Georg von Hahn, *Griechische und Albanische Märchen* (Munich, 1918),
vol. 2, no. 103, p. 157.

novella and a magic tale narrated by two women; and Luria XII and XXIII, an anecdote and a lengthy novella [see above] narrated by two men), with another three uncertain (in Skop. II and VII, same narrator as Skop. I; and Luria VII, with a third male narrator). Only Skop. II and VII, and Luria XXIII contain Jewish markers.

Margaret Mills's analysis of a collection of contemporary oral narratives from Afghanistan[28] suggests that "men tend to tell stories about men, whereas women tell stories about women and men."[29] With respect to Turkish tales, Boratav states that male and female narrators and audiences favor different types of tales;[30] women prefer magic tales and those in which women play a dominant role or which center on a quest for the beloved, while men like realistic, mocking, satirical, moralistic anecdotes or tales of Muslim saints or legendary heroes. He also notes stylistic differences depending on the narrator's gender.[31] The pattern in Crews-Luria-Wagner on the whole tends to support both Mills's and Boratav's observations.

In Crews, twenty-four tales are narrated by females, eight by males. The three without female characters, all male-narrated, are two Djoha stories (Salonika I, II) and one about a lying contest (Bit. VII/Luria III). The other male-narrated tales include two other anecdotes also in Luria: a fake priest (Bit. VI/Luria IX), and an old woman who outwits two clerics (Bit. VIII/Luria VIII); a tale about a magic goose in which male-female representation is about even (Bit. IX); a magic tale in which a youth's wife facilitates the accomplishment of impossible tasks (Skop. IX); and a novella in which a clever wife rescues her naive husband from slavery to another man (Skop. X). Bit. VI, VII, VIII, and IX were narrated by the same man; Skop. IX and X were both told by another man. The style of the anecdotes differs from that of the magic tales and novella, but the latter do not differ in style or fullness of detail from each other or from those of the same type told by women. Female characters predominate in about 90 percent of Crews, some as evil troublemakers or elderly helpers, but more frequently as autonomous actors choosing their husbands, assigning tasks to be accomplished by would-be suitors, or solving problems incurred by their husbands.

---

[28] Mills, "Sex Role Reversals," pp. 187–213.
[29] Ibid., p. 187.
[30] Pertev Naili Boratav, *Türkische Volksmärchen* (Berlin, 1970), p. 343.
[31] Ibid.

In Bit. XV (see above), the heroine escapes her would-be rapist and murderer by a clever stratagem, disguises herself as a raggedy scab-pate with an animal intestine on her head, and eventually shuts all the principals in the story in a room, tells her tale, and unmasks the criminal. As Mark Glazer has pointed out, women as advisors to male heroes are a notable feature of Turkish tales.[32]

Only one Luria tale (XIX, see above) has a female narrator. Eight tales lack female characters, seven have only minor ones, and three have female characters whose function is to act as catalyst for, and to emphasize by contrast, male characters' actions: Djoha and the duck (VI, see above); the peddler whose wife tells him to steal (XIX, see above); and XX, in which a lion learns that humans are more powerful and intelligent than animals by disregarding his mother's advice. Women are major characters in only four tales: an old woman outwits two clerics (VIII/Bit. VIII, see above); a man acquires a house in which a servant dispenses money without limit; his wife has an affair with an oil seller to whom she gives the servant, leaving the husband bankrupt; the wife and lover are found stuck to a lamb (XV); a Jew marries and kills seven women in succession because each is crazier than the last (XXII); and XXIII (see above), the one lengthy, well-developed Luria tale, in which a Jew, after assessing a king's horse, informs the king he is of gypsy origin; the king's mother tells her story, confirming the Jew's intuition.

One man narrates ten of the Wagner tales, and one woman the other four. There are no female characters in four of the male-narrated tales. Of the remaining six, males predominate in one: a youth enters a city inhabited only at night by people who emerge from and return to the sea, one of whom he marries; they move to another city, the woman has a son and dies; the husband, buried alive, escapes with another woman and is aided by three youths, his sons, who emerge from the sea and then return (II). Females predominate in three: a youth courts a Beauty of the World (who is also an ogre), whose parents, particularly the mother, oppose the union; the girl initiates and directs their escape and final release from parental control (IV); a king's son makes advances to a greengrocer's daugh-

[32] Mark Glazer, "Women Personages as Helpers in Turkish Folktales," in *Studies in Turkish Folklore in Honor of Pertev N. Boratav*, eds. Ilhan Boşgöz and Mark Glazer, Indiana University Turkish Studies, no. 1 (Bloomington, 1978), pp. 98–109.

ter, who retaliates each time with a trick of her own; incensed, the prince marries her, intending to kill her, but stabs the sugar dummy she has put in her bed; seeing the red sugar "blood" run out, he regrets killing her; she reveals herself and they embrace (VII). The Sugar Puppet motif occurs also in Bit. I, told by a thirteen-year-old girl, and the differences between the two narratives are notable. In Bit. I, the husband, seeing what he supposes to be his wife in bed, asks, "Was it you who . . ." and with each question, the hidden girl pulls a wire and the marzipan dummy nods. After the "murder," the husband soliloquizes at some length, and when the girl emerges, having extracted his promise not to kill her, the two eat the doll at her suggestion. In two tales the sexes are about evenly represented: a king challenges a youth to win his daughter; with an old woman's help, he enters her bedchamber inside a hollow golden goose and succeeds (V); the queen and the spitting fish (X, see above).

In the four female-narrated tales a woman makes unreciprocated advances to a man who inadvertently kills her; the headless corpse of a woman is discovered; a vizier finds her to be a married woman murdered by thieves whose advances she spurned, and solves the other crime too (I); another version of Luria XV (see above); a poor girl hit by a prince's arrow marries him; when her *birmuelos* magically turn into costly furniture, she denigrates the king's lesser wealth to her husband, who throws her out; the king is impressed by her wealth, so the husband searches for her and asks her to return, which she does (XIII); and the Patience Stone variant (XIV, see above).

Mills also notes that her men's narratives reveal greater interest in sex-role switching than the women's.[33] Crews contains five tales in which women don male apparel and play the roles considered appropriate to the dress, and one in which a youth poses as a girl. In Wagner, a king disguises himself as a Gypsy woman (V) and a girl pretends to be the Devil (VII, see above). Skop. X and the Wagner tales have male narrators. Disguise is a recurring motif in Turkish folktales, stories, and folk theater.[34] Men posing as women seems more frequent, but, as Boratav points out, women posing as men occurs in many folktales with female protagonists.[35]

---

[33] Mills, "Sex Role Reversals," pp. 193 ff.
[34] See Ozdemir Nutku, "Original Turkish *meddah* Stories of the Eighteenth Century," in Boşgöz and Glazer, *Studies in Turkish Folklore*, pp. 166–183.
[35] Boratav, *Türkischer Volksmärchen*, p. 336.

In the view of Israeli folklorist Heda Jason,

> Whether a tale was taken over from another culture . . . or is an inher-
> itance of the same ethnic group . . . is not decisive concerning its "mean-
> ing" today. . . . People generally choose to remember and retell only
> those tales . . . that they "like," meaning that for some reason . . . they
> are appropriate to their culture. . . . The same tale may be told in sev-
> eral cultures. It may function in each of them, but not necessarily
> identically.[36]

Why were the Crews-Luria-Wagner tales appropriate to traditional
Eastern Sephardic culture, and thus appropriated by it? What is the
significance of Jewish markers, or more frequently, their absence?
My remarks here will be largely in the nature of some preliminary
observations.

The tales may be viewed as "stylized presentations of personal
dilemmas"[37] in which the protagonist's "inferior or negative social
and psychological situation"[38] is compensated. Three main themes
emerge which cut across the religious and ethnic boundaries of
Ottoman traditional societies: (1) rich/poor, with its subdivision
poor/good, (and sometimes clever), opposed to rich/bad, and (sometimes stupid) (mainly Luria); (2) courtship and marriage (Crews, and
to a lesser extent, Wagner); (3) the female protagonist (Crews, Wagner
to a lesser extent). Wish-fulfillment is clearly one factor of audience
interest in all three themes.

Of the twenty-three narrators, only three (from Bucharest) were
middle class. The occupations of the eleven Luria males were small
shopkeeper (2), mohel, fruit seller, cheese dealer, rag dealer, butcher,
blacksmith, tinsmith, shoemaker, porter;[39] one of Crews's two main
narrators, from Skoplje, was a washerwoman.[40]

Mark Glazer observes that Cinderella, in desiring to "meet an eli-

---

[36] Heda Jason, *Studies in Jewish Ethnopoetry* (Taipei, 1975), p. 67.

[37] Gerald Thomas, "Other Worlds: Folktale and Soap Opera in Newfoundland's
French Tradition," in *Folklore Studies in Honour of Herbert Halpert*, eds. Kenneth S.
Goldstein and Neil V. Rosenberg (St. Johns, 1980), pp. 343–351.

[38] Mark Glazer, "The Role of Wish-Fulfillment in Märchen: An Adlerian approach," *New York Folklore Quarterly* 5 (1979): 76.

[39] At the time of Crews's and Luria's fieldwork, 75 percent of Monastir's Jews
lived in poverty: Uri Oren, *A Town Called Monastir*, trans. Mark Segal (Tel Aviv
1971), p. 71; see also pp. 55 ff., 70 ff.

[40] Cynthia Crews, "Judaeo-Spanish Folktales in Macedonia," *Folklore* 43 (1932):
196.

gible young man in a socially acceptable context . . . and marry him"
is "adapting to the social structure and the community. . . . This
act . . . transforms her social role, her status and prestige in a society where marriage has status."[41] Although by the late nineteenth
century some Sephardic women were employed outside the home
in domestic service (a fact reflected in Bit. XVI), in workshops, and
in other occupations, they remained subordinate to men, and restrictions on women's activities and social relationships continued for all
classes as both ideal and reality well into the twentieth century.
However, the tales' autonomous female protagonists did partially
reflect social reality in that Sephardic and Turkish women often
exerted considerable influence on their male relatives.[42]

That the polyethnic, multi-religious Ottoman society functioned
well for centuries did not obviate the existence of both a formal and
an informal "pecking order." Muslims and Christians considered
Jews beneath them in the social and political hierarchies, and all
three groups consigned Gypsies to the bottom. In Greek tales, the
most despicable villains are hairless men, Jews, and priests.[43] In non-
Jewish versions of Bit. IX, the evil lover of the youths' mother is
usually a Jew.

Muslim ill-will toward Jews is not reciprocated in Crews-Luria-
Wagner. The Muslim characters (sometimes designated as "Turks"), of
which there are a considerable number, present a variety of "good,"
"bad," and indifferent, and there is no attempt, even indirectly, to
pass judgment on the "bad" as Muslims. It seems to me unlikely to
find Luria XIX, in which a rabbi shames a Jew into returning goods
he stole from a Turk, told by a Muslim about a Muslim stealing
from a Jew. Whatever function the two anticlerical tales (Bit. VI/
Luria IX and Bit. VIII/Luria VIII, see above) assumed in the Greek
Orthodox society in which they originated, as told by Jews they are
a negative comment on an outgroup, although they may also have
functioned as oblique criticism of the rabbinical establishment. The

---

[41] Glazer, "Wish-Fulfillment in Märchen," p. 66.

[42] See Glazer, "Women Personages as Helpers in Turkish Folktales." The autobiography of writer and editor Elia Carmona contains examples of the Sephardic
woman's influence. For a transliterated and annotated edition, see Robyn K. Loe-
wenthal, "Elia Carmona's Autobiography: Judeo-Spanish Popular Press and Novel
Publishing Milieu in Constantinople, Ottoman Empire, ca. 1860–1932" (Ph.D. thesis,
University of Nebraska, 1984).

[43] Halliday, "Subject-Matter of the Folk-Tales," p. 222.

hostile attitude expressed in making the slanderer, would-be rapist, and murderer in Bit. XV (see above) a Christian is unambiguous.

Gypsies in Crews-Luria-Wagner are evil, scheming women punished at the end of the tales (in non-Jewish variants this character is not commonly a Gypsy); the wife's lover in Wagner VIII (see above) and the king's mother in Luria XXIII (see above); who, while portrayed sympathetically, is nonetheless regarded as a social outcast.

The adoption of tales with their Muslim references unaltered reflected, I believe, a sense that the Muslim milieu was in some way a legitimate part of the Jewish environment, and provided a kind of dual viewpoint which enabled Jewish listeners to take what they wished from the narratives while at the same time distancing themselves from them "officially" if need be ("*They* do that; *we* don't").

I would suggest that tales involving Muslims were integrated into Eastern Sephardic culture in the same manner that *romansas* like "La Muerte de Principe Don Juan" and "Las Cabezas de los Infantes de Lara" became traditional Tisha B'Av *endechas*.[44] Despite their Spanish Christian markers, repetition in a setting of shared activity transformed them into signifiers of the Jewish past and present.

If this is the case, then the absence of Jewish references in the majority of the Crews-Luria-Wagner tales is not surprising. They were regarded as part of Jewish life whether or not they were specifically about Jews. Narrators were free to add Jewish markers if they felt that doing so enhanced the tale at a particular time or place. For example, in the variants Luria XV/Wagner VIII, in which a man acquires wealth, his wife takes a lover, and they are discovered stuck to a lamb or goat, husband and wife are Jews in Wagner, but not in Luria.

Exceptions that may prove the rule are Bit. XV and XVI, whose popularity throughout the Balkans and Near East attests to their potent attraction. They endorse deviant behavior (a daughter murdering her mother, a woman allowing the murder of her children in her place) which is, moreover, subversive of the tight social order of rights and obligations within a family (even though, with regard to Bit. XV, implicit in community norms was the idea that a woman's

---

[44] See Samuel G. Armistead, Joseph H. Silverman, and Jacob M. Hassan, *Seis Romancerillos de Cordel Sefardies* (Madrid, 1981), pp. 35–42. See also Samuel G. Armistead and Joseph H. Silverman, "Christian Elements and De-Christianization in the Sephardic 'Romancero'," in *Collected Studies in Honour of Americo Castro's Eightieth Year*, ed. M.P. Hornik (Oxford, 1965), pp. 21–38.

loss of sexual virtue was permanent and condemned her to virtual outcast status, while she could have other children), unlike that of other female protagonists, whose autonomy is employed only in pursuit of the society's accepted goals. While it is true that the Bit. XV and XVI female protagonists do adhere to the norms otherwise, these two acts contain sufficient potential for serious disruption that I suggest their Judaization functioned to protect them from possible censorship by rabbis or other authority figures.

Table 1. Distribution of tale types

Tale type	Total	Crews	Luria	Wagner
Tales of magic	29	19	5	5
Novellas	18	5	8	5
Jokes and anecdotes	16	7	8	1
Religious tales	2	1	0	1
Animal tales	4	0	2	2

Source: Based on Haboucha, "Classification of Judeo-Spanish Folktales," p. xii, table iii.

Table 2. Distribution of tale types: comparison of Crews-Luria-Wagner and Larrea Palacin

Tale type	Larrea Palacin	Crews-Luria-Wagner
Tales of magic	42.0%	43.79%
Novellas	26.98%	33.98%
Jokes and anecdotes	23.18%	9.8%
Religious tales	2.9%	11.11%
Animal tales	5.80%	1.30%

Source: Haboucha, "Classification of Judeo-Spanish Folktales," p. xiii.

Table 3. Distribution of Turkish, Greek,
Persian, and Arabic variants

	Turkish	Greek	Turkish & Greek	Turkish-Greek-Persian-Arabic	Turkish-Greek-Persian	Turkish-Persian-Arabic
Crews	19	18	16	7	–	–
Luria	7	1	2	1	1	–
Wagner	6	4	2	1	–	1

Notes: Persian and Arabic variants in this table are from, respectively, Ulrich Marzolph, *Typologie des Persischen Volksmärchen* (Beirut, 1984) and Ursula Nowak, "Beiträge zur Typologie des arabischen Volksmärchens" (Phil. diss., Freiburg, 1969) as given in Marzolph.

MADAME SARA: A SPIRIT MEDIUM
BETWEEN TWO WORLDS

Isaac Jack Lévy
University of South Carolina

and

Rosemary Lévy Zumwalt
Davidson College

Madame Sara of Istanbul, Turkey, is a spirit medium caught between two worlds. She is firmly rooted in Sephardic tradition, and she draws strength from her Jewish identity, but her work is with the spirits of the dead. Through communication with these spirits, she is able to diagnose disease, prescribe the proper treatment, find lost objects, and remove spells of witchcraft. She is thus both *inside* and *outside* Jewish tradition. This paper will explain how Sara received the gifts of the spirit and how she draws on the traditional curing system of the Sephardim, tying it to her metier as a spirit medium.[1]

"God gave me a gift. This book came to me. Then the jar of water. And then the table which said, 'Lift me'." In this way, Madame Sara of Istanbul describes the sequence in which she received the gifts from the spirit world. Born in Edirne, Turkey, in 1926, to a poor family, Sara was marked as different. As a young child, she felt a force from within and heard voices which told of things to come. She recounts how she used to draw water from a fountain that was located across the street from a Muslim cemetery.

---

[1] The authors conducted research with Madame Sara in Istanbul in March 1990. In addition, we interviewed friends, relatives, and acquaintances of Sara in Istanbul and Izmir, Turkey, as well as in Bat Yam, Herzlia, and Natanya, Israel. Throughout the paper, when Judeo-Spanish words are used, the orthography does not follow that of Castilian, but rather that of the Sephardic. Additionally, the translations of some Judeo-Spanish words differ depending upon the context of their use; e.g., *sikinti* may mean "worry" in one instance, and "fright" in another. For information on spiritualism and mediumship, see Alan Gauld, *Mediumship and Survival* (London: Heinemann, 1982); Alex Owen, *The Darkened Room: Women. Power and Spiritualism in Late Victorian England* (Philadelphia: University of Pennsylvania Press, 1990); Vieda Skultans, *Intimacy and Ritual: A Study of Spiritualism. Mediums and Groups* (London:

Everyone who passed used to pray there. There was a wise man, a person that people would pray to. . . . When I would go to get water, something pulled me to him, and I would speak to him. . . . And this holy man, when I took up this work, the first voice that came to me, came from this man.

This Muslim holy man was Sadik, the spirit who would stay with Sara from that time on.

Sara's powers as a medium came to her even as a young child. As she explained, "From eight years old, I already had these things." She began a story about her early encounter with the spirit, "That day that I heard the voice," and then turned to Isaac and said, "This is very interesting, write this down." She continued:

They took me out of school, and they put me to work. There was no bread, there was nothing. . . . I came from work, my feet all wet, the snow all the way up here [indicates above her knees]. Entirely wet. And dying to eat because we hadn't eaten last night, only a quarter of a piece of bread. . . . I saw my mother, who was near the little hearth, trying to warm herself. "Sarika, have you arrived? . . . Papa did not bring any bread."

Sara turned around to go out in the cold and back to work. To herself, she said,

Ohhh! I would like to find one grosch. One grosch I would like to find because they are selling a halva . . . with figs and sesame inside. Ah! if I could only find it. Where? The snow is up to here [my knees]. "Go this way," like a voice inside. "Go that way. You will find the money." And I entered that street, it was not the street that I usually used. It was not. I went into that street. I found on top of the snow . . . a bag. . . . Now, where should I go? To work? Or home? . . . I went home. "Did you see your father coming?" she said to me. I said, "No, Mama, I found money." "Let's see what it is."

Her mother, a woman of pride and honor, was afraid that Sara had stolen the money. She asked Sara where she had gotten it, and Sara replied, "'Mama, I prayed God to give me a grosch.' And we found inside the bag 300 liras. A lot of money. A lot of liras." Sara said to her mother, "Mama, I found them. Give me a grosch from there." Her mother was reluctant to take even this small amount from the

Routledge & Kegan Paul, 1974); Slater Brown, *The Heyday of Spiritualism* (New York: Hawthorn Books, 1970).

purse, but Sara insisted. She took the money, bought the halva, and returned to work.

> The snow is coming like a blizzard, the wind is terrible. The cold is awful. And I, imagining my mother and my little brothers who were coming from school, they were not going to find the bread, they were not going to find a place to warm up. I said to the *patron* [boss], "Let me go a little earlier, because afterwards I will not find my way, and because my feet are getting wet." "O.K. Go ahead." Four o'clock, I get home. Mama said, "We don't even have coal." I told her, "Give me another four liras from the *bolsa* [money bag]. I will buy it." And I go. I bought the coal. I found some little things that the stores sold under the table. I took them. "Take them, cook them for the children." And Papa came home. We ate. "Where did you get money to eat?" [strong voice] he said to my mother. "Where?" [soft voice] "Where did I find it? Sarika, . . . five groschs she took from her job in advance." What could we say?

Her father quietly told his wife and daughter about "a very rich Jew, tight like everything [who had lost his purse]." Sara asked,

> "Papa, if you found it yourself, what would you have done? Would you have returned it?" And he said, "I would have given it back." "Ahhh!" I said, "If you had lost it and he had found it, would he have returned it to you?" "I don't know, daughter of mine."

That night, the voice spoke to Sara just as she was about to fall asleep:

> You asked for that money. God gave it to you because you are good of heart. This money is your *mazal* [good fortune]. Do not give it back! . . . If you want to test that person, tomorrow go and ask him for some *trushi* [pickles] . . . and see if he gives it to you. If he gives you some, give the money back to him. If not, don't give it to him.

Sara went to the man who had lost the purse. She followed her spirit's instructions, and asked for a little *trushi*. He responded that his wife would not allow him to give any. Sara concluded, "I returned home [without returning the money]."

At the birth of each of her children, Sara was given a special gift from Sadik. For the first of such gifts, she had to suffer: she was paralyzed from *espanto* [fright, fear]. Alone in her house, awaiting her husband's return, she saw an apparition, which she described as "a shadow, tall, tall, that was becoming smaller and smaller, and was coming near me." Sara remarked, "Well, wouldn't you get frightened? A young girl of nineteen or twenty years? There I got paralyzed." The shadow had been the *neshama* [spirit] of Sadik, who had come, as Sara said, "to announce that I was going to give birth to a daughter." Even after the birth, when the paralysis left her, Sara felt unwell. One night, in her dream, Sadik came to her and told her that her power was to be found in the store where the family made brooms. And in the dream, Sara saw the place. The whole family—mother, father, two brothers, one sister, Sara, and her husband—went to the store at night with candles. As Sara's brother, Yakov Sotil of Natanya, Israel, recounted, "We went silently, in order not to make any noise, to dig. We dug for the book. Sadik would talk and only Sara would hear him." Sadik asked Sara for a *korban* [sacrifice], which Yakov provided in the form of a lamb. Yakov concluded, "And the book appeared the next day."

Sara could not read the book, for it was in Hebrew; but with the help of her spirit, she would use it in cures.[2] As her close friend of many years, Diamante Benun of Izmir, Turkey, explained to us, Sara

> would cover herself with a sheet and read. She would cover her face. She used to take her book in her hand, and the pages of the book would turn by themselves. All she did was to hold the book, and the pages would turn to the left and the right at the same time. And suddenly the book would open [to a page]. And wherever it stopped, that's where she read. And she would tell the *goral* [fortune], the *mazal* [fortune].

When Sara's second child, a son, was born, the spirit took the book from her, and gave her a jar of water in its place. Sara's brother, Yakov, explained,

> When the jar came, she *mirar kon la agua* [looked in the water]. Whoever wanted to know something would sit on the floor with Sara. Sara would place the jar in the middle, take the person's ring, throw it in the water. Both people would cover themselves with a sheet. Whoever had a problem would tell Sara, "I want to know such-and-such a thing."

The person who had come for help would hear voices that were not human voices, but would not be able to understand what the

---

[2] Sara had explained that Sadik and her other helping spirits understood other languages. Thus, Sadik, a Muslim holy man, was able to read the Hebrew text.

spirit was saying. Sara interpreted the voices for the person. "On the water," as Yakov recalled, "would appear the shadow of the problem, which could have been a place, a person, or whatever it was. She would explain everything. 'It's a human being,' and she would describe the person, or 'It's an animal,' etc. Only Sara used to see it."

When Sara gave birth to her third child, the spirit replaced the jar of water with a table. Sadik appeared to Sara, and told her to lift the table. She asked him, "How can I do it?" The spirit told her, "Put both hands on the table." She uttered the three words, put her hands where Sadik told her, and the table rose suddenly. Then the spirit told her, "Let your hand go, and touch it with one finger."

Though Sara uses many different forms of seances—from simply lighting a candle in a bowl of water, to covering herself with a sheet, to removing spells of witchcraft—it is the elevation of the table which has gained her the recognition of people from Istanbul to Israel. And Sara is aware of the dramatic power of making the table stand *en pies* [on its feet]. As Sara explains,

> The table rises, stands up. This table moves this way with a little finger [acts out motion], and I, whatever the voice says, I answer to the one in front of me. It tells me the medicine that we are going to administer for the *hazino* [stricken/sick one]. I prepare and administer the medicines, and he is cured.

The table can also confirm a doctor's diagnosis. In the instance of a child who was to be operated on for a tumor of the brain, Sara said, "And my table also said the same thing" [that she should have the operation]. Sara can also advise people about business ventures by consulting the table. During one seance, she warned a man to watch his brother more closely because he was cheating him, and would take the business away from him.[3]

---

[3] In the Western tradition of spiritualism, tables are often the material object through which the spirit speaks to the medium. The celebrated 1848 case of the Fox sisters in Hydesville, New York, involved just such an interpretation of spirit "rappings." A participant observed in a seance conducted by Kate Fox that "The table was moved about the room, and turned over and turned back" (Brown, *Heyday of Spiritualism*, p. 111). The "rappings," or knocks on the table, were said to be a "spiritual telegraph" that could be interpreted by those present, i.e., one knock for no, two for yes. The participants in the seance would call out letters of the alphabet; when the correct letter was mentioned, the spirit would rap. In this way, the

Sara was also saved from a jail sentence by a seance with a table. When there was a military coup in Turkey in 1960, Sara was arrested because the former premier, Adnan Menderes, who had been hanged by the new government, used to come to her for help. As Sara recounts, after three days in prison, she was brought before the judge. She told him that Menderes had come to her to talk about his children, especially about his grandson, who was mentally retarded, and not about affairs of state. She explained, "Look, I am not an *indivina* [diviner]. I am a medium."

> At that moment, . . . as God did to Esther and He led us to Purim, [the judge] said, "I have a nephew . . . who is sick. Could you tell me what is wrong with him?" "Give me his name." And he gave me the name while the table was about to touch the ceiling. I told him that this boy has a stone in the kidney. This stone is moving toward the urinary tract, and it is causing blood. "The stone is large, since he is twelve years old. He cannot remove it. Operation, the doctor will not operate, because the stone is neither inside nor outside [it is in the tract]." "Well, what can we do?" I said to him, "Give him water from parsley. Right away, the stone is going to fall." And the stone broke in five pieces within a period of four days. The stone fell. . . . And now, for this reason, he released me. And he told me, "You're safe." And he told me, "Don't do this kind of work here. Don't do this kind of work in Turkey. Don't do it." And I replied to him, "I have to do it."

Sara also uses the table to call a dead person from the grave. This is done by calling out the name of the person, as well as the mother's name and the place of burial. Sadik then journeys to the tomb and brings back the spirit. Typically, the dead one will come from the grave crying, and in one instance refused to return to the grave.

> Sara said, "Go now." . . . And the father said, "I don't want to go. I am not going to go. I am not going to go, because I want to stay

---

spirit was said to dictate messages through the spirit medium. For a particularly interesting account of such a seance at which Victor Hugo was present when the spirit of his deceased daughter was said to have spoken through a table, see Gustave Simon, *Les tables tournantes de Jersey* (Paris: Louis Conard, 1923), pp. 28–35. Madame Sara's seance with a table, however, differs from the foregoing. There is, for example, no "magnetic circle" of participants who sit, often with the room darkened for a more amenable spiritual ambience, with their fingertips touching the tabletop. Madame Sara herself is the only one allowed to touch the table. Whereas participants in Sara's seances have reported hearing sounds made by the spirit (in the table, chairs, floor), Sara alone is able to interpret what the spirit is saying; and, for the most part, she alone hears the voice of the spirit.

with my children. . . . I'm just not going to go!" Until Sara promised, "I will come another time and I will make you be with your children." And this way, the table set down. Otherwise this table refused to go down, and the father did not want to leave his children.

Madame Sara links her work with the spirit world to her rich knowledge of folk medical cures which have been used for hundreds of years by the Sephardim of this geographical region (the Balkans, the Dodecanese Islands, Greece, and Turkey).[4] A partial list of her traditional treatments includes the use of rue, garlic, raki, *defne* [bay leaves], and *kekik* [thyme]. When asked, for example, if she ever used rue, an important herb in the Sephardic pharmacopeia, Sara responds, "Rue I always use . . . for the evil eye." It was, she explains, especially useful for newly delivered mothers and their babies: "When a pregnant woman gives birth, and she wants to leave the room, and the new baby is left alone, . . . they leave a package of rue, and to the smell it [the spirit] doesn't come. [The spirits] don't touch the baby and the mother." Sara speaks of a sick person, one who is *sikliado* (depressed/in anguish), who cries, and cannot sleep at night. Once she determines that he has not been bewitched, she uses a widely known and much-employed procedure.

> I see him. What does he have? No, it's not an *echizo*. It is not [due to] an *echizeria*. If it is not [witchcraft], what would it be? This person took an *espanto*, a *sikinti* [worry]. I'm going to do something for him. I place for him three small glasses of honey in the window, *a l'aver* [outside nocturnal air]. In the morning, *al sereno* [dew/dawn], we give it to him to drink. Three mornings in a row. . . . Then we give him a bath. All the glasses are washed, and from the water you make a *shorbet* [sweet drink/syrup]. And then we pour it behind him, and I tell him, "*No mires detras. No tornes la kara atras. Te esto echando todo los*

---

[4] For discussion of Sephardic folk medical/magical cures, see Michael Molho, *Usos y costumbres de los Sefardíes de Salónica* (Madrid: Consejo Superior de Investigaciones Científicas, 1950), chaps. 8–9 (pp. 273–306); Abraham Galanté, *Histoire des juifs de Rhodes, Chio, Cos,* etc. (Istanbul: Fratelli Haim, 1935), chap. 24 (pp. 117–127); Rebecca Amato Levy, *I Remember Rhodes* (New York: Sepher-Hermon Press, 1987), chaps. 5 (pp. 62–82) and 6 (pp. 220–232) of the Judeo-Spanish version. See also the following by Isaac Jack Lévy: *Jewish Rhodes: A Lost Culture* (Berkeley: Judah L. Magnes Museum, 1989), chap. 3 (pp. 39–83); "Superstition of the Spanish Jews: Religion or Heresy?" *Southern Israelite* 40, no. 17 (1965): 7–16; "A Domesticated Supernatural: Home Magic of the Sephardim," *Shofar* 3, no. 3 (Spring 1985): 12–19; co-authored with Rosemary Lévy Zumwalt, "The Evil Eye and Power of Speech Among the Sephardim," *International Folklore Review* 5 (1987): 52–59.

males detras" [Do not look back. Don't turn your face back. I'm pouring out all the evils behind you].... We dress him, and that's it.

Isaac asked her if she used, as his grandmother had, *mumia tapada*
[secretly administered mummy], a powder made from the dried bones
of a corpse and/or from the dried foreskin saved from the *brit milah*
[circumcision]. Sara responded that this was used in Izmir, but not
in Istanbul. The procedure, as she explained, was to administer the
mumia in secret to the sick person. While the individual was eating
the *mumia*, which had been concealed in a drink or in an item of
food, those present would say, "*Ke tenga la refua*" [may he have the
cure]. "After twenty-four hours," Sara said, "you tell the sick person, 'The sickness will pass, because I have already given you the
mumia.'" She added, "Last week I went to Izmir, and I gave it to
Julia. She was in great pain. The doctors said that it was cancer. I
said, 'This one does not have cancer. She had great *sikinti* [worry/
espanto]. Let's give her the *mumia*.' And today, Julia called me to
inform me that she is fine."

In another instance, Isaac was describing a cure which he had
seen performed twenty-seven years ago by Sephardic women, originally from Turkey, then living in Atlanta, Georgia, when Sara, with
great confidence, completed the explanation. The transcription of
this portion of the interview follows:

Sara: It happened on the third Friday of the Jewish month. The
moment that the muezzin is going to sing in the mosque. Take
two knives with black handles. And say, "*Deshi el miedo, tomi la
fuersa; Deshi el miedo, tomi la fuersa*" [I discarded the fear, I took
the strength; I discarded the fear, I took the strength.] *Trak, trak*,
the child begins to walk.
Isaac: In Atlanta, they also say, "I wash your evil."
Sara: They pour water.
Isaac: They wash the evil.
Sara: The evil.
Isaac: "I cut your evil."
Sara: To remove your evil.
Isaac: You pass three doors, you kiss the mezuzah. They put her to
sleep.
Sara: And on waking up, would walk.
Isaac: What's all that about? This the spirits tell you? Or do you already
know it?
Sara: That I already know.

Isaac: It's something of the Sephardim, then?
Sara: Umhmm.

When asked about dreams, Sara related several traditional interpretations for specific items:

> The pearl is to cry, the onion is sadness. The fire is enemy. If you
> see a white dog, it is a friend that is going to come. If it is black, you
> are going to have a dark [bad] accident. . . . If it bites, it is removing
> your evil.

Dreams, Sara said, "are like divination." And as so many other Sephardim would tell us, so Sara also emphasized that if one dreamed of something bad, one should wash the hands on waking and say "*Esto yo lo vo ver in bueno*" [This I will see in good fortune]. However, when asked about dreams concerning the moon and the stars, instead of providing the traditional answer, Sara grew somewhat disconcerted, and said, "About the stars, I used to know about them. . . ." Then she invoked her spirit, "I have a Haham. . . . When there are a lot of intricate things in the dreams, I call him and he interprets them, the dreams."

In the above instance, Sara called on a Haham, the spirit of Rav Harbi Bohor, whom she consulted on Jewish matters, in order to save her from the embarrassment of being caught short on her knowledge of the traditional interpretation of dreams. She also calls on her spirits to augment her extensive knowledge of traditional cures. Sara treated a young boy who had a severely infected sore on his leg. His doctor had insisted that the leg must be amputated; but when Sara saw him, she said, "This leg . . . I am going to save . . . for you." First, she cleansed the infected part with peroxide. Then she applied oil which she had purchased from the Turkish spice and herb bazaar, and she covered the sore with threads pulled from a clean piece of cheesecloth. In the morning, Sara removed each thread with, as she said, "doctor's tweezers." This procedure would be repeated four to five times. And as the boy's mother had told the incredulous doctor when he saw the healthy leg, "The wound closed. And the blood began to run." Sara explained, "*Esto es melezina de kaza* [This is medicine of the house]. But still, it was he [Sadik] who showed it to me. He told me to use it, and I used it as a medicine of the house."

In her treatment of a little girl suffering from hair loss, Sara combines a traditional cure with what she calls phototelepathy. At the age of nine, the girl had a very high fever. In Sara's words, "Everything fell out, even the eyebrows, and all the hair on her body, even the little hairs on her arm. She looked like a squash. Doctors, doctors, doctors, doctors [for] years." Someone told the parents to take the child to Madame Sara. As she explained, "I took her. In three weeks, I brought her hair back." Sara had prescribed wine vinegar rinse to be used twice a week, after which calcium was patted on the scalp, and oil made from *defne* [bay leaves] was applied. While the cure is traditional, Sara says that it is "the spirit [who] tells me what medicines to administer." During the night, Sara encloses herself in a room and places a picture of the *hazino* [stricken/sick one] on the floor in front of a burning candle. She then communicates with Sadik concerning each one. If a cure is possible, Sadik prescribes it. Otherwise, the flame goes out. It was during one of these seances that Sara obtained the cure for the young girl.

The spirit also helps Madame Sara in her treatment of those with injured knees and shoulders. Many soccer players in Istanbul come to see Aunt Sara, as they call her, for such cures. As she explains it, there are certain places in the body where water accumulates, and if it is not removed it may turn into meningitis. For the treatment, she places dry towels over the affected part, and, after she has gone into a trance, she kneels by the patient and is covered by a sheet. Sara explains, "I put my hand, and the spirit immediately finds out from where this water is to be drawn, and it is pulled . . . and the water [runs]." The towels are dripping wet. Afterwards when she gets up, she says, "Ouph! I'm O.K. now."

Illness and malaise—infertility, impotence, family arguments, severe depression—can be caused by evil spirits and by powerful spells. Through communication with her spirits, Madame Sara is able to remove *echizos* [witchcraft]. She fills a basin with clear water, covers it with a sheet; and while in trance, after another reads the names of those afflicted, she places the list in the water. When the spirit has had time to travel to the areas where the witchcraft has been done and has brought the objects used to cast the spells, Madame Sara removes the sheet to reveal a basin filled with the items of bewitchment. Among these might be the following: locked padlocks and knotted ropes to tie one's fortune, Hebrew and Islamic amulets to bring bad luck, animal horns, the tail of a pig, and hair from a person to cast the spell. All of these are encrusted with mud from the places where they had been buried. Sara conducted just such a treatment for the ruler of a Middle Eastern country who sent his private plane to fly her to his capital.[5] As Sara described it:

> He was afraid to go out. . . . He wanted to carry out a job, and he felt certain depression right here [pointed at her heart]. He was all tied up. These kinds of feeling make the sick person worse. It keeps increasing until the sick person either commits suicide or becomes insane. Doctors, troubles, these [all the problems] I removed from him. Wherever [the *echizo*] is buried, with the dirt and everything, it comes.

Madame Sara allowed us to observe the ritual to remove an *echizo* which she conducted in the apartment of a rich Turkish woman, whose maid had been having difficulties with her family. Sara ascertained that the source of the problem was the maid's paternal aunt, who had stirred up dissension and discord among her relatives. The other women present, all from the upper class, had also consulted Sara for their problems.

Those who have conducted research on spirit mediums and spirit possession have stressed the notion that ritualized possession states and ritualized communication with the spirits provide a means for women in many cultures to escape otherwise impossible social situations. Vieda Skultans, in *Intimacy and Ritual: A Study of Spiritualism, Mediums and Groups*, saw spiritualism in Wales, and particularly the central role of the spirit medium, as an outlet for women's frustrations engendered by the narrow bonds of the traditional woman's role in the home. In "Mediums, Controls and Eminent Men," Skultans writes, "Spiritualist mediumship has been and is primarily a female vocation." Spiritualism grew, Skultans stresses, out of the sphere of female domesticity, and this is reflected in "both the style and the content of its activities."[6] As an example of this, one should note that the work of the medium is situated in the home, whether it be her own home or that of others. Her powers are often directed toward solving personal problems, often those between family members or lovers. In one of her most important functions, that of

---

[5] To honor Sara, the ruler gave a lavish banquet. Very proud of this, Sara showed us the pictures taken at the party, but requested that we not divulge the ruler's identity.

[6] For spiritualism as a means for women to vent frustration with the traditional women's role, see Skultans, *Intimacy and Ritual*, chap. 4 (pp. 45–60); see also Skultans, "Mediums, Controls and Eminent Men," in *Women's Religious Experience*, ed. Pat Holden (Totowa, N.J.: Barnes & Noble, 1983), p. 16.

curing, the medium's approach is also "domesticated," for she often
uses herbal cures, coupled with the laying on of hands, or what is
believed to be the channeling of the spirit's force through her hands.
Above all, the medium must use her intuitive power, an attribute
which is associated with the stereotypical view of women. And since
most mediums come from a poor or uneducated background, Skultans
concludes that mediumship "could provide women with a livelihood
which was often much better than any they might have otherwise
have had."[7]

Others concur with Skultans. Alan Gauld, in *Mediumship and Survival*,
observes that there are by far more female mediums than male. And
Alex Owen, in *The Darkened Room: Women, Power and Spiritualism in
Late Victorian England*, discusses spiritualism as a validation of "the
female authoritative voice [which] permitted women an active professional and spiritual role largely denied them elsewhere."[8] While
providing women with a channel for self- and spiritual expression,
mediumship does not challenge the basis of the male-female power
structure. Rather, as Skultans observes, "Mediumship . . . capitalizes
on the existing relationships [between men and women] and transfers them to a spiritual plane." Thus, in keeping with such gender
relations, while the medium is usually a woman, the spirit guide,
sometimes referred to as "spirit control," is usually male.[9] Still, though
the spirit might be male, it is the voice of the medium that is heard,
and she does have power.

Madame Sara of Istanbul, Turkey, definitely has her authoritative voice. Ostensibly a Muslim holy man dead for 127 years who
speaks through her, the voice is really hers. This is not to say that
the relationship with Sadik is unimportant, but rather to place the
power where it lies, in the person of Sara. Clearly she feels this
power in herself, and speaks of its growth over the years, nurtured
and guided as it was by the spirits. Sara told about her years of
apprenticeship when she obeyed the spirits:

> I gave them the word that I was going to work, [and] for three years,
> I did not show my hair. I covered it. I did not paint my nails. I did
> not [cut my hair]. I did not put on make-up. . . . For three years, I

[7] Skultans, "Mediums, Controls and Eminent Men," pp. 22–23. For curing by
touch and with the use of herbs, see Gauld, *Mediumship and Survival*, p. 21.

[8] Gauld, *Mediumship and Survival*, p. 22; Owen, *Darkened Room*, p. 6.

[9] Skultans, "Mediums, Controls and Eminent Men," p. 17.

performed this honor for the spirits. When I was about to perform the seance, I would prepare myself. I did not eat. I washed myself.

There came a time when she no longer felt that she had to do the spirits' bidding, rather they assisted her with her seances involving the elevation of the table.

> Now, since I am already very practiced, for twenty years I was their servant. And now there are twenty-one years that they are my servants. Push the table away, they turn it. Bring the table around, they bring it. I pull it, and I tell them, "Don't let it drop." They don't let it fall.

Through the spirits Sara has gained the power which she wished for as a young child when, on her way to school, she said to herself, "Ahh! I would like to become a person who would be recognized [famous] throughout the world."

Madame Sara is truly caught between two worlds, and from this liminal position comes her strength and power. In her own words, Sara explains this: "I [have] a kind of force that I can call the spirits, but I am also a human being like other people." She bridges the world of the spirits and the world of the living, that of the rich and the poor, and of the Jew and the non-Jew. This bifurcation carries over to her own self-view: she is, almost in one breath, of two minds about herself. Apologizing for her lack of education, she would say, "I didn't study, Isaac, I was a daughter of a poor family"; and on another occasion, "Didn't I tell you, if I studied, I would have been a professor like you, Isaac?" Then in the next sentence, she boasted, "I'm bigger than the professor you are."

From an impoverished background, Sara gained power through her ability to commune with the spirits. As she says of Sadik,

> His force is in me, and my force is in him. . . . All this is not because I want to be a big shot. This thing came to me from God. I'm not a big shot, and I don't show any *grandezas* [airs]. . . . I sit with the very poor ones, with the poorest of the poor, and with the very, very rich.

Through her work, Madame Sara has earned the gratitude of a king, a prince, and a prime minister, all of Middle Eastern countries, and she has gained a loyal following in Turkey and Israel. As a dear friend of hers told us,

> You should know that she has in Istanbul the *crema*, multimillionaires. Her clients are Turkish multimillionaires of Istanbul. . . . The presents that they give her. . . . Gold, flowers, bracelets, rings, gems, this is the

kind of presents that they give her. They are so happy with what she has done for them. Of that which she says, of that which she speaks.

But what she desires most is to be recognized by her own people, by the Sephardim. Sara recounts that among the Jewish community she is known as Sara *la indivina* [the diviner] or *la echizera* [the witch]. "And I am not," she emphasizes, "an *echizera*. I am a medium." "And what I would like," she continues, "is for the Jewish people to give me a little *valor*, a little respect and credit." But by her very work, by communing with the spirits of the dead, and by her success, she is thwarted in this desire. Sephardim from Edirne who had known her as a child of a poor family could not fathom her powerful position in Istanbul society. One woman, now in an old-age home in Istanbul, told us of her memories of Madame Sara.

> This woman is from Edirne. Sara, this *indivina* [fortuneteller]. When she was young, she didn't have a father or a mother. . . . There was someone who had a little hut where he sold *pepitas* [seeds]. She was the niece of this one. And in Jewish homes, she was a maid. We hired her as a maid. . . . And she worked in our house. . . . And that's how she grew up, that young lady. And she came here to Istanbul. Afterwards I went for four years to Israel. And there I found out that she was an *indivina*.

In Bat Yam, Israel, we spoke with a man who had known Sara in Istanbul when she was first married. He recalled, "They were very poor. They had children, and they were poor, like many people there. . . . Then we heard that she became an *echizera*." He spoke disparagingly about her work and concluded, "The Messiah came to her? A *hoja* came to her? That's not possible!" In answer to our question about Sara's ostracism by the Jewish community, her friend, Diamante Benun of Izmir, responded, "Well, jealousy has a lot to do with it. They can't tolerate how Sara has reached such a level. In Istanbul, they told me that, 'Sara, what was she? How could she reach this height?' They can't stand it, due to jealousy."

Still, Sara has faith. As she said, "The day will come . . .—write that down—, and someday you will see it. . . . The day will come, [when] even the doctors will come to me to beg me, 'How are we going to cure these patients?' The day will come." And then she concluded,

Look how important *mazal* is. Isaac, you came on a certain journey to teach and to learn things, and to take things with you. You came here for such an opportunity, to the place of the Jews [the *Shalom* newspaper of Istanbul, Turkey], and to ask questions, [and they tell you about me]. Would you imagine such a thing? And . . . after you a thousand people will come. That I already know. Do you understand?

Madame Sara performing a seance with a candle

JUDÍOS Y CONVERSOS EN LA LITERATURA ESPAÑOLA CONTEMPORÁNEA*

PALOMA DÍAZ-MÁS

Universidad del País Vasco

De todos es sabido que, desde su expulsión en el siglo XV, la presencia de los judíos en España ha sido casi nula. Sólo en la segunda mitad del siglo XIX comenzaron a configurarse, tímidamente, los primeros atisbos de comunidades israelitas y aún hoy éstas son exiguas y tienen escasa proyección en la vida general del país.[1]

---

* El original de este artículo fue presentado como comunicación en la Second International Interdisciplinary Conference on Sephardic Studies, organizada por la State University of New York en Binghamton en abril de 1991. Consecuentemente, sólo tiene en cuenta algunas novelas que se habían publicado en España hasta aquella fecha; en los últimos años, ha sido creciente en España el interés por el pasado histórico judío, muy especialmente a raíz de la conmemoración, en 1992, del quinto centenario de la Expulsión. Los efectos de ese interés han sido múltiples: no sólo se han fomentado los estudios académicos sobre historia judía y sefardí, sino que esos estudios están teniendo cada vez mayor proyección en la divulgación a través de publicaciones, cursos, jornadas, ciclos de conferencias, exposiciones, etc; se detecta en los medios de comunicación una mayor atención al tema judío y una mejor documentación sobre él, que redunda en una más cabal información del público en general. También en el ámbito de la creación literaria se ha dejado sentir el creciente interés y la mejor información sobre el tema judío; desde 1992 se han publicado algunas valiosas novelas históricas de tema judío o sefardí: entre ellas cabe señalar *Ahora Rachel ha muerto*, de Gabriel Albiac (Madrid: Alfaguara, 1994), ambientada en época del falso mesías sefardí Sabetay Zví; *Las agujas del Templo*, de Javier Gúrpide (Barcelona: Planeta, 1994), que se desarrolla en la Palestina de la época de Cristo; y, sobre todo, la magnífica novela en catalán *Dins el darrer blau*, de Carme Riera (Barcelona: Destino, 1994), traducida al castellano por la propia autora con el título de *En el último azul* (Madrid: Alfaguara, 1996), que fue Premio Nacional de Narrativa y recrea, con excelente documentación histórica, el último proceso inquisitorial (entre 1687 y 1691) contra criptojudíos mallorquines. En el ámbito de la narrativa infantil y juvenil ha aparecido alguna novela interesante de tema judío, como *El tiempo y la promesa*, de Concha López Narváez (Madrid: Bruño, 1990), que evoca la vida en la aljama de Vitoria en tiempos de la expulsión y constituye una buena y clara introducción a temas y problemas históricos para público juvenil. Entre los autores de origen judío ahora hay que incluir a Daniel Múgica, que ha dirigido sus esfuerzos a la narrativa juvenil en novelas como *Alba y el recaudador de aguas*, *Alba y los cazadores de arañas* y *Alba y la maldición gamada* (todas ellas publicadas por Anaya en 1995), que presentan la novedad—insólita en el panorama literario español—de incluir con toda normalidad a judíos como unos personajes cualquiera de la trama.

[1] Véanse al respecto los datos de mi libro *Los sefardíes: Historia, lengua y cultura*

Sin embargo, el judío ha sido un personaje presente en la literatura contemporánea española; ni que decir tiene que en un país donde la población tiene casi nulo contacto con la realidad judía y escasa información sobre ella (y los escritores no son, por lo general, una excepción), la mayor parte de las veces el judío de la literatura responde más a un estereotipo, a una idealización (positiva o negativa) que al producto de la observación o del conocimiento de su auténtica realidad.

La presencia del judío en la literatura española de finales del siglo XIX y las primeras décadas del XX es relativamente abundante y ha merecido diversos estudios.[2] Desde la guerra civil hasta el final

---

(Barcelona: Riopiedras, 1997, 3ª ed), pp. 238–246 que, aunque se refieren más específicamente a los sefardíes, son extensibles a la práctica totalidad de las comunidades españolas, mayoritariamente de ese origen. De este libro hay versión en inglés: *Sephardim. The Jews from Spain*, trad. de George K. Zucker (Chicago-Londres: The Chicago University Press, 1992).

[2] Sobre los judíos en Benito Pérez Galdós, Vicente Blasco Ibáñez, Pío Baroja y Concha Espina puede verse el libro de A. Benaim Lasry *El judío como héroe de novela. Humanización del personaje judío en algunas novelas españolas de los siglos XIX y XX* (Madrid: 1980). Lo más estudiado han sido sin duda los personajes judíos de Galdós: sobre sus posibles fuentes de información véase S.G. Armistead, V.A. Chamberlin y J.H. Silverman "An Early 20th-Century Characterization of Moroccan Judeo-Spanish: Ricardo Ruiz Orsatti (1905)", *Mediterranean Language Review* 3 (1987): pp. 55–65; R. Ricard "Cartas de Ricardo Ruiz Orsatti a Galdós acerca de Marruecos (1901–1910)", *Anales Galdosianos* III (1968): pp. 99–117; V.A. Chamberlin, "More Light on Galdós' Sephardic Source Materials: A Reply to A.F. Lambert", *Anales Galdosianos*, IX (1974): pp. 167–168; y, del mismo, "The Importance of Rodrigo Soriano's *Moros y Cristianos* in the creation of *Misericordia*", *Anales Galdosianos* XIII (1978): pp. 105–109. Sobre la postura vital de Galdós hacia los movimientos prosefardíes, V.A. Chamberlin, "Galdós and the *Movimiento Pro-Sefardita*", *Anales Galdosianos* XVI (181), pp. 91–103. Sobre la conexión entre la visión galdosiana y la de Américo Castro, S. Gilman, "Judíos, moros y cristianos en las historias de don Benito y don Américo", *Homenaje a Antonio Sánchez Barbudo: Ensayos de literatura española moderna* (Madison: Univ. of Wisconsin, 1981), pp. 25–36; sobre el lenguaje sefardí, los personajes y otros aspectos de judíos y judaísmo en Galdós: J. Casalduero, "Galdós: de Morton a Almudena", *Modern Language Review* 79 (1964): pp. 181–187 y, del mismo, "Significado y forma de *Misericordia*", *PMLA* LIX (1944): pp. 1104–1110; V.A. Chamberlin, "Galdós' Sephardic Types", *Symposium* XVII (1963): pp. 85–100; S.E. Cohen, "Almudena and the Jewish Theme in *Misericordia*", *Anales Galdosianos* VIII (1973): pp. 51–61; D. Lida, "De Almudena y su lenguaje", *Nueva Revista de Filología Hispánica* XV (1961): pp. 297–308; de la misma "El habla de los sefardíes en Galdós", *Galdos Studies* (Londres: Támesis, 1974), pp. 29–33; J. Martínez Ruiz, "Ficción y realidad judeoespañola en el *Aita Tettauen* de Benito Pérez Galdós", *Revista de Filología Española* LIX (1977): pp. 145–179; R. Ricard, "Sur le personnage d'Almudena dans *Misericordia*", en *Galdós et ses romans* (Paris: Institut d'Études Hispaniques, 1961), pp. 51–62; Schraibman, "Las citas bíblicas en *Misericordia* de Galdós", *Cuadernos Hispanoamericanos* 250–252 (octubre 1970–enero 1971): pp. 490–504; S.E. Schyfter, *The Jew in the Novels of Benito Pérez Galdós* (Londres: Támesis, 1978); de la misma, "The Judaism of Galdos' Daniel Morton", *Hispania* 59 (1976): pp.

de la dictadura franquista se extiende un largo período de silencio casi absoluto, durante el cual las figuras judías están prácticamente ausentes de la literatura, más por falta de interés y de conocimiento de los españoles de la época que por otras razones: la España de 1936 a 1975 vive centrada en muy otras preocupaciones, que nada tienen que ver con esa minoría étnica que procura pasar discretamente desapercibida en la sociedad española y que—cuando se trata de la realidad judía de fuera de España—se ve desde el país como algo lejano, de lo que el público hispano no tiene demasiada información (salvo, naturalmente, un selecto grupo de especialistas que se dedica a los estudios hebraicos y sefardíes).[3]

En los últimos veinte años, los judíos han vuelto a resurgir en España como tema literario. No vamos a entrar aquí en las posibles causas de ese resurgimiento (que van desde la mayor apertura y curiosidad de los españoles de hoy por otras culturas y otros países hasta la atención que hoy se presta en España a las culturas locales o minoritarias; pasando, naturalmente, por la mayor libertad de expresión). Unicamente intentaremos hacer una cala en esa presen-

---

24–33; J.B. Vilar, "Galdós y los judíos de *Aita Tettauen*", *Africa* XXIII.358 (octubre 1971): pp. 396–398. En el "descubrimiento" de los judíos por parte de los españoles del pasado siglo influyó sin duda el contacto con ellos a través de la guerra de España con Marruecos y la toma de Tetuán por los españoles en 1860; sobre esa campaña véase el libro de Andrée Bachoud, *Los españoles ante las campañas de Marruecos* (Madrid: Espasa Calpe, 1988); hay también datos interesantes en el libro de Marquina y Ospina citado en la nota 3. Sobre las reacciones ante los judíos que suscitó la campaña en varios escritores, pueden verse el artículo de J.B. Vilar "Filosemitismo y antisemitismo en la obra de Pedro Antonio de Alarcón y otros testigos de la Guerra de Africa", *Hésperis Tamuda* XVII (1976–77): pp. 137–147; y el de Uriel Macías "El primer rencuentro de los españoles con los sefardíes: la guerra de África", *History and Creativity in the Sephardi and Oriental Jewish Communities* (Jerusalén: Misgav Yerushalayim, 1994), pp. 333–351.

[3] La actitud del franquismo hacia los judíos fue ambigua en más de un aspecto: mientras en el discurso oficial se utilizaban expresiones como *la conspiración judeo-masónica*, un pequeño número de funcionarios españoles adoptó actitudes decisivas para el salvamento de judíos en la II Guerra Mundial y para su evacuación de Egipto durante la guerra arabe-israelí de los Seis Días. En el ámbito académico, varias universidades españolas ofrecieron durante la dictadura de Franco estudios hebraicos en sus currícula y en una fecha como 1940 se fundó el Instituto Arias Montano de estudios hebraicos, sefardíes y de Oriente Próximo, dentro de una institución pública de investigación como es el Consejo Superior de Investigaciones Científicas (CSIC); hoy el antiguo Arias Montano sigue funcionando, englobado dentro del Instituto de Filología del mismo CSIC. Para la actitud del régimen franquista con respecto a los judíos pueden verse los libros de Haim Avni *España, Franco y los judíos* (Madrid: Altalena, 1982; es traducción al castellano de un libro originalmente en hebreo); y de Antonio Marquina y Gloria Inés Ospina, *España y los judíos en el siglo XX* (Madrid: Espasa Calpe, 1987).

cia judaica, analizando cuatro novelas de autores españoles no judíos, publicadas entre 1985 y 1991, en las que de una u otra forma se toca el tema de los judíos en España y/o los conversos (conceptos que, además, se confunden con frecuencia en sus obras).[4] Nuestra intención es analizar cómo ven algunos escritores españoles del momento la cuestión judía en España y al judío como personaje, ya que su forma de abordar el tema puede reflejar la mentalidad que el español medianamente culto tiene con respecto a esas cuestiones. Las cuatro novelas tenidas en consideración son las siguientes, por orden cronológico:

- *Los tornadizos*, de Antonio Cascales (Barcelona: Muchnik, 1985): sobre Diego Susón, uno de los primeros penitenciados por la Inquisición sevillana (en 1481). En la ficción alternan la reconstrucción novelada de la vida de Diego Susón con las aventuras de Andrés Baena, un estudiante de época actual que realiza una tesis sobre los hechos en la Universidad de Sevilla, y que tiene una novia (Laura) participando en excavaciones arqueológicas en Israel, justo en el momento en que estalla la Guerra de los Seis Días. Esos dos planos (los judíos históricos y la representación de los judíos actuales a través del Estado de Israel) son fundamentales en la novela.

- *Un sambenito para el señor Santiago*, de Magdalena Guilló (Barcelona: Muchnik, 1986): reconstrucción, novelada pero muy bien documentada—tanto en aspectos biográficos como de cultura judía—de la vida del humanista español Benito Arias Montano (1527-1598), capellán de Felipe II y director de la edición de una famosa Biblia políglota; la autora lo supone conocedor de los ritos judaicos y

---

[4] Excluímos deliberadamente las obras publicadas en España por autores judíos que escriben en castellano (Leopoldo Azancot, Marcos Ricardo Barnatán, Mario Satz), ya que su acercamiento al tema parte del punto de vista judío, y lo que nos interesa aquí es precisamente la actitud de los no judíos. Tampoco tenemos en cuenta obras españolas sobre situaciones o personajes judíos de otros países (como el de la propia Magdalena Guilló *Entre el ayer y el mañana*, Barcelona: Muchnik, 1984, que es una biografía novelada de Theodor Herzl) porque lo que nos interesa es la visión que se ofrece desde España de los judíos de España. Tampoco hemos tenido en cuenta la novela de Angel Vázquez *La vida perra de Juanita Narboni* (Barcelona: Planeta, 1976) porque se sale ampliamente del marco temporal que nos hemos fijado, y además no se centra en la vida de los judíos, sino de los españoles residentes en Marruecos tras la época del Protectorado, aunque en el habla y la biografía de su protagonista (una solterona tangerina) se reflejan con mucho acierto huellas e influencias de su convivencia con sefardíes de Marruecos.

ocasional practicante de ellos, por sus orígenes conversos y su cercanía a círculos criptojudíos sevillanos.

- *Collar de ámbar*, de Mercedes Fórmica (Madrid: Caro Raggio, 1989): una novela casi "rosa" en que un abogado sevillano de baja extracción social y orígenes conversos (Rafael Lobatón) pretende y consigue introducir a su hermana Isabel en los ambientes más aristocráticos de Sevilla, hasta casarla con el hijo de un noble; la trama se complica además con la existencia de círculos criptojudíos y con el descubrimiento de la ascendencia conversa de varios nobles sevillanos. Sorprendentemente, la novela se desarrolla en pleno siglo XX (aproximadamente de los años 20 a los 70) y sin embargo la autora da por supuesto que en la Sevilla contemporánea se da la misma distinción de castas entre cristianos viejos y descendientes de conversos que se producía en los siglos XVI y XVII, lo cual resulta cuando menos chocante y más que discutible.

- *Melibea no quiere ser mujer*, de Juan Carlos Arce (Barcelona: Planeta, 1991): fantasía sobre la composición de la *Celestina* por Fernando de Rojas; el primer auto resulta ser obra de una prostituta de Salamanca de orígenes conversos de quien, naturalmente, se enamora el también converso Rojas. Mientras tanto, el inquisidor Pedro de Mahora busca pruebas para acusar a Rojas de criptojudaísmo.

Pasemos ahora a destacar algunos de los rasgos comunes a tan heterogéneas obras, que quizás arrojen alguna luz sobre determinadas vulgatas que sobre los judíos circulan en ambientes españoles de cultura media.

1. *El marco geográfico*: resulta más que significativo observar que tres de las cuatro obras comentadas—pese a ser de temas muy diferentes e incluso desarrollarse en épocas distintas, que van del siglo XV al XX—tienen alguna relación con Sevilla: sevillanos son Diego Susón y el estudiante que en la novela de Cascales investiga su vida, y que se mueve en ambientes sevillanos vivamente descritos por el autor; en Sevilla (una Sevilla actual bastante irreconocible si se la compara con la realidad) se desarrolla la novela de Mercedes Fórmica; y, aunque la biografía novelada de Arias Montano abordada por Magdalena Guilló se ambienta mayoritariamente en el retiro del estudioso en Aracena (Huelva), acaba con el humanista apartado en la Cartuja de Sevilla y tienen un papel importante en la narración sus contactos con amigos criptojudíos sevillanos. Incluso en las obras de

Cascales y de Fórmica se alude a una misma calle de la ciudad: el llamado Callejón de la Susona, en el cual según la leyenda vivió la hija de Diego Susón y donde—según Fórmica—existía aún en época reciente un lugar de encuentro de criptojudíos. El único que se aparta de la tónica es Arce, y ello por una razón obvia: su protagonista, Fernando de Rojas, vivió históricamente en Salamanca, la Puebla de Montalbán y Talavera de la Reina.

Cabe preguntarse por qué tanta preferencia por la misma ciudad. Naturalmente, en el caso de las obras de Cascales y Guilló viene determinada por el tema elegido, ya que son asuntos históricos. Pero ¿por qué esa preferencia de los escritores por novelar la historia de los judíos y conversos de Sevilla y no, por ejemplo, los de la no menos tópica Toledo, los de Castilla, Extremadura u otros lugares de Andalucía? Cabe apuntar hacia un tópico muy extendido en la opinión española actual: la creencia de que las etnias "semíticas" (moros y judíos) tuvieron mayor arraigo y pervivencia en la zona sur de España, cuya más importante ciudad era y es, precisamente, Sevilla.[5]

2. *Historia y actualidad*: otro hecho significativo es que tres de las cuatro novelas se ambienten en época histórica. El hecho judío hispano parece concebirse como algo perteneciente a la historia y no a la actualidad; apreciación que, entre paréntesis, no resulta descaminada dada la escasa presencia de lo judío en la España actual Sólo la novela de Mercedes Fórmica se ambienta en el siglo XX, pero su visión de este nuestro siglo resulta tan anacrónica que a veces tenemos la impresión de estar leyendo hechos ambientados en el XVII: cuando habla de conversos y criptojudíos, Fórmica traslada a

---

[5] La idea probablemente deriva de que en Andalucía, y concretamente en Granada, estuvo el último reino musulmán de la península. Pero recuérdese que Sevilla había sido conquistada por los cristianos y se había incorporado a la corona de Castilla ya en el siglo XIII. Además, por lo que respecta especialmente a los judíos, su arraigo en los reinos cristianos peninsulares fue, a partir del siglo XII, mayor que en los reinos musulmanes, debido sobre todo al fundamentalismo islámico de los almohades, que produjo una auténtica oleada de emigración hacia los entonces más tolerantes reinos cristianos; por ello es falsa la creencia (también muy extendida) de que los mayores núcleos judíos medievales estaban en la España musulmana: ello puede ser cierto hasta el siglo XI, pero no a partir del XII. Véase al respecto la *Historia de los judíos en la España cristiana* de Yitzhak Baer (Madrid: Altalena, 1981; es traducción del hebreo), en dos volúmenes; y también la *Historia del pueblo judío* dirigida por H.H. Ben-Sasson (Madrid: Alianza, 1988; también traducción del hebreo; hay versión en inglés *A History of the Jewish People*, Weidenfeld and Nicolson, 1976) vol. II pp. 552–554 y 577–579.

la época moderna una serie de esquemas socioculturales propios de épocas históricas (conceptos como limpieza de sangre, conciencia de descender de conversos y el deseo de ocultarlo, práctica del cripto-judaísmo) que son absolutamente inoperantes en la sociedad española actual pero eran muy operativos en la de los Siglos de Oro.

Especialmente significativa es la alternancia de tiempos y lugares en la novela de Cascales: a los judíos *históricos* sobre los que estudia Andrés Baena se contraponen los judíos *actuales* que conoce Laura durante su estancia en Israel. Es decir, los judíos españoles se conciben como algo perteneciente al pasado histórico, mientras que se identifica a los judíos actuales no con las comunidades modernas de España, ni con países de abundante población judía como la cercana Francia o Estados Unidos, sino precisamente con el Estado de Israel. Ello responde a una *vulgata* muy extendida entre el público hispano: que donde están los judíos hoy es en Israel y prácticamente en ninguna otra parte.

3. *Terminología*: pero estamos hablando indistintamente de judíos y conversos, porque en las obras analizadas se utilizan frecuentemente de forma indistinta las palabras y los conceptos *judío, converso* y *cripto-judío* como si fueran sinónimos y equivalentes, o al menos intercambiables. De hecho, las cuatro obras se centran, más que en peripecias y aventuras de auténticos judíos, en los conflictos vividos por los conversos o sus descendientes, a los que los autores suelen llamar *judíos*.

Cascales distingue entre *judíos de ley* y *judíos* simplemente, siendo esto último sinónimo de *conversos* (como también se los llama en la obra). Los personajes de la novela de Arce emplean indistintamente los términos *judío* y *judaizante* para referirse a criptojudíos reales o supuestos (bien es verdad que alguno de los que usa esos términos es un inquisidor, en quien sería verosímil la identificación converso = judío encubierto). Incluso en una novela tan matizada como la de Guilló encontramos (p. 140) una enumeración como: "Simón de Tovar, el biólogo converso, el judío más rico de Sevilla, el marrano que desafiaba a la Inquisición. . . ." Y no digamos ya en la novela de Fórmica, donde se llama *judíos* o—seguramente con intención eufemística—*israelitas*[6] no ya a auténticos judíos o a conversos cripto-

---

[6] La confusión terminológica es la vigente entre la mayor parte del público his-

judíos, sino a los lejanos descendientes de esos conversos en el siglo XX (¡quinientos años después de la conversión!).

En la novela de Fórmica se usa además el término *sefardita* o *sefardí* no como específico para referirse a una familia concreta del judaísmo, sino como sinónimo de judío o israelita. Y ello nos pone en contacto con la consideración de los sefardíes en la mentalidad de nuestros autores: Fórmica, al hablar de los españoles de Sevilla descendientes de conversos, los denomina *sefardíes*, manifestando una identificación entre lo sefardí y todo lo judío hispano[7] (aunque sólo sea lejanamente judío). En la novela de Cascales y en menor medida en la de Guilló la identificación se produce entre los sefardíes actuales postexílicos y los antiguos conversos judaizantes.

Así, Cascales salpica el discurso de sus conversos del siglo XV con citas de oraciones, refranes y canciones documentadas entre los sefardíes de Oriente y Marruecos en el siglo XX,[8] como una forma de dar una pátina de antigüedad y verosimilitud a su lenguaje; quizás sea un mero recurso literario usado como consciente anacronismo, o quizás eco de la creencia de que lo que dicen, cantan o rezan los sefardíes actuales es conservación de lo que ya existía antes de la expulsión, idea muy extendida en la España actual.[9] En la novela, esas citas tienen como contrapunto las canciones sefardíes que Laura

---

pano. En cuanto al término *israelita*, se ha utilizado en la España actual frecuentemente como sinónimo de *israelí* ('ciudadano del Estado de Israel'), sobre todo en los medios de comunicación, aunque ese uso erróneo parece haberse ido corrigiendo en los últimos años. Pero no es infrecuente su uso (lo mismo que la palabra *hebreo*) como eufemismo por parte de personas a quienes *judío* parece una palabra infamante (piénsese que en la lengua coloquial aún se usan términos como *judiada* 'ofensa o agravio que se hace a una persona'). Sobre la terminología de este campo semántico en castellano véase mi libro citado en nota 1: p. 17 n. 1. Por otra parte, la confusión terminológica entre *judío*, *converso* y *criptojudío* nos lleva—aunque por otras vías—al viejo prejuicio inquisitorial de que todo converso es sospechoso de criptojudaísmo y por tanto no existen cristianos convertidos sino judíos encubiertos.

[7] Para la definición del término *sefardí* véase de nuevo mi libro citado en nota 1, pp. 23–25.

[8] Así, en la Andalucía del siglo XV se cantan canciones de boda como "Veinticinco escalones / de plata fina / para que suba la novia / y al año parida" o cantos de ronda como el famoso *Abridme, galanica* (p. 85), se pronuncian bendiciones y oraciones en sefardí ("Bendicho el abastado..." en p. 102, la bendición de la mesa en p. 105) y los personajes dicen refranes sefardíes (como el "más vale vecino que un hermano y primo" de p. 70). El habla de los judíos y conversos medievales tiene a veces hasta rasgos fonéticos del sefardí, como el seseo ("ventisinco" en p. 85), común por otra parte con el andaluz, pero que sólo se señala ocasionalmente en boca de personajes judíos, dentro de citas en sefardí.

[9] Ejemplos de esa idea en mi libro de nota 1, pp. 103–104, allí referido a la lengua judeoespañola.

escucha en Israel de boca de supuestos sefardíes como un taxista "judeoargentino, un sefardita".[10]

También Guilló cita en su novela algunos romances y canciones religiosas sefardíes, como la famosa copla que comienza "Abraham abinu, padre querido" (p. 149); pero en su caso parece más bien un libre recurso de creatividad literaria, ya que la novela entera está salpicada de citas anacrónicas, a la manera de los homenajes cinematográficos.[11]

4. *El retrato del judío*: señalaremos a continuación algunos de los rasgos con que se presenta a los judíos y conversos en las novelas.

4.1. *Marginados y perseguidos*: las cuatro novelas tratan de la situación de los conversos como grupo social perseguido y marginado, sea cual sea la época elegida. No falta en ninguna un mayor o menor protagonismo de la Inquisición como principal responsable de esa marginación. Todos los personajes conversos son seres atormentados, tanto por las propias circunstancias de su vida como por sus recuerdos, con frecuencia relativos a una niñez en la que conocieron directamente las prácticas del judaísmo (así Arias Montano, Diego Susón) o las persecuciones (el propio Susón, Fernando de Rojas); en el caso de Rafael Lobatón, protagonista de la novela de Fórmica, el tormento viene de su triple condición de homosexual reprimido, descendiente bastardo de nobles deseoso de ser reconocido como tal y descendiente de conversos; su contacto con la Inquisición es a través de los árboles genealógicos de la nobleza sevillana, que él contribuye a limpiar de sangre manchada falsificando genealogías.

En todas las novelas se trasluce, por otra parte, una cierta admiración por esa casta marginada: Arce insistiendo en los aspectos relativos a la inteligencia, la creatividad intelectual de los conversos y su independencia de pensamiento, aspectos sobre el que volveremos después; Cascales participa también de la misma idea e insiste además

---

[10] La mayoría de los judíos argentinos son de origen askenazí. Naturalmente, no es imposible que Laura haya encontrado a uno de los escasos descendientes de sefardíes nacidos en Argentina; pero más probable es que la afirmación sea producto de una creencia también muy extendida: que son sefardíes todos los judíos que hablan español . . . aunque lo hablen por ser hispanoamericanos.

[11] Por ejemplo, en pp. 108–110 se desarrolla una paráfrasis del romance castellano de *La condesita* (que también se canta entre los sefardíes), en otro pasaje cita la famosa frase final de *Cien años de soledad*, son frecuentes las citas o alusiones a textos del Siglo de Oro español posteriores a Arias Montano, etc.

en elementos como la solidaridad entre judíos de ley y conversos o la integridad moral de su protagonista Diego Susón; para Guilló la figura del converso atormentado Arias Montano parece encarnar un imposible sincretismo de las dos religiones, aspiración de un espíritu cultivado y liberal; la novela de Fórmica es la más ambigua, pero también en ella parece subyacer una cierta admiración por la capacidad intelectual y la habilidad práctica que ella atribuye a los descendientes de conversos.

En general, Arce, Cascales y Guilló parecen compartir un cierto sentimiento de deuda moral hacia esa casta perseguida, unida al convencimiento de que esos conversos acosados constituían uno de los más fértiles fermentos de la vida social española y que, de no haber sido sofocadas las tendencias—más abiertas, más intelectuales, más libres—que ellos encarnaban, hubiera sido muy otra la historia de España. Es, por tanto, una visión idealizada del converso como fermento fallido de una sociedad distinta; teñida además de cierto sentimiento de responsabilidad colectiva por los sufrimientos y sinsabores de ese grupo social específico.

Frente a ese sentimiento de pertenencia del converso a lo mejor y más esperanzador de la sociedad española, destaca la visión de Mercedes Fórmica: aquí los conversos son vistos más como un cuerpo extraño en esa sociedad, como un elemento ajeno y hasta cierto punto perturbador. Ello acerca la novela a algunos de los más clásicos tópicos antisemitas: por ejemplo, la visión del judío (o converso) como un individuo extraño a la sociedad en la que se inserta, un *extranjero*. Así, los padres de Rafael Lobatón, conversos, se sienten ajenos nada más y nada menos que a la guerra civil española, que no va con ellos (¡y están viviendo en Sevilla!):[12] "La familia Lobatón apenas participó de las vicisitudes de la contienda [. . .] En lo más profundo, Estrella y Rubén se sabían ajenos a las exaltaciones de uno y otro bando" (p. 46).

La misma novela se desliza con frecuencia a otro tópico vinculado al anterior: la percepción de los judíos y/o conversos como una especie de grupo de presión en la sombra, que hace y deshace

---

[12] Recuérdese que fue Sevilla una de las primeras ciudades en unirse al bando "nacional", desde cuya emisora de radio lanzaba el general Queipo de LLano sus soflamas propagandísticas, tendentes a minar la moral de los republicanos. En esos discursos radiados no eran, además, infrecuentes, las alusiones a una conspiración judía mundial y a la guerra civil que estaba desarrollándose como una "cruzada nacional" contra el "judaísmo internacional" (sic).

insidiosamente en la sociedad en la que se insertan, sin integrarse nunca en ella pero manipulándola. Pese a ambientar su narración en la España actual, en la que la presencia judía es mínima y su presión social prácticamente inexistente, Fórmica parece convencida de que han sido los descendientes de conversos (a los que ella llama judíos) los factotum de la vida económica y del tráfico de influencias en la ciudad de Sevilla y quizás en toda España: abundan las alusiones a los "banqueros israelitas", a los matrimonios de interés de cristianos viejos con muchachas de ascendencia judía porque éstas tenían el dinero o a la usura de los judíos; uno de los personajes— un naviero de orígenes conversos-afirma que su negocio sólo pudo sobrevivir gracias a la ayuda económica de las comunidades sefardíes de los Países Bajos, e incluso se llega a afirmar que la desamortización de Mendizábal[13] sólo favoreció a "los hermanos de casta" de ese ministro isabelino "no sabemos si debido al azar o a un proyecto anterior bien calculado" (p. 38). La impresión que se llevaría un lector profano que no conociera España ni su historia y leyera la novela es que Sevilla fue (¡en plena época franquista!) el nido de una conspiración judía universal, donde los descendientes de conversos tenían una poderosísima conciencia de su origen judío y constituían un avasallador grupo de presión. Todo lo cual resulta más sorprendente todavía si consideramos que la autora parece sentir simpatía por esos personajes a los que pinta con tintes tan sesgados.

4.2. *Los conversos como revulsivo social*: en las novelas de Arce, Cascales y Guilló parece subyacer una visión del converso, perseguido y marginado, como una especie de transgresor positivo, un revulsivo social defensor de unas propuestas innovadoras, una especie de levadura (fallida) que se enfrenta a las instituciones de una sociedad anquilosada e intolerante. La misma idea de transgresión y revulsivo se da en la

---

[13] Como es bien sabido, se llamó así por antonomasia a un vasto programa de confiscación de tierras y bienes inmuebles no explotados (pertenecientes en su mayoría a la Iglesia, a la nobleza y a los ayuntamientos) para sacarlos a subasta pública, que fue llevado a cabo en época de Isabel II (concretamente en 1835) por su ministro de Hacienda, Juan de Mendizábal. La operación, que pretendía el mejor aprovechamiento de esos bienes semiabandonados y el dotar de tierras a las clases menos favorecidas, acabó beneficiando a la burguesía adinerada, que pudo hacerse con gran cantidad de bienes inmuebles y terrenos a un precio irrisorio. Esa burguesía serían los "hermanos de casta" (descendientes de conversos, se supone) a los que alude Fórmica, ya que a Mendizábal se le atribuían—con verdad o no—antecesores judíos. Es decir, en la novela de Fórmica se da implícitamente la identificación burguesía adinerada = judíos.

de Fórmica, pero en ella queda la ambigüedad de si la transgresión está vista con tintes positivos o, al contrario, como una especie de peligro de disolución.

Así, el Fernando de Rojas de la novela de Arce (que ha visto quemar a su padre por judaizante) tiene como secreto anhelo burlar a la Inquisición sin más armas que su inteligencia—en una especie de venganza intelectual—, cosa que logra dejando en evidencia a un inquisidor en una escena casi vodevilesca:

> Hacía algunos años que estaba convencido de poder mofarse del Santo Oficio sin riesgo de su cuerpo y, con absoluta seguridad, pensaba que sólo una grandísima burla impune sería capaz de apagar en su cabeza la hoguera en que su padre ardió. Necesitaba jugar contra la Inquisición y se persuadía de que podía abrirle una herida de muerte con una carcajada (p. 16).

El Diego Susón de la novela de Cascales logra superar todas la trabas sociales para encumbrarse a la dignidad de diputado de la alhóndiga sevillana y ejercer su cargo con un rigor y un espíritu de justicia que le costará una denuncia ante la Inquisición por judaizante y, finalmente, el ser quemado. Así que su condena no es tanto por judaizar como por ser un administrador justo en una sociedad corrompida por el clero y la nobleza, aliados en la defensa de sus intereses.

En la de Guilló, la figura de Benito Arias Montano encarna al intelectual guiado por la libertad de pensamiento, obligado a aparentar lo que no es y a reprimir sus verdaderas convicciones (no sólo religiosas, sino muy fundamentalmente intelectuales y morales) por la presión y la represión a la que le someten las fuerzas de la sociedad en la que ha logrado integrarse con gran sacrificio de esas convicciones.

Quizás sea esta última la novela que más certeramente plantea lo que debió ser el drama espiritual de los conversos: la necesidad de optar por la verdad oficial en el plano religioso e intelectual; una opción que implicaba mil renuncias: a los propios orígenes, desde luego; pero también a la posibilidad de conjugar en armonía actitudes intelectuales y corrientes de pensamiento que hubieran podido convivir. El anhelo de Arias Montano en la novela es, por tanto, la convivencia de aparentes contrarios, la apertura de pensamiento que hubiera permitido conjugar una rica variedad de posturas, que hubiera desembocado en fin en la integración de la casta marginada y la convivencia armónica:

cómo podía un converso de la España de Felipe II ser cristiano fiel sin renunciar a su abolengo israelita, cómo podía hacer compatibles el orgullo de ser español y el orgullo de ser judío, cómo participar en la gloria de crear un nuevo mundo más allá de la mar Océana sin renegar del viejo mundo enclavado entre el mar Grande y el Jordán, cómo hacer suyas Lepanto, Pavía, Mühlberg y Otumba sin olvidar Jericó, Gabaón, Adasa y Betulia, cómo conseguir que cada catedral se pareciera a una sinagoga y cada sinagoga a una catedral, y que los cristianos viejos comprendieran la judeidad de Jesús el judío y los cristianos nuevos la hidalguía a lo divino de aquel hombre (p. 137).

El mismo anhelo comparte Diego Susón en la novela de Cascales: un personaje aparentemente cristiano que sigue practicando los ritos del judaísmo, que rompe su compromiso con una judía de ley para casarse con una cristiana, que quiere circuncidar a ese hijo no judío si nace varón, que por piedad acoge a un esclavo indio en contra de los mandatos del judaísmo, que cuando la vieja criada Abigail le incita a pedir prestada la candela para el hogar de su nueva casa la pide a un vecino cristiano y pretende encender con esa llama el fuego de un hogar judaizante.

En la novela de Arce, en cambio, ese conflicto de creencias no se soluciona a través del afán de sincretismo, como en los dos casos anteriores, sino por el desengaño y el descreimiento. Rojas, dividido entre la fe de sus mayores y la impuesta, es incapaz de creer en nada:

> Había elaborado Fernando un sistema incompleto de ideas, al amparo de los furores religioso y antirreligioso que recorrían la vida toda de punta a cabo, que si bien no coincidía con ningún otro sistema aceptado o combatido por la Iglesia, le permitía sobrevivir a sus propias dudas y no enloquecer en medio de todos cuantos parecían conocer, casi de propia mano, los misterios sagrados y la verdad completa de las cosas de este mundo y del otro (p. 43).

y, más tarde, la prostituta Lisona:

> Fernando, tú no crees en la religión cristiana, no crees en la de tus padre tampoco, no crees en nada y eso no ha de ser bueno (p. 129).

En la novela de Fórmica, en cambio, el problema de la división espiritual de los conversos prácticamente ni se plantea: los personajes se mueven fundamentalmente por sus intereses y ambiciones, sin plantearse conflictos morales.

4.3. *El judío intelectual*: si los personajes de las novelas de Arce, Cascales y Guilló son capaces de plantearse tan explícita y analíticamente su actitud ante las contradicciones que viven es en gran parte porque son intelectuales: el estudiante en Salamanca Fernando de Rojas, el humanista Arias Montano son dos casos palmarios; pero también Diego Susón tiene sus veleidades intelectuales, representadas por sus especiales conocimientos matemáticos.

El tópico del judío como persona especialmente dotada para la actividad intelectual está muy arraigado en la opinión española actual. Bien representativa al respecto es la novela de Fórmica, en la que se presenta una Sevilla dividida en dos castas: una aristocrática, que presume de limpieza de sangre, y cuyas dedicaciones principales son "el campo, la caza, los caballos, las mujeres" (p. 19); y otra la de los conversos que eran "médicos, boticarios, practicantes, procuradores de juzgados, recaudadores de Hacienda, comerciantes" (p. 18), entre los que se encontraban los la mayoría de los "escritores y músicos" (p. 19), que estudiaban en la Universidad tanto hombres como mujeres, actitud que propició que también las mujeres cristianas acabasen recibiendo instrucción:

> Hacia 1915 las generaciones femeninas de tales sectores [los cristianos viejos] se incorporaron a la cultura desafiando el prejuicio mantenido por el grupo dominante de ser aquélla signo de judaísmo (p. 20).

Con independencia de lo radicalmente tópica que es la definición de ambos grupos sociales (cuya existencia real en la Sevilla del siglo XX es bastante poco creíble), las visión de Fórmica en su novela manifiesta la pervivencia de un prejuicio secular: el de la identificación de la actividad intelectual como algo propio de castas "manchadas".[14]

4.4. *Magia y misterio entre los judíos*: la otra cara de la moneda la constituye un rasgo que, asombrosamente, convive en varias de las novelas con el concepto del judío (o converso) como racionalista e intelectual: su vinculación con la magia y el esoterismo.

---

[14] El tema está ampliamente recogido tanto en estudios actuales sobre la época como en la literatura de los siglos XVI y XVII. Paradigmática (y profusamente citada) es la réplica que da uno de los protagonistas del entremés de Cervantes *La elección de los alcaldes de Draganzo* que, preguntado sobre si sabe leer, responde que no y que Dios le libre de ello, pues ése es conocimiento "que lleva a los hombres al brasero ['la hoguera de la Inquisición'] y a las mujeres a la casa llana ['prostíbulo']". Aunque en tal afirmación hay mucho de fina sátira cervantina y debía estar pensada precisamente para hacer reír al público con la zafiedad del rústico personaje,

Resulta llamativa tanta insistencia en elementos mágicos relacionados con los judíos, que, por otra parte, viene a coincidir con una curiosa tendencia de los españoles actuales por identificar todo lo semítico (árabe o hebreo) con lo mágico y misterioso.[15]

Así, en la novela de Arce, Fernando de Rojas se nos presenta peligrosamente relacionado con Rodrigo Vara, un estudiante mago y nigromante cuyo asesinato marca el inicio de la acción. En la de Cascales, Diego Susón se relaciona en su juventud con Martín Senén, un misterioso personaje itinerante con algo de mago que le enseña su saber aritmético. En la de Guilló, Arias Montano mantiene conversaciones con "el príncipe de las tinieblas", demonio que se le aparece periódicamente y que tal vez represente los propios demonios interiores del humanista, que discute (¿con el diablo o consigo mismo?) sus contradicciones vitales.

Ideas y fuentes

Como conclusión de este apresurado repaso tal vez sólo podamos indicar una serie de líneas maestras que, a juzgar por las obras literarias analizadas, priman en la concepción de los judíos por parte de una serie de autores españoles. Esas líneas maestras serían:

1) La confusión terminológica (y a veces conceptual) que impulsa a utilizar como sinónimos términos específicos: judío, converso, criptojudío, judaizante, sefardí.

2) La visión del hecho judío español como algo perteneciente a un pasado histórico, con desatención de la realidad actual de los judíos en España. Los judíos actuales, si se les considera, son algo propio de otros países (especialmente Israel). La novela de Mercedes Fórmica constituye sólo aparentemente una excepción, ya que aunque ambienta su historia en el siglo XX las cosas que cuenta corresponderían más bien a la situación social de Andalucía en los siglos XVI y XVII, con lo que el marco temporal contemporáneo se revela como una mera convención.

---

no deja de ser una parodia de la actitud de un cristiano viejo del medio rural con respecto a la instrucción y la formación intelectual.

[15] Recuerdo, por ejemplo, haber visto hace años un ejemplar del *Corán* en una caseta dedicada a obras de esoterismo en la Feria del Libro de Madrid. Y en una librería barcelonesa encontré varios libros sobre historia de los judíos en la sección de "Magia y esoterismo".

3) La conciencia muy viva de las situaciones de exclusión, marginación y persecución que hubieron de vivir los judíos y conversos en la península ibérica, especialmente en los siglos XV al XVII; y el sentimiento de responsabilidad moral de la sociedad española hacia ese colectivo perseguido.

4) La idealización del judío (o, más propiamente, del converso) como persona más preparada intelectualmente, a quien sus desventuras sirven para colocarse en una posición más crítica ante la sociedad. De ahí la recurrente idealización del converso como revulsivo social positivo, que hubiera sido capaz de inducir en la sociedad española una orientación más abierta y tolerante de no habérsele sido brutalmente cercenadas sus posibilidades de expresión y actuación. Esa idealización llega a veces al extremo de "sobrenaturalizar" al converso, poniéndolo en relación con universos considerados como superiores e incomprensibles, aunque irracionales (magia, esoterismo).

Cabe preguntarse de dónde han salido todas estas ideas. Es evidente que algunas son pervivencia de lugares comunes seculares, que circulaban ya en las épocas en que el conflicto converso era más agudo (siglos XV al XVII); otras, adaptación bienintencionada de tópicos de raíz antisemita: en ambos casos se habrá dado una curiosa inversión de los tópicos malintencionadamente calumniosos en *tópicos de simpatía*.[16] En más de una obra—muy especialmente en las de Arce y Cascales—se deja sentir la huella del pensamiento de Américo Castro sobre la convivencia conflictiva e incluso datos y elementos concretos de su obra o de la de algunos de sus seguidores, como Stephen Gilman.[17] Pero la cuestión de la influencia del pensamiento castrista en la configuración de determinadas vulgatas de opinión es tema demasiado complejo como para desarrollarlo precipitadamente aquí, y merecerá atención en otro momento.

---

[16] Sobre los *prejuicios de simpatía*—pero prejuicios al fin—vigentes en la actualidad entre los españoles de a pie, véase mi artículo "Los españoles ante lo judío: Sobre un prejuicio de simpatía", *Raíces* 5 (marzo 1989): pp. 13–16.

[17] Las obras que más parecen haber influído en nuestros escritores son, naturalmente, las más clásicas de don Américo, y muy especialmente *De la edad conflictiva*. Por otra parte, la obra de Stephen Gilman *La España de Fernando de Rojas* ha servido evidentemente como base para buena parte de los datos que maneja Juan Carlos Arce en su novela.

A WINDOW ONTO A "VANISHED WORLD":
SEPHARDIC SALVAGE FICTION
AND THE RHETORIC OF COMMEMORATION*

YAEL ZERUBAVEL

Rutgers University
New Brunswick, New Jersey

In the foreword to *The Second Exodus: A Historical Novel* (1983), Ada Aharoni provides a brief account for her motivation to write this book.

> The Jewish community in Egypt, which was a two-thousand-year-old one, hardly exists anymore. I hope the present book will open a small window onto this vanished society, its traditions, its values, its rich multicolored culture, and its peculiar position as a bridge between the Western and the Oriental. As a former Egyptian Jew who was a witness of the Second Exodus, I have tried to recapture some of the essence, texture, and charm of this vanished world, in the hope that it will be kept alive—not only in me.[1]

The author presents the narrative from the outset as a tribute to the Jewish community of Egypt. This once-flourishing community has not only dwindled down to insignificant numbers, Aharoni warns, but the memory of its unique history, culture, and traditions is now threatened with oblivion. Her references to a "vanished society," a "vanished world" that "hardly exists anymore," create an immediate sense of urgency. They also imply that by responding to this threat, the act of writing becomes the enactment of a rescue mission.

The desire to save a once-thriving culture that is now near extinction distinguishes "salvage literature" from other forms of writing about the past. The salvage approach assumes an irreversible process of decay, disintegration, or contamination that threatens to destroy a traditional culture, soon to disappear without a mark. It also as-

---

* An earlier version of this paper was presented at the Second International Interdisciplinary Conference on Sephardic Studies, SUNY—Binghamton, April 1991.
[1] Ada Aharoni, *The Second Exodus: A Historical Novel* (Bryn Mawr, Pa.: Dorrance, 1983), p. ix.

sumes that through the recording of its last surviving evidence at that critical moment, the "vanishing culture" can be recaptured and preserved for future generations. The very act of salvaging the past through words and images serves as a form of commemoration, the emergent text becomes a literary monument, a symbolic representation of this past.[2]

Salvage rhetoric implies a nostalgic approach to the past and an apocalyptic vision of the future. The past is elevated and romanticized as better, purer, and more authentic than the present, while the future is approached with the foreboding imagery of decay and destruction. As Fred Davis notes, nostalgia often arises in reaction to personal or social crises which threaten the sense of continuity of identity.[3] The acute awareness of the fluidity of the present and the fear that familiar cultural and social forms are about to disappear forever dramatize the importance of documentation as an act of commemoration. A new obsession with recording and preserving the past for future generations has become a feature of modernity. The salvage motif modified the character of autobiographical writing in the nineteenth century, which now "set out to describe circumstances that are altogether vanished"[4] and became central to anthropological research and writing.[5] The invention of the camera and the tape recorder provided new recording technologies which, in turn, reinforced this cultural trend.

---

[2] For other examples of "literary monuments," see Joëlle Bahloul, *La Maison de Memoire* (1992) trans. as *The Architecture of Memory* (Cambridge University Press, 1996), and Lawrence L. Langer, *Holocaust Testimonies* (New Haven: Yale University Press, 1991).

[3] Fred Davis, *Yearning for Yesterday: A Sociology of Nostalgia* (New York: Free Press, 1979), pp. 31–50, 97–116; see also Raymond Williams's remark, in *The Country and the City* (New York: Oxford University Press, 1973), p. 12, that previous generations often appear to have lived in a more pastoral past than the present.

[4] Roy Pascal, *Design and Truth in Autobiography* (Cambridge, Mass.: Harvard University Press, 1960), pp. 55–60. Stefan Zweig's *The World of Yesterday: An Autobiography* (New York: Viking Press, 1943) provides an excellent example of autobiographical writing shaped by a nostalgic view of the past and pervaded by a powerful sense of historical rupture and loss.

[5] For a critique of the salvage approach in ethnography, see George E. Marcus and Michael M.J. Fischer, *Anthropology as Cultural Critique: An Experimental Moment in the Human Sciences* (Chicago: University of Chicago Press, 1986), p. 24; James Clifford, "On Ethnographic Allegory," in *Writing Culture: The Poetics and Politics of Ethnography*, eds. James Clifford and George E. Marcus (Berkeley: University of California Press, 1986), pp. 98–121; the theme of the anthropologist's salvage mission as an expression of the colonialist ethos is further discussed in Renato Rosaldo, "Imperialist Nostalgia," *Representations*, no. 26, Spring 1989, pp. 107–122.

The salvage motif is particularly salient in modern Jewish writing. The processes of secularization and modernization, intensified by the vast waves of Jewish migration in Europe and the Middle East, introduced rapid and fundamental changes to Jewish life. The acute sense of rupture with past communal life and traditions that these processes evoked has been heightened by the collective trauma of the Holocaust. The preservation of the past through the discursive acts of documentation and commemoration has thus become the mission of survivors and students of that past who still retain some access to it before it falls into oblivion. Thus, the salvage rhetoric pervades Jewish ethnography about traditional and contemporary Jewish communities as well as Jewish immigrant literature, and is perhaps most pronounced in writing about the Holocaust.[6]

What happens when the salvage mission is applied to Israeli literature relating to the Sephardic past? More specifically, how is this past represented in a literary work that presents itself as salvage fiction yet subscribes to the Zionist ideology? The salvage approach and Israel's national ideology seem to offer two opposing views of the past from the vantage point of the present: the former romanticizes the pre-immigration past of Sephardic communities as the "authentic" world of tradition that has been lost through dislocation and acculturation, while the latter presents a negative view of the diaspora past as a period of persecution and oppression, resolved by emigration to Israel.

---

[6] On the centrality of the salvage mission to Jewish ethnography, see Barbara Kirshenblatt-Gimblett, "Problems in the Historiography of Jewish Folkloristics" (Paper presented at a conference on Folklore and Social Transformation: A Dialogue of American and German Folklorists, at Bloomington, Indiana, 1988). Aviva Weintraub analyzes the impact of the salvage approach on the visual representation of Jewish life in documentary photo essays and notes the rhetorical use of "the last Jews of . . ." in "Visiting a 'Vanished World': Photography and the Jewish Lower East Side," in *YIVO Annual* 21 (1993): 189–221, special issue on "Going Home," ed. by Jack Kugelmass. For a further analysis of the modern cultural responses to collective historical traumas, see David G. Roskies, *Against the Apocalypse: Responses to Catastrophe in Modern Jewish Culture* (Cambridge, Mass.: Harvard University Press, 1984), and Alan Mintz, *Hurban: Responses to Catastrophe in Hebrew Literature* (New York: Columbia University Press, 1984), esp. pp. 109–269. The discussion of memory and commemoration in Holocaust fiction is further elaborated in Lawrence L. Langer, *The Holocaust and the Literary Imagination* (New Haven: Yale University Press, 1975); James E. Young, *Writing and Rewriting the Holocaust: Narratives and the Consequences of Interpretation* (Bloomington: Indiana University Press, 1988); and Sara R. Horowitz, *Voicing the Void: Muteness and Memory in Holocaust Fiction* (Albany: SUNY Press, 1997).

This study addresses the tension between these two frameworks and its implications for the literary representation of the pre-Israeli past. It analyzes the impact of the salvage and Zionist ideologies on the construction of the narrative, and the significance of the textual representation of the Sephardic heritage for modern Israeli culture. As a first step in the examination of these broader issues in Israeli immigrant literature, the present paper focuses on Ada Aharoni's *The Second Exodus: A Historical Novel* as a case study.

As we have seen, Ada Aharoni's foreword to the novel establishes it as salvage fiction. The author suggests that at this critical moment in history, the Egyptian Jewish past can still be recaptured through the memories of those who once lived in this community, and she thanks other former Egyptian Jews who helped her in *"salvaging important memories and precious information from the past."* The dedication of her work to the memory of her father and the new generations articulates the novel's symbolic role as a monument which carries and shapes the collective memory of the Egyptian Jewish community.

The foreword to *The Second Exodus* also addresses another dimension of the salvaging task, namely, the claim for "authentic representation." As James Clifford argues, salvage rhetoric not only inspires the ethnographic process, but the allegory of salvage is deeply ingrained in the very idea of creating texts that mirror (rather than reconstruct) culture. It suggests that the text can recapture and preserve the past as it was.[7] The challenge of the claim for authentic representation, raised by critics of the salvage approach, is supported by similar observations regarding the nature of autobiographical writing. The study of autobiography suggests that the textual representation of the past necessarily entails a process of selection and rearrangement of "facts" in the creation of a coherent and meaningful narrative. In other words, the past is reimagined and reinterpreted in the actual process of textualization. Thus, modern autobiographical writing exercises and often acknowledges greater freedom in blending fact and fiction.[8]

---

[7] Clifford, "On Ethnographic Allegory," pp. 112–115.

[8] George Gusdorf, "Conditions and Limits of Autobiography," in *Autobiography: Essays Theoretical and Critical*, ed. James Olney (Princeton: Princeton University Press, 1980), pp. 28–48; Pascal, *Design and Truth in Autobiography*, pp. 1–20, 162–195: Susanna Egan, *Patterns of Experience in Autobiography* (Chapel Hill: University of North Carolina Press, 1984), pp. 14–40; Patricia Meyer Spacks, *Imagining a Self: Autobiography and*

"By mixing actual events with completely fictional characters,"
James Young observes, "a writer simultaneously relieves himself of
an obligation to historical authority (invoking poetic license), even as
he imbues his fiction with historical authority of real events."[9] The
fictionalizing techniques may, in fact, add to the writer's ability to
transmit the essence of his or her experiences; but the writer also
needs to establish a documentary authority which would authenticate
the text. By asserting her eyewitness authority, Aharoni reassures the
reader of the historical credibility of her story. The narrative's definition as an eyewitness account in the foreword thus reinforces the
salvage rhetoric within which it is embedded. The generic definition
that the book's subtitle offers, a "historical novel," is incongruent
with this statement and is indeed rather puzzling.[10] Perhaps Aharoni
wished to accentuate the "vanished" character of the past by con-
juring a distancing, mythical image on an event that occurred only
three decades prior to the book's publication.

The salvage rhetoric, then, may be seen as a narrative strategy to
present its role as a literary monument. Having established the inherent limits of representation of such "literary monuments," in defiance
of the salvage rhetoric, the present analysis is not concerned with
an examination of the novel from this perspective.[11] Rather, it attempts
to explore the impact of this ideological orientation on the construction of the commemorative narrative and its representation of
the past.

Novel in Eighteenth Century England (Cambridge, Mass.: Harvard University Press, 1976),
pp. 1–27, 300–315. For recent exploration of the issue of autobiography and fiction
in Hebrew literature, see Alan Mintz, *Banished from Their Father's Table: The Loss of
Faith and the Hebrew Autobiography* (Bloomington: Indiana University Press, 1989);
Menahem Brinker, "On the Question of Autobiographicality in Brenner's Fiction"
[Hebrew], in *Maḥbarot Brenner*, eds. M. Dorman and U. Shavit, nos. 3–4 (Tel Aviv,
1984), pp. 145–172; Yael S. Feldman, "Gender In/Difference in Contemporary
Hebrew Fictional Autobiographies," *Biography* 11, no. 3 (1988): 189–209.

[9] Young, *Writing and Rewriting the Holocaust*, p. 52.

[10] Historical novels tend to assume a greater historical distance between authors
and the periods about which they write. Aharoni, a participant in the historical
event at the center of her novel, clearly lacks the temporal distance implied in the
subtitle.

[11] For historical studies relating to the community, see Norman A. Stillman, *The
Jews of Arab Lands: A History and Source Book* (Philadelphia: Jewish Publication Society,
1979); Gudrun Krämer, *The Jews in Modern Egypt, 1914–1952* (Seattle: University of
Washington Press, 1989); Shimon Shamir, ed., *The Jews of Egypt: A Mediterranean
Society in Modern Times* (Boulder, Colo.: Westview Press, 1987).

The Zionist Message

Despite its professed goal to become a literary monument of the Egyptian Jewish community, *The Second Exodus*, as we shall see below, appears to compromise its salvage mission by its powerful Zionist thrust.

In her foreword, Aharoni accounts for her choice of the main male and female protagonists as follows:

> Inbar and Raoul represent two different aspects of the Jewish people: the Oriental Sephardic Jews from the Arab countries and the Ashkenazi Jews who experienced the Nazi Holocaust. Together they symbolize the unified Jewish people in Israel.[12]

The protagonists thus serve as emblems of ethnicity. The choice of an Ashkenazi Holocaust survivor as one of her two main characters is clearly important for the novel's Zionist message. But Holocaust survivors were latecomers to the Egyptian Jewish community and hence are the least representative of its history and culture. As a result, this choice leads the narrative away from a full engagement in the commemoration of the culture and traditions of the Egyptian Jewish community.

The supremacy of the ideological agenda of portraying Israel's historic role in providing a home for all Jews is conveyed also in the novel's title. The use of the Exodus metaphor, with its powerful historical associations, implies that the symbolic climax of the narrative is not the centuries-long Jewish experience in Egypt, but the departure from that land. The redemptive meaning of Exodus inevitably defines the experience preceding it as negative, turning the disintegration of the Jewish community in Egypt into a welcome development, an act of liberation from oppression.[13] This perspective on the past obviously conforms to the Zionist view of the diaspora, but it stands in sharp contrast to the foreword's nostalgic attitude to the Egyptian Jewish community and the author's lament about the "vanishing" of its traditions.

From the outset of the novel, Inbar, the main Sephardic protagonist, is troubled by her ambiguous identity as a Jew living in Egypt.

---

[12] Aharoni, *Second Exodus*, p. ix.

[13] For further discussion of the meaning of Exodus in Jewish culture, see Yoseph Hayim Yerushalmi, *Zakhor: Jewish History and Jewish Memory* (Seattle: University of Washington Press, 1982), pp. 10–14, 108 n. 5; Michael Walzer, *Exodus and Revolution* (New York: Basic Books, 1985).

At school, Inbar sometimes watched with envy the Egyptian, English, and French girls in the class. They have a country of their own, a culture of their own, a definite identity—not like me, she reflected with a sinking heart. Who am I? What am I? I speak French at home, yet we're not French. I go to an English school, and I'm not English. I live in Egypt, yet I'm not an Egyptian. So what am I?[14]

Although Inbar does not question her Sephardic and Jewish roots, the narrator makes it clear that these do not provide her with an adequate sense of herself. "A deep sudden yearning for a land of her own enveloped Inbar,"[15] and "she played wistfully with the idea of having a country of her own—a culture, language, and heritage of her own, rooted in a little land."[16] Inbar's acute sense of incompleteness denies the fullness and the richness of her life in Egypt and defines it as inherently deficient.

It is, thus, possible to see the narrative structure of *The Second Exodus* as beginning with a fundamental state of "lack," unfolding into a long and trying quest, and ending with its resolution. Inbar's search for identity originates in Egypt and leads her to Israel. It is only upon her arrival in the promised land that the heroine feels instantaneously at home and finds her true sense of herself.

habaita—home! What a beautiful, warm word, Inbar thought. . . . This "home" feeling was the primordial effect Israel had on her from the first moment she left the ship *Moledet* at the Haifa port two days ago.[17]

This plot structure is clearly dictated by (and hence reinforces) the Zionist ideology. In fact, Inbar's experience in Israel could be easily marked by a greater and more acute lack than the one she had suffered in Egypt. As a result of the anti-Jewish measures by the Egyptian government following the foundation of the State of Israel, her communal and familial roots are cut off as she, alone, faces the challenge of accommodating to a new society in Israel. If the novel allows for any lingering "lack" during her first days in Israel, it relates to Inbar's loss of Raoul. When the two lovers finally meet in Jerusalem, her sense of wholeness is complete and the novel reaches a closure in a fully harmonious climax.

---

[14] Aharoni, *Second Exodus*, p. 4.

[15] Ibid., p. 3.

[16] Ibid., p. 4. A story which Inbar writes about her own childhood in Egypt concludes, once more, with her search for a national home (p. 48).

[17] Ibid., p. 125.

In line with the precepts of the Israeli national ideology, the novel embraces the notion that the emergence of a national identity is a total experience that represses and replaces the diaspora Jewish identity. When Inbar begins her new life in Israel, she is, like Raoul, uprooted and disconnected from her past. Once in Israel, both protagonists shed some of their neurotic, "diasporic" characteristics: Inbar rids herself of the obsession with her identity and settles into being herself, and Raoul overcomes his bitterness and modifies his pessimistic outlook on life. *The Second Exodus* does not allow room for the immigrants' struggle to integrate the past with the present. Aharoni's protagonists "glide" into the future without being challenged by strong pulls from their past. Inbar accommodates to kibbutz life and society without misgivings about this process or a sense of loss about her past. And despite his earlier cynical dismissal of Zionism, Raoul resurfaces in Israel a "converted" Zionist, as his highly symbolic new name, Amehad (i.e., "one people"), illustrates. The dramatization of a rupture with the diasporic past sets the stage for the protagonists' successful adoption of an Israeli identity.

Aharoni, a bilingual Israeli writer, wrote the novel in English and published it first in the United States (the Hebrew edition followed two years later).[18] Yet, as the following discussion suggests, *The Second Exodus* is first and foremost an Israeli novel, the meaning of which emerges within the broader context of Israeli literature. In its depiction of the process of assuming an Israeli identity, the novel in fact conforms to the literary norms of the 1940s and the 1950s.[19] It focuses on young protagonists who, like the mythical sabra of the 1940s and 1950s, are free agents, symbolically orphaned from their immigrant parents and redeemed from the diaspora past. If Moshe Shamir's prototypical hero, Alik, was born out of the sea, Aharoni's heroes, Inbar and Raoul, are symbolically reborn during their voyage to Israel. And like the literary heroes of the so-called 1948 generation, these immigrant protagonists emerge in Israel as healthy, positive individuals who, overcoming the psychological scars inflicted by their past, are ready to move on to the future and assume new challenges and social responsibilities.

---

[18] Ada Aharoni, *Yetsiat Mitsraim ha-Sheniya* (Eked, 1985).
[19] Miron, *Arba Panim ba-Sifrut ha-Ivrit Bat Yamenu* (Jerusalem: Schocken, 1975); Nurit Gertz, *Hirbat Hizeh veha-Boker shele-Mohorat* (Tel Aviv: Ha-Kibbutz ha-Meuchad, 1983); Gershon Shaked, *Gal Hadash ba-Siporet ha-Ivrit* (Tel Aviv: Sifriat ha-Po'alim, 1971).

At the same time, *The Second Exodus*'s focus on Egyptian Jews and their immigration to Israel clearly places the novel within the category of ethnic literature, which has recently become increasingly popular in Israel.[20] Published in 1983, it is part of a growing body of literature, often of an autobiographical nature, which explores Jewish life and culture prior to the immigration to Israel. This literary output, in itself, marks a fundamental change in Israeli attitudes toward the Jewish past and Jewish traditions, and is intimately linked to recent changes in Israelis' perceptions of themselves. Israeli literature since the 1960s has challenged earlier assumptions about the redemptive transformation of the diaspora Jew to an Israeli, and has anxiously and critically probed into the latter's character. In the novels of the 1970s and the 1980s, native Israelis often appear as antiheroic figures, the symbolic inversion of their earlier literary counterparts.[21] As part of the reaction against the norms of the 1940s and the 1950s, Israeli literature has also turned to marginalized groups within Israeli society, such as Sephardic Jews, Holocaust survivors, and women. Within this broader development, recent immigrant literature articulates the awakened interest in the pre-Israeli past and examines the immigrant experience in Israel from a critical perspective.

In its professed interest in the pre-Israeli past and focus on a Middle Eastern community, a female character, and a Holocaust survivor, *The Second Exodus* belongs to this new wave of Israeli immigrant literature. Yet, in spite of this appearance, its depiction of the immigrant experience differs dramatically from some other immigrant novels recently published in Israel. This difference is a function of the novel's implicit ideological agenda of highlighting the Sephardic Jews' adherence to Zionism and its mission.

The Second Exodus attempts to dispel a prevalent Israeli view that Sephardic Jews had no choice but to come to Israel, while Ashkenazi

---

[20] This "new wave" in Israeli literature emerged in the seventies. See, for example, Amnon Shamosh, *Aḥoti Kala* (Ramat Gan: Massada, 1974) and *Michel, Ezra Safra u-Vanav* (Ramat Gan: Massada, 1978); Sami Michael, *Be-Ḥofen shel Arafel* (Tel Aviv: Am Oved, 1979); Itzḥak Gormejano Goren, *Kaits Alexandroni* (Tel Aviv: Am Oved, 1979).

[21] See, for example, Aharon Megged, *Ha-Ḥai al ha-Met* (Tel Aviv: Am Oved, 1965); A.B. Yehoshua, *Ha-Me'ahev* (Jerusalem: Schocken, 1977); Yitzḥak Ben-Ner, *Eretz Reḥokah* (Jerusalem: Keter, 1981); Yitzḥak Orpaz, *Masa Daniel* (Tel Aviv: Am Oved, 1982).

Jews left their homes in Europe out of Zionist conviction. In the only confrontation between Sephardic and Ashkenazi Jews in the novel, the young Egyptian Jewish immigrants to Israel emphatically protest when an older Ashkenazi woman articulates this view. While these youths can laugh at other offensive views about Middle Eastern Jews that this kibbutznik expresses, her accusation that they lack Zionist commitment stirs a strong emotional response. The Egyptian Jews refer to their community's long history of Zionist tradition and point out that each one of them had the option of joining members of their families abroad rather than immigrate to Israel.[22]

This point is further enhanced by the portrayal of Inbar, the Sephardi, as the true bearer of Zionist ideology, while Raoul, the Ashkenazi, displays no interest in nationalistic issues until his arrival in Israel. Inbar's experience in the Zionist youth movement guarantees her quick integration into Israeli society. Even the choice of the very modern Hebrew name Inbar (as opposed to a more likely traditional Hebrew name or a foreign name common among Jews in Egypt) projects a contemporary Israeli image onto her life abroad. In contrast, Raoul's name is foreign and clearly marks him as a diasporic Jew.

The Second Exodus attempts to construct a sense of continuity between the Egyptian Jewish past and the Israeli present. In commemorating the past, it selects those aspects of the Egyptian Jewish experience that serve to highlight this ideological message, even when these choices limit or undermine its representation of the Egyptian Jewish community and its multifaceted culture. Even in its depiction of the Egyptian Jewish past, the novel follows the literary norms of the 1940s and the 1950s, focusing on young heroes operating in the social setting of their peers while their immediate family fades into the background. The more formal historical review of the Jewish community, framed in the novel as the protagonist's lecture to her friends in the youth movement, reinforces the primarily nationalist perspective on the Egyptian Jewish past.[23]

At the end, Inbar's Zionist involvement in Egypt, which represents much of the essence of her pre-Israeli experiences, contributes to her emergent Israeli identity. The loss of other aspects of her past

---

[22] Aharoni, *Second Exodus*, pp. 121–125.
[23] Ibid., chap. 7, pp. 58–73.

is silenced in the novel. The Israeli national ideology thus becomes the lens through which one views the Egyptian Jewish community and its disintegration, assigning them to the realm of a buried past.

The Second Exodus *and the Sephardi Identity*

The juxtaposition of the novel's representation of Egyptian Jews' pre-immigrant and immigrant experiences in Israel further helps to clarify its position as a "literary monument." Particularly important is *The Second Exodus*'s portrayal of the experience of "homecoming" in relation to the issue of Sephardic identity. Despite a rather detailed description of her direct experience of Israeli prejudices and misconceptions, this episode concludes with the statement that such disclosures of bigotry did not diminish Inbar's exhilarating experience of homecoming.

> There were several other absurd and painful prejudices in store for her in the Promised Land, especially those pertaining to the Arab Jews—among whom she was automatically classified and labeled as a somewhat second-class citizen. In the eyes of narrow minded people like Pessiah, nothing good could come out of the Arab countries—even their Jews. But there were also many joys, and these joys smoothed over the jagged path. The most important of all was that she felt she was "home" at last, in a way she had never felt in Egypt.[24]

Having satisfied her more fundamental need for a national identity, the protagonist suffers no further problems, even when faced with the unexpected prejudices of veteran Israelis. In fact, Inbar's emergent Israeli identity is depicted as free from any constraints of ethnicity. If back in Egypt Inbar's father alludes to the comparison of an Ashkenazi and a Sephardic girl as comparing a cauliflower with a rose, Inbar finds that in Israel she is "neither a cabbage nor a flower—but just Inbar Mosseri."[25]

It is interesting to compare *The Second Exodus*'s portrayal of "homecoming" with other novels describing the Middle Eastern immigrant experience in Israel during the same period. Such Israeli writers as Shimon Ballas, Sami Michael, David Rabeeya, and Eli Amir reveal

---

[24] Ibid., p. 124.
[25] Ibid., pp. 15 and 124 respectively.

the deep scars that these experiences have left.[26] Their works are pervaded by the immigrants' shock, disappointment, and bitterness at realizing that veteran Israelis of Ashkenazi origin related to them as second-class citizens. Nancy Berg's study of the *ma'abarah* ("transit camp") literature suggests that for some Middle Eastern immigrants, the encounter with Israeli society transformed their experience from a homecoming to an "exile from exile," creating an ironic inversion of the Zionist dream.[27]

Aharoni participates, with the other immigrant writers, in this critique of the ignorance, prejudice, and misconceptions that the Middle Eastern immigrants encountered in Israel; but her strategy in dealing with it is significantly different. The new Hebrew immigrant literature condemns the patronizing, Eurocentric attitude of many Israelis toward Middle Eastern Jews by dwelling on the psychological and social damage it has inflicted on the immigrants and their families. *The Second Exodus* attempts to dispel the validity of this prejudiced view by portraying a highly educated, Western-oriented, urban, middle-class group of Egyptian Jews. The argument here is not against the representation of this class of Egyptian Jews in itself, for the picture Aharoni presents is well grounded, even if incomplete—but rather the ideological thrust of this portrayal. While some other novels are critical of the Ashkenazi hegemony and the prevalent Eurocentric standards that marked the reception of the Sephardic Jews and their traditions by Israelis, this novel implicitly accepts these standards and moves on to demonstrate their applicability to those educated, middle-class Egyptian Jews. By focusing on this group of immigrants and highlighting the "European" aspects of their culture, the richness of the Egyptian Jewish experience is reduced to a scheme that emphasizes homogeneity and continuity rather than diversity and rupture.

One could argue that *The Second Exodus* is different because it does not focus on immigrant life in the *ma'abarah*. But other immigrant novels do not focus on the transit camp experience. For example, both Amir's and Aharoni's works revolve around Sephardic immigrant

---

[26] Shimon Ballas, *Ha-Ma'abarah*; Sami Michael, *Shavim ve-Shavim Yoter* (Tel Aviv: Bustan, 1976); David Rabeeya, *Ḥolmot ve-Loḥamot* (Tel Aviv: Alef, 1979) and *Ohale Nun* (Beer Sheva: Tzorech 1, 1990); Eli Amir, *Tarnegol Kaparot* (Tel Aviv: Am Oved, 1983).

[27] Nancy E. Berg, *Exile from Exile: Israeli Writers from Iraq* (Albany: SUNY Press, 1996).

youths on a kibbutz. While *The Second Exodus* emphasizes the kibbutzniks' welcoming reception of the Sephardic heroine, Eli Amir's *Scapegoat* highlights the tensions between the veteran kibbutz members and the Middle Eastern newcomers. The kibbutzniks' attitude is described as ranging from hostile discrimination to benign patronizing. The young Iraqi protagonist, Nuri, is constantly torn between the desire to become a full-fledged Israeli and accept the kibbutz's values and norms, and his guilt over what he experiences as the betrayal of his parents and the traditional values for which they stand. The young protagonist is struck by the social, economic, and cultural gap between the veteran Israelis, represented by the flourishing kibbutz, and the wretched conditions of the new immigrants who live in the *ma'abarah*. His memories of his family's more secure and comfortable life in Iraq render this realization all the more painful. In this novel, we witness Nuri's struggle to form his identity in Israel by integrating the past and the present, thus resisting the kibbutzniks' pressure to cut himself off from his past.

Thus, while *The Second Exodus* shows the transformative, redemptive nature of becoming "Israeli," other immigrant novels that were written about the same time focus on the pain, frustration, sense of loss, and dilemmas that the immigrants faced in Israel. By ignoring these problematic aspects of the immigrant experience, the novel embraces the Zionist ideology and seems to deny the salvage mission that it sets out to fulfill. And yet, I would like to propose that in spite of this appearance, the salvage and Zionist nationalist approaches collude in silencing the past by the very act of defining its representation as a cultural monument.

Conclusion

The Second Exodus's choice of focusing on the final days of the Egyptian Jewish community serves as the intersecting point of the salvage and Zionist ideological frameworks. Indeed, this particular choice highlights what the two otherwise opposing views of the past share in common.

The basic perception of culture implied by the salvage approach suggests that tradition is a fixed entity that can only erode with the passage of time and under external pressure. The rhetoric of disappearance thus assumes that a traditional culture decays and a communal identity dissolves as new culture and identity are accepted in their place. The salvage mission fulfills the task of preserving the past through the process of textualization. The text captures and "freezes" the past in its supposedly authentic form, which no longer exists outside of its own monument. The text, then, becomes the locus of memory (*lieu de memoire*) of that past.[28]

This aspect of the salvage approach fits in with the Israeli national ideology that advocates the relinquishing of the traditional culture and "ethnic" identity associated with the pre-immigrant period. This view, which was strongly adhered to during the late Yishuv and early state periods but is still pervasive, emphasizes the importance of new immigrants' acceptance of the Israeli life-style, values, and norms in the process of becoming full-fledged members of Israeli society.

If the place of these traditions is located within the domain of "cultural monuments" of a bygone past—relegated to commemorative texts, museum exhibits, or formalized displays of ethnicity—it suggests that these are essentially relics. In other words, this approach implies that the pre-immigrant traditions are no longer an integral part of contemporary Israelis' lives and have survived only through and for their formal commemorations. This view clearly stands in sharp contrast to a more dynamic perception of ethnicity which emphasizes the power of tradition to change in response to a new cultural setting as well as to transform this culture in the process.[29] Indeed, recent studies of Israeli society and culture demonstrate the continuing vitality and transformative abilities of ethnic traditions.[30]

The establishment of "cultural monuments" for Sephardic traditions

---

[28] Pierre Nora, "Between Memory and History: *Les lieux de mémoire*," *Representations*, no. 26 (Spring 1989), pp. 7–25. Nora, who believes that "modern memory is above all archival" (p. 13), claims that "*lieux de mémoire* originate with the sense that there is no spontaneous memory. . . . The defense of minorities, of a privileged memory that has retreated to jealously protected enclaves in this sense intensely illuminate the truth of *lieux de mémoire*—that without commemorative vigilance, history would sweep them away" (p. 12).

[29] Michael M.J. Fischer, "Ethnicity and the Post-Modern Arts of Memory," in Clifford and Marcus, *Writing Culture*, pp. 194–233; Herbert J. Gans et al., eds., *On the Making of Americans* (Philadelphia: University of Pennsylvania Press, 1979); Werner Sollers, *Beyond Ethnicity: Consent and Descent in American Culture* (New York: Oxford University Press, 1986); Mary Waters, *Ethnic Options: Choosing Identities in America* (Berkeley: University of California Press, 1990).

[30] See, for example, Alex Weingrod, *Studies in Israeli Ethnicity: After the Gathering* (New York: Gordon & Breach, 1985); Sholomo Deshen, "Political Ethnicity and Cultural Ethnicity in Israeli during the 1960s," in *Urban Ethnicity*, ed. Abner Cohen (London: Tavistock, 1974), pp. 281–309; Moshe Shokeid, "Cultural Ethnicity in Israel: The Case of Middle Eastern Jews' Religiosity," *AJS Review* 9, no. 2 (Fall 1984): 247–271.

may be acceptable to both the strong salvage impulse of the post-Holocaust era and the Zionist national ideology; but it runs the risk of affirming the very concepts of disappearance and discontinuity which it sets out to battle. Ironically, then, by creating "shrines" for a bygone past, such commemorations of tradition may ultimately result in burying this tradition under the fiction of its monument.

LA TÉMATICA JUDÍA—Y EN PARTICULAR LA SEFARADÍ—EN LA OBRA DE ERNESTO SÁBATO

Mario Eduardo Cohen

Buenos Aires Argentina

Aspectos Biograficos

Ernesto Sábato nace en la provincia de Buenos Aires en 1911, y es el escritor viviente más importante de Argentina.

Entre los multiples premios liberarios obtenidos, podemos citar el Premio Cervantes, otorgado en España en 1984; el Premio al mejor libro extranjero, en París en 1976 (por su novela "Abaddón, el Exterminador"); el Premio Jerusalem, otorgado en Israel en 1989, y tantos más en Argentina, México, Alemania, etc. Su obra ha sido traducida a diferentes idiomas, entre ellos el hebreo.

Egresado universitario y profesor en la ciencia física, a partir de 1943 sustituye con la literatura a aquella actividad, y opta por el arte como modo de afianzar una perspectiva humanista, que considera insuficiente mediante la mera actividad científica. Su primer libro—ensayo—sería "Uno y el Universo", y escribiría también más tarde algunos tros ensayos, tales como "Heterodoxia", "Apologías y rechazos", etc.

Ha sido en el género ficción—novela—en el que logró Sábato trascendencia y proyeccion internacional. En 1951 aparece publicada "El Túnel", su primer novela, escrita en realidad cuatro años antes; en 1961 publica "Sobre héroes y tumbas" (incluye el célebre "Informe sobre ciegos"), y en 1974: "Abaddón, el exterminador".

No ha sido prolífico, pero sí contundent. Feron sólo tres novelas, y en cada una de ellas logra un merecido reconocimiento. Los personajes judíos no faltan en las mismas, siendo junto a Borges, Arciniegas, Octavio Paz de los pocos escritores latinoamericanos que abordan el tema judaico.

Ha cultivado también el género ensayo, siendo un sostenido defensor de los derechos humanos, enérgico humanista y fiscal implacable contra todo atropello de los poderosos para con las minorías. Militante en su juventud en las filas del comunismo, rompera pronto con éstos, denunciando al dogmatismo allí imperante, y convirtiéndose en vigoroso defensor de la democracia política y el pluralismo ideológico.

No sólo se casa—en 1934—con una mujer judía, sino que es permanente luchador v combatiente contra las distintas formas del amenazante antisemitismo. Ha tenido y tiene nuemrosos amigos judíos.

En 1960 tiene una acalorada controversia contra los cenáculos naclonalistas (digamos que con "z")[1] locales, cuando éstos se muestran irritados porque el Estado de Israel captura en Buenos Aires al criminal de guerra nazi Adolf Eichmann, sin previo pedido de extradición. Su artículo "Soberanía para carniceros" definirá con la mayor elocuencia la valiente e íntegra actitud del escritor.

En la década del '70 integra el Comité Internacional por Jerusalem y a su vez enfrenta a la UNESCO cuando este organismo quiso excluir al Estado judío como miembro del musmo: y también es enérgico defensor del Sionismo cuando las Naciones Unidas emitieron una torpe resolución que equiparaba al Sionismo con el Racismo.

Años más tarde, en días aciagos de dictadura militar fue una consecuente voz de denuncia; al asumir el gobierno democrático presidido por el Dr. Alfonsín, Sábato sería designado al frente de la Comisión Nacional sobre Desaparición de Personas—CONADEP—, cuyo informe final sería mundialmente conocido como "Nunca más", titulo del libro que lo expresaba.

Esto le valío el reconocimiento oficial de distintos países que se manifiestan a favor de la democracia y el goce de las libertades públicas por la ciudadanía, siendo homenajeado premiado por su prédica en favor de la dignidad humana, por muchos países, como Italia, Francia, Alemania, etc.

Introducción

La ponencia consiste en un analisis descriptivo en los campos literario, histórico, sociologico y político de la obra de Ernesto Sábato en su relación con el Pueblo Judío, y en particular con los sefaradíes, como parte del mismo. La misma se origina en un trabajo interdisciplinario de investigación realizado en Buenos Aires, y cuyas conclusiones se relejan en la publicación *Sefárdica* No 8, del Centro de Investigación y Difusión de la Cultura Sefaradí, titulada "La temática judía en la obra de Sábato", en octubre de 1990.

---

[1] En la Argentina suelen usar el apelativo de "nacionalistas" muchos filonazis, de ahí el eufemismo popular que los denomina "nacionalistas con zeta".

Recientemente, en octubre de 1990, Salbato interrumpe su alejamiento de los ultimos años en que su salud—y la de su esposa—lo obliga a la pausa, y escribe especialmente para estra publicación académica "Sefárdica"—dedicada a él en su octavo número—, un artículo titulado "Cultura sefaradí: el impulso del origen".

El artículo brinda una aguda reseña de lo que significó la cultura sefaradí en su Edad Oro, citando los preclaros ejemplos de Yehuda Haleví, ben Gabirol y Maimónides.

Sábato halla elementos en esa etapa que nos ayudan a pensar que son posibles las soluciones pacíficas en el Cercano Oriente de la hora actual; nos dice que: "en la España musulmana, se dio quizás el más grande ejemplo, el más hermoso y conmovedor, de la pacífica y fértil convivencia de judíos y árabes", y también que: "Los sectarismos y las violencias de ambas partes deben ser combatidas por todos los hombres del mundo que ansían vivir en el respeto de la grandes culturas". El artículo fue motivado por la vigencia del origen de la cultura sefaradí; y aun inspirado en base a bibliografía tradicional sobre el tema, no actualizada, obtiene—sin embargo—valerosas conclusiones.

Siendo Sábato uno de los pocos autores hispanoamericanos no-judíos en los que encontramos profusión de personajes judíos en sus novelas, pero no encontramos personajes sefaradíes. Aunque sí en sus obras de ensayo discierne acerca de los sefaradí (sea en "Apología y rechazos" en su artículo "Judíos y antisemitas", por citar un ejemplo).

Sábato ha sido uno de los escritores latinoamericanos que mayor comprensión por la prob]emática judía ha demostrado esta comprensión, fruto de su vigorosa postura humanista le valió—entre otros—el Premio Jerusalem, otorgado en Israel, en 1989.

La Convivencia en Sefarad

Puntualiza Sábato[2] que "En la Catedral de Sevilla está el sepulcro de Fernando el Santo, llamado "El gran señor de la convivencia", y la inscrpción, a cada lado, en los cuatro idiomas de la época—latín, árabe, hebreo y español—dice: "Al más leal y el más verdadero y el más famoso y el más esforzado y el mas apuesto y el más granado y el más sufrido y el más humilde", y de no poco

---

[2] "Cultura Sefaradí: el impulso del origen", *Sefardica* (Buenos Aires) 8 (octubre de 1990): 17 a 19.

valor es este homenaje gue mancomuna cuatro lenguas, y que muestra que reyes hubo que legislaron en pro de esta armonía. Así destaca que el "excelso poeta hebreo Yehuda Haleví" haya versificado "no solamente en su lengua sino en árabe y en la lengua vulgar de los cristianos", citando también a su amigo Máximo Kahn cuando afirmase que aquíl fue "el más qrande poeta lírico del judaísmo, pero fue poeta tópicamente castellano", coincidiendo con ona de las más importantes autoridades de la lengua, el erudito Menéndez y Pelayo.

Sábato, en el articulo citado, el ultimo escrito hasta aquí, nos dice también que "el gran centro cultural judaico-arábigo estuvo quizá en aquel portentoso período de los reinos musulmanes en Andalucía, que fueron los verdaderos sucesores de Bagdad, donde brillaron las artes y las ciencias". Y es grande en Sábato la ilusión por un retorno a la convivencia judeoárabe. Sabemos nosotros que este fencómeno que tanto admira nuestro autor fue sólo en algunos momentos de la historia que mancomunó a judíos y arabes en la tierra le Sefarad, y que también hubo otros en los que prevaleció la intolerancia del poder árabe de turno, como por ejemplo durante el dominio de los almohades, o de los almorávides, época en la que el propio Maimónides debería sortear numerosas dificultades.

Recuerda Sábato que "en Córdoba, la Novia de Andalucía y en otras ciudades andaluzas, se desarrolló la extraordinaria civilización que habría de servir de puente entre la cultura helénica y la Europa bárbara", y deposita su fe y vocación humanista en el resurgimiento de la armónica convivencia de pueblos y culturas, para las que Sefarad fuese noble ejemplo.

Y a pocos meses de ingresar en el 500° año del Descubrimiento de América, cobra mucha fuerza la expresión de Sábato al respecto: "no me parece inoportuno recordar que matematicos, astrónomos, geógrafos, y banqueros hebreos hicieron posible el viaje de un marino verosímilmente judío llamado Cristóbal Colón", en un párrafo que concluye recordando a su vez a: "poetas de los más excelsos que produjo el mismo pueblo cuyo destino yo considero sobrenatural: Fray Luis de León, Santa Teresa y San Juan de la Cruz".

Y ya más de veinte años antes[3] Sábato se preguntaría optimista: "porqué en Tierra Santa no habría de reproducirse aquel hermoso

---

[3] Reportaje a Sábato en la revista *Raíces* (Buenos Aires) 2, nr. 10 (Setiembre 1969): 24 a 27.

milagro" al referirse a la época en que judíos y musulmanes convivieron, tal como "en los esplendorosos tiempos de España antes de los feroces Almohades".

Y poéticamente se pregunta si "¿Es muy exaaerada utopía desear la paz y la amistad entre ellos?. ¿Es mucho pedir a la esperanza humana que escuche la utopía de Teodoro Herzl, aquel generoso y noble poeta de la política?"

Legua y Cultura

A definir la cultura sefaradí, Sabato se mostrará seguidor de los lineamientos de Abraham Ieoshúa Herschel,[4] deteniéndose en las obras de pensadores como Maimónides o Spinoza para remarcar el racionalismo sefaradí—en tanto lógico ordenamiento de la materia y del obrar—, que deduce de tales pensadores, diferenciandolo del "estilo askenazí", que se vería más emparentado con el romanticismo aun con el misticismo, en este último caso si pensamos, en Guerschom Scholem, quien nos describiera un "Golem".[5]

El carácter "racionalista" es percibido desde el modo sefaradí de encarar los estudios judaicos en tanto tendencia a desarrollar una equilibrada proporción de la ciencia y la actividad artística, paralelamente a la Torá, como a ese clasicismo aue va Herschel describió en la másica, el carácter y la estructura cultural sefaradita.

Y en su ensayo de 1979, afirma Sábato[6] "la brillante cultura sefaradí, en cierto modo, fue una simbiosis de la tradición judaica y de la civilización musulmana" agregado que "sus realizaciones en medicina y matemática y astronomía, contribuyeron grandemente al desarrollo de la civilización europea moderna."

La cultura sefaradí es visualizada por Sábato—como en Heschel— como simbiosis de la tradición judaica y la civilización musulmana. Así, sostiene también Sábato en "Apologías y rechazos" que: "(la cultura sefaradí) presenta la modalidad abstracta, racionalista intelectual" que se opondría a la "modalidad concreta, intuitiva y

---

[4] Abraham Ieoshúa Heschel en su libro *La Tierra es del Señor*, cap. 3, "Las Dos Grandes Tradiciones".

[5] Artificio que imita a un ser humano, que ha sido creado por las manos del hombre.

[6] "Apologías y rechazos" de Ernesto Sábato (párrafo titulado "Judíos y antisemitas").

mástica del mundo askenazí", concluyendo que "entre ambos hay la diferencia que puede haber entre un clásico y un romantico, entre la arquitectura grecolatina (como sería la sefaradí) y la gótica (como sería la askenazí)".[7] Estas afirmaciones tal vez debamos considerarlas como propias del período de la Edad de Oro del judaísmo español, y por supuesto este armonioso racionalismo sefardita no aparecerá ya en la etapa post-ibérica, por lo que no puede desestimarse que a nuestro autor aquí le haya ganado cierta idealización; pero pocos escritores en nuestro continente han mostrado esta preocupada admiración por la temática judaica como Ernesto Sábato.

A su vez, al relacionar a las lenguas idish y judeoespañol (que Sábato llama "ladino", guiado por cierta difusión que no lo discrimina de su uso sacro), entiende nuestro autor[8] que habría una diferencia favorable a los judíos askenazíes respecto de los sefarditas, debida a la trascendencia adquirida por la literatura de lengua idish; los pensadores sefardíes en la etapa ibérica lo hicieron en hebreo o árabe—mayoritariamente—, y el judeoespañol (que Sábato llama "ladino" aunque sabemos que éste es el idioma que como detalla Jaim Vidal Sephiha, se usa en las traducciones del Tanaj, mientras que "judeoespañol" o "judezmo" sería el nombre más adecuado para la lengua profana) no tuvo posibilidad de expansión en la literatura. Aunque Sábato advierte la importancia del idish como vehículo cotidiano de comunicación, y acá sabemos nosotros que los judíos también mantuvieron al salir de España su lengua, como sorprendiera al propio Sábato en Israel o a Julián Marías al encontrar a una señora de origen judío de Bulgaria, hablar en la lengua adquirida en Sefarad. Citando a Unamuno, Sábato enfatiza asimismo que "la lengua es la sangre del espíritu". En su visita a Israel se esforzó Sábato en hacerle saber a los sefardíes, que no intentasen hablarle en espanol, sino en lengua judeoespañola, aunque lamentó que muchos pensaran que ésta fuese simplemente un "mal castellano". Sábato es defensor de la autonomía cultural, y así como lo fue del voseo en Buenos Aires, también lo ha sido de la lengua original de los sefardíes.

---

[7] Crónica que publica la Revista Hebraica (Buenos Aires), Diciembre 1969, págs. 17 a 21.
[8] Véase "Cultura Sefaradí".

Personajes Judíos en la Literatura de Sábato

La literatura de Sábato es alegórica, pero hay también múltiples personajes judíos (todos ellos askenazíes, cabe aclarar) tomados de la vida real.

A su vez uno de los personajes ("Quique" en "Abaddón, el exterminador") nos hará ver que casi coinciden en número y nombre los socios de la Sociedad Hebraica Argentina con los miembros de la Asociación Psicoanalitica del mismo país[9] con lo que se nos muestra la predilección de los judíos por la ciencia psicológica.

Y tal vez este recorrido inverso, esta obligada reclusión que nos lleva de consciente a inoonsciente es la que nos muestra cuán difícil se hace juzgar la ideología del novelista. Pero si en el campo de las ideas sociales y morales Sábato apuesta por una ética humanista y racional, su literatura de ficción desorienta, y nos muestra cómo ciertos personajes ridículos pueden proclamar sus perogrullescas "verdades", lo cual nos obliga a ponerlas en duda.

Y aquí es donde debe participar el lector. En el género novela Sábato no le ahorrará participación, y en el discurso que nuestro autor hizo llegar a Jerusalem cuando se le concediera el Premio Jerusalem a la Letras 1989.[10]

El carácter disconformista del judío es puntualizado por alguno de sus personajes, y lo señala muy bien Elisa Beatriz Cohen de Chervonagura: "El día que están en paz (en Israel) esto no dura ni un minuto. ¿Te imaginás, Silvia, dos millones de judíos sin una guerra?, dos millones de presidentes de la Repéblica. Cada uno con sus propias ideas sobre vivienda, ejército, educación, lenguaje. Andá, goberná eso. ¿Y el individualismo español?, ¿y el cinismo italiano?", es el párrafo que toma ella de "Abaddón, el exterminador".

Por supuesto que nos interesa enfatizar aquí que muchas veces la construcción de personajes absurdos nos muestra lo vacuo de una pretensión ideológica detenminada, y éste nos parece el caso. Sábato nos enseña personajes de torpes y ridículas obsesiones que visualizan la "amenaza" judía, pero son ellos mismos los que en su patológica

---

[9] Elisa Beatriz Cohen de Chervonagura, "La escritura invisible de Abaddón, el exterminador," *Sefárdica* 8, págs. 63 a 67.

[10] Véase "La temática judía en la obra de Sábato", *Sefárdica* 8, pág. 106; "La función de la literatura es comunicar el saber trágico", discurso pronunciado en Israel durante la entrega del Premio Jerusalem a Sábato. El mismo fue leído, ya que el escritor estuvo imposibilitado de asistir.

expresión y torpe visión denuncian el carácter agresivo y sin fundamento adecuado del antisemita (o antijudío) respecto por la libertad".

Nos dice también María Rosa Lojo[11] que "el componente judío se muestra así (en la narrativa sabatiana) como el factor fundamental en la formación de la Argentina: que es causa, junto con lo español, de la creatividad, pero también de la independencia individual que hace ingobernable al país como país." La autora se ocupa en desgranar los personajes sabatianos que demuestran la inserción del judío como pueblo, en la realidad argentina como en la historia universal.

Nos va a subrayar esta autora que "desde la visión realista y porteña hasta las concepciones misticas y esotéricas de la Historia, los personajes judíos van marcando en la narrativa de Ernesto Sábato una presencia significativa relacionada tanto con el mapa visible de Buenos Aires, como con los hilos simbólicos másocultos y profundos de los textos".

Si la obra de ensayo ha sido siempre de contenido realista—lejana de las abstracciones de Borges—, su novelistica en cambio es más próxima a cierto irracionalismo, sus personajes—y los judíos en especial—no son ajenos a comportamientos paradojales o a veces extravagantes.

El Valor de lo Judio en la Obra Sábato

Como lo expresara muy bien Santiago Kovadloff[12] "(Sábato) ha combatido, además, para lograr que en el mundo cristiano se reconociera la incidencia creadora del judaísmo en su doble dimensión, es decir como expresión de un pueblo y como manifestación de valores constitutivos de lo que el espíritu humano tiene de más preciado" y en esto quizá está resumido el más preclaro espíritu de la obra y la letra de Sábato, y como lo judío desempeña en ésta un papel trascendental. De una obra nacida por y determinada para valores, el judeocristianismo se muestra como guía y faro de principios y fines y como señala Kovadloff "es (Sábato) uno de los contados escritores argenti-

---

[11] María Rosa Lojo, "Personajes judíos en la narrativa sabatiana: de las historias a la Historia," *Sefárdica* 8, págs. 49 a 54.

[12] Santiago Kovadloff, "Lo judío en la ensayística de Sábato," *Sefárdica* 8, págs. 37 a 45.

nos, junto a Borges, en quien las referencias a la cultura judía tienen siempre una fuerza comunicativa visceral, íntima, alejada de todo afán apologético o mera erudición".

Esta visceral comunicación lleva a Kovadloff a señalar oportunamente que "Sábato no se propone inducir el reconocimiento que los judíos "han hecho cosas buenas". Su intención es otra: poner de manifiesto hasta qué punto lo que hoy llamamos *Occidente* tiene en el judaísmo un ingrediente constitutivo sin el cual no sería lo gue es".[13]

Y enfatiza también este autor la presencia de una "labor complementaria de esclarecimeinto que, en torno a la cultura hebrea, ha sabido desplegar Ernesto Sábato como pocos escritores latinoamericanos no-judíos", agregando que "ha trabajado con ahinco por la comprensión del papel de los valores del judaísmo en la constitución del mundo cristiano. Tales valores han sido reconocidos por Sábato como occidentalmente decisivos. En ellos asienta, por lo tanto, buena parte de la condición misma de posibilidad del humanismo que tiene Sábato a una de sus más destacadas conciencias contemporáneas".

Kovadloff defina a Sábato como "minucioso lector de Buber", aseverando que esto le permitió "ver en el judaísmo una espléndida metáfora de la condición humana".

El atributo iconoclasta, la singular rebelión de cada individuo judío no escapan a la obra de Sábato, y Kovadloff[14] al ocuparse de la ensayística en nuestro autor, escribe muy bien que "Sábato ha visto con claridad que el judaísmo enfatiza el papel de la creatividad personal en la preservación del legado tradicional. Advirtió con acierto que, para el judío, la libertad interpretativa es condición "sine qua non" de la comprensión y el respeto a lo heredado".

Ernesto Sábato salió al cruce de quienes pretendieron reducir nuestra civilización a los componentes greco-latinos, afirmando orgullosamente el carácter también judío de la misma, y la decisiva importancia moral que esta característica imprime en la civilización de la América latina.

El tema kabalístico aparece también señalado por distintos autores que se ocupan de la escritura sabatiana, y en "Abaddón, el exterminador" es incluso mencionado Isaac el ciego, considerado padre de la moderna Kabalá.

---

[13] Ibid., pág. 43.
[14] Ibid., pág. 38.

Este aspecto ha sido recientemente tratado por Bernardo A. Chiesi[15] quien refleja en riguroso análisis los componentes de la kabalística y el misticismo judíos en la pluma de Ernesto Sábato. Advierte Chiesi[16] que "el fuego que alumbra en las obras de Sábato es el que arde en el infierno, es el fuego de la conciencia, por eso es un fuego purificador, aun no se vislumbra el paraíso".

Sábato Frente al Antisemitismo

En su obra de ensayo "Apologías y rechazos"[17] sintetiza correctamente Sábato que "no hay nada que hacer: el antisemitismo es de tal naturaleza que se alimenta de cualquier manera. El judío está en una situación tal que cualquier cosa que haga o diga o se diga de él, favorable o desfavorable, sirve en última instancia para avivar el sagrado fuego del antisemitismo", agregando a renglón seguido con perspicaz ironía que "si uno no se ocupa del problema, el antisemita dirá que es porque son indefendiblos, mas si se ocupa, afirmará que algo debe de haber en la raza para que constantemente sea menester su defensa".

Palos porque bogas, palos porque no: a los judíos se les acusa de querer disimular su condición cuando no aparecen distinquiéndose de la masa social, y en su tejido suelen participar con esmero y fidelidad a los principios que la constituyen. Se habla de estos judíos como "asimilados", y los denominados "antisemitas" (aunque más correctamente cabría llamarlos "antijudíos",[18] "denuncian" entonces que sólo se trata de judíos que fingen ser como los demás, que disimulan su verdadero origen.

Y cuando se trata de judíos practicantes. O de quienes escogen sus amistades y pareja en el marco de la microsociedad judía, se denuncia" el automarginamiento de quienes eligen no ser como los demás, de quienes no viven las mismas preocupaciones que el resto de la sociedad en cuestión, y que mal podrían entonces asumir la defensa de los intereses en común, etc.

---

[15] Bernardo A. Chiesi, "Elementos kabalasticos en las novelas de Ernesto Sábato," *Sefárdica* 8, págs. 55 a 61.

[16] Ibid., véase págs. 58 y 59.

[17] "Apologías y rechazos" de Ernesto Sábato. Artículo: "Judíos y antisemitas", págs. 29 a 52 (Buenos Aires: Editorial Sudamerica-Planeta, 1984).

[18] Véase a este respecto: Natalio Arbiser, "La actitud racionalista en el judío diaspórica," *Sefárdica* 8, págs. 93 a 97.

Ernesto Sábato[19] muestra muy bien el carácter irracional de estas críticas (cuando no acusaciones) contra los judíos; si un hombre de ciencia—nos dice Sábato—"encuentra un líquidoque se dilata al congelarse, no dirá que los líquidos se dilatan al congelarse, mientras que cuando un antisemita tropieza con un judío cobarse proclama, de inmediato, que los judíos son cobardes" ...Y define muy bien Sábato que: "se es antisemita a priori, independientemente de toda experiencia: más bien, cuando se produce, la experiencia es forzada en el lecho de Procusto del antisemitismo".

Y señala también que proceden motivados por pasiones e instintos, antes que por razones. Al abocarse a su vez al análisis sartreano en "Réflexions sur la question juive" Sábato critica la postura de aquíl, ya que adjudica al antisemita las características de defnsor de la tierra y lo irracional, frente al judío refugiado por necesidad histórica en el capital, la antítesis antisemitismo-judaísmo, equivaldría a la antítesis feudalismo-capitalismo. Lo que me parece falso". Y afirma también que "Sartre adjudica al antisemita los típicos atributos del espíritu feudal. Ni Ford ni Thyssen participan de ese fetichismo de la tierra, de semejante desprecio medieval por la riguez inmobiliaria Y quién puede poner en duda su antisemitisimo?"

Es más, Sábato puntualiza muy bien que la palabra "banca"[21] es italiana, y que son los italianos quienes a partir de la primer Cruzada (1096) convierten el dineron capital por vez primera, señalando también que: "apenas comenzó el comercio en gran escala, la precaria actividad mercantil de los judíos fue sohrepasada mil veces por el empuje de los italianos". Y concluye nuestro autor sosteniendo que: "de la premisa "muchos judíos aman el dinero" no se puede extraer la conclusión "todos los judíos aman el dinero" y menos todavía "los antisemitas desprecian el dinero" y nos dirá al enumerar a los principales magnates del mundo—que no son judíos—que Henry Ford—uno de tales hombres de fortuna econímica—"no puede soportar la fervorosa ansiedad semita por el dinero". Ansiedad que al parecer quiere sólo para sí. Sábato afirma que: "no es necesario ser judío para ser capitalista y tampoco es suficiente" y que "la condición de judío y de capitalista son rigurosamente independientes".[22]

---

[19] Véase "Apologías y rechazos".
[20] Véase ibid., pág. 35 y sig.
[21] "Banca" = "Banco", en el que se realizan las operaciones.
[22] Véase "Apologías y rechazos", págs. 43 y 44.

La cuestión del judío como sinónimo de hombre de dinero es desvirtuada también por los padecimientos de muchos judíos latino-americanos que comparten hoy la paupérrima situación de sus respectivos países. Hoy mismo en Argentina muchos hogares judíos se ve privados de mandar a sus niños a la escolaridad hebrea por dificulatades económicas.

A su vez el carácter racuonal-irracional es visto en múltiples aspectos en la controversia de Sábato con Sartre, y algunos aspectos propios de la psicologa del judío diaspórico a la luz de conocimuentos de psicología social y psicoanalíticos son desarrollados por Natalio Arbiser,[23] quien afirma que ciertos comportamientos históricos son el producto de realidades que obligaron al judío diaspórico a optar por la mente frente al cuerpo de un modo análogo si se quiere a ese resultado historico que, ante la forzada renuncia a la tierra obliga al judío a ser comerciante o prestamista (pero va sabemos que en el Río de la Plata se dio el llamado caso de "Los gauchos judíos", donde éstos participaron del engrandecimiento agrìcola de la nación, y fueron esforzados colonos).

Y también Kovadloff[24] remarca que: "la lucha de Sábato contra el nazismo es la lucha de Sábato contra el antihumanismo, es decir contra lo que el antihumanismo tiene de irracionalidad encubierta, de falta de racionalidad", mientras considera como buen ejemplo de la racionalidad ficticia a aquílla aue pretendía que Israel siguiese un procedimiento distinto para obtener al criminal de guerra Adolf Eichmann, siguiendo la más clásica metodología del diplomático pedido de extradición, y Sábato no vacilaría en afirmar entonces con toda la energía necesaria, que: "dejémonos de hipocresías, y reconozcamos que en el caso de que Israel hubiese pedido la extra-dición del criminal Eichmann (en vez de proceder a su secuestro) habrían sucedido una de dos variantes: o no habría sido concedida, como en el caso de Karl Klingenfuss, o el señor Eichmann se habría evaporado para siempre".[25]

El encendido verbo y la dúctil pluma de Sábato significaron un valiosísimo aporte para esclarecer a la opinión pública acerca de quiénes eran los que clamaban por un formalismo lega, escudandose

---

[23] Véase Arbiser, "La actitud racionalista".
[24] Véase Kovadloff, "Lo judío en la ensayística", págs. 38–39.
[25] Ernesto Sábato, artículo: "Soberanía para carniceros", Diario *El Mundo* (Buenos Aires), 17 de junio de 1960. Reproducido por *Sefàrdica* 8, págs. 169–170.

en el llamado de la soberanía. Y al ocuparse de las proclamas ideo-lígica del nacionalismo con "z"[26] en nuestro país, es aleccionadora-mente elocuente el párrafo que sigue—y que tomamos de la cita de Kovadloff[27] "el nacionalismo argentino fue en muchos casos, un sub-producto del nacionalismo alemán, lo que sería bastante trágico si no fuera cómico. Bastaría imaqinar, en efecto, la opinión que al doc-tor Rosemberg y al propio Eichmann les habrían merecido los cabe-citas negras, los negros y los mulatos que constituyeron los ejércitos libertadores y que generosamente murieron a lo largo y a lo ancho de nuestra América Latina".

Sábato, Defensor de los Derechos Humanos

Ante la intolerancia, frente al prepotente desvarío del antisemitismo, pocos como Ernesto Sábato han sido consecuentes en la permanente defensa del judío—como de cualquier minoría injustamente aco-sada—; si su vida fue signada por las letras, no menos que por ello se ha asociado el nombre de Ernesto Sábato a la defensa de los derechos humanos. Como es de público saber y de internacional reconocimiento, a la sunción del Primer gtobierno democrático luego de años de dictadura militar, es precisamente Sábato el designado para presidir la Comisión Nacional sobre Desaparición de Personas—CONADEP—, y el producto de esta investigación fue célebre mun-dialmente con la publicación del informe intitulado "Nunca Más".

Cuando en mayo de 1960 el criminal nazi Adolf Eichmann es detenido en Buenos Aires por personal de seguridad israelí, y envi-ado a lsrael para ser allí juzgado, los antisematas se proclaman "defensores de la soberanía" y se escudan en el cuestionamiento del procedimiento, reclamando que las leyes del país han sido burladas, pero obviando que los criminales de guerra nazis habían sido decla-rados en 1945 en el juicio de Nüremberg como criminales contra la humanidad.

La defensa de este sanguinario criminal corre por cuenta de acalo-radas voces del antisemitismo vernáculo, y en el periódico "El Mundo" de Buenos Aires, sendas notas de Sábato: "Soberanía para carniceros"[28]

---

[26] Véase nota 1.

[27] Véase nota Kovadloff, "Lo judío en la ensayística", *Sefárdica* 8, pág. 39.

[28] Véase al respecto mi breve comentario en *Sefárdica* 8, págs. 165 a 167: Mario Eduardo Cohen, "Soberanía para carniceros, un artículo valiente".

y "Viva Eichmann, mueran los judíos!" nos muestran con sobrados motivos a un apasionado combatiente—al tiempo que brillante razonador—contra la mayor de las injusticias, que es la de que los crimanales pretendan ser los justos, tan luego ellos, que precavían a la humanidad de "la amenaza judía", llevarían a cabo la mayor de las matanzas, y escribiría Sábato[29] "será siempre educativo recordar que el crimen más monstruoso que registra la historia se cometió en el país que en la década del treinta al cuarenta era el más adelantado del mundo". Cuestionaría Sábato la actitud del presidente Frondizi, quien pese a su definida vocación democrática, fue mal asesorado y su cancillería acusó al Estado de Israel de una supuesto "violación de la soberanía". Es en este artículo—"Soberanía para carniceros"—en el que ironiza con ácida decepción acerca del razonamiento de nuestra Cancillería, al afirmar que "y bien: el montruo que organizó y dirigió esta operación satánica pudo refugiar en nuestro país como tantos otros de pareja monstruosidad", enfatizando que "la revancha de las víctimas del Holocausto" fue moderada en extremo, y subrayando: "¿Cómo no admirar a un grupo de valientes que arriesgando su vida durante años han buscado por todo el mundo a esos criminales y han tenido todavía la honradez de llevarlos para ser juzgados por tribunales justicieros, en lugar de dejarse arrastrar por un impulso vindicatorioy ultimarlos ahí mismo?"[30]

Y qué brillante es el razonamiento de Sábato cuando refuta el pedido de "respeto por la soberanía" del atribulado coro nazi-fascista, cuando escribe: "aquí está en juego otra soberanía, y es la del ser humano, el supremo derecho a la justicia cuando hay de por medio una masacre y la tortura de un pueblo".

Nos cabe repetir lo que escribiéramos en "Sefárdica":[31] "En "Soberanía para carniceros" se nota la vehemencia y la impetuosidad de un Sarmiento o un Mitre que lucharon por sus convicciones en páginas periodisticas memorables de la historia argentina".

Y tomando la parábola bíblica del Génesis, afirmamos que: "podríamos decir que Sábato fue uno de los diez hombres justos capaces de salvar a una sociedad".

Y no olvidemos que Sábato, que casóse con una mujer judía, viene de una familia que—él mismo nos lo recuerda—"en Argentina como en Italia ha dado sacerdotes y dignatarios de la Iglesia", lo

---

[29] Véase Sábato, "Soberanía para carniceros".
[30] Ibid.
[31] Véase Cohen, "Soberanía para carniceros", *Sefárdica* 8, pág. 166.

que hace mucho más relevante su defensa del judaísmo agredido por los ideólogos del terror, que creen encontrar raíces hebreas en todo aquel que se les cruza para denunciar el espíritu anticristiano y antihumanista de estos nuevos "cruzados" del paganismo nazi.

Así fue tanbo al denunciar a los ideólogos de la barbarie[32] como Rosenberg, Krieck, Larenz o van der Bruck, como a los ofendidos criollos avenidos a defensores del pellejo de los fugitivos criminales, como ese jovenzuelo Casanova Ferro.

Resumiría muy bien Sábato, cuando se le pregunta qué es lo que más detesta en el mundo[33] y responde: "las pasiones menores y vergonzosas, esa hermana despreciable de la prudencia que es la cobardía", y esa cobardía sería tan manifiesta en quiene cansados de prepotear e intimidar a la judeidad local, saltarían a un solo grito a nuevos adalidades de la formalidad legal, no bien uno de los mayores criminales de guerra—ingresado al país como tantos de sus colegas sin tal aprobación legal—, sería capturado y trasladado a Israel para ser juzgado en nombre de la más sagrada de las justicias, la que no puede callar el holocausto de millones de seres humanos a manos de esos Eichmann que pretendían ampararse en las leyes de una nación democrática como la Argentina.

A Modo de Conclusion

Sábato ha sido uno de los pocos escritores latinoamericanos que ha dado un trato especial a personajes judíos en el relato de ficción, mientras que en su tarea de ensayista y pensador ha sido consecuente en la sostenida defensa de los valores judíos del pueblo judío frente a las repetidas amenazas de los prepotentes de turno.

Nostálgico memorioso de un período histórico—el de Sefarad— en que judíos y musulmanes pudieron convivir y crear conjuntamente, idealice tal vez dicha época, que alternó con "los feroces almohades" como él mismo lo admite; pero nos muestra Sábato un optimismo—que algunos quizá califiquen de ingenuo—contagioso por un pronto reencuentro de estos pueblos de milenaria cultura.

A diferencia de Borges, quien solía ser insólito cuando no extra-

---

[32] "Ideólogos de la Barbarie", tituló también Sábato un párrafo de su primer libro *Uno y el Universo*, publicado en 1945.

[33] De las conversaciones de Ernesto Sábato con Carlos Catania, publicadas bajo el título de *Entre la letra y la sangre* (Buenos Aires: Editorial Seix Barral, 1988).

vagante en sus apariciones públicas, profesa Sábato, el culto de la cotidiana lucha por la vigencia de una vida íntegra, y su metodología es siempre la alusión al hecho real, concreto. Allí fuera hombres de carne y hueso padecen, y es por ellos por quien hace oir su voz.

Si en Borges la ironía, la metáfora y la reflexión abstracta eran primeras espadas frente a la torpeza de racistas y verdugos, Sábato no obviaría nunca la lucha frontal, lógica, realista.

Y si en Borges entusiasta admirador de la cultura del pueblo de Israel, valiéndole como argumento para ignorar las pretensiones de los palestinos—que, según el autor del "Aleph"—nada produjeron por la cultura y la civilización—y que éstos históricamente no hicieron sino subsistir, en Sábato la historia grande de la Humanidad también se escribe desde cotidianas y pequeñas batallas por la existencia, y reconoce por ello los derechos de los palestinos.

Siendo también enérgico en su reiterada vocación por defender la pacífica coexistencia de los pueblos, denunciando todo atropello contra la libertad del hombre, Sábato no ha dejado nunca de proclamar a voz en cuello la justa existencia del Estado de Israel.

Más aún, fue integrante de una Comisión por Jerusalem y enfrento las resoluciones de los Naciones Unidas y de la UNESCO, cuando se pretendió equiparar al sionismo con el racismo, o se quiso separar a Israel de estos organismos-madre de la vida institucional en el mundo civilizado. Defensor acalorado de "los sagrados principios de la justicia y la verdad" como entonces los definiera, fue igualmente celoso fiscal de toda dictadura, conbatiendo sin tregua cualquier exceso contra el pluralismo, cualquier intento de demostración antisemita.

Lúcido hombre público, no ha sido hombre de partido alguno, siendo su entrega en pos de la democracia, una bandera inclaudicable.

Queremos concluir esta ponencia, reproduciendo el párrafo final de los fundamentos del dictamen por el que se le concedió en Israel, en el año 1989, el Premio Jerusalem de Letras:[34] "(el Premio es) resultado de su independencia y de su denuncia de violaciones a los derechos humanos en países de opuestos regímenes políticos, vivió muchos años en soledad, hasta convertirse en la voz de la conciencia argentina, una voz escuchada no sólo *en su Patria, sino también más allá de sus* fronteras".

Redacción: Natalio Arbiser

---

[34] Véase *Sefárdica* 8, pág. 101.

TYPOLOGIE DU RÉCIT LÉGENDAIRE
DU SAINT JUDÉO-MUSULMAN AU MAROC

El-Hassane Chrifi-Alaoui

L'hagiographie marocaine a donné une grande quantité de récits légendaires concernant la vie, la mort, les miracles et les oracles des grands Saints patrons et locaux des deux confessions au Maroc, le Judaïsme et l'Islam. Ces récits, notamment ceux qui constituent notre corpus,[1] présentent des éléments homologues aptes à donner, grâce à leur identification, une sorte de typologie de ce genre de production.

Ces éléments homologues qui constituent l'armature du récit se résume dans les aspects suivants; La légende n'est pas une oeuvre d'érudition,[2] elle est formée à partir de plusieurs éléments hétérogènes: récits bibliques, événements historiques, et éléments mythologiques. Malgré cet apanage parfois non conforme aux dogmes des deux religions pratiquées, la légende ne subit aucun contrôle régulier d'une autorité religieuse.[3]

L'espace où elle se dóroulé est sacré, puisqu'il est, d'une part le théâtre des événements et des faits qui s'accomplissent grâce à l'action et à l'intervention du saint. Il est d'autre part symbolisé par des lieux sanctifilés et vénérés, (1) comme la montagne, qui représente le chemin du ciel, le centre de la terre, le lieu de la révélation, le

---

[1] Ce corpus représente des échantillons des grands axes thématiques de l'hagiographie marocaine. Il est constitué àpartir des textes dispersés dans les livres linguistiques, ethnographiques et dans les rapports des missionnaires et voyageurs sur I^e Maroc aux XIXe et XXe siècles.

[2] Après une grande hésitation, on a qualifié nos récits de légendes du fait qu'ils comportent des éléments susceptibles d'identifier la légende:

– comme les légendes nos récits sont présentés comme des récits vrai.
– Ils s'attachent tous à des lieux, et leur création est liée à des faits réels.

[3] Même si les dcux confessions sont d'accord sur le principe que l'agissements, entre autre, sur la nature est réservé pour Dieu, les autorités religieuses n'ont jamais manifesté, en tout cas d'une façon systématique, leur opposition à ce que ces textes attribuent aux saints un pouvoir similaire à celui de Dieu, en plus elles n'ont jamais essayé de censurer ces attributions, malgré leur contradiction avec les deux Livres, hormis les recueils transcrits par des lettres qui les ont soigneusement nettoyés de tous les excès flagrants par exemple: *Salwat al anfas* d'al-Kattani, *Dawhat an-nashir* d'ibn Ashgar, *Momti' al-asma'* d'al Mahdî al-Fâsî. . . .

royaume des prophètes des justes et des saints, (2) la grotte, la caverne ou l'ermitage symbolisant la sollicitude et le dévouement de celui qui les occupe, (3) certains lieux centres producteurs de sacralité, puisqu'ils sont construits ou découverts grâce à une volonté divine, ou tout simplement parce qu'elles présentent les lieux dans lesquels les saints ont vécu ou ont été enterrés. Le temps de même est sacré, le fait de raconter le récit réactualise et restaure le temps dans lequel les saints ont vécu et ont accompli leurs actions et leurs miracles.[4]

Les saints sont répertoriés dans trois catégories différentes:

- La première, celle du Saint patron d'une métropole ou une grande commune est en général un personnage historique bien connu comme kabbaliste, mystique, rabbin, muftí ou simple maître d'une école talmudique ou coranique comme *Ulad zmirru* à Safi, *'Amran ben Diwan* à Wazzan, *Dawid dar'a* à Dar'a, *Sidi Bal 'Abbas* à Marrakech.
- La deuxième, celle du Saint universel, personnage d'une grande renommée spirituelle et dont la célébrité dépasse la frontière de sa localité, tel *'Amran ben Diwan*, *Nissim ben Nissim* et *Ankawa*...
- La troisième, celle du Saint anonyme, personnage mystérieux inconnu, porte le nom de la structure qui l'identifie par exemple: *Mul l'bit* (= le propriétaire de la chambre) à Ayt Sh'ayb Wawizart, *Sadiq laqbibat* (= le saint des petites dômes) à Larache *Mul l'barg* (le propriétaire de la citadelle) à Bizu. Il peut également avoir un nom signifiant l'anonymat tel *Sidi l'mahfi* (= le saint caché), partout au Maroc *Lalla Ġriba* (= la sainte étrangère), *Sidi L'waqí* (= le Saint protecteur), *Sidi Qadi higa*, *Sidi qadi haga*...

Dans le récit le saint est toujours actif, il n'a pas et il ne peut pas avoir un componement passif. Ses activités commence parfois avant sa naissance, il n'a pas d'enfance[5] du fait qu'il ne cesse d'agir et de

---

[4] Cet opération exige du narrateur certaines conditions pour accomplir cet acte délicat el dangéreux à la fois:
- respecter l'intégralité du récit sans rajouter ou enlevez des parties.
- raconter le récit pendant une festivité religieuse, ex. la hillulla ou le musem du Saint, et devant une audience qui sache apprécier et respecter l'histoire.

[5] On a voulu citer cet exemple même s'il ne fait pas parti des textes judéo-musulmans, parce qu'il réunis tous les éléments en questions, qu'on peut trouver évidemment dans notre corpus, mais qui sont éparpillés dans plusieurs textes:
Au village de Lahsun, au moment ou l'enfant (Mulay 'Abdaslam ben Mshish) s'échappant du sein de sa mère, parut en plein lumière, des myriates d'abeilles,

lutter contre: (1) des forces naturelles, comme la sécheresse en envoyant des pluies, des inondations en déplaçant des montagnes ou en creusant des barrages . . ., (2) les grands fléaux et les épidémies, (3) les forces mystérieuses: démons et *jnun*, (4) une force humaine: un saint rival, le Mahzan, sultan, Basha, Qayad, shrif injuste, incrédule et les *rum* (= chrétiens), on peut dire qu'il n'a pas d'existence entant que personne en dehors de l'existence de sa communauté. Sa sainteté est transmise par le lien de parenté, souvent de père en fils, du maître au disciple, ou acquise soit arbitrairement (en général une personne provoquant les bénédictions et le contentement d'un saint), soit chimiquement en avalant unc potion magique, entre autre, l'encre qui a servi à écrire des versets qui peuvent contenir les lettres constituant le nom de Dieu. Son autoportrait que le récit lui donne est un homme juste, très beau et très grand; son visage est lumineux avec une grande barbe blanche, portant un turban et des vêtements verts ou blancs, un grand chapelet en bois sur le coup, un bâton à la main, un oiseau sur l'épaule ou un animal, fréquemment un lion, le suit.

Le saint est capable de prévoir le lieu, et l'heure de sa mort, cette dernière ne l'empêche guère de continuer d'exercer son pouvoir, elle ne peut pas non plus corrompre son cadavre après sa mort, il reste intacte et dégage même des parfums agréables. Quant a ses miracles les actions suivantes peuvent bien les résumer: Devenir invisible ou rendre invisible, faire revivre les morts, discuter avec les morts, se métamorphoser ou faire metamorphoser, déplacer les cites, raccourcir les distances, arrêter le temps, parler avec les plantes et les bêtes, marcher sur les eaux, voler dans les airs, prédire l'avenir et saisir le passé, exaucer les prières, guérir les malades, agir après la mort. . . .

---

accourant des quatres coins de l'horizon, vinrent s'abattre sur Ies chairs molles du nouveau-né, l'enveloppant de toutes parts, enterrant le pauvre petit sous la houle inquiétante d'un grouillement de bestioles noires, aux ailes frissonnantes. Très effrayés, s'imaginant que l'enfant allait être dévoré, les parents poussaient des cris, se tenant prudemment à distance, n'osant intervenir, de peur d'irriter les abeilles. Tout à coup, le grand Mulay Abdalgadar-g-Gilani se montra sur le seuil de la porte. Il rassura la mère, écarta doucement le flot noir des insectes, baisa pieusement les yeux, le front, les oreilles et la bouche du baby prédestiné; puis s'adressant à ceux qui l'entouraient, il prononça à haute voix ces paroles mémorables: "Ma place n'est plus ici. quelqu'un de plus grand que moi vient de naître au Maroc, c'est Mulay Abdassalam, c'est cet enfant. Il sera la gloire de l'islam et du monde. Il n'a pas besoin d'apprendre le Coran, il le sait déjè à la mamelle."

Il était le dernier né d'une famille nombreuse. A l'âge de 15 ans, le jour même de son mariage, des voisins vinrent demander à son pere, le vénérable Sidi Msis, un de ses garçons, pleurant, se lamentant, disant à travers leurs larmes: "Nos fautes illustre patriarche, ont comblé la mesure. Frappées de stérilité depuis plusieurs années, nos terres ne donnent plus de récoltes. Seul un rejeton du Prophète peut les rendre fécondes. Laisse venir donc chez nous un de tes fils. Il sera notre chef protecteur, il ramènera sur nos têtes le courant des bénédictions célestes". Moulèras, *Le Maroc inconnu*, t2 pp. 162–169.

PART FOUR

LINGUISTICS STUDIES

LANGUAGE CHOICE AND LANGUAGE VARIETIES BEFORE AND AFTER THE EXPULSION

ORA RODRIGUE SCHWARZWALD

Bar-Ilan University
Ramat Gan, Israel

Introduction

I would like to present here a panoramic view of the use of languages by the Jews in Spain until the end of the fifteenth century, and by their descendants in various countries from the sixteenth century on. It is my contention that the language varieties used by the Sephardic Jews and their cultural creations were mutually dependent; language type determines and is dependent on the special genres the Jews created.

My discussion is sociolinguistically oriented by features of the message sender and the addressee, the content of the message, and the time and circumstances of communication. The main question is: "Who speaks what variety of what language to whom, when, where and concerning what?" (Fishman 1972, p. 2) in both the written and the spoken modes of communication. All means of language usage will be discussed. The questions to be answered are mainly: In what languages or language varieties did the Jews write/create what in Spain before the expulsion, and in what languages or language varieties did the Sephardic Jews write/create what after the expulsion?

Multilingualism and Diglossia

Languages in Contact

During the course of history Jews have moved within various linguistic societies. Hebrew (biblical and mishnaic) was their basic language, but when they wandered to different places they acquired different languages, keeping Hebrew as their main religious marker. Among these languages were Aramaic, Greek, Latin, medieval local languages like Old Spanish, Old Portuguese, Old French, medieval German, and Arabic, and after the sixteenth century other local modern languages, including Italian, Turkish, Greek, English, French, Slavic languages, and Arabic.

Languages in contact influence each other (Weinreich 1968). Words are transferred from one language to the other. Pronunciation, grammar, and semantics are affected as well.

Diglossia

Multilingualism among Jews is not as simple as it seems. The Jews did not use languages interchangeably for simply any kind of purpose, but rather as in diglossia.

In a diglossic situation, two or more languages or two or more language varieties are used by all the members of a speech community for different purposes: one for formal, religious, polite, educational intercourse; the other for informal, daily, familiar situations (Ferguson 1959). Community members regard the formal variety as the higher and better language, but do not hold the informal one in special esteem.

Literary Genres

In literary evaluation, as in diglossia, we must distinguish between highly evaluated canonical or genuine written literature and nonevaluated folk (oral) literature. The former are learned, serious, valuable cultural innovations cherished and highly valued by the speech community; the latter are light, nonserious, sometimes funny or amusing works. The former tend to be known only by the learned and educated rather than by all members of the speech community; the latter are widely distributed, well known, and fluently used by each and every member. Despite the lack of esteem for them, they are part of the cultural heritage of any speech community.

The valued works were written by individuals in the community. In most cases we are well aware of the identity of the authors. This genre includes scientific and religious literature, poetry, translations of ritual texts, other translations, and other prosaic literature. On the other hand, the innovators of folk literature, such as folk stories, folk songs, ballads, proverbs, idioms, riddles, etc., are mostly unknown.

Jewish Creativity in Muslim Spain

Jews in the Iberian Peninsula were familiar with several languages. Hebrew and Aramaic were consistently their religious and cultural languages, Greek and Latin were used before the Muslim period, and in Muslim Spain they acquired Arabic as well as the Ibero-Romance languages.

Hebrew was always considered the high language of use by the Jew. It was the language of education, prayers, ritual services, and cultural literature. Although not used for everyday speech, it served as a means of formal communication with other Jewish communities. It was the language in which part of the valuable literature was written in Muslim Spain. The most important contributions were as follows:

> *Poetry*: Yehuda haLevi, Moshe ibn Ezra of Granada, Moshe Dgiqatila, Shmuel haNagid, Shelomo ibn Gabirol, Yehuda Alharizi
> *Grammar*: Menahem ben Saruq (*HaMahberet*). Dunash ben Labrat, Abraham ibn Ezra (*Sefer Sahot, Sefer Moznayim*)
> *Dictionaries*: *Sefer haShorashim* of Rabbi David Kimhi (RaDaQ) and of Abraham ibn Ezra
> *Halachic literature*: Shmuel haNagid (*Mavo laTalmud*), Yishaq Alfasi (*Halakot* [*Talmud Qatan*]), Maimonides (*Mishne Tora*)
> *Interpretations of classical texts*: Abraham ibn Ezra, Yosef Kimhi
> *Travel books*: Rabbi Binyamin from Tudela of Navara

Nonetheless, since Arabic was the prestigious cultural language of the non-Jewish world, Jews in Muslim Spain also wrote scientific and philophical works in Arabic, though in Hebrew characters. Jews used this language partly because the terminology had already been set by the Arabs and partly because their audience could have been non-Jewish as well as Jewish. This is a short list of some writers and their books:

> Yona ibn Janah: *Sefer haShorashim, Sefer haRiqma*
> Shelomo ibn Gabirol (= Avicebron): *Meqor haHayim*, a philosophical moralistic book known to the Christian world in its Latin translation as *Fons Vitae* ("The Source of Life")
> Bahyay ibn Paqudah: *Hovot haLevavot*
> Yehuda haLevi: *Sefer haKuzari*
> Abraham Bar Hiyya: works on geometry, astronomy, arithmetic, and geography

Rabbi Abraham ibn Daud from Toledo: *'Emuna Rama*
Maimonides (Moshe ben Maimon = RaMBaM): *More Nebukim* ("Guide
for the Perplexed"), *Sefer haMa'or*

All these texts were known to the Jewish world mainly through Yehuda and Shemuel ibn Tibon's translations into Hebrew.

The third language used in the Iberian Peninsula was Ibero-
Romance. In Muslim Spain its status was relatively weak among the
Jews, but as soon as the Reconquista took place, the linguistic situ-
ation changed.

Jews and Marranos in Christian Spain

The population of Christian Spain included Christians, Marranos,
Jews, and Muslims. The two groups that are of interest to us are
the Jews and the Marranos.

Jews

Since the Jews now needed Arabic less and less, writing in Arabic
ceased, and writing in Hebrew (and Aramaic) was strengthened, especially in the areas of philosophy, religion, law, morals, mysticism,
and exegesis. Jews were also known as scientists, but not much was
written by them at that time in the vernacular. The following is a
short list of some of the well-known writers in Christian Spain:

Rabbi Shlomo (Solomon) ben Abraham Adret (= RaShBA).
Nahmanides (Rabbi Moshe ben Nahman = RaMBaN)
Shem Tov Falquiera
Todros ben Yehudah Abulafia
Shelomo ben Semah Duran
Moshe ben Shem Tov de Leon (author of *HaZohar*, in Aramaic)
Rabbi Yom Tov ben Abraham (= RITBA) from Seville
Shem Tov Gaon from Segobia
Don Vidal (Yom Tov) de Tuluz
Hasdai Cresques (Crescas)
Don Isaac Abravanel
Yosef Albo
Abraham Zacut
Isaac Arama

The vernacular Romance language was acquired by the Jews, but did not have the prestigious status that Arabic had previously enjoyed. Most of the common people acquired the language casually and used it in its colloquial varieties. Because of their unique social and religious background, they probably created special sociolects used selectively by the Jews in each district. Moreover, the attitude toward Ibero-Romance was denigrating, as Latin was considered the model language; and since no normative literary standards had yet been set for writing, very little was created by Jews in Spanish and Portuguese prior to the expulsion e.g. Coplas de Yosef. (See the discussion of Ladino translations below.)

The Kharjas and the Statutes of Valladolid are examples of interactions between the languages in use by the Jews, though they constitute but a minor part of Jewish cultural creativity. Kharjas are concluding verses in Spanish appended to a Hebrew poem (Hitchcock 1977). The combination of languages is systematic, where the rhymes and the metric structure fit. The Kharjas probably belonged to the oral literary tradition, although they were sometimes created by such well-reputed poets as Yehuda haLevi, Moshe ibn Ezra, and Moshe Dgiqatila.

The Valladolid Statutes for the communities in Castile, formulated by the Jewish council in 1432 (April 22–May 2) give additional proof of the interinfluence of Hebrew and Spanish. Although written in Hebrew characters, the text is basically Spanish with an admixture of Hebrew. This short sentence (with the Hebrew words emphasized demonstrates the case: *otro se ordenamos que cual quiere* **qahal yṣ"w** [*yishmerenu ṣuro vego'alo*] *de quince* **ba'ale batim** *sean* **meḥuyavim** *de tener entre si* **malamed tinoqot hagun** *que beze a sus fig'os* **pasuq** ("more we order that each community of fifteen householders be required to have among themselves a respectable teacher who will teach their children Bible"). The use of Hebrew words is not restricted to cultural and religious terms. In addition to the Jewish concepts *qahal, pasuq* (a biblical verse, and by semantic expansion, the Bible or, probably, any Hebrew education), and *yṣ"w* (blessing), we have general terms like *ba'ale batim* along with *mehuyavim* ("required"), *hagun*, and *melamed tinoqot*.

Marranos

The situation was entirely different for the Marranos, who were overtly Christians and concealed their practice of Judaism for fear of their Catholic neighbors and the Inquisition. They secretly observed many Jewish practical laws, such as kosher meats, the Sabbath, Yom Kippur, and Pesah, but, as they could not study the classical literature in Hebrew, did not live in a diglossic situation with Hebrew. Moreover, in order to hide the fact that they were secretly Jewish, their overt linguistic behavior must have complied with the Christian norms. This is why the language of the Marranos had no Jewish markers, but was, rather, the Spanish or Portuguese of their contemporaries. Furthermore, since they did not and could not read Hebrew, they only used translated texts in roman characters following Ladino translation principles already set by their Jewish predecessors for liturgy (see below).

Sefarad I and Sefarad II

Max Weinreich (1973, p. 126) distinguishes two periods in the development of Judeo-Spanish (Dzhudezmo): Sefarad I, before the expulsions from the Iberian Peninsula at the end of the fifteenth century, and Sefarad II, from the sixteenth century on. The expulsions caused the Sephardim to become almost exclusively a diaspora community, with the exception of the Marrano communities (see the discussion at the end of this section).

Sefarad I

The evidence for a special Judeo-Spanish in Sefarad I is difficult to assess, but, as mentioned above, it is obvious that the language was already shaped as a Jewish language before the expulsion. There are some Jewish documents, but their contribution to Judeo-Spanish research is not too significant (Marcus 1962). The existence of the word *malsin* "informer" in Old Spanish proves that the use of Hebrew words by Spanish-speakers was not limited to Jews and Marranos. *Dio* rather than *Dios* is the ancient Jewish word for "God", and *meldar* "read", of Greek origin, is attested to in old pre-expulsion documents (in addition to the Valladolid Statutes and the Kharjas).

The major and most recognizable Jewish component which influenced the spoken variety of Ibero-Romance was Hebrew (and Aramaic). Some words were absorbed into Judeo-Spanish in the given Hebrew tradition (*sedaka* "charity", *misva* "commandment", *pesax* "Pesah"), some were fused into the grammatical structure of Spanish (*sabadear* "keep the Sabbath prayers", *xenozo* "gracious, tender" [from Hebrew *ḥen* "grace"]). Also, the meaning of some Hebrew words changed in Sephardic usage (*xaxam* "rabbi", not just "wise").

Other languages had an influence as well. *Alxa(d)* "Sunday" replaced the Christian (*Dies*) *Dominicus* "the day of the Lord [Jesus Christ]"; and *blanco* "white" also denoted "coal", due to Arabic influence (Weinreich 1973, pp. 147–148).

In addition to these linguistic signs, linguists use two arguments to support the existence of Judeo-Spanish in Sefarad I: (1) Ladino translations of liturgical texts; (2) the similarity between the North African and the eastern Mediterranean communities (Zucker 1988).

Ladino Translations

The first Ladino Bible translations were published in Constantinople in 1547 and in Ferrara in 1553. Other translations of ritual texts were published in the same two cities, as well as in Amsterdam, Venice, Salonika, and a few other places around the same time or shortly after. These Ladino translations were of sacred character and of high value to both the Marranos and the Jewish Sephardic communities. In spite of their dispersion and although published for different populations (Marranos vs. expelled Jews), the principles and the use of certain Hebrew words in the translations are identical. The similarity of grammatical and lexical archaisms is also striking. It is within reason that these translations had already been created in the Iberian Peninsula, as in fact is claimed on the title page of the Ferrara translations, even though they were not printed until just after the expulsion.

North African and Eastern Mediterranean Communities

The linguistic similarities of the Judeo-Spanish spoken by the expelled Jews who settled in North Africa and by those who settled in the eastern Mediterranean are beyond accident.

1. Both communities retained Old Spanish phonetic features: *S* in

ORA RODRIGUE SCHWARZWALD

diSo, paSaro "said, bird" (Sp. *dijo, pájaro*); *Z* in *iZo/fiZo, vieZo* "son, old" (Sp. *hijo, viejo*); *dZ* in *dZusto, dodZe* "right, twelve" (Sp. *justo, doce*); *m* in *mwestro, mwevo* "ours, new" (Sp. *nuestro, nuevo*).

2. Some verb forms are conjugated the same: *kantí, kantates* "I, you [sing.] sang" (Sp. *canté, cantaste*); the conjugation of *ser* "to be" in the present tense: *so/soy, sos/ses/eres, es/e, somos/semos, soS/sedes, son*.

3. Some archaic forms are equally retained in the two communities: *abokarse* "bend"; *agora* "now"; *ambezar* "teach; learn"; *avagar* "slowly"; *eskapar* "finish"; *kamareta* "room"; *kavesal* "pillow"; *kazal* "village"; *mankar* "miss"; *oganyo* "this year"; *tSapeo* "hat".

4. Some innovated forms occur in both communities: *balabay* (masc.), *balabaya* (fem.) "good householder, boss" (from Heb. *ba'al habbayit, ba'alat habbayit* "the owner of the house"); *empesiZo* "beginning"; *trokamyento* "change"; *prestura* "speed"; *araskina* "itch"; *prometa* "promise"; *antSear* "widen"; *alevantar* "stand up"; *amostrar* "show"; *aprovar* "try"; *axenarse* "beautify oneself" (Heb. *ḥen* "grace"); (*gwevo*) *enxaminado* "hard-boiled (egg)" (from Heb. *ḥamin* "[Sabbath] stew"); *dezmazalado* "unlucky person" (from Heb. *mazal* "star, constellation; luck, fate": existing in Cervantes as well, fifty years after the expulsion).

The fact that two communities that had no contact after the expulsion show such a linguistic resemblance is evidence that they both stemmed from the same linguistic source; that is, they probably originated in pre-expulsion Iberian Judeo-Spanish.

Sefarad II

Jews

When the Jews left Spain, they continued to speak Spanish among themselves in a variety of dialects containing a large number of ancient linguistic forms and a number of Hebrew elements. They continued using Hebrew characters for orthography. In the early years of their settlement in the Mediterranean countries they even formed separate congregations and synagogues, but later the language was quite unified.

Once the language was detached from its source, further developments occurred. New words were coined based on the original Spanish structure, and in addition the language changed due to foreign influences. Turkish, Greek, Italian, French, and other languages enriched Judeo-Spanish in very many ways. Hebrew, of course, being the cultural diglossic language, constantly continued to penetrate the language. Here are a few examples:

Turkish: *tSarsi* "market", *kibrit* "match", *musafir* "guest", *kolay* "easy", *tSadir* "umbrella [Trk. 'tent']", *tavan* "roof (also 'God')"
Greek: *fusta* "skirt", *nekotSera* "good housekeeper", *nono, papu* "grandfather", *piron* "fork"
French: *repetar* "repeat", *dezirar* "desire", *suetar* "greet"
Italian: *sigurita* "insurance policy", *adio* "bye", *dirito* "right"
Arabic: *kira* "rent", *tarexa* "duty"
Hebrew: *Savuot/savuo/sevo* "Pentecost", *laSonara(x)* "gossip, evil talk" (Heb. *laSon hara*), *baalaftaxa* "optimist" (Heb. *ba'al* "owner" + *havtaha* "promise"), *sedakero* "beggar; philanthropist" (in different communities) (Heb. *sedaqa* "charity")

Moreover, elements from different morphological sources were fused to create new words. For instance:

azlaxadZi "successful" (Heb. *haslaha* + Trk. + *gi*[adj.])
ladronim "thieves" (Sp. *ladron* + Heb. +*im* [pl.])
xaraganut "laziness" (Sp. *haragan* + Heb. +*ut* [abstract noun])
fulano ben fulano "X" son of "Y" (Arb. *fulano* + Heb. *ben* "son")
adZidear "have pity on" (Trk. *ag'vmak* + Sp. +*ear*)
ramauluk "cheating" (Heb. *ramay, rama'ut* + Trk. +*luk* [abstract noun])
garonudo "glutton" (Heb. *garon* "throat" + Sp. +*udo*)

Marranos

When the Marranos left Spain and Portugal, their language did not carry any Jewish markers, especially if they were second- or third-generation Marranos. Since they did not know Hebrew, they had to learn it after returning to Judaism in the sixteenth and seventeenth centuries. Furthermore, being mainly merchants and financiers, the aristocratic Marranos kept their commercial and diplomatic contacts with Spain and Portugal even after returning to Judaism, so that they continued using the spoken varieties of Iberian Spanish and Portuguese. Therefore, most of their publications in the early years after the expulsion were in Spanish and Portuguese written in roman characters (and sometimes in Latin, the cultural language of the Christian world), rather than in Hebrew.

West and East

The professional literature about Sephardic Jews very often uses the terms "east" and "west" in the taxonomy of the linguistic varieties of postexilic Spanish, but these terms are extremely ambiguous. They are based on sociological, geographical, or dialectal criteria.

Sociological Division

West
The former Marranos, Portuguese and Spanish speakers, who used Ladino, mainly in roman characters, for liturgy, but Portuguese and Spanish for most other purposes. Their most important center was in Amsterdam, but they had other communities in France (Bordeaux, Bayonne), Italy (Ferrara. Venice, Livorno, Florence), Holland (Rotterdam, Amsterdam), England (London), Germany (Hamburg), and the New World in the seventeenth and eighteenth centuries (New York, Brazil, the West Indies).

East
The core of expelled Jews (Judeo-Spanish speakers) in the Ottoman Empire and North Africa, with some Marranos who were absorbed and entirely assimilated in these communities. With a good knowledge of Hebrew, they used mainly Hebrew for their important works, and Ladino and Judeo-Spanish in Hebrew characters for minor writings. Their most important centers were Salonika and Constantinople.

Geographical Division: Judeo-Spanish for All Purposes

Among the eastern communities defined in the preceding section, the following classification is further made: West (*Haketiya*): North Africa (Morocco, Tunis); East: the Ottoman Empire in the eastern Mediterranean (the Balkans, Turkey, Israel, Egypt).

The eastern and western communities in this classification are also linguistically different. The North African western Sephardic communities pronounce /h/, /ḥ/, and /'/ in words of Hebrew or Arabic origin, whereas the eastern communities do not pronounce /h/ and /'/, and /ḥ/ is pronounced as [x]. Also, more Arabic loan-words exist in the North African communities than in the eastern communities, which are loaded with Turkish words.

Dialectal Division

This classification applies within the eastern communities of the Ottoman Empire as defined above: West: Bulgaria. Yugoslavia, Bosnia, Macedonia, Serbia; East: Turkey, parts of Greece, Israel, Egypt. It distinguishes between western communities which retain initial /f/ (of historical *f- > h- > o) and eastern ones that do not (e.g., West: *fazer*, East: *azer* [Sp. *hacer*] "do"; West: *fasta*, East: *asta* [Sp. *hasta*] "until"). Also, final *u* and *i* are typical of the western dialects, whereas the eastern ones have *o* and *e* instead (e.g., West: *fiƷu*, East: *iƷo* [Sp. *hijo*] "son"; West: *verdi/vedri*, East: *verde/vedre* [Sp. *verde*] "green").

Literary Genres and Language Choice

The linguistic distinctions made above between East and West are well reflected in the cultural-literary creations of the Sephardic post-exilic communities and the language varieties used by them. An additional temporal distinction must be drawn between works created before and after the eighteenth century (Kayserling 1890; Grünbaum 1896; Molho 1960).

Marranos

The western Marrano communities published a variety of written texts, mainly in Spanish and Portuguese, but also, to a lesser degree, in Hebrew and Latin. Here is a list of some of the important writers:

Menasseh ben Israel
Immanuel Aboab
Saul Levi Mortara
Isaac Arobio de Castro
Moshe Rephael de Aguilar
Yaacob Yeuda Leon (Templo)
Yaacob Belmonte
Reuel Yeshurun (= Paul de Pena)
Rabbi Jacob Sasportas
Rabbi Ishak de Mathathias Aboab de Fonseca
Joseph Semah Arias
Yshac (Fernando) Cardoso
Don Miguel (Daniel Levi) de Barrios
David Abenatar Melo

Their writings include religious prose and poetry, free translations and interpretations of Hebrew texts, general Jewish and synagogal law, moral texts, polemical treatises, sermons, drama and epics, as well as original or translated nonreligious literature (both prose and poetry). Hebrew was limited to Hebrew grammar books, collections of sermons, and rabbinical literature. The press and the drama created in these communities were mainly in Spanish and Portuguese. Later on, at the end of the eighteenth century and during the nineteenth, these languages were replaced by Dutch, French, English, and other local languages spoken by the descendants of the earlier Sephardim. I do not have much evidence (except for some plays) about the folkloristic creations in this community. I assume that its Iberian roots will be inevitable, once it is studied.

Jews

In the expelled eastern Jewish communities, serious literature was written in Hebrew, with the exception of the Ladino translations, which were elevated to a degree of educational liturgy per se because of their linguistic features. Folk creativity was restricted to the Judeo-Spanish vernacular, a situation which was quite typical of the last generations in Christian Spain. In this respect, Moses (ben Baruk) Almosnino was an exception. He originally wrote *El regimiento de la vida* ("The Management of Life") and *Extremos y Grandesas de Constantinopla* ("The Extremes and Greatness of Constantinople") in (Judeo-)Spanish in Hebrew Rashi script, but his works became famous through their transliteration into roman characters done for the benefit of Christian speakers of Spanish. Most of the rabbinical, educational, moral, and legal works by Moses Almosnino and his contemporaries were written in Hebrew. Rabbi Yaacov ben Habib and his son Levy Habib, for instance, compiled in Hebrew the *Eyn Ya'akov*, a popular collection of talmudic legends; Rabbi Yosef (ben Efraim) Caro wrote his *Bet Yosef* and the classic *Shulhan Aruch* in Hebrew. The responsa literature, although addressed mainly to a Sephardic audience, was also written in Hebrew, although occasionally, in citations of actual cases, Judeo-Spanish wills, expressions, or whole conversations were included in the Hebrew text (e.g., Shmuel de Modena [MaHaRaShDaM]). Moreover, poets like Rabbi Shlomo Alkabez, Rabbi Israel Nagara, Rabbi Nissim Sandgi, and Rabbi Sa'adya Longo wrote poetry in Hebrew. Other mystical literature as well was published in Hebrew (e.g., Moshe Cordobero, Haim Vidal Calabrese). Writings in Judeo-Spanish were quite limited after the expulsion.

Zadok ben Yosef Forman translated *Hovot haLevavot* (written originally in Arabic in Spain) into Ladino as *El deber de los corazones* ("The Needs of the Hearts"), and at the same time an anonymous translation of *Shulhan haPanim* by Yosef Caro was published as *Meza de la alma* ("A Table of the Soul"). These and a few others tried to follow the standards set by the Ladino translations, and since the texts were rabbinical and well approved, so were the translations.

Various changes in the economic, political, and social situation of the Jews caused some decrease in the level of Hebrew education in subsequent generations. The majority of the people spoke Judeo-Spanish, but knowledge of Hebrew steadily deteriorated. At the same time, as trends in the non-Jewish world enabled a number of dialects to attain the status of languages, many Jews began to develop a changed attitude toward the spoken language. Educated Sephardic leaders, grasping the need to elevate the knowledge of the laity, started writing in Judeo-Spanish as well as in Hebrew. The most famous literary work in Judeo-Spanish, although its first author, Yaacob Khuli, calls it Ladino, is *Me'am Lo'ez* ("From a People of Strange Language"). In this masterpiece Khuli (and his successors after his death) assembled biblical commentaries from all the classical sources together with rabbinical commentaries on the Bible from all periods. Later on, rabbinical literature (but not responsa) was also written in Judeo-Spanish (e.g., *Pele Yo'ets* by Yehuda Eliezer Papo, *Seder Tiqun Se'uda* by David ben Moshe Alcalay, *Shelom Yerushalaim* by Yehuda ben Shlomo Hai Alcalay, *Sefer Meshuvat Nefesh* by Shabetay ben Yaacob Vitas), as well as periodicals (from 1865), drama, and poetry. Novels written in foreign languages were also translated into Judeo-Spanish. Hence, starting in the eighteenth century, there was a great outpouring of literary effort in Judeo-Spanish, although, with the exception of *Me'am Lo'ez*, the works produced were of lesser quality than the earlier Sephardic writings in Hebrew.

Preliminary studies in the oral Sephardic tradition excited researchers because of its resemblance to old Hispanic Iberian traditions. More elaborate studies revealed that much had been innovated as a reflection of the local non-Jewish communities in which the Jews lived. The themes, the contents, the music, etc., were Judeo-Spanish adaptations of local folkloristic works.

While North African descendants of the Spanish exiles produced

well-known writings in Hebrew (e.g., Rabbi Abraham Azulay, interpreter of *HaZohar*; David Hasin, the poet; Haim ben Atar, the interpreter), there is no evidence of creative Judeo-Spanish writings among
the western Sephardim. No Judeo-Spanish journal was published in
North Africa, and Ladino translations for their own needs were acquired from Livorno or from Vienna.

The North African communities, however, staunchly retained the
oral Sephardic tradition from medieval Spain. Hundreds of romances,
ballads, *coplas, endechas* (eulogies), proverbs, idioms, and oral musical
traditions were preserved, to the delight of researchers.

These kinds of folk genres were retained in the east as well, but
with stronger local influence.

The Current Situation

The twentieth century brought further linguistic change to the Sephardic world. The western North African Sephardic communities
replaced the Haketiya with Modern Castilian Spanish, while in the
eastern Mediterranean French replaced Judeo-Spanish as the cultural
language. Furthermore, with the formation of separate nationalities
in these regions and the emigration of many Jews to Israel, the local
national languages in each country were established as the languages
of education. Judeo-Spanish became an informal, mundane family
language, spoken at home and kept only for its sentimental value.
The change from a traditional to a secular orientation, the dispersion of Sephardim from their former communities to other areas,
and the destruction of thousands of Sephardic Jews in the Holocaust
resulted in the deterioration of Judeo-Spanish.

At the beginning of this century, several Judeo-Spanish newpapers
and periodicals in Hebrew Rashi letters were still being published
in the Balkans and in Israel, but their number steadily decreased.
In some instances, in any case, substantial portions were printed in
French or Greek, and as time passed, Hebrew type was gradually
replaced by roman type. Current publications in Judeo-Spanish are
the result of some very staunch believers in everlasting Judeo-Spanish
who refuse to face the fact that Judeo-Spanish is dying. Nevertheless,
Sephardic Jews keep on publishing and creating works, in languages
other than Judeo-Spanish, in every literary genre from science to
belle-lettres (e.g., Elias Canetti).

Hebrew-Aramaic Component and Judeo-Spanish Varieties

The use of Hebrew in Judeo-Spanish brings us to the end of this discussion. I mentioned earlier the Hebrew-Aramaic component in Judeo-Spanish. This component gives a clear indication of the variety of language used by the Sephardic Jews, based on the following principles:

1. The more Jewish and religiously oriented the text, the larger the Hebrew-Aramaic component and the more frequent the Hebrew words in it; the less religious the text and the more secular, the smaller the number of Hebrew-Aramaic words.

2. The lower the register (i.e., low informal style), the greater the amount of the Hebrew-Aramaic component and its fusion; the higher the register (high standard, formal style) the fewer the Hebrew words in it and the more they are retained in their Hebrew form.

As an example, over 12 percent of the words and expressions in *Me'am Lo'ez* are Hebrew-Aramaic. A very similar situation exists in other religious texts, whether originally Judeo-Spanish or translated into Judeo-Spanish.

The Ladino translations include a relatively small number of Hebrew words. The number is even smaller in the western Marrano Ladino type of translations. In these, the translators tried to avoid the use of Hebrew words as much as possible.

Nonreligious works include very few Hebrew-Aramaic words. Formal and serious kinds of publications in Judeo-Spanish include hardly any Hebrew-Aramaic component. Humorous works, including folkloristic ones, contain it quite frequently. Hence, political and national Judeo-Spanish periodicals lack any Hebrew-Aramaic elements (with the exception of Hebrew names, dates, and religious concepts). Contrary to this, humorous journals are loaded with Hebrew-Aramaic words, in many cases misspelled in order to reflect the authentic pronunciation of the speakers (Schwarzwald 1990).

The oral folkloristic creations in Sefarad II include a larger Hebrew-Aramaic component than do the older ones which can be traced to Iberian Hispanic tradition. The comparison of romances and *coplas* with Jewish motives and legendary themes to those of a non-Jewish character easily proves this point. The Jewish-oriented works include not only Hebrew names but also other Hebrew words which are not found in non-Jewish themes (e.g., *Avram avinu* "our Father Abraham",

Terah "Terah", *me'ara* "cave", *malak* "angel", *'elbon* "insult", *misriyim* "Egyptians", *nes* "miracle", *go'el* "redeemer, savior").

The same is true of other folkloristic creations. For example, some Judeo-Spanish proverbs are entirely Hebrew, some include Hebrew-Aramaic elements, some are entirely Spanish, and in some the Hebrew background is obvious. To cite an instance: Spanish *cada uno sabe donde le aprieta el zapato* "Everyone knows where his shoe hurts" is retained in Judeo-Spanish as *kada uno save onde le ergwele el sapato*. The proverb *axare eamal veatorax vaikax korax* "someone who likes to enjoy the fruit of somebody else's efforts" (Heb. *'ahare[y] he'amal vehatorah vayyiqah qorah*) is a Judeo-Spanish Hebrew innovation based on the biblical and midrashic literature. The phrase *el santo bindicho el* "The Holy One, blessed be He" is a Spanish reflection of Hebrew *haqadoS baruↂ hu*. The idiom *hoↂ ma i bina i kvoSk enriva* "wisdom and knowledge [building] and a tower on top of them", i.e., "great stupidity" includes the Hebrew synonyms *hoↂ ma* and *bina*. *Bina*, like *kvoSk*, is also a Turkish word for "building". Hence the pun on Hebrew and Turkish gives an entire different meaning. The same principles apply to other folkloristic genres.

Conclusion

I have reviewed above the various languages and language varieties that the Sephardic Jews used in Spain prior to and after the expulsion. I have demonstrated that various factors determined the choice of the languages for various literary purposes: the prestige of the language, the contents of the work, the communities which wrote and created the specific genres, the communities to which the genres were meant to be delivered, the time, and the political and sociological background. All these factors determined not only the choice of a specific language, but also the selection of the language variety within a specific genre.

The following list summarizes our preliminary question: Who speaks what variety of what language to whom, when, where, and concerning what?

> *Who speaks (writes)*: Jews/Marranos
> *What language*: Hebrew/Romance (Spanish, Portuguese)/Judeo-Spanish/
> Latin/local languages
> *What variety*: Formal/informal-colloquial

To whom: Jews/Marranos/non-Jews
When: Sefarad I: Moslem Spain/Christian Spain
Sefarad II: until mid-18th century/after mid-18th century
Where: Spain; East/West
Concerning what: literary genres; Ladino liturgy; Scientific, rabbinical, nonreligious, poetry, etc.; folkloristic stories, songs, proverbs, etc.

References

Ferguson, Charles A. 1959. "Diglossia." *Word* 15:325–340.
Fishman, Joshua A. 1972. *Sociolinguistics*. Rowley, Mass.: Newbury.
Grünbaum, Max. 1896. *Jüdisch-Spanische Chrestomatie*. Frankfurt am Main: Kauffmann.
Hitchcock, Richard. 1977. *The Kharjas: A Critical Bibliography*. London: Grand & Cutler.
Kayserling, Meyer. 1890. *Biblioteca española-portugueza-judaica Dictionnaire bibliographique*. Strassburg: C.J. Trubner (New York: Ktav, 1971).
Marcus, Simon. 1962. "A-t-il existé en Espagne un dialecte judeo-espagnol?" *Sefarad* 22:129–149.
Molho, M, 1960. *Literatura Sefardita de Oriente*. Madrid and Barcelona: Instituto Arias Montano.
Schwarzwald, Ora (Rodrigue). 1990. "Hamilim ha'ivriyot ba'itonut hasfaradit-yehudit beyavan" [The Hebrew words in the Judeo-Spanish press from Greece]. *Proceedings of the Tenth World Congress of Jewish Studies, Division D*, pp. 205–212. Jerusalem.
Weinreich Max. 1973. *History of the Yiddish Language*. Trans. Shlomo Noble. Chicago: University of Chicago Press.
Weinreich. Uriel. 1968. *Languages in Contact*. The Hague and Paris: Mouton.
Zucker, George. 1988. "Was There Judeo-Spanish in Fifteenth Century Castile?" Paper read at the 3rd World Congress on Sephardic and Oriental Jewry, Jerusalem 1988.

THE DEVELOPMENT OF A NORM IN THE ALJAMIADO GRAPHIC SYSTEM IN MEDIEVAL SPAIN

Laura Minervini

Università degli Studi di Napoli Federico II
Naples, Italy

Jewish Graphic Traditions

Multigraphism

Jews represented a remarkable anomaly in medieval European society, where the majority of the population was illiterate.[1] It is well known that literacy, the practice of writing and reading, was relatively widespread among Jews, due to a system of instruction that provided at least the basic knowledge of the Hebrew language necessary to take part in religious services. This anomaly was clearly perceived by contemporaries, as shown by the comment of an anonymous twelfth-century Christian author: "Judeus enim, quantumque pauper, etiamsi decem haberet filios, omnes ad litteras mitteret, non propter lucrum sicut christiani, sed properer legem Dei intelligendam, et non solum filios sed et filias."[2] The anonymous author correctly underlines the essentially religious character of the Jewish primary school, an institution so linked to the synagogue that in many languages of the European diaspora the house of prayer is simply called "the school" (*schola, escola, scuola, Schul*).[3]

The Hebrew alphabet, therefore, was for medieval European Jews the first, and often the only, alphabet they were trained to use. It was used, above all, to write Hebrew, the "Holy Tongue," but was also the language of scholarship (philosophy, science, theology), of

---

[1] Medieval Europe was, however, a literate civilization in the sense that "the knowledge indispensable to the functioning of medieval society was transmitted in writing"; see Bäuml 1980, p. 237.

[2] "The Jew, in fact, although poor, even if he had ten children, would send all of them to school, not for money, like Christians, but in order to understand the law of God, and not only the male children but also the women"; see Graboïs 1980, pp. 838–839.

[3] See Blondheim 1925, pp. 106–110; Graboïs 1980, p. 940.

administration, and of poetry; and it was used, as well, to write in the vernacular languages as they slowly acquired the status of written languages.[4]

Vernacular texts written in Hebrew characters are called *aljamiados* or "written in *aljamía*." Originally the Muslim conquerors of the Iberian Peninsula applied the term *lisān al-ʿaǧam* or *al-ʿaǧamīya* ("the foreign language") to the Ibero-Romance spoken by the local populace. Scholars later applied the term to Spanish texts written in Arabic characters, and then it was extended to any kind of "contamination" between different languages and writing systems. Jewish communities, throughout their peculiar history, have often experienced plurilinguistic and multigraphic situations; but such situations are not exclusive to Jews, since multigraphism, i.e., the coexistence of different writing systems in the same territorial and social environment, has been and is still a common condition in many civilizations.[5]

The Hebrew Alphabet

The communities of the Jewish diaspora employed the square Hebrew script (*kětav měrubba'*), an alphabet derived from the cursive Aramaic of the Hellenistic period, which gradually supplanted the ancient Hebrew writing, coming to a dominant position around the second century B.C.E. In the Middle Ages a number of cursive scripts developed from the square script. The most successful in the European communities was the rabbinic, or Rashi, script.[6]

The Hebrew alphabet, like the other descendants of the proto-Phoenician script, is a purely consonantal writing system based on the syllabic representation of words. Around the eighth century B.C.E. the scribes adopted the Aramean innovation of supplying vowels with consonantal letters. The letters used in Hebrew orthography are *'alef, he, waw* and *yōd*, called *'immōt ha qěrī'ah*, or *matres lectionis* in Latin terminology. It should be noted that *'alef* gradually lost its phonetic strength, being pronounced only in the syllable-initial position. Its

---

[4] The situation, obviously, was completely different in Islamic countries, where most of the nonpoetic literature written by Jews was in Arabic; see Halkin 1963; Blau 1965, pp. 19–24; Goitein 1974, pp. 131–140.

[5] For the phenomenon of Arabic *aljamía*, see Hegyi 1979, 1985.

[6] Rashi is the acronym of Rabbī Šělomoh Yiṣḥaqī, protagonist of the Hebrew renaissance of the twelfth century. Birnbaum (1971, pp. 189–190), opting for a Hebrew terminology, prefers to call *mashaitic* the rabbinic writing.

use for /a/ never gained complete acceptance in Hebrew, where it appears as a vowel letter mostly when it is etymological.[7]

Hebrew passed through several phases of vowel notation. In the Dead Sea scrolls (2nd cent. B.C.E.–68 C.E.) there appears a full development of the *plene* spelling, but in the rabbinic period a conservative reaction pushed toward a more archaic orthography. The process of revision carried on by the Massoretes of Tiberias was mirrored in "the intricate web of variable spellings that lies over and through the entire Hebrew Bible."[8]

To the Massoretes of Tiberias we owe an elaborate system of diacritical signs indicating accents, pauses, musical intonations, and combinatory variants in the pronunciation of some consonants. Some of these signs, together with the vowel letters, were the main devices used in the Middle Ages for writing vernacular languages in Hebrew characters.

Hebrew Aljamía *in Medieval Spain*

General Trends

In medieval Spain, Romance texts in Hebrew characters may be found from the eleventh to the fifteenth century. During this long span of time, the *aljamiado* graphic system developed in two directions. It gradually, but never completely, standardized its choices, fixing some graphical-phonetical equivalences and reducing the fluctuation among different options; and it progressively acquired independence from Hebrew orthography, lightening the burden of interpretation for readers and defining more precisely the sounds of the language.[9]

The Representation of Vowels

Vocalized texts

Texts are seldom vocalized; i.e., they are not provided with the vocalic signs of the Massoretic tradition. Exceptionally, we find some

---

[7] For these problems, see Cross & Freedman 1952, Bange 1971, integrated with Garbini 1969, Scagliarini 1990; for the modern period, see Weinberg 1985.

[8] Barr 1989, p. 2.

[9] The development of the *aljamía* continued in modern times along these lines; see Hassán 1987.

vocalized texts, like the Castilian instructions for the Pesaḥ Seder dating from the late thirteenth century.[10] These short texts appear in a Hebrew *maḥzōr* (festival prayerbook) vocalized by a *naqdan*. The vocalization of *aljamía* is probably due to the same person, who simply extended its operation from the Hebrew to the Castilian text. Since the quantity of vowels is irrelevant in Castilian, long and short vowels freely alternate.[11] The vocalizer also shows some uncertainties with diphthongs and semivowels.[12]

Unvocalized texts

Unvocalized texts indicate vowels by means of *matres lectionis*, following correlations and conventions largely based on Hebrew orthography: *yōd* (<י> = <y>) is used for /i/ and /e/, *waw* (<ו> = <w>) for /u/ and /o/, *he* (<ה> = <h>) for /a/ in word-final position. *'Alef* (<א> = <'>) represents /a/ at the beginning or in the middle of the word; it is often inserted in diphthongs and hiatus to interrupt the sequence of two (or three) vowel letters. It precedes <y> and <w> in words beginning with /i/, /e/, /o/, and /u/. When <y> and <w> appear in word-initial position, they do not have vocalic value: <y> represents the semiconsonantal sound /j/, <w> the fricative consonant /v/ or /β/.

The use of these vowel letters is rather inconsistent in the archaic texts and developed fully only in the fifteenth century. The progression may be observed by comparing the Romance *ḫarǧat* of Mozarabic *muwaššaḥat* by Jewish authors of the eleventh and twelfth centuries[13] with Castilian and Aragonese documents from the 1400s, like the *Taqqanōt* of Valladolid (1432) or the regulations for the

---

[10] Edited by Sirat & Révah 1961 (in this edition the texts are given in transliterated form, without indication of vocalic quantity). Minervini, 1992, I pp. 153–157, II pp. 10–21.

[11] For example, *segol* alternates with *sere* under <y> in קֵידָארֵ, <qyd'ry>, *quedare* (Sirat & Révah 1961, p. 356; Minervini 1992, I p. 154, II pp. 10–11); *qames* alternates with *patah* under <'> in לָא, לֿא, <l'>, *la* (Sirat & Révah 1961, p. 357; Minervini 1992, I pp. 156–157, II pp. 18–19.

[12] For example, *sere* and *yod* under <y> in קֵייֵר, <qyyr>, *quier* (Sirat & Révah 1961, p. 356; Minervini 1992, I p. 154, II pp. 10–11); the sequence of three *patah*s under <'> and <y> in אַיַה, <'yyh>, *aya* (Sirat & Révah 1961, p. 356; Minervini 1992, I p. 154, II pp. 10–11).

[13] Samuel Stern, the first interpreter of the *ḫarǧat*, attributes the lack of vowel letters to the influence of Arabic orthography, where they represent only long vowels; see Stern 1948, pp. 338–339. Without discarding this possibility, the historical development of *scriptio plena* in Hebrew *aljamía* could provide a satisfying explanation.

collection of the meat tax in Zaragoza (1488).[14] At first, when Romance words were scattered in basically Hebrew texts, the *aljamía* borrowed the Hebrew graphic model; words were written as sequences of consonants with some vowel letters, and the interpretative effort of "filling the gaps" rested on the reader's side. Later on, the habit of writing Romance texts in *aljamía* became widespread and the *aljamiado* system separated from the Hebrew, moving toward a fully alphabetical model. Not surprisingly, the few defective writings found in the latest texts belong to the onomastic field, known to be particularly conservative.

It is relevant to observe that not all the vowel letters enjoy the same status. <'> is much more frequently omitted, because of its incomplete acceptance as *mater lectionis* for /a/ in Hebrew orthography and its nature as a tendentially graphic element, disconnected from pronunciation.[15]

Multiple uses of 'alef
Thanks to its lack of phonetic correspondence, <'> is the most dynamic element in *aljamía*. In the first period, when Romance was written in accordance with Hebrew graphic norms, it may represent any vowel. In the *ḥarǧat*, for instance, we find forms like <בֹּאן> = <b'n> = *ben*, <דֹּאלֿיר> = <d'lyr> = *doler*, <אשביליֹה> = <'šbylyh> = *Isbilia*.[16] Later, <'> becomes more closely associated with /a/, but we still find some examples of its original fluctuation in forms like <אֹן> = <'n> = *en*, <מאשטרֹי> = <m'štry> = *maestre* in a Hebrew-Catalan text from Carcassonne (1273–74),[17] <אֹלֿ> = <el> = *el*, <רֹיטֹינֹאר> = <rytyn'r> = *retener* in an Arabic-Aragonese text from Huesca (1305);[18] <גֹואֹרטֹה> = <gw'rth> = *guerta* in a Hebrew text from Calahorra (1333);[19] <אֹשטֹה> = <'šth> = *esta*, <שֹואֹלֿדֹוש> =

---

[14] The *Taqqanōt* have been edited by Moreno Koch 1987 and Minervini 1992, I pp. 181–255, II pp. 54–133. The meat tax regulation was edited by Lacave (1975) and Minervini 1992, I pp. 316–333, II pp. 230–267.

[15] The weakness of <'> as a *mater lectionis* can also be found in other graphical traditions of *aljamía*, e.g., in Judeo-Italian; see Hijmans-Tromp 1989, p. 56.

[16] See Cantera 1949, pp. 205, 220, 225.

[17] See Díaz Esteban 1978, p. 170.

[18] See Alvar & Bosch 1968, pp. 12–13, and Minervini 1992, I pp. 158–159, II pp. 22–23. The Aragonese text is part of a longer document in Arabic. The form <l> appears twice in the text; the first time it has been vocalized with *segol*, the second it is left unvocalized. The form <d'l> = *del* has *segol* under <d>.

[19] See Cantera 1946, pp. 56–57. The word is part of a toponym, *Pontego de la Guerta*.

<šw'ldwš> = *sueldos* in an Aragonese text from Tarazona (1391).[20]

In some of these forms we can actually see the transition of <'> from generic vocalic symbol to multifunctional element. When <'> is established as the graphic representation of /a/, forms like <'sth> or <gw'rth> (where <'> stands for /e/) become opaque, and are replaced by the new writings <gw'yrth>, <'yšth>; here <'> is used as a graphical support of the vowel, which, according to Hebrew norm, cannot appear by itself and must be (at least graphically) carried by a consonant.[21]

In word-final position there is still, in the fifteenth century, a remarkable alternation between <'> and <h> for the representation of /a/ (probably due to the convergence of the Hebrew and Aramaic graphic traditions); <h> is generally more common; <'> is usually found preceded by <y> representing the semiconsonant /j/ or as a graphic element marking the palatalization of /l/, /n/ (see the discussion of liquids and nasals below).

In the case of final -a, there seems to be no linear progression from the eleventh to the fifteenth century. The *muwaššaḥat* clearly prefer <h>, although we can find some cases of <'>, like <ממא> = <mm'> = *m[a]ma*.[22] In the Castilian instructions for the Seder of Pesah, <h> alternates with <'> in the proportion of 30:20, appearing exactly in the same words, like <דִירָה> = <dirah> = *dira*, <דִרָא> = <dira> = *dirá*.[23] The Hebrew documents from Calahorra also present many examples of <'>, like <מריא> = <mry'> = *M[a]ria*, <אינלישיא> = <'yglyšy'> = *iglesia*, <לא> = <l'> = *la*.[24] The last form appears very often in a much later text, the Aragonese process among the Sarfati heirs (Zaragoza, 1465).[25] Therefore we can conclude that the use of <'> or <h> in word-final position was largely dependent

---

[20] The text has been edited by Laredo, Ben Malka, & Cantera 1944, pp. 41–42, transliterated in Latin characters and Minervini 1992, I pp. 166–167, II pp. 32–33. The form <šw'ldwš> could be interpreted as a remnant of the Aragonese diphthongization /o/ > /wa/, *sualdos*. For many reasons that I discuss in my edition, it seems better to consider <w> a graphic representation of /we/.

[21] It is important to note that, while the rule of <'> in word-initial position is (almost) always at work (we even find forms like <"wn> = *aun*, <"y> = *ai*), the rule of the insertion of <'> between two vocalic signs in diphthongs and hiatus is extremely inconsistent.

[22] See Cantera 1949, p. 223.

[23] See Sirat & Révah 1961, pp. 356–357; Minervini 1992, I pp. 154–155, II pp. 10–13.

[24] See Cantera 1946, pp. 47, 56.

[25] Edited by Lacave 1970/71 and Minervini 1992, I pp. 272–313, II pp. 152–227.

on the writer's personal choice. Once again <'> appears as the less standardized element in the *aljamiado* graphic system.

The Representation of Consonants

Aspirated

The Hebrew letters *he* (<ה> = <h>), *ḥēt* (<ח> = <h>), and *ʿayin* (<ע> = <ʿ>) are usually not employed in *aljamía*. In biblical Hebrew these letters, together with *ʾalef*, graphically represented the aspirated consonants, two laryngeal and two pharyngeal. In postbiblical Hebrew the aspirated system collapsed and the distinctions were partially blurred, some phonemes becoming weaker and tending to disappear.[26]

We have already examined the multiple uses of <'>. The other three letters are only found in loanwords from Arabic; for example, <אלקוהילה> = <'lqwhylh> = *alcohela*, <באדיהאש> = <b''dyhas> = *baδehaš*, <אליהראש> = <'lyhr'š> = *alih[a]ras*, <אלגוהאר> = <'lgwh'r> = *aljohar*, <אלחאני> = <'lh''gy> = *alhaje*, <אלעננבר> = <'l'nbr> = *al'[a]nb[a]r*.[27]

Hebrew-Aramaic loanwords are usually written according to their own orthography.[28] An *aljamiado* text is often disappointing from the lexical viewpoint, since the "whole Hebrew" graphic tradition prevails over the "merged Hebrew."[29]

Stops

For the bilabial, alveolar, and velar stops we find the following correspondences: *peh* (<פ> = <p>) stands for /p/; *bēt* (<ב> = <b>) for /b/; *ṭet* (<ט> = <ṭ>) for /t/; *dalet* (<ד> = <d>) for /d/; *qōf* (<ק> = <q>) for /k/; *gēmel* (<ג> = <g>) for /g/. These conventions are

---

[26] The pronunciation of Hebrew is, of course, very different in the different communities of the diaspora; for a general overview, see Morag 1970.

[27] *Alcohela*, *baδehas*, and *al'[a]nb[a]r* are found in a fifteenth-century manuscript; see Crews 1963, pp. 197, 203, 197; Minervini 1992, I pp. 171–172, 178, II pp. 38–39, 48–49. *Alih[a]ras* appears in the Valladolid *Taqqanot* of 1432; see Moreno Koch 1987, p. 95; Minervini 1992, I p. 253, II pp. 126–127. *Aljohar* in a fifteenth-century will from Miranda de Ebro, see Lacave 1986, pp. 274, 277; Minervini 1992, I p. 269, II pp. 148–149. *Alhaje* ('entrails') in the 1488 meat tax collection from the Zaragoza community; see Lacave 1975, pp. 20, 31; Minervini 1992, I p. 328, II pp. 254–255.

[28] The situation is the same in the Arabic *aljamía*; see Hegyi 1978, pp. 305–306.

[29] For the concepts of whole Hebrew and merged Hebrew, see Weinreich 1980, pp. 351–354. We only refer to the graphic tradition, because nothing can be inferred about its pronunciation from an *aljamiado* text.

well established and do not need much discussion; only the <t> and <q> notations deserve a deeper analysis.

These letters, in fact, represent consonants originally pronounced as emphatics, confused in postbiblical Hebrew with their nonemphatic correlates, /t/, *taw* (<ת> = <t>) and /k/, *kaf* (<כ> = <k>). The *aljamía* prefers <ṭ> and <q> for /t/ and /k/, probably because of the fricative pronunciation of the nonemphatic stops in weak position. The Mozarabic *aljamía* makes the same choice, using *ṭā'* <ط> and *qaf* <ق>.

The most archaic texts are uncertain between <k> and <q>, and between <t> and <ṭ>. The *muwaššaḥat* show many instances of <k>, <t>, like <כנד> = <knd> = *c[a]nd*, <כן> = <kn> = *c[o]n*, <דשת> = <dšt> = *d[e]st[e]*, <בשתא> = <bšt'> = *b[a]ste*.[30] Some isolated cases may still be found in the fourteenth century: <מינישתרדור> = <mynyš-trdwr> = *ministra[a]dor* in the Arabic-Aragonese document from Huesca (1305);[31] <הכלונגיש> = <hklwngyš> = *ha-c[a]longes* in a Hebrew text from Calahorra (1317);[32] <אכסטה> = <'ksth> = *aqu[e]sta* in the Hebrew-Castilian inscription in the Puerta de la Reinosa of Aguilar de Campó (1381).[33]

Moreover, /k/ and /t/ are used in Arabic loanwords like <אסוכר> = <'swkr> = *açuk[a]r* and <אלכיתירה> = <'lkytyrh> = *alkiθira*.[34]

Sometimes <q> appears instead of <g> followed by <n>: <שיקנאדה> = <šyqn'dh> = *sicnada*, <דיקנוש> = <dyqnwš> = *dicnas*, <מאליקנו> = <m'lyqnw> = *malicno*.[35] This orthography is probably a reflection of phonemic neutralization of voice distinction in syllable-final position.[36]

---

[30] See Cantera 1949, pp. 205, 207, 215, 217.

[31] See Alvar & Bosch 1968, p. 13; Minervini 1992, I p. 159, II pp. 21–22.

[32] See Cantera 1946, p. 52.

[33] See Cantera & Millás 1956, p. 330; Minervini 1992, I p. 165, II pp. 30–31.

[34] See Crews 1963, pp. 197, 203; Minervini 1992, I pp. 172–174, 178, II pp. 38–43, 48–49. The unknown writer of this medical manuscript was very careful in the reproduction of Arabic words; therefore I prefer to transcribe <כ> and <ת> as <k> and <θ>.

[35] *Sicnada* appears in a Aragonese text from Tarazona (1391); see Laredo, Ben Malka & Cantera 1944, p. 41; Minervini 1992, I p. 167, II pp. 34–35; *dicnos* and *malicno* in the Zaragozan process (1465), see Lacave 1971, pp. 54, 56; Minervini 1992, I pp. 268, 281, II pp. 162–163, 166–167.

[36] But <qn> could also be an attempt at erudite orthography, the <q> not being pronounced at all, as Enrico de Villena suggests: "E aquellas letras que se ponen e no se pronuncian, según es comun uso, algo añaden al entendimiento e sinificación de la dición donde son puestas; aquí pueden entrar magnífico, sancto, doctrina, signo." See Menéndez Pidal 1942, vol. 2, par. 59.

In the fifteenth century, with increasing precision in the graphic rendering of Spanish sounds, <t> was often used in word-final position. It represented, in accordance with its Hebrew pronunciation in weak position, [θ] < [δ] < /d/, i.e., a voiceless fricative interdental sound, the result of devoicing and fricativization of an original voiced dental stop. We find many examples in the longest texts of the period, the Valladolid *Taqqanōt*, the Sarfatī process, and the meat-tax collection in Zaragoza: <סיבדאת> = <sybd't> = *çibda*θ, <מיאיטאת> = <my'yt't> = *meita*θ, <דיבירשידאת> = <dybyrsyd't> = *dibersida*θ, etc.[37] This graphic convention is also followed in the literary masterpieces of Hebrew *aljamía*, Sem Tob's *Proverbios Morales* and the *Coplas de Yoçef*.[38]

The diacritic: fricatives and affricates

The letters <p>, <b>, <d>, and <g> with a diacritical sign represent the fricative consonants /f/, /v/ (or [β]) and [δ]), and the affricates /tʃ/ and /dʒ/ (or [ʒ]). This diacritic, whose origin is probably the *rafeh* of the Massoretic tradition, may appear in different forms, from a point to an oblique or horizontal short line.[39]

The use of the diacritic is extremely inconsistent. It is often lacking on <p>, while it is more frequent on <g>, where it can have a double (or triple) interpretation. A very interesting form is <אִינְקַן> = <'ĭnĕqan> = *inchan*, in an archaic Castilian text from the end of the thirteenth century.[40] Here /tʃ/ is represented by <q> (the diacritic has been omitted), as in the French *aljamiado* system.[41] A unique form of representation of /tʃ/ is <tš> in words like <לִתשֻׁוּנַס> = <litšūgas> = *lichugas*, <לֵתשֶׁה> = <letšeh> = *leche*, <אַסְתְרָאתשׁוּ> = <istere'tšū> = *istrechu*.[42] These words are found in an Arabic-Castilian glossary written in the Hebrew alphabet by an Arabic-speaking Egyptian Jew who clearly ignored the Spanish tradition of *aljamiado* orthography.

The diacritic on <b> is seldom used. It probably represents [β],

---

[37] For *çibda*θ see Moreno Koch 1987, p. 83; Minervini 1992, I p. 241, II pp. 114–115; Lacave 1971, pp. 51, 80; Minervini 1992, I p. 275, II pp. 154–155; Lacave 1975, pp. 15, 25; Minervini 1992, I p. 319, II pp. 234–235. In the very same texts, the result of -*d* may simply be expressed by <t>, <וירד'את> = <wyrd't> = *werdat*; see Lacave 1971, pp. 52, 81; Minervini 1992, I p. 278, II pp. 256–257.

[38] See González Llubera 1935, p. xxiii; 1947, p. 28.

[39] Here the diacritic is represented by <'> preceding the letter. For the diacritic on <s>, see the next section.

[40] See Sirat & Révah 1961, p. 357; Minervini 1992, I p. 157, II pp. 18–19.

[41] See Bannit 1972, p. 54.

[42] See Sheynin 1982, pp. 232, 233, 234.

fricative allophone of /b/, but most texts ignore this notation and only mark the opposition /b/ - /v/, written \<b\> - \<w\>.[43] We find \<'b\> only in fifteenth-century texts: \<מראב׳\> = \<mr'by\> = *m[a]raße(dis)* in the Valladolid *Taqqanōt* (1432);[44] \<דיב׳ו\> = \<dy'bw\> = *deßo*; \<פרובאדה\> = \<prw'b'dh\> = *proßada*; \<מוב׳ינט\> = \<mw'bynt\> = *moßent* in the Aragonese will of Rabbi Senior ben Meir (1439);[45] \<גואיב׳יש\> = \<'gw'y'byš\> = *jueßes*; \<איב׳אשי\> = \<'y'b'šy\> = *ißase*; \<אישקריב׳יר\> = \<'yšqry'byr\> = *escrißir*, in two commercial letters from the Navarro-Castilian frontier at the end of the fifteenth century.[46] More occurrences of \<'b\> may be found in Sem Tob's *Proverbios Morales* and in the *Coplas de Yoçef*.[47]

The diacritical sign on \<d\> is used quite consistently in the fifteenth-century medical manuscript in words like \<פ׳ריאלדאד\> = \<'pry'ld''d\> = *frialdaδ*, \<אישפומאדה\> = \<'yšpwm''dh\> = *espumaδa*, \<טודׄו\> = \<tw'dw\> = *toδo*;[48] \<d\> represents [δ], fricative allophone of /d/, and becomes widespread only in nineteenth-century printed texts.[49]

Liquids and nasals
For liquid and nasal consonants the *aljamía* established from the beginning the following correspondences: *lamed* (\<ל\> = \<l\>) for /l/, *res* (\<ר\> = \<r\>) for /r/, *nun* (\<נ\> = \<n\>) for /n/, *mem* (\<מ\> = \<m\>) for /m/.

It is worthy of remark that \<n\> is often used instead of \<m\> before a bilabial consonants, in forms like \<שיאינפרי\> = \<šy'ynpry\> = *sienpre*, \<אונבריש\> = \<'wnbryš\> = *onbres*.[50] The uncertainty between \<n\> and \<m\> is clearly represented in the case of \<דיזנמברי\> = \<dyzynmbry\> = *dezenmbre*, in a text from Zaragoza (1484).[51] In contrast, in word-final position, \<m\> is constantly used instead of \<n\>

---

[43] The relation among /b/, /v/, and /ß/ in medieval Spanish is the object of different interpretations. For an in-depth analysis of the problem, see D. Alonso 1962, pp. 155–209.

[44] See Moreno Koch 1987, p. 23; Minervini 1992, I p. 188, II pp. 58–59 and passim.

[45] See Minervini 1992, I pp. 259, 283, II pp. 136–137, 140–141.

[46] See Cantera 1971, pp. 314, 315, 316; Minervini 1992, I pp. 335, 337, II pp. 268–269, 272–275.

[47] See González Llubera 1935, p. xxii; 1947, p. 28.

[48] See Crews 1963, pp. 197, 200; Minervini 1992, I pp. 171, 176, II pp. 38–39, 44–45. There are two isolated cases of \<'d\> in Sem Tob's *Proverbios Morales*, difficult to explain; see González Llubera 1947, p. 27.

[49] See Bunis 1974, p. 27.

[50] See Lacave 1971, pp. 51, 80 (MS: fol. 2*v*, line 15), 52, 82 (MS: fol. 3*r*, line 17).

[51] See Minervini 1992, I p. 315, II pp. 228–229.

in the word <שינום> = <sygwm> = *segum*.[52] These graphic fluctuations are explained from the phonetic viewpoint by the processes of consonantal assimilation and neutralization in word-final and syllable-final position, determining an indistinct perception of the point and manner of articulation of the nasal. Similar spellings may be found both in Latin and in the Hebrew graphic tradition.[53]

In Hebrew orthography consonantal doubling is expressed by a point called *dageš ḥazaq*. The Spanish *aljamiado* system never uses this graphic device, probably because /r/, the only Spanish consonant subject to doubling, is transcribed with the letter *rēš*, which in Hebrew may not carry *dageš ḥazaq*. Nor is the spelling <rr> used in *aljamía*, so that /r/ is always represented as simple.[54]

For the representation of alveo-palatal nasal and lateral sounds /ɲ/ and /ʎ/, the *aljamía* chooses digraphic or trigraphic solutions: <ני>, <ניי> = <ny>, <nyy> = ñ, <לי>, <ליי> = <ly>, <lyy> = *ll* (but in the Catalan and Navarro-Aragonese graphic tradition *ny* and *ly*). These kinds of "composed spellings" are unknown to Hebrew orthography and were probably influenced by the writing system of the Latin alphabet.[55]

In Mozarabic *muwaššaḥat* the choice was already established: <פליול> = <plywl> = *f[i]lyal[u]*, <אשביליה> = <'šbylyh> = *Isbilya*.[56] But in later texts we still find some uncertainties: <אקאלה> = <'q'lh> = *aquel[l]a*, <אלי> = <'ly> = *al[l]i*, <מישילוש> = <myšylwš> = *mesil[l]as* in the Arabic-Aragonese text from Huesca (1305); <אקילוש> = <'qylwš> = *aquel[l]as* in a text from Tarazona (1391).[57] In the fifteenth-century there were also some cases of <ll>, clearly influenced by the

---

[52] See, among others, Moreno Koch 1987, p. 53; Minervini 1992, I p. 214, II pp. 86–87. *Segum* occurs also in *Proverbios Morales* and *Coplas de Yoçef*. See González Llubera 1935, p. xxiii; 1947, p. 31.

[53] For the Hebrew graphic representation of the nasal + bilabial sequence in Greek and Latin loanwords, see Segal 1986, p. 33; for the Spanish situation, see Menéndez Pidal 1942, II p. 56.

[54] The Judeo-Italian *aljamiado* system was apparently less influenced by Hebrew orthography, since /r/ is represented both by *rēš* with *dageš ḥazaq* and by *rēš* written twice. See Cuomo 1977, pp. 192, 196–208.

[55] See Hegyi 1981, p. 101; Hassán 1987, p. 129. Mozarabic *aljamía* employs similar spellings, especially for /ʎ/ < Lat. -lj-, -k'l-, -t'l-. See Galmés de Fuentes 1983, pp. 62–67.

[56] See Cantera 1949, pp. 216, 225; I use here Cantera's spelling *ly* instead of *ll*.

[57] For *aquel[l]a*, *al[l]i*, *mesil[l]os*, see Alvar & Bosch 1968, pp. 12–14; Minervini 1992, I p. 159, II pp. 22–23; for *aquel[l]os*, see Laredo, Ben Malka, & Cantera 1944, p. 42; Minervini 1992, I p. 167, II pp. 32–33.

Castilian graphic tradition: <נוללה> = <nwllh> = *nulla*, <נוללאמינט>
= <nwll'mynt> = *nullament*, <אפיללאסיאון> = <'pyll'sy'wn> = *apellaçion*.[58]

Sibilants

In consequence of the contact with Romance languages, the graphic representation of the rich system of Hebrew sibilants has been reanalyzed, with different results in different linguistic areas.[59] The complexity of the sibilant system, the most problematic area of Old Spanish phonology, suggests an extremely cautious attitude in the interpretation of data.

Accepting the traditional description of the system of Old Spanish sibilants, we can posit the following equivalences: *šīn* (<ש> = <š>) represents the voiceless fricative /s/ (<s->, <-ss->, and <-s> in Alphonsine orthography), and its voiced counterpart /z/ (<-s-> in Alphonsine orthography, since phonemic only in intervocalic position); *samek* (<ס> = <s>) represents the voiceless africate /ts/ (<ç> or <c> in Alphonsine orthography); *zayin* (<ז> = <z>) its voiced counterpart /dz/ (<z> in Alphonsine orthography); for the palatal fricative /ʃ/ (<x> in Alphonsine orthography) is used *šīn* with a (frequently omitted) diacritical sign.

Scholars have often wondered why Spanish <ç> and <z>, usually associated with an affricate pronunciation in the Middle Ages, were represented with graphemes pronounced as fricatives in Arabic and in Hebrew: Ar. *sīn* <س> and *zay* <ز>, Heb. *samek* <ס> and *zayin* <ז>. These correlations have sometimes been used to support the hypothesis that affricate sibilants developed into fricatives earlier than generally thought, and were therefore perceived and transcribed as fricatives.

For the Arabic sibilants, the problems has been intensively analyzed by A. Alonso, who focused on the mechanism of selection regulating the system of equivalences.[60] He showed how classificatory

---

[58] *Nulla* and *nullament* are in the Sarfati process (Zaragoza, 1465); see Lacave 1971, pp. 75, 98; 77, 78, 100; Minervini 1992, I pp. 303, 305, 307, 311, II pp. 202–207, 210–211, 218–219; *appellaçion* in the meat tax collection (Zaragoza, 1488); see Lacave 1975, pp. 20, 31; Minervini 1992, I p. 327, II pp. 252–253.

[59] For example, the Talmūd transcribes Latin /s/ with *samek*, but this letter is lacking in French *aljamía* and represents /s/ in the Italian; *šīn* stands for /ʃ/ in Italian *aljamía*, for /s/ in the French; *šadē* is /ts/ and /tʃ/ in Italian *aljamía*, /ts/ in the French, and so on.

[60] See Alonso 1946, with the important integrations of Torreblanca 1982.

processes act to decompose each sound in a number of fundamental features and then choose only some of them that are perceived as particularly meaningful.

The situation of Hebrew *aljamía* is comparable to that of the Mozarabic. This is probably due to the affinity between the Arabic and Hebrew alphabets and to cultural contacts between the two groups. The apical-alveolar feature of Spanish /s/ and /z/ is perceived as relevant and expressed through the transcription with *šīn*, ignoring the voice distinction. The affricate articulation of /ts/ and /dz/ wield to their sibilant quality, emphasized by the choice of *samek* and *zayin*.

The use of <s> for /s/ and /z/ seems to have been established from the beginning. There are only a few exceptions in the medieval documents, like the already quoted form <אכסטה> = <'ksth> = *aqu[e]sta* in the Hebrew-Castilian inscription in the Puerta de la Reinosa of Aguilar de Campó (1381),[61] and the uncommon spellings of the Arabic-Castilian glossary (see above, the section on fricatives and affricates).

The situation is different for *samek* and *zayin*, occasionally replaced with *ṣadē* (<צ> = <ṣ>). This is further evidence of their affricate pronunciation, since <ṣ> is an originally emphatic consonant, often reinterpreted as an affricate among Jews of the Western diaspora.[62]

This letter often appears in toponyms and anthroponyms like <ברצלונה> = <brṣlwnh> = *B[a]rç[e]lona*, <פרץ> = <prṣ> = *P[e]r[e]z*, <מרטיניץ> = <mrtynyṣ> = *M[a]rtinez*, <לופיץ> = <lwpyṣ> = *Lopez*.[63] We can also find several occurrences in fourteenth- and fifteenth-century texts: <ריציונירו> = <rṣywnyrw> = *r[a]çionero* in Hebrew texts from Calahorra (1333);[64] <מאריץ> = <m'rṣ> = *marz* in a Hebrew calendar for the beginning of 1400;[65] <הצאלמידינה> = <hṣ'lmydynh> = *ha-çalmedina* in a Hebrew-Aragonese document from Teruel;[66] <ריגאליץ> = <ryg'lyṣ> = *regaliz* in the Castilian medical manuscript;[67] <נושטיצייא> = <'gwstyṣyy'> = *justiçya*, <פירטיניצין> = <pyrtynyṣyn>

---

[61] See Cantera & Millás 1956, p. 330; Minervini 1992, I p. 165, II pp. 30–31.
[62] See Cardona 1968. Garbell, on the other hand, thinks that in the medieval Spanish pronunciation of hebrew, <s> merged with <ṣ>; see Garbell 1954, p. 670.
[63] For *B[a]rç[e]lona*, see Baer 1929, p. 92 et passim; for the anthroponyms, see Baer 1929, pp. 960–961.
[64] See Cantera 1946, p. 56.
[65] See Pflaum 1961, p. lxv.
[66] Cf. Díaz Esteban 1975, pp. 99, 103; Minervini 1992, I p. 169, II pp. 36–37.
[67] See Crews 1963, pp. 199, 203; Minervini 1992, I pp. 174, 177–178, II pp. 42–43, 46–49.

= *perteneçen*, <לישינצ׳אה> = <lyṣynṣy'h> = *lisençia*, <נראצ׳אה> = <gr'ṣy'h>
= *graçia*, <טריצ׳אה> = <tryṣy'h> = *treçia* in the Valladolid *Taqqanōt*;[68]
<אופיצ׳אל> = <'w'pṣy'l> = *ofiçial* in a Zaragozan public docu-
ment (1484);[69] <ראיץ> = <r'yṣ> = *raiz* in the nineteenth verse of
Sem Tob's *Proverbios Morales*.[70] Moreover, *ṣadē* often occurs, instead
of *samek*, in Navarran *aljamiados* texts.[71]

Conclusions

Writing in *aljamía* means, from the perspective of the dominant culture, writing in a foreign graphic system. Whether the result of a
deliberate choice or of a necessary adaptation, the act of using
"another" alphabet is not a neutral element in the elaboration of
written texts.[72] It represents and emphasizes a formal extraneousness
to the models diffused by the main centers of standardization: the
royal courts and chancelleries, notarial offices, and monastic centers.
In these places there took place an intensive activity of writing and
copying that tended to impose a graphic and linguistic norm. Jews
were not (or were less) exposed to such leveling influences. They did
not have anything comparable to the network of cultural and political institutions that acted so powerfully in the Christian environment.
Their literary tradition was essentially in Hebrew, Romance varieties
representing mostly a *medium* of daily communication.[73]

That is why we prefer to speak about "trends" toward standardization and autonomization of the *aljamiado* graphic system. The
Hebrew *aljamía* never acquired an effective normative force, and its
degree of independence from Hebrew orthography remained extremely
variable. It may be considered the graphical expression of a different
linguistic ideal, an important contribution to the development of
Jewish cultural identity in medieval Spain.

---

[68] Cf. Moreno Koch 1987, pp. 51, 68, 71, 76, 95; Minervini 1992, I pp. 212,
228–229, 235, 252, II pp. 82–83, 100–103, 108–109, 126–127.
[69] See Minervini 1992, I p. 315, II pp. 228–229.
[70] See González Llubera 1935, p. xx; 1947, p. 65.
[71] See Assis, Magdalena Nom De Deu, and Lleal, 1992, p. 22.
[72] See Hegyi 1985, p. 652.
[73] See especially Malkiel 1945, p. 82; 1947, pp. 286–287; 1950, pp. 338–339;
1983, p. 8. Literary texts in *aljamía* are too rare to established a written *koiné*, as
it was hypothesized with Sem Tob's *Proverbios Morales*; see Alarcos Llorach 1951,
p. 255.

References

Alarcos Llorach, E. 1951. "La lengua de los *Proverbios Morales* de Don Sem Tob." *Revista de Filología Española* 35:249–309.

Alonso, A. 1946. "Las correspondencias arábigo-españolas." *Revista de Filologia Hispánica* 8:12–76.

Alonso, D. 1962. "La fragmentación peninsular." In *Encicpoledia Linguística Hispánica*, Suplemento. Madrid.

Alvar, M., and Bosch, J. 1968. "Interpretación de un texto oscense en aljamía hebrea." In *Miscélanea ofrecida a J.M. Lacarra*, pp. 11–22. Zaragoza.

Assis, Y.T., Magdalena Nom De Deu, J.R., and Lleal, P. 1992. Aljamíd romance en los documentos hebraiconavarros (siglo XIV, Barcelona).

Baer, Y. 1929. *Geschichte der Juden im Christlichen Spanien*. Erster Teil: *Urkunden und Regesten*, I, *Aragonien und Navarra*. Berlin.

Bäuml, F.H. 1980. "Varieties and Consequences of Medieval Literacy and Illiteracy." *Speculum* 55:237–265.

Bange, L.A. 1971. *A Study of the Use of Vowel-Letters in Alphabetic Consonantal Writing*. Munich.

Bannit, M. 1972. *Le Glossaire de Bâle*. Introduction. Jerusalem.

Barr, J. 1989. *The Variable Spellings of the Hebrew Bible*. Oxford.

Birnbaum, S.A. 1971. *The Hebrew Scripts*. Leiden.

Blau, J. 1965. *The Emergence and Linguistic Background of Judeo-Arabic: A Study on the Origins of Middle Arabic*. Oxford.

Blondheim, D.S. 1925. *Les parlers judéo-romanes et la Vetus Latina*. Paris.

Bunis, D.M. 1974. "The Historical Development of Judezmo Orthography: A Brief Sketch." *Working Papers in Yiddish and East European Jewish Studies*, vol. 2. New York.

Cantera, F. 1946. "Documentos de compraventa hebraicos de la Catedral de Calahorra." *Sefarad* 6:37–61.

―――. 1949. "Versos españoles en las *muwassahas* hispano-hebreas." *Sefarad* 9:197–234.

―――. 1971. "Cuatro cartas de Laguardia en judeo-español." *Sefarad* 31:313–317.

―――. and Millás-Vallicrosa, J.M. 1956. *Las inscripciónes Hebraicas de España*. Madrid.

Cardona, G.R. 1968. "Per la storia fonologica del *sade* semitico." *Annali dell'Istituto Orientale di Napoli* 28:1–14.

Crews, C. 1963. "A Judeo-Spanish Medical MS (ca. 1400–1450)." *Vox Romanica* 22:192–218.

Cross, F.M., and Freedman, D.N. 1952. *Early Hebrew Orthography: A Study of the Epigraphic Evidence*. New Haven.

Cuomo, L. 1977. "Antichissime glosse salentine nel codice ebraico di Parma, De Rossi, 138." *Medioevo Romanzo* 4:185–271.

Díaz Esteban, F. 1975. "Un documento hebreo inédito de Teruel." *Anuario di Filología* 1:95–108.

―――. 1978. "Un carta hebrea de Carcasona." *Anuario de Filología* 4:165–184.

Galmés de Fuentes, A. 1983. *Dialectología Mozárabe*. Madrid.

Garbell, I. 1954. "The Pronunciation of Hebrew in Medieval Spain." In *Homenaje a Millás-Vallicrosa*, vol. 1, pp. 647–669. Barcelona.

Garbini, G. 1969. "Studi aramaici 2. Le *matres lectionis* e il vocalismo dell'aramaico antico." *Annali dell'Istituto Orientale di Napoli* 19:8–15.

Goitein, S.D. 1974. *Jews and Arabs: Their Contacts Through the Ages*. New York.

González Llubera, I. 1935. *Coplas de Yoçef*. Cambridge.

―――. 1947. *Proverbios Morales de Santob de Carrión*. Cambridge.

Graboïs, A. 1980. "Ecoles et structures sociales communautés juives dans l'Occident aux IXe–XIIe siècles." In *XXVI Settimana di Studio del Centro Italiano di Studi sull'Alto Medioevo. Gli Ebrei nell'Alto Medioevo*, pp. 937–962. Spoleto.

Halkin, A.S. "The Medieval Jewish Attitude Toward Hebrew." In *Biblical and Other Studies*, ed. A. Altman, pp. 233–248. Cambridge, Mass.

Hassán, I. 1987. "Sistemas gráficos del español sefardí." In *Actas del I Congreso Internacional de Historia de la Lengua Española*, eds. M. Ariza, A. Salvador, and A. Viudas, pp. 127–137. Cáceres.

Hegyi, O. 1978. "Observaciones sobre el léxico arabe en los textos aljamiados." *Al Andalus* 43:303–321.

———. 1979. "Minority and Restricted Uses of the Arabic Alphabet: The Aljamiado Literature." *Journal of the American Oriental Society* 99/2:262–269.

———. 1985. "Una variante islámica del español: la literatura aljamiada." In *Homenaje a Alvaro Galmés de Fuentes*, vol. 1, pp. 647–655. Oviedo-Madrid.

Hijmans-Tromp, I. 1989. *Mosé da Rieti: Filosofia naturale e fatti di Dio. Testo inedito del sec. XV*. Leiden.

Lacave, J.L. 1970/71. "Pleito judío por una herencia en aragoneés y carácteres hebreos." *Sefarad* 30:325–337, 31:49–101.

———. 1975. "La carnicería de la Aljama zaragozana a fines del siglo XV." *Sefarad* 35:3–35.

———. 1986. "Un testamento hebraico fragmentario de Miranda de Ebro." *Sefarad* 46:271–279.

Laredo, A.I., Ben Malka, M.H., and Cantera, F. 1944. "Miscélanea de documentos fragmentarios hebraicos." *Sefarad* 4:39–44.

Malkiel, Y. 1945. "The Development of the Latin suffixes *-antia* and *-entia* in the Romance Languages, with Special Regard to Ibero-Romance." *University of California Publications in Linguistics* 1/4:41–187.

———. 1947. "A Latin-Hebrew Blend: Hispanic *Desmazalado*." *Hispanic Review* 15:272–301.

——— 1950. "The Jewish Heritage of Spain (On the Occasion of Américo Castro's *España en su historia*)." *Hispanic Review* 18:328–340.

———. 1983. "Las peripecias luso-españolas de la voz synagoga." *Nueva Revista de Filología Hispánica* 32:1–40.

Menéndez Pidal, R. 1942. *Cantar de Mío Cid*. Madrid.

Minervini, L. 1992. *Testi giudeospagnoli medievali (Castiglia e Aragona)*. 2 vols. Naples.

Morag, S. 1970. "Pronunciation of Hebrew." *Encyclopaedia Judaica*, vol. 13, cols. 1120–1145.

Moreno Koch, J. 1978. *De iure hispano-hebraico: Las Taqqanot de Valladolid de 1432. Un estatuto comunal renovador*. Salamanca.

Pflaum, H. 1961. "Un glosario medico-botanico en judeo-español medieval." *Tesoro de los Judíos Sefardíes* 3, pp. lxi–lxxi.

Scagliarini, F. 1990. "Precisazioni sull'uso della *matres lectionis* nelle iscrizioni ebraiche antiche." *Henoch* 12:131–146.

Segal, M.H. 1986. *A Grammar of Mishnaic Hebrew*. Oxford.

Sheynin, H.V. 1982. "An Unknown Jewish Arabic-Castilian Glossary." *Sefarad* 42:223–241.

Sirat, C., and Révah, I.S. 1961. "Un mahzor espagnol du XIIIᵉ siècle avec des prescription rituelles en castillan." *Revue des études juives* 120:353–359.

Stern, S. 1948. "Les vers finaux dans les *Muwassah*s hispano-hébraïques. Une contribution à l'histoire du *Muwassah* et à l'étude du vieux dialect espagnole mozarabe." *Al Andalus* 13:299–346.

Torreblanca, M. 1982. "La *s* hispanolatina: el testimonio árabe." *Romance Philology* 35:447–463.

Weinberg, W. 1985. *The History of Hebrew Plene Spelling*. Cincinnati.

Weinreich, M. 1980. *History of the Yiddish Language*. New York.

CODE-SWITCHING IN
CONTEMPORARY JUDEO-SPANISH

TRACY K. HARRIS

Bradley University
Peoria, Illinois

Even though all aspects of a language are subject to change, Sala (1961) reminds us that it is in the lexicon where the process of the decline of a language is seen with greater clarity. Disintegration becomes apparent as the number of words diminishes, thus restricting the possibilities of communication. This generally results in frequent borrowings from one (or more) of the in-contact languages which eventually replace the original language. Code-switching, which often occurs in the speech of bilinguals, is generally defined as the alternation of two languages within a single discourse, sentence, or constituent (Poplack 1982, p. 231). However, in the case of Judeo-Spanish this alternation can also occur between more than two languages. Code-switching is one of the most salient characteristics of current spoken Judeo-Spanish. Data on the contemporary language were obtained from studies conducted by the author during the summers of 1978 and 1985 in which native Judeo-Spanish speakers from New York, Israel, and Los Angeles were interviewed. The interview format included samples of free conversation in Judeo-Spanish to determine the extent of code-switching present in the informants' speech. Before presenting the results of the studies I will give a brief background of the informants.

The Informants

A total of ninety-one native Judeo-Spanish speakers or informants were interviewed: twenty-eight from New York, twenty-eight from Israel, and thirty-five from Los Angeles. Of the ninety-one informants, fifty-five were men and thirty-six were women. The majority of the informants—seventy-six, or 84 percent of the total number—were above the age of fifty, and fifty-one (57 percent) were age sixty or above. Only fifteen informants were below the age of fifty, with three being under forty years of age.

The informants' regions of origin were as follows: twenty-three from different areas of Turkey, seventeen from Greece, fourteen from Rhodes, nine from Bulgaria, six from Yugoslavia, seven from Jerusalem, one from Tunisia, and fourteen were born in the United States or Europe with parents from one or more of the above regions. All but seven informants finished high school, and nineteen attended French schools of the Alliance Israélite Universelle in the Balkans. Only 30 percent of the informants were college graduates, and eight had received advanced degrees.

The professions of the informants were quite varied and included (either at the time of the study or before retirement) eleven garment industry workers, nine writers or journalists, five teachers, three college professors, two physicians, two flower shop managers, two professional singers, two secretaries, two accountants, two importer-exporters, seven workers at the Jewish Agency (Sochnut) in Tel Aviv, sixteen housewives, and one of each of the following: grocer, cab driver, telephone operator, graphic artist, cafe owner, sales clerk, shoe shop manager, sheet metal worker, printing shop owner, manager of a brokerage house, dentist, architect, insurance agent, court interpreter, rabbi, cantor, gabbai, radio executive, engineer, historian, millinery designer, escrow officer, folklorist, photo-journalist, office administrator, executive director of a synagogue, and waiter.

The Free Conversation Samples

The informants were asked to speak from three to fifteen minutes on one of the following topics: their childhood, when they came to the United States or Israel (Palestine), their early days in New York, Israel, or Los Angeles, how they met their spouses, their families, or their jobs. If a husband and wife or various family members were being interviewed together, I usually asked them to hold a conversation among themselves.

The speech samples generally fell into the five- or ten-minute range, but many of the informants had difficulty speaking for as long as three minutes. They either did not have the linguistic skills to enable them to speak for a longer period or they said that it was difficult to talk when no other Judeo-Spanish speakers were present to have a conversation. Often I would ask the informants questions in Judeo-Spanish if they were having trouble thinking of something to say.

Thirteen of the informants (15 percent of the total) did not feel competent enough in the language to attempt speaking at all, so they gave no conversation samples.

Types of Code-Switching

The analysis of the conversation samples reveals a great amount of code-switching in the speech of the informants. The lexical interference comes mainly from English and Modern Spanish in the Judeo-Spanish of the New York and Los Angeles informants and from Hebrew, French, and even some Modern Spanish in the speech of the Israeli informants.[1] In the majority of cases a foreign word or phrase is inserted into a Judeo-Spanish sentence and pronounced as it is in the foreign language. Three examples are:

> English: Estavan *delicious*. (They were delicious.)
> French: Mi padre es *banquier*. (My father is a banker.)
> Hebrew: Viaze kon *aviron*. (I traveled by plane.) Hebrew [אווירון]

In the above sentences the English word *delicious*, the French word *banquier*, and the Hebrew word *aviron* were pronounced as they are in English, French, and Hebrew, respectively.

Another type of borrowing occurs when a foreign word is inserted into the language but is given a Judeo-Spanish ending, as in:

> los kayes yenos de pushcart*es* (the streets full of pushcarts)
> Tiene muchas part*es* de Off-Broadway. (He has many Off-Broadway parts.)
> Nunka regret*o* ser sefardi. (I never regret being a Sephardi.)
> Vo return*ar* aki. (I am going to return here.)

In the preceding examples, the Spanish *-es* plural ending was added to the English nouns *pushcart* and *part*. The first-person Spanish present tense *-o* verb ending was added to the English *regret* (or the

---

[1] The influence of Modern Spanish in the language of the Israeli informants was the result of their having lived or extensively traveled in Spanish-speaking countries or of having studied the language.

French verb *regretter* depending on its origin), and the Spanish *-ar* infinitive ending was added to the English word *return* (which is pronounced as in English).

In other cases the English *-s* noun ending is added to Judeo-Spanish or French words, as in:

> Los buro*s* eran aya. (The offices were there.)

Here a variation of the French noun *bureau* is given the English plural ending and pronunciation. Similarly, Spanish words like *komunidad* and *sosiedad* are given the English *-s* ending, as in *komunidads* and *sosiedads* instead of the correct Judeo-Spanish *-es* ending.

The following are examples of code-switching that occurred in the speech of my New York, Israeli, and Los Angeles informants taken from their conversation samples. I have presented examples of interference from English, Modern Spanish, Hebrew, and French and have organized them into various types of switching. I have divided the examples into the two general categories of single words and short phrases versus larger segments, and am emphasizing the lexical (rather than the syntactic) aspects of the language. After each example I have put the translation in parentheses. While reading the examples, notice that most of the switched segments deal with everyday common vocabulary which have Judeo-Spanish counterparts.[2]

Code-Switching with Individual Words and Short Phrases

Dates, Numbers, and Addresses

1. Mi espozo vino aki at *sixteen* en *nineteen sixteen*. (My husband came here at age sixteen in 1916.)
2. Vinimos aki en *October*. Al *December* ventiuno desidimos el kazamiento en la sinagoga en un *hall* en *Bedford Avenue, five ninety-seven Bedford Avenue, Brooklyn, New York*. (We came here in October. On December 21 we decided to get married in the synagogue in a hall on Bedford Avenue, 597 Bedford Avenue, Brooklyn, New York.)

---

[2] I have not included code-switching examples of concepts or objects that did not exist in the same form in the Balkans. Examples are words denoting forms of education like *high school, junior high school, college*, or American concepts or inventions such as *downtown, freeway, ice cream, pie, sandwiches, old age home*), etc.

3. Arrivi en Israel en anyo *mil dix-neuf cent quarante huit.* [French numbers] (I arrived in Israel in the year 1948.)
4. One informant in discussing his desire to sit with his wife and daughters in the synagogue said: Yo me gusta sentar kon mi famiya—no es *fourteen ninety-two.* (I like to sit with my family—it's not 1492.)

Names of Professions

5. El salio *accountant*, my grande *accountant.* (He became an accountant, a very big accountant.)
6 La mande a Paris a estudiar i ya es *teacher.* (I sent her to Paris to study and now she is a teacher.)
7. El yamo a su *lawyer.* (He called his lawyer.)
8. Mi nuera nasio en Mexico y se kazaron por un *rabbi.* (My daughter-in-law was born in Mexico and they were married by a rabbi.)

Names of Places

9. Fuimos para ver este *farm.* (We went to see this farm.)
10. Estuvimos afuera en la *garden.* (We were outside in the garden.)
11. El *toilet* estava en el *hall.* (The toilet was in the hall.)
12. Mi padre estava en el *barber shop* todo el dia. (My father was in the barber shop all day.)
13. Era mi asosiado aki en este *buro* [French *bureau*] (He was my colleague here in this office.)
14. Estuve en *bet holim* [Hebrew בית חולים], serka de Hadera. (I was in hospital near Hadera.)
15. ... asperando kon "*next*" para entrar al *bathroom.* (... waiting to hear "next" in order to enter the bathroom.)
16. Vamos al *beach.* (Let's go to the beach.)

Names of Countries, Nationalities, and Languages

17. Fuimos a *South America.* (We went to South America.)
18. Ya vienen de vez en kuando *the South Americans.* (The South Americans come from time to time.)
19. Todos avlan Ladino o *Arabic.* (Everyone speaks Ladino or Arabic.)
20. Era un eskrivano *français* [French word and pronunciation] *ke era turkofil.* (He was a French writer who was a Turcophile.)
21. Tras esto savia avlar *l'hebreu* [French word]. (After this he knew how to speak Hebrew.)

22. Yo parti de *Salonik* [French pronunciation]. (I left Salonika.) The term *Salonik* (French: *Salonique*) instead of the Judeo-Spanish pronunciation *Salonika* was used by all the Saloniklis (informants from Salonika), thus showing the strong influencs of their French educations.

23. Arrivi kon la vapor de *la Bulgarie* [French pronunciation]. (I arrived by boat from Bulgaria.)

24. Es komo *la Liberty Statue in New York* o *la Tour Eiffel a Paris* [French]. (It's like the Statue of Liberty in New York or the Eiffel Tower in Paris.)

25. Avlamos en *ivrit* [Hebrew עברית]. (We spoke in Hebrew.)

Descriptive Adjectives

26. Es *different*. (It's different.)
27. Era *terrible, disgusting*. (It was terrible, disgusting.)
28. Estavan *delicious*. (They were delicious.)
29. Mi mama fue mas *evoluée* [French] porke los Ashkenazis eran mas *evolues* ke los sefardies. (My mother was more advanced/progressive because the Ashkenazim were more advanced than the Sephardim.)
30. . . . i aya vi las *beautiful* kozas de Amerika. (. . . and there I saw the beautiful things of America.)
31. Bushkamos una koza *suitable*. (We looked for something suitable.)

Common Nouns or Expressions

32. Amanya *the grandson* va venir. (Tomorrow the grandson is coming.)
33. Estuvimos kon la *mishpaha*. [Hebrew משפחה]. (We were with the family.)
34. Tengo muntchos buenos *memories*. (I have many good memories.)
35. No tenemos *paper*. (We don't have paper.)
36. *Sand* no es bueno para ti. (Sand is not good for you.)
37. Tuvimos un *party*. (We had a party.)
38. *The middle one* [referring to a grandson] estuvo en un *play* la otra semana. (The middle one was in a play the other week.)
39. Muzotros dizimos "*Good-bye*" a l'escalera. (We said "good-bye" on the stairs.)
40. La madre de mi papa era komadre i ayudaba kon *baby* kuando una de las mujeres de *harem* tenia un *baby* . . . ke si tenia un *problem* eya le yamo al doktor. (My father's mother was a midwife and she used to help with baby when one of the women of the

harem had a baby . . . that if she had a problem, she called the
doctor.)

41. Los ke vienen de Atena avlan otro Ladino i otro grego ke la djente
ke viene de Yolos. Es komo se dize *"more high class"*. (Those that
come from Athens speak another Ladino and another Greek than
the people from Volos. It is, how do you say, "more high class.")

42. Kuando fuimos a la kaza de eya avia un monton de personas
para dizer *"Congratulations"*. (When we went to her house there
were a lot of people to say "Congratulations.")

43. Kero something *to* komer. (I want something to eat.)

In the preceding examples we see very common words such as *grandson, family, baby, problem, memories, paper, good-bye, congratulations,* and
something, all of which have perfectly good counterparts in Judeo-
Spanish.

Conjunctions, Adverbs and Prepositions

44. Mi papa lavorava en la duana *and* mi mama ayudava al Hadassah
i a los povres. (My father worked in the customs office and my
mother helped at Hadassah and [she helped] the poor people.)

45. Mi papu era haham en la Turkia *but* aya no avia tanto a komer.
(My grandfather was a rabbi in Turkey but there was not so much
to eat there.)

46. Kero merkar livros *aval* [Hebrew אבל] no estan mas baratos. (I
want to buy books but they are not cheaper.)

47. Parti de Rhodesia *because* el situasion [notice gender] no estava
muy buena aya. (I left Rhodesia because the situation was not
very good there.)

48. *So*, vine aki. (So I came here.)

49. Avlan espanyol, *not* ladino. (They speak Spanish, not Ladino.)

50. Este kortijo fue destruido *during* el tiempo de la gerra. (This "court-
yard/neighborhood" was destroyed during the time of the war.)

Idiomatic Expressions, Tags, or Fillers[3]

51. *Aora* [Mod. Spanish], *you know*, no estan aki. (Now, you know, they
are not here.)

52. Akavidate, *believe me*, es verdad. (I warn you, believe me, it's true.)

---

[3] These terms were used by Poplack (1982, p. 244).

53. No savia grego *beklal* [Hebrew בבלל]. (He didn't know Greek at all.)
54. Es *hard to take*. (It's hard to take.)

Judeo-Spanish and Another Language Used to Express the Same Word in the Same Sentence

Silva-Corvalán (1983, p. 82) refers to this kind of shifting as an effort to clarify a message or to make it more precise. This type of switching was very common among my informants. The following are examples:

55. El grande [grandson] tiene un *vapor* y vive en el *boat* en la Marina del Rey. (The oldest has a boat [Judeo-Spanish] and he lives on the boat [English] in Marina del Rey.)
56. Entonses mi kunyado avlo kon su *lawyer*, kon el *avokato* suyo. (Then my brother-in-law spoke with his lawyer [English]), with his lawyer [Judeo-Spanish].)
57. Mi madre vivia kon mi unos kuantos anyos i despues le di gota— *a stroke* i la metieron en el ospital por tres anyos and then *I had*— *tuvi* tres kriaturas. (My mother lived with me for some years and afterwards she had a stroke [Judeo-Spanish]—a stroke [English]— and they put her in the hospital for three years, and then I had [English]—I had [Judeo-Spanish] three children.)
58. Ensenya business an un *adult school*—*eskola de adultos* para business people. (She teaches business in an adult school [English]—a school for adults [Judeo-Spanish] for business people.)
59. Por restriksion de las komidas mi marido *se enfermo*—*se izo hazino* y en 1944 se murio. (Due to lack of food my husband became ill [Modern Spanish]—got sick [Judeo-Spanish], and he died in 1944.)
60. *And* despues no tenia *trabajo*—no tenia *lavoro*. (And afterwards he didn't have work [Mod. Spanish]—he didn't have a job [Judeo-Spanish].)
61. Savemos muy bien el *ivrit*—*el ebreo*. (We know very well Hebrew [Hebrew עברית]—Hebrew [Judeo-Spanish].)
62. Dize *esrim*—*venti*. (I said twenty [Hebrew עשׂרים]—twenty [Judeo-Spanish].)
63. Yo esto kontento lavorar otros 1, 2, o 3 anyos aval no *yoter*—no mas. (I'm content to work another 1, 2, or 3 years but no more [Hebrew יותר]—no more [Judeo-Spanish].)

Elements Larger than a Single Word or Constituent

Complete Sentences

According to Hasselmo (1970), in "unlimited switching" the distribution of the complete sentence or long phrase may vary; it can come
in the middle of the sentence or at the beginning or the end.

64. Despues tuvi un primer tchiko *and he was the most spoiled tchiko ke
    tienes ke ver.* (Afterwards I had a first son and he was the most
    spoiled child that you have ever seen.)
65. Yo avli kon mi amiga Luisa—eya se grandesio en Seattle *and I
    used to go there.* (I spoke with my friend Luisa—she grew up in
    Seattle and I used to go there.)
66. Todos los *ships* ke venian *they (from) all over the world* y savia muchas
    idiomas [notice gender] mi padre. (All the ships that came, they
    were from all over the world, and my father knew many lan-
    guages.)
67. Mi marido se murio *and so I miss him very much.* (My husband died
    and so I miss him very much.)
68. *In fact, in the museum in Seattle in the university,* ay un livro escrito de
    mano de mi papu de *psalms,* kantigas . . . (In fact in the museum
    in Seattle in the university there is a book written by hand by my
    grandfather of psalms, songs . . .)

Different Languages in the Same Sentence

In many instances that have been studied by linguists, code-switching
involves alternations of only two languages. In Judeo-Spanish, however, it often includes interference of two or more languages in the
same sentence, as well as a mixture of all the types of code-switching
previously mentioned. This type of switching was very common
among my informants. Below are six examples:

69. Mi padre avlo en ingles *pero* kon a *heavy accent.* (My father spoke
    in English but with a heavy accent.) Note the use of Modern
    Spanish *pero* instead of Judeo-Spanish *ma* and *a heavy accent* from
    English.
70. Fue en un *bicyclette* a la *tienda* de *Mr.* Barash. (He went by bike to
    Mr. Barash's store.) Note French *bicyclette,* Modern Spanish *tienda,*
    and the English title *Mr.*
71. *Ahora,* te yevo un *picture* de mi *hijo.* (Now I bring you a picture of

my son.) Note the Modern Spanish *ahora* and *hijo* vs. Judeo-Spanish *agora* and *ižo* as well as English *picture*.

72. Yo te dizo ke teniamos muy buen *choir* en el templo *nuestro*. (I tell you that we used to have a very good choir in our temple.) Note the English *choir* and Modern Spanish pronunciation *nuestro* instead of *muestro* with an *m-*.

73. Lo transferaron [notice conjugation] a una *escuela* en Harlem kon tchikos muntcho mas tchikos de los ke tenia *and retarded* tambien, *so* el dicho ke no keria trabajar kon este modo de tchikos porke *he had to sort of babysit for them.* (They transferred him to a school in Harlem with children much younger than those he had and retarded also, so he said that he didn't want to work with these kind of children because he had to sort of babysit for them.) Note the Modern Spanish *escuela* and *trabajar* instead of the Judeo-Spanish *eskola* and *lavorar*; and the final phrase in English.

74. Yo encontre a mi marido de una amiga ke mi madre konosia. *And he* vino a mi ver en mi kaza and despues no tenia *trabajo*. No tenia lavoro *and* despues nos encontremos *and he asked me, well, I'm speaking in English and then we got married after we went for a while* enǰuntos. (I met my husband through a friend that my mother knew. And he came to see me in my house and afterwards he didn't have work. He didn't have a job and after we got to know each other and he asked me, well I'm speaking in English, and then we got married after we went together for a while.) Note *And* and *he* (English); *trabajo* (Modern Spanish) and then the final two sentences in English.

Code-switching occurred in the speech of all of the informants who were capable of speaking in Judeo-Spanish. As the preceding examples show, it ranged from a borrowed word sprinkled here and there in a Judeo-Spanish sentence to partial and complete sentences from the interferring language. However, one important phenomenon must be emphasized. The code-switching which occurred among my Judeo-Spanish informants was not the result of knowing more than one language well, but rather was due to their having insufficient knowledge of Judeo-Spanish.

In contrast to Poplack's studies of code-switching, most of my informants did not engage in what she calls "skilled code-switching," which is characterized by a "seeming unawareness of the alternation between languages," and is not accompanied by false starts, hesitations, pauses, metalinguistic commentary, or repetitions of various segments (Poplack, p. 248). As my examples show, this was not the case with the majority of my informants. Their speech was not only full of pauses, hesitations, commentary, and repetitions, but they also expressed a great awareness of what was not Judeo-Spanish.

Often during the interviews they would correct their errors with comments like "Esto es kasteyano espanyol de Espanya. no es espanyol de muzotros" ("This is Castilian Spanish of Spain, it is not our Spanish"). One informant described something that happened one day with: "Un dia estavamos avlando en la marketa en espanyol de muzotros" ("One day we were talking in the market in our Spanish"). Another informant expressed her frustrations in the following statement, which is a mixture of Judeo-Spanish, Modern Spanish, and English, when she said: "I'm gonna try to use—avlar espanyol ladino because you all know Castellano tambien y sin kerer me konfundo la lengua" ("I'm gonna try to use—speak Ladino Spanish because you all know Castilian also and without wanting to I confuse the language)".

The code-switching that occurred in the speech of my informants probably should be better classified as "code-shifting," a term used by Silva-Corvalán (1983, pp. 71, 81) to describe shifting that occurs when bilingual speakers have to use the language in which they are self-reportedly less fluent or less competent in order to adapt to the language preference of the listener, in this case the interviewer.

In the situation of code-shifting the speaker compensates for insufficient lexical or syntactic knowledge of one of the languages, in this case Judeo-Spanish. This is in opposition to Poplack's (1982) view of skilled code-switching, which appears to require a large degree of linguistic competence in both languages. According to Poplack, skilled code-switching is largely motivated by social and discourse/pragmatic factors, while Silva-Corvalán (1983, p. 85) reports that the primary function of code-shifting has a linguistic communicative function, used when the speaker needs to communicate in a language in which he or she has a limited degree of competence.

Not only did those of my informants who were capable of conversing in Judeo-Spanish resort to code-switching or -shifting, but the extent of the switching was great. There was rarely a sentence uttered by the informants that did not contain some kind of recent borrowing from English, Modern Spanish, French, or Hebrew. And for the most part, the switching occurs in situations where everyday vocabulary is used and has a counterpart in Judeo-Spanish which the informants do not know or cannot remember.

Thus, for 100 percent of the New York, Israeli, and Los Angeles informants capable of conversing in Judeo-Spanish, code-switching or code-shifting is a dominant characteristic of their speech. And since the largest Sephardic communities are presently located in Israel and the United States (New York and Los Angeles being the largest American Sephardic communities), the data suggest that a great amount of code-switching is characteristic of current spoken Judeo-Spanish no matter where and by whom it is spoken in the world today. Even Malinowski's studies in Turkey (1982, p. 15) show that the Sephardic Jews still residing there often code-switch, using a large amount of Turkish and/or French in their speech, that is, if they can still speak Judeo-Spanish at all.

The Significance of Code-Switching

As Poplack (1983, p. 124) has pointed out, code-switching per se is not a phenomenon which is indicative of language death. There is also extensive code-switching in the Chicano and Puerto Rican varieties of Spanish in the United States, and one could hardly say that these dialects are in a state of decline. But even though the generational shift from Judeo-Spanish to English follows a similar pattern to that observed for other immigrant languages in Israel and the United States (Fishman 1972; Malinowski 1983), the case of Judeo-Spanish is different. First of all, there is no home country today where people speak Judeo-Spanish, as is the case for other immigrant languages. This means that there will be no new influx of fluent Judeo-Spanish speakers who can help to revitalize the language as it is spoken in the United States or Israel. Since there are no young Judeo-Spanish speakers left, there is no replacing generation of native speakers.[4] Thus there is rare if any contact with the spoken language.

Moreover, code-switching or -shifting in Judeo-Spanish does indeed show a trend toward language decay, since for the most part, the borrowing occurs in situations where common, everyday vocabulary is used and where good counterparts exist in Judeo-Spanish. This shifting occurs because the informants do not know the equivalent

[4] Today it is rare to find a person under the age of fifty who can still converse in Judeo-Spanish. See Malinowski 1979 and Harris 1979.

words or expressions in Judeo-Spanish, and therefore the replacement with English, Modern Spanish, or Hebrew is necessary to fulfill the function of communication. I might add that there are no Judeo-Spanish texts and very few dictionaries where a Judeo-Spanish speaker could look up terms if he or she so desires. And there are no courses offered which emphasize the acquisition of Judeo-Spanish linguistic skills.[5]

But more important is the fact that the majority of my informants reported that they did not possess good linguistic skills in Judeo-Spanish, and they admitted that they could not speak the language as well as their parents and grandparents. They all felt more comfortable and preferred communicating in English, Hebrew, French, or even Modern Spanish in a few cases, rather than in Judeo-Spanish. The informants admitted this while expressing pride in their Sephardic heritage and the knowledge that Judeo-Spanish is an important aspect of their Sephardic identity. But at the same time, the vast majority of my informants believe that Judeo-Spanish is a dying language, an opinion which is not shared by other immigrants about their respective languages. They are also doing very little to perpetuate the language or to ensure its survival.

Conclusion

Today, as the older generation of Judeo-Spanish speakers diminishes, the switch to English in the United States and to Hebrew in Israel is almost complete. When dying languages such as Judeo-Spanish are accompanied by certain socio-linguistic factors, the role of code-switching or -shifting as a possible stage in the decline of a language is an important issue to be considered.

---

[5] Judeo-Spanish was taught in New York at Columbia University and at New York University in the mid to late seventies by David Bunis and at the University of Judaism (continuing education branch) in Los Angeles by Tracy Harris. It has been taught at Sephardic House by Joe Tarica and a class is presently being taught by Davíd Altabé. In Israel courses are being taught by Shmuel Refael and Erella Gattegno at Bar Ilan University and David Gold at the University of Haifa. David Bunis presently teaches the language at Hebrew Universtiy, and other courses have been offered at Ben Gurion University of the Negev and Beer Sheva University. However, these courses generally either emphasize(d) the reading of religious texts, or were/are concerned with the development of the historical or cultural role of the language, rather than with the acquistion of linguisic skills for conversational purposes.

References

Fishman, Joshua A. 1972. Language maintenance in a supra-ethnic age. In LAN-GUAGE IN SOCIOCULTURAL CHANGE, ed. Anwar S. Dil, pp. 48–75. Stanford: Stanford University Press.

———. 1977. Language maintenance and language shift as a field of inquiry: revis-ited. In LANGUAGE IN SOCIOCULTURAL CHANGE, ed. Anwar S. Dil, pp. 76–134. Stanford: Stanford University Press.

Harris, Tracy K. 1979. The Prognosis for Judeo-Spanish: its description, present status, survival and decline, with implications for language death in general. Ph.D. disserration, Georgetown University: Washington, D.C.

———. 1983. Foreign interference and code-switching in the contemporary Judeo-Spanish of New York. In SPANISH IN THE U.S. SETTING BEYOND THE SOUTHWEST, ed. L. Elías-Olivares, pp. 53–68. Rosslyn, Va: National Clearinghouse for Bilingual Education.

Hasselmo, Nils. 1970. Code-switching and modes of speaking. In TEXAS STUDIES IN BILINGUALISM, ed. G. Gilbert, pp. 179–210. Berlin: de Gruyter.

Malinowski, Arlene. 1982. Aspects of Contemporary Judeo-Spanish in Israel based on oral and written sources. Ph.D. dissertation, University of Michigan.

———. 1982. A report on the status of Judeo-Spanish in Turkey. International Journal of the Sociology of Language. 37:7–23.

———. 1983. Judeo-Spanish language maintenance efforts in the United States. International Journal of the Sociology of Language 44:137–51.

Poplack, Shana 1982. "Sometimes I'll start a sentence in Spanish y termino en español": toward a typology of code-switching. In SPANISH IN THE UNITED STATES, SOCIO-LINGUISTIC ASPECTS, eds. J. Amastae & L. Elías-Olivares, pp. 230–263. N.Y.: Cambridge University Press. Originally appeared in *Linguistics* 18:581–618 (1980).

———. 1983. Bilingual competence: linguistic interference or grammatical integ-rity. In SPANISH IN THE U.S. SETTING BEYOND THE SOUTHWEST, ed. L. Elías-Olivares, pp. 107–129. Rosslyn, Va: Clearinghouse for Bilingual Education.

Sala, Marius. 1961. Observations sur la disparition des langues. Revue Linguistique 6:185–202. Spanish version reprinted in Sala, 1970. ESTUDIOS SOBRE EL JUDEO ESPAÑOL DE BUCAREST, 9–45. Mexico: Universidad Nacional Autonoma de Mexico.

Silva-Corvalán, Carmen 1983. Code-shifting patterns in Chicano Spanish. In SPAN-ISH IN THE U.S. SETTING BEYOND THE SOUTHWEST, ed. L. Elías-Olivares, pp. 69–87. Rosslyn, Va: Clearinghouse for Bilingual Education.

HAQUITÍA AS SPOKEN IN THE BRAZILIAN AMAZON

REGINA IGEL

University of Maryland, College Park

Among all the dialects in use by Jews scattered around the world, Haquitía is the least known. Spoken by Jews of Spanish origin, it is scarcely, if at all, acknowledged in dictionaries or manuals of linguistics, even those related to *judeo-español* languages.[1] Haquitía is essentially a dialect confined to oral communication and accompanied by specific gestures of the hands, the winking of eyes, and certain other facial movements.[2] Therefore, it has the skeptical honor among *judeo-español* dialects of being all the more prone to disappearance along with the demise of its last carriers. Nevertheless, it has been a tool of contact on Brazilian soil, though fragmented and devoid of written documentation, for more than a century. Before that, it was spoken by Jews of Spanish origin in Morocco until the last quarter of the eighteenth century. After the Arab occupation of northern Morocco in 1860, those who immigrated to Brazil from Tangier, Tetuán, Rabat, Salé, Casablanca, and neighboring areas congregated mostly in the Amazon region.

According to Eidorfe Moreira, the Jewish Moroccan immigration to the Amazon basin may have been stimulated by political persecution, among other reasons. The Arab conquest of Mazagão, a Portuguese enclave in northwestern Morocco, in 1768, forced the remaining Jews and New Christians to flee from that region, many in the direction of northern Brazil, paving the way for others who sought a safe refuge in which to live and practice their religion. The financial prospects in the exploration of rubber and other natural

---

[1] Two main Brazilian-Portuguese dictionaries, the *Novo Dicionário Aurélio* and the *Koogan-Larousse*, do not register "Haquitía."

[2] This information was provided by Mrs. Sultana Levy Rosenblatt, who is of Moroccan-Brazilian origin and knowledgeable in Haquitía. Formerly a resident of the Brazilian Amazon basin, Mrs. Rosenblatt still makes use of Haquitía at family reunions and among friends who grew up in the same area. Without her input, this study would not have been possible.

products of the region, such as *sizal, juta*, and nuts, provided an economic incentive as well. And, of course, a geographical factor lay in
the relative ease of crossing the ocean between regions in the same
latitude and adjusting to a new region of parallel climate.[3]

Moysés Benguigui was just seventeen in 1909, when he left his
Salé mellah for Brazil, where he met an uncle who had settled in
Pará.[4] As was the tradition, uncle Azulay Pazuello helped his nephew
with a small loan and sent him off to be a peddler in the Amazon
basin. Many other young Moroccans of the Jewish faith followed
this same pattern for their subsistence, peddling fabrics, tools for
a variety of uses, medicines, and food for the preparation of basic
staples. Further immigration to the area and marriages in the New
World resulted in the fast growth of the Jewish population scattered
throughout the region. Cemeteries with tombstones dating back as
far as 1880 are found in the towns of Moaná, Itaituba, Santarém,
Alenquer, Óbidos, Juriti, and Cametá.

Salesmen and vendors of Arabic descent were also forcing their
way into the Amazon. Moroccan Jews and Arabs were regarded as
a monolithic ethnic group, the "turcos." It was when all were together
that the Moroccan Jews would make use of their Haquitía as a
means of communicating with brevity and wit. A handful of descendants of these first families of expatriates still preserve Haquitía by
resorting to it to make ironic, humorous, or clever comments, "pass-
words" unknown to the outsiders in their presence, who are usually
even unaware of the exchange itself. Its terms penetrate the Portuguese
language as they once did Spanish and Arabic.

The ancestral voices of Haquitía are tied to the many regional
versions of Iberian Spanish used before the expulsion. Its diversified
linguistic coloratura was further embroidered as it encompassed elements of Hebrew, Spanish, and Arabic, and, less extensively, Portuguese
and French. Contrary to Ladino and other *judeo-español* dialects,
Haquitía is virtually used exclusively as a means of oral communication, with the exception of familiar letters or short messages exchanged within the limits of a household or members of an extended
family. Never commonly used as a written medium, it is devoid of

---

[3] Eidorfe Moreira, *Presença Hebraica no Pará* (Belém, 1972), p. 26.
[4] The informant is Dr. Yehuda Benguigui, M.D., the youngest of the eight children fathered by the late Moysés Benguigui. Interviewed in McLean, Virginia,
January 1987.

literary tradition. As used in the Amazon region, the structure of its essential grammar was basically extracted from Old Spanish, and its graphic forms borrowed from the Spanish alphabet.[5]

Haquitía has survived, as have many of the other Jewish-Spanish dialects, because of the need of the Jewish Spanish community to protect its way of life from the prying eyes of non-Jews, in Spain and in Africa. The speakers of Haquitía relied on the weaving of languages to confuse the uninitiated, on the one hand, or to pass undetected, on the other. Having evolved in a politically oppressive situation, it was carried to more tolerant places, such as the many Latin American regions where Moroccans from Tangier and Tetuán settled. Eventually, it lost its raison d'être when the language's carriers felt free of previous restrictions and let their secretive way of communication slowly wane into all but complete neglect.

The origin of the word "Haquitía" itself is a matter of speculation, ranging from a lightweight explanation to a more plausible and scientific one. It has been suggested that the name is due to a rather deprecating nickname invented by Jews from the hinterland of Morocco, who referred to the language spoken by their more educated fellow countrymen as "Hakito language," where Hakito was understood as an abbreviation of Ishaquito, the diminutive of Ishac, as if minimizing the language as it was spoken by "Haquitos." On the other hand, a different approach to the etymology of the word addresses its development from an Arabic root with a Spanish ending that resulted from the verb *haka* ("to talk, chat, narrate"). Other derivations from *haka* are the words *hekaia* or *hekaiata* and the plural form *hekaiat*, their meanings ranging from "happy event" to "witty turn of words" to "smart observation." Clearly, all of these theories concur with characterizations of Haquitía.

Among the less educated, Haquitian words were resorted to when there was a lack of knowledge of the appropriate term in the target language. Because of its extensive use by the less privileged, Haquitian users became stigmatized as uneducated and poor. They

---

[5] A grammar of Haquitía by José Benoliel (Tangier, 1888–1937), the only one known to this date, was published in bulletins by the Real Academia Española (n.d.) with the title "Dialecto Judío-Hispano-Marroquí o Hakitía." It had a second edition as a booklet in Madrid in 1977 (no information on publishing house available). Abraham R. Bentes, originally from Pará, translated and incorporated the bulletin edition in his book *Os Sefardim e a Hakitia*, 2nd ed. (Belém: By the author, 1981).

were also called *desmazalados* ("luckless"), a word which was incorporated into Portuguese as *desmazelado*, meaning "sloppy," "negligent," or "sickly." The combination of the Hebrew root *mazal* and the prefix *de* is obvious in the formation of this word, whose variant *desmazalado* also found its way into Spanish. Nevertheless, the more educated and sophisticated evoked Haquitía when there was a conscious need to preserve blessings in the language heard from their predecessors, or for emotional expressions, such as lamentation and scorn, as well as for irony and when scolding children.

Today, Haquitía is used almost solely by those who are in their mid-sixties and older. It survives mostly through the exchange of scant words, proverbs, blessings, and the punch-lines of familiar jokes. It creeps into conversation among the descendants of Moroccans in the Amazon through isolated words (e.g., *go*, an exclamation or curse, as in *Go por los moros!*) or along with picturesque comments that usually are intended to win a smile of approval from another person who also understands the dialect. Examples of this are the expressions *zamá* in *Se casou com traje de noiva, zamá la-asba . . .* ("She married dressed as a bride, however . . .") and *Ahlas*, as in *Ahlas . . . cuide-se, pare de falar* ("Watch out, don't say more").

Words from the Hebrew take on different meanings in Haquitía. For example, *haber* (from the word for "friend" in Hebrew) turned into "lover" with a derogatory tone, as in *Eles estao habereados* ("they are paramours"). Another example is the word *hatuná* ("wedding") used as a synonym for "drunkard," as in *Ele está hatuná* ("He is drunk").

Though Ladino speakers can claim that they know and use these words too, this does not deter Haquitía users in their thoughtful efforts to preserve these expressions when they do it with a twist of humor and irony. As a reflection of its colorful vocabulary, which mirrors the circumstances lived by its carriers, Haquitía speakers tend to express feelings through metaphor and allegory. A light-hearted illustration of this tendency is evident in the story of the lady who complained of a headache to her doctor: ". . . *que tenía un martío en cada sién y un xaqqor en la cabesa*" (*martío* = "hammer"; *xaqqor* = "ax"), "She felt a hammer in her temples, and an ax on her pate"). The doctor, less interested in the rhetorical characterization of the language, replied that the matter was more in the field of a blacksmith than his.[6]

---

[6] Bentes, *Os Sefardim e a Hakitia*, p. 262, s.v. "Martío."

Sentimentalism is the only reason for the preservation of Haquitía as a way of oral exchange in the Amazon today. With respect to the number of people speaking it, it has stagnated, being for all practical purposes limited to the cities of Manaus and Belém. Its circulation is limited to the occasional utterance of fragmented sentences—witty words, proverbs, blessings, and jokes—among members of the less than fifty families that still remember it. The future of Haquitía is doomed. The new generation of descendants of the Spanish Moroccan Jews does not acknowledge it and is, for the most part, even unaware of it.

Jewish assimilation, of course, is a strong factor in the neglect of Haquitía, and the generations born in Brazil are totally ignorant of the language. Many families have wiped it out altogether for fear of being confused with Moroccans of a lower class. There is one note of cautious hope, however, which might make this a premature obituary: In France, an association called Mabat-Francia, composed of Sephardim who originated in the former Spanish Morocco, has founded an Atelier de Haketía, because, in the words of one of its advocates, *el judeo-español hablado por los judíos de Tangier, Tetuán y otras ciudades de esta región [y que] ahora está en vías de desaparición* ("the *judeo-español* spoken by the Jews of Tangier, Tetuán and other cities in this region is [also] close to disappearance").[7]

Nevertheless, the ever-shrinking population of Sephardim in the Amazon region, who previously included Haquitian words in their conversation, has not passed this ability on to their descendants. As a means of oral communication which flourished because of oppressive circumstances, the dialect holds the dubious characteristic of being doomed to oblivion now that those conditions have ceased to exist. Its main appeal, that is, the wit, humor, and veiled sarcasm that bloom in conversations during stressful times, has become unnecessary in an open society. Ironically, Haquitía has lost its raison d'être in the Amazon region. It has become an object of reverence, dusted off from time to time by those who still remember it.

---

[7] Moshe Shaúl, Moshe Liba, and José Luis Najenson, *Judeo-Español*, Separata Hispanorama, organ des Deutschen Spanishchlehrerverbands, 38 (Israel: Instituto Central de Relaciones Culturales Israel-Iberoamerica, España y Portugal, November 1984), p. 37.

GROWING UP IN A POLYGLOT
SEPHARDIC HOUSEHOLD

Joy Zacharia Appelbaum

Hackensack, New Jersey

If you are familiar with the conflicts of the Hatfields and the McCoys, the Capulets and the Montagues, the Litvaks and the Galitsianos, chances are you have yet to learn about the *Kastorialis* and the *Monastirlis*—Sephardic Jews who took refuge in two neighboring communities of the Ottoman Empire after their expulsion from Spain.

Monastir, now called Bitola, is situated at the junction of the borders of Yugoslavia, Albania, and Greece, the very center of Macedonia. Surrounded by mountains, it rests in a deep valley and is divided by the swift Dragor River. Prior to the Balkan Wars and the demise of the Ottoman Empire, it enjoyed a key role as an international trading center of agricultural products and fine handicrafts. It was also known for its cattle grazing, tanning, and rubber industries. Bulgars, Rumanians, Greeks, Serbs, Albanians, Turks, and Jews pleasantly coexisted, abiding by a three-day weekend—one day for each of the three religions represented. Through World War I, the largest Jewish community in Macedonia existed here. Bitola (its Slavic name) is now part of Yugoslavia.

Kastoria, a somewhat smaller town, is located in the mountains of Macedonia, south of Monastir. It features a lake of 11 square miles that is known as a resort area and for its fisheries. Designated the fur-trading center of Europe since the seventeenth century, this mountainous marketplace is the destination for an assortment of merchandise that even includes Russian sable pelts. Indeed, the once predominantly Jewish fur business of New York City is now run by non-Jewish Greek furriers, primarily from Kastoria. Kastor Furs, whose advertisements regularly appear in high-fashion magazines, is just two brothers from Kastoria. Before World War I, the town had several synagogues and three yeshivot with a chief rabbi. As in Monastir, practically all vestiges of its Jewish community were destroyed by the four-year Nazi occupation during World War II. All Jews remaining were transported to Auschwitz. Prior to World War I and the demise of the Ottoman Empire, however, relations between Jew and Christian were tolerable, with the chief rabbi and the Greek Orthodox bishop presiding over their respective communities. Kastoria is still the seat of a Greek Orthodox metropolitan bishopric.

Although no battles were fought between Jewish *Kastorialis* and *Monastirlis*, no blood was shed, and a goodly portion of each group "intermarried" with the other, their verbal feud continues until today wherever they may live. While they now share the same neighborhoods and synagogues in the United States, Israel, and South America, the very mention of one group to the other is bound to bring a grimace and the *sotto voce* derogatory comment: *montanyeros!* ("hillbillies!").

Each group complains persistently about the other's command of Judeo-Spanish, insisting that its version is the more scholarly jargon; One says *harina* instead of *farina* for "flour." The other insists that *scola* and not *scolia* is the proper word for "school." If you are capable, then one group says you are *potente*, while the other will label you *capacho*. "Oh heavens!" is *barminan* in one town, and *barminyan* in the other.

A simple sentence can contain many variations, such as *La hija yeva una rida en la aldikera de su fusta* or *La fija yeva una riga en el giep de su falda* ("The daughter carries a handkerchief in the pocket of her skirt").

Polemics can ensue over the use or abuse of a single word, and everyone is convinced that he is correct. (I say *he* instead of *she* because women were not supposed to get involved in such meaningful debates.)

Of course, the two clans are in total agreement that the *ajenos* ("strangers, foreigners") speak even worse Judeo-Spanish, although they (*los ajenos*) may come from more cosmopolitan communities, such as Rhodes, Izmir, Salonika, or Istanbul. Had not some of their homegrown *Monastirli* and *Kastoriali* scholars, such as Shlomo Molcho, Rabbi Yosef ben Lev, and Rabbi Abraham ben Yehuda di Buton, received recognition from these larger communities?

Then there are the *Yanyotis*, the Greek Jews from Janina (Ioannina), who don't speak Judeo-Spanish at all and, therefore, are considered *gente baja* ("low people"). The men were to be avoided as marriage partners at all costs, reputed as being *escasos* ("stingy").

Of course my two aunts who happened to marry *Yanyotis* were very fortunate because their husbands were the exceptions that proved the rule. Uncle Chaim was a thief in business; even the labor unions were afraid to deal with him. But he was the most generous of husbands. Uncle Samuel, also not to be trusted among businessmen, always put his family first and was an excellent provider.

But the *Yanyotis* are not as bad as the *Yiddishim* or *Ziggizooks*, as the Ashkenazic Jews are called, who were commonly referred to as *fediendo* ("rotten"), especially their women. If your son married a *Yiddisha*, he would rue the day! These overbearing women, who not only handled the household accounts, often participated in the family business. They were pushy and domineering. Besides, your grandchildren would never be named for you, since the Ashkenazim only name after the dead. If, on the other hand, your daughter married an Ashkenazic man, this was good. Ashkenazic men were so browbeaten by their mothers and sisters, that they could feel very compatible with a more docile, homebound Sephardic woman.

The *Yiddishim*, however, are not as bad as the Syrians. They are the worst of all! The Syrians and other groups of Mizrachi Jews are simply *gorsus* ("evil"). If your family members get mixed up with them, you will never see them again! These people have their own tight community and demand total conformity. Of course, they are all rich and your relative will live well, as long as a child is produced almost every year. How they earn their money is another story! They are all horse thieves in their hearts!

Growing up Sephardic instilled a strong sense of identity and overwhelming confusion at the same time. I knew we were different from Jews who did not speak Spanish, yet those who spoke Greek, French, or Italian attended our synagogues, and those who spoke Yiddish, German, or Arabic did not. It seemed that among those who did speak Spanish there was never total harmony or trust. Outsiders frequently think of the Sephardim as a homogeneous entity and refer to them as clannish, but within their ranks there are many divisions and distinctions. In *Sephardim in Twentieth Century America: In Search of Unity*, Joseph M. Papo aptly described my dilemma:

> Throughout their centuries-long sojourn in the Ottoman Empire, the Sephardim had maintained a fierce pride in their Sephardic identity, and upon their arrival in America the immigrants had to face the realization that the established American Sephardic community, dating back to the 17th century, did not recognize them . . . as fellow Sephardim. Ashkenazi immigrants, in their turn, mistook the swarthy Sephardim . . . for Arabs and Turks, so that the Sephardim had to work at proving

their very Jewishness. But the most difficult and most persistent challenge confronting them was to overcome their internal differences.

As Great-Uncle Angelo Uriel used to say, "*Todos son gallos*" ("They are all roosters" [i.e., leaders]).

The Sephardim formed many groups, stemming from their or their parents' hometowns, that began as friendship and burial societies. Some founded small synagogues that eventually combined with other Sephardic congregations or, unfortunately, faded away. Clubs were formed, such as the Broome Street and Allen Street Boys' clubs, the *Pashas*, and the Masonic Abravanel Lodge, which finally crossed confining geographic boundaries. But a *Kastoriali* still had *Kastoriali* children and grandchildren, as did the *Monastirlis*, *Rhodeslis*, *Izmirlis*, and *Saloniklis*.

My paternal grandfather, Chief Rabbi Isaac Menahem Zacharia, was fortunate to come to America in 1916, preceded by his three oldest sons, who brought the family over. As the *haham bashi* (chief rabbi) from Kastoria, it was hoped that his arrival would help establish a Beth Din (board of rabbis) to improve the cohesiveness of the disparate Sephardic groups through religious unity. Because there is only traditional Sephardic observance—no divisions among Orthodox, Conservative, and Reform denominations—religious restrictions do not interfere with the formation of such a governing body. Congregation Hessed ve Emeth de Kastorialis, founded in 1910 even before my grandfather's arrival, and Congregation Ahavat Shalom de Monastir, established in 1907, were the first to approve of this plan, despite their age-old separate identities.

Unfortunately, my grandfather passed away prematurely in 1925, after establishing the secular as well as the religious authority of the Beth Din. The Beth Din continued in existence until 1959, but had lost most of its power by 1939, due to internal politics. The constant demographic shifting of congregations and inconsistent economic conditions prevented the assembling of another Beth Din.

The lay Central Sephardic Jewish Community was then organized in 1941, in an attempt to create a single umbrella organization devoted to enhancing Jewish education, coordinating activities, and providing a united front. The original, fragmented societies, however, were afraid of losing their autonomy and would never sufficiently come together to make the unification successful. Had they successfully organized themselves, their history in our country as a viable force in America's Jewish community might have been quite different.

One more component that complicated my nurturing was the Italian Jewish strain from my mother's side. My maternal grandmother's family had lived in Florence for many generations before moving to Istanbul for reasons of professional advancement in the Hapsburg Empire's diplomatic service. Their Judeo-Spanish was sprinkled with Italian, their menus with Italian foods; their women were better educated and more liberally treated. This branch of the family was equally comfortable among Jews and among non-Jews, although they did not condone intermarriage. They made an indelible impression on me because, in addition to being able to speak in the appropriate languages with the Spanish, Greek, and Turkish merchants in our area, they could also converse with the Italians and, the Germans (due to the Hapsburg Austrian connection). While exposed to the schools of the Alliance Israélite Universelle in Istanbul, where they now lived, they preferred that the girls be tutored at home in a variety of academic as well as domestic-science subjects; sons were sent to Prussian military schools. The family manifested minimal Ottoman influence, other than their knowledge of languages, foods, and religious traditions. Because of the aforementioned differences, distrust and resentment existed between the two sides of the family, especially among their women. The education of women was a very controversial subject.

On the few occasions when large representations from the two sides of the family were present, there was a certain amount of awkwardness. The Italian side would call me *Gioia*, and the others, *Julica*. (Neither nickname was used by my parents.) Their different Judeo-Spanish dialects went something like this:

La nona mete el fostan en el almario de la camareta.
La mana mete el vestido en el raf de la alcoba.
("The grandmother puts the dress in the closet of the bedroom.")

When I first studied Spanish formally in high school, I was amazed to learn that so many words used regularly at home were not of Spanish origin at all. This made taking examinations very challenging. Studying verb conjugations with my father did more harm than good. For example, *traer*, "to bring"; Castilian, *traje, trajiste, trajo*; dialect, *trushe, trushiste, trusho*.

I was allowed to attend college, an out-of-town college at that, in spite of the Ottoman side of the family. They cautioned my father against it, claiming that I would lose my virginity, and possibly worse than that, if he let me go. Against their admonitions, he was persuaded by our Ashkenazic friends and neighbors whose daughters were already attending universities. Mind you, he was not particularly happy about it, but he agreed.

As it turned out, my mentor at Brandeis University was Dr. Denah Levy Lida. She encouraged me to compose a dictionary/grammar and cultural sourcebook of the Judeo-Spanish dialect of the Jews of Kastoria. My father and his family were delighted, but interviewing them was a unique experience. They were very self-conscious about the fact that what they spoke was a dialect and not modern Castilian. Frequently, they would try to correct themselves and give me the Castilian instead of their own word. I had to convince them that what I wanted was *their* language.

In the meantime, the other branches of the family felt offended at being left out. They also wanted to contribute and would offer their versions of a word or expression. It was a delicate situation. Of course, each group insisted that its dialect was the most authentic.

As the older generation has passed on and fewer of the Old World traditions are observed, the differences among my many cousins from each side of the family are now more regional than historical. I still see heavy traces of their parental teachings, however, and chuckle at loyalties to and prejudices from the past that continue to linger.

TEXTS, CONTEXTS, AND SUBTEXT IN THE JUDEO-SPANISH BIBLICAL BALLAD OF *AMNÓN Y TAMAR*

MESSOD SALAMA

Memorial University of Newfoundland
St. John's, Newfoundland

Valued for its ability to preserve archaic texts that otherwise were lost or became scarce in the Iberian Peninsula, the "extraordinario carácter conservador" of the Sephardic *Romancero*, in Menéndez-Pidal's terms, has long attracted the attention of Hispanists and Sephardic scholars alike.[1] This emphasis on the philological and text-oriented approach, coupled with the comparativist and historical perspectives, has lessened the importance of the context and setting in which Judeo-Spanish balladry developed, flourished, and managed to survive without interruption for the last five hundred years. More and more, however, studies dealing with the significance of oral transmission and variants have rectified the static perception of the Sephardic *Romancero*, but they have not yet fully explored its originality and independence.[2] As Meir Benardete, a respected authority on Sephardic studies in the United States, rhetorically pointed out at the beginning of this century:

> ... ¿es justo afirmar que las canciones de los judíos españoles tienen un interés puramente hispánico? El que hayan seguido siendo cantadas durante más de cuatro siglos lejos de la madre patria permite suponer que, en un momento dado, asumieron una función propia en las pequeñas teocracias mediterráneas de los desterrados de 1492.[3]

---

[1] R. Menéndez-Pidal, "El romancero sefardí, su extraordinario carácter conservador," in *Essays on the History and Cultural Contribution of the Jews of Spain and Portugal*, ed. R.D. Barnett (New York: Ktav, 1971), vol. 1, pp. 552–559.

[2] An important contribution in this particular field is R. Benmayor's investigation. See the introduction to her *Romances judeo-españoles de Oriente, Nueva recolección* (Madrid: Catedra-Seminario Menéndez Pidal, 1979) and "Social Determinants in Poetic Transmission: The Sephardic Romancero," in *The Sephardi and Oriental Jewish Heritage*, ed. I. Ben Ami (Jerusalem: Magnes Press, 1982), pp. 246–260.

[3] M. Benardete, *Hispanismo de los sefardíes levantinos* (Madrid: Aguilar, 1963), p. 12.

Better than any other type of Judeo-Spanish ballads, the group of *romances* based on the Hebrew Bible stand in sharp contrast to their original Spanish counterparts in number of texts, versions, homogeneity, and wealth of incorporated material.[4]

Although an analysis of the various *Cancioneros, Silvas,* early collections of *romances,* and *pliegos sueltos* (broadsides) exhibits a wealth of biblical ballad compositions in sixteenth- and seventeenth-century Spain, few of these managed to become popular, let alone traditional. Most of them, in fact, never succeeded in achieving the expressed desire of one well-known collector, Lorenzo de Sepúlveda, who hoped that some of his ballads, including biblical ones, would eventually be sung.[5] Menéndez y Pelayo has pointed out the abundance of this type of *romance* in sixteenth-century Spain,[6] Sancha was able to gather a rich corpus of religious songs.[7] Scholars have noticed the paucity of biblical ballads in the modern Spanish oral tradition and compare it with the copious repertory of the Sephardic *Romancero.*[8]

In his correspondence with R. Menéndez Pidal, José Benoliel pointed out that contrary to what was believed, these particular songs were "tan populares como los otros y por una curiosa supersticion, cuando se principian a cantar es obligatorio acabarlos, las judías antiguas no bromean con estas cosas y tiene gracia el tono y aire solemnes que asumen cuando cantan estos romances."[9] To the biblical *romances* that are known to us, Benoliel added *Samsón y Dalila* and the *romance* of *La venta de Joseph,* but none of these have been recorded so far in the Judeo-Moroccan tradition. Another early erroneous assumption is that of the authorship of these ballads. Benoliel

---

[4] M. Salama, "The Biblical Ballads of the Sephardim: A Literary and Linguistic Study" (Ph.D. diss., University of Toronto, 1982).

[5] A. Rodríguez-Moñino, ed., Lorenzo de Sepúlveda, *Cancionero de romances* (Seville, 1584). *Edición, estudio, bibliografía e índices* (Madrid: Castalia, 1967). For an assessment of Sepúlveda's collection, see also R. Menéndez-Pidal, *Romancero hispánico (hispano-portugués-americano y sefardí)* (Madrid: Hernando, 1928), vol. 2, p. 118.

[6] M. Menéndez y Pelayo, *Antología de poetas líricos castellanos* (Madrid: Hernando, 1928), vol. 1, p. xix.

[7] J. de Sancha, ed., *Romancero y cancionero sagrados: colección de poesías cristianas morales y divinas,* vol. 35 (Madrid: Biblioteca de Autores Españoles, 1950).

[8] M. Alvar, *Poesía tradicional de los judíos españoles* (Mexico City: Porrua, 1971), p. xi. For a comprehensive review of the first edition of this book, see S.G. Armistead and J.H. Silverman in *Romance Philology* 22 (1968): 235–242.

[9] Menéndez-Pidal, "Catálogo judioespañol," in *Romances de América y otros estudios* (Madrid: Espasa-Calpe, 1972), p. 129.

hinted that these biblical *romances* could have been composed by Spanish Jews.

> Yo tengo muy posible el que varios romances mucho tal vez de lo que se parece, de asuntos histórico o caballeresco o simplemente novelesco sean de composición judía, pues no escasearon poetas judíos en España, ni de menor envergadura que sus colegas cristianos. Quien compuso . . . *el sacrificio de Isaac* bien podría componer el romance de Tamar.[10]

M. Alvar added that these songs are postexilic and implied that they were composed in the Sephardic communities of the diaspora. ". . . en buena lógica los hemos de creer posteriores a la expulsión: de otro modo vivirían en la tradición española."[11] This hypothesis does not seem implausible. Some popular ballads, such as *La consagración de Moisés* (á-o) ("The Consecration of Moses") and *El paso del Mar Rojo* (á-o) ("The Crossing of the Red Sea"), do not have Spanish counterparts and may have well been composed by Sephardic poets. Furthermore, there is an extraordinary number of *cantares* or songs and long poems written by Spanish-speaking poets and *hazanim* in all corners of the diaspora. In the same vein, D. Catalán thought that the ballad of *El idólatra de María* ("The Idolater"), with its anti-Christian and anti-Marian feelings, may have originated among Spanish Jews in the diaspora or was secretly sung by Spanish Jews in the Iberian Peninsula prior to 1492.[12] An examination of the religious ballad repertoire balladry of the Crypto-Jews of Portugal also reveals a vibrant poetic activity.[13]

A scrutiny of the *pliegos sueltos* (broadsides), *Cancioneros*, or *Silvas* show, however, that these biblical *romances* are also known in the Christian Spanish tradition. Furthermore, the original sources of the Sephardic versions are precisely these very Spanish texts which were transmitted to Sephardic communities of the diaspora well after 1492.

Of the few authentic octosyllabic biblical *romances* which are found

---

[10] From a letter of Benoliel to R. Menéndez-Pidal found in the Archivo Menéndez-Pidal.

[11] Alvar, *Poesía tradicional*, pp. xi f.

[12] D. Catalán, *"El idólatra de María. Judaísmo frente a Cristianismo,"* in his *Por Campos del Romancero* (Madrid: Gredos, 1970), pp. 270–280.

[13] Amilcar Paulo, *Romanceiro criptojudaico. Subsidos para o estudo do forclore marrano* (Braganza: Escola tipográfica, 1969); S. Schwarz, *Os Cristãos{{os novos em Portugal no Século XX* (Lisboa: Empresa Portuguesa de Livros, 1925): E. Cunha Azevedo; *O Sefardismo no Cultura Portuguesa* (Porto: Paisagem, 1974).

in the Eastern and Western Sephardic ballad repertoire, only two
survived in the Peninsular modern oral tradition. There are few
versions of *El sacrificio de Isaac*, mostly confined to the Northern and
Castilian-Leonese traditions, but more than two hundred versions of
the ballad of *Amnón y Tamar* have been collected, making it one of
the most popular traditional songs in the pan-Hispanic *Romancero*
after *Gerineldo, Delgadina, la condesita y la boda estorbada*, and few other
ballads.[14] With the exception of a few remote regions (Isla de la
Gomera, Tenerife), this *romance* is found everywhere in Spain. Its
evident popularity emerges from the treatment of the taboo subject
of incest, a powerful theme which arouses great curiosity not only
because it sets the conflict between nature and culture but also because of the character of the crime. This transgression belongs to
the category of *nefandum* (rape, incest, sodomy) (from the Latin *nefandus*,
ne + *fandus* = "not to be spoken"), meaning "the unspeakable, un-
mentionable," or *l'indicible*, a transgression which is so horrendous or
so unnatural (*contra naturam*) that it cannot be uttered. As expressed
by Amnon in one of the Golden Age dramatic adaptations by Tirso
de Molina, *La Venganza de Tamar* ("Tamar's Revenge") (1621–1624):

> Oh, my dear sister
> I can't, I fear to trust my heart.
> I was about to tell you all,
> but not. Please go. Better to die
> than speak of it.
>   (II.525–29)[15]

The law of silence is also expressed in Calderón de la Barca's *Los
Cabellos de Absalón.*

> Si yo, divina Tamar
> mi pena decir pudiera;
> si capaz de mi voz fuera
> el pesar de mi pesar,
> si me pudiera explicar
> solamente a ti (¡ay de mi!)
> lo dijera; y siendo asi

---

[14] For a study of these ballads of incest, see M. Gutiérrez Estevez, "El incesto
en el Romancero popular hispánico. Un ensayo de análisis estructural," 2 vols.
(Ph.D. thesis, Universidad complutense de Madrid, 1981).

[15] J. Lyon, ed., *Tirso de Molina: Tamar's Revenge (La Venganza de Tamar)* (England:
Aris & Phillips, 1988), p. 121.

que a tu te lo callo, cree
que a nadie se lo diré
pues no te lo digo a ti
    (vv. 361–370)[16]

It is not surprising, therefore, that the word "incest" does not appear
explicitly in any version of the ballad. Although the need to cir-
cumvent the story is essential, the necessity to report it is most compelling and even irresistible. Paradoxically, however, the *romance* of
Amnón y Tamar flourished in a rather subversive way. As with other
related ballads of incest (*Delgadina, Silvana,* and *Blancaflor y Filomena*),
Menéndez Pidal confessed collecting them with a certain *fastidio*
("weariness"). Menéndez y Pelayo stated equally that "aparecen con
estéril abundancia que causa tedio," its theme is considered variably
as "brutal y repugnante," "bárbaro," or "antipático."

   In the Sephardic tradition the ballad of *Amnón y Tamar,* although
confined to Morocco, reveals the greatest number of versions of any
biblical ballad. Its popularity seems to transcend religious boundaries. In a rather hyperbolic statement Benoliel observed that "el
romance de Tamar y Amnón [es] tan conocido en todo Marruecos
que hasta las moritas lo cantan,"[17] surmising quite naively that this
is due to the fact that performers ignore that "que hay muchos
[romances] extraídos del mismo fondo bíblico, como *el sacrificio de
Isaac, el pasaje del Mar Rojo, El nacimiento y muerte de Moisés,* y *La venta
de Joseph.*"[18]

   Similarly the ballad also overcame age limits in Mexico. M. Díaz
Roig is reported to have collected it among children. Furthermore,
ballads of incest, including *Amnón y Tamar,* form an integral part of
the so-called *romances infantiles,* or children's repertoire.[19] Ironically,
however, Benoliel deliberately omitted any version of the *romance*
in his vast collection.[20] Like some of his contemporaries, and for

---

[16] H. Fuad Giacoman, ed., *Estudio y edición crítica de la comedia los cabellos de Absalón
de Pedro Calderón de la Barca* (University of North Carolina, Department of Romance
Languages, 1968), p. 77.

[17] Quoted by Menéndez-Pidal, "Romancero judioespañol," p. 129.

[18] Stated in a letter sent by J. Benoliel to R. Menéndez-Pidal, found in the
Archivo Menéndez-Pidal.

[19] M. Díaz Roig, *Estudios y notas sobre el Romancero* (Mexico City: El Colegio de
México, 1986), p. 218n.

[20] J. Benoliel, "Dialecto judeo-hispano-marroquí o hakitía," *Boletin de la Real
Academia* 13 (1926): 209–233, 342–363, 507–538; 14 (1927): 137–168, 196–234,
357–373, 566–580; 15 (1928): 47–61, 188–223; 32 (1952): 255–289. All these articles

reasons of aesthetic and social decorum, Benoliel modified and eliminated a number of passages which he deemed tasteless or simply
uncharacteristic of Sephardic culture.

The restriction imposed upon the story of Amnón y Tamar is
not, however, a modern or exclusively Jewish phenomenon. Milá y
Fontanals censored similar ballads of incest, such as *Delgadina*, in his
Romancerillo catalán.[21] Often in an effort to project an antiseptic view
of folklore or to purify and whitewash certain aspects of Sephardic
culture, scholars eliminated offensive material.[22] As such, we have
few texts which are considered risqué or belong to the category of
romances picarescos or *vulgares* like the irreverent *Paipero* or *Fray Pedro*.[23]
It is not surprising that in her linguistic studies among Jews from
the Balkans, C. Crews observed:

> Vu leur stricte éducation morale, leur vie de famille pure et les soins
> qu'ils mettaient à échapper à l'ire du Seigneur, il n'est point étonnant
> que les Juifs aient évité tout mot obscène. Il sont allés plus loin: par
> une espèce de tabou réligieux, ou euphémisme . . . les Juifs évitent les
> mots qui évoquent des idées de mort, de méchanceté, de noirceur.[24]

From time immemorial rabbinical authorities were torn between the
compelling need to use the episode from I Samuel 2:13 as an illustration of selfish love and the potential dangers that may derive from
misinterpretations of the episode. It is significant that out of the
fifteen Torah texts censored by the rabbinical authorities, five of
them are about incest, and the pericope of Amnon and Tamar has
a prominent place. Although the biblical episode itself cannot be altered and expurgated because of the immutability of the Torah, it
has to be treated with great caution. The talmudic tractate of Megillah
4:10 indicates that "the stories of David [II Sam. 11:2–17] and
Amnon [II Sam. 13:1–4] are neither read nor translated,"[25] while

---

were conveniently collected as a single volume by J. Benazeraf (Salamanca: Copistería
Varona, 1977).
    [21] M. Milá y Fontanals, *Romancerillo catalán. Canciones tradicionales* (Barcelona, 1882).
    [22] W.P. Zenner, "Censorship and Syncretism: Some Social Anthropological
Approaches to the Study of Middle Eastern Jews," in *Studies in Jewish Folklore*, ed.
Frank Talmage (Cambridge, Mass.: Association for Jewish Studies, 1980), pp. 377–394.
    [23] The song of *Paipero*, because of its sexual connotation, is often sung at most
joyful gatherings.
    [24] C. Crews, *Recherches sur le judeo-español dans les pays balkaniques* (Paris: Librairie
E. Droz, 1935), p. 18.
    [25] R.I. Epstein, ed., *The Babylonian Talmud, Seder Mo'ed in Four Volumes*, vol. 4
(London: Soncino Press, 1938), p. 151.

the Tosefta recommends that "the story of Amnon and Tamar is read and translated."[26]

The reader may be confused by these two apparently contradictory statements; this cryptic opposition is discussed further in the Gemara:

> The story of Amnon and Tamar is both read and translated. Certainly! You might think that [we should forbear] out of respect for David. Therefore we are told [that this is no objection].[27]

and quickly resolved:

> The accounts of David and Amnon are neither read nor translated. But you just said that the story of Amnon and Tamar is both read and translated? There is no contradiction; the former statements refers to where it says "Amnon son of David," the latter to where it says "Amnon" simply.[28]

These restrictions are not applied because of the incest theme. As pointed out in the same Gemara, similar episodes are not banned.

> The story of Lot and his two daughters is both read and translated. Certainly! You might think that [we should forbear] out of respect for Abraham. Therefore we are told [that this is no objection].[29]

Several factors could have influenced this type of unusual censorship and apprehension. Respect for the *avot* ("fathers") is a powerful motivation in rabbinical exegesis, and the offensive incidents connected with King David reflect badly not only on him but also on the Messiah. Furthermore rabbis were rather weary of a literal translation of these texts and of the interpretations introduced by the *metarguman* ("translator"). Finally, the warning in the mishnaic tractate Hagigah (2:1) concerning decorum and the desire not to put wrong ideas into weak minds or the risks in discussing the different degrees of incest are partly responsible for these restrictions.

The moral exemplum provided by the biblical story did not, however, escape rabbinical authorities and Christian theologians. In *Pirké Avot* (5:16), the most popular didactic and aggadic tractate of the

---

[26] J. Neusner, ed., *The Tosefta Translated from the Hebrew, Second Division, Mo'ed (The Order of Appointed Times)* (New York: Ktav, 1981), p. 296.

[27] *Babylonian Talmud*, vol. 4, p. 153.

[28] Ibid., pp. 153–154.

[29] Ibid., p. 152.

Mishna, the passion of Amnon is seen as an equivalent of *loco amor*, or carnal love.

> All love that depends on a [transient] thing, [when the] thing ceases [the] love ceases; and [all love] that depends not on a [transient] thing, ceases not forever. Which is the [kind of] love that depends on a [transient] thing? Such as was the love of Amnon for Tamar. And [which is the kind of love] that depends not on a [transient] thing? Such as was the love of David and Jonathan.[30]

Contrasted with this type of love is that of David and Jonathan.

Similar teachings are echoed in Spain. The Beato Juan Avila shows that Amnon's love is a destructive force that knows no boundary.

> ¿Quién se fiará de parantesco, leyendo la torpe caída de Amon con su hermana Thamar; con otras muchas tan feas y más, que en el mundo han acaecido a personas que las ha cegado esta bestial pasión de la carne, por cercanas que fuesen en parentesco.[31]

Juan Luis Vives, a biblical scholar and a descendant of *conversos* in both the maternal and the paternal lines, in his *Instruction of a Christian Woman*, brings the episode of Tamar as an *exemplum horrendum* illustrating the Fall of Princes through lust and a standard illustration of incest.[32]

In the Judeo-Spanish vernacular from Morocco, or Hakitía, an echo of the biblical episode seems to have survived in the rather enigmatic expression *llamad a Tamar*, meaning, "go or call upon Tamar."[33] It is difficult to see the connection with the scriptural sources and to ascertain whether the name is associated in any way with the character of the ballad, or with the other Tamar of the similarly censored and explicit sexual encounter of Judah and Tamar in Genesis. Neither J. Benoliel, who recorded it,[34] nor his Brazilian translator, Abraham Bentes, supplied an explanation. This phrase, however, is used in moments of despair, upon facing the realization

---

[30] J. Israelstam, *The Babylonian Talmud: Seder Nizikin in Four Volumes*, IV, *Aboth* (London: Soncino Press, 1935), p. 70.

[31] L. Sala Balust and F. Martin Hernández, eds., *Obras completas del Santo Maestro Juan de Avila, Edición crítica*, vol. 1, p. 439.

[32] Quoted by I.S. Ewbank, "The House of David in Renaissance Drama: A Comparative Study," *Renaissance Drama* 8 (196?): 22.

[33] R. Benazeraf, ed., José Benoliel, *Dialecto judeo-hispano-marroquí*, p. 120.

[34] Abraham R. Bentes, *Os Sefardim e a Hakitía* (Río de Janeiro: Mitograph Editora, 1981), A. Bendayan de Bendelac, *Voces jaquetiescas.* Caracas: Biblioteca popular Sefardi, 1990, p. 102.

of the inevitability of a certain happening and of the futility of resorting to a higher authority. It may also reflect the tremendous feelings of powerlessness and frustration of these female characters. Therefore, in spite of the censorship imposed on the story by its taboo theme, and against the serious apprehensions of rabbinical authorities, the story of Tamar found a receptive and wide audience in the Sephardic communities of Morocco through the *romance*.[35]

It seems that this popularity was intrinsic to the very nature of the story, its oral transmission and possible didactic dimension. In a seminal essay dealing with the four functions or effects of folklore, William Bascom showed that folklore maintains the stability of a culture, and there are four ways in which it fulfills this role. Through the first function, entertainment, the individual finds an escape from the restrictions imposed by society. The second function legitimizes cultural activities through rituals and institutions for those who perform and participate in them. Thirdly, folklore has a didactic character. The fourth function, which is the most relevant for our study, contributes to maintain conformity and accepted patterns of behavior.[36]

Through these four functions, folklore has the dialectical ability to apply social pressure and at the same time to play a vital role in transmitting and maintaining the institutions of a culture. Conversely, folklore forces the individual to comply with certain rules, but at the same time it supplies socially approved outlets and escapes for the very same repressions and restrictions which these institutions impose upon the individual. Folklore, therefore, is able to mediate conflicts, mitigate contradictions, and offer limited means of expression. Writing about texts similar to the story of Amnon and Tamar, Bascom added that "folklore reveals man's frustrations and attempts to escape in fantasy from repressions imposed upon him by society, whether these repressions be sexual or otherwise and whether they result from taboos on incest or polygamy."[37] The popularity of the ballad of *Amnón y Tamar* can be explained, therefore, through the functions

---

[35] For a bibliography on this *romance*, see S.G. Armistead et al., *El Romancero judeo-español en el Archivo Menéndez-Pidal Catálogo-índice de romances y canciones* (Madrid: Cátedra-Seminario Menéndez-Pidal, 1978), vol. 1, pp. 216–217. For a number of these versions, see M. Alvar, "Amnón y Tamar en el romancero," *Vox Romanica* 15 (1956): 241–258; and *El romancero, Tradicionalidad y pervivencia* (Barcelona: Planeta, 1974), pp. 389–398.

[36] W. Bascom, "Four Functions in Folklore," in *The Study of Folklore*, ed. A. Dundes (Englewood Cliffs, N.J.: Prentice-Hall, 1965), pp. 279–298.

[37] Ibid., pp. 290–291.

that the ballad fulfills in society among performers and public alike.

In spite of the multiple restrictions imposed upon the *romance* by the sacred nature of its scriptural sources, its taboo theme, the gender of the performers, mostly female, and the contexts of the performance, the romance of *Amnón y Tamar* broke its scholarly mold and became a collective legacy of the ordinary people. If the story was allowed to be told and recreated by generations of singers, the restrictions on the linguistic level are most evident through the oral transmission of the ballad. The constant use of euphemisms reveals the pressure imposed on the *romance*. These euphemisms have been almost unanimously identified by linguists as characteristic of "women's language" or "language of the powerless."[38] They are an integral part of the strategies of coding used by certain groups in order to protect them from the dangerous consequences of directly expressing or exposing certain messages deemed subversive.[39]

One clear illustration refers to the meal prepared by Tamar for Amnon, who was feigning illness. The Second Book of Samuel mentions the word *lebibot*, or dumplings in the shape of hearts (13:6).[40] This term is variously translated in Spanish medieval and Judeo-Spanish Bibles as *escalphaduras* (Alba Bible),[41] *buñuelos* (Amsterdam edition),[42] *fojaldres* (Llamas;[43] E.J. 4),[44] and *hojuelas* (Nácar-Caluinga, Casidoro de Reina)[45] and is in line with folk medicine and beliefs. Chicken and chicken soup are seen as therapeutic and are often associated with an aristocratic meal. Therefore, in the Spanish ver-

---

[38] R. Lakoff, *Language and Woman's Place* (New York: Harper & Row, 1975); William M. O'Barr and Bowman K. Atkins, "'Women's Language' or 'Powerless Language'?" in *Women and Language in Literature and Society*, eds. S. McConnell-Ginet et al. (New York: Praeger, 1980), pp. 93–110; D. Spender, *Man Made Language* (London: Routledge & Kegan, 1980).

[39] J.N. Radner and S.S. Lanser, "The Feminist Voice: Strategies of Coding in Folklore and Literature," *Journal of American Folklore* 100 (1987): 412–425.

[40] P. Kyle McCarter, Jr., ed., *II Samuel: A New Translation with Introduction, Notes and Commentary* (New York: Doubleday, 1984), p. 322.

[41] A. Paz y Melia, ed., *Biblia traducida del hebreo al castellano por Rabi Mosé de Guadalfajara* (1422–1433?) *y publicada por el Duque de Berwick y de Alba* (Madrid: Imprenta Artística, 1920), I.

[42] Joseph, Iacob, Abraham de Salomón Proops, eds., *Biblia en dos colunas, Hebrayco y español* (Amsterdam, 5522 [1762]).

[43] P. José Llamas, *Biblias medievales romanceadas, Biblia medieval romanceada judio-cristiana*, vol. 1, p. 450.

[44] O.H. Hauptmann and M.G. Littlefield, eds., *Escorial Bible I.J.4*, vol. 2 (Madison: Hispanic Seminary of Medieval Studies, 1987), vol. 2, p. 67.

[45] *La Santa Biblia, Antiguo y Nuevo Testamentos* (London: Sociedad Bíblica Trinitaria, n.d.), p. 255.

sions the biblical meal becomes an *ave* ("bird"), *palomino* ("young pigeon"), *paloma blanca* ("white dove"), *pichón* ("squab"), *pechuga de una pava* ("turkey breast"), or *taza de caldo* ("chicken bouillon").

In the Judeo-Spanish versions there is unanimity. All the texts show a *pechuguita de pava* (the "Jewish penicillin"), yet a reconstruction of the earliest prototype of the ballad by M. Alvar reveals that the original word would have been *polla* or *pollita* ("pullet") as it appears in a few versions.[46] Nonetheless this term has completely disappeared in the Sephardic versions simply because the word acquired an obscene meaning and is one of the many names given to the male sexual organ in certain regions of Spain, including Andalusia.[47] This substitution fits perfectly with M.L. Wagner's remarks about the language spoken by Sephardim in the Orient. He observed that

> Con todo rigor se evitan las palabras de pedrisión "perdición", como se llaman las palabras sucias. En vez de las palabras significativas de las partes naturales se emplean casi exclusivamente palabras enfemísticas o translaticias. El miembro viril no se denomina nunca con las expresiones usuales en España; se dice: fulana, la kosa negra, la koza feya y vulgarmente: la mía, la tuya, la suya o la d'abaso, la d'en medio . . .[48]

Other types of euphemisms occur with the rape scene. Rabbi Moshé Arragel de Guadalajara in his *Biblia de Alba* (1432), like most of the translators, used the term *afligio*, but the Peninsular versions of the ballad completely skip over the scene with an excellent *saber callar a tiempo* ("To know when to keep silent"). The sexual act is left to the imagination of the public. Yet the singers did not spare details within the parameters of what is considered permissible. The horror of the crime is described with a simple "hizo de ella lo que quizó," an expression which may be considered a "ridiculously mild euphemism,"[49] but nonetheless a faithful translation of the biblical verse and an expression which refers to serious violations that threaten the very essence of society (Gen. 20:9, 29:26).[50]

---

[46] Alvar, *El romancero*, pp. 195–196.

[47] V. León, *Diccionario de Argot español* (Madrid: Alianza, 1983), p. 128.

[48] M.L. Wagner, *Carácteres generales del judeo-español de Oriente* (Madrid: Hernando, 1930),

[49] See S.G. Armistead and J.H. Silverman, eds., *The Judeo-Spanish Ballad Chapbooks of Yacob Abraham Yona* (Berkeley: University of California Press, 1971), p. 124.

[50] McCarter, *II Samuel*, p. 322.

This attenuation, however, seems to comply with a general tendency in the Judeo-Spanish *Romancero* to mitigate acts of violence. Although some Sephardic texts are more tame in their description, most versions seem to emphasize it. The details vary from

> Tiróla la mano al pecho y a la cama la arronxara
>
> (Larrea Palacin 45:15)[51]

to the more extreme:

> La ha puesto el puñal al pecho, pa' que no se revolcara
>
> (Alvar 39:16)[52]

The reason for the intensification of violence and the demonization of Amnon is deliberate and reveals once more the importance of female singers in the reorientation and restructuring of the ballad. The women who were transmitting these *romances* of incest could hardly be indifferent to the plight of the female victims and to a problem of such vital importance for them. The terse and brief description of King David's reaction toward his daughter and apparent lack of concern may have seemed unfair to these Sephardic female singers. David's indifference will therefore be compensated by the empathy of the performer toward the victim. The role of Tamar in the biblical episode acquires a greater visibility, and her precarious vulnerability is emphasized. His mood is duly captured with an intensifying anaphora:

> Triste saliera Tamar, triste saliera y mal airada
>
> (Anahory 6:16)[53]

The need for revenge becomes imperative, and her anguished voice and lament are clearly heard. In the precise and particular language of the ballad a Sephardic version indicates that:

> tres gritos diera Tamar siete cielos aburacara
>
> (Armistead and Silverman: 17)[54]

---

[51] A. de Larrea Palacín, *Romances de Tetuán* (Madrid: Consejo Superior de Investigaciones Científicas, 1952), vol. 1, pp. 130–131.

[52] Alvar, *El romancero*, p. 391.

[53] O. Anahory Librowicz, *Florilegio de romances sefardíes de la diáspora (Una colección malagueña)* (Madrid: Cátedra Seminario Menéndez-Pidal, 1990), p. 34.

[54] S.G. Armistead and J.H. Silverman, "Romancero antiquo y moderno, dos notas documentales," *Annali Istituto Universitario Orientale Napoli* 16 (1974): 246, later

The growing protagonism of Tamar, which is not indicated in the biblical episode, is an illustration of how female predominance in the transmission of a genre that was essentially and primarily passed from mother to daughter, had a determining factor in molding and reshaping the *Romancero*. As pointed out by D. Catalán,

> Dado el papel preponderante que en la transmisión del romancero viene teniendo la mujer desde hace siglos (debido al carácter fuertemente "matriarcal" de nuestra cultura popular oral), los romances que actualmente se cantan o recitan representan, sin duda, un enjuiciamiento del mundo referencial que ha de considerarse en buena parte como espresión de una perspective femenina. El romancero tradicional moderno constituye una de las más importantes creaciones literarias en que la mujer tiene una voz más destacada posiblemente que la del hombre.[55]

The gender factor is of capital importance, not only for the portrayal of female characters in the *romances novelescos* but also in the selection, survival, and popularity of certain themes that were relevant to women's life. T. Catarella stated that

> the *romancero* ... tells of a female-centered world with female main characters. It centres on the most dramatic events of human life and stresses the dynamics of human relationships. These ballads deal with seduction, betrayals, rapes, poisonings, incests, infanticides and murders and are populated by evil mothers-in-law, faithless lovers, wife-abusing husbands, rejected children, murdered innocents and incestuous relatives. The constant and consistent repetition of these themes leaves no doubt as to their relevance for ballad singer and ballad audience alike. Clearly the *romancero*, and particularly the *romancero novelesco*, is a women's genre par excellence.[56]

The historical ballads, or *romances de asunto histórico-nacional*, ceased to have great interest for these performers. Their *valor moticiero*, or informative and propaganda value, disappeared. Furthermore, the urban make-up of the Sephardic populations did not provide opportunities

---

reprinted in their *En tomo al romancero sefardí (Hispanismo y balcanismo de la tradición judeo-española)* (Madrid: Seminario Menéndez-Pidal, 1982), pp. 96–101.

[55] D. Catalán, *Catálogo general del Romancero, Teoría general y metodología del romancero pan-hispánico; Catálogo general descriptivo*, I.A. (Madrid: Seminario Menéndez-Pidal, 1984), p. 21.

[56] T. Catarella, "Feminine Historicizing in the *romancero novelesco*," *Bulletin of Hispanic Studies* 67 (1990): 332.

to sing ballads while sharing common agricultural tasks, as in the Iberian Peninsula. As observed by E. Rogers.

> ... the change of the social class that sustained the tradition and possibly a shift in the ratio of singers from men to women caused a loss in interest in songs of heroes or adventurous journeys and nurtured the intimate ballad of courtship, jealousy, adultery, murder or other events that had a correlation in the experience of a village dweller.[57]

The traditional ballad of *Amnón y Tamar* is a late composition of the eighteenth century. Menéndez-Pidal wrote: "También debe ser tardío el origen y la tradicionalidad de *Tamar y Amnón* . . . es el romance bíblico más difundido, si bien no parece ser conocido entre los sefardíes de Oriente lo cual arguye contra su antigüedad."[58] M. Alvar is more specific: "Acaso tengamos que fijar su llegada a Marruecos en la segunda mitad del siglo XVIII."[59]

The first known Spanish traditional version was recorded in 1885 in Asturias, and none of the earlier ballad texts from the fifteenth and seventeenth centuries which deal with same biblical episode is related directly to the Sephardic and modern Peninsular versions. It must have been transmitted to the Sephardic communities of northern Morocco after the conquest of Tetuán in 1860. The hypothesis that the ballad was composed by a Jewish poet, as Benoliel claimed, has to be discarded. A *morisco* authorship, as claimed by Menéndez Pelayo, is also to be rejected. The Spanish scholar wrote that "puede ser obra de algun judío o morisco como puede indicarlo la anteposición del artículo *al* al nombre de Tamar."[60] The change from Tamar to Altamar, however, is very typical of the constant reelaborations found in traditional poetry, which *vive en variantes*. The use of the article *al* can be a reminiscence of the Arabic one or the pejorative and insinuating form, as in *La Cava* (*al kahba* = "the prostitute"). As pointed out by Benoliel, "[es] más facil reconocer la adulteración de Tamar en Altamar por aquella tendencia que todos los pueblos tienen de asimilar vocablos extrajeros a los propios con que más se parecen."[61]

---

[57] E.R. Rogers, *The Perilous Hunt: Symbols in Hispanic and European Balladry* (Lexington: University Press of Kentucky, 1980), p. 118.

[58] Menéndez-Pidal, *Romancero hispánico*, I, 345.

[59] Alvar, *El romancero*, p. 239.

[60] M. Menéndez y Pelayo, *Antologia de poetas líricos castellanos* (Madrid: Hernando, 192?), vol. 10, p. 197.

[61] Quoted from a letter of J. Benoliel to R. Menéndez-Pidal and found in the Archivo Menéndez-Pidal.

In contrast with the Judeo-Spanish texts, the Peninsular versions are far removed from the biblical sources of *Tamar y Amnón*. Among the Sephardim, familiarity with the Scriptures and reverence for the biblical writings prevented performers from radically modifying the episode. Sephardic performers seem to have in mind the twice-repeated rule of Deuteronomy: "You shall not add anything to what I command you or take anything away from it, but keep the commandments of the Lord your God that I enjoin upon you,"[62] and "Be careful to observe only that which I enjoin upon you; neither add to it nor take away from it."[63]

Such factors did not exist in Spain. The tradition of biblical scholarship was violently interrupted in the seventeenth century. Inquisitorial censorship and attacks on the Bible in the vernacular were common, and the fear of Judaizing added further apprehension. Therefore, while the initial verses of the Sephardic versions retain faithfully the names of the protagonists and the setting,

un hijo tiene el rey David que por nombre Amnon se llama,

(Bénichou: I)[64]

in a number of the Spanish versions Amnon becomes:

Un rey moro tenía un hijo que era príncipe de España

(Alvar 87:1)[65]

and the crime therefore takes place in Granada.

The strategic importance of this initial verse triggers a series of unending correlative and phonetic associations. The substitution of "un rey moro" for King David is of an ideological nature. The Moor, in the Spanish popular mind, was a feared enemy capable of committing every kind of sexual crime. Marco de Guadalaxara, in his *Memorable expulsión y Iustíssimo destierro de los moriscos de España* (1613), wrote that "[Los Moriscos] dejaban las mujeres viejas, o feas, que tenían, y se casaban con otras más mozas y más hermosas, y algunos se casaban con primas hermanas y aun con hermanas."[66] This belief

---

[62] Deut. 4:2, from W. Gunther Plaut, ed., *The Torah: A Modern Commentary* (New York: Union of American Hebrew Congregations, 1981), p. 1339.

[63] Deut. 13:1, from ibid., p. 1423.

[64] P. Bénichou, *Romancero judeo-español de Marruecos* (Madrid: Castalia, 1968), p. 113.

[65] Alvar, *El romancero*, p. 393.

[66] Quoted by José María Perceval, "Asco y asquerosidad del morisco según los apologistas cristianos del Siglo de Oro," *La Torre* 13 (1990).

survived until the Romantic period, when the taste for Orientalism and exotism allowed the exploration of certain taboo themes to be attributed to Moorish characters.

Traditional poetry is not preoccupied with historical and geographical accuracy. In the Christian Peninsular versions, the name of Tamar changed almost systematically to Altamar and by folk etymology to Altarmares ("high seas"). Consequently, the rape occurs in *Ultramares* ("overseas"), while they are *navegando* ("sailing") and even in an *automovil*. Likewise, the name of Amnon, because of his association with his sister, switched to Altamor, Altomoro, Amor, Timón ("helm"), and through maritime association to Bergantín (a two masted-vessel). There is no end to this series of *sinrazones*, or nonsenses.

In some cases, by means of thematic linking, Amnon becomes Tarquino, the rapist of Lucrecia (from another ballad of rape)[67] or Tranquito, Ataquino (from the verb *atacar*, "to attack"), Paquino, Pepito, Periquito, or the more paradoxical Tranquilo ("peaceful, calm") in spite of his aggressive nature. In the Sephardic versions such onomastic playfulness is absent. The only variant for Amnón is Abón (García Figueras 1), Ablón (Alvar 1:1), or Hablór (Bennaim 15:17) due to the mention of the verb *hablar* ("to speak").

Similarly, the unstable Spanish denouements, which range from the intervention and sanction of the union by the pope to the birth of the illegitimate child, the suicide of Tamar, or her confinement to a convent, are systematically rejected as unproper or unsuitable by Sephardic singers. More faithful to the Book of Samuel, they retained the revenge of Absalom,

> Antes qui arraye el sol, tu sangre sera derramada
>
> (Armistead and Silverman: 21)

reestablishing, therefore, the concept of poetic justice. One unique text from Alcazarquivir concludes with the formulaic happy ending so common in the Sephardic *Romancero*. The line

> No son los tres dias pasados las ricas bodas se arman
>
> (Martínez Ruiz 46:20)[68]

---

[67] On the ballad of *Tarquino y Lucrecia*, see S.G. Armistead and J.W. Silverman, eds., *Romances judeo-españoles de Tánger recogidos por Zarita Nahón* (Madrid: Cátedra-Seminario Menéndez-Pidal, 1977), pp. 69–70.

[68] J. Martínez Ruiz, "Poesía sefardí de carácter tradicional (Alcazarquivir)," *Archivum* 13 (1963): 137–138.

seems to be a migratory verse, borrowed from another *romance* on a related theme. Although there is no biblical or midrashic basis for such an ending, a similar denouement appear in the ballad of *El robo de Dina* ("The Rape of Dinah").[69] The presence of this concluding line in both *romances* may be fortuitous or the product of oral transmission. On the other hand, the similarities between Dinah and Tamar, the nature of the sexual crime committed against them, and certain common features in both stories are rather striking.

The *romance* of *Amnón y Tamar* reveals the dynamic tensions which characterize the Sephardic *Romancero*. In spite of the restrictions imposed upon the biblical episode and the nature of its oral transmission, the Sephardic performers were able to negotiate around these limitations and popularize a text which was aesthetically and morally acceptable to their audiences. In the process they shifted the focus of the biblical narrative, they eliminated the political dimension of the story, and they gave more prominence to the victim, emphasizing her despair and identifying with her. The ever-going midrashic enterprise was once more accomplished, with poetic devices borrowed from the poetic language of the Spanish ballad and a solid knowledge of the biblical material.

---

[69] On the ballad of the Rape of Dinah, see Armistead and Silverman, *Judeo-Spanish Ballad Chapbooks of Yacob Abraham Yona*, pp. 116–128; M. Salama, "And I Whither Shall I Carry my Shame," *Pe' 'amim* 51 (1992): 4–26.

PART FIVE

MUSIC AND ART

PIYYUT MELODIES AS MIRRORS OF
SOCIAL CHANGE IN HARA KEBIRA, JERBA

RUTH DAVIS

University of Cambridge
Cambridge, England

Jerba is a Mediterranean island lying just off the southeastern coast
of Tunisia. According to popular tradition it was the land of the
lotus eaters in Homer's *Odyssey*, and its paradisic reputation in myth
has some reflection in truth. It is a fertile island on a desert latitude, populated by a heterogenous mixture of Berbers—many of
whom belong to the heretic Kharajite sect, Arabs, black Africans,
and an ancient Jewish community whose origins are believed to pre-
date the destruction of King Solomon's Temple in 586 B.C.E. Until
the globally related social and political upheavals of recent decades,
these disparate religious and ethnic groups coexisted peacefully in
an economy based on fishing, farming, various crafts, and trade.[1]

The Jews are concentrated in two villages distinct in personality
and reputation: Hara Kebira ("big Jewish quarter") lies on the out-
skirts of Houmt Souk, the island's main port and market town, while
Hara Sghira ("little Jewish quarter") nestles among olive groves in
the open countryside, some seven kilometers inland. In local legend,
Hara Kebira is the younger settlement, associated with migrations
from the west during the past few hundred years; it is also the more
worldly, excelling in scholarship. Hara Sghira, in contrast, is the ho-
lier community, linked directly with the original migrations from the
east. It was traditionally inhabited exclusively by Cohenim,[2] and its
principal synagogue, standing slightly apart from the village, is the
miraculous Ghriba (Arabic: "lonely one" or "stranger"), whose foundations allegedly contain a stone, a door, and various other artifacts
originally belonging to the Jerusalem Temple. Venerated by Muslims
as well as Jews, the Ghriba attracts pilgrims from the Tunisian mainland, Libya, and beyond, most spectacularly for the festival of Lag

---

[1] The principal crafts are weaving, pottery, and, among the Jews, jewelry making.
[2] I.e., descendants of the priestly caste of the Temple.

B'Omer in the early summer, when islanders and foreigners, Jews, Muslims, men, women, and children gather there to celebrate with ritual spectacles and processions accompanied by music-making.[3]

In the spring of 1929, the German musicologist Robert Lachmann visited Jerba in order to discover whether the alleged age of the Jewish community was reflected in its musical traditions. He focused on the community of Hara Sghira, whose relative isolation, he believed, would have acted as a buffer against alien influences. Lachmann's conclusions, however, were negative; Jewish music on Jerba, he maintained, displayed no more ancient characteristics than Jewish music on the mainland (1940, p. 1; 1978, p. 28). Nevertheless, his pioneering research remains valuable, not only for the richness and originality of its ideas and methods, and its broader musicological significance, but also as the first comprehensive documentation of this particular community's musical culture.[4]

The music of Hara Sghira was purely vocal, since the rabbis forbade the mere presence of musical instruments there.[5] Lachmann recorded three types of repertory differentiated by language, subject matter, musical character, and social function; namely, liturgical cantillation, festival songs (piyyutim), and women's songs. The first two repertories, based on written Hebrew texts. were performed exclusively by men; the last, in the Judeo-Arabic vernacular, was sung only by women. The piyyutim are associated with specific religious

---

[3] The annual pilgrimage to the Ghriba falls into the North African tradition of the hilula (lit. "marriage," i.e., the reunion of the soul with its Maker occurring at the death of a famous rabbi), which is generally celebrated by a pilgrimage either to the rabbi's tomb or to a substitute local shrine. The festival of Lag B'Omer coincides with the hilula of the celebrated second-century rabbi Shimon Bar Yochai, who was buried at Miron in the Galilee. A detailed account of the celebrations at the Ghriba and their significance is given in Udovitch and Valensi 1984, pp. 125–131.

[4] Lachmann's research was first published posthumously and incompletely (only nine of the twenty-two musical examples were included) in English translation, in 1940. A complete edition in the original German, edited by Edith Gerson-Kiwi, was published in 1978. In her foreword, in English and German, Gerson-Kiwi summarizes Lachmann's research and places it in its historical and musicological context. References in this article give both sources.

[5] In most Jewish communities, musical instruments are banned from the synagogue (in contrast to the rich instrumental tradition of the Temple) but allowed in other contexts. The extreme position taken by the rabbis of Hara Sghira at first threatened to jeopardize Lachmann's research, since the community mistook his Edison phonograph with its horn for a musical instrument. It was only after special expiatory prayers had been offered, on the payment of a fee, that the machine was eventually accepted (1940, p. 2; 1978, p. 28).

holidays and family festivals, such as weddings or circumcisions; the vernacular songs focus on festive events, biblical and other themes relating to women.

Lachmann attributed to each repertory a particular relationship to the music of the Tunisian-Arab environment. The cantillation was, within the limitations of its genre, loosely related to the *maqamat* (melodic modes) of Tunisian urban music; the women's songs, in contrast, belonged to the modally undifferentiated sphere of rural Arab music, while the *piyyutim* represented the various *maqamat, iqa'at* (rhythmic-metric cycles), and styles of Tunisian urban music; individually, they reflected classical, popular, Ottoman, and in one case, Lachmann hypothesized, specifically Jewish influences. He noted, however, that the actual melodic repertory of the *piyyutim* was unique (1940, p. 57; 1978, p. 126).

Like liturgical cantillation, the *piyyut* (lit. "poem") is a genre common to all Jewish communities, but far more versatile. Sung in the synagogue and at home, in worship and in festivity, *piyyutim* are incorporated in the standard liturgy, inserted spontaneously at climactic points in the service, and sung purely for entertainment at communal and family celebrations.

The *piyyut* repertory for any given community is open-ended in both word and tune. Certain texts are known throughout Judaism; however, many are confined to specific communities or regions, and in either case their melodies, as Lachmann observed, generally reflect local traditions. Sung by the entire congregation or domestic gathering, providing entertainment for the community at large, the tunes are necessarily simple, attractive, and easily memorable, requiring neither specialist expertise from their performers nor connoisseurship from their audience. Effectively, they are the community's popular musical tradition. Throughout Judaism, the melodies of well-known songs in the vernacular have been adapted to Hebrew texts, and secular texts have often served as models for new Hebrew poems set to the same tunes. It would have been unusual, therefore, if the Jews of Jerba had cultivated an entirely distinctive melodic repertory, as Lachmann's findings suggested.

In 1978 I spent three months in Jerba researching the music of the Jews of Hara Kebira.[6] Inevitably, the social and musical conditions

---

[6] My research was partly sponsored by the City University of Amsterdam, where I was a graduate student. The subsequent writing-up was sponsored by a Leverhulme

I found there were radically different from those Lachmann described in Hara Sghira nearly fifty years before. The founding of the State of Israel in 1948, Tunisia's independence in 1956, and her alignment with the Arab camp against Israel, had provoked waves of mass emigration, mostly to Israel and exceptionally to France.[7] In 1929, Lachmann reported 3,500 Jews in Hara Kebira and 1,500 in Hara Sghira; at the time of my visit the figures had dropped to around 800 and 300 respectively. At first, the homes of those who had emigrated remained empty; then in the late sixties, Muslim immigrants from the mainland began to move in. The mutual trust established between Jerban Jews and Muslims through centuries of peaceful but separate coexistence was not automatically extended to the newcomers, who compound religious and cultural differences with economic ones. The Muslims generally emigrated to find relief from poverty; conversely, it tended to be the wealthier Jews who stayed behind. A mosque now stands at the entrance of the "Jewish Quarter," whose name has officially been changed to As-Sawani ("the gardens"),[8] and the most pervasive religious sound during my stay was the strident recording of the *muezzin* crackling through the air five times a day.

The first substantial intrusion of modern values occurred in the 1940s, when Zionist emissaries from Palestine introduced modern Hebrew as a secular language and established a secular Hebrew education to supplement the traditional religious training of the yeshivot.[9] Boys and girls are taught in separate buildings, and it is clearly the latter, previously denied any formal schooling, who have benefited most from these innovations. Free from the conflicting demands of the yeshivot, the girls devote more time to secular studies than their brothers, and while it is increasingly common for boys to terminate their schooling at the age of fourteen, shortly after their bar mitzvah, many girls continue to attend the Hebrew school until their marriage.

European Studentship. The choice of village was determined by the Free University of Amsterdam and the Tunisian government, which were jointly responsible for the broader research program in which I was participating.

[7] In general, Jews from Tunis and the north, who had come under French cultural influence during the protectorate, emigrated to France, while those from the south, where the French influence was weaker, veered toward Israel.

[8] Hara Sghira has been renamed Riyad ("meadow, garden").

[9] The Zionist initiative was welcomed by the Jerban rabbis, who had previously

The girls' school also provides a framework for various other religious and social activities, including music-making. Since women in Jerba, as in other Oriental communities, are barred from worship in the synagogue, the girls hold daily services in the classroom instead;[10] and they celebrate the Sabbath and other holidays in the school and its inner courtyard with readings, songs, and games. Meanwhile, their brothers play football outside.

Their musical repertory on these occasions comprises modern, secular Israeli songs, reflecting European musical traditions, and *piyyutim* set to Ashkenazi and Ladino melodies, which are sung by the entire gathering without instruments. The dissemination of these foreign repertories on Jerba is continuously boosted by contacts with Jewish communities abroad, and some of the new melodies have also been introduced into synagogue and domestic worship, supplementing the traditional Jerban tunes.

Secular education has been followed by electricity, running water, cars, and the contraceptive pill. Whereas previously, a newly wedded wife would automatically have moved into her husband's home, finding her typically inferior position in the extended-family hierarchy, nowadays young couples are increasingly building separate, European-style villas, their interiors modeled on pictures from glossy Parisian magazines. Modern European fashions have replaced traditional costume among the younger generations; and while married women continue to keep their heads covered according to religious propriety, they use multicolored silk scarves instead of the characteristic red headpiece worn by their elders.

Since the late sixties, the development of a coastal *zone touristique*, spawning a string of luxury hotels and discotheques, has opened up

---

resisted attempts by the Alliance Israélite to establish a French education there. In most cases, the modern Hebrew schools continued to provide the only source of secular education for Jewish children: one hour daily for the boys, and two hours for the girls. At the time of my visit, most families were still boycotting the free government schools on their doorstep (there is a primary school in Hara Kebira and a lycée just outside), even though Jewish children are exempt from religious classes. As a result, most of my informants were illiterate in Arabic and spoke only a smattering of French. In general, families were more willing to send their daughters to the Tunisian schools than their sons, whose time was considered better spent in the yeshivot and, later, in lucrative employment.

[10] The girls told me that they were originally taught to read the service in 1972 by the daughter of the director of the modern Hebrew school, on her return from studies in yeshivot abroad. They literally read rather than chant the liturgy; cantillation on Jerba is still exclusively the domain of men.

new cultural, including musical, horizons; and an international air-
port on the island has facilitated communications with relatives abroad.
The annual Lag B'Omer celebrations at the Ghriba, traditionally
occasions for the exchange of musical repertory, have become a focal
point for family reunions, and a touristic bonanza as pilgrims arrive
on charter flights via Paris and the island's main hotels turn kosher
for the week.

The most intrusive threat to traditional culture has come from the
mass media. Transistor radios arrived in the 1960s, and television
followed close at heel, bringing contemporary European lifestyles and
values directly into the home and, reinforced by commercial records
and cassettes, providing continuous exposure to an ever-changing
spectrum of Tunisian, Middle Eastern, and European popular music.

Many of the popular Arabic media songs have been absorbed into
the community's live repertory, and are typically performed at weddings and other festive occasions by an ad hoc band of male musicians hired specially for the event. At the wedding celebrations I
attended, the band was led by Jacob Bsiri, chief Jewish musician
of Jerba, who sings and plays the *'ud* (Arab lute);[11] he was joined
by fellow Jews on the *darbuka* (goblet drum) and *tar* (tambourine),
and the band was augmented by Muslims playing violin and accor-
dion. The instrumentalists doubled as chorus and were electronically
amplified. The festivities took place in the courtyard of the groom's
home, where a platform had been erected for the musicians; they
sat on chairs facing their audience at a table laden with *bucha* (traditional Jerban spirits made from figs). Below them, the courtyard
was filled with male guests feasting at tables, while the women were
crushed, mostly standing, against the walls.

Certain occasions, such as the last night of wedding celebrations
following the ceremony, or the Lag B'Omer celebrations at the
Ghriba, were considered holy, and the secular repertory was banned
by the rabbis. Instead, a reduced band of Jewish musicians performed *piyyutim*, often to the same tunes as the Arabic songs.

When professional musicians were absent, live and recorded music
would sometimes compete. At the women's celebrations I attended
for a bride's henna ceremony, a cluster of guests sat in the court-

---

[11] Bsiri is a wealthy merchant from Hara Kebira, descended from a family of
musicians; he is regularly hired to perform at Jewish and Muslim weddings on Jerba
and the mainland.

yard singing Arabic songs, clapping and beating the *darbuka*, while beside them a record player was blasting out a continuous stream of French popular songs. No one, apart from myself, seemed bothered by the contradiction; and while I desperately tried to readjust my microphones to pick up the live music, the rest of the guests chatted and helped themselves to refreshments, apparently oblivious of the music altogether.

I found no evidence that the popular European songs promoted by the island's hotels and discotheques had been assimilated into live performances, or that their melodies had been adapted to Hebrew texts, although this type of repertory was well represented in private record collections. It appeared that the only European melodies sung in any communal context were the Israeli songs and *piyyutim*, which had been introduced with Hebrew texts.

Nor did I find any evidence of a repertory corresponding to Lachmann's women's songs. My informants insisted that the Jewish women of Hara Kebira had traditionally sung the same vernacular songs as their Muslim neighbors, which were also sung by Jewish and Muslim men. The only difference was in their accompaniment: the men played a variety of instruments, while the women were restricted to the *darbuka*. I did, however, record a particular genre of Judeo-Arabic songs performed by Jacob Bsiri and other male musicians at the Lag B'Omer celebrations at the Ghriba. Despite their language, these songs were referred to as *piyyutim*, and they were set to similar types of Tunisian and Middle Eastern melodies.

Not all the musical differences between my research and Lachmann's are necessarily linked to the social changes that have occurred on Jerba since his visit. According to my informants, the rabbis of Hara Kebira, unlike their counterparts in Hara Sghira, never banned musical instruments outside the synagogues. Jewish musicians have traditionally played a prominent role in Tunisian urban music; moreover, regular trading contacts would have ensured constant exposure to musical currents on the mainland, including Tunis. The influx of Jewish refugees from Tripolitania around the turn of the century provided a boost to the musical life of the capital; and the 1930s and 1940s saw an upsurge of popular Tunisian Jewish musicians, most famously the female singer Habiba Msika and the singer/composer Sheikh el-Efriat. Songs by these and other Jewish musicians of their generation, in Arabic and Franco-Arabe (the French-Arabic dialect), were vigorously promoted by the newly emerging record industry, and at the time of my visit, they were still performed by the Jews of Hara Kebira. My informants were vague about the origins of this repertory on Jerba; however, it is feasible that these and other Arabic songs had been imported from the mainland well before the arrival of mass media on the island.

Six Piyyutim *from Hara Kebira*

Just as the six *piyyutim* Lachmann recorded in Hara Sghira represented various stylistic tendencies within Tunisian urban music, so those of Hara Kebira, fifty years on, reflected in addition certain foreign Arab and European musical traditions that had been absorbed into the community's live repertory. And while the *piyyutim* of Hara Sghira merely displayed typical characteristics of the secular traditions with which they were associated, certain *piyyutim* of Hara Kebira were identified, whether by the performers themselves or by others outside the community, with particular songs in the vernacular.

Examples 1–6 represent five *piyyutim* set to a total of six melodies, paired with their corresponding secular songs.[12] Exs. 1A, 2A, etc., designate the *piyyutim*, Exs. 1B, 2B, etc., the secular songs, and lower-case letters indicate their texts alone.[13] Ex. 7 illustrates the *maqamat* of Exs. 1–4. In all six examples, musical transcription(s) with text underlay are followed by the texts in both original script and transliteration, with rhyme schemes shown in upper-case letters. Where the quality of rhyme is identical in both versions, the corresponding letter is underlined.

The transcriptions of all six *piyyutim* and the Arabic song Ex. 3B are taken from my field recordings, which are referenced according to tape number, track, and date.[14] Sources for all twelve examples are given after each song title, below. In all cases, the musical transcriptions give a complete round of each melody with its corresponding portion of text(s), i.e., one or two strophes and/or refrain,

---

[12] The relationships between the Hebrew and Arabic versions of Exs. 1, 3, and 4 are discussed in a previous article (Davis 1986).

[13] I am grateful to Isaac Mazouz, Israel Elia, and Yehoram Ten Brink for their help in transcribing the *piyyut* texts of Exs. 3 and 4, and to Habib Gouja for his help in transcribing the corresponding Arabic texts

[14] The complete collection of my field recordings is kept in the Etnomusicologisch Centrum Jaap Kunst, Vakgroep Muziekwetenschap, Universiteit van Amsterdam.

or in Exs. 1B and 2B, one line. In general, the transcriptions represent the opening of each song; the exception, Ex. 4B, is taken from a commercial cassette recording in which the verses are elaborated by repetitions, choral responses, and solo improvisations; in this case the transcription represents the simplest rendering, i.e., the last verse and preceding refrain.

Musical examples 1, 2, and 4 are analytical transcriptions. In Exs. 1 and 2, where individual melodic phrases are ordered differently within each pair of songs, corresponding phrases are indicated by upper-case letters, with primes denoting variants. In Ex. 4, where the ordering of phrases is unchanged, corresponding phrases are presented in vertical alignment. Musical examples 3, 5, and 6 are virtually identical in the Hebrew and the vernacular versions.

The Jews of Hara Kebira described the *piyyut* melodies of Exs. 1–4 as traditional. They volunteered no vernacular sources for Exs. 1A and 2A, nor for Exs. 5A and 6A, which had been imported from Israel. However, they were familiar with the Arabic versions of Exs. 3 and 4, which were frequently sung at wedding celebrations.

On my return from Jerba, I played my recordings to several young Jews from Tunis who had recently arrived in London, including Cantor Isaac Mazouz. These informants were familiar with the *piyyutim* Exs. 1A and 2A, which they maintained were sung to the same traditional melodies in Tunis, and they recognized the imported examples 5A and 6A; one identified the Ladino source Ex. 5B as a Sephardic song from Israel. However, none knew the *piyyutim* Exs. 3A and 4A, although they were all familiar with their corresponding Arabic versions. Both songs represent foreign musical traditions, and in neither case was there a written source for the Hebrew text, suggesting that the *piyyutim* were recent additions to the repertory. In both examples, the Hebrew and Arabic texts are closely related structurally, and in Ex. 3 (as in Ex. 6) there is also a clear relationship in meaning. In sum, it is feasible to suppose that these particular *piyyutim* were modeled on the Arabic songs, and composed recently in Jerba.

In 1982–83 I revisited Tunisia, this time to research the classical repertory, or *ma'luf*, in and around the capital. I took the opportunity to play my Jerba recordings to some of my Muslim colleagues, who identified sources from the *ma'luf* for Exs. 1A and 2A. I was not aware that the Jews of Hara Kebira performed this repertory, which was traditionally cultivated in the northern parts of the country and has generally had only token support from the media. However, my Muslim informants were unanimous in attributing to Tunisian Jews generally a key role in the transmission of the *ma'luf* both in secular contexts and, adapted to Hebrew texts, in sacred ones. In both examples 1 and 2, the melodic transfer between the Hebrew and Arabic versions involves considerable variation and rearrangement of individual phrases, thus masking the overall melodic correspondence.

Musical Examples

Ex. 1A: *Enos notsar ve khal nivra.* 8, 1: 8/6/78.

Ex. 1B: *Muwashshah "'Asfarat 'ashiya" btayhi, nubat al-asba'in.*
        Al-turath al-musiqi al-tunisi [The Tunisian musical heritage], vol. 7 (Tunis: Ministry of Cultural Affairs, n.d.), pp. 12 (text), 31 (music).

The *piyyut*, in praise of the Torah, is typically sung by the congregation when the Torah is taken from the ark and carried in a procession around the synagogue. Sung to the same melody in the synagogues of Tunis, the text is the first item in the *diwan Kol Yacov* (Jerba, n.d.), where it is attributed to the celebrated eighteenth-century rabbi from Hara Kebira, Aharon Perez. The present example was sung with *'ud* accompaniment by Jacob Bsiri in the courtyard of his home, with his baby granddaughter playing audibly in the background.

The vernacular source was identified by Muslim musicians in Tunis. The *btayhi* is the first of the five characteristic rhythmic-metric genres of the Tunisian *nuba*. There are in total thirteen *nubat*, each belonging to a different *maqam*, which constitute the core repertory of the Tunisian classical tradition known as the *ma'luf*. According to popular belief, this repertory was originally imported by Muslim and Jewish refugees from Spain from the twelfth to the fifteenth centuries.

Ex. 2A: *Tsor mishelo achalnu.* 1/5: 21/7/78.

Ex. 2B: *Zajal "Raaityu l-riyada," maqam hsin al-'usayrin.*
        Al-turath al-musiqi al-tunisi [The Tunisian musical heritage], vol. 2 (Tunis: Ministry of Cultural Affairs, 1967), text and music, pages not numbered.

The *piyyut* is traditionally sung at the Sabbath table, in thanksgiving for the meal. The present example was sung by Rabbi Attourgi in a private house in Houmt Souk.

The *Zajal* was identified by Muslim musicians of Tunis. Excluded from the thirteen *nubat*, its rhythm, *mukhames*, identifies it as a later addition to the *ma'luf* composed during Ottoman rule.

Ex. 3A: *Goeli ya, el melekh neeman.* 8/4: 8/6/78.
Ex. 3B: *Ya ma ya ghaliya.* 6/1: 8/6/78 and 18: 4/7/78.

The *piyyut* prays for the redemption of the Jewish people in the diaspora, and affirms their trust in God's faithfulness. Like Ex. 1A, it is typically sung by the congregation when the Torah is removed from the ark and carried in a procession around the synagogue. In the present example it was sung with *'ud* accompaniment by Jacob Bsiri in the courtyard of his home, in the same session as Ex. 1A. The *piyyut* has no written source.

The vernacular song, in which a woman vows to remain faithful to her lover despite his many betrayals of her, is traditionally sung at Jewish and Muslim weddings. I recorded two sources. In the first, it was sung by a Jewish woman in her home, accompanied by her two daughters and a Muslim friend on the *darbuka*; the three girls join in the refrain.[15] In the second, it was sung by Jacob Bsiri accompanied by a mixed band of Jewish and Muslim musicians (see above, p. 482 for line-up) on the penultimate night of the celebrations for a Jewish wedding, held in the groom's home. The transcription was taken from the earlier source.

My Jewish informants from Hara Kebira associated the song with a female Jewish singer named Dalel who was apparently popular in Tunis in the 1930s. However, Muslim musicians from Tunis maintained that the song was originally imported to Tunis at the beginning of the twentieth century by Jewish refugees from the Fezzan region of Libya. They identified the *maqam* with its flattened fourth and sixth degrees as the Libyan *saba* in contrast to the Tunisian *hsin saba* with its neutral fourth and ascending sixth degrees (see Ex. 7 iii).

---

[15] My female informants in Hara Kebira requested that they not be identified by name.

Ex. 4A: *Shalom nasim be'eretz.* 4, 4: 7/6/78.

Ex. 4B: *Andik bahriya, ya rais.* Commercial cassette SODACT: TCMP 338 featuring songs performed by Wadi Essafi, bought in Tunis.

The *piyyut* is a joyful description of the Promised Land, typically sung at the Lag B'Omer celebrations at the Ghriba by a band of Jewish musicians led by Jacob Bsiri. In the present example it is sung by Jacob Bsiri alone, accompanying himself on the *'ud* in the courtyard of his home. The *piyyut* has no written source.

The vernacular song in the Middle Eastern *maqam bayati* (Tunisian *hsin*) represents a woman addressing her lover, a captain of a ship, as she awaits him on the shore. The Jews of Hara Kebira associated the song with the Lebanese singer Wadi Essafi, who had apparently performed it on a recent visit to Tunisia. His recording was widely available on cassette and frequently heard on the radio. Muslim musicians in Tunis, however, maintained that the song was in fact originally sung by the Egyptian Abdul Wahhab and imported to Tunis on commercial records in the 1930s, where it was taken up by Jewish singers of the time, including Habiba Msika.

Ex. 5A: *Tsur mishelo achalnu.* 14, 8: 28/6/78. Same *piyyut* as Ex. 2A, sung to a different melody.

Ex. 5B: Ladino song *Los bilbilicos cantan.* Leon Algazi, *Chants Sepharadis* (London: World Sephardi Federation, 1959), music and text, p. 54.

The *piyyut* was sung in my home in Hara Kebira by Yossi, a jeweler. My landlord's daughter, who was visiting from Israel, came to listen and, recognizing the *piyyut*, joined in.

The secular version was first identified for me by Yehoram Ten Brink.

Ex. 6A: *Lecha dodi likrat calah.* 3, 2: 31/5/78.

Ex. 6B: *Etz ha rimon.* Shlomo Kaplan, ed., *Sh'demati: Selected Songs by Yedidya Admon-Gorochov*, Nissinov Music Library, no. 192 (Israel: Education & Cultural Center of the Histadrut, n.d.), music and text. pp. 20–21.

Liturgical *piyyut*, text by Solomon ha-Levi Alkabets, in which the Sabbath is welcomed as a bride; the analogy is extended to the

Jewish people, who are exhorted to rise up from their suffering and rejoice. The *piyyut* is traditionally sung by the congregation in the synagogue on the eve of the Sabbath; in Jerba, it is also sung by the young girls at their service in the modern Hebrew school. In the present example it was sung by a young girl in her home.

The Israeli song, identified by Jehoram Ten Brink, describes the scent of a pomegranate tree in the Holy Land, compares the people of Israel to a bride, and welcomes them back to their land. The text is attributed to the Ukrainian poet Yaakov Orland, who emigrated to Palestine in 1921. The Ukrainian composer, Yedidyah Admon-Gorochov, emigrated to Palestine in 1906, where he took the Hebrew name Admon.

References

Davis, Ruth. 1986. "Some Relations Between Three *Piyyutim* and Three Arabic Songs." *Maghreb Review* 11, 5–6, pp. 134–144.
Lachmann, Robert. 1940. *Jewish Cantillation and Song in the Isle of Djerba*. Jerusalem.
———. 1978. *Gesange der Jüden auf der Insel Djerba. Posthumous Works* II, ed. Edith Gerson-Kiwi. Yuval Monograph Series VII, Jerusalem.
Udovitch, Abraham L., and Valensi, Lucette. 1984. *The Last Arab Jews: The Communities of Jerba, Tunisia*. New York: Harwood Academic Press.

Appendix

Ex. 1A

Verse 1
enos notsar ve khal nivra'
havu cavod ve tif'arah
ve tnu hosen 'oz la Torah
yir'at yehovah tehorah
larukhah va kol ushmurah
mipnimim hi' yekarah
ye'ot kal shirah vezimrah

Refrain
lichvod Torah hadurah

Rhyme scheme

Verse 1	Verse 2	Verse 3
a	b	d
a	c	c
a	b	d
a	c	c
a	a	a
a	a	a
a	a	a

Ex. 1B
'asfarat 'ashiya, fi bustanin badi
wasaqi l-humaya, badar bil-qati
wat-tuyur hamiya, bisawtin rafi

Rhyme scheme
    a, b
   (a), b
    a, b

Ex. 2A

Refrain
Tsur mishelo achalnu. barachu emunai
shavanu ve hotarnu. cidbar adonai

Rhyme scheme
    a, b
    a, b

Verse 1

hazan et alama. roaynu aviynu
ochainu et lachma. ve yana shatiynu
alcen nodeh lishma. unehalala bepiynu
amarnu ve aniynu ayn cadosh cadonai

Verse 1	*Verse 2*
c a	d a
c a	d a
c a	d a
a b	a b

raaitu l riyada wa-qad labis, thauban jadid min nuwwar
hallahu banafsajuh wa-as, habaqun ma' l-jullanar
idha tashammu lanfas, taquiu miskun wa atar

Rhyme scheme

  (a) b
   a   b
   a   b

Ex. 3A

Verse 1

go'eli ya
el melekh ne'eman go'eli ya
el melekh ne'eman
go'eli ya
ga'al ben hagvirah hayefihfiyah

Refrain

melekh ne'eman

Rhyme scheme

   a
   b a
   b
   a
   a
   a

Ex. 3B

Verse 1

ya ma ya ghaliya
li nahsibik khawan ya ghaliya

li nahsibik khawan
ya ma ya ghaliya
ya shmatat el-'adwan fik u fiya

Refrain
li nahsibik khawan

Rhyme scheme
   a
   b a
   b
   a
   a
   b
   a
   b a
   b
   a
   b a
   b

Exs. 4A & 4B

Ex. 4A

Refrain
ve 'andi cirah, be'eretz
gefen puriyah, be'eretz
yahad nehalel yah, be'eretz
ve nashir shirah, be'eretz

Verse 1
shalom nashim, be'eretz
hadesh ne'urim be'eretz
ve yashvu 'ahim, be'eretz
ve ya'ir orah, be'eretz

Rhyme scheme
   a b
   a b
   a b
   a b
   c b
   c b
   c b
   a b

Ex. 4B

Refrain
'andik bahriya, ya rais
sumru was sharqiya, ya rais
wal-bahru kwals, ya rais
wa saill habibi, ya rais

Final verse
dakhlik ya nawl'sh-shamali
iran al-hawa qad 'alaya
min al-ghurbah lakhira 'alay ball
'ayam zamani wa layall ba'lda 'alay ball,
                                    ya rais

Rhyme scheme
   a b
   a b
   b b
   c b
   d
   e
   d
   d b

Ex. 5A

Refrain
Tsur mishelo achalnu. barachu emunai
shavanu ve hotarnu. cidbar adonai

Verse 1
hazan et olamo. roaynu aviynu
achainu et lachma. ve yayna shatiynu
alcen nadeh lishma. unehalalo bepiynu
amarnu ve aniynu. ayn cadosh cadonai

Rhyme scheme
   a b
   a b

Verse 1	*Verse 2*
c a	*d a*
c a	*d a*
c a	*d a*
a b	*a b*
	. . . etc.

Ex. 5B
Los bilbilicos cantan
Saspiran del amor
Y la pasion me mata
Muchigua mi dolor

Los bilbilicos cantan
En ei arvoi de la flor
Debasa se asentan
Los que sufren del amor

Rhyme scheme
    a
    b
    (a)
    b
    a
    b
    a
    b

Ex. 6A

Refrain
lecha dodi likrat calah
penay shabat nekabelah

Verse 1
shamor vezachor bedibor echad
hishmianu el hamyuchad
adonai echad ushmo echad
leshem utiferet helitehilah

Rhyme scheme
    a
    a

Verse 1	*Verse 2*
b	*c*
b	*c*
b	*c*
a	*a*
	. . . etc.

Ex. 6B
etz harimon natan raycho
bayn yam hamelach ve yericho
shav chomati gedudech mindad
shav tamati dodech midod

Otzrot ofir utsri gilad
rechev mitsrayim shalaiti lach bat
elef hazemer etleh lach magen
min hayor ad hayarden

> *a*
>
> *a*
>
> *b*
>
> *b*
>
> *c*
>
> *(c)*
>
> *d*
>
> *d*
>
>   . . . etc.

BACK TO THE FUTURE: NEW TRADITIONS IN JUDEO-SPANISH SONG

JUDITH R. COHEN

York University, Toronto

Innovation, change, continuity, and stability are the stock-in-trade of the ethnomusicologist. Most ethnomusicologists today no longer automatically posit and lament the "persistent and repetitious 'disappearance' of social forms at the moment of their ethnographic representation" or restrict their concerns to a tradition's "past, not its present or future," to quote James Clifford (1986, pp. 112–113). Indeed, as Adelaida Reyes Schramm has recently said (1990, p. 4), "Surface change no longer signifies loss of identification"; a music can be "transplanted" and "still remain itself."

Change and innovation in Judeo-Spanish song, however, have received little attention from scholars.[1] The time-honored passion of Hispanists for the *romance*—and their corresponding lofty disregard for most other genres—has a musical counterpart in the preoccupation with seeking links between the Judeo-Spanish and the early Spanish *romances*. As well, so few ethnomusicologists have concentrated on Judeo-Spanish song that they have had to lay the groundwork for studies of change by providing studies of the recent past.[2] Whatever the factors, there are significant differences in the images of Judeo-Spanish song held by scholars, performers, consumers, and tradition-bearers.

Shiloah and Cohen's (1983) refreshingly unsentimental typology of the dynamics of change in Israeli oriental music—"museumized," "concertized," "ethnic fine," etc.—is a promising approach. However, while the authors make a crucial distinction between internal and external audiences, any discussion of contemporary Judeo-Spanish song demands a further distinction: between internal and external

---

[1] There have been some exceptions to this; e.g., Katz 1980, Arbeteta 1974, and Seroussi 1990.

[2] For links to early Spanish music, see Etzion and Weich-Shahaq 1988*a*; for life-cycle songs, see Weich-Shahaq 1979–80 and 1989.

performers. While Judeo-Spanish song is hardly unique in being in the throes of major changes, it is unusual in that such a high percentage of its mediated performances are by outsiders to the tradition, precisely the area most neglected by scholars.

With such numerous and various "transplants," one must ask whether Judeo-Spanish song does indeed "remain itself." This paper surveys the kinds of changes in Judeo-Spanish song performance made by both insiders and outsiders, and includes observations by tradition-bearers on some of these changes. The data are drawn from my own observations, as well as from questionnaires and interviews with performers and tradition-bearers. My aim is not to evaluate any specific performance, but rather to move toward an understanding of how changes are conceptualized, put into practice, and received.[3]

Insiders, Outsiders, and "Informants"

Informants for scholarly studies have traditionally been drawn mostly from insiders, while the general public's knowledge is gleaned largely from outsiders or semi-insiders. Informants for this study were drawn from among tradition-bearers, performers both insider and outsider, scholars, audience members, and other persons involved with Judeo-Spanish song.

The terms "insider" and "outsider" are used here descriptively, and not judgmentally. "Insider" will refer, simply, to someone who has grown up in the tradition. Tradition-bearers are insiders; they may or may not also be performers. "Insider private performers" refers to those who sing for themselves, family, or the researcher only. "Insider community performers" may also perform in a community setting—for example, synagogue services or Golden Age groups. "Insider public performers" are those who regularly perform for varied audiences, usually for a fee. While insiders perform in any of these contexts, "outsiders" usually refers only to "public" performers. To place my own role in context, besides my academic involvement, I am an outsider performer who has performed for

[3] This represents the preliminary findings of a two-year postdoctoral fellowship project which includes questionnaires distributed to performers, scholars, and audience members involved in Judeo-Spanish music, funded by the Social Sciences and Humanities Research Council of Canada, whose support I gratefully acknowledge.

many years with Gerineldo, an otherwise insider group specializing in tradition-based renditions of Moroccan Judeo-Spanish songs.

Types of Change

I propose to examine changes within two main categories: concepts and behavior; and musical traits. This will be familiar to any ethnomusicologist as an adaptation of Merriam's (1964) now-classic "sound, behavior and concept" categories. The first group includes such parameters as notions of authenticity, identity of the performers, repertoire and canon formation, context and function, transmission and dissemination. The second group looks at melodic and rhythmic traits, vocal style, texture, instrumentation, movement, and the words of the songs (which I will call, simply, "text," though of course "text" is used more broadly). It should be understood that this survey of changes is not and cannot be an exhaustive one.

Concept and Behavior

Authenticity
The most radical change in performance practice would be, of course, the total disappearance of the tradition, in fact a fairly rare phenomenon. One often thinks of an archetypal "authentic" rendition of a Judeo-Spanish song in terms of a "classical model": a woman in pre-mass media Morocco rocks her grandchild to sleep singing a *romance* replete with fetching archaisms and alluring Merovingian roots. But how "authentic" would this have sounded to a fifteenth-century Spaniard? Who would enjoy listening to it and/or perpetuating it in this form in the late twentieth century? By no means all of the informants I have interviewed so far—including tradition-bearers. When the demise of the tradition is lamented, the mourning is usually for this incontestably doomed "classical model," which perhaps should not be thought of as synonymous with the tradition as a whole. Is it productive to assume a definition of authenticity and then use an "authenticity quotient" as a major criterion for determining the value of a performance?

Performers

Perhaps the most dramatic change is in the identity of the performers. Considered in global perspective, performance changes in
Judeo-Spanish song are no more dramatic than those in other traditions. However, they are unusual in that their mediated dissemination takes place largely through outsiders, who are responsible for
most of the major changes. Questions of "legitimacy" arise. Which
is the more important, the nature of the changes or the identity of
the changers? Who is really an outsider or an insider? Is an Ashkenazi
Jewish singer more an outsider to the tradition than a Spanish folksinger? Is a Moroccan insider performer more an outsider to the Eastern Mediterranean tradition than a non-Jewish Turkish singer?

Canon and repertoire, context and function

The "canon" of Judeo-Spanish song is seen differently by different
groups. To the Hispanist, it has often meant the *romances*, the ballads, and, secondarily, life- and perhaps calendar-cycle songs. To the
general public, it often means lyric songs, usually from the Eastern
Mediterranean repertoire—or whatever the performers choose to present to them, with or without labels. For the Eastern Mediterranean
tradition-bearer, Moroccan ballad versions are often "not Jewish,
they're Spanish." For Moroccans, the canon is composed of "our
songs," those which are "*los nuestros*," even if they use a Spanish folk
tune as the musical vehicle for the misadventures of long-defunct
peninsular nobility.

Twentieth-century compositions have been mostly in the genres
least favored by academic attention: parodies, topical and recreational
songs, love songs, Zionist songs, and, in the case of Flory Jagoda,
new calendar-cycle songs. Wedding songs and, especially, *romances*
have remained a closed canon. They also receive the most academic attention, and are the genres whose survival and perpetuation
are the most threatened.[4] Repertoire depends largely on context and

---

[4] Some of Flory Jagoda's compositions have become popular among both (eastern Mediterranean) insider and outsider performers; her recordings are being re-
issued by Global Village Music (New York). Los Pasharos Sefardíes (Istanbul) have
recorded two songs with lyrics by Avner Perez and music by group member Selim
Hubes (Cassette 4). See also Rosa Zaragoza's settings of medieval Judeo-Catalan
wedding advice to "Ladino" tunes (Rosa Zaragoza, *Cançons dels Jueus Catalans, Cançons
Jueu-espanyoles* [Madrid: Saga, SEC541, 1987], side 1). Local community-based compositions, often parodies or topical narratives, are rarely discussed in the literature;

function. In the "classical" model, certain songs were sung while
swinging on *matexas*, others while rocking a child. Others were related
to specific stages in the life or calendrical cycle. Selection of repertoire on the part of tradition-bearers is now, of course, also influenced
by the investigator's own agenda. *Endechas* (laments) are a case in
point; normally, they are sung only at a ritual or personal time of
mourning. Recently, a Tetuani tradition-bearer sang one for me;
when I asked him about appropriateness, he remarked somewhat
guiltily that if his wife had been home she would have said not to
sing it. He then added that a week earlier, during Passover, he would
not in fact have sung it, as that was a time of celebration. On further reflection he concluded, with evident relief, that because this
session took place during the period of the *'Omer*, a song of mourning could in fact be sung.

Formal performances are a fairly new context. They replace traditional functions with aesthetic or practical concerns, especially the
need to provide variety. Too large a serving of *romances* is generally
deemed indigestible for all but specialized "gourmet" audiences; there
is a prudent tendency to ration out the "heavier" songs, padding
them well with lighter material for an *ensalada* effect, to borrow a
term from Renaissance music. Religious constraints and traditional
gender roles may be affected. Insider and outsider public performers differ somewhat in approach; insider groups may not follow traditional gender roles slavishly, but they do tend to give them more
attention than outsider groups; for example, liturgical songs sung by
men, wedding songs by women.

Even when the performers are insiders, there are major differences
in context and function. The first shift, from the private or communal to the public domain, has been followed by one which recalls
Jacques Attali's observations regarding "repetition" and "representation." Attali (1977) posits that in an earlier stage, repetition—
meaning recorded versions of performances which can be repeated
indefinitely—was aimed at supporting representation, the live setting.
The opposite, he suggests, is now the case. Live performances are
aimed largely at repetition; you are what you record and sell. Insider
and outsider public performers of Judeo-Spanish will often do sev-

---

see my dissertation (Cohen 1989, pp. 175–187); also Seroussi (1990). Western art-
music-style choral or other compositions based on Judeo-Spanish songs are not considered here.

eral "takes," sometimes dubbing in extra parts or dubbing out mis-
takes until they have a "good take." Tradition-bearers may also
repeat a song several times at the researcher's request, but the versions are kept, rather than discarded as in the studio, and are analyzed as variants—there are no "bad takes."

Transmission and dissemination
Direct person-to-person oral transmission, featuring gradual osmosis,
is no longer the principal means of transmission. However, one must
remember that written transmission of texts is nothing new. Referring
to an old copybook of ballads written out in an aunt's old-fashioned,
elegant handwriting, or jotting down more words for a friend at a
Golden Age meeting are logical sequels to the old broadsides and
chapbooks.

Written musical notation is almost never used by insider private
or community performers, and, to my knowledge, only rarely by
insider public performers. By contrast, it has been till extremely
recently the main resource of most outsider performers.

Secondary orality is probably now the most important means of
transmission. Its main disadvantage is, of course, that the listener
hears the same ornaments, rhythmic subtleties, etc., every time, so
that these become fixed as standards. Also, the transmitter has no
specific awareness of the receiver, or, more accurately, is aware only
of the researcher and recording equipment; this also influences the
rendition. Another problem is that of outsider groups learning songs
from recordings of other outsider groups, themselves working from
inaccurate transcriptions; perhaps one could call this "tertiary orality." Even with its drawbacks, secondary orality is a vast improvement over reliance on written transcriptions. The recent involvement
of some scholars in making archival material and their own expertise available to performers is the next-best thing to "organic" transmission, with the added perks of narrowing the gap between scholars
and performers and adding a positive practical dimension to scholarly research.

The video *Trees Cry for Rain*[5] contains a scene with another variation
on secondary orality: an outsider performer is learning a song from
a tradition-bearer. As she sings, adding chordal accompaniment on

---

[5] Rachel Amado Bortnick, Bonnie Burt Productions (California, 1989), 30 minutes VHS.

a guitar, the tradition-bearer (who is the narrator) stops her and corrects her pronunciation. The camera then zooms in on the singer picking up a pencil and writing down the correction in a notebook; when she sings the song again, the tradition-bearer's comment is, "Beautiful!" Direct transmission from insider to outsider and a combination of oral and written transmission are witnessed by the audience, who also learn a little through this visual "secondary orality". The zoom-in on the hand holding the pencil and the final approving comment let the audience know that the insider approves of at least this particular outsider's efforts.

Secondary orality is not restricted to outsiders; tradition-bearers in this and, it must be remembered, countless other traditions do not scorn learning new songs or refreshing their memory through recordings.

Dissemination

Recording and concertizing would not effectively disseminate Judeo-Spanish songs without marketing. Though systematic marketing is recent, as are, of course, videos about the tradition, commercially released recordings go back to the beginning of the recording industry. As this topic requires a study in its own right, I will merely touch on it, to point out that, for better or for worse, business agents, media producers, critics, music festival organizers, and others all have important effects on Judeo-Spanish song. The visual images projected through record, cassette, and CD graphics also help shape the image of the tradition, especially the public's association of it with exoticism and/or early music, but that is another story for another time (see Cohen 1990 and 1989, pp. 119–123).

Musical Traits

Melodic, rhythmic, and structural changes

Tradition-bearers change little in the areas of melody, rhythm, and structure. A dramatic change in some formal interview settings is the total absence of melody when informants recite texts; such renditions are still valued because the researcher is primarily interested in the words, or, as in the case of a recent study, because the recitation provides useful information about underlying rhythm concepts (Armistead et al. 1986, p. 31). Etzion and Weich-Shahaq (1988*b*) report that younger tradition-bearers tend to sing in a more definite rhythm, speculating that media influences may be a factor in this. During field recording sessions, tradition-bearers often make some changes; for example, deliberately omitting repeated lines or refrains.

Insider public performers may standardize melodic and rhythmic elements, often as a result of adding instrumentation to traditionally unaccompanied songs. Outsider performers have, in general, only recently begun to learn some of their material from live or recorded sources. Especially when working from transcriptions, their interpretations of melody, mode, rhythm, tempo, to say nothing of vocal style, are often imperfectly understood, or even totally at odds with the song as usually performed. Even when using documentary recordings as models, outsider performers may unwittingly strive to duplicate a rendition which happens to be atypical, perpetuating it in performance or recordings. Ornamentation may be technically impressive, but rarely sounds like the *floreo* so important to tradition-bearers. Structural changes may include such innovations as inserting a recited portion into a sung rendition.

From listening to recordings, attending concerts, and interviewing performers, it seems clear that, while insider performers are concerned with authenticity (as they see it), outsider performers consciously focus on each individual song as a separate musical entity, relying on their own training and sensitivity to recreate it. For the tradition-bearer, while ornamentation, tempo, and other aspects are important, recognizing a melody as the "right one" is often the crucial criterion for approval. "*Está bien,*" commented one woman singer, "*yo la canto así.*" A Tetuani well-versed in synagogue music listened to my cassette of an insider performer singing a well-known *piyyut* (hymn). On the cassette, the singer performs one verse in southern, rather than northern, Moroccan style. Mystified, the tradition-bearer finally decided that the singer must be "Syrian or Turkish," though in fact he knew him! When the northern Moroccan melody returned, he commented, "*Esa [voz] es la* 'real one.'"

Singing style

An obvious problem in determining changes in singing style is the advanced age of most traditional singers, making changes in timbre, tessitura, tempo, and phrasing difficult to assess. An elderly singer may be using subtle phrasing or may simply be short of breath. A woman may have sung in a higher range as a young girl, especially if she has smoked for any length of time. Insider public performers, logically enough, usually have a vocal timbre typical of their culture. However, among outsiders, singing style, especially timbre, is probably the element furthest from the traditional style. It usually reflects their musical training or background: Western art music; Spanish, Israeli, Ashkenazi Jewish, North American "folk music"; cantorial style; or, particularly popular recently, an "early music" style. This is often in a high tessitura, especially for women, frequently using the sort of "white" timbre which has become popular in the past decade or so of early music performance practice (and which I sometimes think of as "neo-virginal" or "aspiring angel" style).

In general, singers are far more resistant to altering their vocal production than to mastering new instrumental techniques or complex pronunciation systems. Some tradition-bearers who listened to my sample tape found it difficult to discuss vocal style, ignoring the question altogether no matter how it was phrased, and reverting to melody recognition and pronunciation. Others commented that it sounded like "church singing"; another observed that "*la voz es muy educada; no tenemos la voz afinada*," though such comments were not necessarily meant as adverse criticism.

Texture
Vocal harmony is seldom used by insider *or* outsider performers, except of course in choral settings, though instrumental arrangements may involve some polyphonic elements. Among insiders, Ester Roffé (Morocco/Venezuela) adds some unexpected choral effects to some songs, and Flory Jagoda (Sarajevo/Washington, D.C.) uses some parallel thirds, reflecting one of the musical styles of Yugoslavia. The Oziel family (Tangiers/Toronto) have harmonized some a capella *piyyutim* (Hebrew hymns).

Use of instruments
There are few changes in the use of instruments among insider private performers. One group of Moroccan women living in Israel recorded several wedding songs using castanets, a practice which tradition-bearers I interviewed unanimously agreed was atypical. (A sample of this was imitated almost exactly by the outsider performing group Voice of the Turtle, illustrating my earlier point about the vagaries of secondary orality.)[6]

---

[6] Weich-Shahaq 1979–80 and Voice of the Turtle, *Bridges of Song: Music of the*

Insider community performers may use Western instruments, such as violin or piano. When one elderly *paytan* from Tangiers, living in Toronto, sings or plays violin for a traditional *noche de la novia* ("bride's night"), his son accompanies him on the synthesizer; he commented to me that this saves a lot of money because one needn't hire several musicians. Instruments of the host culture which are useful or are symbols of the mainstream culture's power are often selected (as is the case with borrowed melodies).

Insider public performers may use instruments more discretely than outsiders, but they do use them, sometimes in contexts where they would not normally be heard. Outsider performers use an eclectic array of instruments, and apply them more or less indiscriminately to different genres, sometimes performing purely instrumental versions of a song. As is the case with vocal technique, performers often display considerable virtuosity.

Electronic technology also implies changes. Overdubbing, reverb, and other studio recording techniques add new dimensions to recorded renditions; and, even in live performances, the sound system and hall acoustics influence vocal production, balance, and other factors.

The mere presence of instruments, of course, alters performance style, standardizing starting pitches, sometimes precluding the use of microtones, and perhaps even altering the structure of a song by adding instrumental interludes where there would typically be no break between stanzas.

Far from objecting to the use of instruments, tradition-bearers have been known to complain when performers present too many a capella numbers. One man, who helps lead the liturgical singing in his congregation, responded when asked specifically, "*No creo que el instrumento cambie el valor de la canción. La hace . . . más bonita, que si la letra no la cambia . . . uno puede tocar con la guitarra, otro con el violín, otro con el laud: el fondo, la base e' la misma, no?*" Or, more succinctly, a woman tradition-bearer from Tangiers supported instrumental innovations because, after all, music is "*pour les oreilles.*"

Spanish Jews of Morocco (Titanic Records Ti-189, 1990). For insider public performances of the Moroccan repertoire, see Gerineldo, *Chansons traditionnelles judéo espagnol,* vols. 1–4.

Movement

Movement in Judeo-Spanish song is traditionally associated either with domestic tasks, swinging on the *matexa*, dancing while singing wedding songs, or expressive hand gestures. It is relatively rare for movement to be deliberately incorporated into formal performances, but there are notable exceptions, both in gesture and in movements formally designated as dance.

Dance movements are part of at least two groups' performance repertoires: Gerineldo, an insider group, and Voices of Sepharad, an outsider group. The former's concerts include short sequences from traditional women's wedding dancing; and its Judeo-Spanish musical theater productions incorporate traditional gesture sequences related to the scenes of daily life, from stylized ones such as wedding processions to those related to domestic tasks and everyday speech and song. These movements, especially facial and hand gestures, are necessarily exaggerated for the stage. Voices of Sepharad features a dancer trained in both modern and Yemenite dance; her blend of flamenco, Middle Eastern, and other dance forms is an integral part of their performances.

Movement, ranging from traditional to highly stylized and contrived, is important to D. Raphael's video *Song of the Sephardi*. Rebecca Amato Levy, a tradition-bearer from Rhodes, and her friends and family, produced a home video (not for general distribution) which includes both *à la turca* dancing to Sephardic songs and movements of domestic tasks, such as sewing and serving traditional coffee and pastries. Mrs. Levy herself, when I interviewed her, observed repeatedly that the Turkish insider group Los Pasharos Sefardíes was remarkable not only for its singing style but for its traditional gestures.

Movement and gestures function simultaneously as a reinforcement of identity for insider audiences and a nonverbal partial translation for non-Hispanophones.

Manipulation of the text

Many competent scholars have discussed changes in texts by tradition-bearers, and this complex subject will not be treated here. In relation to performance, during a fieldwork session tradition-bearers may decide to omit refrains or repeated lines, thereby both shortening the text and altering the song's structure. Or they may ask to see a printed version of the text to refresh their memory, and end up singing a version partly read, partly remembered. Insider public performers make relatively few changes. The most common are singing verses in a prearranged order and shortening/condensing long songs for non-Hispanophone publics or recording convention. The presence of highly religiously observant audience members may prompt omissions in certain bawdy wedding songs, or an insider public might stimulate spontaneous insertions. Other changes reflect, for example, the de-christianization process common to renditions by tradition-bearers. One of Gerineldo's singers, during a rehearsal, contributed to this process without ever having heard of it, while rehearsing the *romance La mala suegra*; two other members collaborated on altering certain phrases in the nineteenth-century narrative *Sol la Sadika*, to avoid possible offense to Muslims.[7]

While insider public performers may standardize traditional pronunciation, outsiders may seriously mispronounce certain vowels and consonants, or even go too far in the opposite direction in the effort to project a "pure" pronunciation. Others strive to imitate regional pronunciations, using several different ones in the same concert or recording. Text underlay in particular is often treated atypically by outsider performers. For the tradition-bearers I interviewed, pronunciation and enunciation were almost inevitably crucial criteria for performance evaluation.[8]

Both insider and outsider performers semidramatize dialogue songs, usually with a male and a female singer "taking roles." While this is not traditional in Sephardic balladry, it does have parallels in *romance* balladry; for example in a version of *Gerineldo* collected in Trás-os-Montes, a male and a female singer perform the ballad in alternating dialogue (*Portugal: Chants du blé*). One insider performing group that answered my questionnaire reported that they sang songs in dialogue form, and elsewhere stated repeatedly that they presented the songs authentically, implying that this is not a change from outside but a natural development.[9]

---

[7] In *La mala suegra*, the vocalist asked if she could substitute "a mi padre y a mi madre" for "Jesu Cristo y mi madre." Among the changes made to *Sol la sadika* was the elimination of the phrase "no fiarse en ninguna mora." These changes were all made during rehearsals in which I participated as a group member.

[8] Cf. Hirshberg (1990, p. 84) on the Karaites: ". . . insistence on accurate text setting . . . appears to prevail over melodic features."

[9] Karen Gerson of Los Pasharos Sefardíes, questionnaire.

Conclusion

Changes, both deliberate and otherwise, are more common among outsider performers, though by no means absent from insider public or even private renditions. Insider private and community changes are the least frequent, and usually occur within the parameters of musical behavior and concept, rather than in specific musical traits. Insider public changes occur in both main categories, but rarely in areas which tradition-bearers consider crucial: pronunciation, and use of traditional texts and tunes. Outsider changes, as one might expect, are the most widespread and numerous. Tradition-bearers often tolerate and even welcome and enjoy changes as long as *"la melodía está bien y la letra es clara,"* to quote one woman singer from Tangiers. Their instantaneous recognition of a performer's "otherness" does not by itself imply rejection; in fact, they have sometimes expressed pride that musicians from the mainstream culture pay serious attention to their music.

Finally, all this must be seen in perspective. Change is not new in the Judeo-Spanish or any other tradition—and it could be even more dramatic in this era of "worldbeat" and "ethnopop." The "Phantom of the Ofra," as the *Canadian Jewish News* dubbed her, does not yet have a counterpart in Judeo-Spanish song, nor does the klez-jazz fusion. For the worldbeat audience, all musics are theoretically sacred but nothing specific is sacred; all can be appropriated in a sort of cultural neocolonialism. Certainly not all "outsiders" who try to revitalize Sephardic song, incorporating musical innovation, achieve successful "transplants"; but neither do they deserve such sweeping dismissals as "ejecuciones cada una peor que la anterior" (Hassán 1986, p. 35).

It could well be argued that performers have a responsibility to present at least a portion of their repertoire in traditional style, to show the public where the tradition is coming from, as well as the directions it is going in. But treading water is not ultimately a solution. An insider community performer, speaking of *piyyutim*, reminded me of the injunction to sing "new songs," as well as old, of praise. David Harris, an outsider performer, wrote, "It's incumbent on all of us who are passionate about [Judeo-Spanish song] to make it dynamic."[10] If this now-fragile tradition is to continue its long his-

---

[10] "New songs of praise" (*shirim hadashim*) comment: interview with Samuel Oziel,

tory of migration, adaptation, and survival, all changes should certainly not be embraced with indiscriminate enthusiasm. But assessing their validity means examining them as musical interpretations, as a component of "world music"—and as contributions to a tradition which has always been less subject to change than open to it.

Musical Examples

I am including two musical examples of change out of many possible ones.

1. *Desde hoy, la mi madre (La despedida de la novia)*
This is a Moroccan wedding song transcribed in three versions. The first is from the singing of Alicia Bendayan (Tetuan/Israel), as recorded on Weich-Shahaq, *Judeo-Spanish Moroccan Songs for the Life Cycle*. The second is from the singing of Joaquín Díaz, a Spanish folksinger and collector, who, while he did not state his source on the recording, had access to a much earlier recording of Mrs. Bendayan's version, recorded by Manuel Alvar in the 1950s (*Temas Sefardíes*, p. 36). I recorded the third from an elderly Tangiers woman living in Montreal, Canada, who stated that she had learned it from the Díaz recording. Though she had not heard the first recording, her rendition is closer to it, particularly in ornamentation and tempo, than it is to Díaz's. This also illustrates the idea of tertiary orality suggested earlier.

2. *Morenica a mi me llaman*
This is a very popular wedding/love song from the Eastern Mediterranean repertoire, with a text which can be traced to early Spanish poetry.
    a. Victoria Rosa Hazan: recorded from this legendary Turkish Sephardic singer in 1977, by Robin Greenstein, at the Brooklyn Sephardic Home for the Aged. This version is similar to others I have heard sung by tradition-bearers. It is the only one of the four to employ percussion.
    b. From the four-volume anthology *Chants judéo-espagnols* by Isaac Levy (vol. 1, p. 26). This transcription, like many from this anthology,

Toronto, March 1991. David Harris comment: from my "Performers Questionnaire," completed in April 1991.

MUSICAL EXAMPLE 1: *Desde hoy, la mi madre* (*Despedida de la novia*) (Morocco)
(OST-original starting tone)

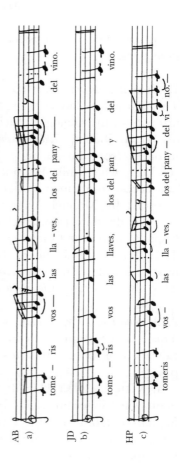

MUSICAL EXAMPLE 2: *Morenica a mi me llaman* (eastern Mediterranean)
(OST-original starting tone)

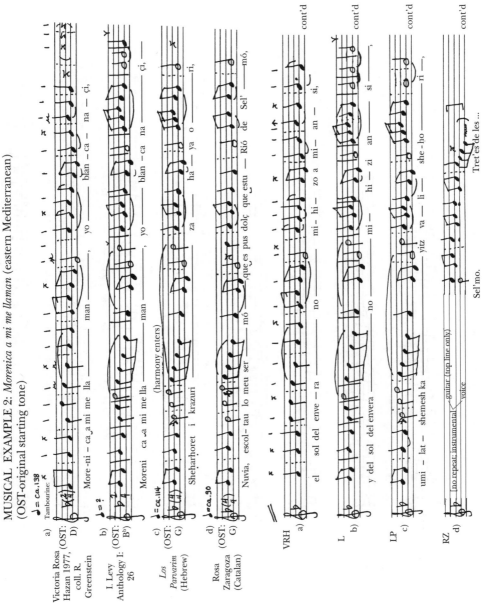

(*Morenica* cont'd)

served as the prototype for many outsider performances. Note the regularized tempo, simplified melodic line, and omission of the Greek words *mavromatia mou* ("dark eyes").

c. From *Los Parvarim: Judeo-Español Songs* (CBS 62947, n.d.). Apparently based on the Levy transcription, there are minor melodic and rhythmic changes, but note especially the two most startling alterations: the change of language from Judeo-Spanish—arguably the strongest identifying feature of the repertoire—to Hebrew; and the use of Western harmony. Also, there is a change in gender; the song is obviously in the voice of a woman, and is here sung by a male duo.

d. Rosa Zaragoza: *Cançons dels Jueus Catalans* (Saga SEC541). Tertiary—or further—orality; this is obviously based on the Parvarim version, even to the same instrumental interlude. However, the text once again changes languages; Zaragoza has set medieval Judeo-Catalan words to it, adapting them to fit the melody, and also changing the original Hebrew within the Catalan text to Catalan, and even borrowing words from another poem (Riera i Sans 1974, pp. 55–61). The instrumental accompaniment, while it takes the Parvarim arrangement as a starting point, adds Renaissance-style counterpoint.

References (Print and Recording)

Arbeteta, Letizia. 1974. "Raíces de la canción sefaradí y problemas de su interpretación a propósito de un disco de Sofía Noel." *Cuadernos hispano-americanos* (Madrid) 287:490–497.

Armistead, Samuel G.; Silverman, Joseph A.; and Katz, Israel J. 1986. *Judeo-Spanish Ballads from Oral Tradition*, vol. 1. University of California Press.

Attali, Jacques. 1977. *Bruits*. Presses Universitaires de France., Clifford, James, and Marcus, George, eds. 1986. *Writing Culture*. University of California Press.

Cohen, Judith R. 1989. *Judeo-Spanish Songs in the Sephardi Communities of Montreal and Toronto*. UMI.

———. 1990. "The Medieval Sephardic Fusion Song." Paper presented at the 1989 Medieval Studies Congress, Kalamazoo, Michigan.

———. 1995. "Just Harmonizing it in their Own Way: Changes and Reactions in Judeo-Spanish Song", *Revista de Musicologia* 6/3: 1578–1596.

———. 1996. "Pero la voz es muy educada: reactions to Evolving Styles in Judeo-Spanish Song Performances," *Sephardica: Hommages Haim Vidal Sephiha*, ed. Winifred Busse, Marie-Christine Varol, Berlin, Peter Lang, pp. 65–82.

Etzion, Judith, and Weich-Shahaq, Shoshana. 1988a. "The Spanish and Sephardic Romances: Musical Links." *Ethnomusicology* 32, no. 2:1–67.

——— and ———. 1988b. "The Music of the Judeo-Spanish Romancero: Stylistic Features." *Anuario Musical* 43:221–225.

Greenstein, Robin. 1979. *La Serena: A Collection of Ladino Songs*, New York: American Jewish Congress (booklet & cassette).

Hassán, Iacob. 1986. "Los Sefardíes como tópico." *Raíces* 1.
————; Romero, Elena; and Díaz-Más, Paloma. n.d. *Temas Sefardíes del Cancionero Sefardí*. Ministry of Culture (Spain) (booklet & two cassettes).
Hirshberg, Jehoash. 1990. "Radical Displacement, Post-Migration Conditions and Traditional Music." *World of Music* 32, no. 3:68–86.
Katz, Israel Joseph. 1980. "Stylized Performances of a Judeo-Spanish Traditional Ballad: *La mujer engañada*." In *Studies in Jewish Folklore*, ed. Dov Noy and Frank Talmage, pp. 181–200. Cambridge, Mass.: Association for Jewish Studies.
Levy, Isaac. 1959–73. *Chants Judéo-espagnols*. 4 vols. London: World Sephardi Federation.
Los Parvarim. n.d. *Judeo-Español Songs*. CBS 62947.
Merriam, Alan. 1964. *The Anthropology of Music*. Northwestern University Press.
Portugal: Chants du blé et corenmuses de berger. Ocora MU 219, 1980/82.
Riera i Sana, Jaume. 1974. *Cants de Noces dels Jueus Catalans*. Barcelona: Curial.
Schramm, Adelaida Reyes. 1990. "Music and the Refugee Experience." *World of Music* 32, no. 3:3–21.
Seroussi, Edwin. 1990. "The Growth of the Judeo-Spanish Folksong in the 20th Century." *Proceedings of the Tenth World Congress of Jewish Studies, Division D*, 2:173–180. Jerusalem.
————. 1993. "New Directions in the Music of Sephardic Jews," in Ezra Mendelsohn, ed., *Modern Jews and their Musical Agendas, Studies in Contemporary Jewry, an Annual* 9, Hebrew University/Oxford University Press, pp. 61–77.
————. 1995. "Reconstructing Sephardi Music in the 20th Century: Isaac Levy and his *Chants Judeo-Espagnols*," in *The World of Music* 37/1, pp. 39–58.
Shiloah, Amnon, and Cohen, Erik. 1983. "The Dynamics of Change in Jewish Oriental Ethnic Music in Israel." *Ethnomusicology* 27, no. 2:227–252.
Weich-Shahaq, Shoshana. 1979–80. "Wedding Songs of the Bulgarian Sephardi Jews." *Orbis Musicae* 7:1–107.
————. 1989. *Judeo-Spanish Moroccan Songs for the Life Cycle*. Jerusalem: Jewish Music Research Center.

THE IMAGE OF MOSES
IN THE SPANISH HAGGADOT

ZEFIRA GITAY

Ben-Gurion University
Beer-Sheva, Israel

The creation of a visual image combines artistic creativity with intuition and intellectual power.[1] When an artistic exemplum is being portrayed, it can be executed either as an imitation of nature or as a reflection of a written text, translating the words into a visual medium.[2] However, with figures based upon a specific literary text like the Bible, artists find themselves in a difficult position due to the characteristic features of written texts, and of the biblical narrative in particular. The written word may elaborate on physical descriptions or backgrounds—matters that the artistic image cannot translate into visual images. Moreover, the Bible is very concise regarding contextual information, dwelling mainly on the plot and its message. The biblical narrator limits the descriptive details to whatever is necessary for the written discourse, elaborating and expanding only when he intends to emphasize a specific point or to clarify a specific concept.[3] The missing information, which pertains to descriptions of the characters as well as to the landscape, has to be supplemented by later commentaries and midrashic material.[4] As a result, the biblical narrative invites expansion,[5] serving as a fertilizing catalyst that evokes the artistic imagination and opens the door for a variety of literary details and artistic expressions. The purpose of biblical visual works of art, then, is beyond the aesthetic

---

[1] Rudolf Arenheim, "The Plea for Visual Thinking," in *The Language of Images*, ed. W.J. Mitchell (Chicago: University of Chicago Press, 1980), p. 176.

[2] Meyer Schapiro, *Words and Pictures* (The Hague: Mouton Press, 1973), p. 9.

[3] Erich Auerbach, *Mimesis*, trans. R. Trask (Princeton: Princeton University Press, 1967), p. 11.

[4] Schapiro, *Words and Pictures*, p. 11.

[5] Auerbach, *Mimesis*, p. 15.

experience,[6] since the goal is to interpret the message in order to deliver it via an artistic medium.[7]

Following the poetics concept of the precise and condensed biblical narrative, we realize that there are certain exceptions, mainly regarding the character of Moses. The narratives about Moses do not omit the details but instead, as in a modern novel, furnish specific biographical information regarding his life. This information is not concentrated in one specific text, but is spread almost throughout the Pentateuch (except, of course, the Book of Genesis). In addition to providing an account of Moses as a leader struggling with his people and with God, the Bible also tells us about his private life. The narrative enables us to reconstruct an almost complete picture of his life-cycle: his birth (Exod. 2:1 ff.), his rescue from execution by Pharaoh (Exod. 2:5–10), his early years in Egypt (Exod. 2:11–14), his escape to the desert (Exod. 2:15), his meeting with his future wife (Exod. 2:16–21), the nomadic years in the desert (Exod. 3:1 ff.), his sons (Exod. 2:22; 4:24–26), his return to Egypt (Exod. 4:18 ff.), his relationship with his brother and sister (Num. 12:1 ff.), his later meeting with his father-in-law (Exod. 18), and his death (Deut. 34).

The many stories about Moses and the overall biographical account they make possible portray him as an unusual leader and a unique biblical character. Naturally, the Bible's atypical portrayal of so outstanding a figure has been a consistent source of artistic inspiration. Each and every episode or image has played an important role in the crystallization of the image of the leader. Thus the relationship between the biblical episodes and the actual image of Moses—as an individual who participated in various activities concerning Egypt and the exodus—are combined together. Eventually, even in biblical times, the figure of Moses came to be shaped as an idealized image far beyond the concrete individual.[8]

And there has not arisen a prophet since in Israel like Moses, whom the Lord knew face-to-face; none like him for all the signs and the wonders which the Lord sent him to do in the land of Egypt, to Pharaoh, and to all his servants and to all his land. And for all the

[6] Erwin Panofsky, *Meaning in the Visual Arts* (Garden City, N.Y.: Doubleday, 1955), p. 10.

[7] Ananda K. Coomarswamy, *Christian and Oriental Philosophy of Art* (New York: Dover, 1956), p. 93.

[8] Pierce Rice, *Man as Hero* (New York: Norton, 1987), p. 5.

mighty power and all the great and terrible deeds which Moses wrought in the sight of all Israel.[9]

As a rule, visual artists, whether painters or sculptors, narrow down the subjects of their illustrations and focus on one or two specific episodes. In focusing on the image of Moses, this task is made difficult and complex by the numerous significant events in his life. Nonetheless, it is essential, because from the artist's perspective, the episode chosen is the illustrative component that condenses the story of Moses into one incident.[10] Selecting from the vast body of literary material, the artist depicts the most significant and characteristic features of the portrayed event or image.

As for the representational details of the story, the artist need not be bothered by the question of whether the image bears an accurate resemblance to the reality of what is depicted. Even in their own time it was no longer possible to obtain a realistic description of the image and its environment.[11] As a result, many artistic expressions portray figures like Moses in a variety of fashions, techniques, styles, and expressions; and all of them tend to describe a heroic, symbolic figure. Thus, writes D. Norman:

> Since Moses is one of the world's greatest heroic figures, it is by no means surprising either that he should be portrayed in a Persian miniature of the fourteenth century, or be almost universally admired—and often depicted—even to the present day.[12]

However, Norman warns:

> There is the ever-present danger, nonetheless, that images deriving at second- or third-hand from distant cultures may become merely formalized, decorative objects. It is equally possible that we shall simply give lip service to what they are attempting to make us realize. Only if a work of art—whether created in the remote past, or in our time—profoundly moves us, illuminating what has not hitherto been revealed

---

[9] Deut. 34:10–12.

[10] The reason is that the artistic medium does not enable the artist to dwell on his canvas or stone at length, whereas words enable the writer to illustrate a rich composition that includes more then one incident. Hence, physical limitations can dictate the characteristic features of a visual artistic creation.

[11] E.H. Gombrich, J. Hochberg, and M. Black, *Art, Perception, and Reality* (Baltimore: John Hopkins University Press, 1973), p. 79.

[12] Dorothy Norman, *The Hero: Myth/Image/Symbol* (New York: New American Library, 1966), p. 131.

to us; only if it expresses authentic affirmation and wonder, can it have significance.[13]

That is to say, artists who intend to use Moses as their artistic inspirational source, need to take into consideration not only the physical image, but, no less significantly, the impact of this image in its cultural and religious matrix.

However, the image of Moses that expresses authentic affirmation and religious wonder seems, by its heroic nature, to narrow down the various opportunities created by the biblical narrative for a variety of artistic creations. The point is that such an idealized image requires a specific iconographic symbol. The viewer, confronted with the visual image, has to be able to identify the image by its attributes.[14] The portrayal of Moses as a symbolic figure could, of course, have been based on any number of episodes in his life. The most significant event in his life, however, was the receiving and giving of the Torah and his exposure to God on Mount Sinai (Exod. 19–20). Thus the image of Moses as the lawgiver who receives the Law directly from God became the most commemorated depiction; the penultimate expression of timeless and placeless religious affirmation.[15]

Focusing our attention on the period of the Renaissance, with Michelangelo's statue of Moses (1513–15) as its peak, we note Vasari's comments: ". . . so dazzling and resplendent does it appear and so perfectly has Michelangelo expressed in the marble the divinity that God first infused in Moses' most holy form."[16] The impact of Michelangelo's Moses went beyond a mere artistic creation even in his own time.

The question is, What iconographic symbolism did the artists dwell upon in their portrayals of Moses? Was it primarily based upon the biblical text, or was it merely an artistic invention? The most popular image in portrayals of Moses was Michelangelo's, Moses the

---

[13] Ibid.

[14] As we have been taught, for instance, by classical tradition, where the depiction of Aphrodite takes place at the moment of her emergence from the sea, and that of Dionysus while he is carrying his wine glass, so that each figure has its own attribute that identifies it for the viewer, so as to avoid confusion between different images. Thus, for instance, King David might be depicted as sitting on a throne with a harp in his hand, referring to the popular images of him as king and psalmist.

[15] In regard to the meaning of myth, see Coomarswamy, *Christian and Oriental Philosophy of Art*, p. 45.

[16] Giorgio Vasari, *Lives of the Artists* (London: Penguin Books, 1965), vol. 1, p. 345.

lawgiver. This image is rooted in the biblical text, but not in the original version of the Hebrew Bible.

Michelangelo's Moses is horned. What was the source for the depiction of the horns? The Hebrew text describing Moses' descent from the mountain with the commandments uses the words *vekaran or panav* ("the skin of his face shone").[17] However, the Hebrew word *krn*, here translated as "shine," has another meaning, "horn" (as a noun but not as a verb in the Hebrew version), which has been adopted in the Latin Vulgate translation.[18] Here the verb *karan* is translated as *cornuta*, i.e., "horns."

Interestingly enough, this view was also held by Jewish commentators, and most especially by Rashi, the great Jewish exegete of the eleventh century in France, whose commentaries also influenced non-Jewish biblical interpretation.[19] Rashi writes as follows in his explication of the phrase *karney or* ("rays of light"): "*And it came to pass when Moses went down [from Mount Sinai] . . . that the skin of his face beamed . . .* is an expression connected with the word 'horns,' and the phrase [is used here] because light radiates from a point and projects like a horn."[20] Thus, Rashi interpreted this Hebrew word as having a dual connotation that goes beyond the mere philological meaning of *krn* to provide a theological dimension.

The Vulgate translation and the theological exegesis of *krn* as horns or rays of light have been depicted by artists from the eleventh century on, becoming the normative format, in the Western artistic tradition, for portrayals of Moses as the lawgiver.[21] At the same time, it is necessary to point out that artistic portrayals in the Eastern Church—the Byzantine hegemony—lack any visual illustration of the horned Moses. The Eastern approach may have its literary roots in the Septuagint Greek translation of the Bible.[22] Here the same Hebrew verb, *karan*, is translated as *dedoxastai*, "glorified." As a result, the

---

[17] Exod. 34:29 (Revised Standard Version).

[18] The Latin translation of the Bible by St. Jerome in the fourth century.

[19] See Chaim Pearl, *Rashi* (New York: Grove Press, 1988).

[20] *Pentateuch with Targum Onkelos, Haphtaroth and Rashi's Commentary*, trans. M. Rosenberg and A.M. Silbermann (New York: Hebrew Publishing Co., 1935), vol. 2, p. 196.

[21] And see the study on the question of Moses' horns by Ruth Melinkoff, *The Horns of Moses in Medieval Art and Thought* (Berkeley: University of California Press, 1970), pp. 5–6. Melinkoff detects the earliest visual exemplum of the horned Moses in English illuminated manuscripts like the Aelfric Paraphrase (Canterbury, 1050).

[22] The Jewish translation of the Bible into Greek in the third century B.C.E.

portrayal of a horned Moses would have been irrelevant wherever the Latin translation was not in use.[23]

Calling attention to the Jewish artistic illumination of Moses, we ask whether the Hebrew text had a direct influence on the artists, or whether they relied on a common artistic vocabulary, an exemplum dictionary, that served each and every one for the portrayal of the image of Moses. The question is complicated, since the Jewish artistic tradition tended to avoid elaborate illustrations of images.[24] Therefore, the issue is where, and if at all, one might find visual images of Moses in Jewish artistic expressions, and whether one can trace their literary sources.

Obviously, the biblical narrative of the exodus is the appropriate text for depiction. However, the Book of Exodus itself was not often illustrated, while the story of the exodus has been recited regularly during the annual holiday of Passover. For this purpose a specific text was composed, serving as a guideline to the festival that celebrates the exodus. This text, called the Haggadah, i.e., "the saying," includes prayers and stories that enlighten the exodus. The material is recited at the Seder on Passover eve.

In the beginning, the Haggadah was not regarded as an entity in its own right. On the contrary, in the eleventh and twelfth centuries it was a part of the prayerbook.[25] During the thirteenth and fourteenth centuries, the popularity of the Haggadah increased, and it was crystallized as a self-contained text transmitted in an authoritative version. As such, the Passover Haggadah was extracted from the complete annual cycle of prayers in the Siddur and produced as an independent text. It became one of the most popular Jewish books, since it was used in the family's private domestic rituals performed on the holiday of Passover.

As a personal and domestic object used at home and not in public, the Haggadah was much less subject than the public prayerbook to Judaism's restrictions on and prohibitions of illustrations. Moreover,

---

[23] Melinkoff, *Horns of Moses*, p. 138.

[24] One might refer to the sparse usage of imagery in the Jewish tradition in light of the Second Commandment, "You shall not make for yourself a graven image" (Exod. 20:5).

[25] In the eleventh century the Haggadah was included in the Siddur of Rav Saadiah Gaon and in Mahzor Vitri; in the twelfth century it was included in the *Mishne Torah* of Maimonides. And see *Encyclopaedia Judaica* (1971), s.v. "Haggadah," vol. 7, cols. 1093 ff.

as an item in the private domain, this text lent itself to the expression of personal taste, thus opening the door for artistic creativity.[26] Indeed, with the appearance of printed Haggadot in the sixteenth and seventeenth centuries, the popularity of the Haggadah increased, for wider distribution was now possible, as was the inclusion of artistic illustrations.[27] Naturally, the many editions of the Haggadah used in Jewish homes did not limit their focus to the liturgical and prayer components, but provided elaborate instructional material designed to appeal not only to the leader of the Seder but to the children.[28]

The Haggadah was richly illuminated in the various countries where Jews settled. In the most established communities, there were two main schools of Haggadot, the Spanish and the Ashkenazi. In both of them, one finds a strong emphasis on visual images taken from the midrashim, the traditional commentaries of the rabbis, rather than a reliance on the biblical text.[29] This approach may have been anchored in the Haggadot themselves, where one is expected to comment and also interpret. However, there are several differences, and I would like to dwell on one exception: the full-page illuminations.

In the Spanish Haggadot, such as the Golden Haggadah or the Sarajevo Haggadah, from the fifteenth century, the illustrations are full-page miniatures. Most of them are divided horizontally into two framed sections or into four compartments, each depicting a different episode.[30] The Ashkenazi Haggadot, however, lack this extensive illumination of the biblical narrative, focusing more on the ceremonial and the folk customs.[31]

The artistic tradition of depicting whole scenes is not inserted into the body of the text of the Haggadah, but precedes it, as the Sarajevo Haggadah demonstrates. The illustrations of the Sarajevo Haggadah contain episodes from all five books of the Pentateuch: from Creation (Genesis) to the death of Moses (Deuteronomy). There are, for the most part, two illustrations per page. All together there are thirty-four pages, followed by fifty pages of text. In addition, the written

---

[26] Ibid., col. 1095.

[27] For example, the Haggadah and its commentaries, such as the *Zevach Pesach* by Isaac Abarbanel of 1506, had 120 editions. Yosef Hayim Yerushalmi, *Haggadah and History* (Philadelphia: Jewish Publication Society, 1975), pp. 22–23.

[28] Bezalel Narkiss, *The Golden Haggadah* (London: British Library, 1977), p. 9.

[29] Chaim Raphael, *A Feast of History: A Drama of Passover Through the Ages* (London, 1972), p. 122.

[30] Narkiss, *The Golden Haggadah*, p. 21.

[31] For instance, see the illustrations of the Birds Haggadah, from 1300.

pages themselves are illustrated with diminutive floral motifs, echo-
ing the Gothic art of the twelfth and thirteen centuries. Most of
these illustrations are inserted along the written text, or interlaced
and woven in elaborate patterns that decorate the singular letters,
words, or phrases of the text.

The Gothic period was characterized by numerous illuminated
manuscripts of Scripture and of religious texts in general. The techniques of producing illuminated manuscripts flourished under the
patronage of the French court. Nonetheless, until the thirteenth century most of the manuscripts were of religious content. As the social
and economic situation changed, bringing about the growth of urban-
ism, artistic creativity also benefitted. There were now more patrons
who were able to foster and increase the number of workshops for
artistic manuscripts, which now illustrated secular texts as well as
religious ones. This new development in art was quite influential,
and did not exclude Jewish artists who were employed by princes
or their courts, especially in Spain.[32]

In regard to Jewish patrons commissioning religious manuscripts,
the question, therefore, is, What kind of artist would be employed?
There were two alternatives: either a Christian artist or a Jewish artist.

If the artist was a Christian, the patron might have had to tell
him what sort of illustrations he wanted. If the artist was Jewish, the
patron did not need to give him detailed instructions, yet the results
were not guaranteed. The Jewish artist could employ the conventional iconography as well as the style of his place and time, not
excluding the Christian model. However, he did not have to, since
he could also use specifically Jewish artistic traditions. Thus, one
needs to inquire about the artistic vocabulary used by the artists of
the period, its nature and literary sources.

We find, for instance, that the illustrations of the Reynolds Haggadah
(Catalonia, 14th cent.) seem to follow the artistic tradition of the
wall paintings of the Dura-Europos Synagogue of the third century.[33]
Such a long continuity of visual imagery may lend support, according to H. Rosenau, to the theory of a Jewish pictorial development,
partly submerged in later times, but reappearing in the Spanish

---

[32] *Encyclopaedia Judaica*, s.v. "Haggadah," vol. 7, col. 1098.
[33] Helen Rosenau, "Notes on the Illuminations of the Spanish Haggadah in the
John Rylands Library," *Bulletin of the John Rylands Library, Manchester* 36, no. 2 (March
1954): 481.

Haggadot.[34] B. Narkis, in his commentary on the Golden Haggadah, sheds light on this artistic process: "It seems more and more obvious that an early Hellenistic Jewish model fashioned not only the Early Christian Western and Eastern Biblical cycles, but also the middle Byzantine representations."[35]

A Jewish artistic tradition was the source of a later, specifically Christian artistic development. Through the early Christian and Byzantine periods, certain Jewish artistic elements entered into the biblical representations of Western Europe from Carolingian times onward. Consequently, Jewish artists of the Gothic period must have had direct access to an early Jewish biblical artistic cycle, which either survived independently or had been continuously copied throughout the existence of different Jewish elements in Christian art in various places and styles.[36] Thus concludes C. Roth: "The illustration of the Sarajevo Haggadah preserves more faithfully than any other document now extant the traditions of the illuminated Jewish Bible codices that existed in Antiquity."[37]

The Sarajevo Haggadah reflects a long Jewish artistic tradition. In regard to Moses, it glorifies in numerous episodes the important events of his image, such as his childhood, his leadership, and his role as lawgiver. Many of the episodes illustrated are not mentioned in the biblical text, but they can be found in later midrashic material. The question now is, What determined the artist's choice of episodes? Was the artist fascinated by the midrashic legends that elaborated and commented on the biblical text, or was it simply that he preferred to use as sources the popular midrashic material that served as an artistic lexicon?

There is another alternative. The Jewish artist was familiar with the content and character of the Haggadah as a text elaborating on the midrashic legendary literature rather than on the biblical narrative itself. In regard to Moses, this artistic approach, which takes into consideration the nature of the Haggadah, sheds light on the illuminations in the Sarajevo Haggadah. The artist decided not to include an image of Moses in the body of his Haggadah. Instead he created a unique framework that, on the one hand, did not

---

[34] Ibid., p. 483.
[35] Bezalel Narkis, *The Golden Haggadah* (1970): p. 34.
[36] Ibid., p. 67.
[37] Cited in Raphael, *Feast of History*, p. 108.

contradict the lesson of the Haggadah, while on the other, it enabled readers to elaborate and glorify Moses' heroic deeds. The artist accomplished this by isolating his portrayal of Moses from the body of the Haggadah, inserting it at the beginning as an entity in itself.

This artistic solution also explains why Moses, in our Spanish Haggadah, does not appear as a hero or as an overwhelming figure on the opening page (as was the case in later versions, such as the Amsterdam Haggadah, 1695). He is depicted as a human being, with no specifically heroic or symbolic features.

In conclusion, I propose that the Spanish Sarajevo Haggadah was created by a Jewish artist who was well familiar with the content of the Haggadah and did not confine himself to the artistic technique of illuminating the manuscript.[38] The content and meaning of the Haggadah text had eliminated the power of a literary description of the heroic figure of Moses. As a result, the artist of the Sarajevo Haggadah composed a unique way to illuminate the image of Moses without offending the text. He does indeed tell the biblical story in conjunction with the Haggadah, but not as an integral part of it. By compiling all the visual imagery as an independent entity, he made it an appendage to the written text, and not beyond it. Thus the illuminations of Moses supplement the text, but by no means replace its original religious intention.

---

[38] Even though the artists served the Spanish court, they did not simply follow the more fashionable trend of imitating their environment but preserved their own tradition and exercised it in their illuminations of the Haggadah.

THE SEPHARDIC WOMAN'S HEAD-DRESS IN SPAIN AND IN THE OTTOMAN EMPIRE

Batsheva Goldman-Ida

Tel Aviv Museum of Art

This presentation deals with a certain head-dress prevalent among Jewish women in the Kingdom of Aragon, more specifically in Barcelona and its environs, in the mid-fourteenth century, which appears among Jewesses in the Ottoman empire some five hundred years later. Salonika women interviewed recently attributed the head-dress worn during the Ottoman period in their area to a tradition stemming from Spain.[1] Does this head-dress attest to a preservation throughout many centuries of a Sephardic tradition or is there some other explanation for the astonishing similarity?

A glance at the Passover meal scene in the Rylands Haggadah, one of a group of Catalonian manuscripts of the mid-fourteenth century relevant to our discussion, falls on the figure of a woman. A close look (fig. 1) reveals what appears to be a bonnet worn over a scarf which also encircles the chin. The same head-dress may be seen in other contemporary manuscripts.[2]

The head-dress conforms to a style prevalent in the late thirteenth century when the *couvre-chef*, a type of light cloth with which women covered their hair in various ways, underwent a change. In 1280, it

---

Note: The dating of the Catalonian manuscripts has taken into account Metzger, note 3 below, pp. 303–05.

[1] Esther Juhasz, ed., *Sephardi Jews in The Ottoman Empire, Aspects of Material Culture*, exh. cat., Jerusalem, The Israel Museum, 17 May–22 October 1989, New York, Jewish Museum, Spring 1990, p. 145: "In light of . . . the claim of the women of Salonika that it originated in Spain."

[2] "The Seder table," *Barcelona Haggadah*, Kingdom of Aragon, probably Catalonia, 1350–60, London, British Library, Add. 14761, fol. 17v; "Eating the Passover Meal," *Brother Haggadah*, perhaps Valencia (then in the kingdom of Aragon), c. 1330, London, British Library, Or. 1404, fol. 7v, lower register, right, and "When coming from the synagogue," fol. 8r; "The Seder Ceremony," *Sister Haggadah*, Aragon, c. 1350, London, British Library, Or. 2884, folio, 18r. Illustrated in Narkiss, Bezalel, *Hebrew Illuminated Manuscripts in the British Isles*, pt. 1: *The Spanish and Portugese Manuscripts*, Jerusalem 1982, Part Two: Plate LX, ill. 209, p. 65; Plate CI, ill. 295 (b), p. 106; and Plate CII, ill. 296, p. 107; Plate LI, ill. 188, p. 56 respectively.

passed over the head to be fastened under the chin, and was crowned with a sort of standing starched band called a *tourret*.[3]

A detailed description of the 14th century head-dress or *tocado* has been given by Miguel Angel Motis Dolader.[4] Characterizing the head-dress as one reserved for Festivals, typical of the upper class, and specifically of married Aragon Jewesses, it is described as a linen roll—covered by a gilt band with crimson stones—which encircled the face, coming under the chin, and leaving the neck uncovered. This band was embellished with a small bonnet-shaped ornament (*bonetillo*) of three rings enriched with gilt edging (*galón*) at the top of the forehead. The hair was hidden behind the back in a cloth sac or coif, a kind of hair net consisting of a gold-thread mesh (*crespina*) with pearls, from which hung a veil of silk gauze. (fig. 2)

There is one interesting facet which recurs in this group of Catalonian manuscripts: The Biblical picture cycles which precede the *Haggada* in this group show a different head-dress on the Biblical heroines than that found on the Jewish wife at the Passover meal table. This is true of the two Jewish midwives being instructed by Pharaoh in the *Golden Haggadah*. (fig. 3) These women wear a softer head-dress where the scarf encircles the chin, but also hangs loosely on the sides to the shoulders. This head-dress may be related to a development towards the end of the twelfth century where the cape hood was detached to form an independent head-dress. The hood was attached to a closed neck scarf, the *camail*, which women wore open, hanging free on the shoulders. It might point to an earlier prototype for the Biblical cycle in this group, or may indicate a lower social status. Motis Dolader relates this head-dress to one prevalent in the Cantigas of Alfonso X of Castille but in use for everyday wear during the period in question. This is contrasted with the *tocado*

---

[3] Francois Boucher, *A History of Costume in the West*, John Ross, trans., London 1970, 2, pp. 184–5, and Lucy Barton, *Historic Costume for the Stage*, Boston 1963, 3, p. 138. See also Mendel and Thérèse Metzger, *Jewish Life in the Middle Ages: Illuminated Manuscripts of the 13th to the 16th Centuries*, New York 1982, pp. 111–14.

[4] Miguel Angel Motis Dolader "Los Judio Oscenses en La Plena y Baja Edad Media," in Angelina García, *Los Judios de la Corona de Aragón en los Siglos XIV–XV, De Sefarad*, Generalitat Valenciana 1988/89, pp. 115–130. This differs from and likely supercedes Metzger's definition of "Costume of the Spanish Jews in the 1330s: . . . a *couvre-chef* fastened under the chin like a *mentionnière*, and a very small bonnet with two layers of piping," in Metzger, op. cit., fig. 165, p. 116. See also, Miguel Angel Motis Dolader, *Coleccion: Mariano de Pano y Ruata, Los Judios en Aragón en la Edad Media (Siglos XIII–XV)*, Aragon 1990, p. 121.

which is a head-dress for festive attire, specific to the Aragon Jewesses of the period.[5]

It would not be unusual to find Jewish women retaining a style of half a century previous as a traditional head-dress. It is surprising however to find the same style worn by an Iraqui married woman in the early twentieth century. (fig. 4) Farḥa, the daughter of Rabbi Ezra Reuven Dangoor wears a small, rectangular bonnet, the *topi*, topped with a gold plaque (*tasa*) and egg-shaped ornament (*joza*), from which hangs a tassel. Across the front of the *topi* is an embroidered rectangular piece of cloth, the *chiati*. A scarf, the *lecheg*, encircles her chin.[6] In the period just before, a low, ornamented cap was worn. Later, when the head-dress changed to a headscarf (the *shaksa*), the chin scarf (*lecheg*) was retained.

Iraq is here considered for purposes of comparison since, although the Judeo-Spanish tongue was not spoken in Iraq, the area was part of the Ottoman Empire in the nineteenth century, and also because there are artistic reasons to suspect a cross-cultural influence from this area on Spain. For instance, in a synagogue scene from the *Barcelona Haggadah*, a Torah scroll held aloft is encased in a cylindrical checkered metal case ending in a conical crown. In material, design and proportion it corresponds to the kind of Torah scroll in wide use throughout Iraq and parts of the Middle East, in the 19th century, likely made by a Baghdadi silversmith.[7] Iraqui ceremonial objects in use during the 19th century can be related to pieces described in literature as early as the 10th century. Other objects, such as drinking vessels, relate in form to periods even earlier. Thus, the retention of an ancient form in the 19th century is not without precedent, as far as Iraq is concerned.

In this regard, a case for different cultural traditions in Catalonia

[5] Angelina Garcia, op. cit., p. 121. For purposes of comparison of two head-dress styles (appearing in the same illustration) see: *Roman de la Violette*, mid-fifteenth century, Paris, Bibliothèque National, ms. fr. 24376, folio 5 illustrated in Boucher, op. cit., ill. 394, p. 208.

[6] Aviva Muller-Lanset, "On the History of the Costume of Jewish Women in Baghdad," *Studies in the History of the Jews of Iraq and their Culture*, vol. 1, Or Yehudah 1981, p. 216, ill. 3. [hebrew]

[7] "*Hallelujah* in a synagogue," *Barcelona Haggadah*, Kingdom of Aragon, probably Catalonia, 1350–60, London, British Library, Add. 14761, folio 65v, in Narkiss, op. cit, Plate LXXIII, ill. 241, p. 78. Torah Scroll case, Basra, Iraq, 1904, in Y.L. Bialer, *Jewish Life in Art and Tradition: Based on the Collection of Sir Isaac and Lady Wolfson Museum, Hechal Shlomo Jerusalem*, London-Jerusalem-New York, 1976, p. 105.

in the fourteenth century may be attested to from another synagogue scene, this time in the *Sarajevo Haggadah*, where the Torah scroll is enclosed in a cloth mantle and topped with a round, metal crown, similar to those used in the tradition of Sephardic communities in Turkey, Holland and Italy until today.[8] The tradition of the head-dress in these 14th century manuscripts, however, are consistent throughout.

Could the 19th century Ottoman head-dress also be a continuation of a medieval style? When we turn to a Salonika Jewess from the early nineteenth century, (fig. 5) the resemblance is striking. The only deviation appears to be the long, narrow, rectangular scarf-sleeve or snook enclosing the braided hair on either side or down the back.

Although the Salonikan bonnet is sometimes called *tocado*, as were the head-dresses in Spain, the myriad of head-dress styles spanning the 500 year period shows no continual tradition through time. A pertinent development for our discussion are the conical and truncated cone head-dresses which became prevalent in parts of Europe, notably the Court of Burgundy and the Netherlands, in the fifteenth century. (fig. 6) While not to be found in Spain, an adapted version, without a chinstrap, and with a long veil attached to the upper part, is later worn by Jewesses in 16th century Italy (fig. 7) and crossed the sea to North Africa, notably Algeria and Tunisia. They relate to that basic element later found in the 19th century Ottoman head-dress—a truncated cone cap. The early 19th century Izmir *tocado* is a small skullcap with an ornamented band on the forehead encircling the head. A kerchief gathers the hair under the cap. There is no chinstrap. The head-dresses of Jewesses in the Ottoman Empire in the 17th–18th centuries feature a totally different type of head-dress, such as a metallic disc cap, while other 19th century head-dresses consist of a spherical, layered covering—the *hotoz* or *halabi*.[9]

---

[8] Synagogue Scene, *Sarajevo Haggadah*, probably North Spain, c. 1350, p. 34, lower register, in Cecil Roth, *The Sarajevo Haggadah*, Beograd 1967. [hebrew] Ottoman Torah Case, Crown and Shield, Ottoman Empire, 19th century, and Italian Dressed Torah, 18th century, both The Israel Museum, Jerusalem, in Grace Cohen Grossman, *Jewish Art*, China 1995, p. 96 and opposite p. 91 respectively.

[9] Osman Hamdy Bey, *Les Costumes Populaires en la Turquie en 1873*, Istanbul 1873; M. de Ferriol, *Recueil de cent estampes représentant différentes nations du Levant*, Paris 1714; Scarce, Jennifer, "Principles of Ottoman Turkish Costume," *Costume* 22, 1988, pp. 13–31; see also Juhasz, op. cit.

Fig. 1. "The Passover meal," *Rylands Haggadah*, Aragon, c. 1330, Manchester, John Rylands University Library, Ms. Ryl. Hebr. 6, folio 19v, detail: lower register, left. Reproduced by courtesy of the Director and University Librarian, the John Rylands University Library of Manchester.

Fig. 2. Costume of the Jewess of the upper class for the holidays, 14th century, watercolour illustration by Letizia Arbeteta, detail of head-dress, seen from side, in Angelina García, *Los Judios de la Corona de Aragón en los Siglos XIV–XV, De Sefarad*, Generalitat, Valenciana 1988/89, p 124.

Fig. 3. "Pharoah Ordering the Midwives," *Golden Haggadah*, Catalonia, c. 1320–30, London, British Library, Ms. Add. 27210, folio 8v. By permission of The British Library.

Fig. 4. Farḥa, married daughter of Rabbi Ezra Reuven Dangoor, Baghdad, c. 1910, photograph, detail, in Meir Benayu, ed., Rabbi David ben Salman Sassoon, *Masa Bavel* (Travels to Babylonia), Jerusalem 1955, ill. no. 46, p. 289. See also Shaul Nawi and his wife, in Abraham Hayyim Twena, *Babylonian Jewry—the Exiled and the Redeemed*, Ramleh 1981, p. 170.

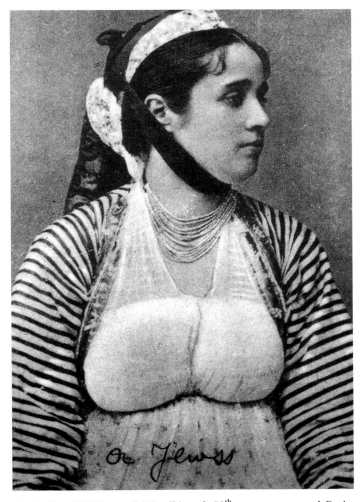

Fig. 5. "Jewish Woman," Saloniki, early 20th century, postcard, Paris, Gérard Lévy Collection, in Esther Juhasz, ed., *Sephardi Jews in The Ottoman Empire, Aspects of Material Culture*, exh. cat., Jerusalem, The Israel Museum, 17 May–22 October 1989, New York, Jewish Museum, Spring 1990, ill. 38, p. 151.

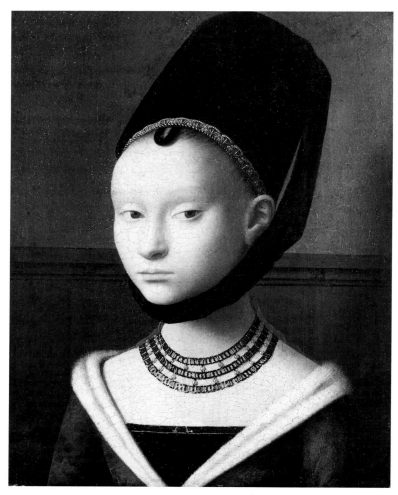

Fig. 6. Petrus Christus, *Portrait of a Girl*, mid 15th century, Berlin, Staatliche Museen, Preußischer Kulturbesitz, Gemäldegalerie, cat. 532.

Fig. 7. *Hebrea*, Rome, 1602, etching, London, British Museum, in Alfred Rubens, *Jewish Costume*, London 1973[2], ill. 193, p. 138.

There may be one final explanation for the small bonnet or *tocado* which defies our hopes of describing a continuous Sephardic tradition—a historical reason for the prevalence of a small bonnet in the 19th century in the Ottoman Empire.

With the beginnings of modernization, the Sultan's Decree of 1829 regulated a red felt truncated conical cap—the *fez* or *tarbush*—which became the recognized headwear among men. Initially regulated in the army, it filtered down to the rest of society. Still, religious leaders continued to wear the traditional turban (as may be seen in fig. 4).[10] From that time on, women throughout the Ottoman Empire—be it Iraq, Salonika, or Turkey—chose to wear a smaller version of the *fez*, a small bonnet. It may well have been this decree which brought the latter day 19th century women's head-dress so close to that of their 14th century sisters. Incidently, the use of the *fez* among women in the 19th century was not limited to Jewish circles: It appears in regions of Greece and among the Christian women of Iraq as well.

Thus, despite an initial impression of a close parallel, the careful analysis of the elements of the head-dress in both periods indicates important differences. As we have seen, the *bonetillo* of the 14th century head-dress is much smaller than the 19th century versions of the *fez*—really more an ornament than a hat. Further, the distinctive tying under the chin is, in the 14th century, part of the *rollo* or roll with its *bonetillo* ornament, while in 19th century Iraq, for example, it is a separate scarf, the *lecheg*, as are the other elements of the head-dress.

The myriad of styles which followed the Judeo-Aragon period does not substantiate a hypothesis wherein a costume tradition was upheld through time. However, the survival of the *verbal* definition of the head-dress as *tocado* may be considered and warrants further inquiry.

---

[10] N.a., "The History of the Style of Eastern Costume," الهلال *Al-Hilal*, newspaper, year 16, issue no. 2, 1 November 1907, pp. 80–90 and 1908, pp. 149–153 [Arabic], where according to the latter, p. 149, the headgear *fez* (or *tarbush* as it is referred to) was relegated initially as part of the modernization decrees of Ali Pasha Mahmet (1805–1840), the red color was chosen, and this continued under Abd al-Majid Sultan (1839–1861), but the specific truncated conical hat we refer to as *fez* was introduced by Abd-al-Aziz Sultan (1861–1876), that is, in the late 19th century, and it was called at the time *aziziyan*. The author of the article states that it is still prevalent in his period (1907–08). See also, Scarce, Jennifer, "Turkish Fashion in Transition," *Costume* 14, 1980, p. 146, note 12.

Thanks for their helpful assistance in translation to, in Arabic, Dr. Shaul Sehaiyek, Tel Aviv, who pointed out to me the *Al-Hilal* newspaper articles, and, in Spanish, to Fanny Levy of the Helena Rubinstein Art Library at the Tel Aviv Museum of Art. Special thanks to Prof. Yedida Stillman for her support and encouragement throughout.

PART SIX

CONCLUSION: EDUCATION AND
THE FUTURE OF SEPHARDIC STUDIES

THE SEPHARDIC HERITAGE IN THE JEWISH CURRICULUM: CURRENT PRACTICES AND FUTURE DIRECTIONS

Tamar Frank

Cincinnati, Ohio

Recognizing that scholarly research and academic presentations are too often divorced from the communities that could nurture and benefit from them, the organizers of the Second Sephardic Studies Conference at SUNY Binghamton included a panel dealing with the presence of Sephardic content in university and pre-college education. Participants in this panel discussed the roles of the university, Jewish day and supplementary schools, and museums in helping to educate the community. The lively discussion period following the presentations showed that such issues do, indeed, engage academics, who share many of the concerns of other educators in trying to win a place for Sephardic Studies in a Jewish or Jewish Studies curriculum.

This paper deals with a survey of Jewish educators carried out during the first months of 1990 and sponsored by the Maurice Amado Foundation, which inaugurated its Sephardic Education Project in 1989. The Project's long-term goal was to increase awareness and appreciation of the Sephardic heritage on the part of the North American Jewish community. While the Sephardic Education Project supported a variety of different educational initiatives, ranging from musical programs and museum exhibitions to academic conferences and publications, a particular concern was the education of Jewish youth. This survey was to be the first step towards implementing a variety of educational initiatives, and was intended to ascertain current curricular content and educational methods, and to assess needs and preferences for the future.[1]

Sephardim comprise perhaps 8% of North American Jewry. Since their numbers are so small, it is not surprising that Sephardic customs

---

[1] The Sephardic Education Project lasted for six years, 1989–1995. This paper, originally presented in April 1991, was updated in November 1995.

and history are so little known and so little studied. That such a
situation is predictable, however, does not make it desirable. Given
the large numbers of Sephardic Jews in Israel, where they are a majority, and given the historical importance of the Sephardic communities and the richness of their traditions, the North American
ignorance of things Sephardic is unfortunate. Educators and students
of public policy have come to realize that, in today's "shrinking
world" or "global society," even those who comprise the majority in
their own communities would do well to understand minority and
foreign cultures. This approach is even more relevant to minorities
within a minority community; instead of fostering divisiveness with
ignorance or prejudice, the Jewish community could grow stronger
through an appreciation and understanding of the many strands of
Jewish tradition.

It is a cliché that non-Ashkenazic Jewish communities and practices are not represented in Jewish curricula. Even some respondents
to the survey cited this common wisdom: "If you intend to show
that there is a 'weakness' in knowing about Sephardic Judaism—
we *all* know this is accurate;" "If the point was to prove that Sephardic Jewry is not included in a big way in most schools, you
will succeed." In his 1987 rabbinic thesis, Bruce Greenbaum examined in some detail the portrayal—or, too often, the neglect—of
non-Ashkenazic Jewry in the textbooks most often used in Reform
religious schools.[2] The textbooks were not, with a few exceptions,
designed exclusively for Reform Jewish schools, so that the results
of Rabbi Greenbaum's study may be taken as descriptive of most
texts used in American and Canadian Jewish schools.

His findings about the lack of Sephardic content in the texts are
discouraging, because they also point to an educational vicious circle: the textbooks contain little material about non-Ashkenazic Jewry,
so that even an educator who is eager to include these communities in a curriculum is stymied by a lack of appropriate materials.
Few teachers have the time or resources to present material that is
not included in the textbooks they are asked to use. Respondents
to the survey commented on this problem: "This is an area about

---

[2] Bruce D. Greenbaum, "Towards an Integration of Non-Ashkenazic Jewish
Studies into the Program of North American Reform Jewish Religious Schools: A
Textbook Analysis and an Experimental Curriculum," (Cincinnati: Hebrew Union
College).

which there is little material available—we thus do very little;" "I would like to see more units taught about Sephardic Jewry in our classrooms, but we're having trouble finding materials suited to the elementary grades;" "there is precious little on Sephardic Judaism available." An issue of the *Pedagogic Reporter* devoted to the teaching of Sephardic Jewry (January 1987) emphasized the importance of teaching such material, yet was able to offer little in the way of available resources for teachers.[3]

The Foundation was interested in obtaining more concrete information about current educational practices and goals. Despite the fact that "we *all* know" about the lack of non-Ashkenazic content in the classroom, it was deemed desirable to find out what material is actually taught. For example, a few of the books surveyed by Greenbaum did contain some sections about Sephardic communities and history; might such material be used in the classroom? A number of films and recordings dealing with Sephardic topics are available; were these used? The survey was intended to find out which aspects of Sephardic culture and history are currently taught in American and Canadian Jewish schools, and also to pinpoint the curricular areas in which some Sephardic content might be introduced. In addition, the educators were asked to indicate their preferences for materials and methods. It was hoped that the results of

---

[3] Some of the items mentioned are certainly excellent resources. *A Treasury of Sephardic Laws and Customs*, by Rabbi Herbert C. Dobrinsky of Yeshiva University (New York: Ktav and Yeshiva, 1986, with teacher's guide), for example, is an outstanding collection of material, but would be hard to use as a textbook with any but the most advanced and knowledgeable students. While the list of films and books in this issue is worth careful perusal, what is striking is how few can actually be used as teaching tools.

This situation has changed somewhat: in 1991, the Coalition for the Advancement of Jewish Education (New York) published a four-part series, *Our Story: the Jews of Sepharad*. One part, *The Whole Sephardic Catalog: A Resource Guide*, by Carolyn Starman Hessel, is a substantial bibliography which lists both popular and scholarly publications, classroom materials, and films. The other parts of the CAJE series itself include lesson plans, a workbook, outlines and discussion guides. This series was sent to the entire membership of CAJE when it was published, and copies of the booklets were available for purchase. Although the materials have not won universal approbation, classroom teachers were, in general, enthusiastic about its accessibility and ease of use.

Another publication which has garnered much applause is *The Melton Journal*, vol. 26 (Autumn 1992), "Celebrating the Sephardi Spirit." It contains a variety of articles on Sephardic studies, written with educators in mind. For educators of another sort, Jane Gerber's book, *Sephardic Studies in the University* (Madison, NJ: Fairleigh Dickinson, 1995) includes essays and syllabi to aid university teachers.

the survey might be used prescriptively; that is, that educators and designers of educational materials might be able to use the survey results in planning and implementing new curricular materials.

The survey was mailed to the American and Canadian members of the Coalition for the Advancement of Jewish Education (CAJE), and also to the heads of Bureaus of Jewish Education,[4] as well as to the staffs of several independent day schools. In all, 3480 surveys were mailed out. A total of 233 completed forms were returned. In addition, 25 responses were received from people who were not able to fill out the forms but were interested in the issues involved: teachers and directors of adult education programs, co-ordinators of family education programs, writers, musicians, and rabbis. (The CAJE mailing list includes many community professionals who, despite an interest in Jewish education, would not have been able to complete a questionnaire directed at principals and teachers. In fact, those teachers who deal primarily with Hebrew language would also not have been able to complete the form.) A return rate of 7.4% seems to indicate a positive level of interest in the issue of non-Ashkenazic curricular content.[5]

The first section of the questionnaire dealt with specific curricular areas: holidays, history, life-cycle, ethnic communities, the land of Israel, religious life, values. The respondents were asked to indicate, grade by grade, whether certain topics were emphasized. The areas selected were those in which it was felt to be possible to insert Sephardic content; such areas as biblical history or geography of the biblical world were therefore excluded. History of the medieval and post-medieval periods was broken down into smaller units to indicate units in which Sephardic content is found or could be included.

As might have been expected, those areas dealing specifically with Sephardic content or with non-Ashkenazic content are stressed much less than other topics. Even where the question did not use the terms "Sephardic" or "non-Ashkenazic", but referred instead to "different Jewish communities," the percentage of respondents who said the

---

[4] I am grateful to Caren Levine, of the National Education Resource Center of Jewish Education Services of North America (JESNA), for her help.

[5] The participants in the survey, then, were not randomly selected; in addition, the survey was self-administered. Nevertheless, the results are interesting, with implications that will be discussed in the last section of this paper.

material was "emphasized" was low. So, for example, "holiday customs and observances of non-Ashkenazic Jews" are little taught in most grades (0–30%), although holiday customs and rituals in general receive a great deal of attention (55–90%). This pattern can be seen throughout the responses: "the synagogue" is a focal point for most respondents in many grades, while "synagogues of various communities" receive short shrift. Life-cycle customs are taught in many classrooms, but only a small number highlight life-cycle customs in "different Jewish communities."

A more positive note is struck under the heading "Ethnic Jewish Communities:" we see that "Sephardic Communities" are emphasized by 40–50% of teachers in grades 5–high school. It should be noted, however that the figures for most of the ethnic communities are much lower: Jews from Arab lands, and Persian and Indian Jews are mentioned far less (most under 30%). In the lower grades, these communities hardly figure at all (6–17%). Sephardic Jewry, then, fares somewhat better than other ethnic Jewish communities, but this aspect of the curriculum seems not to be particularly important. Some educators seem to feel that children in the early grades are not ready for cross-cultural material. So, for example, a first-grade teacher who writes,

> I'm only familiar with the grade I teach (1). The children aren't ready to differentiate [between Ashkenazim and Sephardim]; however, this sounds like a good idea for 4th grade as a lead-in to Jews in America.

Other teachers, however, have a different view:

> Since I am Sephardic and have a number of Sephardic students, I teach holidays and blessings to my kindergarten by combining customs of both groups [Sephardic and Ashkenazic].

Another teacher writes,

> I taught a pilot course called "famous Jewish personalities" to the 3rd and 4th grades. It was extremely difficult to find anything written on their grade level. I emphasized discussion regarding positive contributions of people like Maimonides and the Golden Age of Spain because so often we only hear about tragedies in Jewish history.

Experts in secular education who have been grappling with problems of multicultural and intercultural education have found that an early start on such issues is both possible and necessary if the materials and approach are geared to the right level;[6] it seems advisable for Jewish educators to pursue this approach.

In studying the Land of Israel, ethnic groups and their settlement in the State receive some attention in junior high school and high school (63–75%), although "ethnic contributions to the State of Israel" are featured much less (55–58%). This difference might be indicative of a cultural bias; that is, the helping hand extended by a Western-oriented state to "unsophisticated" refugees (such as the Yemenites of "Magic Carpet" or the Jews of Kurdistan) is emphasized, while the cultural contributions of those non-Western immigrants are downplayed. One fifth-grade text that is always mentioned with approbation in this context is *One People, Many Faces* by Shira Simchowitz, published by the World Zionist Organization in 1986; it deals with three representative Jewish communities, Yemen, Poland, and Morocco. Nevertheless, there is a widely recognized dearth of material: ". . . we have little up-to-date material in this area;" "we would really like *very* much to have some resources for teaching Sephardic culture."

American Jewish history fares badly in general. Even in grades 7–12, only 65% of respondents said that any aspect of American Jewish history is stressed. The different communities of origin of these Jews or the customs they brought with them are mentioned even less. Perhaps the study of American Jewish history, together with the study of the ethnic groups who came to America, could be introduced into the context of other units: life cycle, for example, values, or contemporary issues.[7]

The questionnaire continued with a section on family education, an area of Jewish education that is growing in importance. This topic was felt by the Foundation to be significant, since many schools, community centers, and synagogues offer family education programs that could be designed to include some Sephardic content.

Of our 233 respondents, 131, or 56%, indicated that their school or synagogue had some type of family education program; four were

---

[6] One well-known example is the design of "Sesame Street" (Children's Television Workshop), which incorporates a number of multicultural themes in a format aimed at pre-schoolers.

[7] An exemplary textbook, *America: The Jewish Experience* by Sondra Leiman (Union of American Hebrew Congregations), appeared in 1994, and has already been adopted by a number of schools. Engagingly written, it integrates material about Sephardic Jews throughout. Teachers and middle-school students alike have responded enthusiastically to it.

involved in setting up new programs, and a number of the letters we received expressed interest in family and adult education. The definition of a "family education event or project" seems to be as inclusive as possible; responses ranged from student/parent classes or "learn-ins" to festivals and communal dinners. Most of the programs listed by respondents were centered on Shabbat or holiday events. Thirty percent listed Shabbat dinners and services, havdalah services, retreats or kallot, an Oneg Shabbat or Melave Malka, or a Shabbaton. Holiday workshops and events were listed by 57%: a Tu bi-Shevat Seder, Lag b'Omer picnic, Megillah reading followed by Purim carnival, Hanukkah dinner or party, a model seder or family seder, workshops to prepare for various holidays, special family services for holidays, and even a special Selihot workshop were among the programs listed.

Classroom programs were listed by only 15% of respondents, but some of these programs seem very substantial, meeting on a regular (monthly) basis. Some are occasional ("learn-ins;" all-day special events; "bring an older relative to class day"), while others, such as regular discussions on tefillot, or an annual kallah based on a study theme, or a parent-child study or lecture series, are designed with a program of study in mind. On the other hand, events such as an "Israel Faire", simulations of a Jewish wedding or immigration experience, and family history projects are much less programmatic, and seem designed primarily to involve parents and children together in some Jewish activity. A number of programs are geared towards social action—projects to help the homeless, for example—while others are cultural in orientation (concerts, Jewish Book Day, cultural arts programs). A number of programs are designed for pre-Bar and Bat-Mitzvah youngsters and their families, while others focus on problems of the teen years: discussion groups on AIDS, cults, teen suicide, intermarriage, anti-Semitism.

Despite the diversity in the nature of these programs, it seems clear that family involvement in educational programs and projects is an important aspect of Jewish education. It should be borne in mind that the nature of a family program depends, to some degree, on the nature of the community, and while some schools or congregations will have a good response to a "kashrus workshop", other communities will feel the need to have a "Chanuka program at the same time as Christmas". Certain types of programs can be planned for diverse groups, of course, and as the idea of family education takes firmer hold, materials or programs designed for family study and participation will become more important.

This flexibility about the nature of teaching tools or educational experiences, so readily applied to family education, can have another benefit: that of reaching non-affiliated families, those who might attend a film or visit a museum, but who do not send their children to religious school. A "hands-on" children's museum in Los Angeles, My Jewish Discovery Place, has found that it serves both affiliated and unaffiliated families with its exhibits and programming. The museum is very sensitive to multicultural issues, and has incorporated material on Sephardim and Oriental Jewish communities both into its permanent displays and its well-attended public programs.

The materials and methods sections of the questionnaire were of interest to the Sephardic Education Project diagnostically: if new curricular materials, including Sephardic content, are to be designed, what types of materials do teachers prefer to use? What would they use most frequently?

The overwhelming preference—71%—is for self-contained materials, that is, kits which include both teacher guide and student materials in one package. In a number of cases, principals and education directors indicated that while they preferred "materials that allow a range of choice" or even "preferred to do some outside reading" they liked to have self-contained materials available for their teachers. One respondent, who does not teach but directs a teacher-resource center in a metropolitan area, says that "self-contained materials (kits) are what *teachers* prefer." It seems clear that modular units are more readily usable by teachers who may not always have the necessary background or preparation time for material they are required to teach.

Respondents were asked to rate materials for frequency of use. Not surprisingly, the favorite was "Teacher-made materials" (80%). "Worksheets" were second (73%), followed by a variety of other materials, including workbooks, audiotapes, and maps. It is clear that educators have few preconceptions about the types of material that they consider appropriate or effective for classroom use, and that they are willing to try almost any teaching tool that would prove to be effective. Games, videotapes, films, filmstrips—all find their way into most classrooms at some point. A teaching tool that was not rated for frequency of use was that educational staple, the textbook. Respondents were asked to list the major textbooks used in their programs, but the questions focussed on non-textbook materials. While it is desirable to encourage textbook authors and publishers to build a multicultural attitude into their publications, non-textbook materials are clearly of great importance.

A second section on materials and methods listed eight types of materials and activities and asked respondents which they were currently using and which they would like to have. One interesting result was that while computer games were then the least used— only 33%—they were the outstanding choice for "would like more materials," at 80%. Many schools did not yet have computers for classroom use, and could not use games or other software; the schools were, however, interested in acquiring computer equipment for student use.[8] Teachers find the games to be an effective tool because they are so appealing to the students, yet can be designed to convey a wealth of information. Plays and dramatic activities, now used by 74% of respondents, are still a favorite, and teachers are looking for more materials of this sort (71%).

A trend toward the "hands-on" aspect of education is evident in the preference for artifacts/objects, third on the list (64%). Children enjoy tactile objects, reproductions of artifacts, or lessons with tactile components such as costumes or models to build, a fact that museum educators have long realized. A number of projects have incorporated this idea into kits. Perhaps the first series of these was assembled by the Los Angeles Bureau of Jewish Education, whose Sephardic Family Heritage Project had kits that could be borrowed by schools.[9] Each kit was designed to represent one Sephardic or Oriental Jewish community (Moroccan or Persian, for example), and contained a videotape, some objects characteristic of that community, some recipes and craft projects for children to make, a characteristic

---

[8] Computer use in the classroom is clearly an area where change could be expected during the years 1991–95, and a follow-up study would be of some interest. To my knowledge, other than *Beyond the Sambatyon: The Myth of the Ten Lost Tribes* (a CD-ROM disc assembled by Beth Ha-Tefutsoth and released in 1995 by Creative Multimedia) which includes much material on far-flung Jewish communities, no electronic material on Sephardic or Oriental Jewry is readily available.

[9] The project was assembled under the supervision of Karen Lebow. Her article, "The Sephardic Family Heritage Project" [*Pedagogic Reporter*, 37:4 (January, 1987), 3–5], was written during the planning stages. She was responsible for much of the community involvement that made the project successful. The Sephardic Family Heritage Project was supported by many organizations, including the Los Angeles BJE and the Maurice Amado Foundation.

costume, a "family album" of snapshots, and a teacher's guide. The kits, boxed in trunks, were used by teachers in a variety of ways. The project, which received a great deal of community support, was quite successful for a while. A similar project, carried out with Maurice Amado Foundation support, is the "Sephardic Travelling Trunk" program of the Dolores Kohl Jewish Teacher Center in Wilmette, Illinois. These trunks were tested with schools and community groups in the Chicago area, and have also been shipped to other midwestern cities.

Other educators, particularly museum educators, have used "hands-on" methods and tools to great effect. The Skirball Museum in Los Angeles has assembled kits of objects and documents, which are used, together with workbooks, to teach both public and Jewish school-children about German and Polish immigration to the United States. The Skirball staff is now creating a "Sephardic learning cart," incorporating some of these ideas, for use in their new facility. In Chicago, the Spertus Museum developed and tested a "Museum-in-a-Box" kit dealing with the history and music of the Sephardic Jews. Another recent project of this type is "Artifacts Tell Stories about Sephardim and Jews of the Middle East," an artifact-based curriculum designed by the educational staff of the Jewish Museum in New York.

Finally, respondents were asked about an independent unit dealing with Sephardic culture. Would they use such a unit? For which grade level? What subject emphasis is preferred? What length unit would they prefer? The response was overwhelmingly positive: 62% yes, 35% maybe, and 3% no. The grades preferred by 31–34% of respondents were the middle school grades, 6–8, with grade 5 and High School as second choices (23% and 22% respectively). Most respondents preferred a 3 or 4 week unit to a full quarter or term (7+ weeks); responses favoring the latter option were mostly for grades 7 and up. The preferred emphasis was, first, history (58%), then life cycle (44%), then customs, with an emphasis on holidays (37%). A variety of other topics, such as literature, folktales, arts and crafts, food, and music were also mentioned. Respondents also indicated that they would like material presented in a form that would make it easy to compare and contrast Ashkenazic and Sephardic practices. A number of respondents wanted materials that they could use in the context of a unit on Israel or Jews in other lands. Some of the respondents' comments here are detailed:

What might be most useful and effective in the early (primary) grades could be an introductory unit on Sephardic culture emphasizing history, geography, artifacts, and music (approx. 2 weeks). Then in connection with each holiday, we could include Sephardic rituals and customs, foods, songs, crafts projects. This would reinforce and elaborate upon the introductory unit.

There would probably be a lot of interest in a 3–6 week unit for 1992 for all grade levels on the Sephardic communities of Spain and Portugal—*not* on the Inquisition, but on the community's contributions—poetry, ritual, art, prayer, etc.

In fact, several educators commented on the need for emphasis on positive contributions and cultural material, rather than on tragic or lurid stories of the Inquisition; one respondent also wrote that "it's important to emphasize that Jews and Arabs *did* have some positive peaceful interactions at some time in history!"

An area that was not explored in the survey but which was of great interest to the Sephardic Education Project is the area of adult education. A number of responses were received from educators who work with adults and college youth. The questionnaire was not directly relevant to their concerns, but they were interested in the results of the survey and in discussing possibilities for new materials or methods. Once again, it is important to think of educational opportunities and methods that do not rely on the conventional classroom: museum exhibits together with their public programming; recordings, films, or videotapes together with print materials that could act as discussion or study guides; popular books or thematic issues of periodicals that move people to think about and discuss important issues—all of these become valuable educational tools.[10]

It should be kept in mind that the respondents who completed and returned the questionnaires are those most likely to be interested, for whatever reason, in learning and teaching about Sephardic

---

[10] Through the Foundation's granting program, a number of these options have already been developed. For example, the National Center for Jewish Film at Brandeis University assembled a film series, "A Modern Lens on Sephardic Jewry," accompanied by a discussion guide, that is available for rental; the Center has also created a package of videotapes dealing with Sephardic Jews. The early music group, Alhambra, under its leader Isabelle Ganz, has completed a recording of Sephardic music, much of it newly transcribed from folklore archives. The Jewish Museum, in addition to its "Convivencia" exhibition and catalogue of 1992, has created a family visit guide, which can be used by visitors to the Museum's core exhibition.

Jewry. Many indicated this interest in the comments section, and many gave their names and addresses so that they could receive the results of the survey, as well as prototype materials for testing in their schools or classrooms. These educators are the ones who are interested in trying an independent unit on Sephardic culture, and who indicate that they have been searching for materials about non-Ashkenazic communities to use with their classes. While other Jewish educators may not be uninterested in Sephardic history and culture, new educational materials would have to be particularly appealing or effective to make their way into many classrooms.

Most Jewish educators see their students only for a few afternoons and Sunday morning every week, if that often; curricula are crowded and time is short. The day schools also feel a great time pressure because of their commitment to teach a full curriculum in both Jewish and secular studies. Thus, any new subject must be introduced in such a way that it enhances, rather than displaces, material that is already present and felt to be necessary. One respondent touched on this problem by saying that "with very limited time for actual teaching of pertinent material in curriculum [the presentation of] innovative material [is] hampered." Another, who thinks that "the variety of traditions among Jews of various origins needs to be taught more widely" says also that "the restrictions of a full and tightly organized curriculum and a limited number of hours of instruction per week make teaching [new material] difficult." A good solution would be one that combines educator awareness, teacher training, and new materials of a type that would be appealing to teachers and principals.

It should be noted that the problems of integrating non-Ashkenazic, and particularly Sephardic, materials into today's Jewish curricula represent only a small portion of the problems besetting Jewish education in North America.[11] Nevertheless, if Jewish education is to undergo a "systemic change," according to the suggestions made by an influential investigative body,[12] it is important to build in a multicultural perspective from the outset. The American public is now aware of the push for multiculturalism in public school and univer-

---

[11] See for example H. Himmelfarb, "A Cross-Cultural View of Jewish Education," in H. Himmelfarb and S. Della Pergola, eds., *Jewish Education Worldwide: Cross-Cultural Perspectives* (Lanham: University Press of America, 1989), pp. 3–41.

[12] The Mandel Commission, convened in 1988. The Commission's report is published as *A Time to Act* (Lanham: University Press of America, 1991), p. 21.

sity education. Too often, the benefits, and indeed, the necessity, of this approach are lost in squabbles over which historical figures to include, over which group is "empowered" and at whose expense.[13] Yet despite the pettiness of some of these controversies, the importance of the main point must not be lost. Just as many ethnic groups have contributed to the formation of American history and culture, so many ethnic groups have contributed to the richness of the Jewish heritage. An awareness of the history and traditions of non-Ashkenazic Jewry can only enhance an understanding of any aspect of Jewish life and culture.

Because approaches to multiculturalism have been so widely discussed and tried both in North America and abroad, it is possible that Jewish educators could learn from the experiments of others. The literature on this subject, vast and still growing, provides a bewildering assortment of perspectives and methods.[14] Nevertheless, some ideas, themes, and methods could be adapted and incorporated. As the need for this emphasis is recognized, more educators and curriculum planners make use of these models and strategies.

It is important to realize that educational change takes time: not only must suitable materials be developed, but educators must be made aware of the need to use them and must be trained in their effective use. We have seen that many educators are, indeed, eager to include Sephardic Jewry in their curricula. Now that educational materials are becoming more readily available, it is to be hoped that the interest in multicultural education will intensify the trend that gained momentum with the Quincentennial commemorations of 1992.

---

[13] *The New York Times* (September 18, 1991, p. A17) reported on a controversy in the Oakland, California schools under the headline "A City's Determination to Rewrite History Puts its Classrooms into Chaos." This is simply one example of the dilemmas caused by hastily-imposed and poorly-understood approaches to multiculturalism. The headline indicates the way in which these problems are widely regarded.

[14] A computer search of the ERIC (Education Resources Information Center, a bibliography assembled under the auspices of the U.S. Department of Education) under "Multicultural Education" turns up literally hundreds of entries within the period 1986–1990 alone, on subjects ranging from language teaching to art and even mathematics education, dealing with all ages from preschool through college.

INDEX

BRILL'S SERIES
IN JEWISH STUDIES

1. COHEN, R. *Jews in Another Environment.* Surinam in the Second Half of the Eighteenth Century. 1991. ISBN 90 04 09373 7
2. PRAWER, S.S. *Israel at Vanity Fair.* Jews and Judaism in the Writings of W.M. Thackeray. 1992. ISBN 90 04 09403 2
3. PRICE, J.J. *Jerusalem under Siege.* The Collapse of the Jewish State 66-70 C.E. 1992. ISBN 90 04 09471 7
4. ZINGUER, I. *L'hébreu au temps de la Renaissance.* 1992. ISBN 90 04 09557 8
5. GUTWEIN, D. *The Divided Elite.* Economics, Politics and Anglo-Jewry, 1882-1917. 1992. ISBN 90 04 09447 4
6. ERAQI KLORMAN, B.-Z. *The Jews of Yemen in the Nineteenth Century.* A Portrait of a Messianic Community. 1993. ISBN 90 04 09684 1
7. BEN-DOV, N. *Agnon's Art of Indirection.* Uncovering Latent Content in the Fiction of S.Y. Agnon. 1993. ISBN 90 04 09863 1
8. GERA, D. *Judaea and Mediterranean Politics,* 219-161 B.C.E. 1998. ISBN 90 04 09441 5
9. COUDERT, A.P. *The Impact of the Kabbalah in the Seventeenth Century.* The Life and Thought of Francis Mercury van Helmont (1614-1698). 1999. ISBN 90 04 09844 5
10. GROSS, A. *Iberian Jewry from Twilight to Dawn.* The World of Rabbi Abraham Saba. 1995. ISBN 90 04 10053 9
12. AHRONI, R. *The Jews of the British Crown Colony of Aden.* History, Culture, and Ethnic Relations. 1994. ISBN 90 04 10110 1
13. DEUTSCH, N. *The Gnostic Imagination.* Gnosticism, Mandaeism and Merkabah Mysticism. 1995. ISBN 90 04 10264 7
14. ARBEL, B. *Trading Nations.* Jews and Venetians in the Early Modern Eastern Mediterranean. 1995. ISBN 90 04 10057 1
15. LEVENSON, D. *Julian and Jerusalem.* The Sources and Tradition. 1996. ISBN 90 04 105441
16. MENACHE, S. (ed.). *Communication in the Jewish Diaspora.* The Pre-Modern World. 1996. ISBN 90 04 10189 6
17. PARFITT, T. *The Road to Redemption.* The Jews of the Yemen 1900-1950. 1996. ISBN 90 04 10544 1
18. ASSIS, Y.T. *Jewish Economy in the Medieval Crown of Aragon, 1213-1327.* Money and Power. 1997. ISBN 90 04 10615 4
19. STILLMAN, Y.K. & STILLMAN, N.A. (eds.). *From Iberia to Diaspora.* Studies in Sephardic History and Culture. 1999. ISBN 90 04 10720 7
20. BARKAI, R. *A History of Jewish Gynaecological Texts in the Middle Ages.* 1998. ISBN 90 04 10995 1